Under the General Editorship of

JESSE W. MARKHAM

Princeton University

Houghton Mifflin Adviser in Economics

Readings in United States Economic and Business History

EDITED BY:

Ross M. Robertson, *Indiana University*

James L. Pate, *Monmouth College*

HOUGHTON MIFFLIN COMPANY • BOSTON

New York   Atlanta   Geneva, Illinois
Dallas   Palo Alto

35096

EDITOR'S INTRODUCTION

All disciplines have their history. So do the special phenomena for which each discipline has been particularly fashioned. In some areas of intellectual inquiry, possibly mathematics, the history may be relatively incidental to the substance. In others, the history and the discipline itself are so interrelated that each is an integral part of the other.

Economics, as in the case of all other social sciences, is inseparable from the economic and business affairs that make up economic history. For example, much of the theoretical work on the welfare implications of monopoly was stimulated by the historical fact that in the last quarter of the nineteenth century corporate enterprise in capitalistic economies demonstrated a high propensity to monopolize. And the Keynesian revolution was in response to, and made relevant by, the "Great Depression" of the early 1930's and its attendant wholesale unemployment. Economic theory completely divorced from these historical facts is sterile. The facts divorced from economic theory lose much of their meaning.

In this volume of readings Professors Robertson and Pate provide a selection of articles and documents that greatly enrich our understanding of economics and business. While the selections are designed primarily to meet the needs of students in American economic history, they should be of equal interest to the general economist and historian. Many, such as St. Thomas Aquinas' essay on usury, have long since taken their place among the classics. Some selections, notably the late Professor Joseph Schumpeter's penetrating article, "Economic Theory and Entrepreneural History," still possesses a freshness that keeps it on current reading lists in general economics and business. The reproduction of important original documents pertaining to vital economic issues is a genuine innovation in a volume of readings all will appreciate. The original text of such documents as the Navigation Act of 1651 and Justice Marshall's famous Dartmouth College decision may not be the sort of selections students and teachers refer to every day, but when they do need them, they find it time consuming to gain access to them without such a source as this.

Finally, a word should be said about volumes of selected readings generally. More and more, in large part because the students entering colleges and universities are becoming brighter and brighter, professors are assigning materials that deal in depth and variety with issues and problems which because of the constraints of space are not fully covered in traditional textbooks. As the reading list grows, the burden on library facilities, especially the reserve desks, grows heavier and heavier. Wisely conceived volumes of readings immeasurably lighten the burden. The selections included in this volume have met the test of nearly thirty years of teaching and the approval of the numerous students who have read them. Teachers of economics and economic and business history will be grateful to the authors for making such an excellent variety of material available to them and their students in such convenient form.

Princeton University   Jesse W. Markham

PREFACE

This book of readings has emerged from nearly thirty years of teaching. It is clearly designed for beginning students in American economic history, though advanced undergraduates and graduate students should find it helpful. Professor Pate and I have aimed at enriching the beginner's fare rather than providing advanced topics for seminar discussion.

Achieving a proper balance among the traditional parts of a course in American economic history is a formidable and unsettling task. We finally decided upon a substantial list of articles on methodology in the hope that we could convey to the student a sense of the change that has occurred over the past half-century. As a consequence, some teachers may feel that we have slighted this topic or that — labor, transportation, finance — and specialists in different historical periods may feel that their favorite half-century was slighted. We simply plead that we did our best to achieve balance while meeting two or three other major objectives.

One thing we tried to do was to make this volume as entertaining as possible. Most college sophomores are convinced that history is a bore. The unfortunate fact is that it very often is, and students might cite some of these very selections in support of their opinion. Nevertheless, "The Medieval Legacy" as Herbert J. Muller describes it in his limpid prose or "The First Months in the Log Cabin" from John Ise's autobiographical novel are attractive and poignant vignettes. The story of Dr. Gesner's kerosene and the recollections of the year of the old folks' revolt will evoke a little nostalgia even for students born well after the end of World War II.

More important, perhaps, is the embellishment of standard textbooks at points where students often encounter difficulties. In the interest of effective communication, those who undertake the task of providing the narrative of economic history find themselves required to take a position. Effective history writing like effective history teaching often demands that a presentation *not* be dispassionate, that it take a position deemed legitimate after all evidence is weighed. Yet beginning students should quickly be exposed to the pleasures of intellectual controversy, and we have tried wherever possible to present two sides of arguments even though the very latest research seems to have resolved the contention one way or another.

We must confess that some of the following selections are, almost by definition, unexciting. These are the documents appended to Parts Three through Six. Most of these legislative and judicial bits and pieces are cited in standard textbooks in our field and mark critical beginnings or turning points in our economic history.   Yet nothing brings them into the student's consciousness like reading the original text.   In the original, the Land Ordinance of 1785 becomes something more than abstract talk about principal meridians and base lines.   The Chinese Exclusion Act is no longer a sectional oddity, but a shocking expression of late Nineteenth Century political opinion.   The National Labor Relations Act emerges as a major effort towards stabilizing the performance of the American economy rather than an attempt to relieve the plight of the workingman.

The marketplace will in time tell us whether we have produced a useful textbook.   In the meantime, we express our thanks to the students who indicated their consumer preference for these particular readings.

Indiana University   Ross M. Robertson
Monmouth College   James L. Pate

CONTENTS

PART ONE / Methodology

1. Business History and Economic History, *Arthur H. Cole* 3
2. On the Philosophical Method of Political Economy,
   Thomas Edward Cliffe Leslie 6
3. On the Study of Economic History, *W. J. Ashley* 9
4. The Rise and Development of Economic History, *N. S. B. Gras* 10
5. New Tools for the Economic Historian, *E. A. J. Johnson* 12
6. Economic History: One Field or Two? *Carter Goodrich* 18
7. The Professors Discover American Business,
   Harold F. Williamson 25
8. Letter to an Industrial Historian 35
9. The Businessman and Business History, *August C. Bolino* 37
10. Aspects of Quantitative Research in Economic History,
    L. E. Davis, J. R. T. Hughes, and S. Reiter 42

PART TWO / The Emergence of Capitalism

11. Law in History, *Edward P. Cheyney* 52
12. Just Price in a Functional Economy, *Bernard W. Dempsey* 54
13. Of Cheating, Which Is Committed in Buying and Selling,
    Thomas Aquinas 64
14. Of the Sin of Usury, *Thomas Aquinas* 68
15. Florence: Turbulent City of Individualism, *Miriam Beard* 73
16. The Medieval Legacy, *Herbert J. Muller* 77
17. Capitalism and the Reformation, *P. C. Gordon Walker* 84
18. The Mathematical Principles of Natural Philosophy,
    Isaac Newton 99
19. Economic Theory and Entrepreneurial History,
    Joseph A. Schumpeter 101

ix

PART THREE / The Colonial and Early National Period

20. The Colonial Period, *J. Potter* — 112
21. Colonial Commerce, *Charles M. Andrews* — 122
22. The Economic Relations of Boston, Philadelphia, and New York, 1680–1715, *Charles Nettels* — 140
23. Thomas Hancock, Colonial Merchant, *Edward Edelman* — 149
24. The Case of the Planters of Tobacco in Virginia, & Co. — 159
25. An Economic Interpretation of the Constitution of the United States, *Charles A. Beard* — 165
26. Charles Beard and the Constitution, *Robert E. Brown* — 167

DOCUMENTS

27. Navigation Act of 1651 — 172
28. Tea Act, July 2, 1767 — 175
29. The Quebec Act, June 22, 1774 — 178
30. Articles of Confederation — 179
31. The Land Ordinance of May 20, 1785 — 181
32. Northwest Ordinance, July 13, 1787 — 183

PART FOUR / The American Economy Between the Revolution and the Civil War

33. Economic Validity of the Safety-Valve Doctrine, *Clarence H. Danhof* — 189
34. The Economic Cost of Slaveholding in the Cotton Belt, *Ulrich B. Phillips* — 195
35. The Economics of Slavery in the Ante Bellum South, *Alfred H. Conrad and John R. Meyer* — 204
36. The Legend of Eli Whitney and Interchangeable Parts, *Robert S. Woodbury* — 208
37. Dr. Gesner's Kerosene: The Start of American Oil Refining, *Kendall Beaton* — 220
38. International Capital Flows and the Development of the American West, *Douglass C. North* — 233

DOCUMENTS

39. The Land Act of 1796 — 241
40. McCulloch v. Maryland — 242

41. The Trustees of Dartmouth College v. Woodward
(Justice Marshall) 244

42. The Trustees of Dartmouth College v. Woodward (Justice Story) 248

43. The Land Law of 1820 249

44. Pre-emption Act of 1841 250

45. Gibbons v. Ogden (Justice Marshall) 251

46. Andrew Jackson's Attitude Toward the Bank in 1829 255

47. Jackson's Veto of the Bank Bill, July 10, 1832 256

48. Commonwealth v. Hunt, 1842 257

49. Coinage Act of 1837 258

50. Independent Treasury Act, 1846 259

PART FIVE / The Transition from Agriculture to Industry, 1865–1920

51. The Homestead Law in an Incongruous Land System,
Paul Wallace Gates 262

52. The First Months in the Log Cabin, *John Ise* 273

53. A Quantitative Approach to the Study of Railroads in American
Economic Growth: A Report of Some Preliminary Findings,
Robert W. Fogel 282

54. St. Louis as a Central Reserve City: 1887–1922,
Ross M. Robertson 306

55. The Legend of the Robber Barons, *Thomas C. Cochran* 316

56. Development, Diversification and Decentralization,
Alfred D. Chandler, Jr. 327

DOCUMENTS

57. Homestead Act, 1862 349

58. The Pacific Railway Act, 1862 349

59. The National Bank Act, 1864 350

60. Coinage Act of 1873 352

61. Desert Land Act of 1877 352

62. Chinese Exclusion Act, 1882 353

63. The Gold Standard Act of 1900 354

64. Report of the Pujo Committee, 1913 355

65. The Sherman Anti-Trust Act, 1890 356

xii   *Contents*

PART SIX / America and the Problems of Economic Maturity, 1920 to the Present

66. The Growth of American Unions, *Irving Bernstein*   359

67. The Great Crash, *John Kenneth Galbraith*   375

68. The Year of the Old Folks' Revolt, *David H. Bennett*   388

69. The International Monetary System — Its Evolution and the Problems Ahead, *Frederick L. Deming*   394

70. Thurman Arnold, Antitrust, and the New Deal, *Gene M. Gressley*   406

71. A Note on Professor Rostow's "Take-off" into Self-sustained Economic Growth, *Douglass C. North*   418

72. Eight Tycoons: The Entrepreneur and American History, *J. R. T. Hughes*   423

DOCUMENTS

73. National Industrial Recovery Act, 1933   436

74. The Clayton Anti-Trust Act, 1914   436

75. The Transportation Act of 1920   437

76. Coolidge's Veto of the McNary-Haugen Bill, 1927   438

77. Norris-Laguardia Anti-Injunction Bill, 1932   439

78. The Agricultural Adjustment Act, May 12, 1933   440

79. Reciprocal Trade Agreements Act, 1934   441

80. The National Labor Relations Act, 1935   442

81. Labor Management Relations Act of 1947   443

PART ONE

◻ Methodology

In the following selections, several topics are held up to the light and examined. The writers — some long dead, some still active and vigorous — are of course trying to convey their notions of what economic history and business history are all about and how these subjects can most fruitfully be studied. But observe how over the last several decades ideas about the uses of economic history have changed. Writing in the latter part of the Nineteenth Century, T. E. Cliffe Leslie argued that economic history was simply a type of economic analysis — to be distinguished from the "a priori" method that he so obviously distrusted. On the other hand, Professors Davis, Hughes, and Reiter — expressing the views of many contemporary economic historians — come close to saying that economic history serves the primary function of providing data for the economic theorist.

A second theme seems to have preoccupied economic historians for twenty-five years or a little more. Writing in the early 1940's, Professor Johnson was clearly more concerned than Professors Ashley and Gras about the importance to historical study of quantitative as distinguished from qualitative methods. No one would argue that we have found a substitute for historical judgment. Yet Professor Goodrich implies what Davis, Hughes, and Reiter make explicit, that a rewriting of economic history is going on as a consequence of new developments in data processing and statistical interpretation of data.

The student of business history may be somewhat astonished to discover that between economic and business history there is no clear-cut line of distinction as he may once have thought. Some teachers like to say that business history corresponds to microanalysis in economics and that economic history corresponds to macroanalysis. While such a distinction may have its uses, the line between the two studies — if indeed there is one — is fuzzy at

1

best. Actually, a field of study, new or old, encompasses what its students wish to include in it. In the passages that follow, some of the younger historians, two old pros, and the man who pioneered the field examine the values, tangible and intangible, of business history. Each takes a different view, and each casts a different light on current problems of research and writing. Like economic history, business history is in flux, changing to meet the needs of the people who use it. □

❖ 1 ❖

Business History and Economic History *

ARTHUR H. COLE

The ensuing remarks are addressed to two topics which seem to me important: (a) what conflicts, if any, are there between business history and economic history; and (b) how can research in the two areas be mutually helpful . . .

Differentiation seems to me to hold advantages, even as the development of
specialized libraries has its good points. In both cases, there is the enthusiasm
of the active proponents and the capacity to grasp more fully the details of a
restricted field. But in both cases there is also the likely danger that each specialty will look too exclusively inward upon itself rather than outward toward
the rest of the world: outward toward the whole breadth of historical research
and writing or toward the whole library system of a university or a community . . .

The point that I would make today is emphatically that economic history
profits richly from all scholarly research and writing in this younger field; and
the implication, sometimes voiced, that economic historians are emotionally
antagonistic or feel superior to business data or to business history is something which surely I should like to challenge.

Like the business historian, any of us who calls himself an economic historian is concerned with company histories and biographies of businessmen.
The business historian wants to know more about the growth of corporate
government, about the adoptive process in technological change, about the
processes of business decision, about the causes of business failures, about the
role of innovation in business success, and a score of other matters connected
with the contribution of businessmen to economic progress and to cyclical
movements. And, as Mr. Gras with others has advocated, we need more case
studies. We cannot safely build conceptual schemes of any considerable
scope with so few bricks as we at present possess.

We need studies of the business institutions and their functions at selected
periods of the past, studies that I think of as cross-sectional in time. Writing
business or economic history without such surveys is both difficult and potentially dangerous. It is somewhat comparable to writing the political party
history of a nation without knowledge of the changing structure of its government. I look on such surveys as providing maps so that those engaging in

* Taken and adapted from Arthur H. Cole, "Business History and Economic History,"
The Journal of Economic History, Vol. 5, Supplement, December 1945, pp. 45–50. Used
by permission.

3

longitudinal inquiries — longitudinal in time — will be conscious of the area through which they are traveling.

Again, the studies of individual companies and individual businessmen, together with a knowledge of the changing environment of business institutions and other appropriate data, should lead to histories of specific business functions: marketing, personnel administration, maintenance of public relations, and so on. For some of these studies, it seems indeed unnecessary to wait for the preparation of numerous histories of individual enterprises or enterprisers . . .

We need histories of changing business thought, both the study of the opinions of particular leading or typical businessmen — like that in which Richard C. Overton is now engaged — and that of businessmen in general over series of decades — a subject that has stimulated Thomas C. Cochran's imagination now for some years . . .

When we progress beyond these four categories or types of studies in business history — biographies of individual enterprises or businessmen, cross-sectional surveys, histories of particular business functions, and histories of business thought — I find myself somewhat puzzled; I am doubtful whether business history can advantageously proceed to more general or broader summaries. Of what would a regional, and industrial or a national business history consist? On what central thread or group of threads would such a history be hung?

Possibly a *region* would be found to have a religious or racial individuality or variant social values sufficiently potent to affect the development of specific business functions or business operations in general in a manner to differentiate it from other parts of a given country — at least for some periods of time. I have in mind the Quaker businessmen in the Philadelphia area or perhaps the Scandinavian farmer-entrepreneurs in the Middle West as presenting possibilities of this sort. Likewise, the force of local custom or the mere fact of physical distance between business communities might affect the evolution of particular business functions in given regions or localized industries.

To be sure, there are threads on which partial industrial or national histories of business might be strung. One is the sharing of stimulus to economic progress between business and government. Lately we have got into the habit of thinking of government solely as a regulating or restraining force; but this aspect of governmental action was not always so prominently displayed. Nor is it all-pervasive today: as witness the T.V.A. and its sisters and brothers, or wartime research on atomic energy. Business has been generally — though not universally — a dynamic force; but it shares this character with government over the whole history of the past. Perhaps here we should have in mind Mr. Innis' oft-tendered injunction that we should think in terms of "political economy," not in those of economics or business alone.

Another basis for the development of a fairly broad theme, largely out of business phenomena, is the history of entrepreneurship: the changing character of participants, changing methods, incentives, distributions of risks and the like. The economic historians themselves have manifested some interest in this subject, although admittedly not the attention that the topic deserves: as, for example, in the biographical studies of the Fuggers or, very recently, John D. Rockefeller or Andrea Barbarigo, or the histories of the great English companies. Perhaps adequate treatment has had to await research within the field of business technology itself; that is, until the conduct of business affairs ceased to be considered wholly an art and came to be regarded at least in part as a science. Only further research can determine whether Adam Smith was or was not justified in writing about "the mean rapacity, the monopolizing spirit of merchants and manufacturers" — that is, in treating the businessman as an object not worthy of study — and whether Ricardo did well in spurning the outline of the entrepreneurial function supplied by Jean Baptiste Say.

The history of entrepreneurship differs from business history, at least as I grasp the nature of the latter, chiefly in merging the business into the whole process of economic change. Mr. Gras has defined business history as "primarily the study of the administration of business units of the past,"[1] or, again, as "the story of the systematic and continuous effort to make adjustment to labor situations, market conditions, community feelings, swings in general business, and trends in political thinking."[2] In a history of entrepreneurship, the "administration of business units" would be studied to find out what changes or innovations in that administration have meant for society. Similarly, in entrepreneurial history, the business leader would be viewed not as merely making "adjustment" to what may for some purposes be regarded as external forces, but as being an integral and highly important part of those forces. He is one half of the "labor situation"; he is one of the forces at work, he himself must be subjected to analysis. In this way an economic historian becomes keenly interested in all the scholarly productions that have flowed or that may in the future flow from research in the area of business history.

Such analyses of development — the relative role of business in economic development of the history of entrepreneurship — may seem to the business historian, however, as smacking much too much of economic history. I must confess that they do possess that savor; but the question that I would raise is whether that propensity is not inevitable; whether, in any broad treatment of business evolution, the central theme introduced to give it significance is not necessarily external to business itself. Even a history of business management, possibly that of particular business functions, seems to need some nonbusiness talisman to differentiate the important from the trivial . . .

Now perhaps we are ready to consider reciprocity. If business history can supply highly important new data for economic history, what can the latter

---

[1] N. S. B. Gras and Henrietta M. Larson, *Casebook in American Business History* (New York: F. S. Crofts and Company, 1939), p. 3.

[2] "Are You Writing a Business History?" *Bulletin of the Business Historical Society,* XVII (October 1944), p. 77.

provide that would be of value to those working in the field of business history? Of course, the business historian actually can, and does, employ practically any and all data garnered by the economic historian: such as population movements, changing governmental policies, technological advances, and cyclical movements. Perhaps, in addition, the economic historian can prepare certain primarily business studies more objectively and in a broader framework than can those who are closer to business experience and business sentiment. I have in mind such an investigation as I have already mentioned, the history of business opinion, to which we might add a history of public relations or even a history of industrial relations. Again, economic historians can contribute to advance in business history by inquiries into the history of the corporation, business failures, commercial law, or the theories of profits. Obviously, these are all closely affiliated to, if not included within, the area of research which I think of as the history of entrepreneurship. I have in fact been so audacious as to hope that, here in the history of entrepreneurship, business historians and economic historians could find an intellectual tract which both might cultivate in mutual good will. Surely research in that tract requires knowledge of both business and economic developments . . . ◻

❖ **2** ❖

On the Philosophical Method of Political Economy *

THOMAS EDWARD CLIFFE LESLIE

. . . In order to form any approach to an adequate estimate of the influence of human desires on the amount of wealth, it must surely be evident that we need an investigation, not only of the motives and impulses which prompt the acquisition of wealth, but also of those which withdrew men from its pursuit, or give other directions to their energies. What abstract political economy has to teach on this subject is stated by Mr. Mill in his *Essay on the Definition and Method of Political Economy*, and also in his logic, as follows: . . .

'Political economy is concerned with man solely as a being who desires to possess wealth. It makes entire abstraction of every other human passion or motive, except those which may be regarded as perpetually antagonizing principles to the desire of wealth, namely, aversion to labour, and desire of the present enjoyment of earthly indulgences. These it takes to a certain extent into its calculation, because these do not merely, like other desires, occa-

* Taken and adapted from Thomas Edward Cliffe Leslie, "On the Philosophical Method of Political Economy," *Essays in Political Economy*, Second Edition, Hodges, Figgis & Co. Ltd., Dublin, 1888, pp. 163–90. Originally published in *Hermathena*, Vol. ii., 1876.

sionally conflict with the pursuit of wealth, but accompany it always as a drag or impediment, and are therefore inseparably mixed up in the consideration of it.' Abstraction has here clouded the reasoning of the most celebrated logician of the century. Had Mr. Mill looked to actual life, he must have at once perceived that among the strongest desires confounded in the abstract 'desire of wealth' are desires for the present enjoyment of luxuries; and that the aversion to labour itself has been one of the principal causes of inventions and improvements which abridge it. Frugality, as Adam Smith has observed, has never been a virtue characteristic of the inhabitants of England; commodities for immediate consumption and luxuries have always been the chief motives to exertion on the part of the bulk of the English population. The love of ease is the motive which has led to the production of a great part of household furniture, and is one of the chief sources of architecture.

'A great part of the machines,' says Adam Smith, 'made use of in those manufactures in which labour is most subdivided, were originally the inventions of common workmen, who naturally turned their thoughts towards finding out easier and readier methods of performing it . . . One of the greatest improvements (in the steam engine) was the discovery of a boy who wanted to save his own labour.' By what logical principle, moreover, can economists justify the admission of 'two antagonizing principles' into their theory while excluding or ignoring others? In fact, no economist has ever been able to limit his exposition in this manner. Mr. Mill, in his own *Principles of Political Economy*, follows Adam Smith in including in his doctrine of the causes which govern the choice of occupations and the rates of wages and profits, many other motives, such as the love of distinction, of power, of rural life, of certain pursuits for their own sake, of our own country, the consequent indisposition to emigrate, &c.

The real defect of the treatment by economists of these other principles is, that it is superficial and unphilosophical; that no attempt has been made even to enumerate them adequately, much less to measure their relative force in different states of society; and that they are employed simply to prop up rude generalizations for which the authority of 'laws' is claimed. They serve, along with other conditions, to give some sort of support to saving clauses — such as 'allowing for differences in the nature of different employments,' *caeteris paribus*, 'in the absence of disturbing causes,' 'making allowance for friction' — by which the 'law' that wages and profits tend to equality eludes scrutiny. Had the actual operation of the motives in question been investigated, it would have been seen to vary widely in different states of society, and under different conditions. The love of distinction or social position, for example, may either counteract the desires of wealth, or greatly add to their force as a motive to industry and accumulation. It may lead one man to make a fortune, another to spend it. At the head of the inquiry into the causes on which the amount of the wealth of nations depends is the problem, what are the conditions which direct the energies and determine the actual occupations and pursuits of mankind in different ages and countries? A theory surely cannot be said to interpret the laws regulating the amount of wealth which takes no account, for instance, either of the causes that make arms the occupation of the best part of the male population of Europe at this day, or, on the other hand, of those which determine the employments of women.

Enough has been said in proof that the abstract *a priori* and deductive method yields no explanation of the causes which regulate either the nature or the amount of wealth. With respect to distribution, it furnishes only a theory of exchange (or of wages, profits, prices, and rent), which will be hereafter examined. The point calling for immediate attention is, that such a theory, even if true, must be altogether inadequate to explain the distribution of wealth. One has but to think of the different partition of land in England and France, of the different partition of both between the two sexes, of the influence of the State, the Church, the Family, of marriage and succession, to see its utter inadequacy. Take land, for example. Sir Henry Maine has justly observed that exchange lies historically at the source of its present distribution in England to a greater extent than most modern writers on the subject seem aware. The purchase and sale of land was active, both in the Middle Ages and in the age of the Reformation; and the original root of the title of the existing holder, in a vast number of cases, is a purchase either in those ages or since. But it is only by historical investigation that we can mount up in this manner to purchase; and the present distribution of land, descending from such a source, is none the less the result of another set of causes, among which that great historical institution, the Family, which has never ceased to be one of the chief factors in the economy of human society, holds a principal place.

The truth is, that the whole economy of every nation, as regards the occupations and pursuits of both sexes, the nature, amount, distribution, and consumption of wealth, is the result of a long evolution, in which there has been both continuity and change, and of which the economical side is only a particular aspect or phase. And the laws of which it is the result must be sought in history and the general laws of society and social evolution. □

On the Study of Economic History [*]

W. J. ASHLEY

. . . There reigns just now a spirit of tolerance and mutual charity among political economists such as has not always been found within their circle. It is not that we have returned to the confident dogmatism and unanimity of the last generation, — of the period which extended from the publication of John Stuart Mill's treatise to the sounding of the first note of revolt in Cliffe Leslie's essays. It is rather that, though there are still marked divergencies, the followers of one method no longer maintain that it is the *only* method of scientific investigation; that, on the other hand, the believers in induction now recognize more fully the value of deduction; that the most abstract sometimes refer to facts and the most concrete occasionally make use of abstraction; and, what is far more important, that they are inclined, whatever their own turn of thought may be, to let others alone who walk not with them, or even to cheer them on their way in the benevolent hope that they may arrive at something worth the getting. It has now become almost a commonplace even with economists of the older school that students may usefully be led to work in different ways, owing to "varieties of mind, of temper, of training, and of opportunities." [1] . . .

It would be idle to deny that the hopes which were entertained by the younger men of the "historical" or "inductive" school in Germany some twenty years ago, and by Cliffe Leslie and more recently by Dr. Ingram among English writers, have not hitherto been realized. They looked for a complete and rapid transformation of economic science; and it needs only a glance at the most widely used text-books of today to see that no such complete transformation has taken place. Of this disappointment a partial explanation may be found in the fact that the historical economists were still so far under the spell of the old discipline as to continue to conceive of economics under the forms made familiar by the manuals. They still had before their eyes the customary rubrics of Production, Distribution, and Exchange; they still handled the sacred terms Value, Supply, Demand, Capital, Rent, and the rest, — terms which, to use Oliver Wendell Holmes's phrase, were just as much in need of depolarization as the terms of theology; they still looked forward to framing "laws" similar in character, however different in content, to the "laws" in possession of the field. Aiming, as they unconsciously did, at the construction of a body of general propositions dealing

---

[*] Taken and adapted from W. J. Ashley, "On the Study of Economic History," *The Quarterly Journal of Economics*, Harvard University Press, Vol. VII, No. 1, January 1893, pp. 115–36. Used by permission.
[1] Marshall, *Principles* (2nd Ed.), p. 92.

with just the same relations between individuals as the older school had given its attention to, it was natural that they should fall back on the use of that deductive method which is certainly of service for the analysis of modern competitive conditions, although they had begun by unnecessarily rejecting it. And thus the "methodological" arguments of the orthodox may seem to have gained an easy victory.

I shall attempt to show later that this is not an adequate version of the matter; that during this period the historical movement has been slowly pushing its way towards its own true field of work. Even in its relation to current economic teaching, it has performed a work of vital importance. It has been no mere aberration, passing away and leaving no trace; nor is it quite a complete account of it to say that it has contributed useful elements which have been incorporated in the body of economic science. It has done more than this: it has changed the whole mental attitude of economists towards their own teaching. The acceptance of the two great principles — which are but different forms of the same idea, — that economic conclusions are *relative* to given conditions, and that they possess only *hypothetical* validity, is at last a part of the mental habit of economists. The same is true of the conviction that economic considerations are not the only ones of which we must take account in judging of social phenomena, and that economic forces are not the only forces which move men. It need hardly be said that all this was recognized *in word* long ago; but it may be left to the verdict of those who are conversant with the literature of the last generation whether these convictions were really underlying and fruitful parts of daily thought, as they are now tending to be. The remark, indeed, is not out of place in passing that, although this salutary conversion may be discerned among professional economists, it has hardly taken place so completely as one could wish with the educated public, and that historical zealots may still do good service in insisting on these well-worn platitudes. □

❖ **4** ❖

The Rise and Development of Economic History *

N. S. B. GRAS

Economic history is the story of the various ways in which man has obtained a living. It is, indeed, a segment of the history of civilization, comparable with political, ecclesiastical, legal and literary history. But because of the fact that in the long run the economic segment necessarily influences or even

* Taken and adapted from N. S. B. Gras, "The Rise and Development of Economic History," *The Economic History Review*, Vol. I, No. 1, January 1927, pp. 12–34. Used by permission.

largely determines the others, it is commonly held to be the most fundamental part of human history, though many people do not like the implication. As is the case with most of our sciences, economic history was born late . . .

The oldest historians were not interested in economic history. They were commonly priests, concerned with priestly things. Their approach to life was antithetical to economic history. They turned from the actualities of this world to the supposed conditions and influences of another existence. A comet, an earthquake, or an eclipse was to them a social, not a natural, phenomenon. The nearest to worldliness that such historians usually attained was to record the death of a high priest, or a potentate friendly or unfriendly to priests, or a famine carrying off part of the flock; or later to note the interplay of diplomatic and political forces, usually treated in brief fashion. With the secularization of history-writing in town economy, whether in the ancient or the medieval period, came an interest in the mundane for its own sake. But still it was political, not economic, history that was considered worthy of record, though general economic situations did force themselves into the story at certain places.

History is a jade who periodically renews her vigour by marrying oncoming youths. When History was wedded to the youthful Economic Interest, without banns and without heralds, our Economic History became a reality. But first we must account for Economic Interest itself, at least as expressed in literary form. When men began to reflect upon the business of getting a living, we know not. It is clear, however, that in the stage of town economy, when writing was employed, thoughts on things economic began to be set down, though not from the historical point of view . . .

But we must hasten on to Adam Anderson, for he is a major prophet in the book of economic history. From Adam to Adam there was no one like Adam — that is, from the father of man to the father of economics there was no one like the father of commercial history. At least two of the Adams were Scotsmen. And for what had Scotland done all its starving, if not to produce such distinguished workers in the economic field? Comment on the historical work of Adam Smith is needless: the historical chapters of *The Wealth of Nations* are still among the most illuminating discussions of economic development that exist in English . . . Adam Anderson wrote two thick volumes, expanded after his death by Macpherson and others into four. The work first published in 1764, was entitled *An Historical and Chronological Deduction of the Origin of Commerce*. Critical of his secondary resources, but without a conscious philosophy of history, this clerk of a London counting-house had set out to write a genuine history — that is, a chronology of commerce from the Flood to his own time, from Noah's precious cargo to the East Indian fleet returning with their spices and their calicoes, or, more exactly, from the Creation to the end of the Seven Years' War. He emphasized trade, manufacture, colonies, a large population, a favourable balance of trade, money and an increasing standard of living . . . Economic history is now launched with wine of a respectable vintage. It is called commercial history, but it is as inclusive as much that has since passed for economic history. Although Anderson occasionally rationalized where he had no knowledge, still he strove to give the facts as he could unearth them from his copious London library. He knew the works of Werdenhagen, Evelyn, Bishop Huet and many others. Their efforts constitute the first dawn, his the morning of economic history. ◻

◇ **5** ◇

New Tools for the Economic Historian *

E. A. J. JOHNSON

I

Archeologists assure us that organized social life has existed on this earth for about two hundred and fifty thousand years. How millions of people have sought to satisfy their wants over this tremendous span of time is the acknowledged province of economic history. Yet, for lack of records, the gild of economic historians must, for the most part, confine their attention to the last one per cent of this time span; indeed the great bulk of research in economic history is devoted to the last one-tenth of one per cent of the archeologists' two hundred and fifty thousand years of social history. Even then the economic historian is utterly overwhelmed with facts. He who essays to write the economic history of the United States, for example, must depict as best he can the economic activities of people for more than a hundred and fifty years, farmers, merchants, manufacturers, wage-earners, rentiers; men, women and children in all walks of life, in all variety of occupations. The task is utterly staggering. An army of economic historians would be required to write a complete economic history of the United States; a regiment at least to write a faithful factual account of a single industry.

The economic historian circumvents these difficulties in two ways: by disregarding a great many facts and by generalizing about others. By either procedure he distorts historical reality. This distortion is not peculiar to economic history; it is the eternal problem of all historiography. Hence, although every historian must attempt to increase the factual base upon which he builds his account of the past, he must also find suitable methods for generalizing about historical events. For each branch of history, therefore, efforts have to be made to perfect appropriate methodology; from this necessity, the economic historian, for all his reliance on facts, cannot escape . . .

* Taken and adapted from E. A. J. Johnson, "New Tools for the Economic Historian," *The Journal of Economic History*, Vol. 1, Supplement, December 1941, pp. 30–38. Used by permission.

There is no reason why the economic historian need confine himself to any comprehensive variety of systematic economic theory; he must use any theoretical tools that promise to be helpful. His task is to depict the evolution of wealth-getting and wealth-using activities; hence he perforce must envisage some productive process, some distributive process, and some consumptive process. But all these processes are constantly being altered in the time-sequence flux of history: agriculture is mechanized, transport becomes more efficient, the proportions in which the factors of production are combined change with technological innovations; meantime marketing devices (both technical and organizational) modify the distributive machinery of society.

I am speaking about economic theory. Sociological theory also has a place in the economic historian's tool-box, although I must frankly admit that I am somewhat impatient with the recent fashion toward an excessive reliance on sociological theory that alleges that the time-sequence of economic events is definitely divisible into stages. Perhaps other branches of history can be truthfully described by the technique of periodization; but economic history in its major operational aspects is discontinuous to a very limited extent. Moreover, where clean-cut divisions into time-periods are discernible, the discontinuity has more often a political than an economic origin. The prohibition of chattel slavery, for example, did no doubt constitute a demarcation point in economic history; but the termination of a slave system cannot be regarded as something wholly economic, however great the economic consequences of such a governmental decision may have been.

Sociological theory has a place in economic history when used with great care; for very obviously economic activity is only a fraction of a larger set of sociological activities, and economic history must therefore be related constantly to the larger social process. But whereas political shifts can be violent, and whereas religious beliefs can be altered by evangelical waves, the mundane business of making a living is a pretty continuous thing. Whether ministries fall or whether the palace revolution is successful, the cows must be milked, the fields must be plowed, and the sheep must be sheared. Regardless of the decisions of a synod of churches, people must have food, clothing, and houses. The business cycle, which is a sociological phenomenon, does seem to have a real power to introduce a noticeable degree of discontinuity in economic activity, and hence the statisticians can properly be considered as supplying one body of theory extremely useful to the economic historian.

For dealing with quantitative data, the economic historian must, therefore, employ the tools which have been so skillfully devised by that remarkable gild of enthusiastic tool-makers, the statisticians. Unfortunately, only a very recent portion of economic history is adequately statistical to permit the employment of these intricate tools; and hence the economic historian must muddle along as best he can when dealing with most chapters of economic history prior to the last quarter of the nineteenth century. It is true that little by little, as a consequence of painstaking research, the statistical series are being elongated; but it is a vain hope to believe that if we are only patient we shall someday have adequate quantitative data. For the long, backward reach of economic history we shall never have enough statistical data to allow us to use the tools of the statisticians. We must therefore grope our way, using limited quantitative data and the much more abundant qualitative data; aided meanwhile by any usable theoretical tools.

II

What theoretical equipment can the economic historian put into his tool-box? Unlike the statistician, he can find few precision instruments of a delicate and sensitive character. Unlike the economic theorist he cannot employ refined logical methods simply because he cannot impound all troublesome items in that bottomless *caeteris paribus*. He must always deal with "stubborn and irreducible facts." Yet, as I have already said, he is actually confounded by factual detail unless he can determine by some theoretical blue-print what facts to concentrate upon and what facts to disregard. Thus, although almost every text-book on American economic history tells us that Squanto taught the Pilgrim Fathers how to plant corn, I doubt whether this is a particularly important fact. If, in contrast, it could be demonstrated that most New England farmers discovered that, in terms of man-hours of labor expended, the corn yield was fifty per cent greater on the average than the wheat yield, that would be, for economic history, a significant fact. For here the emphasis would be rigidly economic: a concern with the experiential historical process whereby scarce means were employed to maximize the output of food.

How can productivity be measured in a non-statistical age? and even more important, how can changes in productivity brought about by technological progress be measured? For agriculture, some answers to these questions may be found in Leo Rogin's *Farm Machinery in Relation to the Productivity of Labor,* a book which is much more than a recital of evidence. It is at once a set of findings and a method, inasmuch as it shows how very meager quantitative evidence can, if properly understood, throw a flood of light on one of the most important of all industries. Moreover it reveals the essential continuity of the quest for greater productivity, and although there are ladder-like technological improvements in the history of the productivity of farm labor, there are few demarcation points which would justify a periodization of agrarian economic history . . .

Improved farm machinery, however, is not heaven-sent; it is invested, built, and put into use. What is called for, clearly, is some working hypothesis which will explain why creative powers emerge, how ideas can be translated into technology, and why technology of an improved variety comes into general usage. Any satisfactory dynamic analysis of economic history, therefore, involves a theory of invention and a theory of diffusion. Along with Rogin must be placed Usher's *History of Mechanical Inventions,* especially that generalized theory developed in the first two chapters. For without this general theory, the remarkable progress of agricultural machinery or any other technology becomes merely a random collection of seemingly heroic events unexplained except by mysterious forces such as Yankee ingenuity or the influence of the frontier. A theory of invention, however, is not enough. Knowledge does, after all, diffuse itself throughout society; and just here, sociological theory of an essentially genetic nature becomes valuable. The processes of cultural transference have been studied in many contexts by anthropologists and historians. Rostovtzeff's essay on "Parthian Art and the Motive of the Flying Gallop " [1] illustrates how essentially similar environment led to the appearance of essentially similar intellectual achievements, whereas the writings of V. Gordon Childe demonstrate the complicated processes of cultural diffusion.[2]

With an empirical method for analyzing changes in productivity plus a general theory of invention and a working concept of the process of diffusion, the economic historian can, I think, begin asking some important questions about the history of agriculture. Productivity and its relation to technology, however, will not explain agrarian economic history. For in spite of the indelible pictures of rural self-sufficiency painted by novelists like Daniel Defoe and Knute Hamsun, agriculture is an enterprise rather intimately related to markets. Access to markets involves transport costs; hence agriculture, like all other enterprises, is tied up with the efficiency of transport. Here again the economic historian is surfeited by facts; about stagecoaches and corduroy roads; about inclined planes and Tom Thumb engines. Unguided by theoretical desiderata, the monographs on transportation too often degenerate into quaint, nostalgic, accounts of bull-whackers and uncomfortable railway carriages.

III

Oddly enough neither the historians nor the economists have offered any very useful suggestions about how the economic importance of transport can be determined. That theory was supplied by a British engineer, J. Edwin Holmstrom, in an analysis of the "Morphology of Transport," an incisive appraisal of the comparative goods-moving potentiality of various methods of transport now in use in various parts of the world.[3] By setting up comparative hypothetical, continuous, goods-moving arrangements, Holmstrom was able to show that a continuous stream of pack animals has a limited advantage over a continuous stream of porters and that a continuous parade of ox-wagons has no tremendous advantage over a column of pack animals. The

---

[1] *Independence Convergence and Borrowing* (Cambridge, 1937), 44–57.
[2] See, especially *The Danube in Prehistory* (Oxford, 1929).
[3] *Railways and Roads in Pioneer Development Overseas: A Study of Comparative Economics* (London, 1934).

surprisingly modest differentials depend, however, upon an arbitrary factor which Holmstrom calls the "fraction of availability," in other words the relative share of total men, pack animals, or oxen that could be devoted to transport without crippling all other economic activities requiring men, burros, or oxen. In spite of this theoretical weak-spot, Holmstrom's theory is an invaluable tool for the economic historian. Horse-drawn wagons on surfaced roads show a really great advantage, while steam railways are revealed as genuinely revolutionary in their two thousand fold potential advantage over primitive forms of transport. Holmstrom's theory abundantly justifies Clapham's insistence that the advent of the steam railway really transformed modern economic life.

J. M. Clark's *Economics of Overhead Costs* and other studies of invariable cost factors have been extremely helpful to economic historians in their wrestle with multitudinous facts. But Holmstrom has revealed that several important considerations have been disregarded by students of transportation. Because wagon roads employed, before the advent of the automobile, slow-moving tractive power, and because roads could be built by incremental investment, a road system tends normally to create a network of transport agencies. In contrast, the railway (and to some extent today, automobile roads) create axes. In one case economic development will be peripheral, in the other linear. Furthermore, because of the long-haul economy, an accentuation of economic progress will occur at the poles of the railway axis. An awareness of this tendency toward economic polarization is imperative for the economic historian. Professor Gates, in his excellent study of the *Illinois Central Railway*, realized that polarizing influences were operative. But I suspect that Holmstrom's theoretical tools would have made it possible for Gates to have shown much more clearly why Chicago became a metropolis and Cairo did not.

IV

Holmstrom's emphasis on the net-work of roads indicates the geographical basis for another very important problem of economic history, especially in the pre-railway age. Unsurfaced roads place a rather rigid limitation upon the mobility of people. East of the Mississippi and north of the Ohio, villages are seldom more than seven or eight miles apart. The historical explanation is simple enough: the speed of transport determined the location of markets. It did more than that, however; by restricting buyers in adjacent areas to market towns, slow moving transport created spatial monopolies and quasi-monopolies.

The entire history of local business enterprise is explicable in terms of the theory of oligopoly and monopolistic competition. Consider, for a moment, the organizational structure of an American country village, let us say, in 1850. What enterprises were to be found? A general store, a blacksmith shop, a grist-mill, a tannery — certainly these. Probably also a cooper's shop, a cobbler's shop, and a cheese factory. Each of these enterprises possessed some degree of monopoly power. If prices were too high for nails or harness at the general store, farmers could trade in other villages. But only at a transport disadvantage; one which might more than offset the higher prices at the nearby store. Oligopolistic factors were omnipresent.

In a general way we can envisage this typical scheme of things by the aid of modern economic theory. Partly as a result of quasi-monopolistic incomes, there emerged a limited number of well-to-do businessmen in every American village, financially capable of making sizable local investments, of lending money on local farm mortages or of speculating in western lands. They were the propertied people who formed the local bank, built the new cotton mill, or brought the railway. Their profits, originating in partial monopolies, presently flowed out into wider areas, thus hastening the rate of capital formation in the entire nation . . .

The whole history of the American trust movement needs to be reviewed in terms of modern economic theory. The older literature assumed for the most part that monopolistic power stemmed from control over supply. Yet in the entire configuration of our trust movement, I suspect that monopsony was fully as important as monopoly . . .

V

About general locational theory, I need say little. It has become an indispensable tool for every economic historian. And for all its abstractness we must go back to Alfred Weber's theory for the basic concepts and for unambiguous terminology. Many more case studies need to be made before the theory can be perfected . . . We need only re-examine some of our first-rate older industrial monographs to appreciate how much better these studies could have been if their authors had had at their disposal suitable tools for dealing with industries in the process of migration.

VI

Year by year the number of tools available to the economic historian is increasing. The theory of money and credit, for example, has made notable advances and as a result provided economic historians with new equipment. It is nonetheless distressing to see how much work in economic history is still haphazard and planless. Facts are gathered assiduously with little appraisal of whether they actually throw much light on economic development. Like the geologist, the economic historian must go about his work with his pockets full of hypotheses. For there is so much to do if we are ever to have a more complete understanding of the past that we cannot afford to waste our time collecting unimportant data. As economists we should employ our scarce time, energy, and resources for the most important tasks. We should not be beguiled by the fascination of antiquarian details. We must visualize the major problems of production in relation to basic economic desiderata: we

must see them historically in terms of productivity, of least-cost approximations; we must trace the processes of capital formation — local and national;
the changes in income streams — earned and fortuitous.   We must try to
show how an enterprise system has worked with the aid of more or less governmental subvention and restrained by more or less governmental regulation.
We must give more attention to the history of consumption and to the effects of changes in consumption upon the entire structure of the economy.

All these tasks must be visualized in a theoretical way.   All can be advanced by employing the most efficient theoretical tools at the disposal of the
economic historian.   There will be enough factual searching to do once the
areas that require study have been charted. ◻

❖ 6 ❖

Economic History: One Field or Two? *

CARTER GOODRICH

Is Economic History one subject or two?   The question has been posed twice
during the present century, each time by the growth of a vigorous body of
research concerned with economic changes over time but developed largely in
isolation from conventional economic history.   In each case the new work
was quantitative in method, and the result was the phenomenon of two separate bodies of scholarship — the one written in prose and calling itself economic history, the other written mainly in figures and calling itself by another
name.

The first of these quantitative innovations was the systematic study of business cycles, particularly as developed under the auspices of the National Bureau of Economic Research.   Though its leading figure was Wesley Mitchell,
whose own first writing was in economic history, the study of business cycles
developed greater and greater separateness from conventional economic history precisely as it succeeded in refining its own methods.   An early publication of the Bureau, Willard Thorp's *Business Annals*, used much the same
materials that economic historians have always used, such as contemporary
newspaper accounts.   Later, as the cycles students were able to perfect a
greater and greater number of time series, their work consisted more and more
of the analysis and manipulation of the figures themselves, and they found
less and less occasion to make use either of the writings of economic histori-

* Taken and adapted from Carter Goodrich, "Economic History: One Field or Two?"
The Journal of Economic History, Vol. XX, No. 4, December 1960, pp. 531–38.   Used
by permission.

ans or of the conventional sources of economic history. The separation has been much less complete in studies of business fluctuations in Great Britain, perhaps because the use of time series has not reached the degree of elaboration practiced in the United States and perhaps also because there has been a closer connection between the work of economic historians and economic theorists. The notable recent books of R. C. O. Matthews and J. R. T. Hughes represent what Matthews calls the "quantitative-historical method" making use of what he describes, half apologetically, as "literary" as well as statistical evidence.[1] In the United States, however, the study of business cycles and conventional economic history are for the most part carried on in separate compartments, though the presidential address of Arthur F. Burns to the American Economic Association makes a notable contribution to general economic history in analyzing the changing impact of the business cycle on the economy.[2]

The second new body of scholarship is that described under the still more recent rubric of Economic Growth. Its origin lies in the current interest in the problems of economic development, and its primary and original purpose was to contribute to an understanding of these problems by the quantitative analysis of past economic growth, with particular emphasis on "estimates of national income, wealth and their components."[3] In 1940, as you will recall, the Social Science Research Council sponsored a Committee on Research in Economic History which made a notable contribution to the advancement of our profession. In the nineteen-fifties, the Social Science Research Council sponsored a Committee on Economic Growth which has subsidized research in the new area, organized conferences, and published their results. With this encouragement, a significant body of material has already appeared and further research is flourishing.

For economic historians, the rise of this newer field poses a more disturbing question than did that of cycle study. The latter after all occupied an area of inquiry which was of great practical and theoretical importance but which was well defined and clearly delimited. Its principal concern was with the isolation and analysis of a recurrent and persistent phenomenon of capitalistic society, the business cycle. The changes in which it was most interested, at least in its purest form, were oscillations around an equilibrium or trend line. The study of continuity and of patterns of regularity is, of course, just as legitimately a part of economic history as the study of change; yet it is true

[1] R. C. O. Matthews, A *Study in Trade-Cycle History, Economic Fluctuations in Great Britain, 1833–1842* (Cambridge: Cambridge University Press, 1954), esp. p. xiii. J. R. T. Hughes, *Fluctuations in Trade. Industry, and Finance, a Study of British Economic Development, 1850–1860* (Oxford: Oxford University Press, 1960). As the subtitle indicates, Hughes is concerned with growth as well as fluctuations.

[2] Arthur F. Burns, "Progress Toward Stability," *American Economic Review*, L (March 1960), 1–19.

[3] Simon Kuznets, "Notes on the Study of Economic Growth," Social Science Research Council, Items, XIII (June 1959), p. 13.

that economic historians have been on the whole more interested in the analysis of changes in economic institutions. The quantitative changes with which they have been most concerned have been long-run rather than short-run, trends rather than fluctuations, and typically cumulative of irreversible rather than cyclical in character. But it is precisely with these changes, or at least with one major variety of them, that Economic Growth is concerned. Moreover, the difficulty of distinguishing between the fields of Economic History and Economic Growth is further confounded by the fact that the work appearing under the new title is no longer entirely confined to the use of quantitative methods. Witness the recent publication of a symposium entitled "The Role of the State in Economic Growth." [4] Could any subject be closer to the work of many members of our guild? If the study of major economic changes, and their analysis in terms of institutional factors, are not the central business of economic history, it is hard to see what our business is. If these are tasks that can be done better by scholars operating under another banner, is there any remaining purpose for us to serve?

The challenge is a serious one. Perhaps economic historians of the traditional sort are indeed the handloom weavers of a new intellectual revolution. But before we abdicate in favor of the students of Economic Growth and before we join the march into the electronic factories, there are certain questions that require consideration. Two in particular have been defined by the committee that planned this morning's program. The first concerns the promise and the potentialities of the quantitative analysis of economic change, whether applied to the study of "growth" or to other historical problems. What is the new strength that can be added by use of modern quantitative methods, and what are their limitations? The second concerns the adequacy and appropriateness for economic historians of the concept of Economic Growth. Can it properly be regarded as furnishing either the sole or the central organizing principle for the analysis of economic change? The first of these questions will be examined by the Purdue University team of Lance Davis, J. R. T. Hughes, and Stanley Reiter, and the second by Barry Supple of McGill University. My function is only to introduce the discussion, and I should like to do so by stating the issues in a somewhat different form: What, if anything, have the students of Economic Growth contributed to the understanding of economic change that economic historians of the more conventional sort had failed to supply? What contributions toward such understanding, if any, can be made only by economic historians using qualitative as well as quantitative methods?

A first essential is to recognize the elements of strength and promise in the work on Economic Growth. Its outstanding virtue is that it is related to a major problem, that of economic development. Its efforts to measure past economic growth are a direct outgrowth of the overriding current interest,

---

[4] Hugh G. J. Aitken, ed., *The Role of the State in Economic Growth* (New York: Social Science Research Council, 1959).

theoretical and practical, in devising methods for the deliberate encouragement and promotion of economic growth,, particularly in the underdeveloped
countries. By contrast, it must be admitted that a considerable part of what
has passed as economic history appears to have been written with little explicit relationship to any economic problems at all; and it is possible to think
of works in our field that are hardly more than chronicles or even collections
of curiosa. But the strength and significance of work in economic history has
always depended on the degree to which it was related to economic generalizations, to the great issues of economic organization and policy. Today there
appears to be something of a consensus within our profession that the question of economic development offers the most stimulating central theme, the
greatest promise of fruitful synthesis of theory and history, and the largest
possibility that economic historians may make a useful contribution toward
the improvement of public policy.[5]

Even more obvious is the strength of the work in Economic Growth in its
use of the quantitative method. Scholars in the field have found new data
by diligent and systematic search, have constructed new and relevant time
series, and have developed new methods with great ingenuity. At the same
time similar contributions to quantitative method and materials have been
made by economic historians who do not consider themselves students of
"growth." In the case of most of this work, on the part of either group, the
scholar of less quantitative bent can only applaud and accept. Where he has
been in the habit of saying "largely" and "mostly" and the statistician demonstrates that the proportion is really 25% or 90%, the historian's obligation
is clear: He must either change his adverb or substitute the more significant
figure. When Hughes and Reiter present complete figures on the first 1,945
steamships, there is no longer any excuse for attempting to date the rise of
steam, or the substitution of iron for wooden vessels, on the basis of scattered descriptive materials.[6] But this is the kind of use of quantitative materials that economic historians have always made. Recall, for example, the
famous passage in Clapham's *Economic History of Modern Britain*, he makes
painstaking use of the census figures to demonstrate how small a sector of the
British economy was quickly revolutionized by the industrial revolution. But
recall also what Clapham did when he wished to compare the levels of income in various countries and no one had compiled the figures of national
income; so told that American and Canadian rags brought the highest
price and Italian and Greek rags, the lowest, he presented this as his evidence

[5] A vigorous recent statement of this position is contained in Hugh G. J. Aitken, "On
the Present State of Economic History," *Canadian Journal of Economics and Political
Science*, XXVI (February 1960), pp. 87–95. An earlier discussion took place at the Williamstown meeting of the Economic History Association, at which W. W. Rostow described the study of economic development as "the most natural meeting place of theory
and history" and "the major common task . . . of economists and historians." *Journal of
Economic History*, XVII (December 1957), pp. 509–523, 545–553.
[6] J. R. T. Hughes and Stanley Reiter, "The First 1,945 British Steamships, *Journal of
the American Statistical Association*, III (June 1958), pp. 360–381.

on relative standards of living.[7]   Economic historians have always rested heavily on economic arithmetic.   They will doubtless learn, perhaps with some lag, to make use of economic algebra and economic calculus.   But I trust they will also continue to use their wits, like Sir John Clapham, when they need answers that the quantitative methods do not supply.

A third virtue of the work in Economic Growth is its bold application of the method of comparison between countries.   Economic historians have talked a good deal about the importance of comparative studies and the insights they should provide.   Recall, for example, the discussion at our Williamstown meetings under the leadership of Sylvia Thrupp and W. T. Easterbrook.[8]   But the students of Economic Growth have been more enterprising than most of us in actually undertaking such comparisons.   The book on "The Role of the State" brings together papers applying a common set of questions to ten countries or regions.   One major part of the program of the Committee on Economic Growth "is to produce for a number of foreign countries comparable series of long-term records of economic growth." [9]   As one example of the insights obtained by this comparative method, I should like to cite the demonstration by Bert F. Hoselitz and Simon Kuznets that "the supply of agricultural land per capita is much lower in most underdeveloped countries today" than it was in the countries of Western Europe, and *a fortiori* in the United States, on the eve of their industrial revolutions.[10] This is a sobering observation and one of great significance in assessing the prospects of development.

Yet there remain certain points to be considered before economic historians can agree to abdicate in favor of the new discipline of Economic Growth. In the first place, economic historians cannot accept its limitations either as to time or to subject matter.   For Economic Growth the past is prelude, or at best "preconditions," to a single apocalyptic event, which used to be called the industrial revolution and is now called the take-off into self-sustained economic growth.   Everything before this lies in an indifferentiated limbo, a sort of economic B.C.   But this will not satisfy the intellectual interests of those members of our guild who are curious about the course of economic life in primitive societies, in a "distributive economy" like ancient Egypt, in Greece or Rome, or in the Middle Ages.   Not all students will be willing to regard

---

[7] J. H. Clapham, *An Economic History of Modern Britain, the Early Railway Age, 1820–1850* (Cambridge: Cambridge University Press, 1926), Preface and Chapter II; *The Economic Development of France and Germany, 1815–1914*, 3rd edition (Cambridge: Cambridge University Press, 1928), p. 407.

[8] *Journal of Economic History*, XVII (December, 1957), pp. 554–602. See also Carter Goodrich, "The Case of the New Countries," in Douglas F. Dowd, ed., *Thorstein Veblen, A Critical Reappraisal* (Ithaca: Cornell University Press, 1958).

[9] Kuznets, "Notes on the Study of Economic Growth," p. 13.

[10] Simon Kuznets, "Underdeveloped Countries — Present Characteristics in the Light of Past Growth Problems," an unpublished paper prepared for the University of Texas Conference on Economic Development, 1958, p. 3, citing Bert F. Hoselitz, "Population Pressure, Industrialization and Social Mobility," *Population Studies*, XI (November 1957), pp. 122–135, esp. Table 1.

the history of the "hydraulic economy" of China as mere preface to the Big Push of the Chinese Communists.[11]

Nor is the economic development the only general question with which economic historians have been or should be concerned. Much of the classic work in the field has been devoted to the study of the relations between technological and economic changes on the one hand and social structure and political alignments on the other. The objective of increasing per capita income — however vital it appears in the face of the poverty and the aspirations of the developing countries — is not the only valid end of economic policy. Other issues involving human values and other effects of economic changes — on the distribution of income between individuals and classes, on stability or instability of employment, on the quality of the working life and on personal relations within industry — have provided central themes for economic historians in the past. A considerable body of the work in the field has indeed been devoted not to the triumphs of economic development but to an appraisal of the social costs incurred in the process of the industrial revolution. Not all economic historians will be willing to accept the limitation to concern with a single issue of policy, and members of the profession must remain free to act as critics as well as celebrants of economic progress.

Even economic historians who are primarily concerned with a study of the recent past and of its implications for the present and future, and who accept for our own day the primacy of economic development as a central theme, will find that the quantitative method has distinct limitations. This is true even in the description of economic growth. Figures of income and production, however cleverly devised, will tell only part of the story; and this is particularly true of the decisive changes by which a fully pecuniary economy replaces an older order based largely on production for subsistence and barter. Since by its nature one of these societies produces abundant figures and the other does not, a quantitative statement of the difference between the two must rest very heavily on the method of imputation.

What is more important is that attempts to deal with causation, to consider what factors lead to development in one situation and stagnation in another, necessarily become qualitative in their nature. Encouragement of national income accounting in the developing countries, and the use of such techniques as input-output analysis, may be of great practical value in assisting these countries to formulate their objectives and to test their results. But they will not of themselves tell why some programs succeed and others fail. The western economist who goes to an underdeveloped country on a mission of technical assistance quickly discovers that the most stubborn obstacles in

[11] For definition of "distributive economy," see Karl Polanyi, Conrad M. Arensberg and Harry W. Pearson, eds., *Trade and Market in the Early Empires* (Glencoe, Ill.: The Free Press, 1957).

For definition of "hydraulic economy," see Karl A. Wittfogel, *Oriental Despotism, a Comparative Study of Total Power* (New Haven: Yale University Press, 1957), esp. Chapter II.

the way of increased production are matters of deep-rooted habit and customs and social attitudes, and many of the academic students of economic development have come to ask their questions in similar terms. What are the factors that produce what Arthur Lewis calls "The Will to Economize?" [12] What makes for the spread of the pecuniary calculus? Under what circumstances will the masses of the people see economic advancement as a real possibility? What factors make for resistance or receptivity to technological change and to the unfamiliar disciplines of factory and office? What determines the balance of savings against conspicuous consumption? Under what circumstances will business and especially industrial leadership acquire the prestige held by the older occupations of government, war, religion, and landed proprietorship? What are the sources of vigorous entrepreneurship, private or governmental?

None of these questions can be answered solely in quantitative terms. No doubt they are difficult to answer in any terms at all, but it must be emphasized that questions exactly like these have been explored by economic historians in their attempts to explain the transformation of the western world. Such studies, indeed, form a large part of the corpus of traditional economic history. Consider for example the contributions of Werner Sombart on the spread of bookkeeping and accountancy, of Max Weber and R. H. Tawney on the Protestant Ethic, or of Schumpeter and the enterpreneurial school on the nature of business leadership and innovation. The President of our Association has recently provided a specific example of the application of historical method to a developmental problem by asking Puerto Rican businessmen of today questions quite similar to those which he asked of the letters and journals of the American railroad leaders of the nineteenth century.[18] The attempt to understand the conditions of economic progress in the developing countries will require the full and sensitive application of the insights and methods that have been devised by the economic historians of the past, together with imaginative use of the newer contributions of sociology and anthropology. What is needed in the study of economic development is a broadening of the range of inquiry rather than a narrowing to purely quantitative method.

I asked at the beginning of this paper whether economic history was to be thought of as one field of inquiry or two. No one, I am sure, would wish to impose a single orthodoxy of method. I should, however, regard it as a tragic waste of intellectual resources if the present lines of division among students of economic change were to harden into the establishment of two separate and non-communicating disciplines. Economic historians of the more conventional sort have great need of the stimulus provided by the stu-

---

[12] W. A. Lewis, *The Theory of Economic Growth* (London: George Allen & Unwin, 1955), esp. Chapter II.

[18] Thomas C. Cochran, *The Puerto Rican Businessman, a Study in Cultural Change* (Philadelphia: University of Pennsylvania Press, 1959), and *Railroad Leaders, 1845–1890, the Business Mind in Action* (Cambridge: Harvard University Press, 1953).

dents of Economic Growth with their concentration on a major problem, their powerful use of quantitative techniques, and their emphasis on comparative study. But the students of Economic Growth have, I believe, no less need of the insights and the methods of the economic historians who write prose, who use "literary" as well as statistical source, and who attempt to understand the infinite variety of social factors that determine the complex processes of economic development. □

✧ **7** ✧

The Professors Discover American Business *

HAROLD F. WILLIAMSON

In itself the discovery of business by the professors is hardly newsworthy. Academic writing on the subject, especially by economists, began at least two hundred years ago in France and England. In the United States a somewhat sporadic interest in business and businessmen became more intensified after 1900, as an increasing number of economists, political scientists, sociologists, psychologists, and even psychiatrists began to explore the subject.

In recent years a new group of scholars has "discovered" American business. They are the business historians or business biographers who have already made noteworthy contributions to a better understanding of American business. Undoubtedly their most important influence is through that teaching in schools and colleges which deals with business and businessmen. They are also affecting other disciplines by showing the importance of adding a time perspective to their findings; that economic principles, for example, need to be put into a proper historical setting before adequate policy conclusions can be drawn.

Of equal significance is the fact that not only have the business historians discovered American business, but American business has discovered the business historians. Businessmen are becoming increasingly aware of the contributions that histories of their own concerns can make to a better general understanding of business. They have also found that such histories can do much to acquaint their customers, employees, and management personnel with the nature of their operations, how the company got where it is, the reasons for its policies, and its place in the industry and the economy. They have come to recognize a common interest with the business historians in

* Taken and adapted from an address, "The Professors Discover American Business," by Harold F. Williamson before the Northwestern University Associates, Northwestern University, Evanston and Chicago, Illinois, about 1956. Used by permission of the American Economic Association.

contributing to knowledge and are willing to work out the problems this type of research involves.

FROM MUCKRAKER TO SCHOLAR

To a very considerable extent the first and frequently the most lasting impression held by Americans about business comes from courses in American history. Until quite recently these impressions have tended to reflect an incomplete and inaccurate account of the history of business and businessmen in the United States. This point was well brought out in 1943 by Stanley Pargellis, Librarian of the Newberry Library in Chicago, in an address to the Newcomen Society on the subject, *The Judgment of History on American Business*. By way of illustration, Dr. Pargellis called attention to a currently popular book called *Documents in American History*, described by the publishers as containing "the fundamental sources" of American history and as being a "larger and better balanced collection than any predecessor." Included were famous state papers, great speeches, key pronouncements of diplomacy, leading Supreme Court decisions, and important political platforms. For the post-Civil War period this collection included such items as the Resolutions of the National Grange, the Preamble of the Constitution of the Knights of Labor, Henry George on the Single Tax, the platform of the Populist Party, Bryan's Cross of Gold Speech, the platforms of the Socialist and the Progressive parties of 1912, excerpts from the 1915 Pugo committee report on monopoly, Wilson on the New Freedom, the Preamble of the Industrial Workers of the World, La Follette's platform of 1924, leading decisions in industrial labor matters since Munn vs. Illinois, and the various acts of the New Deal. But there was ". . . not one single document which gave the attitudes, the arguments, the economic and political philosophy of businessmen." As Dr. Pargellis pointed out,

> . . . If an uninformed but intelligent stranger, ignorant of American or other history, should read the story in these documents alone, he would necessarily have to deduce, from such apparent unanimity of opinion, that the enemy against which all these different groups were arrayed, *i.e.*, corporate wealth, was, in the words of the Springfield grange of 1873, "detrimental to the public prosperity, corrupting in (its) management, and dangerous to republican institutions"; he would have to admit that the various adjectives used to describe this "invisible and intolerable power," such as "poisonous," "plundering," "merciless," "unprincipled," "extortionate," "cruel," "greedy," were justified by the noticeable absence of any defense.[1]

The reasons for this kind of an emphasis are not difficult to determine. The first important writing about American businessmen began around the turn of the century when a group of journalists, tagged by Theodore Roose-

---

[1] Stanley Pargellis, *The Judgment of History on American Business*, A Newcomen Address, 1943, p. 10.

velt as the "muck rakers," began to turn out their "best sellers." Ida Tarbell's *History of the Standard Oil Company* and Gustav Myers' *The History of Great American Fortunes*, for example, became minor classics. In best journalistic style, these authors not only picked the more colorful personalities for treatment but pointed up the more lurid aspects of their careers — business and personal — for discussion. It was not long before the term "robber barons" became an accepted part of our vocabulary. Strictly speaking, of course, the products of this school of writers were not business histories. They were highly personalized accounts of individuals whose more mundane business activities were largely ignored.

It was about this same time that American historians began to move away from their previous preoccupation with political and military events to a consideration of the economic and business factors that have affected our history. It was perhaps inevitable that the writers of textbooks and the teachers should draw upon the works of the muckrakers for information about how business operated in the United States. It made for much more dramatic presentation of material to identify a Rockefeller, a Carnegie, a Fisk, a Drew, or a Gould as individuals or prototypes responsible for the shortcomings of a business and industrial society which was undergoing tremendous change.

But even more important in affecting the writing and teaching of American history was the lack of material which a conscientious scholar could draw upon to give a more accurate account of American business. There was the work of the economic historians who were giving increased attention to the nature of American economic development, our adoption of mass production and mass marketing methods, our emphasis upon technology, the increases in productivity of labor, and a general expansion in living standards. But these were not enough to offset the impressions gained from the journalistic approach. Dealing principally with entire industries or the economy as a whole, the accounts of the economic historians were especially weak in giving any realistic picture of operations of the individual firm. Questions such as how it raised its capital, managed its finances, handled its labor, changed its production methods or marketing procedures, and in general adapted its policies to changing circumstances were relatively neglected.

One of the principal difficulties faced by scholars who might have wished to explore this aspect of business was the lack of access to the records which would enable such a story to be told. Census data, court cases, government hearings, newspaper and magazine accounts were readily available. But the business records, the raw material for a more accurate and objective evaluation of American business practices, were largely untouched. In part this was the result of the attitude of business managements who felt that their records should not be made available to outsiders. In part this was due to a lack of appreciation on the part of scholars of the significance this type of research might have.

It was not until the 1930's that the first real start was made toward filling in these gaps in our knowledge by the writing of business biographies, the histories of individual business concerns. Appropriately the leadership came from the Harvard Business School where Professor Gras started the Harvard Studies in Business History. Beginning in the 1940's, other educational institutions such as New York University, Indiana, Michigan, Stanford, and Northwestern joined Harvard in encouraging members of their faculties to do this kind of research.

"PUFFERY" IS NOT HISTORY

Free lance writers, public relations firms, advertising agencies, and company personnel soon joined the academicians in writing about individual companies. They added very considerably to the list of over nine hundred " business history titles " received by Dun and Bradstreet's library up to mid-1952, most of them published since the end of World War I.[2]

In terms of contributing to a better understanding of business operations, this list is less impressive than it sounds. A breakdown of the nine hundred titles shows that the bulk of the items noted were brief pamphlets or illustrated brochures. They contain little more information than biographical sketches of executives and descriptions of the products and services of the company involved. They fall into the class of institutional advertisements but by no stretch of the imagination can they be considered business histories.

Of the titles reported by Dun and Bradstreet covering the period since 1945, there were, however, over seventy-five book-length histories. Some twenty of these were prepared by experienced economic or business historians, while the remaining fifty-five were written by free lance journalists, by personnel within the company's organization, or by consulting firms which undertook to provide authorship for this purpose. Whatever virtues the products of this second group of writers may possess, I doubt very seriously that on the whole they contain very much which contributes to a better understanding of the operations of American business. They are quite likely to be characterized by book reviewers, scholars, and the general public as "puff jobs," not to be taken seriously as authentic sources of information.

It is the rare executive or company employee who, however well qualified he may be on technical grounds, has the objectivity to write a thoroughly unbiased account. The free lance journalist usually concentrates on colorful episodes and personalities, seldom pushing his analysis beyond the superficial aspects of the business.

The so-called "popular" or "puff histories" may have some value in public relations, but as one of my colleagues has pointed out, these books usually go to stockholders and others who are already staunch friends of the company and "the very small public who buy expensive books that will both entertain

---

[2] James H. Soltow, "The Business Use of Business History," *The Business History Review*, Vol. XXIX, No. 3 (September 1955), p. 227.

and put them to sleep of an evening." One executive at least felt that his company's popular history impressed stockholders much less than the free lunch and liquor at the annual meeting at which the book was distributed.[3]

It is the business histories prepared by well-qualified authors working under conditions that insure the objectivity of their analysis and with full access to the business records of the business concerns involved which are making the real contribution to a better understanding of American business.[4] They are the sources which conscientious students and writers of American history are drawing upon for more accurate information on this important phase of American development. This information has already begun to affect the teaching of American history. As American history is a popular course, with individual classes having up to a thousand members, the multiplied effects of this exposure are impressive. Business historians are also supplying new insights on the working of business over a period of time, which economists and allied social scientists are incorporating in their thinking.

THE MAINTENANCE OF STANDARDS

To be successful, this relatively new approach to the study of American business by business historians requires the solution of a number of problems that affect both the authors and the companies involved.

For one thing, business history writing is time consuming and expensive. Barring planned or accidental destruction, the business records of a firm or corporation which has been in operation for fifty, seventy-five, or one hundred years, may run into hundreds of thousands or even millions of individual items. Only a fraction of these items needs to be examined individually for the purposes of a history, but their selection, processing, and the preparation of the final manuscript may well take the time of the author and a small staff from one to three or four years to complete.

While their ranks are increasing, the number of persons qualified to take on the responsibility for this kind of work is still relatively small. The principal author must have the kind of training and experience which will enable him to identify and analyze the major factors — both internal and external — which have influenced the company's development. Without losing the objectivity of an outside observer, he must have a sympathetic understanding of the circumstances and reasons that led to major policy decisions by the man-

---

[3] Soltow, *op. cit.*, p. 235.

[4] Some of the better known works of this type are Thomas Cochran, *The Pabst Brewing Company*; Boris Emmet and John Jeuck, *Catalogues and Counters, A History of Sears-Roebuck and Company*; George S. Gibb, *The Saco-Lowell Shops: Textile Machinery Building in New England, 1813–1949*; Ralph W. Hidy, *The House of Baring in American Trade and Finance: English Merchant Bankers at Work, 1763–1861*; Ralph M. Hower, *The History of an Advertising Agency: N. W. Ayer & Son at Work, 1869–1949* and *History of Macy's of New York, 1858–1919: Chapters in the Evolution of the Department Store*; and Thomas R. Navin, *The Whitin Machine Works Since 1831: A Textile Machinery Company in an Industrial Village*.

agement. While he cannot become an expert in all phases of a particular business, he should be able to ask the right questions and to incorporate the answers into the history.

Actual costs of preparing a scholarly history will depend on a number of variables such as the size of the firm, the nature of its business, the time span covered, and the volume of its records. In practice the amounts involved have ranged from around $10,000 for a small, short-lived concern, $20,000 to $50,000 for intermediate or larger companies, to a figure reported in excess of $500,000 for the multi-volume history of Standard Oil of New Jersey.

The financing of business histories has come and probably will continue to come from companies interested in having their histories prepared. This method of financing means that both the scholars and educational institutions which undertake such research must avoid any suspicion that "he who pays the piper calls the tune." They must make sure that projects are carried out under conditions which will permit the final product to meet the accepted academic standards of being both objective and a contribution to knowledge.

Among educational institutions provision for maintaining these standards are typically provided by the type of agreement worked out at Northwestern University under the guidance and supervision of a faculty committee appointed by the president. Among other items the standard agreement between Northwestern University and the individual company provides that

> It is understood that in conducting this research and in preparing the manuscript, the authors will enjoy the independence accorded to all scholars in the University world. This includes access to all records pertaining to the period included in the study, and the freedom to judge the relevance of evidence, to make interpretations, and to publish the findings. . . . If any disagreement should arise concerning either the facts or the interpretations of the data which cannot be resolved by consultation with the management, then a footnote will be added to the manuscript stating the Company's disagreement and the reasons for its position.

These provisions may strike some as being too much of a one-way street; they may feel that the accompanying "Letter to an Industrial Historian," reprinted from *Punch,* is less of a satire than the editors intended. It is true that the decision to turn over the business records of a firm to outsiders who are free to evaluate and interpret their historical significance requires a considerable faith in the integrity, ability, and judgment of the researchers involved. But those who are willing to make such an arrangement are assured that the end product will largely escape criticism of bias, censorship, or lack of objectivity so frequently leveled at sponsored research and the so-called "popular or puff" histories.

USES OF A BUSINESS HISTORY

The small but growing number of business histories prepared under arrangements substantially like those followed by Northwestern, gives evidence of the "discovery" of business historians by businessmen. Far from viewing the former as intruders, businessmen are making it possible for scholars to push their explorations under highly favorable circumstances.

A recent survey covering some thirty-nine companies which had published full-length histories showed that a desire to make information available to scholars ranked next to public relations as the most important reason for having their histories written.[5] In general it may be noted that when the management thought principally in terms of public relations, the books were written by free lance authors or company personnel. With few exceptions these histories were not used for any other purpose. It was found, however, that the more scholarly works were also useful in public relations. One company, for example, felt that an unbiased account of its activities would counteract the effects of a prior publication highly critical of its founder. Several companies expected their histories to be of assistance in relations with the public in communities where its plants were located, to combat local criticisms of "outside control."

This survey indicated several other uses to which carefully prepared company histories had been put. A number reported that they had given or made copies of their histories available to employees. In many instances it was felt that the result had been an increase in the employee's pride and interest in the company and a better understanding of management problems.

Most companies distributed their histories to customers or in the case of banks to principal depositors, or by insurance companies to agents. A number reported that they felt this distribution helped explain particular company policies to the members of the groups who received their histories. Some were able to draw interesting and colorful advertising copy from their histories.

The other major use to which these histories were put, and perhaps the most important single purpose they can serve for management, has been as a guide to management policies and for training management personnel. One of the most valuable assets of any business is never listed in its books of account, although it may be reflected in the market value of its stock. This unlisted asset is the experience of the organization's key executives. To be able to profit from past experience and to appreciate the circumstances affecting major policy decisions, is as important to the business or corporate entity as to the individual. But this is an asset that may easily be lost or dissipated. Those members of management whose experience is most valuable are often too busy with current problems to impart their knowledge to others. Preoccupation with day-to-day affairs makes orderly and systematic formula-

[5] Soltow, *op. cit.*, p. 229.

tion of this information difficult. Casual recollections are frequently inaccurate as time tends to magnify the decisions which were sound and minimize those which turned out badly. Myths about the organization's past become accepted as reality.

A carefully prepared, well documented company history can do much to preserve the corporate memory. It will record both the triumphs and mistakes of management in the past, it will help explain when and why many current policies were adopted, it will indicate to a younger generation how the company survived depressions, and adapted to changing economic and social conditions. To all persons associated with the business, shop workers, supervisors, and junior executives, it should explain how the company got where it is and its place in the industry and the economy. At a time when American business is increasingly concerned with personnel relations and management training, it could well be that a carefully prepared company history is worth the cost for this purpose alone.

LESSONS LEARNED FROM BUSINESS HISTORIES

And what have the professors learned from their discovery and explorations of American business? What conclusions can they draw from the carefully prepared histories of individual concerns? One result has been an addition to the knowledge of the development of parts of the American economy which have been relatively neglected, the story of companies and their managements that never made the headlines by being involved in a major strike, by appearing before a congressional committee, or being indicted for violation of the anti-trust laws. The histories of the Whitin Machine Works, the Saco-Lowell Shops, and the Bucyrus-Erie Company, give us a better understanding of the problems faced by capital goods producers. Several studies of banks have added to our understanding in that area, although the role of commercial banks in the middle west in the nineteenth century has yet to be told. The history of Macy's and Sears-Roebuck have contributed to a better understanding of merchandising, as has the history of N. W. Ayer & Son in the field of advertising. This list could be multiplied, even though there are many areas in which the first company history has yet to be written.

Even in fields much better known there have been notable contributions. Several good accounts have shed new light on the land practices of American railroads. Others have indicated that roads like the Santa Fe and Burlington, for example, followed a different evolution than the Erie under Gould. The forthcoming histories of Standard of New Jersey, Standard of Indiana, and the Shell Oil Company, should do much to give new perspective to the growth of the petroleum industry.

We have also made some discoveries on a different level. It is clear, for example, that there are two especially critical phases in the life span of an individual business organization.   One comes at the start, when the casualty rate is high.   In the case of the Northwestern Mutual Life Insurance Company, this came when two of its insureds were killed in a train wreck and the president had to borrow from a bank to pay claims amounting to $3,500.

The second critical phase involves what may be termed the institutionalization of the business, when it is organized in such a way as to provide guides or policies for management decisions and a program for management training and succession.   The effectiveness of institutionalization may be put to the test when the founder of an organization turns over his job to his successor. Or it may come later, as in the case of Winchester, when the third generation of family management was unable to meet the challenge of the job, and the company passed into the hands of a management group which attempted with disastrous results to follow the Liggett drug store methods in the distribution of guns, ammunition, and hardware.

Another discovery which has come in part from business history is the importance of other variables than those traditionally used by economists in evaluating business operations.   Here the models used by economists have proved quite inadequate.   Essentially static in nature, they have emphasized cost-price-output relationships almost to the exclusion of such other factors as product line, innovation, and the time element.   The result has been that much of the reasoning, and a great deal of the anti-trust legislation, based upon these theories is often quite misleading.   Not uncommonly the practices of individual concerns at a given time are in response to technological or demand conditions inherited from the past.   It has been found, for example, that firms often fail to adjust prices to changes in demand or cost because they fear the impact which such changes may have on their markets in the future.   Agreements on price — tacit or formal — are not always accompanied by a lack of vigorous competition on other levels.   This does not mean that economists are ready to abandon their concern about restrictions of competition or that they are willing to concede there is little to worry about in this regard.   But on the other hand, they have found that the term "competition" is a much more complex thing than had long been supposed and that apparently anti-social business practices may stem less from conscious invidious intent by businessmen than from attempts to adjust to market situations in which businessmen find themselves.   This discovery has led to a re-examination of the nature of competition by economists, the courts, and the government.   Professor Kenneth Galbraith's recent book on *Countervailing Power*, in which he argues that big business and vigorous competition are not incompatible, represents one result of a new orientation.

There are many other discoveries that might be mentioned, such as the role that aggressive business management has played in our economic growth, a greater appreciation of the complexities of operating a large business concern, the circumstances under which it may be advisable for a firm to be a follower rather than a leader, and of particular importance, the fact that twentieth century business standards and ethics are a far cry from those which were acceptable in the nineteenth century.

These examples illustrate a few of the results which have already emerged from a preliminary exploration of the historical aspects of American business. They indicate the great promise this type of research holds for a better and more complete understanding of this complex and important subject, a promise which can be realized by the continued cooperation between scholars and businessmen.

■ **Suggested Procedure for the Preparation of a Company History** [6]

1. *Selection of the Author.* If the history is to be an objective, well documented account of the company's growth, the selection of the author should be made in consultation with recognized scholars or educational institutions engaged in this type of historical research.

2. *Record Survey.* As a preliminary step, before any final arrangements with the author, a survey should be made of the company records to determine whether they are adequate for the preparation of the history.

3. *Agreement between Authors and the Company.* Among the more important items which should be covered in the agreement are:

    a. Terms under which the author is to prepare the history.

    b. Provision for working space and facilities at the company.

    c. The designation of a company officer to serve as liaison between the author and company personnel.

    d. Agreement on a "cut-off" date for a full historical account. It may well be that for many reasons the company will not wish to have published a detailed account of its history during recent years.

    e. Provision for review of the manuscript by designated company officer or officers and its return to the authors within a reasonable length of time.

4. *Internal Publicity.*

    a. All personnel of the company should be notified that the history is being prepared and be urged to cooperate with the author and his staff.

    b. Personnel should be encouraged to call attention to any documents or material such as diaries, journals, reports, *et cetera*, of historical interest which may not be in the company's archives.

    c. Provision should be made for interviews with older or retired employees. □

---

[6] These suggestions are based upon experience at Northwestern University in the preparation of a number of company histories.

Letter to an Industrial Historian *

KERN AND GALLOWGLASS LTD.

R. *Gibbons, Esq., Ph.D., M.A.,*   Quality Hardware and Plumbers
Porterhouse College,   Sundriesmen
Umbridge University   GATH WORKS, S.E. 35

250TH ANNIVERSARY HISTORY

DEAR MR. GIBBONS, — May I say, first of all, that the Board wish me to congratulate you upon the truly remarkable research that you have carried out for the 250th Anniversary History of Kern and Gallowglass? There are, however, a few criticisms of a very minor nature that they wish to make.

Generally. The History appears to be rather longer than was envisaged. By "full book-length" the Board had in mind the generally accepted meaning of the phrase: enclosed with this letter for your guidance is a copy of *Favourite Weekly* (which please return at your convenience) in which, as you will observe, a Full Length Book is given away.

In reducing your MS the following notes may be of assistance.

pp. 2–26. Cut drastically. It is surely of little interest that the Founders of the Company first became acquainted in the Fleet Prison.

pp. 30–35. Omit. It was never proved.

p. 36. *"unmitigated and unprincipled scoundrels."* Substitute "somewhat unorthodox and high-spirited personalities."

pp. 40–96. The Company's part in the collapse of the *South Sea Bubble* is irrelevant and might throw doubt on the financial acumen of the present Board. Omit.

pp. 107–125. The Board feels that the previously unrecorded letter from Lord Nelson attributing Admiral Byng's loss of Minorca to inferior products of this firm should remain unrecorded. Not only was the affair no business of Lord Nelson's, occurring as it did before he was born, but in view of the fact that this highly controversial letter has now been unfortunately mislaid they feel that it is possible that you have misread the contents and they would hesitate, as a matter of historical principle, to publish such an important letter without adequate documentation. The Chairman, who recently spent a holiday in the neighbouring island of Majorca, feels this particularly strongly. Omit.

pp. 132–137. *Grant of Royal Warrant under Geo. III.* Delete all references to the insanity of the monarch.

pp. 195–199. *Loss of Royal Warrant under Geo. IV.* The instability of the Prince Regent's character should be emphasized.

* (C) PUNCH), London. Used by permission.

p. 242. *"Virtue was its own reward — supplemented by a dividend of* 120 *per cent."* An unfortunate phrase. Omit. Emphasis should be laid, rather, on the provision at this period of Model Dwellings for Protestant Communicant Artizans.

pp. 249–268. *Siege of Sebastopol.* What the soldiers said is not evidence! Omit.

No page. *The Bronze Medal* awarded to the Company at the International Exhibition at Clermont-Ferrand in 1872 appears to have been overlooked.

pp. 275–296. *South African War.* The Company is hoping to expand its trade with the Union. Rewrite, omitting all reference to Boers.

No page. Some reference should be made to the close personal friendship with the Crown of our Directors Sir Harry Wormwood and Alderman Isaac Bagshot. (A photograph of them in the Royal Party at Ascot is available for illustration.)

pp. 301 *et seq.* All references to the close personal friendship with the Crown of Mrs. Phœbe Gallowglass should be omitted.

pp. 320–340. *World War I.* Much more emphasis should be laid on the events leading up to the raising of our late Chairman to the Style and Honour of Baron Kern of Stamford Hill. The far-sighted provision of inexpensive metal tea-pots for Government offices contributed incalculably to the maintenance of "morale" on the "home-front."

pp. 345–352. *Shareholders' Protection Association.* Omit entirely all references to this body. They can only revive ill-feeling.

pp. 358–393. *World War II.* "Blitz" of London, so-called German Atrocities, War Trials, etc., etc. Drastically revise. Such harmful and biased references cannot but cause unnecessarily hard feelings at a time when Germany is being welcomed back into her traditional place in the ranks of Democracy . . . They must also adversely effect the efforts of our subsidiary Company — Kern und Galgenstein AG — to secure a footing in the British market. More stress should be laid on the Company's contribution to the "War Effort." (In this connection the Chairman's Governmental appointment as Controller of Funeral Bakemeats appears to be treated unduly lightly.)

p. 398. The suggestion that Christmas should have any particular religious significance is irrelevant. Not only might it cause offence to our agnostic customers but it would severely handicap our Retailers' Yuletide Sales Drive which, it is intended, shall in future commence in August. Omit.

These cuts should make it possible to include a verbatim report of our Chairman's speech at the last Banquet of the Quality Hardware Manufacturers Mutual Benefit and Price-Fixing Association.

Yours sincerely,
Tom Girtin, *Secretary* ◻

❖ 9 ❖

The Businessman and Business History *

AUGUST C. BOLINO

Recently there has been a tremendous upsurge in the number of business histories emanating from the nation's presses. The Dun and Bradstreet list for 1952 shows that two-thirds to three-fourths of the 900 titles in their compilation were published since the end of World War II.[1]

Not only are more and more of these histories being printed, but most of them are favorable in their attitudes toward the businessman. When compared with the traditional, prejudiced, and usually unrealistic notions of the journalists, economists and historians of the past, this reconsideration of the business leaders of our time is very remarkable.

The prejudices against the business life are very old. Christ Himself admonished the Pharisees to render to Caesar what are Caesar's, and since that time many individuals have interpreted this to mean that we must eschew all things that are material. There is abundant evidence to show that in all ages the businessman was held in ill-repute. The Medieval man who made his living at business was thought to be "immoral," and he could only atone for this debased occupation by giving alms and by becoming a connoisseur of the arts.[2] Shakespeare had his Shylock, Molière had his "Would-Be Gentleman," Napoleon contemptuously applied Adam Smith's description of the English as a nation of shopkeepers to his neighbors across the Channel, and of course, the Victorians never talked about money. The industrial revolution affected countries in different ways because of these institutional barriers to expansion. For example, French economic growth was impeded in the nineteenth century because the French considered business a stepping stone to the civil service. Businessmen were placed at the bottom of the scale of the bourgeoisie and the best talent turned to law, medicine and government. In the United States and in Germany these attitudes did not exist to the same degree and economic progress was very rapid in both countries. But this economic achievement created the very forces which were to produce an anti-business element in our society. Increased production led to increased capital accumulation and a greater concentration of wealth and economic power. The emphasis on economic progress at the expense of social progress fathered the "muckraking movement" in the early years of the twentieth century which

* Taken and adapted from August C. Bolino, "The Businessman and Business History," *Commerce and Finance*, Number 3, February 1, 1958, pp. 1–3. Used by permission of the author and publisher.

[1] A *List of Business Histories in the Business Library, Dun and Bradstreet, Inc.*, 1 September 1952 (New York: Dun and Bradstreet, Inc., 1952).

[2] For a fourteenth century case dealing with the conflicts between business leadership and producing culture, see Stanley S. Miller, "Business and Fear of Materialism," *Bulletin of the Business Historical Society*, XXVI (September, 1952), pp. 107–121.

resulted in a spate of business histories that were so emotionally conceived and so biased that the businessman has not yet fully recovered from the blows delivered by Ida Tarbell, Lincoln Steffens, Thomas Lawson, and Upton Sinclair. That businessmen needed to be criticized is irrefutable, but that they deserved the kind of treatment they got is uncertain.

The most unfortunate result of this aspect of the reform movement was the creation of a feeling of mistrust between businessmen and the intellectuals. The businessmen felt that the historians were always teaching that businessmen were hypocritical, selfish and unscrupulous.[3] Some historians assumed that all business deals were shady. They completely neglected the role of the "robber barons" in furthering the economic development of the United States. Professor Steirgerwalt states that "When American Historians have not belittled the businessman they have neglected him," and he attributes this neglect to a disinterest or a lack of qualifications to write an objective history.[4] It is the job of competent business historians to right the scales if they need righting. The historian and the businessman must work together to record the differing opinions in our society. The businessman will get his dues only if he allows the objective recorder to evaluate his role in the community.

Here, then, is the bridge that spans the great chasm that was created in an earlier era. As Professor Hidy said:

> . . . if the historian can produce an accurate objective history of the functioning of big business in America, he may aid in a more rational formulation of public policy. Voters may show more discrimination and judgment in the selection of representatives. Politicians may use business less as a whipping boy and may sponsor legislation which recognized the place of the large unit in American economic and social life.[5]

This need for better balanced and relatively unbiased information on the business subject partly explains the resurgence of business history today, but other important reasons may be cited: (1) European firms had been for years commissioning anniversary histories, (2) the New Deal attitudes compelled foresighted businessmen to turn to scholars to right the public relations balance, (3) the trend towards national planning created an interest in how firms had acquired their present dimensions, and (4) tax regulations are conducive to generous subsidizations of business historians. "Indeed we may label the fifty-two per cent corporate income tax as among the historians' best friends." [6]

[3] For some prejudiced notions on business, see Henrietta M. Larson, "Danger in Business History," *Harvard Business Review,* XXII (Spring, 1944), pp. 316–327.

[4] A. K. Steigerwalt, "The Boom in Business History," *Michigan Business Review,* IX (January, 1957), p. 25.

[5] Ralph W. Hidy, "Importance of the History of the Large Business Unit," *Bulletin of the Business Historical Society,* XXII (February, 1948), p. 6.

[6] The quotation and the four reasons are taken from George S. Gibb's "Introduction" in Lorna M. Daniell's, *Studies in Enterprise* (Boston: Harvard University, Graduate School of Business Administration, 1957).

Business history deserves the emphasis that it is receiving today. Business has penetrated American Society to an extent unequalled anywhere in the world and it is the duty of businessmen to help preserve the record of this achievement. This does not mean a "blind amassing of facts in isolation." Business history aims at providing "the empirical data upon which a better judgment of the businessman's role in the past can be based." [7] More specifically, business history is the study of the operation and administration of business in the past. Its fundamental objectives are to make clear the changes which have occurred in policy, control, and business management and to give explanations for these changes.[8]   As such, business history becomes "the study and appraisal of man's reaction to the challenge of a business opportunity, with the focal point the process of individual or group decision-making." [9] This interpretation of business stresses the social aspects of the businessman and it is in line with the recent emphasis in business literature on the non-economic forces affecting economic growth. Undoubtedly, the profit motive is still the dominant incentive for expansion, but few will now deny that other factors shape business decisions.[10]

ADVANTAGES TO MANAGEMENT

Of what use is a business history to a business manager? Generally we may say that it would help management in dealing with problems of administration, training of executives, and maintaining good relations with employees, customers, and the general public. These require additional comment.

1. *The problems of administration.* The business historian can help solve many policy questions. The following only suggest possible aids. What is the optimum size of business unit? How big is too big? Do the answers vary from industry to industry? Has the large unit abused its economic power? What is the best price policy? Is it true that the quasi-monopolist can give better service, better-quality goods at a lower price than can the more competitive firm? Here a history of Standard Oil, General Motors, General Electric, American Shoe Manufacturing, or Alcoa may be of great value.

[7] W. Woodruff, "History and the Businessman," *Business History Review*, XXX (September, 1956), p. 251.

[8] Henrietta M. Larson, "Business History: Retrospect and Prospect," *Bulletin of the Business Historical Society*, XXI (December, 1947), p. 173.

[9] Richard C. Overton, "Can the Records Manager Help the Business Historian," *Business History Review*, XXIX (September, 1955), p. 211.

[10] In the last few years, social scientists have made great efforts to synthesize the theories of business growth. This has resulted in many interdisciplinary volumes that stress psychological motives of business. W. W. Rostow is a pioneer in this field; his *The Process of Economic Growth* (New York: W. W. Norton and Co., 1952) makes investment a function of political and social factors as well as capital yields. See also: Karl F. Helleiner, "Moral Conditions of Economic Growth," *Journal of Economic History*, XI (Spring, 1951), pp. 97–116; Norman S. Buchanan, and Howard S. Ellis, *Approaches to Economic Development* (New York: The Twentieth Century Fund, 1955); and Thomas Easterbook, "Uncertainty and Economic Change," *Journal of Economic History*, XIV (1954), pp. 346–360.

Another business management problem is "What is the best way to manage a subsidiary?" Standard Oil of New Jersey allows the subsidiaries a free rein and this system works well. But would it work equally well for all types of firms? Professor Raymond DeRoover offers an example of how the business historian can help the man of business. In his book, *The Medici Bank*, he tells how the Medici controlled managers of distant branches, and he covers all the problems of centralization and decentralization and the responsibilities of the head office and the branches.[11] The businessman of today would find that his problems have much in common with those of Cosimo and Lorenzo de'Medici and that he could perhaps use the same technique in meeting those problems.

2. *The training of executives.* A business history can also be used as a part of a training program. It will provide young executives with an immediate source where they can learn of the evolution of company policy, the progressiveness of the company, its community relations, and its civic responsibility.[12] Nothing but gain can come to executives who have an acquaintance with accurate business histories, placed in their proper political and social milieu. Someone once said that "who knows only his own generation remains always a child," and this seems particularly applicable to business executives. They must observe the dynamic nature of business and its successes and be aware of the need for flexible, dynamic policies and good management methods.

3. *Relations with employees and the public.* Many companies are distributing complimentary copies of their histories to all employees. Most firms at least provide supervisory personnel with histories where they are available. Firms can also use histories for advertising purposes in two ways: first, the histories can be given to all customers (some companies print inexpensive editions to donate to schools and libraries) and second, several companies use historical items from their business histories as the framework for present-day advertising copy. United States Steel, General Electric, and General Motors have been doing much in this area using the television medium. The results of the survey conducted by Soltow give some indication of the reasons why firms authorized the writing of business histories. The replies of thirty-nine executives are reported in table 1.

Corporations, then, ought to set up some sort of mechanism to facilitate historical research, and they should where possible commission that a business history of their firms be written. But what is the cost of a business history? The writer knows of only one survey which gives at least a hint of the answer. Mr. Soltow's findings, based on 33 responses, are reported in table 2.

These figures are for fairly large corporations and include all expenses to the company for writing and publication of from 2,000 to 150,000 copies.

---

[11] *The Medici Bank: Its Organization, Management, Operations and Decline* (New York: New York University Press, 1948).

[12] See James H. Soltow, "The Business Use of Business History," *Business History Review*, XXIX (September, 1955), pp. 227–237.

█ TABLE 1   Reasons for Authorizing and Publishing a Company History

Reasons	Number
1. Institutional publicity	26
2. Willingness to make information about the company available for scholarly and educational purposes	11
3. For use in relations with employees	8
4. To provide background for supervisory employees	7
5. For use in relations with customers	6
6. No benefits of any kind expected	2

(Since some responders gave more than one reason, the sum exceeds 39.)

Source: Soltow, *op. cit.*, p. 229.

█ TABLE 2   The Cost of Business Histories

Type of History	Number of Companies Reporting Costs of					
	$10,000 or less	$11,000– 20,000	$21,000– 30,000	$31,000– 50,000	$51,000– 75,000	$76,000 and up
Popular	1	3	2	3	—	2
Scholarly	2	2	7	2	3	3
Written by Executives	–	1	1	1	–	–
TOTALS	3	6	10	6	3	5

Source. Soltow, *op. cit.*, p. 236;

The popular or "puff" histories are much more expensive and many feel that they create more ill will than good. One insurance company spent $150,000 for a history by magazine writers while a competitive company had a better, more objective history prepared by a scholar for only $20,000. For a pair of merchandising companies, the respective figures were $175,000 and $54,000.

THE HISTORIAN'S ROLE

Historians have done much to improve the record-keeping of corporations. The business history movement was founded (and is perhaps still centered) at Harvard University in the twenties. Through the efforts of Edwin Gay, Norman Gras and Henrietta Larson there developed a school which was dissatisfied with the generalizations of economists on business growth. By studying the administration of past businesses, they stressed the growing importance of the business civilization. The pace of the movement quickly accelerated: The American Council of Learned Societies, with the Social Science Research Council, set up in 1929 a Joint Committee on Materials and Research. The American Library Association established the Committee on Archives in the thirties, and the Committee on Research of the Economic History Association was created in the next decade. During the winter of

1945, the New York Committee on Business Records was organized to teach businessmen how to arrange their records and to foster the access of scholars to records.[18] Two years later the Business History Foundation was incorporated (nonprofit) under the laws of New York. It has supported several projects, given grants-in-aid, and underwritten publication of business histories.

To conclude, the businessman's role in society is in process of reassessment by business historians. Men of business cannot expect to have a favorable "press" and good public relations unless they allow *competent* economists to review the record of business periodically.

Corporations must make it possible for the historians to acquire data, whether this be by opening the records to scholars or by donating historical items to universities and archives. There are many advantages which accrue to companies from business histories. The obvious public relations and advertising advantages are greatly outweighed by the chief reason for the existence of business histories: that is, the management policies which emerge out of these histories and which serve as tools for effective future administration and organization of business. The historian cannot go it alone in this field; he must have the cooperation of the nation's business leaders. □

✧ **10** ✧

Aspects of Quantitative Research in Economic History *

L. E. DAVIS, J. R. T. HUGHES, AND S. REITER

1

If we are successfully to relate our work with the main body of Economic History, we must be able to show the fundamental relationship between quantitative analysis and more conventional methods of economic historians. The historian reconstructs events of the past, and with them attempts to understand the institutions and modes of behavior associated with those events. He seeks to construct a consistent story revealing the fundamental nature and meaning to us of the past, thus creating insight into the past and understanding of it — something considerably beyond a mere account of what probably

---

[18] For some of the results of the Committee see Thomas C. Cochran, "The Economics in a Business History," *Journal of Economic History*, V, Supplement (December, 1945), pp. 54–65.

* Taken and adapted from L. E. Davis, J. R. T. Hughes, and S. Reiter, "Aspects of Quantitative Research in Economic History," *The Journal of Economic History*, Vol. XX, No. 4, December 1960, pp. 539–47. Used by permission.

happened. However, this story must be based upon, and be consistent with, the reconstructed events of the past, "what probably happened."

This view of historical study is a familiar one and, in fact, almost any working historian would accept it as a definition of his activities. What has this view to do with quantitative methods in economic history, and how does quantitative economic history differ from non-quantitative writing in economic history? The answer lies partly in the nature of the materials from which the reconstruction is to be made, and partly in the technique employed to analyze these materials. First, each society generates its own accounts of, and commentaries upon, contemporary affairs, as well as its own histories of the past. This class of materials can be more or less explicitly labeled historical writings. Second, in the course of its characteristic processes each society generates a body of artifacts, debris left behind in time. The processes of economic life, for example, produce masses of receipts, books of account, legal documents, tax returns, and various kinds of rolls, lists, and records; and these materials can be used to reconstruct the past. Such a reconstruction is analogous to the process frequently employed by archeologists who utilize the surviving debris of an ancient city to provide materials for understanding the civilization that built it and lived there. Characteristically, this material consists of a mass of individual items, each of which contains a relatively insignificant piece of information. This collection, originally generated for purposes other than historical study, usually requires reorganization and analysis to enable the information contained to be brought to a form useful to the historian. That is, the information must be organized on some principle and made the basis of inferences about the past, a task familiar to the historian, but that also contains the essential elements of a statistical problem.

If we had at hand every item of the kind under consideration (for example, every warehouse receipt issued in New York State between 1870–1900), we would face the task of formulating meaningful questions with which to confront these data, and of organizing the data to bear on these questions. Thus we might be interested in the geographical distribution of warehouses, in the time-shape of business activities, in the commodity composition of consumption, or in the profitability of warehousing, and each question would require a different method of systemization and analysis. We must, therefore, first formulate a statistical-historical model in terms of which historical meaning can be given to the observations. Having formulated such a model, we are still confronted with a large collection of observations that must be statistically summarized and described. We shall have more to say later about the problems of data processing.

In fact, however, since we generally do not have the complete collection of all observations of a given land, but rather only a sample of the surviving ones, the study of the historical process is even more complicated. For in addition to the question of analysis and systemization, we must also decide, on the basis of the observations at hand, what the whole collection would reveal if we had access to complete information. **This last is the problem of statistical inference.**

In brief, the logical structure necessary to make historical reconstructions from the surviving debris of past economic life essentially involves ideas of history, economics and statistics. The offspring of such an act of interdisciplinary miscegenation calls for a name worthy of it; at Purdue the resulting discipline has been labeled "Cliometrics."

II

An examination of the literature of economic history indicates that, while the qualitative stream in the discipline has usually been the larger, there has been from earliest times a significant and respectable flow of quantitative work. The political arithmeticians — Graunt, King and the like — as early as the seventeenth century were trying to infer from data an explanation of some aspects of economic history.[1] In 1851 William Newmarch produced his pathbreaking study on the circulation of bills of exchange — a study that, in statistical sophistication (given the knowledge of the time), is the equal of anything produced more recently.[2] At yet a later date, F. W. Taussig's *History of the Tariff*, and still later, the work of Arthur Cole (as represented both by his work on the evolution of the American foreign exchange market and with W. B. Smith, *Fluctuations in American Business 1790–1860*), were attempts to infer the state of the world of the past from quantitative information.[3] The National Bureau of Economic Research, although not much given to interpretation, has produced a vast amount of quantitative information that others could use, and the works of some of their authors (Kuznets, for example) certainly fall within the category of quantitative economic history.[4]

[1] See, for example, Charles D'Avenant, *An Essay Upon the Probable Method of Making a People Gainers in the Balance of Trade* (London, 1699); John Graunt, *Natural and Political Observations Mentioned in a Following Index and Made Upon the Bills of Mortality* (London, 1662); Gregory King, *Natural and Political Observations and Conclusions Upon the State and Condition of England 1696* (London, 1810); Charles H. Hull, ed., *The Economic Writings of Sir William Petty* (Cambridge, Mass., 1899).

[2] William Newmarch, "An Attempt to Ascertain the Magnitude and Fluctuations of the Amount of Bills of Exchange (Inland and Foreign) in Circulation at One Time in Great Britain, in England, in Scotland, in Lancashire, and in Cheshire, Respectively, During Each of the Twenty Years 1828–1947, Both Inclusive; and Also Embracing in the Inquiry Bills Drawn Upon Foreign Countries," *Journal of the Statistical Society of London*, XIV (1851), 143–92.

[3] Frank W. Taussig, *The Tariff History of the United States* (New York and London: G. P. Putnam's Sons, 1888); Walter B. Smith and Arthur H. Cole, *Fluctuations in American Business 1790–1860* (Cambridge, Mass.: Harvard University Press, 1935); Arthur H. Cole, "Seasonal Variation in Sterling Exchange," *Journal of Economic and Business History*, II (Nov. 1929), 203–318; Arthur H. Cole, "Evolution of the Foreign Exchange Market of the United States," *Journal of Economic and Business History*, I (1928), 384–421.

[4] See, for example, Simon Kuznets, *National Product Since 1869* (New York: National Bureau of Economic Research, 1946); or Simon Kuznets, *Secular Movements in Production and Prices; Their Nature and Bearing Upon Cyclical Fluctuations* (Boston and New York: Houghton Mifflin, 1930); or "Long-Term Changes in the National Income of the

More recently excellent work combining economic theory and quantitative methods can be found in R. C. O. Matthew's *A Study in Trade Cycle History* and in what is perhaps the most notable recent study of this kind, the paper of Conrad and Meyer on slavery in the ante bellum south.[5]

Nonetheless, the total amount of work in the field is small. Why? Is it because quantitative work is unrewarding? We think not. The dearth of quantitative economic history can probably be traced to two factors: first, the extraordinary effort that has been necessary in the past to sift and classify quantitative information; and second, the relatively recent development of statistical theory and techniques capable of handling these problems. Let us examine each of these problems in turn.

III

Recently developed computing equipment has opened to economic historians the possibility of performing prodigies of data-processing and statistical calculation. Where the archeologist can dig with spade and hard labor into the mounds of the past to unearth artifacts, the economic historian needs power shovels and bulldozers to move the mountains of paper records. The power shovels and bulldozers are now available to economic historians, but these developments in the analysis of data by machine processing methods have scarcely been applied to the more significant questions of economic history. We need to recognize that data-processing at last provides us an opportunity to study the kinds of problems that, because of the unwieldiness of the purely mechanical processes of computation, have long been cast aside.

There is nothing novel or revolutionary in the problems themselves. There have always been problems in which masses of data had to be "processed" by one means or another; the early work on index numbers by Jevons and Sauerbeck are well-known examples of such large-scale computations. Another, and better, example of early data-processing is to be found in the work of one of our most illustrious predecessors, William Newmarch. His work is a particularly germane example of the nature of data-processing problems.

Newmarch's celebrated survey of the circulation of bills of exchange in Great Britain, one of the most brilliant contributions to the British monetary-policy debate of the mid-19th century (although not one which noticeably affected policy, interestingly enough), and subsequently, one of the pieces of historical evidence most often used in the study of century monetary phenomena, appeared in 1851.[6] Anyone who has processed data will experience a distinct "shock of recognition" when he first reads Newmarch's paper. New-

---

United States Since 1870," *Income and Wealth of the United States Trends and Structure*, Series II, pp. 10–246.

    [5] Robert C. O. Matthews, *A Study in Trade Cycle History; Economic Fluctuations in Great Britain, 1833–1842* (Cambridge, England: University Press, 1954); Alfred H. Conrad and John R. Meyer, "The Economics of Slavery in the Ante Bellum South," *Journal of Political Economy*, LXVI (April 1958), 95–130.

    [6] Newmarch, "Circulation."

march obtained a sample "at hazard" of the total bill circulation. The sample size was 4,367 inland and foreign bills with a nominal value of £1,216,974. From each bill he took three pieces of information, or a total of 13,101 separate pieces of numerical information. On the basis of this data and the stamp-tax returns on bills of exchange for Great Britain and certain subdivisions, Newmarch was able to compute an estimate of the total bill circulation. In his computation only three arithmetic operations were required once the initial classification and organization of the data had been done. Such a study by present-day computing standards would not be cumbersome. In "The First 1,945 British Steamships," for example, there were 13 initial observations per ship, or 25,285 separate pieces of numerical information on 1,945 punch cards.[7] Once on the cards, the actual computing (far more extensive than was Newmarch's) of tonnages, estimated speeds and the index of transport capacity was not a particularly tiresome job. But in Newmarch's case, one hundred years ago, 13,101 separate pieces of information to be classified, summed, averaged, and the results used to convert stamp-tax yields into aggregate value figures was an enormous undertaking. After explaining his ingenious methods to his audience, Newmarch noted that the final operations were: . . . clearly a mere matter of calculation; but I confess that, if I had foreseen, before I undertook the task, the extent and severity of the labour it would impose, I am not at all certain that I should have ventured upon the inquiry.[8]

That data-processing on this scale was done so long ago with quill pens instead of electronic computers underscores our main point. It is only the absence of machinery which is novel in the Newmarch story, not the presence of a data-processing problem. Some kinds of historical problems are by nature data-processing problems. In the past they have too often (but perhaps understandably) been neglected simply because too much labor was involved. Today, with the purely mechanical computational problems much reduced, economic historians have the means to study these questions. In particular, these new techniques will permit the opening of new sources that, while always in existence, have heretofore been largely closed to research because of the magnitude of the task involved. First, business records that hold many of the answers to questions concerning early 19th century American development can be made available to the study of broader questions than the history of a single business. While corporate letters, minutes and like documents have long been utilized in business history, the labor involved in organizing sales slips, time cards, and the like, has frequently prevented their use in producing data on prices, output, investment, and employment that would be more useful to the economic historian. Second, largely unorganized government data existing in committee and bureau reports could be brought

---

[7] Jonathan R. T. Hughes and Stanley Reiter, "The First 1,945 British Steamships," *Journal of the American Statistical Association*, LIII (June 1958), 360–81.

[8] Newmarch, "Circulation," p. 149.

together in manageable shape. And third, even correspondence, long a bug-a-boo of historians, could, perhaps, be better analyzed by data-processing techniques together with some form of content analysis. Both economics and economic history stand to gain enormously if this work is done wisely.

Our work at Purdue along these lines is, we hope, only the beginning of extensive data-processing work in Economic History. Since 1957 five data-processing studies in Economic History have been produced at Purdue. In all of our studies we have developed entirely new statistical series which are now readily available as "building blocks" for other economic historians to use in their studies. Our main results from these five papers may be briefly summarized.

In "Sources of Industrial Finance: The American Textile Industry, A Case Study," one hundred seventy-five observations on each of eight financial variables were brought together in a multiple regression model. The analysis of this data indicated that heretofore economic historians had tended to overstate the role of retained earnings in 19th century American corporate finance and understate the role of borrowed capital. In addition, the analysis indicated, as might be suspected, that the importance of loans grew concomitantly with the development of the capital markets and that a firm's capital structure was responsive to short-term changes in the capital markets, output and employment.[9]

In "Stock Ownership in the Early New England Textile Industry," data-processing techniques were used to systematize some 3,782 separate stock accounts (representing the equity holdings of at least 854 individuals and firms in eleven textile mills) to uncover the trends in stock ownership over the period 1829 to 1859. The analysis indicates, first, that while mercantile capital represented a large proportion of the investment, the transfer from mercantile to industrial capital appears to have been slower than has been generally assumed. Second, that there was a considerable degree of backward integration with textile merchants and mercantile firms contributing a significant block of capital. Third, that financial intermediaries made a substantial contribution to the finance of new industry. And fourth, that out-of-state and foreign investors made no significant investments.[10]

In "The First 1,945 British Steamships," the growth of the British steam merchant marine up to 1860 was chronicled and measured in detail, by type of propulsion and build. It was shown that not only was this development more rapid than had previously been thought, but that the transport capacity of the fleet grew more rapidly than did the tonnages to the extent that it could have played the powerful role in overseas earnings which had been as-

---

[9] Lance E. Davis, "Sources of Industrial Finance: The American Textile Industry, A Case Study," *Explorations in Entrepreneurial History*, IX (April 1957), 189–203.

[10] Lance E. Davis, "Stock Ownership in the Early New England Textile Industry," *The Business History Review*, XXXIII (Summer 1958), 204–22.

signed to it by contemporaries, and which had been heavily discounted by modern scholars.[11]

In "The New England Textile Mills and the Capital Markets: A Study of Industrial Borrowing 1840–1860," 2,385 industrial loans were systematized by machine techniques in order to provide some new information about the ante bellum capital markets. The analysis produced a new series of interest rates independent of the frequently-cited Bigelow estimates. It seemed to indicate that a theory of a sectored money market better explains the term structure of rates than does the more classical Lutz-Hicks expectation theory, and it presents some new data of the relative importance of various types of lenders in the composition of this lender group.[12]

Finally, in "A Dollar Sterling Exchange 1803–1895," data processing techniques permitted us to organize 2,789 bills of exchange and, from the bill prices, to deduce a series of pure exchange rates. In addition to this new series, the analysis indicates that exchange rate stability did not always characterize "the gold standard"; instead, it is only after 1875, when transportation, communications, and the money markets had evolved into near-modern form, that exchange stability became common. Finally, the paper casts further light on the development of the foreign exchange market and the rise of the major foreign exchange houses — a subject previously explored by Arthur Cole.[13]

IV

We now turn our attention briefly to statistical inference. Broadly speaking, statistical inference refers to a body of techniques that permit the user to garner with some confidence a knowledge of certain characteristics of populations on the basis of observations from these populations. For example, Newmarch's estimate of the average value of all bills based on the average of the sample drawn is a statistical inference. In that case the unknown quantity (called a parameter) is the average of all bills. In the Hughes and Reiter paper on the first 1,945 steamships, a more elaborate, but essentially similar, technique was employed to estimate the speed and carrying capacity of the ships from a knowledge of other related facts about them.

In other cases the unknown quantity of interest might be, for example, a measure of dispersion, or the largest observation in the population. Inference of this kind can achieve remarkable accuracy, more accuracy sometimes than that yielded by an attempt to count an entire population. This was the case in World War II when Allied estimates, based on the serial numbers of samples of German military equipment observed in battle, proved to be more accurate than the information supplied to the German government

[11] Hughes and Reiter, "1,945 Steamships."

[12] Lance E. Davis, "The New England Textile Mills and the Capital Markets: A Study of Industrial Borrowing, 1840–1860," *The Journal of Economic History* XX (March 1960), 1–30.

[13] Lance E. Davis and Jonathan R. T. Hughes, "A Dollar Sterling Exchange 1803–1895," *Economic History Review* (August 1960).

from production records, and in addition, were available much sooner than the data derived from the latter source.[14] Further, there are techniques for the study of relationships among various observable quantities, ranging from simple regression analysis to highly elaborate statistical schemes for detecting the presence of association between one pair of variables in the presence of many other associations or influences. A simple multivariable regression model, for example, was used in the study of textile financing previously cited to sort out the effects on corporate finance of firm age and historic time.

Before closing this desperately brief discussion of statistical inference, we should point out that one ought not to have too narrow a concept of the phenomena subject to quantitative analysis. It is, of course, obvious that observations, given in the form of numerical quantities such as money amounts or physical units of output, are subject to quantitative analysis. However, the possibilities of quantification go much further than this. Any phenomena whose occurrence may be noted or counted is quantifiable, and, in addition, coding sometimes permits apparently non-quantitative phenomena to be quantified. Thus, attitudes, opinions, and perceptions are studied with the aid of quantitative techniques by psychologists. Content analysis of written material provides another example of the usefulness of an extended notion of quantification. In our study of 19th century exchange rates we coded proper names, origins and points of payment of the bills. Thus "quantified," the mass of information could be handled and yielded us important evidence of the development of specialization in the exchange market.

V

We are not suggesting in this paper that there is to be a "new" economic history which will render non-quantitative economic historians technologically unemployed. It should be obvious that we regard ideas from statistics and data-processing as natural aspects of problems of historical study. It should also be obvious that the historian's special knowledge and viewpoint is essential to the useful employment of quantitative methods. Our main point is that modern statistical techniques and computing equipment make possible the intensive exploitation of a vein of historical materials that was perforce only little worked in the past; and that if even a few economic historians would take the time to learn even a little of these new techniques, the 1960's could easily prove the most productive years in the history of the discipline. On the other hand, if the discipline chooses to remain completely in the literary tradition, we can see small hope for anything but a continual rehashing of the already existing sources and a continuation of the century-long cleavage that should soon disappear if the economic historian is able to provide the economists with new data and new interpretations of the process of economic life. ◻

[14] W. Allen and Harry V. Roberts, *Statistics, A New Approach* (Glencoe, Illinois: The Free Press, 1956), p. 20.

PART TWO

□ The Emergence of Capitalism

The heterogeneity of material in the following pages suggests the massive intellectual problem confronting whoever would explain the emergence of capitalism. The student may be comforted to recall that these readings are calculated to increase his comprehension of the phenomena that accompanied the emergence of modern business and not to give a current, orderly account of them. That account must be left to textbook and teacher.

This section begins with Edward P. Cheyney's famed essay, Law in History, partly as a caution against too ready acceptance of a particular environment or a particular event as a historical cause. As the late Father Dempsey makes clear, the notion of "just price" gained acceptance because it provided a benign form of price control during half a millennium when the price mechanism could not yet be trusted to allocate resources. The businessmen of late medieval Florence and Genoa were a major activating force; similarly, the medieval legacy of a bourgeois class, so well remarked by Professor Muller, can account in part for an emerging capitalism. Just as important were what men thought, particularly about God and about God's relation to the natural world. The article on capitalism and the Reformation suggests that the cause-effect relationship of a reformed church and an acquisitive society was not as pat as Weber and Tawney once made it out to be. On the other hand, the spreading influence of scientific thought, particularly that of the towering intellectual figure, Isaac Newton, has probably received far too little emphasis in most accounts of the development of economic life in the early modern period.

The late Professor Schumpeter suggests in closing how change and the entrepreneur are related. What he says is relevant to both the world of mid-Twentieth Century and that of medieval Florence. This last essay, even in its abridged form, should both whet the appetite for more Schumpeter and provide a continuing thread for future reading and discussion. □

Law in History *

EDWARD P. CHEYNEY

On the morning of the tenth of August, 1588, the last and most eventful day of the running fight of the English fleet with the Spanish Armada, the wind blew steadily from the southwest. As the day wore on, it rose to the force of a gale; the Spanish ships as they emerged from the harbor of Calais, unmanageable and harried by the English, drove northward before the wind, past the mouth of the Scheldt, for which they were bound, and through the North Sea, till after a long and stormy course around Scotland and Ireland, broken and scattered, they regained the Spanish and Portuguese harbors. If the wind on that critical day had blown from some other quarter the Invincible Armada might have justified its name and effected the invasion of England. What an overwhelming influence on the course of events to be exercised by a mere vagary of the weather!

In the year 1527, Henry VIII was approaching the "dangerous age" of forty. He was ill-at-ease. His somewhat irregular marriage seemed unblest. He had no living children except one little girl and she was in frail health. Early in that year a young lady came to court, black-eyed, vivacious, charming. With striking contemporaneity the king began to express doubts of the validity of his marriage with Catherine and to give evidence of having fallen in love with the new maid of honor. The story is a familiar one, in which the personal and public elements are indistinguishable. The unsuccessful negotiations with the pope, the divorce, the marriage with Anne, the statutory separation of the Church of England from Rome, the dissolution of the monasteries, the regulation of the Church by the State, changes in practice and doctrine, followed rapidly upon one another, till the whole course of the official English Reformation was run. What an enormous influence on the course of history to be exercised by the wayward passion of one human being!

In the middle of the fifth century a wild band of Orientals under the leadership of Attila the Hun, "the Scourge of God," swept through Gaul and Italy, burning, slaying, and plundering. They depleted populations, overthrew governments, desolated provinces, reduced to utter confusion the already wasted Empire. What an impression on history made by the destructive sweep of a barbarous horde through a civilized country!

Just a thousand years later, in 1347 and the years following, a new disease swept across Europe, the bubonic plague, the "Black Death," as it has been

---

* Taken and adapted from Edward P. Cheyney, *Law in History and Other Essays* (New York: Alfred A. Knopf, Inc., 1927), pp. 1–7. Used by permission.

called. It was more devastating than the armies of Attila. High and low, old and young, clergy and laity, fell before its onset, till in many regions it is estimated that within a year one-half the population died instead of a twentieth, as in ordinary years. Great economic and social changes took place during these years. Serfdom passed rapidly away, monks and nuns in the monasteries and even the secular clergy deteriorated, one form of Gothic architecture was abandoned and gave place to another. Such wide and varied effects on the course of history have been attributed by historians to this most fatal of recorded epidemics . . .

It is by this time quite sufficiently evident that I have been giving some almost chance examples of what are apparently great historical effects flowing from causes of a relatively simple, individual, casual character; a turn of the weather, an onset of ill-regulated royal passion, a fortuitous invasion by a fierce army or a destructive epidemic . . .

But are these statements of cause and effect true, or are the appearances deceptive? Have these events and personalities really had the influence on the course of history so easily and naturally attributed to them? A hasty re-examination of the instances I have taken may suggest the need of a more adequate explanation. Although the wind blew from the southwest on the tenth of August, 1588, it did not blow adversely for the Spaniards through the whole eighteen years of the Elizabethan war. Yet Spain never successfully invaded England. Moreover, as we compare the two countries it becomes doubtful whether, even if Spanish troops had landed on the shores of England, any serious influence would have been exerted on the general course of the history of the two countries. Spain, over-strained by too ambitious undertakings, unsupported by adequate economic resources, deficient in statesmanship, was an anemic giant, holding her predominance in Europe with a constantly slackening hand. England, of youthful vigor, hardening Protestantism, rapidly increasing wealth, an exhilarating sense of her own nationality, was of almost unlimited, if undisciplined, powers, and was especially resistant to all forms of foreign control. Whether a Spanish or an English wind blew on a certain day really made little difference. England was bound to remain independent of Spain.

Can anyone believe there would have been no Reformation in England in the sixteenth century if Henry VIII had not fallen in love with Anne Boleyn? As we follow the stream of English history downward toward 1527, evidence of an approaching religious struggle is visible on every hand. There was much native heresy. The influence of Luther was active at Cambridge, in London, and through the eastern counties while Henry VIII was still living happily with Catherine and writing essays in support of the Pope. The monarchy was becoming constantly stronger and threatening to come into conflict with the old claims of the Church to semi-independence. Many of the monasteries were bankrupt and could have continued to exist but a little longer at best. Change was in the air; economic change, political change, intellectual change. Is it likely the Church alone would remain unchanged? A breach with the medieval Church took place in all the northern countries of Europe. Would England have been an exception? I think it is safe to say that the Reformation would have occurred in England at about the time it did and about in the form it did, if Henry VIII had never seen Anne Boleyn, indeed if Henry VIII had never lived . . .

So it is with the other instances. How little occasion the modern historian engaged in tracing the fall of the Roman Empire and the transformation of Roman institutions in the fifth century finds even for a mention of Attila! Every successive student of social and economic change in the fourteenth century gives less consideration to the "Black Death," and more to that gradual, obscure, and almost imponderable disintegration of the early medieval type of society which gave its character to that period . . .

These great changes seem to have come about with a certain inevitableness; there seems to have been an independent trend of events, some inexorable necessity controlling the progress of human affairs. If a hundred instances were taken instead of five or six, all would show the same result. Examined closely, weighed and measured carefully, set in true perspective, the personal, the casual, the individual influences in history sink in significance and great cyclical forces loom up. Events come of themselves, so to speak; that is, they come so consistently and unavoidably as to rule out as causes not only physical phenomena but voluntary human action.

So arises the conception of *law in history*. History, the great course of human affairs, has not been the result of voluntary effort on the part of individuals or groups of individuals, much less of chance; but has been subject to law. □

❖ 12 ❖

Just Price in a Functional Economy *

BERNARD W. DEMPSEY

The current recrudescence of corporate economy bestows importance on historical analogies hitherto neglected. Medieval economy combined a corporate and functional concept of economic society with political ideals close kin to American constitutional principles. But at present, very incorrect notions of just price, widely accepted, preclude an objective examination of medieval economic theory by American economists. Just price is here examined in its historical sources, the Roman law and the writings of Augustine; development is then traced by quotation from the leading medieval thinkers. Just

* Taken and adapted from Bernard W. Dempsey, "Just Price in a Functional Economy," *American Economic Review*, Vol. XXV, No. 3, September 1935, pp. 471–86. Used by permission.

price thus appears as an integral part of a consistent social philosophy and properly applied as a workable general principle.

I

When the record of economic history is viewed in its full length, that lack of a system which we call the system of individualism is seen to be a recent episode. Historically speaking, only the last century and a half have endeavored to live an economic life without organization or control; and even within that century and a half, individualism has never held the field uncontested. Since the war, as is perfectly evident, the nineteenth century individualistic mood has been replaced by a powerful twentieth century trend toward a corporate economy. Moreover, the economists of the English-speaking world who do not like the Hegelian outlook of Stalin, Mussolini and Hitler, face this world of facts under a severe handicap with the postulates of their own system challenged on various scores.

In all the years of economic activity, and all the types of economic organization before and since the brief day of liberalism, one only attempted to combine the ideas that "all men are by nature equal"; [1] that the state is for man and not man for the state; [2] and that there is a measure and a limit and a norm for government interference with individual effort. [3] When we are being pushed into a corporate economy, an historical example of a system that could maintain those three objectives is worthy of consideration. Any economy based on such theory, however faulty in practice, can in our present situation be profitably studied. From this emphasis on principle, it should be clear that we shall not describe the archaic external trappings of medieval economic life, upon which undue emphasis has been placed by enthusiasts and critics alike. The question is one of radical economic principles, not of gargoyles or stained glass windows.

Yet the American economist does not consider the medieval system of economic thought a fruitful field of study. The reason is that he approaches the subject with a fundamental misconception; at the mere mention of just price or objective value, the matter is closed. Regardless of practical considerations, a concern for objective truth would alone justify a re-examination of basic medieval economic concepts. There are few subjects in the field of social science upon which misinformation can be more readily obtained. Scholastic philosophy has recently enjoyed a renascence, both in development as neo-scholasticism, and in historically accurate studies. That the fruit of these studies has not penetrated into the economic world is evident from the fact that it was possible, as late as 1928, to reprint pages 90–96 of Dr. Lewis H. Haney's *History of Economic Thought,* with the statement among others that:

---

[1] Thomas Aquinas, *Summa Theologica,* 2a 2ae quaestio 104, ad 5um.
[2] Thomas Aquinas, *De Regimine Principum* (De Regno) Lib. 3, cap. ii.
[3] Thomas Aquinas, *Summa Contra Gentiles,* Lib. 3, cap. 71.

The general notion appears to have been that value is absolute, and objective, and independent of price.[4]

Nor can much be said for Dr. James Westfall Thompson's summary save that it is in harmony with the tall gratuities found elsewhere in his volume. Relying on a second-hand quotation from Thomas Aquinas, through an unidentified Miss Davidson, Dr. Thompson commits himself to the unequivocal position that:

> The Church's concept of value was something absolute and apart from value in use and value in exchange, something independent of supply and demand, something intrinsic and fixed.[5]

Even so carefully objective an investigator as Dr. Norman S. B. Gras is able to remark of medieval economics rather complacently:

> It was assumed that there was such a thing as an objective value, something inherent in the object rather than in the minds of the buyer and seller. We now have had enough experience and have made enough examination of the problem, of course, to know that no such value ever existed.[6]

Medieval schoolmen are frequently criticized for their lack of scientific method, though Hugo Grotius felt that:

> Whenever they are found to agree on moral questions they can scarcely be wrong, they who are so keen in discovering the flaws in each other's arguments.[7]

But whatever may be said for the methods of the schoolmen, one can scarcely approve of the critical technique of the writers cited above or indeed of most writers in English on this subject. In such case, it behooves us to let the schoolmen speak for themselves, and thus to remove the principal misconception which has prevented modern writers from seeing in realistic perspective the medieval organic economy which is the only historical analogy which can now be of service to us. Our present purpose is to look the bogey of just price squarely in the eye, and thus to clear the air. Around the correct conception of just price, we shall then seek to sketch some of the leading principles of scholastic economic organization. The space devoted to the question of price is objectively disproportionate but the disproportion is necessary under the circumstances. . . .

IV

The Dark Ages, if there were any such, offer us little new on price and value save the work of the canonists properly so-called who lie beyond the

---

[4] Haney, *op. cit.*, p. 90.

[5] Thompson, *Economic and Social History of the Middle Ages,* New York, 1928, pp. 697–698.

[6] Gras, "Economic Rationalism in the Late Middle Ages," *Speculum,* viii, 3, July, 1933, p. 305.

[7] Grotius, *De Jure Belli et Pacis,* reproduction of the edition of 1646, Washington, 1916, pages unnumbered (17).

scope of this present writing. The next writer of importance to whom we turn is Albertus Magnus (1193–1280), a Suabian of the noble family of Bollstadt, teacher at Paris and Cologne, bishop of Ratisbon and founder of the theological tradition of the Dominican order. Albert, though one of the few writers who quotes neither the commentary of Paulus, nor the famed passage of Augustine, is on his own grounds an advocate of just price. He is commenting on the *Ethics* of Aristotle:

> There is accordingly always a just mean between gain and loss. This mean is preserved when in a voluntary contract the antecedent situation is equivalent to the consequent, that is to say, before and after the contract. A couch, for example, prior to the contract had a value of five; if one received five for it, the situation consequent to the contract is equal to that which was antecedent. No one can complain that he has been in any way injured thereby.[8]

> Such exchange, however, does not take place through an equality of the things exchanged but rather according to the value of one thing in relative proportion to the value of the other with due regard for the need which is the cause of the transaction.[9]

This "need" of which Albert speaks includes not only my personal need of this particular object but also and more significantly the need which all men have of living in society and of exchanging with one another the products of their labor, if human life is to be carried out on a level in any way proportionate to human capacity and dignity. My need is included, to be sure, but the principles of justice involved derive from the general nature of human needs in society, as the writer proceeds to show in the continuation of the passage cited above.

> According to this analysis, the carpenter ought to receive the product of the tanner and in turn pay the tanner that which according to a just exchange is his. . . . And when this equality is not preserved, the community is not maintained, for labor and expense are not repaid. For all would, indeed, be destroyed if he who makes a contract for so much goods of such a kind, does not receive a similar quality and quantity. For the state cannot be built up of one type of workers alone. Properly, therefore, these things are exchanged not absolutely but with a certain comparison to their value according to use and need. Otherwise, there would be no exchange.[10]

To this end, money was invented, that community life might be facilitated and preserved through just contracts which, through the device of money, are made both easier and more just:

> Wherefore all exchangeable goods are properly priced in money and thus there will always be exchange. . . . While there is exchange, there is also a com-

---

[8] B. Alberti Magni, *Opera Omnia*, Paris, 1891, vol. vii, *In Librum V Ethicorum*, Tract. 2, cap. 7, no. 30.
[9] *Ibid.*, cap. 9, no. 31.
[10] *Ibid.*, cap. 9, no. 31.

munity. Now money equals all exchangeable goods just as the unit of a ruler by addition and subtraction equals all things ruled. We have just said that without an exchange of products there will be no community life. But community life cannot be unless the products are reduced to proportionate equality. . . . And this is the reason why the first and primary measure of all exchangeable goods (money, to wit) was of necessity invented.[11]

Lest his doctrine be misunderstooood, Albert is careful to explain how what he says fits in with the traditional scholastic doctrine of immutable essences and final values with reference to a last end. Time has shown the wisdom and need of the warning.

. . . In a certain way, natural objects are immutable, as for example, with regard to those first principles by which man is ordained for the good and the true, for these are imprinted on humankind and do not change. However, the use of these things when applied in practice varies with many customs and institutions. Thus, although with the gods every just thing is precisely so and in absolutely no degree otherwise, for with the gods nothing suffers change; with us, however, an object is by nature in a certain sense changeable, for whatever is human is changeable, and as this is the case, so there is in human justice an element that is of nature and an element that is not.[12]

These citations manifest an intimate connection in the writer's mind between just price and social organization. Because men must live in community, because life can be sustained only by mutual exchange of products for the subvention of mutual needs, the contracts arising from these exchanges must be equitable. And if they must be fundamentally equitable, the expression of that basic equity in money must be a just price. The process, as a whole, is radically a social phenomenon arising from man's need for life in society, and his inability adequately and congruously to develop his personality alone; "the commonwealth cannot be built up of one type of workers alone." Albert is talking not only of a division of labor but more particularly of the organic interrelation arising from this specialization of function. Because exchange is socially necessary, money is socially necessary, and because both money and exchange are designed to serve the development of persons in community, the quantitative determination of price is necessarily social. Prices must be equitable because all of the functional groups are necessary to each other and live in mutual interdependence. By fair exchange manifested in a fair price, is progress made and the commonwealth maintained.

Had Albertus Magnus no greater claim to distinction than his part in the intellectual formation of Thomas Aquinas (1225–1274), it should be enough. Master and pupil are both Doctors of the Church, and the works of Thomas are rightly regarded as an epitome of medieval thought. Before we turn to the question as to whether Thomas thought that value and price were exclu-

[11] *Ibid.*, cap. 10, no. 36.
[12] *Ibid.*, Tract. 3, cap. 1, no. 49.

sively objective, it is necessary to consider briefly the structure of the society in which these transactions would take place.

That human societal relations are natural and, therefore, both normal and normative is axiomatic in the work of Thomas Aquinas as indeed in all scholasticism. The principle of Aristotle, "Man is by nature a social animal," [13] is cited almost every time a social topic is discussed. Out of the innumerable places in Thomas's vast works that touch upon social analysis, we limit ourselves to a few which indicate in what manner he regarded society, economic society included, as organic.

Economic need is one of the most powerful motive forces impelling to social organization, in the mind of Aquinas as well as in that of Albert.

> "Man is naturally a social animal." This is evident from the fact that one man does not suffice for himself if he lives alone because the things are few in which nature makes adequate provision for man, since she gave him reason by means of which to provide himself with all the necessities of life such as food, clothes, and so forth, for the production of which one man is not enough. Wherefore man has a natural inclination to social life.[14]

In a totally different connection, and in a different work, after an introduction which is almost *verbatim* with the above, Aquinas continues:

> Just as one man has various members by which he functions in various capacities, all ordered to supply any need, since all functions cannot be supplied by one member, so the eye sees for the whole body and the foot carries the whole body. Likewise, in what pertains to all mankind, one man is not able to do all the things which are needed in a society, and, accordingly, different people properly work at different tasks.

But since in Thomas's thought, order and liberty when properly conceived are not exclusive notions but complementary ones, he explains:

> This diversity of men in different functions, happens, in the first place, by divine providence which has so distributed the types of men that nothing necessary for life will ever be found wanting. But this also comes about from natural influences by which different men have different inclinations for this function of that manner of life.[15]

The thought is also developed by an analogy from the animal world, the division of labor in the bee-hive.

> For, as many things are needed for man's livelihood for which one man is not sufficient for himself, it is necessary that different things be done by different men, that some, for instance, should cultivate the land, that some build houses, and so forth.[16]

[13] Aristotle, *Nichomacean Ethics*, Book I, c. 7.
[14] Aquinas, *Summa contra Gentiles*, Book III, c. 85.
[15] Aquinas, *Quaestiones Quodlibetales*, Quodlibetum 7um, quaestio 7, art. xvii, ad corpus.
[16] Aquinas, *Summa contra Gentiles*, Book III, c. 134.

All of which may thus be summarized:

> In civic relationships, all men who belong to the same community are regarded as one body, and the whole community as one man.[17]

A division of labor, therefore, is fundamental in Aquinas's idea of social organization and progress:

> For the welfare of human society, many things are necessary; divers offices are done better and more expeditiously by divers persons than by men singly.[18]

But, though there be a division of labor, competition as a ruling principle is far from his mind. Scholastic economic organization is pre-eminently one of non-competing groups.

> In the temporal commonwealth, peace departs because the individual citizens seek only their own good. . . . Rather through diversity of function and status is the peace of temporal commonwealths promoted inasmuch as thereby there are many who participate in public affairs.[19]

When there is combined with this organic concept of economic society, the scholastic doctrine on private property, which cannot be here elaborated, we achieve a conclusion which sounds odd to modern ears.

> All particular goods which men procure are ordained for the common good as for their end.[20]

And we come also to that fundamental notion of the basic community of goods which the institution of private property is to promote and not impede.

> And, therefore, the division and appropriation of goods that proceeds from human law cannot come in the way of man's need of being relieved out of such goods. . . . To use the property of another, taking it secretly in a case of extreme need, cannot, properly speaking, be characterized as theft.[21]

In the economic society of which Thomas had practical experience, these diverse functions and various tasks and offices and duties of which he speaks were carried out not by isolated individuals but by well-defined *universitates* and *corpora*, gilds, in other words, each of which was an organ of the state for fulfilling some requisite of community life. Thomas was no advocate of the modern "monolithic" state, ruled with high hand from above. Association took place naturally on many levels.

> Since there are various grades and orders in these communities, the highest is that of the commonwealth which is ordained to procure by itself a sufficiency of goods for human life.[22]

[17] Aquinas, *Summa Theologica*, 1a 2ae, quaestio 81, art. 1, ad corpus.
[18] Aquinas, *Summa Theologica*, 2a 2ae, quaestio 40, art. 2, resp.
[19] Aquinas, *Summa Theologica*, 2a 2ae, quaestio 183, art. 2, ad 3um.
[20] Aquinas, *De Regimine Principum*, Book I, c. 15.
[21] Aquinas, *Summa Theologica*, 2a 2ae, quaestio 66, art. 7.
[22] Aquinas, *In Libros Politicorum*, prologus.

Thus, though the state has a proper regulatory office, these lesser associations should be left to carry out their organic functions freely within the limits of justice.

The optimum in any government is that things should be provided for according to their own measure for in this does the justice of an administration consist. Accordingly, it would be against the principle of human government if men were to be prevented by the governor of the commonwealth from carrying out their own functions, unless perchance for a brief time because of some emergency.[23]

From this brief sketch, of necessity inadequate,[24] we wish to point out those factors in Thomas's analysis which bear on our present problem. The state is a natural society within which flourish many lesser coördinate societies, each enjoying within its own sphere an ordinate autonomy, all, however, designed through coöperation to serve the interests of the persons who compose the state, and all attaining these ends through an observance of justice which regulates those acts of men which concern a second person.

With these observations in mind, what Thomas has to say on the subject of just price becomes more intelligible. On the origins of money and exchange, he comments approvingly upon the words of Aristotle,[25] but a fuller discussion is given elsewhere.

To the end that exchange be just, as many shoes should be exchanged for a house, or for a man's food, as the labor and expense of the builder or farmer is greater than that of the tanner because, if this be not observed there will be no exchange, nor will men share their goods with one another. . . . This one thing which measures all other things is, in truth, the need which embraces all exchangeable goods insofar as all things are referred to human needs. *For things are not valued according to the dignity of their natures,* otherwise a mouse which is a sentient thing would have a higher price than a pearl which is an inanimate thing. This is manifest because, if men had no needs, there would be no exchange. . . . In other words, insofar as the farmer, whose function is the provision of food, is more necessary than the tanner whose function is the provision of shoes, by that amount in numerical proportion must the work of the tanner exceed that of the farmer so that many shoes are exchanged for one measure of grain. . . . Moreover, it is true that money also suffers the same as anything else. . . . That is to say that it has not always the same value but ought, nevertheless, to be so instituted that it have greater permanency in the same value than other things.[26]

If, however, this reciprocity is absent, there will be no equality of the things exchanged, and thus men are no longer able to dwell together. . . . All the

23 Aquinas, *Summa contra Gentiles,* Book III, c. 71.
24 Among the many writings on the political thought of Thomas Aquinas few compendious statements will be found to excel the work of Dr. Clare Q. Riedl of Marquette University, "The Social Theory of Thomas Aquinas" in *Philosophy of Society,* Philadelphia, 1934. For a scholastic interpretation of general modern "value" theory see, *Philosophy of Value* by Leo R. Ward, of the University of Notre Dame, New York, 1930.
25 Aquinas, *In Primum Librum Politicorum,* lect. 7.
26 Aquinas, *In Decem Libros Ethicorum,* Liber V, lect. 9 (italics inserted).

crafts would be destroyed if each would not receive an amount proportionate to that which he produced.[27]

In the light of these considerations of the natural and all-inclusive mutual interdependence of men, of the close articulation of all parts of the community for the maintenance and progress of all, and of the necessary observance of justice if these ends are to be obtained, the jejune remarks of Thomas in the passage usually cited from his works in this connection, acquire a fuller meaning.

> Buying and selling were instituted for the common good of both parties since each needs the products of the other and vice versa as is evident from the Philosopher. But what was introduced for the common utility ought not to bear harder on one party than on the other, and therefore, the contract between them should rest upon an equality of thing to thing. The quantity of a thing which comes into human use is measured by the price given, for which purpose money was invented, as said. Therefore, if the price exceeds the quantity of the value of the article, or the article exceeds the price, the equality of justice will be destroyed. And, therefore, to sell a thing dearer or to buy it cheaper than it is worth, is, in itself, unjust and illicit. . . . The just price of things, however, is not determined to a precise point but consists in a certain estimate. . . . The price of an article is changed according to difference in location, time, or risk to which one is exposed in carrying it from one place to another or in causing it to be carried. Neither purchase nor sale according to this principle is unjust.[28]

Elaborate demonstration that scholastic writers are not concerned with an absolute, immobile, intrinsic value should, in the light of the quotations given, be quite superfluous; for "things are not valued according to the dignity of their natures." Value rests upon a kind of estimate, not of the buyer and seller alone, but of the whole community. This is true because man is social by nature and for him production and progress are possible only in association. That society which arises through this association is a commonwealth in the fullest sense of the word, and will flourish only when all its parts are sound. By the production of a useful commodity, man makes his contribution to the commonweal for which contribution he expects a reciprocal support. Because social relations are governed by justice (which we do not here prove, but assume as axiomatic in scholasticism, or in any other civilized philosophy) the exchange must take place according to the community's estimate of the social utility of the two products because the producer who expects sustenance from society in return for his labor, by performing his function in the social organism, has earned his right to a just return. The factors which will normally determine the community estimate of social utility are labor, cost of materials, risk and carriage charges. . . .

[27] *Ibid.*, lect. 8.
[28] Aquinas, *Summa Theologica*, 2a 2ae, quaestio 77.

VI

Scholastic writers demanded a just price because purchase and sale is a social transaction and social transactions are governed by justice. Purchase and sale is a social transaction because man is social by nature, and only through exchange is he able to provide himself with congruous sustenance. Man is a person with the right and obligation to develop and perfect his personality. But this he can do only in society. The two societies in which he invariably seeks and finds the proper medium for development are the family and the state, which are for this reason called natural societies. Among the functions of the state, one of the principals is the procuring of economic prosperity for its members, yet, for this purpose the state is not directly equipped. Men, ever social in tendency, in this as in everything else, lean naturally toward association for the more efficient fulfillment of their material needs, and the state achieves its purpose by fostering, protecting, or, if need be, restraining these associations. Functional associations of this sort are not absolutely indispensable to social life as are the family and the state but they are requisite for a healthy commonwealth for which reason they are called quasi-natural societies. They stand lower than the family and the state but above the purely conventional society like a joint stock corporation or a club.

The achievement of prosperity is patently a coöperative enterprise to which each producer brings his labor as his means of production and his title to subsistence. For the protection of that right and the improvement of those powers, it is natural that man should associate with all, owners or workers, who function in the same industry where each makes his contribution, whence each receives his sustenance. Such associations are the economic organs of the body politic; they are the vertical girders furnishing structural balance in the social edifice along with the horizontal, geographical, political framework. The exchange of the increased product made possible by the diversification of function must take place at a fair price, else the commonwealth will suffer. In an organism, the diminution of function in one organ means a diminution of function in all. When society permits transactions at other than just prices, it is cutting off its nose to spite its face, or is enacting the ancient pantomime of the hands that would not feed the lazy stomach.[29]

In such an organization of society, the tension of class conflict, which is unnatural and philosophically as well as practically inhuman, is relieved because men, on a basis of what they are, stand united according to what they do, not divided according to what they have or have not. There is achieved, not a sterile and futile socialization of goods, but a natural and fruitful socialization of men. □

[29] The application of scholastic principles to modern economy will be found in the five volume work of Heinrich Pesch, S.J., *Lehrbuch der National Ökonomie*, Freiburg, 1907. Pesch was a pupil of Adolph Wagner, and Spann rates his work as "the most comprehensive economic treatise in the German language."

Of Cheating, Which Is Committed in Buying and Selling *

THOMAS AQUINAS

We must now consider those sins which relate to voluntary commutations. First, we shall consider cheating, which is committed in buying and selling: secondly, we shall consider usury, which occurs in loans. In connection with the other voluntary commutations no special kind of sin is to be found distinct from rapine and theft.

Under the first head there are four points of inquiry: (1) Of unjust sales as regards the price; namely, whether it is lawful to sell a thing for more than it is worth? (2) Of unjust sales on the part of the thing sold. (3) Whether the seller is bound to reveal a fault in the thing sold? (4) Whether it is lawful in trading to sell a thing at a higher price than was paid for it?

FIRST ARTICLE

Whether It Is Lawful to Sell a Thing for More than Its Worth?

We proceed thus to the First Article: —

OBJECTION 1. It would seem that it is lawful to sell a thing for more than its worth. In the commutations of human life, civil laws determine that which is just. Now according to these laws it is just for buyer and seller to deceive one another (Cod., IV., xliv., *De Rescind. Vend.* 8. 15); and this occurs by the seller selling a thing for more than its worth, and the buyer buying a thing for less than its worth. Therefore it is lawful to sell a thing for more than its worth.

OBJECTION 2. Further, That which is common to all would seem to be natural and not sinful. Now Augustine relates that the saying of a certain jester was accepted by all, *You wish to buy for a song and to sell at a premium,* which agrees with the saying of Prov. XX. 14, *It is naught, it is naught, saith every buyer; and when he is gone away, then he will boast.* Therefore it is lawful to sell a thing for more than its worth.

OBJECTION 3. Further, It does not seem unlawful if that which honesty demands be done by mutual agreement. Now, according to the Philosopher (*Ethic.* viii. 13), in the friendship which is based on utility, the amount of the recompense for a favour received should depend on the utility accruing to the receiver: and this utility sometimes is worth more than the thing given, for instance if the receiver be in great need of that thing, whether for the purpose of avoiding a danger, or of deriving some particular benefit. Therefore,

---

* Taken and adapted from The *"Summa Theologica"* of St. *Thomas Aquinas,* Part II, Question LXXVII literally translated by fathers of the English Dominican Province (London: Burns, Oates & Washbourne Ltd., 1929), pp. 317–33. Used by permission.

in contracts of buying and selling, it is lawful to give a thing in return for more than its worth.

On the contrary, It is written (Matth. vii. 12): *All things . . . whatsoever you would that men should do to you, do you also to them.* But no man wishes to buy a thing for more than its worth. Therefore, no man should sell a thing to another man for more than its worth.

I answer that. It is altogether sinful to have recourse to deceit in order to sell a thing for more than its just price, because this is to deceive one's neighbour so as to injure him. Hence Tully says (*De Offic.* iii. 15): *Contracts should be entirely free from double-dealing; the seller must not impose upon the bidder, nor the buyer upon one that bids against him.*

But, apart from fraud, we may speak of buying and selling in two ways. First, as considered in themselves, and from this point of view, buying and selling seem to be established for the common advantage of both parties, one of whom requires that which belongs to the other, and vice versa, as the Philosopher states (*Polit.* i. 3). Now whatever is established for the common advantages, should not be more of a burden to one party than to another, and consequently all contracts between them should observe equality of thing and thing. Again, the quality of a thing that comes into human use is measured by the price given for it, for which purpose money was invented, as stated in *Ethic.* v. 5. Therefore, if either the price exceed the quantity of the thing's worth, or, conversely, the thing exceed the price, there is no longer the equality of justice: and consequently, to sell a thing for more than its worth, or to buy it for less than its worth is in itself unjust and unlawful.

Secondly, we may speak of buying and selling, considered as accidentally tending to the advantage of one party and to the disadvantage of the other: for instance, when a man has a great need of a certain thing, while another man will suffer if he be without it. In such a case the just price will depend not only on the thing sold, but on the loss which the sale brings on the seller. And thus it will be lawful to sell a thing for more than it is worth in itself, though the price paid be not more than it is worth to the owner. Yet if the one man derive a great advantage by becoming possessed of the other man's property, and the seller be not at a loss through being without that thing, the latter ought not to raise the price, because the advantage accruing to the buyer, is not due to the seller, but to a circumstance affecting the buyer. Now no man should sell what is not his, though he may charge for the loss he suffers.

On the other hand if a man find that he derives great advantage from something he has bought, he may, of his own accord, pay the seller something over and above: and this pertains to his honesty.

REPLY OBJECTION 1. As stated above (I.–II., Q XCVI., A. 2) human law is given to the people among whom there are many lacking virtue, and it is not given to the virtuous alone. Hence human law was unable to forbid all that is contrary to virtue; and it suffices for it to prohibit whatever is destructive of human intercourse, while it treats other matters as though they were lawful, not by approving of them, but by not punishing them. Accordingly, if without employing deceit the seller disposes of his goods for more than their worth, or the buyer obtain them for less than their worth, the law looks upon this as licit, and provides no punishment for so doing, unless the excess be too great, because then even human law demands restitution to be made, for instance if a man be deceived in regard of more than half the amount of the just price of a thing.

On the other hand the Divine law leaves nothing unpunished that is contrary to virtue. Hence, according to the Divine law, it is reckoned unlawful if the equality of justice be not observed in buying and selling: and he who has received more than he ought must make compensation to him that has suffered loss, if the loss be considerable. I add this condition, because the just price of things is not fixed with mathematical precision, but depends on a kind of estimate, so that a slight addition or subtraction would not seem to destroy the equality of justice.

REPLY OBJECTION 2. As Augustine says (ibid.) *this jester, either by looking into himself or by his experience of others, thought that all men are inclined to wish to buy for a song and sell it at a premium. But since in reality this is wicked, it is in every man's power to acquire that justice whereby he may resist and overcome this inclination.* And then he gives the example of a man who gave the just price for a book to a man who through ignorance asked a low price for it. Hence it is evident that this common desire is not from nature but from vice, wherefore it is common to many who walk along the broad road of sin.

REPLY OBJECTION 3. In commutative justice we consider chiefly real equality. On the other hand, in friendship based on utility we consider equality of usefulness, so that the recompense should depend on the usefulness accruing, whereas in buying it should be equal to the thing bought . . .

FOURTH ARTICLE

Whether, in Trading, It Is Lawful to Sell a Thing at a Higher Price than What Was Paid for It?

We proceed thus to the Fourth Article: —

OBJECTION 1. It would seem that it is not lawful, in trading, to sell a thing for a higher price than we paid for it. For Chrysostom says on Matth. xxi. 12: *He that buys a thing in order that he may sell it, entire and unchanged, at a profit, is the trader who is cast out of God's temple.* Cassiodorus speaks in the same sense in his commentary on Ps. lxx. 15, *Because I have not known learning,* or *trading* according to another version: *What is trade,* says he, *but buying at a cheap price with the purpose of retailing at a higher price?* and he adds: *Such were the tradesmen whom Our Lord cast out of the temple.*

Now no man is cast out of the temple except for a sin. Therefore, suchlike trading is sinful.

OBJECTION 2. Further, It is contrary to justice to sell goods at a higher price than their worth, or to buy them for less than their value, as shown above (A. I.). Now if you sell a thing for a higher price than you paid for it, you must either have bought it for less than its value, or sell it for more than its value. Therefore this cannot be done without sin.

OBJECTION 3. Further, Jerome says (Ep. ad Nepot. lii.): *Shun, as you would the plague, a cleric who from being poor has become wealthy, or who, from being a nobody has become a celebrity.* Now trading would not seem to be forbidden to clerics except on account of its sinfulness. Therefore it is a sin in trading, to buy at a low price and to sell at a higher price.

On the contrary, Augustine commenting on Ps. lxx. 15, *Because I have not known learning,* says: *The greedy tradesman blasphemes over his losses; he lies and perjures himself over the price of his wares. But these are vices of the man, not of the craft, which can be exercised without these vices.* Therefore trading is not in itself unlawful.

I answer that, A tradesman is one whose business consists in the exchange of things. According to the Philosopher (*Polit.* i. 3), exchange of things is twofold; one, natural as it were, and necessary, whereby one commodity is exchanged for another, or money taken in exchange for a commodity, in order to satisfy the needs of life. Suchlike trading, properly speaking, does not belong to tradesmen, but rather to housekeepers or civil servants who have to provide the household or the state with the necessaries of life. The other kind of exchange is either that of money for money, or of any commodity for money, not on account of the necessaries of life, but for profit, and this kind of exchange, properly speaking, regards tradesmen, according to the Philosopher (*Polit.* i. 3). The former kind of exchange is commendable because it supplies a natural need: but the latter is justly deserving of blame, because, considered in itself, it satisfies the greed for gain, which knows no limit and tends to infinity. Hence trading, considered in itself, has a certain debasement attaching thereto, in so far as, by its very nature, it does not imply a virtuous or necessary end. Nevertheless gain which is the end of trading, though not implying, by its nature, anything virtuous or necessary, does not, in itself, connote anything sinful or contrary to virtue: wherefore nothing prevents gain from being directed to some necessary or even virtuous end, and thus trading becomes lawful. Thus, for instance, a man may intend the moderate gain which he seeks to acquire by trading for the upkeep of his household, or for the assistance of the needy: or again, a man may take to trade for some public advantage, for instance, lest his country lack the necessaries of life, and seek gain, not as an end but as payment for his labour.

REPLY OBJECTION 1. The saying of Chrysostom refers to the trading which seeks gain as a last end. This is especially the case where a man sells something at a higher price without its undergoing any change. For if he sells at a higher price something that has changed for the better, he would seem to receive the reward of his labour. Nevertheless the gain itself may be lawfully intended, not as a last end, but for the sake of some other end which is necessary or virtuous, as stated above.

REPLY OBJECTION 2. Not everyone that sells at a higher price than he bought is a tradesman, but only he who buys that he may sell at a profit. If, on the contrary, he buys not for sale but for possession, and afterwards, for some reason wishes to sell, it is not a trade transaction even if he sell at a profit. For he may lawfully do this, either because he has bettered the thing, or because the value of the thing has changed with the change of place or time, or on account of the danger he incurs in transferring the thing from one place to another, or again in having it carried by another. In this sense neither buying nor selling is unjust.

REPLY OBJECTION 3. Clerics should abstain not only from things that are evil in themselves, but even from those that have an appearance of evil. This happens in trading, both because it is directed to worldly gain, which clerics should despise, and because trading is open to so many vices, *since a merchant is hardly free from sins of the lips* (Eccles. xxvi. 28). There is also another reason, because trading engages the mind too much with worldly cares, and consequently withdraws it from spiritual cares; wherefore the Apostle says (2 Tim. ii. 4): *No man being a soldier to God entangleth himself with secular businesses.* Nevertheless it is lawful for clerics to engage in the first mentioned kind of exchange, which is directed to supply the necessaries of life, either by buying or by selling. □

✧ **14** ✧

Of the Sin of Usury *

THOMAS AQUINAS

We must now consider the sin of usury, which is committed in loans: and under this head there are four points of inquiry: (1) Whether it is a sin to take money as a price for money lent, which is to receive usury? (2) Whether it is lawful to lend money for any other kind of consideration, by way of payment for the loan? (3) Whether a man is bound to restore just gains derived from money taken in usury? (4) Whether it is lawful to borrow money under a condition of usury?

* Taken and adapted from *The "Summa Theologica"* of *St. Thomas Aquinas,* Part II, Question LXXVIII, literally translated by fathers of the English Dominican Province (London: Burns, Oates & Washbourne, Ltd., 1929), pp. 317–33. Used by permission.

FIRST ARTICLE

Whether It Is a Sin to Take Usury for Money Lent?

We Proceed thus to the First Article: —

OBJECTION 1. It would seem that it is not a sin to take usury for money lent. For no man sins through following the example of Christ. But Our Lord said of Himself (Luke xix. 23): *At My coming I might have exacted it,* i.e. the money lent, with usury. Therefore it is not a sin to take usury for lending money.

OBJECTION 2. Further, According to Ps. xviii. 8, *The law of the Lord is unspotted,* because, to wit, it forbids sin. Now usury of a kind is allowed in the Divine law, according to Deut. xxiii. 19, 20 *Thou shalt not fenerate to thy brother money, nor corn, nor any other thing, but to the stranger:* nay more, it is even promised as a reward for the observance of the Law, according to Deut. xxviii. 12: Thou shalt fenerate to many nations, and shalt not borrow of any one. Therefore it is not a sin to take usury.

OBJECTION 3. Further, In human affairs justice is determined by civil laws. Now civil law allows usury to be taken. Therefore it seems to be lawful.

OBJECTION 4. Further, The counsels are not binding under sin, But, among other counsels we find (Luke vi. 35): *Lend, hoping for nothing thereby.* Therefore it is not a sin to take usury.

OBJECTION 5. Further, It does not seem to be in itself sinful to accept a price for doing what one is not bound to do. But one who has money is not bound in every case to lend it to his neighbour. Therefore it is lawful for him sometimes to accept a price for lending it.

OBJECTION 6. Further, Silver made into coins does not differ specifically from silver made into a vessel. But it is lawful to accept a price for the loan of silver vessel. Therefore it is also lawful to accept a price for the loan of a silver coin. Therefore usury is not in itself a sin.

OBJECTION 7. Further, Anyone may lawfully accept a thing which its owner freely gives him. Now he who accepts the loan, freely gives the usury. Therefore, he who lends may lawfully take the usury.

On the contrary, It is written (Exod. xxii. 25): *If thou lend money to any of thy people that is poor, that dwelleth with thee, thou shalt not be hard upon them as an extortioner, nor oppress them with usuries.*

I answer that, To take usury for money lent is unjust in itself, because this is to sell what does not exist, and this evidently leads to inequality which is contrary to justice.

In order to make this evident, we must observe that there are certain things the use of which consists in their consumption: thus we consume wine when we use it for drink, and we consume wheat when we use it for food. Wherefore in suchlike things the use of the thing must not be reckoned apart from the thing itself, and whoever is granted the use of the thing, is granted the thing itself; and for this reason, to lend things of this kind is to transfer the ownership. Accordingly if a man wanted to sell wine separately from the use of the wine, he would be selling the same thing twice, or he would be selling what does not exist, wherefore he would evidently commit a sin of injustice. In like manner he commits an unjustice who lends wine or wheat, and asks for double payment, viz. one, the return of the thing in equal measure, the other, the price of the use, which is called usury.

On the other hand there are things the use of which does not consist in their consumption: thus to use a house is to dwell in it, not to destroy it. Wherefore in such things both may be granted; for instance, one man may hand over to another the ownership of his house while reserving to himself the house, while retaining the ownership. For this reason a man may lawfully make a charge for the use of his house, and, besides this, revendicate the house from the person to whom he has granted its use, as happens in renting and letting a house.

Now money, according to the Philosopher (*Ethic.* v. 5; *Polit.* i. 3) was invented chiefly for the purpose of exchange: and consequently the proper and principal use of money is its consumption or alienation whereby it is sunk in exchange. Hence it is by its very nature unlawful to take payment for the use of money lent, which payment is known as usury: and just as a man is bound to restore other ill-gotten goods, so is he bound to restore the money which he has taken in usury.

REPLY OBJECTION 1. In this passage usury must be taken figuratively for the increase of spiritual goods which God exacts from us, for He wishes us ever to advance in the goods which we receive from Him: and this is for our own profit not for His.

REPLY OBJECTION 2. The Jews were forbidden to take usury from their brethren, i.e. from other Jews. By this we are given to understand that to take usury from any man is evil simply, because we ought to treat every man as our neighbour and brother, especially in the state of the Gospel, whereto all are called. Hence, it is said without any distinction in Ps. xiv. 5: *He that hath not put out his money to usury*, and (Ezech. xviii. 8): *Who hath not taken usury.*

They were permitted, however, to take usury from foreigners, not as though it were lawful, but in order to avoid a greater evil lest, to wit, through avarice to which they were prone according to Is. lvi. II, they should take usury from the Jews who were worshippers of God.

Where we find it promised to them as a reward, *Thou shalt fenerate to many nations*, etc., fenerating is to be taken in a broad sense for lending, as in Eccles. xxix. 10, where we read: *Many have refused to fenerate, not out of wickedness*, i.e., they would not lend. Accordingly the Jews are promised in reward an abundance of wealth, so that they would be able to lend to others.

REPLY OBJECTION 3. Human laws leave certain things unpunished, on account of the condition of those who are imperfect, and who would be deprived of many advantages, if all sins were strictly forbidden and punishments appointed for them. Wherefore human law has permitted usury, not that it looks upon usury as harmonizing with justice, but lest the advantage of many should be hindered. Hence it is that in civil law it is stated that *those things according to natural reason and civil law which are consumed by being used, do not admit of usufruct, and that the senate did not (nor could it) appoint a usufruct to such things, but established a quasi-usufruct,* namely by permitting usury. Moreover the Philosopher, led by natural reason, says (Polit. i. 3) that *to make money by usury is exceedingly unnatural.*

REPLY OBJECTION 4. A man is not always bound to lend, and for this reason it is placed among the counsels. Yet it is a matter of precept not to seek profit by lending: although it may be called a matter of counsel in comparison with the maxims of the Pharisees, who deemed some kinds of usury to be lawful, just as love of one's enemies is a matter of counsel. Or again, He speaks here not of the hope of usurious gain, but of the hope which is put in man. For we ought not to lend or do any good deed through hope in man, but only through hope in God.

REPLY OBJECTION 5. He that is not bound to lend, may accept repayment for what he has done, but he must not exact more. Now he is repaid according to equality of justice if he is repaid as much as he lent. Wherefore if he exacts more for the usufruct of a thing which has no other use but the consumption of its substance, he exacts a price of something non-existent; and so his exaction is unjust.

REPLY OBJECTION 6. The principal use of a silver vessel is not its consumption, and so one may lawfully sell its use while retaining one's ownership of it. On the other hand the principal use of silver money is sinking it in exchange, so that it is not lawful to sell its use and at the same time expect the restitution of the amount lent. It must be observed, however, that the secondary use of silver vessels may be an exchange, and such use may not be lawfully sold. In like manner there may be some secondary use of silver money; for instance, a man might lend coins for show, or to be used as security.

REPLY OBJECTION 7. He who gives usury does not give it voluntarily simply, but under a certain necessity, in so far as he needs to borrow money which the owner is unwilling to lend without usury.

Other Scholastic Texts Concerning the Just Price

Corpus juris canonici, Decretales: Canon *Placuit, in I,* lib. III, tit. 17, c. 1:

It pleases us that parish priests admonish their flocks to be hospitable and not to charge more to wayfarers than what can be gotten by selling in the market.

Albert Magnus, St. (1193–1280), *Commentaria in IV Librum Sententairum*, dist. 16, art. 46:

> However the just price is what a commodity may be worth according to the estimation of the market at the time of the contract.

Alfred O'Rahilly, "Notes on Thomas Aquinas, III. St. Thomas on Credit," *The Irish Ecclesiastical Record*, 5th series, XXXI (1928), pp. 159–168:

> For if Tuscan merchants, bringing cloth (into Italy) from the fair of Lagny, have to wait for payment until Easter and, therefore, sell their cloth for more than it is worth in the public market, there is no doubt that it is usury. However, if they sell it not at more than its worth, yet at more than they would accept if they were paid cash, there is no usury.

San Bernardine of Siena (1380–1444), *De Evangelio Aeterno*, Sermon 33, art. 2, cap. 7, part. 2, s 5:

> If, however, I am asked what price is just in buying or in selling, I answer: the just price is the one set according to the estimation of the current market, that is, according to what the goods sold are worth commonly at present in the market. Because according to Hostiensis and Raymondus of Pennaforte the just price is set with reference to the time of the contract without considering whether one sells for less what has been bought for more, or vice versa, whether more is offered.

San Bernardine of Siena, *De Evangelio Aeterno*, Sermon 33, art. 2, cap. 5 (on price discrimination):

> Fifth, it is not licit to trade by taking into consideration the circumstances of the person with whom one deals and to sell wares dearer to wayfarers than to merchants or residents, dearer to rustics of ignorants than to well-informed citizens, or dearer to the simple than to the astute.

Cardinal Cajetan (1468–1534), *Comments on Summa theologica* of St. Thomas, II, ii, qu. 77, art. 1 (Leonine ed., VI, 149):

> The just price of goods is that one which is now obtainable from the buyers, presupposing adequate knowledge and in the absence of all fraud and coercion.

Luis de Molina, S.J. (1535–1601), *De Justitia et Jure*, Tract. 2 (*De contractibus*), disp. 348. s 4:

> A great concourse of buyers, more at one time than another, and greater avidity increases price; but paucity of buyers decreases price.

John Duns Scotus (1265–1308), *Quaestiones in librum quartum Sententiarum*, dist. XV, qu. 2, No. 22:

> . . . hence (the merchant) can justly receive a price corresponding to his trouble or industry beyond what is required for his own needs and the support of his family, and thirdly, beyond this something to cover his risks. □

❖ 15 ❖

Florence: Turbulent City of Individualism *

MIRIAM BEARD

While the role of the Jews in the evolution of modern capitalism has received exaggerated emphasis in the popular mind, including that of Professor Sombart, the prodigious share of the Italians in forming business practices and concepts has been correspondingly underestimated. In England and America, for a variety of reasons, misconceptions about Italy are particularly abundant; the Anglo-Saxon tends to view Italy through a roseate haze, as the home of a passionate and impractical people, devoted to art and religion rather than to profit-making. Yet in the past, Italy was in fact the scene of pagan revolt against clerical restraints on trade; at an extremely early date, it produced capitalistic methods of industrial and financial exploitation and some business dictatorships which exhibited many of the characteristics of present-day Fascism.

The sweet illusion respecting the nature of the old Italian commercial life, which was implanted in the British mind by William Shakespeare, was still further strengthened in the nineteenth century by other writers like George Eliot and especially by John Ruskin, the great social critic who conjured up the most magical visions of medieval Italian society, out of his own imagination and without benefit of research. Ruskin was the son of a conservative wine-merchant whose journeys in wine-growing regions brought the impressionable youth to Italy; there Ruskin found in Italian relics of art a message of social salvation for England, then undergoing the most shocking early phases of the Industrial Revolution. Inspired by the matchless beauty of Florence and Venice, Ruskin returned to look at the North of England, blackened and defiled by soot and slag; much to the chagrin of his parent, he attacked the machine as the destroyer of human dignity and denounced the then sacred doctrine of laissez faire as a mere pretext for untrammeled greed.

Many Victorians accepted Ruskin's vision of Italy for the same reasons. Another recalcitrant son of a business man, William Morris, escaped the paternal brokerage office and devoted himself to spreading the gospel of the gilds and handicrafts. The aesthetes known as "Pre-Raphaelites," who followed the leadership of Ruskin and Morris, helped to nourish the legend of a pure and lofty old Italy, a kind of lost Garden of Eden, in which venders and makers of goods had dwelt peacefully together as happy gild-brothers, united in "honest Christian faith and vital craftsmanship," unspoiled by vulgarities of commercial mass-production.

* Reprinted from A *History of Business* by Miriam Beard by permission of The University of Michigan Press. Copyright © by University of Michigan 1938.

These enthusiastic "mediaevalists" urged England to hush her wheels and give heed to her soul. Preaching regeneration through observing the sublime example set in the "Age of Giotto," they did have a decided influence in deflecting the course of English capitalism. They aroused consumers to demand some aesthetic values in the products of the machine. And they focused attention on the worst evils of industrialism so stridently that many Englishmen, when they read about the spiritual serenity of the old Italians, felt abashed at their own earthy greed. But compelling and useful as this wonderful myth appeared, it was without documentary foundation.

At the time Ruskin began to study art in Italy in the 1830's, little was known of economic history in Europe. The origins of the machine, of competitive individualism, of scientific rationalism, of factory organization, had not yet been traced back by French and German scholars to mediaeval days. The dust of centuries still lay thick upon the yellowed documents in the archives of the old towns. What a herculean task had yet to be performed in deciphering and evaluating these manuscripts, may be judged from the fact that a single business house in Italy, that of Francesco Datini, who died in 1410, left records filling 97 yards of shelf, and besides, a correspondence of 140,000 letters.

Without such material at his disposal to reconstruct the actual background of early Italian life, Ruskin had to rely mainly on the evidence of his eyes. Gazing upon the portraits of Italian merchants, he was delighted with their "healthy serenity" of mien, and announced "I see no hypocrisy in their countenances." He inferred that "a deep and constant tone of individual religion" had lent "a peculiar dignity to the conduct even of their commercial transactions." In his "Ariadne Florentina," Ruskin declared that the innocent Italians had repudiated, "with universal contempt and malediction," the nefarious practice of receiving interest until the fifteenth century, and had left usury to Jews. For this assertion, Ruskin adduced no proof except Shakespeare's "Merchant of Venice." And he advanced none at all for his claim that it was the wicked Germans of Augsburg who at length corrupted this paradise of simplicity.

Art, argued Ruskin, can only spring from a "good society"; Florence and Venice were more beautiful than Manchester or Liverpool; hence they must have been more virtuous. How could Venice, "fair city of graceful arcades and gleaming walls," appear like a white "vestal from the sea," if she had not known "a depth of devotion, in which lay all her strength"? Whence came the radiance in the paintings of the Florentine Giotto, if it was not the reflection of a nobler social scheme?

In Ruskin's youth, his countrymen supposed, some with pride and a few with contrition, that they had invented the machine. They would have scouted as ridiculous the idea that Englishmen had ever been forced to learn, from a parcel of foreigners, how to make money. Least of all, would they have believed that their old tutors had been Germans and Italians. Both Germany and Italy had fallen into such poverty and apathy by the

1830's, that they no longer seemed capable of ever having invented anything rational or profitable.

Germany at that period had reverted to bucolic simplicity. A casual visitor there would not have guessed that, in the 1400's, she had been famous as a "land of machines" and miraculous contrivances. Nor would anyone have supposed that, in just a few decades, by the 1870's, she could suddenly regain her old ingenuity and, at one bound, overleap England again in technological skill.

Similarly unimpressive at that day was Italy, exhausted by Napoleonic exactions. Her people, wrapped in rags and dwelling amid ruins, seemed lazy and superstitious to the British. It was natural to suppose, as Ruskin did, that their ancestors must have been even more childlike and oblivious to material advantages. It was easy to set up a fictitious ideal society in that sunlit scenery.

Ruskin did not realize, when he fled to Italy from the filth and noise of England's "Black Triangle," that he was not escaping industrialism, but was actually making a pilgrimage to its cradle. The sources of the evils he most deplored at home lay in those two mellow towns which exerted the strongest fascination over him, Venice and Florence. Venice was founded, like Liverpool, upon the slave-trade. Florence, in the age of Giotto, was already a mediaeval Manchester, bringing raw materials from afar, making them up by highly complex processes, and distributing them throughout Europe more cheaply than the craftsmen of other places could afford to do. Led by a malicious Fate, therefore, Ruskin, burning with desire for a society built on social justice and aesthetic rapture, fixed his ideal society in the very country, the exact cities, and even the precise period, in which capitalism unfolded its early buds.

Florence and Venice were in fact the two most irreligious cities in mediaeval Italy. Their relations with clerical Rome, however, were far from similar. While Venice carefully retained the forms of faith, her government was constantly clashing with the Holy See. Florence, on the contrary, was usually on the side of Rome officially, for she was the chief banker of the Popes and supported them against the claims of the German Emperors. But privately the Florentines were extremely pagan and boasted their kinship with the classic past; more than any other men of Italy, they assisted in the revival, or Renaissance, of the Greek and Roman culture.

Both Florence and Venice had ties with pre-Christian antiquity and the Infidel Turk. Venice restored to Europe much of the business lore which had been preserved in Constantinople and Alexandria from Roman times. Florence also had relations with these sites of classic culture. The monks and nuns who came from Alexandria to Florence in the thirteenth century and set up spinning and weaving establishments belonged to an Eastern sect, the Humiliati, which maintained that ascetics should support themselves by business and not by begging. This view of business as compatible with spirituality, so characteristically Alexandrian, easily took root by the

Arno. Florentine connections with Constantinople were established much later, but they were profitable ties, for after the Grand Turk took that city in 1453 the Florentines obtained formal trading privileges in the Golden Horn. The Turk feared Venice and Genoa, suspecting that they had designs upon his territories as well as his markets, and welcomed the Florentines by preference. At once jealous Venice thought of fighting Florence, but the wily Florentine, Cosimo de' Medici, skillfully drained Venetian banks of their gold and thus withdrew the sinews of war from the rival.

Despite the papal bans upon such unholy intercourse, the two cities struggled for the trade of the Infidel. Florence had marketed her cloth abundantly through Venetian merchants in the Near East until at last she established direct connections with the Turks. Neither city for a moment intended to abandon this illicit traffic. Venice dealt with the Infidel without apology. But Florence justified her actions by appealing to pagan philosophy; it was hardly an accident, as Doren points out, that Cosimo de' Medici was founding his Platonic Academy to foster the spirit of the heathen thinkers, while he was extending the hand of friendship to the Turk.

Moreover, Florentine rebellion against Rome had traditional roots. Florence lies in that region of Italy called Tuscany after the race of powerful Etruscan merchants, foes of the Romans, who lived there in very ancient times. Though the Etruscans finally surrendered to the Roman sword, they never succumbed to Roman agrarian views, but continued to struggle against Roman dominance with the subtle methods of finance, until at last the masterful financier, Maecenas, who, as Horace declares, boasted his descent from Etruscan monarchs, managed to place Octavian on the throne as the first Emperor of the Roman world. Maecenas, the power behind this throne, reaped rich harvests in Egyptian real estate and, becoming Prefect of all Italy, was a virtual ruler of the Italian people.

Resistance to Rome continued under another guise in the last years of the Empire, when Christianity was spreading from the Roman center. Roman Christianity was agrarian rather than commercial; its hierarchical order was founded upon agriculture as the most stable basis for society. Furthermore the Roman Church declared that the world was ruled by Divine Plan and not by chance and competition. St. Augustine denounced the Etruscan deity, Fortuna, as a dangerous creature whose whims destroyed social order, and he warned her devotees, the ambitious merchants, against attempting to hurt the heavenly scheme by adherence to her cult. Naturally this conception of life was coldly received by the Etruscans; Schillman states that the market-town of Florence was particularly loath to tear down pagan statues. One of the last places in Italy to accept Christianity, it held out until after the new faith was official. Though dethroned formally, the goddess Fortuna, the beloved, continued to dwell in the hearts, if not on the altars, of her commercial followers. ◻

16

The Medieval Legacy *

HERBERT J. MULLER

Offhand, even the enduring achievements of medieval men are melancholy reminders of their lost cause. Their cathedrals give Europe its most hallowed charm and dignity but are ghostly in their silence, forlorn in their isolation from the civic life that once swirled through and about them. (A medieval ghost might be more horrified by the tourists strolling their aisles with guidebooks than he was by the lovers who made them a trysting-ground, or the students who played dice on their altars.) Their great universities — one of the most original of their unconscious creations — remain centers of learning, but of a heretical, worldly kind of learning; their 'cleric' has dwindled into clerk. Their aristocratic ideals of romantic love have become the stock in trade of a vast, vulgar industry, cheap entertainment for the masses they disdained. Offhand, their descendants have made a mockery of all their grandiose aspirations. We might only hope that they sleep well after the fitful fever of their lives; for they grew more despairing as their age waned, and they would hardly be proud of the civilization they sired.

Yet we may be proud of them. We owe our being to their restless striving, their eagerness to experiment and adventure — in particular to the ardor for learning, beauty, and fullness of life that made the twelfth century a profounder, more wonderful renaissance than the official Renaissance. Because we have gone on to build a vastly different world we may forget our kinship, and because we are now prone to their despair we may be seduced by the fond legends of their humble piety; but we owe them something better than sentimental fondness. In a time of confused aims, and much mean endeavor, we may profit by recalling the reality of their idealism, the power of their belief in things unseen. We may escape the easy cynicism that denies such realities, and thereby strengthens the power of unprincipled business and political leaders.

For all its corruptions, Christianity in the Middle Ages was never a mere opium for the masses. It was a truly spiritual force, among the most powerful that have made history. It was the mainspring of the great revival that enabled the barbarians of the West to surge ahead of proud Byzantium. The Gothic cathedrals alone testify to a religious exaltation that has never been surpassed, even in the intensely religious East. Secular life was also enveloped in this exaltation, always colored by it, at times fired by it. The very corruptions intensified the spirituality, for they stirred constant indignation, reawakened conscience, and led men back to purer versions of the Christian

* From *The Uses of the Past* by Herbert J. Muller. Copyright 1952 by Oxford University Press, Inc. Reprinted by permission.

ideal. And perhaps the purest was actually realized by St. Francis and his band of brothers, at the turn of the thirteenth century. A century later St. Francis might have been burned at the stake as a heretic, because of his sublime disregard of dogma; but at this moment, which may be considered the apex of the Middle Ages or of Christianity itself, medieval man was able to find the perfect expression for his simple absoluteness, and in the midst of corruption to realize his impossible idealism. The message of St. Francis was pure love and joy — a continuous, radiant spiritual gladness born of a real love for all earthly creatures and things, and an utter indifference to all earthly cares and pains. He forgave God and man for everything, except only the pride of the schoolmen.

St. Francis is not the complete Christian, since he cared nothing for reason, knowledge, and the whole classical heritage. At the same time, he knew nothing of Gregory the Great's terrible fears of the world, the flesh, and the Devil. He could achieve his kind of perfection because by this time medieval men had sufficiently mastered their heritage to take liberties with it. While they retained Gregory's legacy — even elaborating upon it with Germanic and Celtic superstitions, introducing new hordes of gnomes, goblins, witches, and werewolves to a demon-infested world — they also made it over in their own image. To the cult of the Devil they added the complementary cult of the Virgin. To Roman order they brought Germanic ardor and lust for life. They reclaimed patristic Christianity emotionally and imaginatively, through grand symbolism, making poetry of its dogma, realizing in their cathedrals the community of God and men that they so painfully sought to demonstrate in their theology. Their art is the token of their supreme achievement, which was to humanize Christianity. In various ways they approached a religious ideal that could satisfy the whole man, making him at home in both the natural and the social world, fulfilling his needs for truth, beauty, and goodness. If this Christian humanism cannot be called the essence of the medieval spirit, which was always prey to a gross worldliness and neurasthenic other-worldliness, it was at least a real element of this spirit. For us, I think, it is the most valuable element of the medieval legacy.

An obvious example is the ideal of universality. Although it was a narrower ideal than that of the Roman Stoics, embracing only the true believers, it was less provincial than the patriotic ideal that superseded it. Medieval men tended to regard themselves first of all as Christians; they had their share of local pride and jealousy but relatively little of the violent national prejudice that now splits the West. They were at least free from racial prejudice, persecuting men for their beliefs rather than the color of their skin. The deplorable intolerance they bequeathed was less irrational than modern forms.

No less pertinent is medieval economic theory. As Christians, they naturally considered business a subordinate means to the serious business of the good life, and naturally sought to bring it under the rule of Christian morality. St. Thomas Aquinas, among others, worked out their cardinal principle of the 'just price': instead of charging whatever the market will bear, and thereby taking advantage of the needs of fellow-Christians, producers and merchants should charge just enough to cover the costs of their labor. (As R. H. Tawney points out, 'the last of the Schoolmen was Karl Marx'; for they provided the basis of his labor theory of value.) Later thinkers made the just price more elastic, recognizing the complex variables that affect value, but they still agreed that prices could never be left to the discretion of the seller, since this would simply encourage extortion. They also agreed that speculation, or buying and selling for gain, was an unpardonable sin. They even continued to condemn interest on loans: to extract a guaranteed pound of flesh, without labor of one's own, was contrary to nature, Aristotle, and God. In all this the schoolmen were hopelessly impractical, and seem more so because their theory was so contrary to medieval practice, especially the practice of the papacy. They were naive enough to believe that business morality might be secured by the mere formation of sound moral principles. But they were never so naive as to believe that morality would be promoted, and the good society achieved, by glorifying the profit motive. 'If it is proper to insist on the prevalence of avarice and greed in high places,' Tawney concludes, 'it is not less important to observe that men called these vices by their right names, and had not learned to persuade themselves that greed was enterprise and avarice economy.' [1]

Political theory was less humane. While it proclaimed the high duties of rulers, it provided little freedom for the ruled and little protection against misrule; and St. Thomas himself justified the institution of serfdom on economic grounds. Nevertheless medieval culture contained the seeds of democracy. They flowered briefly in the Italian city-states, fertilizing the soil of the Renaissance; they produced such enduring growths as the common law and parliamentary institutions of England. The Church, moreover, offered a high career that was open to the lowliest men — at least half of the medieval popes were humbly born. And both clerics and nobles kept pronouncing a stereotyped principle of equality: a highly theoretical equality which they made no effort to realize in social life, and which amounted to little more than the melancholy sentiment that all men are equal before death, but which some common men took seriously. Medieval peasants began to claim rights that the peasants of Byzantium hardly conceived. 'At the beginning we were all created equal,' proclaimed John Ball; 'it is the tyranny of perverse men which has caused slavery to arise, in spite of God's law.' Ball was properly hanged,

---

[1] Some respectable types in modern America may find themselves in the lowest circles of Dante's hell. He regarded sins of fraud as worse than sins of violence because they were deliberate and cold-blooded, sins against the mind and soul of man; so he reserved his more horrible punishments for flatterers, seducers, fortune-tellers, hypocrites, evil counselors, et cetera. This company — somewhere below the murderers — would now be swelled by advertisers and publicity men.

drawn, and quartered, but the authorities could not kill his dream of 'equal liberty, equal greatness, equal power.'

Even the celebrated religious achievements of the Middle Ages have a humanistic significance that conventional piety has obscured. Art was a far more vital force than it is today because it was not fine art. Gothic art was essentially a folk creation, springing from the common people, expressing a common aspiration and joy in creation; it was not monopolized by an elite. (Hence it seemed 'barbarous' to a later age, which set up aristocratic canons of taste and moved art from the workshop to the salon, studio, lecture hall, and finally the museum.) From the outset it broke away from the rigid formalism of Byzantine sacred art, and its progress was toward freedom, exuberance, and naturalism. Sculpture gradually overcame the orthodox suspicion of the evil body; painting took to a realistic treatment of religious subjects. The work of Giotto, the first great painter, expressed a frank pleasure in the flesh and the natural world, and amounted to an open repudiation of asceticism and spiritual abstraction. The more exuberant humanism of the Renaissance was a continuation of the medieval trend, not a sudden rebellion.

Similarly with medieval theology. While its immediate aim was to establish orthodoxy, and its most apparent accomplishment was the official theology of the Roman Catholic Church, its inspiration was a faith in human reason, and its most significant accomplishment was its contribution to the whole adventure of thought. In spite of themselves, the schoolmen established the value of doubt and even of heresy.

One reason why the Dark Ages were dark was that there was no thought worthy of the name of heresy.[2] With the first glimmerings of light man began to question Gregory the Great's legacy of blind faith. As early as the tenth century Berengar rebelled against authority in the name of reason. (Disunity, one might say, was the first sign of the famed medieval unity.) Then St. Anselm proclaimed his motto, 'I believe in order to understand,' and made a new effort to understand, producing his noted ontological argument for the existence of God. Peter Abelard was much bolder, maintaining that one can believe only what he understands, and that it is ridiculous to preach to others what one does not understand. With Abelard the renaissance of the twelfth century came into full swing. He discovered that the Church Fathers were not infallible guides, listing in his *Sic et Non* some hundred and fifty propositions on which they flatly contradicted one another. He was nevertheless confident that the true faith was perfectly reasonable, and therefore believed in the positive value of doubt; he thought that even heretics

[2] The striking exception is John Scotus Erigena in the ninth century — one of the rare isolated geniuses in the history of culture. While recognizing the authority of the Bible, Erigena held that reason was its source and did not need its support: 'true religion is true philosophy.' His declaration of independence had little influence at the time, however; and when his true philosophy caught the attention of the Church several centuries later, he was condemned as a heretic.

should be reasoned with instead of tortured. Above all, he had a passion for knowledge, insisting that all knowledge was good. He accordingly fell a victim to the pious obscurantism of St. Bernard, the still more impassioned champion of orthodoxy. As a saintly skeptic, Bernard was less horrified by Abelard's specific heresies than by his general assumption that sacred truths should not be accepted unless they are comprehensible; and he got Abelard officially condemned and disgraced. Yet the future belonged to his victim.

Students had flocked to Paris from all over Europe to listen to Abelard. He had much to do with the rise of the University of Paris, which became the great center of theology. Before long the spiritual progeny of Abelard were poring over Aristotle, who had been discovered through the translations of heathen Arabs and Jews. Inflamed by his passion for knowledge, they persisted in studying Aristotle even though ecclesiastical authorities had properly condemned his philosophy as heretical. The triumph of Abelard was sealed when Thomas Aquinas came to the University of Paris. St. Thomas carried to a magnificent conclusion his effort to substitute rational principles for mere appeal to historic authority. Although he acknowledged that certain revealed truths, such as the existence of angels, could not have been discovered by reason, he never wavered in his insistence upon making God as rational as he himself was.

St. Thomas began the hard way, with the dangerous admission that the truth of Christianity or even the existence of God cannot be taken for granted — it seemed self-evident only because of custom. He supplemented the Platonic intuition inherited by Christian theology with the empirical principle of Aristotle. 'The origin of our knowledge is in sense,' he stated, 'even of those things that are above sense.' He therefore opposed the teaching of St. Augustine that knowledge of the natural world is unimportant, or that Scripture tells us all we need to know about it. 'The truth of our faith,' he declared, 'becomes a matter of ridicule among the infidels if any Catholic, not gifted with the necessary scientific learning, presents as a dogma what scientific scrutiny shows to be false.' False ideas about God's handiwork would naturally lead to false conclusions about God himself. Believing that Aristotle's philosophy contained the essential truth about the natural world, St. Thomas made his bold effort to reconcile it with Christianity. He capped his work by an extraordinarily patient, thorough application of the method of Abelard. In his *Summa Theologica*, designed for 'beginners,' he stated honestly some ten thousand 'Objections' to Christian doctrine, and as honestly tried to meet them.

For his own age, in short, Thomas Aquinas was a modernist, or even a radical. Shortly after his death the archbishops of Paris and Canterbury formally condemned his heretical 'materialism'; and it took his Dominican order fifty years of politics to get him canonized. It is this radical spirit that gives enduring significance to his system. The system was indeed a marvelous synthesis of 'science and sanctity,' wrought with remarkable zest, patience, and acumen, unsurpassed in the history of thought for its combination of imaginative breadth, intellectual rigor, and loving care in detail; but its equilibrium was even more delicate and precarious than that of the Gothic cathedrals. Later schoolmen pointed out basic inconsistencies, and with the rise of science the whole foundation of the elaborate structure was undermined. Today the philosophy of Aquinas is a kind of historical curiosity for most of those outside the Catholic Church and the University of Chicago; and most ordinary Catholics, if they tried to read him, would likely find much of his thought unintelligible or irrelevant. Yet there is nothing curious or irrelevant about his essential faith — his grand conviction that the true faith could and should embrace all knowledge, all truth from all sources.

Hence the real curiosity — the tragic irony — is that the revolutionary philosophy of St. Thomas Aquinas has become the very symbol and stronghold of conservatism. When the pioneers of science, still informed by a pious spirit, made revolutionary discoveries about God's handiwork, one might have expected the Church of Aquinas to welcome this natural knowledge, or at least to avoid the ridicule of infidels by revising dogmas that 'scientific scrutiny shows to be false.' Instead, it chose to stand on the dogmas. Though it lost the historic battle that ensued, it continued to betray the spirit of Aquinas by stubbornly resisting the new knowledge. And even more demoralizing than the endless conflict was the deepening confusion. Philosophy, science, and religion, which Aquinas had united, now broke apart and went their separate ways, to produce the hodgepodge of thought and feeling that constitutes the state of mind of most literate Christians today. All in all, the boldness and the integrity of St. Thomas Aquinas provide a melancholy perspective on contemporary Christianity. The orthodox flatly reject the 'higher criticism,' refusing to permit any rational criticism of the Canon that is the basis of their faith. The liberals suffer from the lack of any consistent philosophy, smuggling in traditional beliefs they wish to preserve by talking of symbolism, but evading the intellectual import duties on their symbols. The modern clergyman, lamented the Reverend Kirsopp Lake, is apt to have 'a lower standard of intellectual honesty than would be tolerated in any other profession.'

THE FAILURE OF THE MEDIEVAL IDEAL

According to Henry Adams, the Virgin was bankrupt by 1300: the precarious structure of medieval faith had collapsed, and the ideal unity was no more. According to Toynbee, the religious wars of the sixteenth century signaled the breakdown of Western Christendom, though he also stresses the spiritual debacle of the papacy in the thirteenth century. Catholic historians usually minimize this debacle and picture the Reformation as the great tragedy, attributing it to the greed of princes, the pride of heretics, or simple perversity; Hilaire Belloc went so far as to say that 'the breakdown of our civilization in the sixteenth century . . . was an *accident.*' Protestants naturally deny this apparent lapse of Divine Providence, and tend to view the Reformation as a great liberation. My own liberal, humanistic bias would lead me to stress the good that came out of the breakdown of feudalism and absolutism. Yet this good was also implicit in the Middle Ages — the breakdown was not sudden or accidental. The more impartial of modern historians picture Western history from the dawn of the Middle Ages through the Reformation as a drama that had logic and continuity but no definite climax or curtain fall, and that was neither pure tragedy nor simple success story. The issues of this drama are still live, open, and ambiguous.

Now, the chief disruptive force in the medieval world was quite unconscious. Medieval writers commonly divided society into those who work, those who guard, and those who pray, omitting merchants and townsmen; but it was these men without status — an anonymous 'middle' class — who made over the whole society. They developed the money economy that undermined the feudal system, helping the peasants to emerge from serfdom and the kings to dominate the barons. Just why they proved so much more enterprising than their bourgeois forebears in the Greco-Roman world, or in any other civilization, Marxist theory does not explain. At least they did not embark on a conscious class war against those who guarded and those who prayed; generally they were medieval enough to revere the ideal fictions, and bourgeois enough to be content with their material gains. But the fact remains that they were the most vigorous, resourceful class, and therefore rose to power. While the nobility played at tournaments, the bourgeoisie played the leading role in the great historic events that secularized and then revolutionized Western civilization — such key events as the invention of printing, the discovery of America, the Reformation, the rise of science, the growth of republicanism, and the Industrial Revolution.

In general, the rise of a bourgeois, urban civilization — at first commercial, then industrial, and then increasingly nationalistic and imperialistic — is doubtless the major theme of Western history, and the locus of our major problems. We may accordingly note that medieval Catholicism contributed to the continuity of this story. Sombart thought that the great working order of the Benedictines laid the foundations of capitalistic enterprise by dignifying work and instituting the fixed, orderly, punctual life, which now seems very natural even though men naturally rebel against it. Their rule — practiced in forty thousand monasteries — exemplified the bourgeois ideal of being 'as regular as clock-work.' (The mechanical clock itself was a medieval invention.) Later churchmen contributed more directly to the development of finance, since the Church was by far the greatest financial enterprise of the age. Few have heard of Fra Luca Pacioli, the inventor of double-entry bookkeeping; but he has probably had much more influence on human life than has Dante or Michelangelo.

For our philosophical purposes, however, the rise of bourgeois is not the main issue of the Middle Ages. If economic forces make history, non-economic motives make it significant; and such motives created the unique glory of the medieval renaissance. They made its history a religious drama. The main theme of this drama was the effort to establish a Christian society, united by a catholic faith. The failure of this effort was genuinely tragic, since it was an ideal effort on a grand scale. But out of reverence for human idealism we again need to view the tragedy with some ironic reserve, aware that the grand effort was born in conflict with Eastern Christendom, that it was nourished by ignorance and illusion, that all along it involved radical contradictions, and that it never achieved real harmony or peace.

Since we are cursed by self-consciousness, and are prone to think how happy is a people without a history or a sociology, we might begin by recalling the perils of innocence. 'Every sin arises from a kind of ignorance,' wrote St. Thomas Aquinas. 'A man's will is secure from sinning only when his understanding is secured from ignorance and error.' This alone might serve as the epitaph of the Middle Ages. ◻

17

Capitalism and the Reformation *

PATRICK GORDON WALKER

I

Until the early twentieth century the relationship between the Reformation and capitalism was really no problem at all. Almost as old as Protestantism itself was the truism that "among the Reformed the greater their zeal, the greater their inclination to trade and industry, as holding idleness unlawful." [1] There was virtual agreement on the facts; Protestants and Catholics were only concerned to draw different consolation from the common observation that "usury was the brat of heresy." [2] Marshall may be taken as typical of these views, which prevailed down to our own day.[3]

The bombshell was dropped by Max Weber at the beginning of this century in a brilliant development of an idea suggested to him by W. Sombart in his 1902 edition of *Der Moderne Kapitalismus*. Sombart here proclaimed as the guiding force in the evolution of capitalism and the modern world the "Spirit of Capitalism," which consisted in the pursuit by the individual of

---

* Taken and adapted from P. C. Gordon Walker, "Capitalization and the Reformation," *The Economic History Review*, Vol. VIII, No. 1, November 1937, pp. 1–19. Used by permission of the author and publisher.

[1] Quoted. R. H. Tawney, Foreword to Weber's *The Protestant Ethic and the Spirit of Capitalism* (English translation, 1926).

[2] Quoted. R. H. Tawney, *op. cit.*

[3] Marshall, *Principles of Economics*, p. 742.

gain for its own sake, in exact calculation, and the rigorous rationalisation of every department of life. Max Weber in his *Protestant Ethic and the Spirit of Capitalism* (1904–5) found a personal vehicle for this capitalist spirit in the Calvinist and the Puritan and demonstrated with ingenuity the causal connection between the doctrine of Calvinism and the inculcation into its adherents of the capitalist spirit. . . .

My purpose is to show that Weber has led the whole body of historians, both adherents and opponents, down the wrong path in the study of one of the most important problems of modern European history; that the methods of enquiry used by both sides in the controversy *must* lead to false results; and finally that the only solution is to take a new method and a new point of departure.

II

Weber created a special method of enquiry and argument for the purposes of his study of Protestantism. This method has been tacitly taken over by his main assailants, who have not attempted to destroy it but rather to turn it against its creator. Critics like Tawney and Sée have suggested only minor modifications and cautions. The consequence has been that the problem of the Reformation as a sociological phenomenon has been coloured and, in my opinion, vitiated by a method which has been so easily accepted that its implications and assumptions have been hardly realised.

The most striking aspect of the Weber method is the use of an abstract definition of capitalism. The particular definition was arrived at as follows. It was assumed, after Sombart, that there was an eternally valid quality of mind, abstracted from, and independent of, any particular period or place of history, which was called the "Capitalistic Spirit"; and that a society was capitalist in so far as this spirit could be found in it. In order to give this spirit authentic letters of credit it was related to human nature. Brentano considered it as equivalent to human nature; Weber, as a development triumphing over its earlier form; Sombart, as at the same time a subjugation of human nature, over whose departure he romantically lingered, and as identical with human nature.[4] Such an assumption was bound to be arbitrary and external to problems of past history; in this case, it reflected faithfully nineteenth-century *laissez-faire*. The result was a concentration upon the individual and upon emancipation. Attention was focused upon the emancipated individual, upon economic individualism, as the sole and eternal need of capitalist society at all periods, as the sole and eternal test of whether a society was capitalist or not.[5]

[4] W. Sombart, *Quintessence of Capitalism* (1915), pp. 13, 202, 205, 239.

[5] For example: Brentano based his criticism of Weber upon an assessment of the comparative emancipation brought to the individual by the Renascence and the Reformation. See also O'Brien (*Economics of the Reformation*) and H. M. Robertson (*The Rise of Economic Individualism*).

This particular definition of capitalism in terms of the emancipation of the individual (in common with all such abstract definitions) springs from a very serious misconception concerning the vital historical distinction between changes in quantity and changes in quality. The Weber method has silently concentrated search upon the discovery of changes in quality, in kind; of a new and distinct attitude of mind in individuals, unlike any preceding attitude. Once this attitude can be isolated and pinned down, we are told, then we have the beginning of the spirit of capitalism and hence the origins of capitalism itself.

This is a gravely misleading method of approach. The distinction between changes in quality and changes in quantity is an unreal one. If historians looked for changes in quantity, in degree, they would find that "changes in quality" only in fact result from changes in quantity. This holds good both for changes in ideas and social outlook, as well as for changes in economic organisation (without for the moment postulating any connection between the two).

Let me put it like this. Social outlook can only be changed, *e.g.* from feudal to bourgeois, by a sufficiently powerful bourgeois *bloc* in the society, not by the mere presence of individual capitalists. The simple discovery of a feudal or a bourgeois outlook in an individual can mean nothing by itself; for ideas the same in kind must produce very different results according to their social context. They may be isolated and socially insignificant, or they may be dominant and colour and control their whole society. Somewhere between these two stages will come a period of time in which the outlook of the society will be altered in kind; but the alteration will have been brought about by simple changes in the relative social importance of the ideas in question, that is to say in the numbers and strength of the people holding the ideas. In the same way, changes in economic organisation will occur gradually but will, if they continue, reach a point at which they are strong enough to necessitate a radical alteration of the whole economic organisation of the society in which they occur. Qualitative changes in society, thus, can only result from preceding changes in quantity; changes of quality are nothing else but a certain stage of intensity reached by preceding changes in quantity. The absolute distinction between the two is misleading.

Yet this absolute distinction lies at the root of the method used by both sides in the Weber controversy. It receives clear expression in Pirenne; he accepts the distinction, but denies that the change of quality which is necessary for Weber's theory occurred at the moment postulated by Weber. He is writing of capitalism in the Middle Ages and in modern times and says: "Il n'y a là qu'une différence quantitative, non une différence qualitative, une différence d'intensité, non une différence de nature." [6] This attitude underlies all those criticisms of Weber that attempt to show that there was nothing new in sixteenth-century capitalism, either in its organisation or in the spirit

[6] H. Pirenne, *Les Périodes de l'histoire sociale du Capitalisme* (1914), p. 9.

of those at its head. Weber in defending himself against such charges did not abandon the method but merely drew his definitions finer and distinguished in kind between unscrupulous money-makers, who have existed at all times, and the true bearers of the capitalist spirit in the sixteenth and seventeenth centuries. Indeed, he was forced into the question-begging of which Brentano and Sée accused him. Weber was precluded by his method from arguing that the change of quality necessary to his theory *resulted* from the quantiative changes noticed by his critics.

If we penetrate behind the rigid distinction drawn between changes of quality and quantity we come upon the heart of the matter and find the explanation why Weber used the method he did and why he is unable to escape from abstract definitions and qualitative categories. The whole apparatus of the method results from an approach which Franz Borkenau [7] has called "isolierendkausal" and which Henri Sée perhaps sought to indicate when he said that Weber's method was "unilatéral." [8] What is meant is the simplification of the enquiry down to the tracing of the effects of *one* isolated historical factor upon some historical development. Sombart and Weber admit in effect to the use of this method when they say that they are not unaware of other factors outside their chosen one. Others use the method against Weber, showing the effects upon the Reformation of other factors taken in isolation (war, luxury, the Jews, the Price Revolution, the Renascence State, etc.), in an attempt to depreciate the importance of Weber's particular factor.

Now, this method of isolation may lead and has undoubtedly led to important discoveries; it is a valuable method for making partial and limited enquiries. But it cannot serve as a method for an interpretation of the total historical problem of a period or a movement. The inter-relation between the factors must be lost; for the fatal and always false assumption of *ceteris paribus* must be made. The difficulty cannot be overcome by multiplying the use of the method, for distortion is inherent in it.

The major defect, however, is the inevitable failure to discover or even enquire into the historical causes of the factors whose influence the method is used to investigate. The question of the cause of the Reformation has hardly been broached at all in the whole Weber controversy. And this is no accident. Weber set out to disprove the materialist conception of history; and, within its own limits, the unilateral method can easily, indeed inevitably, be made to do this. Weber in effect asks, Did the Calvinist ethic and attitude to work precede and largely influence the application of this ethic in the capitalist world? [9] Weber, for all his critics, showed the answer to be substantially Yes. The conclusion must be that ideas that came to birth in the mind effected economic and material developments and not vice versa.

[7] F. Borkenau, *Der Übergang vom foedalen zum bürgerlichen Weltbild* (1934).
[8] H. Sée, "Dans quelle mesure puritains." etc., p. 58.
[9] F. Borkenau, *op. cit.*

Such conclusions are inevitable from the way the question is put; for if Weber starts with Protestantism as a datum and has merely to examine its development and its social repercussions, he cannot, within the framework of his enquiry, go behind this datum. His type of argument can throw no light at all upon the validity of the materialist conception of history, because it is debarred from facing the vital problem of the origin of the ideas whose reaction upon the material world it is engaged in discovering. Some of Weber's critics have side-tracked the issue by finding sufficient material explanations for the evolution of capitalism, without bringing in the Reformation at all; but they find that they are forced to dismiss the Reformation as an historical accident without causes.[10] Others have found an alternative "spiritual" cause for capitalism, either in Catholicism or in some secular spirit of mind; but these, like Weber, do not find a cause for their spiritual factor. Others still, like Sombart or Robertson, do both these things, and find mixed spiritual and material causes for capitalism. As far as the problem of the Reformation is concerned, all of them treat it in the same way, either directly or invertedly. This is the fundamental reason why Weber's method has been productive of some important discoveries but cannot be used to solve the whole problem of the cause and effects of the Reformation.

A tree may be known by its fruit. Some of the hair-splitting to which the controversy has degenerated must be attributed to the pugnacity and perversity of historians; but much of it is the natural result of the method. Take for instance the fierce debates about the birth-year of capitalism. If Weber based his theory upon the close-dating of a change in kind in the outlook of the European mind, it was inevitable that his opponents would push this dating back to a point where it was no use to him. Sombart, Pirenne and others did this with moderation; it was left to L. Brentano to find that the Fourth Crusade already disclosed "a veritable orgy of modern capitalism";[11] indeed he admitted that in this sense there was really no date behind which you could not find the origins of capitalism. Brentano at least had the merit of reducing the argument to absurdity. Another source of hair-splitting is the extreme over-simplification of the manifold Reformation movement that results from the Weber method. Owing to the abstraction of the problem, each author concentrates his theories and researches upon one single consequence of the Reformation movement. If the Reformation is reduced to a movement with all its consequences in one direction, it is then easy enough for both sides to find all the ammunition they need in the rich and variegated elements that are for convenience grouped together as the Reformation. The Weber method is constitutionally incapable of taking account of the *variety* of the Reformation.

Another significant fruit of the method is the way in which it has concentrated upon the seventeenth and subsequent centuries. This is the first mo-

[10] *e.g.,* L. Brentano and H. M. Robertson (see p. 2 above).
[11] L. Brentano, *Die Anfaenge des modernen Kapitalismus*, p. 33.

ment at which Protestantism begins to show any significant signs of behaving in the way Weber wanted; in consequence he coolly left out the vital first century during which the Reformation established itself and caused the most stir. Other historians have equally concentrated on some special period, pre-sixteenth century if they are against Weber, post-sixteenth century if they incline his way. The curious result has been that a controversy about Protestantism has hardly touched the Reformation in the first great century of its establishment. Similarly, the theory has found no place for Luther. Although Weber found some of his deepest ideas best illustrated in Luther, although Calvin looked to Luther as his master, Weber was prepared to agree with his enemies that Luther was part of the Middle Ages and therefore outside the world with which he was dealing.

Clearly a new method of approach is needed. What is it to be? The method I propose to follow is simple; I shall abandon all abstract, cast-iron definitions, and get away from the psychology of the isolated individual, and from the obsession that all that the capitalist individual ever needed was emancipation, escape from discipline. Instead, I shall approach the problem as a social one; ask what were the social and economic needs of society at the time of the Reformation; and then examine how far the Reformation (amongst other factors) was a response to these needs.

In spite of my strictures on abstract definitions I have already used the word "capitalism"; it is too useful as a shorthand symbol to forgo. Wherever I use it, it is not as a *definition* of the psychology of individuals but as a description of a type of social organisation. I shall use "capitalist" to describe a society which is preponderantly a money-economy, in which workers labour for wages and in which employers own and control the means of production and decide to what use they shall be put by a calculus of profits. Anything that makes for the spread and establishment of such an economy out of pre-existing feudal conditions, I shall describe as advancing capitalism.

III

There is one immediate obstacle to be cleared away, which was a stumbling-block to Weber; namely the existence of capitalism in fifteenth-century Europe before the occurrence of the Reformation. It is no use trying to define this capitalism out of existence by dismissing its leaders, as Weber does, as mere unscrupulous money-makers; or as exceptions, as Sombart does of Jacob Fugger and his saying "Let me earn as long as I am able." [12] Even by Weber's own psychological standards the way of life of north Italy, as described by Sombart [13] (who, as usual, is on both sides of the controversy) and Brentano,[14] was capitalist; L. B. Alberti with his "Holy Economy" and his saying "Whoso loses no time can accomplish almost everything" and Lo-

[12] Sombart, *Quintessence of Capitalism*, p. 158.
[13] Sombart, *Quintessence of Capitalism* and *Der moderne Kapitalismus*.
[14] L. Brentano, *op. cit.*

renzo da Vinci with his list of Sins are exact counterparts of Franklin, on whose "Little Book" and "Time is money" Weber builds so great a superstructure. Nor was this capitalism confined to north Italy; it stretched across the Alps into the mining areas of south Germany and the manufacturing districts of north-west Europe and into the cities along the Rhine and the Danube.

The non-occurrence of a Reformation in these circumstances throws light on the problem of the Reformation when it did occur. Capitalism in the late fifteenth century could by no means be made compatible with contemporary Catholicism, which was intertwined with the law, thought, needs, and property of feudalism; and which must inevitably go down if the social basis and presuppositions on which it had built were destroyed by capitalism. But there were factors which made a working compromise possible. In north Italy capitalism was triumphant over a small, compact area; whereas beyond the Alps even the most developed cities were isolated, a mere fringe of town-civilisation against a vast feudal and rural background. In the words of H. Sée, at the end of the fifteenth century even "Antwerp was an islet in a society founded mainly on landed property." Thus, Rome had behind her the strength of vast social responsibilities in Europe beyond the Alps, where capitalism was isolated and where a predominantly feudal society needed catholic protection. Moreover, since north Italian capitalism had never had to impose itself rapidly upon a large feudal area, it had evolved into a society of City-States instead of into a single nation with a capital; therefore, as a system of society, it lacked political force against Rome. Rome, for her part, had come to rely upon Italian capitalism to finance her huge undertakings.

In these circumstances, it was inevitable that the comprehensive doctrines of usury (elaborated in the thirteenth century as a safeguard against the first steps of capitalist advance) should be qualified by subtle exceptions which made the necessary modifications in her practice but did not destroy her doctrines. The Church "a dû favoriser les banques italiennes, dont il avait besoin, et peu à peu composer avec l'esprit du siècle, à mesure que les conditions économiques se transformaient." [15] Here was the reason for the exceptions and qualifications to the doctrine of usury, qualifications which the Church could afford to make and which the slowly developing and small-scale capitalism of north Italy and northern Europe, for its part, was prepared to accept. The pagan Renascence permitted a sufficient "solvent of traditional restraints." [16] Even then, there occurred with Savonarola a beginning of what might have ended in an Italian Reformation. Savonarola parallels in many ways Calvin; he put his genius at the disposal of the patriot party, just come to power in Florence; he helped to discipline the middle and lower class; he purged the constitution of its democratic features.

On the heels of this, not the first, abortive attempt at the Reformation,

[15] H. Sée, *op. cit.*
[16] R. H. Tawney, Foreword to Weber's *Protestant Ethic.*

came the real thing at last at the other end of Europe. The intruding factor was the Price Revolution, the effects of which were enormous. It speeded up the economic development of Europe into an Industrial Revolution (of which all subsequent have been in the family). The sixteenth century became the age of water-power; cranes, pulleys, pumps, coal for heating, gunpowder, and innumerable inventions in particular industries transformed the productive capacity of Europe.[17] The driving force behind this industrial expansion was the profit-inflation caused by prices rising faster than wages, which then formed a very high part of the costs of production. Europe was introduced to the age of manufacture (in the strict sense as opposed to mecanofacture). These improvements hastened the displacement of north Italy by the north-west of Europe as the commercial and manufacturing centre of the continent. Therewith the position of Rome as against capitalism was reversed; the area for which Catholicism was socially necessary became less important than the area dominated by capitalism; Rome was suddenly put upon the defensive.

But this was not all. The Industrial Revolution brought with it the displacement of the class-system on which the Roman Church was based by another class-system that grew out of the first. The bourgeoisie, which had been a middle class under feudalism, had to break forth from its social and political subordination and from its self-imposed restrictions (the gilds) and become a ruling class. This involved the transfer of blocks of feudal property to the bourgeoisie for exploitation by capitalist instead of feudal methods of production; the destruction or conversion to new ends of feudal law and ideology; the absorption or ruin of the feudal upper classes; and, finally, the supplanting of the feudal working-class by a class of wage-earners.

Above all, the Price Revolution meant that all these problems needed urgent and immediate solution over large parts of Europe which had received insufficient slow and gradual preparation for them.

I have to show how these circumstances gave rise to the Reformation.

IV

It has often been pointed out that the Reformation was a great ascetic movement within Catholic Christianity. Weber's description of the Reformation as intramundane asceticism, as a taking of the Catholic ascetic outside the monastery walls into the world, has been generally accepted. It is important to see how far this description provides an explanation of the origin of the Reformation.

The Christian ascetic had already played a vital part in the evolution of

---

[17] See, *e.g.* Sombart, *Der moderne Kapitalismus;* H. Grossman, "Die gesellschaftlichen Grundlagen der mechanistischen Philosophie u. die Manufaktur" (*Zeitschrift für sozialforschung.* 1935. Heft 2) and J. U. Nef, "The Progress of Technology and the Growth of Large-Scale Industry in Great Britain, 1540–1640," *Economic History Review,* v (Oct. 1934).

Catholicism. The ascetic ideal had driven man to effort and (often un-conscious) economy in the slow medieval struggle for mastery over material conditions; the Church, in order to retain its hold, had had to make itself the custodian of this ascetic and, in the process, had transformed Christianity into its peculiar western European form. But there was a definite limit to the powers of the Church to embrace the ascetic within her system. The magical powers of the priest, on which was grounded the sacerdotal hierarchy, depended upon the *non-ascetic*, worldly peasantry which formed the social background of medieval Catholicism; this peasantry and normal feudal society was only capable of intermittent effort and needed the powers of the priest to recover man from mortal sin, etc. The basis of the ascetic, however, was the notion that man could struggle and triumph without lapses; that it was within his own abilities, without the magical aid of priest, to save himself. These two standards of morality were incompatible; if the Church were to make room within her system for the growth of the ascetic, and yet preserve the priestly powers and hierarchy, she must strictly canalise the ascetic and confine it to monastic walls and orders outside the world. She must main-tain a double standard of morality.

The Catholic system, therefore, depended upon an equilibrium between incompatible elements; and her marvellous philosophy was built upon the synthesis of opposites, such as free Will and divine Omnipotence, Aristotle and the Bible. But the equilibrium could never be maintained; for alongside the monastery, in the lead of economic advance, was the town, with a mode of life which was unlike the peasant's and which, with its ideals of saving and steady, unrelaxing effort, was a form of the ascetic. Accompanying the eco-nomic advance of Europe, there were therefore repeated demands for the re-newal, widening, and generalisation of the ascetic; and in order to prevent the formulation of lay concepts of the ascetic, the Church was forced from time to time to widen and renew her own formulation. But the widening of the ascetic came ever nearer heresy and was increasingly difficult for the Church to control; for each extension threatened to destroy the double stand-ard of morality and put in its place a single ascetic standard, to which all men would be expected to comply. If the ascetic came out into the world, it would destroy the basis of the magical powers of the priesthood, namely a lower standard of morality for the ordinary man than the standard demanded by the ascetic; and, with it, the whole Catholic hierarchy and the balanced theology upon which it rested.

The dangers of this development had been revealed in the thirteenth cen-tury. Already St. Benedict had "adumbrated, if he did not actually reach, a condition of things in which the distinction between the monk and the world had been reduced to the smallest possible dimensions, *compatible with its existence at all.*" [18] Then "the mendicant orders drove the ascetic out into the

---

[18] K. E. Kirk, *Vision of God* (1932), pp. 121–22 (my italics).

fullest relations with the world." [19] At the same time the dangers of the lay ascetic were pressing; the associations of pious laymen "found themselves almost unwittingly drawn into heresy. Many sects were led by degrees to discard the ministry and the sacraments of the Church and substitute their own rites." "By the beginning of the thirteenth century Christianity was in danger of disruption." [20]

The Reformation, regarded as a movement within Western Christianity, was a second and more successful attempt to carry the ascetic beyond the danger-point for Catholicism. The forms for the ascetic were at hand: the monastery and the sect (the Ghetto, also a cradle of the European ascetic, would not be available for a Christian movement): the appropriate doctrines were also at hand within the equilibrated Catholic theology. But, as the thirteenth century had shown, any further development of the ascetic would take it out of the monastery into the world, there to join the strengthened Sects. The foundation of the Catholic priesthood would be destroyed; the conception of human nature would be changed. Both these results would find theological expression in a re-statement and re-emphasis of certain parts of Catholic theology, especially Predestination and Original Sin.[21] The re-emphasis would be heresy, for it would overset the vital equilibrium of Catholic doctrine.

It can therefore be said that the Reformation, being an ascetic movement, was bound to disrupt the Church and rend its theology. But this does not wholly solve (as is implied by Troeltsch or K. E. Kirk) the problem of the cause of the Reformation. It does not explain why an ascetic movement occurred at this moment; nor why a movement *within* Christianity came about; nor why just these elements in the Catholic tradition and none of its other ideas were so developed; it does not explain why such a development occurred at just this moment and in some places, but not in others.

The attempts to explain the origin of the Reformation in terms of the inner logic of Christianity, as if Christianity were bound from the beginning to develop just as it did and just at the right moment, are so far from successful that they force one to the conclusion that there must have been another factor at work, external to Christianity, which impinged upon it and brought out of it results that were, sure enough, conditioned by the Christian tradition, but could not have been caused by it. When Europe at the time of the Reformation is surveyed the only force capable of working such results seems *prima facie* to have been the pressure of the social needs suddenly posed by the Price Revolution. The Price Revolution brought these problems upon Europe with a speed that was totally unexpected, and with an urgency for which there had been no gradual preparation.

[19] K. E. Kirk, *op. cit.*
[20] *op. cit.*, p. 151.
[21] Troeltsch, *Die Bedeutung des Protestantismus für die Entstebung der modernen Welt* (1924), p. 39 ff.

To prove this assumption it is necessary to examine the Reformation in detail and to go further into the nature of the social problems facing parts of Europe at this time. So far I have taken the Reformation as a single, undifferentiated movement; and there is a sense in which such a treatment is justified. There was an underlying similarity running through all the parts of the Reformation, just as there was a basic similarity in the problems set by the Price Revolution, wherever it transformed the European economy. On the other hand, within this basic similiarity lay a great variety of appurtenant but not identical lesser movements. There are amongst others three factors, without which it seems to me impossible to account for these known subdivisions within the Reformation:

1. The social problem, presented by the Price Revolution, was really a problem with two parts. The first need was primary accumulation, that is to say the accumulation of capital into sufficiently large units to permit the new methods of production by means of water-power, pumping, and enclosure; all of which were beyond the capacity of the previous scale of capital accumulation. In conditions like those of Colbert's France it would be possible for the State to make capital available; but, in the early stages of capitalist advance, the better and perhaps the only way was by an extension of the methods and mentality of the bourgeois merchant. That meant by private enterprise; which again meant a large-scale transfer of feudal capital into the private hands of the advancing bourgeoisie. The second, subsequent, and really basic need was the acclimatisation of the classes of capitalist society into the new positions made necessary by the results of primary accumulation. The proportions in which these needs were present would affect the nature of the responses to the social needs of the time, amongst which I am claiming the Reformation as one of the most important.

2. The dual problem that was posed by the Price Revolution was partly a political one; this was especially true of the problem of primary accumulation. The Reformation with its development of the ascetic to the point of heresy would naturally join any state that wished to transfer feudal property, for "ecclesiastical property had been the bulwark of the traditional system of landownership"; [22] and the state, for its part, would join forces with a movement aimed at the heart of the Roman system. The problem of the acclimatisation of the new classes was also, but to a less extent, a political one. The form of the Reformation would, thus, be affected by the particular forms of government and local political problems in different countries. Without organisation into nations, Europe would not have reached her actual degree of economic development; the Reformation, therefore, had to occur in and accommodate itself to a system of nations. The relationship between Reformation and state would also partly depend on whether the concrete problem of primary accumulation or the ideological problem of class-acclimatisation was the more pressing.

[22] K. Marx, *Capital* (C. and E. Paul Edition), p. 799.

3. The pressure exerted by the Price Revolution, moreover, was not equal throughout its course. The Price Revolution occurred in two phases. The first, lasting from about 1520–40/50, was relatively mild and was limited to two areas: (*a*) Germany with the Netherlands, under the influence of the expansion of production in Saxony, Austria, and the Tyrol: [23] (*b*) Spain, particularly Andalusia,[24] under the influence of the first imports from America. From 1521–40 Mexico sent no more silver to Europe than the product of the single mining district of Schwarz, Tyrol; [25] and there was little if any re-export from Spain into the rest of Europe. Prices in these two areas seem to have risen by about 20 per cent. The second phase of the Price Revolution was introduced by the discovery of Potosi (1545), Zacatecas (1548), and Guanaruato (1558), and by the application of the mercury amalgamation process, invented in 1557. American silver poured into Europe; the production of German mines fell off; the silver spread from Spain to the manufacturing centres in the north-west. This import and the consequent rise of prices lasted for about a century, varying in different countries. But each successive increment of silver was a smaller percentage of the total circulating stock and the major shock of the inflow was limited to the first years, *i.e.* between the years 1545–80 (rather later in England).

These two phases controlled the economic importance of various parts of Europe. From 1520–40 the leading areas were Spain (which inherited no strong middle class from the Middle Ages) and Germany (which had a strong feudal bourgeoisie). From 1545–80, both Spain and Germany fell away, and the lead was taken by England, the Netherlands, and parts of France and Scotland. The parallelism between these areas and the areas of the Reformation is striking; as also the parallelism in time between the first phase of the Price Revolution and Luther (both about 1520–40); and between the second phase and Calvin (both about 1545–80).

If it can be shown that the actual Reformation can only be explained in the light of these factors, it will go a long way towards establishing that the Reformation was rooted in the material conditions of the time and examination of the various parts of the Reformation will also explain (what we have not yet ascertained) why the Reformation was an ascetic movement.

We may call the two phases of the Reformation, Lutheran and Calvinist, though neither phase was entirely represented by the man after whom it is convenient to name it.

The concrete results of the Lutheran phase, including the violent period of Anabaptism, were destruction of the Catholic hold upon the middle and lower classes, and sanction for the seizure of Catholic and feudal property. On the whole, the religious movement was subordinate to the state, except in Germany, where the absence of a political head who could give expression

[23] Wiebe, *Die Preisrevolution der XVI u. XVII Jahrbunderte* (1895).
[24] E. J. Hamilton, *American Treasure and the Price Revolution in Spain* (1934).
[25] Wiebe, *op. cit.*, Tables.

to national feeling allowed religion at first to give the lead to the secular powers.

The second stage of the Price Revolution meant that Germany could not lead the capitalist revolution. The initiative passed to England, the Netherlands, the industrial parts of Scotland, France and Switzerland; the very parts where the second, Calvinist, phase of the Reformation took root. The problem of primary accumulation was already partly solved and the chief problem now became class-acclimatisation. This problem was very urgent; the bourgeoisie had to exchange its subservience for the will to govern, it had grave economic and political tasks ahead; the working-class had to exchange its loose, extensive labour [26] for disciplined, regular and organised work. These great changes in mental outlook had to be solved quickly enough to keep pace with the Industrial Revolution.

It is here that the Weber method leads most astray. Weber saw enough of the truth to force him into a contradictory position. He could describe the Reformation as an ascetic movement, as one that made the piece-wage system workable; [27] yet he could also conceive of it primarily as a movement bringing nothing but economic liberation from all restraint. Clearly capitalist society was individualist as opposed to feudalism; it was based on private enterprise; it needed individualism to cloak the class-structure of society, which was nearer the surface than in feudalism; it thought mechanistically in terms of quantities rather than *a priori* in terms of qualities, both of matter and of mankind.[28] In the same way capitalism could only come into existence if it broke through the feudal ideas, which had become restrictions upon it as a system of society. Hence, if the Reformation was a chief ideological expression of capitalist society at this stage, it must be shown to have been both individualist and emancipating. But this does not imply that it must preach licence from all restriction for each separate individual. The pressing need was the opposite; the *disciplining* of individuals to the ends of a new society, which was breaking forth out of feudalism and was basically individualist in its social outlook. The urgent need was a re-statement of the ascetic that was deeply embedded in the Christian tradition; an ascetic so interpreted that it would inculcate by discipline the necessary social attitudes. Both the bourgeoisie and the wageworkers must be submitted to this ascetic according to the ends each had to serve.

It was natural that Calvin should stress the ascetic, that he should erect into first principles the Original Sin and Predestination which Luther had kept increasingly in the background. The chief results achieved by Calvin were (1) the rigid division into Elect and Reprobate (which also had been

---

[26] See *e.g.*, Sombart, *Quintessence of Capitalism*, p. 19.

[27] M. Weber, *Protestantische Ethik*, etc. (2nd German edition, 1922), p. 42.

[28] F. Borkenau, *op. cit.* See also criticism by H. Grossman, "Die gesellschaftlichen Grundlagen der mechanistischen Philosophie" (*Zeitschrift für Sozialforschung*, iv, Heft 2, 1935).

latent in Luther) and the Sovereignty of the State (which Hobbes later deduced from the same premises).[29] And (2) the need for incessant goodness; if a Calvinist sinned, he could not recover by the magical aid of the priest; a single sin was sufficient sign that he had been damned from eternity. It was to achieve this second result, which was in fact the setting out of a single-standard of morality in place of the Catholic double-standard, that Calvin had to make his main theological innovations. It was because this change was involved that men disputed so bitterly on points of academic dogma. The effect of these doctrines in social terms was that the capitalist class-structure was both justified (from eternity) and obscured by the stress upon the individual's spiritual behaviour as the sole criterion of social division; and that the correct social ethic and methods for its enforcement were ready-made for self-imposition amongst the Elect, and, if necessary, coercive imposition upon the Reprobate.

The Calvinist system thus provided for the lower-class; but in some parts (notably Holland and later England) the lower-class was powerful enough to play its own part. By now it had lost its early Anabaptist hope of violent emancipation; capitalism was firmly enough established to make labour within the system the only road. The result was that Menno Simon, the complementary contemporary of Calvin, was able to win the Anabaptists back to their earlier non-resistance. He preached an ethic suitable for the working-class and therefore similar to that which Calvin preached for the Reprobates; but the Anabaptist retained his silent protest of withdrawal from the affairs of a wicked world; he lacked the Calvinist's interest in politics, his belief in a strong state and his desire to have that state as his servant. From the amalgam of Calvinist and Anabaptist resulted Puritanism, a vague attitude of mind covering every gradation from the obscure sect to the prosperous Calvinist; and with no fixed internal boundaries, for the Protestant ethic led to worldly success and so, often, to the progress of the successful Protestant up the rungs of the social ladder of Puritanism.

Such was the real spirit of capitalism needed by capitalist society and inculcated by the Reformation. Had the Reformation really produced the libertine "spirit of capitalism" it would have endangered, not advanced, capitalism.

V

Puritanism was clearly an influential factor: the magic mirror described by Tawney, reflecting back the narrow, arid qualities that led the Puritan to success in this world. It set men striving after new virtues, that yesterday had been vices, rather than their actual achievement. But such a superhuman struggle necessarily left a real impress; apart from moral attitudes, Puritan society saved money and developed novel notions of interest; [30] it developed

---

29 F. Borkenau, *op. cit.* Chapters on Calvin and Hobbes.
30 H. Hauser, *Les débuts du capitalisme* (1925), Ch. 2.

a special attitude towards colonisation; [31] and naturally evolved the Puritan Sunday as the only way of securing regular intervals of rest in peoples avidly devoted to work as the highest end.

But, though Puritanism was thus bound up with capitalism in the sixteenth century, the relationship between Protestantism and capitalism is not eternal and absolute. The Reformation was the product of peculiar circumstances; it could occur only against the background of Christendom, in a civilisation of nations, and under the stress of the special and urgent problems posed by the Price Revolution. From the beginning of the seventeenth century, Protestantism began to lose its special functions and therewith its spiritual position. Two sets of factors brought this about. First, as the class-acclimatisation which was the highest task of the Reformation was gradually accomplished, Protestantism had to yield ground to other activities which became more important; above all, it had to give place to the secular State and to science.[32]

Secondly, Protestant societies had no monopoly of the advance of capitalism. The Reformation was necessary for the vital first advance in the sixteenth century; but once this advance had been safely made, other countries could follow in the tracks and "step over the Reformation." In such circumstances, certain social devices became important, especially the military-bureaucratic State (*e.g.* Colbert's France), that were closed to Protestantism, with its depreciation of State and court service.[33] Protestantism ceased to have a monopoly of world-capitalist advance and this lowered the prestige it was already losing in its homes; wide concessions were made to the State and to the individual businessman, which Protestantism would have scorned to make in its heyday. Protestantism, of course, has retained considerable social importance; in Protestant countries it is bound up with the achievement and the thought-texture of capitalism. But it is noteworthy that the Reformation was the culminating ascetic revival of Christendom; all subsequent revivals have been Protestant, but of steadily decreasing social significance.

To draw the arguments together. The Reformation was a movement divided into two chronological phases, corresponding to the two phases of the Price Revolution; it was also divided laterally throughout its course into Church and Sect; the emphasis shifted from the problem of primary accumulation to the problem of class-acclimatisation; and there were the expected relations to the State. The movement was diverse and blind, but wonderfully related in its parts; innumerable leaders, Calvin, Menno Simon, Luther, Melancthon, Martyr, Melchior Hoffman, Bucer, Olivetan, and a host of oththers, each played his part, though his only guide was his private conscience;

---

[31] A. J. Toynbee, *Study of History*, vol. i, pp. 211 ff.

[32] B. Hessen, "The Social and Economic Roots of Newton's Principia" in *Science of the Cross Roads* (1931).

[33] E. Beins, *Die Wirtschatsethik der Calvinistischen Kirche der Niederlande, 1565–1650* (1922), p. 117.

behind these was a mass of anonymous followers, each in his own eyes choosing his adherence according to the logic and reasonableness of his particular leader. The inescapable conclusion is the same that we drew from an examination of the inner logic of Christianity, namely that the Reformation was the reaction to a force external to itself. The genius of leaders, the devotion of followers, even apparent accidents, were not so much independent forces controlling the destinies of the Reformation as factors that were present or called into being and made use of by a force greater than themselves. The Reformation corresponded in its various parts so closely to the social needs created by the Industrial Revolution, its effects (if properly conceived) were so apt, that in my submission we are entitled to say that our *prima facie* supposition that the Industrial Revolution was the external force we were looking for is now proven.

The Reformation was not the cause of capitalism; rather it was the result of needs created by capitalist advance at a particular place and time. *For this reason*, once it was in existence and throughout its various stages and forms, the Reformation played an indispensable part, amongst other factors, in the triumph of European capitalism over difficulties that had threatened to overwhelm it. ◻

◇ **18** ◇

The Mathematical Principles of Natural Philosophy *

ISAAC NEWTON

Since the ancients (as we are told by Pappus) made great account of the Science of Mechanics in the investigation of natural things; and the moderns, laying aside substantial forms and occult qualities, have endeavoured to subject the phenomena of nature to the laws of mathematics; I have in this treatise cultivated Mathematics, so far as it regards Philosophy. The ancients considered Mechanics in a twofold respect; as rational, which proceeds accurately by demonstration, and practical. To practical Mechanics all the manual arts belong, from which Mechanics took its name. But as artificers do not work with perfect accuracy, it comes to pass that Mechanics is so distinguished from Geometry, that what is perfectly accurate is called Geometrical, what is less so is called Mechanical. But the errors are not in the art, but in the artificers. He that works with less accuracy, is an imperfect Mechanic, and if any could work with perfect accuracy, he would be the most perfect Mechanic of all. For the description of right lines and circles, upon which

* Taken and adapted from Sir Isaac Newton, *The Mathematical Principles of Natural Philosophy*, Vol. I. Printed for Benjamin Motte, at the Middle-Temple-Gate, in Fleet Street, London, 1729, pp. A–A4. Translated into English by Andrew Motte.

Geometry is founded, belongs to Mechanics. Geometry does not teach us to draw these lines, but requires them to be drawn. For it requires that the learner should first be taught to describe these accurately, before he enters upon Geometry; then it shews how by these operations problems may be solved. To describe right lines and circles are problems, but not geometrical problems. The solution of these problems is required from Mechanics; and by Geometry the use of them, when so solved, is shewn. And it is the glory of Geometry that from those few principles, fetched from without, it is able to produce so many things. Therefore Geometry is founded in mechanical practice, and is nothing but that part of universal Mechanics which accurately proposes and demonstrates the art of measuring. But since the manual arts are chiefly conversant in the moving of bodies, it comes to pass that Geometry is commonly referred to their magnitudes, and Mechanics to their motion. In this sense Rational Mechanics will be the Science of motions resulting from any forces whatsoever and of the forces required to produce any motions, accurately proposed and demonstrated. This part of Mechanics was cultivated by the ancients in the Five Powers which relate to manual arts, who considered gravity (it not being a manual power) no otherwise than as it moved weights by those powers.

Our design not respecting arts but philosophy, and our subject, not manual but natural powers, we consider chiefly those things which relate to gravity, levity, elastic force, the resistance of fluids, and the like forces whether attractive or impulsive. And therefore we offer this work as mathematical principles of philosophy. For all the difficulty of philosophy seems to consist in this, from the phenomena of motions to investigate the forces of Nature, and then from these forces to demonstrate the other phenomena. And to this end, the general propositions in the first and second book are directed. In the third book we give an example of this in the explication of the System of the World. For by the propositions mathematically demonstrated in the first books, we there derive from the celestial phenomena, the forces of Gravity with which bodies tend to the Sun and the several Planets. Then from these forces by other propositions, which are also mathematical, we deduce the motions of the Planets, the Comets, the Moon, and the Sea. I wish we could derive the rest of the phenomena of Nature by the same kind of reasoning from mechanical principles. For I am induced by many reasons to suspect that they may all depend upon certain forces by which the particles of bodies, by some causes hitherto unknown, are either mutually impelled towards each other and cohere in regular figures, or are repelled and recede from each other; which forces being unknown, Philosophers have hitherto attempted the Search of Nature in vain. But I hope the principles here laid down will afford some light either to that, or some truer, method of Philosophy.

In the publication of this Work, the most acute and universally learned Mr. Edmund Hally not only assisted me with his pains in correcting the press and taking care of the schemes, but it was to his solicitations that its becoming publick is owing. For when he had obtained of me my demonstrations of the figure of the celestial orbits, he continually pressed me to communicate the same to the Royal Society; who afterwards by their kind encouragement and entreaties, engaged me to think of publishing them. But after I had begun to consider the inequalities of the lunar motions, and had entered upon some other things relating to the laws and measures of gravity, and other forces; and the figures that would be described by bodies attracted according to given laws; and the motion of several bodies moving among themselves; the motion of bodies in resisting mediums; the forces, densities, and motions of mediums; the orbits of the Comets, and such like; I put off that publication till I had made a search into those matters, and could put out the whole together. What relates to the Lunar motions (being imperfect) I have put all together in the corollaries of prop. 66. to avoid being obliged to propose and distinctly demonstrate the several things there contained in a method more prolix than the subject deserved, and interrupt the series of the several propositions. Some things found out after the rest, I chose to insert in places less suitable, rather than change the number of the propositions and the citations. I heartily beg that what I have here done may be read with candour, and that the defects I have been guilty of upon this difficult subject may be, not so much reprehended as kindly supplied, and investigated by new endeavours of my readers. ◻

❖ **19** ❖

Economic Theory and Entrepreneurial History *

JOSEPH A. SCHUMPETER

In the areas of economic theory and entrepreneurial history, I shall present a brief survey of the history, within economic literature, of the notions that economists have formed at various times on the subject of entrepreneurship and economic progress.

In the field to be discussed, as in others, early economic analysis started from the notions evolved by common experience of everyday life, proceeding to greater precision and refinement of these notions as time went on. From the first, the businessman was a familiar figure that did not seem to call for elaborate explanation at all. The particular forms of business enterprise that every particular environment produced — the artisan, the trader, the moneylender, and so on — took a long time in merging into the general concept of businessman. But by the end of the 17th century this modest generalization

* Reprinted by permission of the publishers from Joseph Schumpeter, "Economic Theory and Entrepreneurial History," CHANGE AND THE ENTREPRENEUR, Research Center in Entrepreneurial History, Cambridge, Mass.: Harvard University Press, 1949.

was pretty much accomplished. It is, however, worth noting that at least from the beginning of the 15th century on, the scholastic doctors in their economics had a very definite idea of the businessman and his functions, and that in particular they distinguished clearly between the specific *industria* of the merchant and the *labor* of the workman.

The same applies to the laic successors of the scholastic doctors, "the philosophers of natural law," and still more to all those pamphleteers of the "mercantilist" age that laid the foundations of classic economics. Cantillon's work, which is usually, though not quite correctly, described as the first systematic treatise on economics, then introduced the term "entrepreneur." It is worth our while to note that Cantillon defined this entrepreneur as the agent who buys means of production at certain prices in order to combine them into a product that he is going to sell at prices that are uncertain at the moment at which he commits himself to his costs. I think that this embryonic analysis was not infelicitous. Besides recognizing business activity as a function *sui generis*, it emphasizes the elements of direction and speculation that certainly do enter somehow into entreprenuerial activity. Like most of Cantillon's ideas, including the idea of the *tableau économique*, this one was accepted by the physiocrats as a matter of course. Since directly and through the physiocrats Cantillon's teaching continued to be known in France, it seems fair to say that J. B. Say only continued the French tradition by developing this analysis further. In this he was greatly helped by the fact that, knowing from experience what business practice really is, he had a lively vision of the phenomenon which most of the other classic economists lacked. With him, then, the entrepreneur is the agent that combines the others into a productive organism.

It could be shown that this definition might be expanded into a satisfactory theory of entrepreneurship by analyzing what this combining of factors really consists of, and that Say himself did not do much with it beyond stressing its importance. Let us note in passing, however, that he put the entrepreneur into the center of both the productive and the distributive theory which, though it is disfigured by many slips, first adumbrated the analytic structure that became fully articulate in the Austrians. Still more clearly the nature and importance of entrepreneurship were perceived by Jeremy Bentham. It is a curious fact (curious, that is, considering the tremendous influence that Bentham exerted in other respects) that his views on this subject — which were not fully given to the public until the posthumous publication of his collected works — remained almost unnoticed by professional economists.

In spite of the great influence of the physiocrats and of Cantillon upon Adam Smith, English thought took a quite different line. To be sure, Adam Smith repeatedly talked about the employer — the master, the merchant, and the undertaker — but the leading or directing activity as a distinctive function played a surprisingly small role in his analytic scheme of the economic process. His reader is bound to get an impression to the effect that this process runs on by itself. Natural law preconceptions led Adam Smith to emphasize the role of labor to the exclusion of the productive function of designing the plan according to which this labor is being applied. This shows characteristically in his turn of phrase that asserts that "capitalists" hire "industrious people," advancing them means of subsistence, raw materials, and tools, and letting them do the rest. What the businessman does in the system of Adam Smith is, therefore, to provide real capital and nothing else: the identification of the capitalist's and the entrepreneur's function was thus accomplished. Let us note: first, that this picture of the industrial process is entirely unrealistic; but that, considering the prevalence at Adam Smith's time of the putting-out system, and also for other historical reasons, this identification was then less absurd than it became fifty years later; and that Smith's authority explains why it survived so well into times that presented different patterns. Since capital, according to Adam Smith, is the result of saving, and since providing capital is the only essential function of the businessman, the latter's profits was essentially interest to be explained on the lines of either an exploitation or an abstinence theory. Adam Smith elaborated neither, but no doubt suggested both.

With Ricardo and Marx the processes of production and commerce are still more automatic. The designing, directing, leading, co-ordinating function has practically no place at all in their analytic schemata. To avoid misunderstandings, let me emphasize that there is no doubt but that, if pressed, both Ricardo and Marx (and this goes for a majority of the writers of the classic period) would certainly have recognized the importance of entrepreneurship or business management or however they would have called it, for the success or failure of the individual concern. But it is possible to recognize this and to hold, nevertheless, that for the social process as a whole individual differences in this respect are of no great moment. John Stuart Mill who, at an early age, had experienced the influence of Say, abandoned Ricardianism in this as he did in other points. He emphasized the function of direction in the productive process and went out of his way to say that very often it required "no ordinary skill." His perception of the importance of entrepreneurial activity shows among other things in the fact that he regretted that there is no good English word for the French "entrepreneur." But this was all. When we observe that he analyzed the entrepreneur's profits into wages of management, interest on owned capital, and premium of risk, we wonder why he should not have been content with the perfectly good English term "business management," which was in fact to satisfy Marshall. For, after all, his entrepreneur does a type of non-manual work that does not essentially differ from other types, and therefore reaps a return that is analogous to wages. There should be no need for a distinctive term.

Just as the understanding of the phenomenon of rent of land was facilitated by the English land system that showed up the distinction between the owner of land and the agricultural producer with unmistakable clearness, so the distinction between the entrepreneur and the capitalist was facilitated in the second half of the 19th century by the fact that changing methods of business finance produced a rapidly increasing number of instances in which capitalists were not entrepreneurs and entrepreneurs were not capitalists. Though the owner-manager remained for a time still the ruling type, it became increasingly clear that a link between owning and operating the physical shell of industry is not a necessary one. Economists accordingly began to emphasize distinctions between the two functions and to devote more attention to the specifically entrepreneurial one. Fundamental change in the analytic set-up was very slow, however. Among other things, this shows in the survival of the risk theory of entrepreneurial profit. If providing the capital is not the essential or defining function of the entrepreneur, then risk bearing should not be described as an essential or defining function either, for it is obviously the capitalist who bears the risk and who loses his money in case of failure. If the entrepreneur borrows at a fixed rate of interest and undertakes to guarantee the capitalist against loss whatever the results of the enterprise, he can do so only if he owns other assets with which to satisfy the creditor capitalist when things go wrong. But, in this case, he is able to satisfy his creditor because he is a capitalist himself and the risk he bears, he bears in this capacity and not in his capacity of entrepreneur. To this point I shall return below. The economists, therefore, who went on to emphasize the entrepreneurial function more and more, such as Francis Walker in the U.S., Marshall in England, Mangoldt and others in Germany, added very little to its analysis.

Two lines of thought that issued in distinctive theories of entrepreneurial profits as distinguished from interest should not go unmentioned. Mangoldt, following up a generalization of the rent concept that may be traced to Samuel Bailey, defined the particular element of total receipts that goes to the entrepreneur as a rent of ability. The underlying idea is very plausible. All current disturbances of the economic process, the whole task of adaptation to ever changing situations, impinges primarily upon the heads of business concerns. Obviously this is a very personal task of which some people acquit themselves very much better than others. There is a common-sense impression to the effect that there is such a thing as a distinct business ability, which includes aptitude for efficient administration, for prompt decision, and all that sort of thing; and it is very generally recognized in spite of some votes to the contrary (in this country, mainly from economists of Veblenite persuasion) that successful survival of difficult situations and success in taking advantage of favorable situations is not merely a matter of luck. The concept of a rent of ability expresses the element involved quite well. Again the cognate idea that business decisions in a world that is full of uninsurable risks ("uncertainty") will in general produce results that diverge more or less widely from the expected ones and thus lead sometimes to surplus gains and sometimes to losses, is one that common experience presses upon us very strongly. This idea may be but need not be added to the element of business ability and is of course, still more obviously, not quite the same as the element of risk: but we need not stress these relations. So far as I know, Bohm-Bawerk was the first to make use of this notion for the purpose of explaining entrepreneurial profits as distinct from interest. But this line of thought culminates in the work of Professor Knight.

It does not seem far-fetched, however, to analyze the entrepreneurial function in a different direction which moreover leads to a result that comprises also some of the elements of other theories. I shall try to convey this analysis by starting from two different standpoints. The first standpoint to start from is given by Say's definition of the entrepreneurial function. If production in the economic, as distinguished from the technological, sense consists essentially in transforming or combining factors into products, or as I have put it above, in providing the design of production, then we certainly have in this combining or planning or directing activity a distinct function before us. But this function would be an exceedingly simple matter and essentially a matter of administration if the combinations that have been carried into effect in the past had to be simply repeated or even if they had to be repeated subject to those adaptations which common business experience suggests in the face of conditions that change under the influence of external factors. Administrative or managerial activity of this kind, however necessary, need not be distinguished from other kinds of non-manual labor; but if we confine Say's definition to cases in which combinations that are *not* inherited from the past have to be set up anew, then the situation is obviously different and we do have a distinctive function before us. Naturally, to some extent, even current decisions contain elements that have not been contained in inherited routine. There is, therefore, no sharp dividing line between entrepreneurial activity in this restricted sense and ordinary administration or management, any more than there is a sharp dividing line between the *homo neanderthalis* and the types which we recognize as full-fledged human beings. This does not, however, prevent the distinction from being possible and useful. And the distinctive element is readily recognized so soon as we make clear to ourselves what it means to act outside of the pale of routine. The distinction between adaptive and creative response to given conditions may or may not be felicitous, but it conveys an essential point; it conveys an essential difference.

The other standpoint from which to get a realistic understanding of the entrepreneurial function comes into view when we try to analyze the nature and sources of the gains that attend successful entrepreneurship. This can be done in many ways, for instance, by analyzing the sources of a sufficient number of industrial fortunes. We find immediately that industrial activity in established lines and by established methods hardly ever yields returns that are much greater than is necessary to secure the supply of the factors required. Furthermore, we find that the earning capacity of almost any industrial concern peters out after a time that varies from a few months to a few decades. And, finally, we find that the great surplus gains are in general made in new industries or in industries that adopt a new method, and especially by the firms who are the first in the field. These propositions await scientific investigations in order to be fully established, but are strongly suggested by universally known facts.

If then we have, on the one hand, a distinctive function and, on the other hand, a distinct return on the exercise of this function, we can start with the task of conceptualization. First, we need a word. I have myself suggested that the word "entrepreneur" be harnessed into service, but it is quite clear, of course, that since this "entrepreneurial function" is not a neologism other meanings are bound to creep in. I should, therefore, have no objection to some such expression as "business leader" or simply "innovator" or the like. The essential thing is the recognition of the distinct agent we envisage and not the word.[1] Secondly, in applying our conception to reality we find, as we do in other cases, that real life never presents the function in and by itself. Even the English landlord is not merely the owner of a natural agent but does various other things besides. In the case of the entrepreneur it is even difficult to imagine a case where a man does nothing but set up new combinations and where he does this all his life. In particular an industrialist who creates an entirely new set-up will, in a typical case, then settle down to a merely administrating activity to which he confines himself more and more as he gets older. On the other hand, the entrepreneurial element may be present to a very small extent even in very humble cases and in these the entrepreneurial function may be all but drowned in other activities. It will be seen, however, that while this makes it difficult to deal with entrepreneurship irrespective of the other types of activity of the same individual and while Professor Cole is therefore quite right in emphasizing the necessity of considering business activity as a whole, the distinctive element and its *modus operandi* should not and need not be lost from sight.

Thirdly, since entrepreneurship, as defined, essentially consists in doing things that are not generally done in the ordinary course of business routine, it is essentially a phenomenon that comes under the wider aspect of leadership. But this relation between entrepreneurship and general leadership is a very complex one and lends itself to a number of misunderstandings. This is due to the fact that the concept of leadership itself is complex. Leadership may consist, as it does in the arts, merely in doing a new thing, for instance, in creating a new form of pictorial self-expression, but in other cases it is the influencing of people by methods other than example that is more important. Take, for instance, the phenomenon that we call the ability of

---

[1] The difficulty of naming our function is of course greatly increased by the fact that such words as "management" or "administration" from which we are trying to distinguish our function have with many authors also caught some of the meanings that we wish to reserve for the term "entrepreneur."

being obeyed. Here it is not so much example as a direct action upon other people that matters. The nature and function of entrepreneurial leadership, its causes and effects, therefore constitute a very important subject of investigation for our group.

Fourthly, the distinctive return to entrepreneurship presents difficulties of its own. It is certainly a return to a personal activity. In this sense we might be tempted to call it a form of wages as has in fact been done in the past by many economists. Furthermore, it is clear that if all people reacted in the same way and at the same time to the presence of new possibilities no entrepreneurial gain would ensue: if everybody had been in a position to develop the Watt condenser, prices of products to be produced with the new steam engine would have adjusted themselves instantaneously and no surplus over costs would have arisen for the firm of Boulton and Watt. Therefore, entrepreneurial gain may also be called a monopoly gain, since it is due to the fact that competitors only follow at a distance.[2] But if we called it either wages or monopoly gains we should be obscuring very important characteristics that do not apply to other wages or to other monopoly gains. Moreover, the entrepreneurial gain does not typically consist, and in any case does not necessarily consist, in a current surplus *per se*. If a man, for instance, sets up a new industrial organization such as United States Steel, the value of the assets that enter into this organization increases. This increase no doubt embodies, at least ideally, a discounted value of the expected surplus returns. But it is this increase in asset return itself rather than the returns that constitute the entrepreneurial gain, and it is in this way that industrial fortunes are typically created — another subject to be investigated.

Finally, as has been often pointed out, the entrepreneurial function need not be embodied in a physical person and in particular in a single physical person. Every social environment has its own ways of filling the entrepreneurial function. For instance, the practice of farmers in this country has been revolutionized again and again by the introduction of methods worked out in the Department of Agriculture and by the Department of Agriculture's success in teaching these methods. In this case then it was the Department of Agriculture that acted as an entrepreneur. It is another most important point in our research program to find out how important this kind of activity has been in the past or is in the present. Again the entrepreneurial function may be and often is filled co-operatively. With the development of the largest-scale corporations this has evidently become of major importance: aptitudes that no single individual combines can thus be built into a corporate personality; on the other hand, the constituent physical personalities must inevitably to some extent, and very often to a serious extent, interfere with each other. In many cases, therefore, it is difficult or even impossible to name an

---

[2] The rate of speed at which competitors follow is another very important point for our research program, as are the means at the disposal of the successful entrepreneur for holding his own against would-be competitors (patents and other practices).

individual that acts as "the entrepreneur" in a concern. The leading people in particular, those who carry the titles of president or chairman of the board, may be mere co-ordinators or even figure-heads; and again a very interesting field of research opens up into which I do not wish to go, however, since this problem is in no danger of being forgotten.[3]

We have now briefly to advert to the relation that exists between economic change (usually called economic progress if we approve of it) and the entrepreneurial activity. At present there is, as has been stated above, a whole range of differences of opinion on this subject that extends from a complete or almost complete denial of any importance to be attached to the quality of leading personnel to the equally reckless assertion that the creative individual is nothing less than everything. It need hardly be pointed out that most of these opinions carry the stamp of ideological preconception. It is no doubt part of our work to put provable results into the place of such ideologies. The fundamental question is one of fact, but the necessity of a theoretical schema to start with is nevertheless obvious. I submit that the material under observation may be classed into two masses: on the one hand, there are the given data of the physical and social (including political) environment and, on the other hand, there are the observable reactions to these environmental conditions. But it is better perhaps to include those facts that may be independently observed concerning the quality of leading personnel among the conditions in order to display the interrelation between this and the other factors and to emphasize from the first that on principle there are never any causal chains in the historical process but only mutual interaction of distinguishable factors.

We can then attempt to construct an analytic model of the mechanism of economic change or else, for different countries and periods, different such schemata or models. Let us, in order to visualize this method, consider for a moment the situation that existed in England around 1850. A unique set of historical conditions had produced a uniquely able political sector, the bulk of the members of which hailed from a distinct social class. This sector, while very efficient in certain respects, was entirely unfit and unwilling to undertake anything that we now call economic public management or economic planning. Neglecting for the rest of the agrarian sector, we find industry, trade, and finance substantially left to themselves; and if we add a number of other unique historical circumstances we are pretty much able to draw the picture of economic change that is in fact drawn in the ordinary textbook of economic

---

3 It is extremely interesting to observe that for a long time and occasionally even now economic theorists have been and are inclined to locate the entrepreneurial function in a corporation with the shareholders. However little the individual small shareholder may have to do with the actual management or else with the entrepreneurial function in the corporation, they hold that ultimate decision still lies with them to be exerted in the shareholders' meeting. All I wish to say about this is first, that the whole idea of risk-taking in this way takes on a further lease of life and, second, that such a theory is about as true as is the political theory that in a democracy the electorate ultimately decides what is to be done.

history. In this process of change it is possible to identify a number of factors and events that are entirely impersonal and in some cases random. But looking more closely we see not only that these factors do not determine outcomes uniquely but also that they do not tell us how the actual changes such as the tremendous increase in exports actually came about. In order to make headway with this problem we must investigate how the thousands of individuals actually worked whose combined action produced these results. And for this purpose it is useful as a first step to assume all the environmental factors to be constant and to ask the question what changes we might expect under this assumption. We immediately see that simple increase of population and of physical capital does not constitute the answer. It is not simply the increase of the existing factors of production but the incessantly different use made of these factors that matters. In fact, much of the increase in factors and particularly of physical capital was the result rather than the cause of what we may now identify as entrepreneurial activity. What we observe is rather a behavior pattern, possibly supplemented by a schema of motivation; a typical way of giving effect to the possibilities inherent in a given legal and social system both of which change in the process; the effects of entrepreneurial activity upon the industrial structure that exists at any moment; the consequent process of destruction and reconstruction that went on all the time. All these things may be conceptualized in a more or less complicated schema, every item of which has to be nourished with facts and corrected and amplified under their influence. And this is all.

I shall add, however, that in investigations of this kind the notion of an economic process that merely reproduces itself and shows neither decay nor progress has been found to be of considerable use. It is called the stationary state, and plays two distinct roles in economic theory. On the one hand, economists, ever since Adam Smith and perhaps earlier times, have envisaged the possibility that the energetic advance they were witnessing would some day subside into what we now call a stagnating or mature economy. John Stuart Mill differed from Ricardo not in his expectation that a stationary state would one day emerge but in the optimistic view he took of its features — a world without what he considered an unpleasant bustle, a world much more cultured and at ease than the one he observed. Now, as everybody knows, this "stagnationist thesis" has emerged once more, but it has emerged with two differences. First, the stationary state is by some authors not looked upon as something that looms in the far future but as something on which we are actually about to enter. Let us note in passing that the experiences of the crises 1929–1932 may have a lot to do with the emergency of this frame of mind. Secondly, a problem has arisen which did not worry the classicists at all. Smith or Ricardo did not anticipate any particular difficulties that would arise from the very process of settling down into stationality: rates of change would converge towards zero in a slow and orderly way. But our modern stagnationists anticipate difficulties in this process of settling down.

Keynes in particular anticipated that habits of saving to which equally strong or still stronger propensities to invest corresponded would run on in spite of the fact that there would be no longer any investment opportunities left. With everything indicating now that a new period of unheard-of "progress" is at hand it might be thought that we need not greatly worry about this. But I do not think that we can entirely overlook the problem and history's contribution to it. □

PART THREE

□ The Colonial and Early National Period

There are many reasons why a robust, rapidly expanding population was an important attribute of colonial America, and the recently published researches of Mr. Potter, English expert on American demographic history, throw new light on the subject. Next comes an examination of colonial commercial activity, the preoccupying economic pursuit of the colonists. In our allocation of scarce page resources, we have devoted much the greater portion of this part's share to extending the reader's feeling for the activities of the great merchant class that, after all, largely directed the destinies of the colonies. But the plaint of the tobacco planters in Virginia, heard for more than two centuries from colonials in the tobacco-growing South, is here presented in unusually poignant form. At the conclusion of the readings proper, there is provided the gist of the argument between two opposing views of the importance of economic phenomena in influencing the formation of the Constitution.

Concluding these readings on the colonial period are several documents that should serve as useful references for those who like to do some reading in original sources but who do not have ready access to them. For example, the student has read a great deal about the Navigation Acts and their influence on Anglo-American commercial relationships, but it is unlikely that many students have had an opportunity to read a navigation act. Similarly, the Tea Act, a major precipitant of revolution, and the Quebec Act, which helped to bring the Southern landholders forcibly into the conflict, should be read for their flavor and for a personal evaluation of their meaning. To comprehend the difficulties of a new nation, the student really ought to read the Articles of Confederation, which for so many years loosely bound the American people. Finally, the great Land Ordinance of 1785 and the Northwest Ordinance of 1787 should be read in the original; for the one prescribed an orderly movement into the West, and the other made it certain that new states would not themselves be in colonial subjection to old ones. □

❖ 20 ❖

The Colonial Period *

J. POTTER

The Malthusian postulate, that the American population doubled every twenty-five years, would have required an average decennial increase of 32 per cent. The first question then is whether the evidence for the colonial period provides support for the assumption of such a rate of growth.

The statistical records for the seventeenth and eighteenth centuries are very limited. Some colonial governors, especially in the North, conducted enumerations of the population, usually at the behest of the British government. These are too sporadic in occurrence, restricted in scope, and unreliable in content, however, to provide anything like a complete picture of the demographic history of the colonial period. Consequently much weight has often been placed on the observations of contemporary Americans like Judge Samuel Sewell and Benjamin Franklin, or the impressions of European travellers like Peter Kalm or Jean de Crèvecoeur. While such literary evidence can clearly not be ignored, it is no substitute for detailed quantitative information.

Various estimates have, however, been made of the colonial population. The first 'official' estimates were contained in the 1850 Census (pp. xxx–xxxi). The statistics most usually quoted in more recent writings are those which appeared in 1909 in a publication of the Bureau of the Census, *A Century of Population Growth*, written by the Chief Clerk of the Bureau, W. S. Rossiter.

Rossiter gives estimates of total colonial population and of the total population of the separate colonies by decades from 1620 to 1780. Valuable though these figures are, they leave large areas of uncertainty. Above all, the absence of reliable immigration figures makes it impossible to distinguish natural increase from growth due to immigration.[1] Similarly it is not until the First Census of 1790 that separate figures are available for white and coloured. Rossiter's figures are aggregate and do not distinguish between these two very different groups. Finally, information about internal migration in the colonial period is slight, and not at all comparable with that available from the

---

* Taken and adapted from J. Potter, "The Colonial Period," *Population in History*, eds. D. V. Glass and D. E. C. Eversley (London: Edward Arnold (Publishers) Ltd., 1965), pp. 636–46. Used by permission of author and publisher.

[1] It is acknowledged that the use of the word 'immigrant' in this context is probably anachronistic. Colonial Americans still thought and spoke of themselves as 'emigrants' from the old country, not 'immigrants' into the new. The word 'immigrant' appears to have been an Americanism first used about 1790, but not in general use until the fourth decade of independence, i.e. towards 1820.

Censuses from 1850 on. Without much more knowledge of these aspects of colonial population it is very difficult to put Malthus to the test.

Rossiter's estimates, and calculations based upon them, are presented in Table 1. It is seen from Table 1(d) that the total American population increased between 1700 and 1790 at an average rate of 34.5 per cent per dec-

■ **TABLE 1   American Population in the Eighteenth Century**

• (A) ESTIMATED TOTAL POPULATION (000)

		1700	1710	1720	1730	1740	1750	1760	1770	(1775–6)	1780	1790
New England	New Hampshire	6	7.5	9.5	12	22	31	38	60	(81)	85	142
	Massachusetts	70	80	92	125	158	180	235	299	(339)	363	476
	Rhode Island	6	8	11	17	24	35	44	55	(58)	52*	69
	Connecticut	24	31	40	55	70	100	142	175	(198)	203	238
	Total	106	127	152	209	274	346	459	589	(676)	703	925
Mid-Atlantic	New York	19	26	36	49	63	80	113	185	(193)	240	425
	New Jersey	14	20	26	37	52	66	91	110	(122)	137	184
	Pennsylvania	20	35	48	65	100	150	220	275	(308)	372	493
	Total	53	81	110	151	215	296	424	570	(623)	749	1,102
South Atlantic	Maryland	31	43	62	82	105	137	162	200	(255)	250	320
	Virginia	72	87	116	153	200	275	346	450	(504)	565	822
	North Carolina	5	7	13	30	50	80	115	230	(247)	300	395
	South Carolina	8	13	21	30	45	68	95	140	(170)	160	249
	Georgia						5	9	26	(33)	55	83
	Total	116	150	212	295	400	565	727	1,046	(1,209)	1,330	1,869
TOTAL		275	358	474	655	889	1,207	1,610	2,205	(2,507)	2,781	3,930†

• (B) DISTRIBUTION OF POPULATION (PER CENT)

		1700	1710	1720	1730	1740	1750	1760	1770	(1775–6)	1780	1790
New England	New Hampshire	2	2	2	2	2	3	2	3	(3)	3	4
	Massachusetts	25	22	19	19	18	15	15	14	(14)	13	12
	Rhode Island	2	2	2	3	3	3	3	3	(2)	2	2
	Connecticut	9	9	8	8	8	8	9	8	(8)	7	6
	Total	39	35	32	32	31	29	29	28	(27)	25	24
Mid-Atlantic	New York	7	7	8	7	7	7	7	8	(8)	9	10
	New Jersey	5	6	5	6	6	5	6	5	(5)	5	5
	Pennsylvania	7	10	10	10	11	12	14	12	(12)	13	13
	Total	19	23	23	23	24	24	26	25	(25)	27	28
South Atlantic	Maryland	11	12	13	13	12	11	10	9	(10)	9	8
	Virginia	26	24	24	23	22	23	21	20	(20)	20	21
	North Carolina	2	2	3	4.5	6	7	7	10	(10)	11	10
	South Carolina	3	4	4	4.5	5	6	6	6	(7)	6	6
	Georgia								1	(1)	1	2
	Total	42	42	45	45	45	47	45	46	(48)	47	47
TOTAL		100	100	100	100	100	100	100	100	(100)	100	100

* In parts (C) and (D) the population of Rhode Island in 1780 is taken as 60,000, in view of Sutherland's figure of 58,228 from a Rhode Island census of 1774.
† In part (A) the grand total population for 1790 of 3,929,625 includes 35,691 persons in Tennessee not listed in the sectional figures.

■ **TABLE 1 (cont.)**

- (C) DECENNIAL INCREASE (000)

		1700 –10	10– 20	20– 30	30– 40	40– 50	50– 60	60– 70	70– 80	80– 90
New England	New Hampshire	1.5	2	2.5	10	9	7	22	25	57
	Massachusetts	10	12	33	33	22	55	64	64	113
	Rhode Island	2	3	6	7	11	9	11	(5)	9
	Connecticut	7	9	15	15	30	42	33	28	35
	Total	21	25	57	65	72	113	130	(122)	214
Mid-Atlantic	New York	7	10	13	14	17	33	72	55	185
	New Jersey	6	6	11	15	14	25	19	27	47
	Pennsylvania	15	13	17	35	50	70	55	97	121
	Total	28	29	41	64	81	128	146	179	353
South Atlantic	Maryland	12	19	20	23	32	25	38	50	70
	Virginia	15	29	37	47	75	71	104	115	257
	North Carolina	2	6	17	20	30	35	115	70	95
	South Carolina	5	8	9	15	23	27	45	20	89
	Georgia					5	4	17	29	28
	Total	34	62	83	105	165	162	319	284	539
TOTAL		83	116	181	234	318	403	595	576	1,149

- (D) PERCENTAGE DECENNIAL INCREASE

											AVERAGE
New England	New Hampshire	25	27	26	83	41	23	58	41	68	44
	Massachusetts	14	15	36	26	14	31	27	21	31	24
	Rhode Island	33	38	54	42	46	26	25	9	17	32
	Connecticut	29	29	38	27	43	42	23	16	17	29
	Total	20	20	38	31	26	33	28	21	30	27.5
Mid-Atlantic	New York	37	39	36	29	27	41	64	29	77	42
	New Jersey	43	30	42	41	27	38	21	25	34	34
	Pennsylvania	75	37	35	54	50	47	25	35	32	43
	Total	53	36	37	42	38	43	34	31	47	40.1
South Atlantic	Maryland	39	44	32	28	31	18	24	25	28	30
	Virginia	21	33	32	31	38	26	30	26	45	31
	North Carolina	40	87	130	67	60	44	100	30	32	66
	South Carolina	63	60	44	50	51	40	47	14	56	47
	Georgia						80	189	112	50	108
	Total	29	41	39	36	41	29	44	27	41	35.3
TOTAL		30.0	32.7	38.1	35.7	35.8	33.4	37.0	26.1	41.3	34.5

i) The above data are transcribed or calculated from W. S. Rossiter, "A Century of Population Growth" (US Bureau of the Census), pp. 9–10. The column headed '(1775–6)' is from S. H. Sutherland, "Population Distribution in Colonial America," p. xii.

ii) For the years 1770–90, separate figures are available for Maine, Vermont, Delaware, Kentucky (1780–90) and Tennessee (1790). For the earlier years Maine is included with Massachusetts, Vermont with New York, Delaware with Pennsylvania, and Kentucky with Virginia. This grouping is used throughout in the table above, for simplicity of presentation. This has introduced, however, a small inaccuracy, especially in the sectional totals, for the years 1770–90, as the following revision of the percentage distribution table will show (cf. (B) above).

■ TABLE 1 (cont.)

	Maine	Vt.	Mass.	Total New England	New York	Penn.	Total Mid-Atlantic	Va.	Total South Atlantic	Ky.	Tenn.	Total East-South-Central
1770	2	1	12	28	7	11	24	20	48			
1780	2	2	11	27	7	12	24	19	48	1		1
1790	2	2	10	26	8	11	24	19	47	2	1	3

ade.[2] This rate of growth conforms closely with that of the first half of the nineteenth century down to 1860. Population increase in the eighteenth century was apparently uneven; particularly rapid growth is found in the 1720's, 1760's and 1780's (the last of these being the decade with the fastest rate of growth in America's history); particularly slow growth is found in the 1700's, 1710's, 1750's and 1770's.

Similarly, there is an unevenness of growth between region and region. It appears from Table 1(b) that New England as a whole failed to maintain its share of the population, declining from 39 per cent of the total in 1700 to 26 per cent (note ii) in 1790; the decline was most pronounced in Massachusetts, whose share fell from 25 per cent to 10 per cent (note ii), but Connecticut also shows a decline which is especially sharp after 1760. Both the middle and the southern colonies increased their share, from 19 to 24 per cent, and from 42 to 47 per cent respectively. The rise in the share of the South mainly depended on the rapidity of the growth of the Carolinas, which offset the fall in the Virginian percentage.

It may be noted that, of the colonies which appear in part (d) of the Table to have particularly high growth rates,[3] Georgia and the Carolinas included an important slave element, and also, in this period, a significant group of white immigrants; Pennsylvania and New York were also immigrant-receiving areas in the eighteenth century. At the other end of the scale the New England colonies were relatively unattractive to white immigrants in the eighteenth century; but even if immigration is assumed to have been negligible, the indicated rates are probably below the natural rate of growth as a result of net emigration from the area.

Before these first approximations could be made any more accurate it would be necessary to know the respective contributions made to colonial population growth by (i) the importation of salves, (ii) white immigration, (iii) natural increase of white population and (iv) internal migration.

[2] The decennial average of 34.5 per cent is of course dependent on the arbitrary choice of 1700 as the starting date for the calculation. Still using Rossiter's estimates, but with different starting dates, the decennial averages become: 1660–1790, 34.0; 1670–1790, 34.3; 1680–1790, 34.1; 1690–1790, 33.8; 1700–90, 34.5; 1710–90, 35.0; 1720–90, 35.3; 1730–90, 34.9. The difference created by the use of different starting dates is thus not more than one per cent.

[3] The appearance may be in part deceptive, of course, because of the different starting-points.

On the first problem, a starting point may be found in the Census of 1790 which distinguishes white and non-white population, as shown in Table 2. Thus in 1790 there were just over 750,000 Negroes in the newly created USA, either imported as slaves themselves or descendants of imported slaves. The number of slaves in America in 1700 is not known; it is generally assumed to

■ **TABLE 2**   **Structure of the American Population in 1790**

		White (000)	Free Non-White (000)	Slave (000)	White %	Non-White %	Distribution of White Population %	Distribution of Non-White Population %
New England	Maine	96	0.5	none	99	1	3	
	New Hampshire	141	0.6	—	99	1	4	
	Vermont	85	0.3	—	99	1	3	
	Massachusetts	373	5	none	99	1	12	
	Rhode Island	65	3	1	94	6	2	
	Connecticut	232	3	3	97	3	7	1
	Total	992	12	4	98	2	31	2
Mid-Atlantic	New York	314	5	21	92	8	10	3
	New Jersey	170	3	11	92	8	5	2
	Pennsylvania	424	7	4	97	3	13	2
	Total	908	15	36	95	5	29	7
South Atlantic	Delaware	46	4	9	78	22	1	3
	Maryland	209	8	103	65	35	7	14
	Virginia	442	13	293	59	41	14	40
	North Carolina	288	5	101	73	27	9	14
	South Carolina	140	2	107	56	44	4	14
	Georgia	53	0.4	29	64	36	2	4
	Total	1,178	32	642	64	36	37	89
East-South-Central	Kentucky	61	0.1	12	84	16	2	1.5
	Southwest Territory	31	0.4	3	91	9	1	0.5
	Total	92	1.0	15	86	14	3	2
USA		3,171	60	697	81	19	100	100

have been small, in the range 5,000 to 20,000. Importations between 1700 and 1790, however, probably amounted to between 250,000 and 300,000. The inflow was uneven, the biggest decennial importation being in the 1760's when about 75,000 were imported. It may be assumed that practically all these went to the South Atlantic colonies; in other words the increase of 319,000, or 44 per cent, shown by the southern colonies in that decade contains an importation of perhaps 70,000 slaves, the increase otherwise being about 35 per cent (Table 3, columns 16 and 17).[4]

An attempt is made in Table 3 to estimate the population growth rates

[4] These assumptions are based on figures cited in Rossiter, *op. cit.*, p. 36.

■ TABLE 3 American Population Growth in the Eighteenth Century with Allowance for Imported Slaves

	1	2	Total 3	4	5	6
	Total Population in Base Year (000)	Total Increase (000)	Assumed Total Importation of Slaves (000)	Increase without Slave Import (000)	Col. 2 as % of Col. 1 %	Col. 4 as % of Col. 1 %
1700–10	275	83	10	73	30.0	26.8
1710–20	358	116	20	96	32.7	24.0
1720–30	474	181	25	156	38.1	32.8
1730–40	655	234	25	209	35.7	31.9
1740–50	889	318	25	293	35.8	32.9
1750–60	1,207	403	35	368	33.4	30.5
1760–70	1,610	595	75	520	37.0	32.3
1770–80	2,205	576	20	556	26.1	25.2
1780–90	2,781	1,149	20	1,129	41.3	40.6
1700–90			255		34.5	30.8

Maryland		Virginia		North Carolina	
7	8	9	10	11	12
Assumed Slave Import (000)	Percentage without Slave Import	Assumed Slave Import (000)	Percentage Increase without Slave Import	Assumed Slave Import (000)	Percentage Increase without Slave Import
1.5	34	4	15.	1.5	10
3	38	8	24	3	43
3.8	29	10	23	3.8	102
3.8	23	10	24	3.8	54
3 8	27	10	32.5	3.8	53
5.3	14	14	21	5.3	37
11.4	16	30	21	11.4	90
3	23	8	24	3	29
3	27	8	44	3	31
	25		25		50

South Carolina		Total South Atlantic		
13	14	15	16	17
Assumed Slave Import (000)	Percentage Increase without Slave Import	Assumed Slave Import (000)	Total Percentage Increase	Percentage Increase without Slave Import
1.5	44	9	29	22
3	39	18	41	29
3.8	25	22.3	39	29
3.8	37	22.5	36	28
3.8	42	22.5	41	36
5.3	32	31.5	29	23
11.4	35	67.5	44	35
3	12	18	27	25
3	54	18	41	39
	35			29

when allowance is made for the increase caused by slave imports. The calculations are obviously very crude and the findings can be no more than a rough approximation. Two rather arbitrary assumptions are made: the figure used of total slaves imported (just over 250,000) is a low one, but it is 'allocated' to the different decades roughly according to the estimates quoted by Rossiter. Secondly, it is assumed that throughout the eighteenth century the geographical distribution of the imported slaves was the same as the distribution of the non-white population in the Census of 1790.[5]

With this adjustment made for slave importation, the average decennial increase of the total population falls from 34.5 to 30.8 per cent. If the first two decades are excluded as being the most conjectural, the fall is from 35.3 to 32.5 per cent. The greatest effect is naturally seen in the figures for the southern colonies whose calculated rate falls from 35.2 to 29.4 per cent. Revised in this way, the southern rate of growth more closely resembles the New England average of 27.5 per cent. Within the south, North Carolina, where just under three-quarters of the population was white in 1790, still shows a particularly high rate of growth.

The growth rate derived by this calculation includes the natural increase of the slave population. An estimate of the rate of growth of the white population only may be made via a different route. If it is assumed that there were 25,000 non-whites in America in 1700 — probably a high figure — then the increase in the white population in 90 years was from 250,000 to 3,171,000, which would require an average decennial growth of 32.5 per cent; an assumption of 5,000 non-whites in America in 1700 gives a decennial growth for the white population in the same 90 years of 31.5 per cent.

In view of the irregularities from decade to decade, such century-long averages are of course only of very limited value. But with due reservations, the findings to this point are as follows: average decennial growth of whole population from all causes, between 34 and 35 per cent; average decennial rate of growth of whole population, with allowance for importation of slaves, between 30.8 and 32.5 per cent; average decennial rate of growth of white population, in the range 31.5 to 32.5 per cent. This suggests that during the eighteenth century the total white population in America did increase at roughly the Malthusian rate.

Viewed regionally, there are considerable variations. Of those provinces with a white population of over 90 per cent, New Hampshire, New York and Pennsylvania are still significantly above the 32 per cent level, Rhode Island and New Jersey are very close to 32 per cent while Massachusetts and Connecticut are significantly below 32 per cent. There are three possible explanations of these disparities: immigration, internal migration and differences

---

[5] The 'allocation' by decades is based on Rossiter, *op. cit.*, p. 36, the figures assumed for the first two decades being the most doubtful. The geographical allocation used is: Virginia, 40 per cent, Maryland, 15 per cent, the Carolinas, 15 per cent each, total South Atlantic, 90 per cent.

in natural increase. It is tempting to suppose that these regional differences may be quite simply explained: that Massachusetts and Connecticut are low because of emigration from these regions to other parts of America; that New Hampshire, New York and Pennsylvania are high because of immigration from Europe and from other parts of America; and that Rhode Island and New Jersey represent something like the norm at the Malthusian 32 per cent.

One would like to be able to substantiate, or refute, this conclusion with data on colonial immigration. Benjamin Franklin, at any rate at mid-century, seems to have attributed a major role in American population growth to immigration, but without any statistical basis for his assumption. 'This quick Increase,' he wrote in *Poor Richard Improved*, 'is owing not so much to natural Generation, as to the Accession of Strangers. . . .' Nevertheless, Franklin went on to argue, natural increase is greater in America than in Europe.

> 'I believe People increase faster by Generation in these Colonies, where all can have full Employ. . . . For in old settled Countries, as England for instance, as soon as the Number of People is as great as can be supported by all the Tillage, Manufactures, Trade and Offices of the Country, the Overplus must quit the Country, or they will perish by Poverty, Diseases, and want of Necessaries. Marriage, too, is discouraged, many declining it, till they can see how they shall be able to maintain a Family.' [6]

Thus Franklin linked the lower rate of natural growth in Europe directly with migration to America. In his *Observations* of 1751 he carried this further. In America there were more marriages, younger marriages (he suggested that a marriage age of 20 was average), and more children per marriage.

> Hence, marriages in America are more general, and more generally early, than in Europe. And . . . if in Europe they have but four births to a marriage (many of their marriages being late) we may here reckon eight, of which, if one half grow up, and our marriages are made, reckoning one with another, at twenty years of age, our people must at least be doubled every twenty years. . . . The great increase . . . is . . . not always owing to greater fecundity of nature, but sometimes to examples of industry in the heads, and industrious education; by which the children are enabled to provide better for themselves, and their marrying early is encouraged from the prospect of good subsistence.[7]

Regrettably, it seems impossible to assess with any degree of reliability or accuracy the number of immigrants in the eighteenth century. The sources

---

[6] *The Papers of Benjamin Franklin*, iii, p. 440. *Poor Richard Improved* (1750). Franklin was then 44 years of age.

[7] B. Franklin, *Observations Concerning the Increase of Mankind* . . . (1751), clauses 7 and 19. On the age of marriage, Franklin's guesses both about the age of marriage and about the average number of children per marriage have some support in calculations by F. S. Crum based on the selective evidence of genealogical records (Frederick S. Crum, 'The Decadence of the Native American Stock. A Statistical Study of Genealogical Records,' *American Statistical Association*, vol. xiv, Sept. 1914. See also note 50).

of information are few and the estimates made by students of the period vary widely. The usual assumptions are that, while the absolute numbers entering America from Europe in the eighteenth century were far greater than in the seventeenth century, immigrants nevertheless constituted a smaller proportion of total population than in the later seventeenth century; and that the flow varied greatly over time, being small in years of war in Europe and encouraged by the return of peace. But beyond these generalities most of the leading writers both on migration and on colonial history refrain from committing themselves to quantitative assessments.

One of the highest estimates of colonial immigration is that cited by the eminent historian of the colonial period, C. P. Nettels. This writer asserts that 'the eighteenth century was pre-eminently the century of the foreigner: in 1760 the foreign-born represented a third of the colonial population.' [8] This would imply the presence of over half a million immigrants and in the context of the quotation Nettels does not appear to include Negro slaves in this figure. Even if one 'spread' these arrivals over as much as fifty years and made no allowance for deaths, this would require an average annual immigration of over 10,000 (or 100,000 per decade) between 1710 and 1760; it would also account for almost half the total population increase, of 1.2 millions, in that same period. If such immigration figures could be definitively established, they would play havoc with the usual assumptions about the natural growth of population in colonial America.[9]

At the other extreme, one finds the view that immigration was insignificant, with a suggested figure of about 10 per cent foreign born in 1790. This is, however, a mathematical solution unsupported by historical evidence, reached by applying an assumed birth rate of 55 to the total population of 1.2 millions in 1750, giving about 66,000 annual births; from this it is deduced that the immigrant contribution was slight.[10]

[8] C. P. Nettels, *The Roots of American Civilization* (New York 1938), p. 383. The history of this notion is itself interesting. In making his assertion Nettels gives a footnote reference to a group of articles by Max Farrand in *The New Republic*, 1916, especially 'A Nation of Immigrants,' 9 Dec. 1916, p. 148. If we trace it back still further, Farrand in this passage is seen to be quoting directly from Edward Channing's *History of the United States*, where Channing stated 'About one-third of the colonists in 1760 were born outside of America.' Farrand does not give the reference but this passage is found to be an isolated sentence in vol. ii of Channing's *History* (New York 1908), p. 492. Channing explains his statement in a footnote on the same page, citing as his sources Benjamin Franklin, *Works*, iv, 24, and the work by Edward Wigglesworth referred to in footnote 3 of this chapter. Neither source gives a satisfactory statistical foundation for Channing's statement.

Farrand supports his own view with the well-known passage from Crèvecoeur's *Letters from an American Farmer* (1782): 'What is an American? They are a mixture of English, Scotch, Irish, French, Dutch, Germans and Swedes. From this promiscuous breed that race, now called Americans have arisen. . . .'

[9] If the half million foreign born are assumed to have arrived within the 30 years prior to 1760, this 'spread' would account for well over half the probable total population increase in those three decades.

[10] W. H. Grabill and others, *The Fertility of American Women* (New York 1958), pp. 8–9. Grabill contrasts these assumed births of 66,000 with an assumed annual net immigration of about 4,000. If a much lower birth rate of 35 is assumed, however, this

Such is the width of the gulf in possible interpretations created by the lack of reliable data of immigration. Can one go any further than to point out the apparent coincidence between the decades of most rapid population growth (1720's, 1760's and 1780's) and the decades of high immigration? [11]

The balance of probability, on the evidence known to the author, seems to suggest a total immigration, additional to imported slaves, of about 350,000 between 1700 and 1790 (though it must be emphasized that this is little more than a shot in the dark).[12] If we use this figure as a hypothesis, a calculation similar to that used in Table 3 reveals a rate of natural increase for the white population of slightly over 28 per cent per decade.[13] Assuming a concentration of the immigrants in certain known areas, especially Pennsylvania, North Carolina, Georgia and to some extent New York, some of the disparities in the rates of growth between colony and colony disappear (but of course this procedure involves to some extent assuming what one seeks to prove). If about 100,000 of these immigrants, for example, settled in Pennsylvania, then the rate of growth for that colony was not 43 but under 30.

An extremely approximate calculation may be made to assess the birth rates and death rates required to satisfy the assumptions made earlier about the size of the white population, at different assumed levels of immigration. The possible combinations which emerge from such a calculation are as follows:

Assumed White Immigration 1700–90	Assumed White Birth Rate	Resultant White Death Rate (approx.)
350,000	35	11
	45	21
	55	31
600,000	35	13
	45	23
	55	33

would have produced about 42,000 births, a figure which might be reconcilable with 10,000 annual arrivals in the middle of the century. It is possible that immigration tended to lower the birth rate, owing to the later age of marriage of immigrants; see J. P. Monahan, *The Pattern of Age at Marriage in the United States* (Philadelphia 1951), pp. 73–75. It should be noted however that the evidence for this view is taken largely from the second half of the nineteenth century.

[11] Marcus Hansen, the pioneer historian of migration, speaks of the migration of the 1760's, especially after the final defeat of France, as 'the greatest of all colonial migrations,' by M. L. Hansen, *The Atlantic Migration* (Harvard 1945), p. 51. This inflow came after the date mentioned by Nettels.

[12] This figure is based on the sporadic glimpses, based especially on ships' lists, to be found in such works as Abbot E. Smith, *Colonists in Bondage* (1947), Warren B. Smith, *White Servitude in Colonial South Carolina* (1961), and from Marcus Hansen. It implies a somewhat lower immigration than that suggested by the Beards who estimate an influx of 750,000 Europeans between 1660 and 1770. C. A. and Mary R. Beard, *The Beards' Basic History of the United States* (1944), p. 17.

[13] Of course if a higher immigration figure is assumed the calculated natural increase falls. An immigration of 600,000 between 1700 and 1790 gives a natural increase figure of just over 25 per cent per decade.

If the lower immigration figure is accepted as the more likely, then three combinations of birth rates and death rates would produce the given population growth. The balance of probability seems to suggest the second combination, or a mid-point between the second and the third, with a birth rate of 45–50 and a moderate death rate of 20–25 per thousand. The death rate of 30–31 required by the assumption of as high a birth rate as 55 seems rather implausible.

In the absence of further evidence, the findings of this section have to remain hypothetical. Let it simply be repeated at this point that there can be no definitive picture of American demographic history in the eighteenth century until the problem of immigration has been satisfactorily solved. ◻

◇ **21** ◇

Colonial Commerce *

CHARLES M. ANDREWS

As a rule trade and commerce in their various manifestations, as features of American colonial history, have been considered of minor importance by our historians and relegated to the obscurity of a few supplemental paragraphs. No writer has placed them in the same rank with government, administration, and social development, or has deemed their consideration essential to a proper understanding of the conditions under which our colonies were founded and grew up. Yet it is a well-recognized fact that during the greater part of our colonial period commerce and the colonies were correlative terms, unthinkable each without the other. As an underlying factor in colonial life, commerce was of greater significance than it is to-day in the life of the United States, for some of the most vital aspects of our early history can be understood only when construed in terms of commercial relationship, either with England or with some of the other maritime powers of the period which were finding their strength and prosperity in colonial and commercial expansion.

In the domain of history a shift in the angle of observation will often bring into view new and important vistas and will create such new impressions of old scenes as to alter our ideas of the whole landscape. In the case of colonial history this statement is peculiarly true. Viewing the colonies as isolated units of government and life, detached in the main from the larger world of England and the Continent, leads us to ignore those connections that constituted the colonial relationship in which commerce played a most important

* Charles M. Andrews, "Colonial Commerce," *The American Historical Review*, Vol. DD, October 1914, pp. 43–51. Used by permission. A paper read in the conference on colonial commerce at the meeting of the American Historical Association in Charleston, December 30, 1913.

role. The older view is natural because it is easily taken and satisfies local interest and pride; the newer point of observation is more remote, less obvious, and more difficult of attainment. Yet it is the only view that enables us to preserve the integrity of our subject and so to comprehend the meaning of our history. The thirteen colonies were not isolated units; they were dependencies of the British crown and parts of a colonial empire extending from America to India. They were not a detached group of communities; on the contrary they were a group among other groups of settlements and plantations belonging colonially to five of the European nations, Portugal, Spain, Holland, France, and England, and their history was influenced at every point by the policies and rivalries of these maritime powers. The age in which they reached their maximum of strength as colonies was one in which the colonial relationship was highly developed and the feature of subordination to a higher authority an integral and dominant characteristic. Such an interpretation of colonial history is not a scholar's vagary, a matter of theory and hypothesis to be accepted or rejected as the writer on colonial history may please. It is historically sound, preserving the proper perspective, and preventing in no way the following out to the uttermost detail the local activities and interests of the colonists themselves.

The reason why this colonial relationship has been so persistently ignored in the past is not difficult to discover. The period of our history before 1783 has been construed as merely the ante-chamber to the great hall of our national development. In so doing writers have concerned themselves not with colonial history as such, but rather with the colonial antecedents of our national history. This form of treatment is common to all our histories, even the very best, because all limit their scope to the thirteen colonies, which formed but part of the colonial area and are segregated for no other reason than that they constituted the portion out of which the United States of America grew. In our text-books, not excepting the very latest, the colonial period is frankly presented as an era of beginnings, and stress is laid upon ideas and institutions that were destined to become dominant features of the nation's later career. With this mode of presenting the subject we may not quarrel, but it seems almost a pity, now that we are becoming such a nation of text-book writers, that the children of the country cannot be set upon the right way of understanding what the colonial period really means. Dealing with thirteen colonies, searching among them for the conditions under which were laid the foundations of the great republic, and treating those conditions as but preliminary to the history of the United States will never enable the writer to present an honest or complete picture of colonial life or to analyze successfully the causes that provoked revolution or rendered independence inevitable.

In one respect the colonial period is fundamentally different from that of our national history. For one hundred and seventy-five years, the people who inhabited the American seaboard were not members of an independent and sovereign state, free of all control except such as they exercised for themselves. Legally, they formed dependent and subordinate communities, subject to a will and authority higher than themselves and outside of themselves. This state of dependency was a reality and not a pretense. At least, the members of the British Parliament deemed it so, when in 1733 they rejected a petition from the assembly of Massachusetts as "frivolous and groundless, an high insult upon his Majesty's government, and tending to shake off the dependency of the said colony upon this kingdom, to which by law and right they are and ought to be subject." At least the British executive and administrative authorities deemed it so, when by a thousand acts and through hundreds of officials in the colonies they endeavored to maintain the royal prerogative and to carry out the British policy of making English subjects the sole carriers of the whole British commerce and of appropriating and securing to England and her subjects "all the emoluments arising from the trade of her own colonies." The British merchants took this view, when they could say, as Stephen Godin asserted in 1724, that "it were better to have no colonies at all unless they be subservient to their mother country." Certainly the colonists deemed it so, when by their very restlessness under restraint they betrayed the reality of the ties that bound them. No act of the colonists, either individual or collective, can be traced to a conscious expectation of future citizenship in an independent republic. No aspect of colonial resistance to the royal authority was ever due to any definite belief that an independent nation was in the making. There is nothing to show that a colonist ever allowed visions of such a future to influence the course of his daily life. To the colonist there was no United States of America in anticipation, and there should be none to the student of colonial history to-day. The subject should be dealt with for its own sake and not for its manifestations of self-government and democracy; and the eye of the scholar should look no further ahead than to its legitimate end, the close of a period, the era of revolution, war, and independence.

It may be stated as a general principle that studying a period of history with its later manifestations before us is apt to lead to perversions of historical truth. With notions of the present in mind we approach certain landmarks of our early history in much the same spirit as that in which older writers approached Magna Carta. Most of us make too few allowances for the differences of mental longitude between the present and the past, and fail to realize that our thoughts were not the thoughts of our forefathers and our institutions were not the institutions they set up. The colonial period is our Middle Ages, and he would be rash who interpreted the thoughts of that time in the light of later views as to what democracy ought to be. There are traces and important traces of radical notions in matters of government in our colonial period, for our colonies were settled during a century of unrest in religion and politics; but these notions were not the characteristic or the generally prevalent ideas that governed colonial action. It is not profitable or scholarly to single out these manifestations, to study them apart from their surroundings, and to classify them as representative and typical of the period in which they appeared. I am afraid that the majority of the colonists listening to some modern comments upon the early institutions of New England and Virginia, would have replied in somewhat the same fashion as Maitland pictures William Lyndwood replying to questions on the "canon law of Rome":

> I do not quite understand what you mean by popular liberties and this thing that you call democracy. I am an Englishman and I know the liberties that I enjoyed in England. But these were class liberties, to be understood in the light of the law and of the rights of the crown and parliament; they are not what you mean when you talk about popular rights and liberties in a democratic republic. You mean equal liberties for all, including the mass of the people. But that is something we do not want, for that would admit all men of whatever station, property, or faith to equal privileges in society, church, and state, and such a philosophy of government is one in which only a dreamer would believe.

In truth, we have arrived at this idea of what our forefathers thought, by selecting certain documents and incidents, from the Mayflower Compact to the Declaration of Independence, and from Bacon's Rebellion to the various riotous acts of the pre-Revolutionary period; and, construing them more or less according to our wishes and prepossessions, have wrought therefrom an epic of patriotism satisfying to our self-esteem. We love to praise those who struggled, sometimes with high purposes, sometimes under the influence of purely selfish motives, against the authority of the British crown. But this, in an historical sense, is pure pragmatism. It is not history, because it treats only a part of the subject and treats it wrongly and with a manifest bias. It does not deal with what may be called the normal conditions of the colonial period. It ignores the prevailing sentiment of those who, however often they may have objected to the way in which the royal authority was exercised and to the men who exercised it, lived contented lives, satisfied in the main with the conditions surrounding them, and believing firmly in the system of government under which they had been born and brought up. It misunderstands and consequently exaggerates expressions of radical sentiment, and interprets such terms as "freedom," "liberty," and "independence" as if, in the mouths of those who used them, they had but a single meaning and that meaning the one commonly prevalent at the present time. It relegates to a place of secondary importance the royal prerogative and the relation with England, which beyond all other factors dominated the lives and actions of a majority of the colonists. Without an understanding of the relationship with England, colonial history can have no meaning. Before we can treat of colonial self-government, of the growth of democratic ideas, of the conflict between the colonies and the mother-country, and of the westward movement, we must know what England was doing, according to what principles she acted, and how these principles found application in the colonial world that stretched from Hudson

Bay to Barbadoes. Only in this way can we deal with our own colonial problems, and only in this way can we answer those subordinate but important
questions, why did not the West Indies and the Floridas revolt, and why did
the Canadian colonies remain loyal to the mother-country.

This preliminary statement is necessary in order to explain the attitude that
I shall take in regard to the subject under consideration here. One period of
our history, that from 1690 to 1750, has long been recognized as a neglected
period, and it will continue to be neglected as long as we treat colonial history
merely as a time of incubation. Now just as an important period has suffered
neglect from failure to make a radical change in our point of view, so an important phase of colonial history has suffered similar neglect from a similar
cause. I refer to the subject of colonial commerce. The many divisions of
this fundamentally important topic have lain hitherto strewn about over the
pages of colonial history, veritable *disjecta membra*, without proper unity and
co-ordination, and without that grouping of principal, subordinate, incidental,
and extraordinary features, which taken together disclose the paramount significance of the whole.

Any study of colonial commerce should begin with a thorough grounding
in the commercial policy of England from the beginning of the colonial period, and a thorough understanding of the place of the colonies, not only in
England's commercial scheme, but also in the schemes of other maritime
states of the European world. England's relations with the colonies were primarily commercial in character, not only because of the wide expanse of water that separated the mother-country from her outlying possessions, but much
more because from the beginning to the end of the legal connection, England's interest in the colonies was a commercial interest. British merchants
and statesmen valued the colonies just as far as they contributed to the commercial and industrial prosperity at home; and they actively promoted and
upheld legislation that brought the colonies within the bonds of the commercial empire. Commerce was, therefore, the cornerstone of the British system.
Naturally other interests, legal, political, institutional, religious, and military,
assumed large proportions as the British colonial system was gradually worked
out: but in the ultimate analysis it will be found that the building up of
strong, self-governing communities in America and the West Indies was a
contributory rather than a primary object, furthering the commercial aims of
British merchants and statesmen through the establishment of vigorous but
dependent groups of producers and consumers; for England was bound to protect and develop the sources of her wealth and power. England valued her
colonies exactly as far as they were of commercial importance to her, and it
was no accident that the terms "trade" and "plantations" were joined in the
same phrase as the title of the British boards of control, or that in the same
title "trade" took precedence over "plantations." The commercial history of
every colony, without exception though not all in the same measure, was affected by this policy of the mother-country, who, possessing plenary author-

ity, was able to enforce to no inconsiderable extent the policy that she laid down. A study of colonial commerce carries us at once, therefore, into the very heart of that most fundamental of all colonial questions, the relation of the colonies to the sovereign power across the sea.

If we limit our observation to a single colony or to the group of thirteen colonies, as we are more or less bound to do when dealing with colonial history as prefatory to that of the United States, we get an imperfect view of our subject, if, indeed, that can be called a view at all which is taken at such close range. Commerce thus seen appears to be an interesting, but not particularly conspicuous, feature of colonial life. Settlement, government, politics, religion, war, and social life generally have taken precedence of it in the narratives of our writers. If not ignored or treated as an issue of only local or minor consequence, it is used as a convenient text for moralizing on the unwarranted part which a government can take in interfering with the free and natural development of a high-spirited and liberty-loving people. As a rule such an attitude is due to the unprofitable habit of studying colonial history with our ideas warped and distorted by standards of judgment derived from the Revolutionary and national periods, a habit that is formed when colonial history is studied from the wrong end. Mr. Beer is showing us how to correct that habit, and his volumes are teaching us what can be done when the right vantage-point is sought for and attained. We are now beginning to learn that what we call colonial commerce was but part of that ocean-wide commercial activity of England and her merchants which stands as England's most vital possession of the last two centuries, and thus was concerned with a larger world of obligations and opportunities than that embraced by the thirteen colonies. Construed in this way, colonial commerce grows in dignity and rank and yields to no other phase of our history in the influence it has exercised upon the life of the period to which it belongs.

In presenting our subject from this standpoint, we must in the first place acquire a sound knowledge of the commercial ideas of the period, of mercantilism and the self-sufficing empire in all aspects of their development, and we must exhibit a sympathetic attitude toward views and opinions that had as legitimate a right to a place in the commercial and political thought of the seventeenth and eighteenth centuries as have corresponding but different views and opinions a right to exist to-day. We must study understandingly the conditions under which these commercial ideas came into being, and must analyze thoroughly and carefully all orders, proclamations, statutes, and instructions that represent official utterances upon these points; the minutes of subordinate councils and boards; and the letters, pamphlets, and memorials of private persons that contain expressions of individual opinion. Furthermore, we must follow in all their ramifications, in all the colonies dependent on the authority of the British crown, the attempts, whether successful or unsuccessful, to apply these regulations to the actual business of commerce. The Navigation Acts were but the most conspicuous of hundreds of official declarations, defining the limits within which colonial commerce could be carried on; yet even now we understand but imperfectly the influence of those acts upon our colonial history and the extent to which they were obeyed.

In tracing the effect of the Acts of Trade and Navigation, we shall meet with a series of institutions in the colonies that played a continuous and active part in the every-day life of the colonists, and we shall find that as yet scarcely one of these institutions has been made the subject of any comprehensive treatment. The Navigation Acts gave rise to the plantation duty, the collectors and surveyors of customs, and the naval officers, and involved the intricate question of salaries and fees; they brought into existence the courts of vice-admiralty with their complements of officials, their procedure under the civil law, their claims of jurisdiction, and their time-honored antagonism to the courts of common law which had already and everywhere been set up in America. We shall find that the machinery for the control of colonial commerce, thus set in motion, gave added duties, not only to existing departments and boards in England — a subject of no little importance in itself for colonial history — but also to the governors of every colony without exception, and to the admirals and commanders of ships of war engaged before 1713 (and even after that date on account of West African pirates and Spanish *guardacostas,* in the work of convoying fleets of merchant ships back and forth across the Atlantic); of looking after affairs in Newfoundland, where civil control was vested in an admiral-governor; and of interfering, long before the famous interferences of 1760 to 1765, to prevent illegal trade and the traffic in uncustomed goods. As we follow on in our study of colonial commerce, we meet with the attempts to set up ports of entry in Virginia, Maryland, and elsewhere for the discharge and lading of ships and the checking of illegal trade, and with the complicated problems of embargoes, chiefly in times of war, of the impressment of seamen from colonial vessels in England and from colonial ports in America for the manning of the royal ships, and of the issue of passes, provided by the Admiralty under special treaties between England and the Barbary States, great numbers of which were used in America by American-built ships to guard against capture by the Barbary cruisers, most dangerous of whom were the Algerine pirates. We are concerned with the question of privateering and the issue of letters of marque, and also with that of prizes, the establishment of special prize courts, and the disposition of ships captured in war. We are concerned also with the question of coast defense in America, the employment of frigates and smaller vessels for the guarding of individual colonies, and with the whole subject of piracy, including the efforts made through the navy, the colonial governors, and specially commissioned courts erected for the purpose, to suppress these marauders of the seas. Indirectly, we are concerned with England's attempt to persuade the colonies to produce naval stores for the use of the royal navy, an attempt which played an important part in the industrial history of the continental colonies, especially in New England; and we are also concerned with England's determination to control the supply of masts from the northern American forests, by means of special officials, notably the surveyor-general of the woods and his deputies, whose business was very obnoxious to the northern colonists.

Furthermore, the attempts of the colonists to evade the restrictions that England laid down for the control of navigation and commerce not only resulted in the seizure of scores of ships, their condemnation and sale, and the arousing of a great amount of ill-will and hostility, but they were also responsible, and often directly responsible, for events of political and constitutional importance, such as the loss of the Massachusetts charter, the consolidation of the northern colonies under Andros, the temporary control of Maryland and Pennsylvania by the king, and the unsuccessful efforts, lasting nearly half a century, to unite the proprietary and corporate colonies to the crown. These are important events in colonial history and can all be traced immediately or remotely to the demands of England's commercial policy.

Continuing this subject in its further ramifications, we find it leading us on into other aspects of the life of the colonies. Commerce influenced the passing of colonial laws; provoked the king in council to disallow colonial acts, because under the statute of 1696 the colonists were forbidden to have any "Laws, Bye-Laws, Usages or Customs" that were in any way repugnant to the terms of the act, and because the colonial governors were forbidden "to pass any laws by which the Trade or Navigation of the kingdom [might] in any ways be affected," [1] brought about appeals to the High Court of Admiralty

---

[1] *House of Lords Manuscripts*, new series, II. 483–488, 494–499 (1696–1697); C. O. 5: 1364, pp. 474–476; *Acts of the Privy Council, Colonial*, vol. II., § 1271 (1717); C. O. 324: 10, pp. 443–454, 456–497 (1722); *Acts of the Privy Council, Colonial*, vol. III., § 58 (1724); C. O. 5: 1296, pp. 120–130; *Acts of the Privy Council, Colonial*, IV. 763–764 (1766).

Dr. O. M. Dickerson, in commenting on this paper at the Charleston meeting, expressed his belief that seventy-five per cent of the "vetoes" of colonial laws must be explained on other than commercial grounds. Until the royal disallowances have been collected and their contents analyzed, we are hardly in a position to speak very positively about their numerical proportions, but after studying with considerable care those in print and in manuscript relating to all the colonies for the entire colonial period, I am convinced that Dr. Dickerson's percentage is too high. Dr. Dickerson must have failed to realize that scores of disallowances apparently concerned with other than commercial matters are found on closer inspection to have a trade motive somewhere lurking in them. This is particularly true of all that deal with financial legislation. But after all can we determine the place of trade and commerce in colonial history by simply counting the number of laws passed and disallowed that deal with this subject? I think not. The colonists had frequent warnings that legislation affecting trade or discriminating in any way against British merchants or British commodities would not be tolerated, and the governors were expressly instructed to veto such laws. It would be surprising, therefore, if any large number of such laws had been passed wittingly by the colonial legislatures. We can obtain a much more accurate estimate by studying the motives underlying British policy in this respect, as seen in the reports of the Board of Trade and of the Council Committee. Among the reasons for disallowance that stand out above all others are two: the impairment of trade and the infringement of the royal prerogative. Many of the other reasons are technical as having to do with the legal aspects of the case, and none of them to anything like the same degree represent the fundamental principles governing the relations of mother-country and colonies as do the two named above. In 1766

from the courts of vice-admiralty in America, and in a few cases at least from the common law courts in the colonies to the Privy Council. It gave rise to the thousand and one complicated phases of international finance, involving mercantile dealings and transactions, currency, credit, and exchange, gold, silver, copper, and paper money, bills of exchange and rates of exchange, the drift of bullion from colony to colony, and above all that question, sometimes most difficult to answer in the case of individual colonies, of the balance of trade. It touched very closely the attitude of the Board of Trade, the Privy Council, and Parliament toward bills of credit and colonial banking, a phase of our early financial history that has nowhere been studied in its entirety. As we continue to the uttermost reaches of this subtle and penetrating force, we find ourselves in the very centre of colonial life, discovering unexpected traces of its influence upon other phases of colonial activity that seem at first sight far removed from the sphere of the Navigation Acts and all their works.

Thus we see how large is the field within which the commercial policy of England operated and how deep and far-reaching were the effects of this powerful agent in shaping the development of colonial history. In the aggregate, the results of this policy, which England by virtue of her sovereign authority was endeavoring to force upon the colonies, constitute an impressive picture, the details of which are so interwoven with the general life of the colonies as to be inseparable from it. From the historian they deserve and are capable of such treatment as will furnish an orderly and logical presentation of this neglected phase of our history.

Turning now to the second part of our general subject, we shall see that colonial commerce, quite apart from its connection with England's policy, was a dominant interest of the colonists themselves. There is danger lurking in the new point of view we are taking, the danger of giving exaggerated treatment to governmental policy and neglecting those parts of the story that represent colonial activity and private enterprise. We are right in taking our stand in the mother-country and in following thence the diverging lines of governmental influence in the colonies themselves. But when once these features of our subject have been outlined there still remains another and equally important group of subjects to be studied, the actual commercial and industrial conditions in the colonies and the extent to which these conditions reacted upon the policy at home. British governmental policy on one side and colonial organization and development on the other are but the complementary parts of a common subject. Each is incomplete without the other, and neither can be fully understood unless the other has been adequately and impartially presented.

To the colonists in America a commercial and trading life was the natural

---

the Board of Trade itself summed up the leading motives controlling the disallowance, as "the Commerce and Manufactures of this country," "Your Majesty's Royal Prerogative," and "the Authority of the British Parliament." It will be noticed that trade and commerce are mentioned first. *Acts of the Privy Council, Colonial*, V. 43.

accompaniment of their geographical location. The colonists did not confine their interests, as do most of our historians, to the fringe of coast from Maine to Georgia. They ranged over a larger world, the world of the North Atlantic, a great ocean-lake, bounded on the east by the coast of two continents, Europe and Africa, and on the west by the coast of a third continent, America. On the northeast, the British Isles occupied a vantage-point of great commercial and strategic importance, while within the ocean area were scores of islands, massed chiefly along the southwestern border or off the coast of Africa, from the Bahamas to Curaçao and from the Azores to the Cape Verde Islands, which held positions of the highest importance for purposes of trade and naval warfare. It is an interesting fact that the British island colonies, and still more those of France, Holland, and Denmark, have been mere names to the students of our history; and it is equally significant that no atlas of American history displays in full upon any of its maps the entire field of colonial life. The American colonists were not landsmen only, they were seafarers also. They faced wide stretches of water, over which they looked, upon which hundreds of them spent their lives, and from which came in largest part their wealth and their profits. Though migration into the interior began early, nearly half the eighteenth century had spent its course before the American colonists turned their faces in serious earnest toward the region of the west. Though the lives of thousands were spent as frontiersmen and pioneers, as many crossed the sea as penetrated the land, for colonial interstate commerce was not by land but by water. In the shaping of colonial careers and colonial governments, sea-faring and trade were only second in importance to the physical conditions of the land upon which the colonists dwelt. No one can write of the history of Portsmouth, Salem, Boston, Newport, New Haven, New York, Philadelphia, or Charleston, or of the tidewater regions of Maryland, Virginia, and North Carolina, without realizing the conspicuous part that commerce played in the lives of those comunities and regions. Even within the narrower confines of their own bays and rivers, the colonists of continental America, particularly of the northern part, spent much of their time upon the water. They travelled but rarely by land, unless compelled to do so; they engaged in coastwise trade that carried them from Newfoundland to South Carolina; they built, in all the colonies, but more particularly in New England, hundreds of small craft, which penetrated every harbor, bay, estuary, and navigable river along a coast remarkable for the natural advantages it offered for transit, transport, and traffic by water; and they devoted no small part of their time and energies as governors, councillors, and assemblymen to the furthering of a business which directly or indirectly concerned every individual, and which became more exigent and effective as the numbers of the colonists increased and their economic resources expanded.

In elaborating this phase of our subject we are called upon to deal with certain aspects which, though inseparable from the larger theme, are more strictly colonial in their characteristics and connections. I refer to staple products, shipping, trade routes, and markets, and in close connection with these are the various aspects of commercial legislation in the colonies themselves. A study of staple products demands that we survey the entire agricultural and industrial history of the colonies from Hudson Bay to Surinam, and enter upon a discriminating analysis of the economic importance of their chief products from furs to sugar and from fish to lime-juice. A study of shipping for the purpose in hand demands that we find out where ships were built, what was their tonnage, and how they were manned, and acquire some knowledge of the fitness of certain types of vessels for ocean, island, and coastwise service, according to their size and rig. The study of trade routes, one of the most varied and tangled of problems, demands that we determine the customary routes with all their variations, examine the reasons why these routes came into being, analyze the conditions attending traffic by these routes, and follow each route from port to port, as far as descriptions, logs, and registers will allow, instead of being content to see the captains and masters sail out into the unknown and return from the unknown, with very indefinite ideas as to where they had been and what they had done there. A study of markets requires that we have some fairly exact knowledge of the staple demands of other countries and colonies than our own, of the conditions under which our colonial staples were distributed, and of the nature of the commodities that other countries could offer to the captains and supercargoes wherewith to lade their vessels, either for the return trip, for the next stage of a long voyage that might cover many countries, or for the kind of huckstering business that many masters engaged in, going from port to port as they saw opportunities for profit.

Having presented these general features of this phase of our subject, I should like to state somewhat more exactly what I have in mind, and to discuss at somewhat greater length topics which, though commonly classed as economic, are in no way the peculiar property of the student of so-called economic history. First of all as to staple products. In the far north, from Hudson Bay to Nova Scotia, Maine, and New Hampshire, furs, fish, and lumber predominated. These same staples were also of importance to central and southern New England, in addition to whale-fins and whale-oil, but the main products here were agricultural, including live-stock, naval stores, and also a great variety of provisions, many in their natural state and other dried, salted, and pickled, with some articles of wooden ware, among which were jocularly classed the wooden clocks and nutmegs of Connecticut. New England differed from her neighbor colonies to the immediate southward, not so much in the character of the staples exported as in the possession of large numbers of shipping ports through which she sent her surplus products to the world outside. New York, including within its area of supply Long Island, Westchester County, and the Hudson and Mohawk river valleys, exported a similar variety of domestic staples, with a greater amount of bread-stuffs and peltry, but lagged behind such towns as Salem, Boston, Newport, and Philadelphia in the extent of her export business. Though sharing with Albany and Perth Amboy the trade of the region, she surpassed all the others as an entrepôt for re-exported commodities from the tropical colonies. Philadelphia was wholly absorbed in commerce, and early became the main port, with Burlington and Salem as subsidiary, through which the farmers of Pennsylvania and West New Jersey and the tobacco raisers of Delaware sent their supplies. She specialized in wheat, beef, pork, and lumber, and during colonial times was the greatest mercantile city of the colonial world. She raised almost no staple suitable for export to England and did but a small re-exporting business. As she drew practically all manufactured commodities from England, the balance of trade in that direction was heavily against her. Thus we have in one group what are commonly known as the "bread colonies," possessed of diversified staples, similar in many cases to those that England produced for herself.

South of Mason and Dixon's line we enter the group of single staple colonies, in which the export was confined to a single commodity or to a small number of commodities. Maryland and Virginia raised very little except tobacco until after the middle of the eighteenth century, when the export of grain, largely to the West Indies, marked the beginnings of trade with the tropical colonies and laid the foundations of the prosperity of Baltimore and Norfolk. North Carolina in the seventeenth century was relatively unimportant as an exporting colony, supplying only tobacco to New England traders who shipped it to England; but afterward, particularly in the southern section, from the plantations along the Cape Fear River, she developed a variety of staples, live-stock, naval stores, and provisions, and entered upon a considerable exporting activity. South Carolina was a long time in finding her staple industry, but the enumeration of rice in 1704 shows that out of the diversified commerce of the earlier era had come the one product that was to be the chief source of her wealth. In the eighteenth century rice, indigo, naval stores, furs, cypress, and cedar made up the bulk of her cargoes. Among the island colonies, Bermuda and the Bahamas, having no sugar and little tobacco, played but little part in the commercial life of the colonies. But with the West Indies — Jamaica, Barbadoes, and the Leeward Islands — we are face to face with that group known as the "sugar colonies" which formed till 1760 the leading factor in England's commercial scheme. Conspicuous among colonial staples were the products of these islands, sugar, molasses, and rum, with a small amount of indigo, cotton, ginger, allspice, and woods for cabinet work and dyeing purposes, some of which came from the mainland of Honduras. The contrast of the "bread colonies" and the "sugar colonies" forms one of the leading features of colonial history, and in their respective careers we have the operation of forces that explain many things in the course of colonial development.

With shipping we deal first of all with the actual extent of the ship-building industry, regarding which at present we have no very exact statistical information. Weeden has given us for New England an admirable, though rather miscellaneous, collection of facts that stand badly in need of organization. All the leading towns of the North had dock-yards and built ships, and many of the smaller towns on sea-coast and navigable rivers laid the keels of lesser craft. So rapidly did the business increase that New England after 1700 was not only doing a large carrying trade on her own account, but was selling vessels in all parts of the Atlantic world — in the southern colonies and in the West Indies, Spain, Portugal, and England. The golden age of New England ship-building was during the first third of the eighteenth century, and so rapid was the growth of the business that in 1724 English shipwrights of the port of London would have had a law passed forbidding the New Englanders to build ships or compelling them to sell their ships after their arrival in England. But here the colonists scored, for, as the counsellor of the Board of Trade said, the English ship-builders had no remedy, since by the Acts of Navigation the shipping of the plantations was in all respects to be considered as English-built. Later the business fell off, the centre of the ship-building activity moved north to northeastern Massachusetts and New Hampshire, and the English builders ceased to be concerned. New York, too, had her ship-yards, as had northern New Jersey, that of Rip Van Dam occupying the water front on the North River in the rear of Trinity churchyard; and Philadelphia, the chief ship-building city in America, in the years between 1727 and 1766, built nearly half the entire number that were entered in the ship-registry of the port during those years. In the South ship-building was less of a negligible factor than has commonly been assumed. Maryland in 1700 had 161 ships, sloops, and shallops, built or building along the Chesapeake, and some of these were large enough to engage in the English trade. Virginia built chiefly, but not entirely, for river and bay traffic, and North Carolina, though hampered by the want of good ports and harbors, made ship-building one of the established industries of the colony. South Carolina carried on her great trade with Europe chiefly in British bottoms and during the eighteenth century had scarcely a dozen ships at any one time that belonged to the province. Among the island colonies only Bermuda and the Bahamas played any part as ship-builders; while the others, early denuded of available timber, remained entirely dependent on outside carriers.

In size, the New England built vessels were mainly under 100 tons, with a large proportion of vessels of less than 20 tons, in which, however, ocean voyages were sometimes made. Occasionally vessels were built of 250 and 300 tons, and a few, monster ships for those days, reached 700 and 800 tons. Gabriel Thomas tells us that ships of 200 tons were built in Philadelphia, but the largest ship entered in the register mentioned above was of 150 tons, with others ranging all the way down to 4 tons. The Maryland lists mention vessels of 300 and 400 tons built in that colony, but the number could not have been large. In 1767 a vessel of 256 tons was offered for sale before launching in Virginia.

Five varieties of vessels were in use: (1) ships and pinks, three-masters with square rig; (2) snows and barks, also three-masters, but with one mast rigged fore-and-aft; (3) ketches, brigs, and brigantines, with two masts but of different sizes, combining square rig with fore-and-aft, and schooners, a native American product, with fore-and-aft rig on both masts, though in its development the schooner often carried more masts than two, without change in the cut of the sails; (4) sloops, shallops, and smacks, single-masters carrying fore-and-aft sails; and (5) boats without masts — hog-boats, fly-boats, wherries, row-boats, and canoes. Bermuda boats were conspicuous among colonial vessels, because rigged with mutton-leg sails. No statement regarding relative numbers can be made until far more information has been gathered than exists at present, but the proportion of three-masters, two-masters, and single-masters was somewhat in the ratio of one, two, and three. Of the numbers of seamen we know as yet very little.

Turning now to the complicated question of routes, which criss-crossed so bewilderingly the waters of the Atlantic, we can, I think, group the courses without difficulty, if we keep in mind the nature of supply and demand and the requirements of the Navigation Acts.

The first determining factor was the requirement that all the enumerated commodities — tobacco, sugar, cotton, indigo, ginger, fustic and other dye woods, and later cocoa, molasses, rice, naval stores, copper, beaver and other skins — be carried directly to England, or from one British plantation to another for the supply of local wants, whence, if re-exported, they were to go to England. This requirement gives us our first set of trade routes. The chief staples of all the colonies from Maryland to Barbadoes were carried to England in fleets of vessels provided by English merchants that during the days of convoys went out in the early winter, about Christmas time, and returned to England in the spring. The providing of naval protection in times of war was a matter of constant concern to the Admiralty, while the gathering of vessels and the arranging of seasons was one of concern to the merchants. After 1713 when convoying became largely unnecessary except to the West Indies, individual ships sailed at varying times, frequently returning from Maryland or Virginia as late as the end of August. We may call this route back and forth across the ocean between England and her southern and West Indian colonies the great thoroughfare of our colonial commerce. It was regular, dignified, and substantial. Out of it grew two subsidiary routes, one from New York and New England with re-exported commodities to England, and one from South Carolina and Georgia to southern Europe under the privilege allowed after 1730 and 1735 of exporting rice directly to all points south of Cape Finisterre. Thus we have a series of direct routes from nearly all of the American colonies converging upon England and one route from South Carolina and Georgia diverging to any point south of France, but generally confined to the Iberian Peninsula and the Straits. Along these routes were carried a definite series of commodities, raised, with the exception of naval stores and beaver, entirely in colonies south of Pennsylvania. To this commercial activity must be added the traffic in these same commodities among the colonists themselves, a service chiefly in the hands of the northerners, who carried tobacco, rice, logwood, and sugar from the southern and West Indian colonies to their own ports and there either consumed them, re-exported them to England, or in the case of sugar and molasses worked them over into rum and shipped the latter where they pleased.

When we consider the export activities of the northern colonies, we find ourselves involved in a more varied and complicated series of voyages. First, all the colonies north of Maryland, except Pennsylvania, had a certain but not very extensive trade directly with England. They carried in greater or less quantities an assortment of furs, fish, rawhides, lumber, whale-fins and whale-oil, naval stores, wheat, wheat flour, hops, and a little iron, though the largest amount of exported iron came from Maryland and Virginia. They also re-exported tobacco, sugar, molasses, rum, cocoa, hard woods, and dye woods. All these they carried in their own ships as a rule, and because their own products were not sufficient to balance what they wished to buy, they frequently sold their ships also to English merchants. Salem, Newport, and New York were the chief centres of the English trade. Secondly, the northern colonies carried on a very large trade in non-enumerated commodities with the countries of Europe. To various ports, from the Baltic to the Mediterranean, they sent quantities of "merchantable" fish, lumber, flour, train oil, and rice and naval stores before they were enumerated, chiefly to Spain, Portugal, southern French ports, and Leghorn, the mart of the Mediterranean. A few ships appear to have crept through the Sound into the Baltic; others, very rarely, went up the Adriatic to Venice; and in the case of a few enterprising merchants, notably John Ross of Philadelphia, vessels were sent to India and the East, though in 1715 New England reported no trade there, only a few privateers having occasionally "strol'd that way and [taken] some rich prizes."

The bulk of the northern trade, however, was not with Europe but with the West Indies and with the other continental colonies. The ramifications of this branch of colonial commerce were almost endless, the routes followed were most diverse, and the commodities exported included almost every staple, native or foreign, that was current in the colonial world. Philadelphia and New York traded chiefly with the West Indies and concerned themselves less than did New England with the coastwise traffic; but the New Englanders, in their hundreds of vessels of small tonnage, went to Newfoundland and Annapolis Royal with provisions, salt, and rum, to New York, the Jerseys, Pennsylvania, Maryland, Virginia, North Carolina, South Carolina, Bermuda, and the Caribbee Islands, peddling every known commodity that they could lay their hands on — meats, vegetables, fruits, flour, Indian meal, refuse fish, oil, candles, soap, butter, cider, beer, cranberries, horses, sheep, cows, and oxen, pipe-staves, deal boards, hoops, and shingles, earthenware and wooden ware, and other similar commodities of their own; and tobacco, sugar, rum, and molasses, salt, naval stores, wines, and various manufactured goods which they imported from England. They went to Monte Cristi, Cape François, Suri-nam, and Curaçao, to the islands off the coast of Africa, commonly known as the Wine Islands, and there they trafficked and bargained as only the New Englander knew how to traffic and bargain. It was a peddling and huckstering business, involving an enormous amount of petty detail, frequent exchanges, and a constant lading and unlading as the captains and masters moved from port to port. Sometimes great rafts of lumber were floated down from Maine, New Hampshire, and the Delaware, and not infrequently New England ships went directly to Honduras for logwood and to Tortuga and Turks Island for salt.

Let us consider the return routes. With the southern and West Indian colonies the problem was a simple one. The merchant ships from England went as a rule directly to the colonies, generally laden with English and Continental manufactured goods that according to the act of 1663 could be obtained by the colonists only through England. They followed usually the same route coming and going, though occasionally a ship-captain would go from England to Guinea where he would take on a few negroes for the colonies. Maryland seems to have obtained nearly all her negroes in that way.

But with the northern colonies, where the vessel started in the first instance from the colony, the routes were rarely the same. A vessel might go to England, huckstering from port to port until the cargo was disposed of, and then return to America with manufactured goods. It might go to England with lumber, flour, furs, and naval stores, then back to Newfoundland for fish, then to Lisbon or the Straits, then to England with Continental articles, and thence back to the starting point. It might go directly to Spain, Portugal, or Italy, trying one port after another, Cadiz, Bilbao, Alicante, Carthagena, Marseilles, Toulon, Leghorn, and Genoa, thence to England, and thence to America. It might go directly to the Wine Islands and return by the same route with the wines of Madeira and Fayal and the Canaries, though it was a debatable question whether Canary wines were not to be classed with Continental commodities and so to be carried to America by way of England only. It might go to Spain or Portugal, thence to the Wine Islands, thence to Senegambia or Goree or the Guinea coast for beeswax, gums, and ivory, thence back to Lisbon and home by way of England; or, if it were a slave ship, it might go to the Guinea coast, thence to Barbadoes, and home, or as was probably common, to Barbadoes first, thence to Africa, thence back to the West Indies and home, with a mixed cargo of negroes, sugar, and cash. Frequently the captain sold his cargo and even his ship for cash, and if he did this in Europe, or in England to London or Bristol merchants, he would either return with the money or invest it in manufactured goods, which he would ship on some homeward-bound vessel, returning himself with his invoice. With the New Englander, and to a somewhat lesser degree with the New Yorker and Philadelphian, the variations were as great as were the opportunities for traffic.

In this brief statement, I have given but a bare outline of a difficult and unworked problem in colonial history. Did time allow I should like to consider certain supplemental phases of the general subject that are deserving of careful attention. These are, first, the methods of distributing colonial commodities in England and Wales and of sending them into the interior, into Scotland, and into Ireland; secondly, the character and extent of the plantation trade with Ireland and Scotland directly, a matter of some interest and a good deal of difficulty; and thirdly, the re-exportation of tobacco, sugar, and other tropical and semi-tropical products from England to the European Continent. But upon these subjects I can say nothing here. One topic must, however, be briefly discussed, the question of illicit trade and smuggling.

The nature of the smuggling that went on during our colonial period is very simple, though the extent of it and the relation of it to the total volume of colonial trade is very difficult to determine. It is doubtful if satisfactory conclusions can ever be reached on these points, owing both to the lack of evidence and to its unsatisfactory character. For the most part smuggling took three forms: first, direct trade in enumerated commodities between the colonies and European countries, and participated in by English, Irish, American, and West Indian ships, trafficking to Holland, Hamburg, Spain, Portugal, Marseilles, Toulon, and other Mediterranean ports; secondly, a direct return trade to America or the West Indies, without touching at England as the law required, and participated in by the same ships, carrying the dry goods, wines, and brandies of Europe. The latter traffic had many aspects, for it included the trade between American British colonies and American foreign colonies, in which enumerated commodities, or in many cases non-enumerated commodities, were exchanged for European goods, purchasable at St. Eustatius, St. Thomas, or Curaçao, or at Monte Cristi in Hispaniola. There can be little doubt that this trade attained considerable proportions and was one of the channels whereby brandies, cocoa, silks, linens, and the like came into the colonies. There was much smuggled liquor drunk in the West Indies, and many were the damask gowns and silk stockings worn; and I fear that there were many things enjoyed in Newport, Boston, and Philadelphia that came either directly from France or by way of the foreign West Indies. Indeed, it seems to have been a common practice for ships of nearly every continental colony to go to Curaçao and return with European dry goods and cocoa.

Thirdly, there was a trade of the northern colonies with the foreign West Indies, in which a vessel would carry a general cargo to Jamaica or Barbadoes, sell all or a part of it for cash — gold or light silver — pass on to the French colonies of Guadeloupe, Martinique, or Santo Domingo, or to the Dutch colony of St. Eustatius, and there buy, more cheaply than at Jamaica, Barbadoes, or the Leeward Islands, their return cargo of sugar and molasses. There was nothing strictly illegal about this traffic, unless the northern trader laid out a part of his cash in European dry goods and smuggled them into the colonies by one or other of the many contrivances so well known to all West Indian traders; but it was injurious to the British sugar colonies in depriving them of a part of their market and draining them of much of their cash. It became illegal, however, when, after the passage of the Molasses Act, expressly designed to prevent this traffic, the Northerner evaded the duties imposed by this act on foreign sugar and molasses. Then if he brought in foreign sugar and molasses without paying the duty and on the same voyage stowed away hidden bales of Holland linens and French silks, casks of French brandies, and pipes of claret, he committed a double breach of the law. Lastly, if we were to go into the problem of illicit trade in all its phases, we should have to consider a certain amount of petty smuggling off Newfoundland, in Ireland, and at the Isle of Man, and by way of the Channel Islands; but upon these points our knowledge is at present very meagre.

A useful addition to this paper would be a statement regarding our sources of information, in manuscript in England and America, and in print in a great number of accessible works. There is an immense amount of available material in the form of correspondence, accounts, registers, lists, reports, returns, log-books, port books, statements of claims, letter-books and the like, which, though often difficult to use, are all workable and illuminating to the student who has organized his plan of treatment in a logical and not a haphazard fashion. The subject is a fascinating one, and the more one studies it, the more important and suggestive it becomes. I cannot believe that the future will show such a disregard of its significance as the past has done, for when its place is once recognized and its influence determined, colonial history will become not only fuller and richer, but also more picturesque, and the life of the colonists will appear as broader and more varied. And just as the local field will be enlarged and extended, so will the place of the colonies in the British and European systems of commercial empire be given its proper setting, and the balance between things imperial and things colonial will be restored. Only when such balance has been sought for and attained will the way be prepared for a history of the colonial period that is comprehensive in scope, scientific in conception, and thoroughly scholarly in its mode of treatment.

◆ **22** ◆

The Economic Relations of Boston, Philadelphia, and New York, 1680–1715 *

CURTIS NETTELS

A principal feature of the history of early America is a rising standard of living. As a class the colonists left Europe in order to improve their economic position in life; they desired not only to maintain the standard to which they had been accustomed but also to raise that standard as far as possible. This necessitated the importing of a large variety of familiar commodities that could not at first be produced profitably in America. Paint, glass, tools, fine cloth, gunpowder, arms, medical supplies, books, instruments, wines, superior household articles — these were only a few of the indispensable things that the primitive economy of the colonies did not afford. The distributing of these imports throughout the mainland provinces was the central feature of intercolonial trade. The story of this distribution furnishes the best clue to economic contacts existing between various regions — to the balance of trade and the movement of coin, to banking and credit relations, and to colonial indebtedness and a great deal of social and economic strife.

The merchants of England sent their goods to five regions on the continent: New England, New York, Pennsylvania, Virginia-Maryland, and South Carolina. In the Virginia-Maryland area, such goods went directly to the consumer in exchange for produce that could be sold in England; in the other colonies they went first to a central port, and there found an independent colonial distributor who carried them throughout the surrounding country. These distributing centers were Boston, New York, Philadelphia, and Charleston. Each supplied a definite area with the commodities it needed and took off the surplus products which that area produced. In the intercourse between two of these cities the one enjoying the dominant position was the one furnishing the other with transportation and European goods. The high cost of such goods (occasioned by freight charges and merchants' profits) meant that the balance of trade generally favored the distributing center rather than the country districts. The deficit was in part made up by means of such coin as the farmers obtained, and partly by means of bills of exchange drawn on outside credits. Beyond this the deficit assumed the shape of indebtedness. Thus the city distributor combined the several rôles of merchant, carrier, banker, and creditor.

Of these four centers, Boston at the close of the seventeenth century stood

* Taken and adapted from Curtis Nettels, "The Economic Relations of Boston, Philadelphia, and New York, 1680–1715," *Journal of Economic and Business History*, Vol. III, February 1931, pp. 185–215. Used by permission.

head and shoulders above the others. Its commercial supremacy did not arise from manufacturing, since it possessed a widely extended commerce before it exported cloth, ironware, or other products of its own making. Nor did its leadership arise from the agricultural resources of Massachusetts. It is true that Randolph found the farmers prospering in the sale of their produce, but their profits grew out of a large local demand and an inadequate supply. Andros observed in 1690 that "The Massachusetts Collony tho Considerable for Number of Townes and Inhabitants and well Scituated for Trade, is One of the Smallest and poorest Tracts of Land, and Produces least of any of the other Collonys for Exportation, Noe wheat having Grown but blasted there for about Thirty years past, nor have they of Cattle or other grains beyond their own Consumption. . . ." From time to time the assembly prohibited the exportation of local products such as wool, hides, skins, grain, beef, pork, and flour, because the supply for domestic use was insufficient. When Quary was buying provisions for the British West India fleet, he found that grain could be bought most cheaply in New York and Pennsylvania. In 1711 the supplying of the Canada expedition disclosed a shortage of provisions in Boston, and eventually they had to be procured at New York. The estimates of Banister in 1715 indicate the trend of Massachusetts trade. Exports of farm produce amounted to £113,000, whereas the province derived £491,000 from the sea. The limits of the land resources of Massachusetts forced the settlers to find wealth elsewhere — in the fisheries, in ship-building, and in the carrying trade.

Geographically, Boston enjoyed the favored position for serving the colonies as the carrier of their products. It had the best approach to Newfoundland, where fish, European goods, coin, and bills of exchange were obtained. It was the logical center for supplying the needs of the fishermen who went out from Salem and Marblehead to fish in the waters off eastern New England and Nova Scotia. Likewise, it was well placed with reference to New Hampshire, and hence could market New Hampshire's lumber in the settlements to the south. From the middle colonies, the provision country, it easily secured cargoes of foodstuffs for the West India trade. Virginia and Maryland were not far away, and the Leeward Islands and Barbados could be reached as readily as from Philadelphia or New York. The products of these places sought European markets, either directly or indirectly. Colonial commerce was an ocean-borne, outgoing commerce, rather than a continental, inland traffic. Its profits arose from the furnishing of settlements scattered along the coast, not from supplying a thickly settled interior. And as this commerce centered in England, Boston again held the advantage. Its location made it a natural stopping point for ships bound to the colonies from England or southern Europe. It became the distributing center of European goods, and the rendezvous of ships sailing under convoy from the northern colonies in time of war. The freight costs of the Atlantic voyage were so high, and the returns which the bread colonies could procure so meager that the goods had to be assembled in one place by small vessels before the larger ocean-going ships took them on board. Boston was by far the best assembling point for the scattered produce which the northern and middle colonies sent to the markets of the Old World.

Boston of course did not lack a hinterland of its own. The size of the population of New England at the turn of the century is rather difficult to ascertain. Official reports in 1708 and 1709 would have it appear that all the New England settlements contained not more than 85,000 souls. At this time Dudley computed that there were 150,000 people living between Pemaquid and the Delaware. Bancroft's estimates for 1689 assign 75,000 to the New England colonies, 30,000 to New York and New Jersey, 12,000 to Pennsylvania and Delaware, only 75,000 to the Chesapeake colonies, and 8,000 to Carolina. Whatever the exact figures, it is clear that Boston in the early eighteenth century was the most favorably situated of the principal port towns to act as the exchange center for the larger part of the population of the colonies.

One great advantage over the other colonies lay in the shipping both built and owned in Massachusetts. Bellomont found in 1700 that the colony had 264 vessels, 194 of which belonged to Boston. He thought Boston possessed more good ships than Scotland and Ireland combined. A few years later, after six years of war, the number had fallen to 200, but these vessels employed 1,000 seamen. Moreover, the ships owned in the colony give no index of its actual shipping, in view of the fact that vessels built there were commonly loaded with cargoes and sold on the maiden voyages. In two years, 1715–16, the ship-builders of New England turned out 308 vessels, most of which came from the Bay colony.

"The Bostoners," said Bellomont, "may be said to be the carriers to most of the other Plantations." Rhode Island in 1688 did not own more than five small vessels, and in 1708 less than thirty, employing but 140 seamen; Connecticut in the former year possessed only nine, and in the latter not more than twenty, the number of seamen then engaged being about 100. With respect to the number of vessels, New York probably had not more than half as many as Massachusetts. Maryland owned but a fraction of the shipping that carried on its trade. Virginia in 1708 had no vessel exceeding 150 tons, and only six ships and ten lesser craft. All these vessels and "the open shallops which carry tobacco for the ships and sometimes trade from one River to another" employed only 200 seamen. South Carolina in 1708 reported only ten or twelve vessels and not above "Twenty sea faring men who may be Accounted Settlers . . . in the Province."

It seems likely that Massachusetts possessed half the carrying capacity of colonial-owned shipping. This condition prevailed at a time when the distribution of goods by land was far more costly than transportation by sea. What one writer says of Maryland is true generally — that the "chief means of communication between the different parts of the colony and between the colony as a whole and the outside was by water." [1]

These influences favoring Massachusetts were re-enforced by other assets — principally by the fact that its merchants had been the first to arrive on the colonial scene, and hence derived the advantages of priority in establishing their trade. Their aggressive, enterprising spirit also helped them to retain their position. "It is the great care of the Merchants," wrote Randolph, "to keep their Ships in constant employment, which makes them seek all ports and places to force a trade, whereby they abound with all sorts of Commodities." [2] . . .

Sailings between Boston and England were so much more frequent than sailings from New York that New York carried on a great deal of its correspondence with Europe through Boston. Bills of exchange drawn in New York on England were often handled by Boston merchants. Thus the New York governors who drew on the Crown made their bills payable to New York merchants and the latter endorsed them to Bostonians, who then sent them to London for collection. By this process the New York trader settled his account with Boston merchants for European and other goods, and the latter received the means of purchasing in England.

At times the New Yorkers were not altogether happy in their intercourse with Boston. One source of friction sprang from the whale fishery of eastern Long Island. The towns of Southold, Southampton, and Easthampton, which carried on this fishery, had been settled by New Englanders. They showed a decided preference for Boston merchants when it came to selling their whale products and buying manufactured goods. This irked the New York merchants not a little, because they lost a very valuable means of making payment for English goods, as well as a market for the wares they had for sale at New York.

A second cause of trouble grew out of the provision trade. The spokesmen of the New York merchants complained that Boston merchants carried away from New York in payment for European goods all the heavy pieces of eight and other coin they could lay their hands on. They took this money to Boston where they cut a third of the silver from the coin, and then sent back the clipped pieces to buy grain at New York. The Bostoners refused to buy flour but insisted on exporting grain to Boston and there manufacturing their own flour. By this process, Boston was underselling New York flour in the British West Indies, and New York had found its source of coin was drying up. Were it not for the trade with Surinam and Curaçao, New York would be able to obtain no heavy coin at all.

[1] Morriss, *op. cit.*, p. 9. Weeden, *op. cit.*, vol. i, p. 260, gives data on New England freight charges. A shipment of wheat, Northampton to Boston via the Connecticut River, cost 1s. 8d. (1s. from Northampton to Windsor by land and 8d. from Windsor to Boston by water).

[2] British Museum, Additional Manuscript.

These two factors led to an attack in New York on the Boston trade. The assembly first levied a duty of ten per cent on European goods imported into New York from another colony. Governor Dongan explained that this act aimed to prevent the Long Islanders from buying and selling at Boston. When he found that they ignored the act, he ordered that every ship trading to or from the various parts of the province should first enter or clear at the port of New York. The ten per cent duty continued in force until early in the term of Lord Cornbury. This unworthy governor allied himself for a time with the merchants, and labored with the assembly to secure laws directed against the Boston trade. His program called for the re-establishment of the ten per cent duty; moreover, he wanted to pass an act to discourage the exporting of grain and to encourage the exporting of flour. He would place a special tax on rum and spirits imported indirectly from the West Indies, and furthermore would set up legal devices to prevent the clipping of New York's coin. All these proposals rested on his view that the practices of the Boston merchants were undermining the prosperity of New York.

Cornbury, however, could not get these measures enacted. But his policy was pursued by his successor, Governor Hunter. The duties on imports became involved in the larger controversy in the province over the revenue. Finally, in 1713, Hunter secured duties on European goods, rum, and wine when imported from another colony. Later acts in May, 1715, provided for a duty of five per cent on all English goods imported by way of Boston. Wine, distilled liquor, and cocoa were to pay twice as much when coming from Boston as when shipped directly from the place of their production. And all Boston ships importing directly from the West Indies were required to pay a duty of 3s. a ton. Thus the Boston trade was taxed either way — whether the goods came straight from the West Indies or indirectly by way of Boston. . . .

The province of New York divided its interest among three major pursuits: the raising of grain, the traffic in furs, and the driving of a sea-going commerce throughout the colonial trading area. The distribution of these activities was described in 1684 by the New York town officials: "the Manufacture of Flower & bread . . . hath been And is the chief support of the Trade & Traffique to and from this Citty & Maintainance of its Inhabitants in all Degrees . . . all other parts of this Province have some particular Advantage & way of Living as Long Island by husbandry & whaling; Esopus being the fatt of the Land by Tillage, Albany by Indian Trade & Husbandry, This City No other advantage or way of Living but by Traffique & Dependence one on Another chiefly upheld by ye Manufacture of Flower and bread." [3] Bellomont found New York to be "the growingest town in America." It maintained a regular trade with Albany: in 1687 there were six or seven vessels employed in this river traffic. Naturally, the town was the metropolis of the province for

---

[3] Petition of the mayor, aldermen, and Council of New York, 6 April, 1684, C. O. 5:1041, No. 4 (xv).

distributing English goods and other imports, and for assembling grain and furs for outgoing ships. Most of the townspeople were either merchants, millers, bakers, coopers, or seamen.

"The Trade of this Province," wrote Lord Cornbury, "consists cheifly of flower, and Biskett, which is sent to the Islands." By an early executive order, the making and packing of flour and bread had been confined to the port city. But about 1680, several flour mills had sprung up in the various parts of the province, thus threatening the monopoly of the city merchants, who thereupon secured a re-issue of the order prohibiting the operating of bolting mills or the packing of flour outside the city limits. The country flour-makers did not abide by this order, and in 1683 Governor Dongan had to instruct the sheriffs to seize all flour bolted and packed in the country districts. However, when the province secured its assembly, that body, representing mainly the farming communities, authorized that any person might engage in bolting, baking, and packing. At this time the assembly refused to pass any other measures until this free flour act was accepted. It was charged that Governor Fletcher took £400 for his assent to the law.

From this time (1695) the town officials made repeated efforts to recover the monopoly. The equally spirited opposition of the farmers suggests that they had not been at all satisfied with the scheme of selling their grain through the merchants of New York alone. In 1700, the city officials adopted an ordinance placing heavy duties on flour and biscuit imported into the city from the outlying settlements. The assembly then refused to pass any money bill until the obnoxious order was repealed. Bellomont wrote that the "City Members were as obstinate for maintaining their Ordinance, so that the money bill was very near miscarrying." Finally, however, he persuaded them to revoke the offending order. Cornbury, on the other hand, took the side of the merchants. He suggested that the city be given as many representatives in the assembly as all the other parts of the province combined. Then the free bolting act might be repealed. But this was not done, and the city did not recover its monopoly rights.

The city spokesmen presented their case in vigorous terms. They attributed the growth of the port to its early privileges. Two-thirds of the townspeople, they said, depended for their livelihood on the flour and bread trade. Formerly New York was the granary of America, having 40,000 bushels of wheat on hand. But after the free bolting act, the city often could not get enough grain for the needs of its own inhabitants. The city stood on the verge of a decline: bolters and coopers were leaving; and the province was in danger of losing its trading center. Moreover, the quality of New York flour had been maintained under the city monopoly through a scheme of inspection easily enforced by the town officials. When bolting became general, regulations and inspections were impossible. The country bolters mixed Indian corn with their wheat, and the city merchants had to do likewise in order to compete with their rivals. New York flour got a bad name in the West Indies;

it was said that its sale price there, which had formerly been higher than that of Pennsylvania flour, fell to 5s. in the hundred below the Pennsylvania product after the passing of the free bolting act. In the old days New York had received only heavy pieces of eight from the West Indies; now the decline of the flour trade had greatly diminished the supply of that valued commodity.

The views of the city leaders are of more than passing interest. They emphasized the value to the province of a trading and manufacturing center that would simplify the collecting of the revenue and lessen the task of inspecting the colony's export products. The centering of those products in one place enhanced their value in foreign markets, and the metropolis made possible a locally-owned shipping that freed the province from outside dictation of the prices of goods it bought and sold.

The merchants of New York naturally regarded East New Jersey as a part of their trading area. They fought with resolution for the control of this region. In the early days New York had been the metropolis for the Jerseys, but in 1685 the officials of the city were complaining that its trade had fallen off one-third as the result of the separation of those territories from New York. The trouble with East New Jersey grew out of heavy permanent duties that had been levied on New York's import and export trade. The proprietors of East New Jersey desired to establish a town of their own through which the trade of their province would be carried on. Accordingly, they declared Perth Amboy a free port and allowed vessels to bring in goods and to export the country's produce without paying any duties whatsoever. New York refused to accept these measures, and established an official at Perth Amboy to collect the same duties that were payable at New York. Later, all vessels trading to New Jersey were forced to come into New York in order to make the payments there. New York justified itself on two grounds. Inasmuch as goods imported into Perth Amboy paid no duties, they could be carried across into New York, there to undersell the wares imported by New York merchants. Likewise, commodities for the fur trade could be sent to the Indians more cheaply via New Jersey, and the furs returned to Perth Amboy where they paid no export duties such as were in force at New York. In spite of these arguments, the proprietors of East New Jersey resented strongly any interference with their trade. They asserted that an independent commerce was essential to the development of their colony, and that the prospect of a free port had been the major inducement leading them to invest their money. New York had no right to impose duties on the trade of East New Jersey because the people of the latter had never given their consent to the offensive measures.

This conflict became one of the main factors leading to the re-uniting of New Jersey and New York. When the proprietors of East New Jersey offered to surrender their claims to the government of their province, they demanded emphatically that it should be allowed a free port and the right to import and export without touching at any other place. On this basis, they yielded their claims in April, 1702. The policy pursued by England thereafter was that of allowing a free trade to Perth Amboy but also of insisting that the same duties be paid in New Jersey that were paid in New York.

The currency standards that prevailed in New York extended likewise to East New Jersey, for the latter province put into effect the evaluation of foreign coin adopted by its northern neighbor. In 1708, Cornbury wrote that New Jersey had no direct trade with England. East New Jersey bought its European goods from New York and sent thither its grain and other products. Nor did East New Jersey have much trade with other parts of the continent. Of the shipping of the province, Cornbury wrote, "the last year some of the Inhabitants built a sloop and fitted her out to sea, she had made a Voyage to Barbados and that is all the Vessels that belong to the Eastern Division, except wood boats that bring firewood and pipe staves to New York." East New Jersey had no native products that might serve as returns for England; thus in 1694 when the colony sent £400 to New York for colonial defense its remittance consisted of silver coin.[4]

It was stated by New York officials that in the years before 1685, New York was the mart for Pennsylvania, West New Jersey, and the Delaware counties. But the growth of Philadelphia altered this condition. As early as 1687 Governor Dongan complained that New York was losing the tobacco trade of the Delaware to Philadelphia, and that Pennsylvania was engrossing the fur trade at the expense of the older colony. New York's hardships and expenditures in defense of the colony greatly benefited Pennsylvania, yet the latter colony gave practically no assistance. Pennsylvania placed a higher value on pieces of eight than New York; this was thought to have attracted light money and settlers to the southern province. Cornbury also believed that the fact that the Pennsylvania trade paid no duties caused people to go there in preference to New York. By 1698, the trade of Pennsylvania was found to be nearly equal to that of New York; and the former colony was buying very little from the latter. . . .

When Penn laid out the city of Philadelphia he intended that it should become the trading center of his province. This it speedily did. As settlement pushed up the Delaware and Schuylkill rivers, the inland farmers sold their products and bought supplies through Philadelphia traders. The city grew by leaps and bounds. It maintained regular markets and fairs, built imposing wharves along the water-front, and domiciled a group of hardy Scotch and English merchants. By 1700, it stood at the center of a settled area which produced an abundance of grain and livestock — a fertile, prosperous, growing country. In the beginning Penn had placed great emphasis on trade, and the colony's economic policy and the spirit of its institutions were alike conducive to free intercourse with the outside world. The location of the city,

---

[4] Cornbury to Board of Trade, 1 July, 1708, C. O. 5:970, no. 77; *Col. Recs.*, Pennsylvania, 23 May, 1694, vol. i, p. 459.

together with its splendid harbor facilities, made it the natural shipping cen‑ ter for the farms along the Delaware.

The tobacco exported by Philadelphia came from the three lower coun‑ ties. In 1696 Quary noted a considerable production there which he thought yielded a fourth of the produce of the province. Three years later he found a great increase; the province had flooded the West India markets with pro‑ visions; now it was turning to tobacco. The crop of 1699 had amounted to four times that of any previous year. Not enough ships were available in June, 1700, and in 1702 the assembly of the lower counties declared that they had that year freighted ten vessels for England. The exports from Pennsyl‑ vania in the period 1698–1704 totaled 1,482,488 pounds. The tobacco was marketed by the merchants of Philadelphia, who in turn supplied the farm‑ ers with goods they needed. This relationship accounts in part for the deter‑ mination of the lower counties to maintain their own assembly rather than accept representation in the Pennsylvania legislature.

West New Jersey soon came within the trading sphere of Philadelphia. In 1693 the assembly of that province declared that "it has been found very in‑ convenient that money in this Province hath differed in value from the same coin current in our Neighbouring Province of *Pennsylvania*." It was there‑ fore enacted that the schedule of foreign coin values then prevailing in Penn's colony should extend likewise to West New Jersey. Lord Cornbury later ob‑ served that West Jersey imported all its European goods from Philadelphia and sent thither its surplus grain. It owned not a single vessel, and had no trade with any other place than Philadelphia.

After the reunion of the Jerseys in 1702, the two parts of the province con‑ tinued to use different money standards. That of East Jersey — the official standard of the province — was derived from New York; that of West Jersey from Philadelphia. Consequently, when public dues were collected in West New Jersey, the accounts were first stated in Pennsylvania money. But when remittance was made to East New Jersey, the sums had to be converted into New Jersey money. Though West Jersey belonged politically with East Jer‑ sey, commercially it belonged to Pennsylvania. . . .

Three factors determined the relative importance of the colonial towns, namely, ship-owning, the distributing of foreign goods, and the marketing of local produce. The profits of carrier and middleman gave the towns a favor‑ able balance of trade in their exchanges with the farming communities. This produced a movement of coin and bills of exchange to the commercial cen‑ ters. Judged by these factors, Boston clearly outdistanced its rivals. It owned the most shipping, served as the principal emporium for distributing the ex‑ pensive European goods, and used most of its ships, not for supplying Massa‑ chusetts alone, but for marketing the surplus produce of other colonies and for providing them with foreign goods. This trade made Boston the coin center of the continental colonies. Both New York and Philadelphia, though they possessed an independent commerce, were also tributary to Boston. The country localities felt more or less dissatisfied with their condition — a feeling that arose largely from the exporting of their coin to the trading centers. The attempt to prevent this accounts for many provincial quarrels. Each of the colonies desired a plentiful supply of coin for its own use. Yet the need of European goods was equally insistent. Since the supply of both was limited, the colonies faced a real dilemma. The difficulties that Boston, Philadelphia, and New York met in paying for their purchases in England likewise confronted the country districts in their intercourse with those colonial towns.

✧ 23 ✧

Thomas Hancock, Colonial Merchant *

EDWARD EDELMAN

It is the purpose of this essay to sketch briefly the career of Thomas Hancock, uncle of John Hancock, the bold signer of the Declaration of Independence, for what it reveals of the business conditions and commercial practices found in American foreign and domestic trade during the decades just previous to the Revolution. Few salient facts about this merchant are known, and the only account of his life which deserves mention is a brief, laudatory biography by Staples.[1] This old-time merchant's experiences so clearly reveal typical problems with which American business men of his class had to contend that a study of his activities may succeed in supplementing the very general discussions which now make up most of the existing works in this field.

Thomas Hancock was born and bred in seaboard Massachusetts, just outside of Boston. One of his ancestors is known to have been in Cambridge at as early a date as 1634, and his father, John Hancock, son of Nathaniel the cordwainer, was settled as minister at Cambridge Farms, later Lexington, in 1698. In the small, one-story Hancock house in Cambridge Farms, Thomas was born on July 13, 1703; and grew up in a family of five children, his oldest brother being the Rev. John Hancock, father of John Hancock of Revolutionary War fame.

It is likely that there was little in his father's experience to tempt his young, ambitious son to the ministry, as the Rev. John Hancock had for a long time struggled to live in a respectable fashion on a yearly salary of £45 in depreciated currency. While his two sons, John and Ebenezer, were pre-

---

* Taken and adapted from Edward Edelman, "Thomas Hancock, Colonial Merchant," *Journal of Economic and Business History*, Vol. I, 1928–1929, pp. 77–104. Used by permission.

[1] C. A. Staples, "Sketch of the Life of Hon. Thomas Hancock, A Native of Lexington," *Proceedings of the Lexington Historical Society*, vol. ii (1905), pp. 5–18. A. E. Brown, *John Hancock, His Book* (Boston, 1898), and Lorenzo Sears, *John Hancock* (Boston, 1913), include important information about Thomas Hancock.

pared for the ministry at Harvard, Thomas was not sent to college. Instead, when less than fourteen years of age, he was sent to Boston on July 1, 1717, as apprentice to Samuel Gerrish and Sarah, his wife, to learn "the Art and Trade of a Book-binder." In the shop at the lower end of Cornhill, the lad was indentured to serve them seven years, but they were obliged by the agreement to ". . . teach instruct, & inform or cause to be taught and informed the Said Apprentice; finding for and to him the Said Apprentice, Meat, Drink, Washing and Lodging, as well in Sickness as in health . . ." until July 1, 1724.[2]

Apparently, as soon as he had completed his term of service, he sailed for the British Isles, for in the summer of 1724 he was at Plymouth, England. Shortly after his return he was established in a shop of his own on Ann Street, near the Drawbridge, selling and binding books for the trade. Perhaps his former master helped him to secure sufficient credit for this venture. It is possible, also, that he had accumulated a little money during his period of apprenticeship. In any event the stock necessary for the opening of his small bookstore was probably worth much less than £100 lawful money, and it is likely that he started his business career with no greater amount of assistance than this.

His business aptitude and untiring energy won him success from the start. In 1725 or 1726 he was able to hire Isaac Woody, a bookbinder, agreeing to pay him "Fifty-Pounds per annum by four Even and Equal payments in the year until . . . Two-years be ended — ."[3] Three years later he had advanced to a point where he could become party to a contract with Benj. Gray, a Boston bookseller, under which Gray was to sell about three thousand books belonging "to Hancock . . . out of his [Gray's] Shop in Boston for the best Profit and advantage of the sᵈ. Thomas Hancock. . . ." He allowed Gray a commission of only 6 per cent for the disposal of the books.[4] During this same year he instructed one of his English agents, Sam Storke, to have some books printed for him in London, while at about the same date he sent a detailed order to another London firm, adding in a characteristic way, "directions to put up such new things [books] as are valuable."[5]

Meanwhile, during this early period of business expansion, Hancock's London agents were carrying the financial burden devolved upon them because he was operating with such a meager supply of capital. The very fact that he was buying through so many agents in London may indicate that he was attempting to spread his debts. How deeply Hancock was engaged in these years is not disclosed by the evidence which now remains. We do know, however, that by the fall of 1728, Storke, his principal agent, was refusing to

[2] "Indenture of Thomas Hancock," *Bostonian Society Publications*, vol. xii, (1915), pp. 99–101.
[3] Articles of Agreement between Hancock and Woody, January 11, 1925 (?), Lexington Hist. Soc. Mss., B–105–837.
[4] Agreement between Hancock and Gray, July, 1728, in Hancock Mss.
[5] Osborne & Co. to Hancock, August 6, 1728, *ibid.*

deliver goods on Hancock's order, demanding that someone else account to him for them before they were sent; and Thomas Cox of London invited him to send cash immediately for his entire debt, as he had promised.

Hancock's business aspirations were by no means confined to his new bookshop, the "Bible and Three Crowns," which he probably opened in 1729. Indeed during that same year we find him extending his activities into an entirely new type of business, shipping fourteen hogsheads of rum to Joseph Shepheard, his agent at Bonavista, Newfoundland, and ordering him to invest part of the proceeds in a quantity of codfish from the season's catch on the Grand Banks. Though he suffered a loss of £16 17s. 8d. on this purchase of fish, Hancock was only temporarily deterred from advancing his interests by commencing a general shipping business.

The development of his export ventures came with such rapidity immediately after 1730, that it is difficult to explain where he secured the funds to finance his extensive transactions. Perhaps his choice of the fair Lydia Henchman as his wife was an influential factor. An intimacy that had begun in the old Brattle Street Church, and had deepened during months of constant attendance at Sunday services, resulted in his marriage, on November 5, 1730, to Lydia, the daughter of Daniel Henchman, a prosperous wholesaler and retailer of books and general merchandise.

Hancock in no wise remained exclusively concerned in foreign trade and book dealing at this time. Indeed in 1728 he became one of the five organizers of a paper mill. The group of partners, headed by Daniel Henchman, and including Benjamin Faneuil, Gillam Phillips, and Henry Dering, received a charter which gave them "the sole privilege and benefit of making paper within this province [Massachusetts] . . . during the term of ten years." They were to make "merchantable, brown paper," "printing paper," and "merchantable writing paper." [6] Leasing a paper manufactory, which had been built twenty years before "on the Milton side of the Neponset river, seven or eight miles from Boston," they began operations in 1730; [7] and within a few years were said to be making paper "to the value of two hundred pounds Sterling yearly." [8]

But his partnerships in trading enterprises assumed far greater importance. Shortly after his marriage he formed a partnership with William Tyler, another Boston merchant, with the object of exporting codfish and whalefins on their joint account. Hancock's papers reveal that the partners shipped cod-

[6] *Acts and Resolves of the Province of Massachusetts Bay*, vol. ii (Boston, 1874), Acts of 1728–1729, chap. xvii, pp. 518–19.

[7] L. H. Weeks, *A History of Paper Manufacturing in the United States, 1690–1916* (New York, 1916), p. 21; Joel Munsell, *Chronology of the Origin and Progress of Paper and Paper-Making* (Albany, 1876), p. 37.

[8] W. B. Wheelwright, *New England's Pioneer Paper Makers* (typewritten copy in Massachusetts Historical Society Library), pp. 3, 39. After about ten years the mill was sold by the partners. It did not finally discontinue operations until torn down in 1839. It appears from Hancock's correspondence that at a later period he was interested in an iron mill and a potash works.

fish from Nantucket to the firm of Laxminter & Barrow at Bilbao, Spain, as early as 1731; and that Tyler was a partner in the majority of his exporting ventures from that date until 1738, though practically all imports came in on their separate accounts.

Various enterprises were jointly undertaken by the partners. They shipped "Train Oyle" and whalebone to London in considerable quantities.[9] They consigned on their own "account and risque" Indian corn, staves, flour, New England rum, white sugar, tobacco, and cider to their agents at St. Johns, Newfoundland.[10] They invested their funds in shares in sloops. In 1735 and 1736 they constructed the ship "Industry."[11] Moreover, when they had sufficient bills of credit they bought vessels, and within a few years controlled a small fleet. When the risks were greater than usual, or matters could be arranged more advantageously with the aid of others, they expanded their partnership to take in one or two business associates. In 1734 John Erving joined with them in shipping dry codfish from St. Johns; and two years later Tyler, Richardson, and Hancock imported "Tafetty," French linens, sweet oil, "Script holland," Holland duck, and other articles by way of Cadiz.[12] This same year they were associated with Captain Henry Atkins in the purchase of a three-eighths' share in the expected profits from Joseph Snow's whaling voyage to the northward. . . .

With characteristic foresight, Hancock refused to undertake highly speculative enterprises alone, even after he had enough money to finance them. In the years directly following 1740 his exports to Europe appear to have been of less importance, and were not often financed with the aid of partners. But the valuable Newfoundland supply was handled differently. When the "catch" was far below normal, cargoes were unsaleable at Placentia, Bonavista, or St. Johns; and because of this, each large consignment to those points was in the nature of a speculation. It was primarily for this reason that Henry Atkins was concerned with him in practically all the major shipments of molasses, rum, shoes, and other supplies made to these points during the forties. It is possible also that he required the former sea captain because of his intimate knowledge of the needs of the fishermen; but this factor must be discounted, for it is clear that the astute Hancock dispatched a number of small consignments to Newfoundland on his own account.

Hancock's largest single article of export was whale oil. He was with Tyler in a speculation in oil in the early thirties, and by 1740 was making sizable shipments every season. Though unable to buy during the war years, he was back in the market in that precious interval of peace that extended from 1748 to 1754. The settlement of Halifax, however, made large demands upon his resources in those years; and it was not until after 1761, when the

[9] Account of sales, Wilks to Tyler and Hancock, February 8, 1731/2, May 7, 1731, July 8, 1732, and others, *ibid.*
[10] Bill of lading signed by Atkins, May 4, 1734, *ibid.*
[11] Bill for Ship "Industry," Bulfinch, May 17, 1736, *ibid.*
[12] Account of goods from Cades, 1736, *ibid.*

seas were quite clear again, that he and his partners began to make big thousand barrel shipments, rivaling those of the great William Rotch of Nantucket.

Monthly and seasonal variations in the price of oil were so considerable as to make ventures of this type unusually hazardous, especially as the arrival of several hundred barrels at London often upset the whole market. Yet Hancock's dealings in whalebone, potash, and logwood were almost as risky. With this situation prevailing, temporary partnerships were arranged for all purchases of considerable size, and all means, legitimate or illegitimate, were resorted to, in order to meet competition. London news was distorted so that competitors would hold their ships in port until too late, and great efforts were made to beat the Nantucket oil schooners across the Atlantic.

But the problem of gauging the market and postponing the disposal of Hancock's goods until they could be sold most profitably was chiefly in the hands of his agents. These men were frequently his partners in the trade. Their shares of the cargoes were often nine-sixteenths, a half, seven-sixteenths, or a third of its total value, the last named more commonly being the proportion they desired to hold. Hancock or another American partner purchased the cargo, and loaded it on board a sloop which was often owned in common with the London agents. His foreign agents paid the entry fees, warehoused the commodities, sought out buyers, and did not complete the transaction until they had credited the accounts of Thomas and the other partners, according to their respective divisions of the proceeds.

Early in his career as an exporter Hancock was brought into contact with his first important general agent in London, Francis Wilks. This probably came about through the agency of Hancock's partner, the well-known merchant, William Tyler. Wilks was soon acting for him in independent, as well as partnership, matters, and continued as Hancock's principal English agent until 1742. Hancock employed several other firms as his agents during this same period, but their services were of a less important nature. Wilks' demise in 1742 caused a complete break in the management of Hancock's English affairs, and possibly left him temporarily embarrassed. The firm of Bourryau & Schaffer immediately succeeded Wilks. After 1745 we find frequent dealings with Benjamin Horrocks. As early as 1744 Hancock was dealing with Sedgwick, Kilby & Barnard of London, and by 1749 Kilby & Barnard had become his chief foreign agents; in which capacity they ably represented him until his death.

These agents were great commission merchants. They not only handled Hancock's shipments to European ports, but also, and this was their major function, purchased any articles that he might desire for his wholesale and retail trade, for the government supply, or for his personal use. Hancock bought some articles, however, only through special agents. Books were ordered from Thomas Longman, Sam Storke & Company, or John Osborne & Company; John Rowe's specialty was paper (though he sometimes sent books; and novelty hardware and cutlery came from Elisᵃ. and Jarvis Maplesden of London. . . .

Thomas and Adrian Hope at Amsterdam and Martin Dubrois Godet at St. Eustatius, an island in the West Indies, were agents primarily interested in furthering Hancock's smuggling ventures. The Dutch firm was a well-established commission house. It is likely that at times they sold legal cargoes which Hancock sent them from America. It was only when they shipped goods of European or East India manufacture to Hancock, John Erving, the Quinceys, or other colonial merchants that their actions became questionable.

There were two ways by which Hancock received contraband shipments from Holland. It seems to have been possible at times for a vessel to return directly to Boston, carrying a consignment from Amsterdam, without entering the cargo at an English port. The second mode of illegally running in a shipment is the more interesting. Hancock would write the Hopes, commissioning them to buy paper, rope, twine, linseed oil, Russia duck, Holland duck, linen, pistol powder, chinaware, wine, tea, or other commodities, and ship them to Godet, at the Dutch Island of St. Eustatius, where free trade was allowed to the ships of all nations. The difficulties involved in smuggling goods from Amsterdam are partially described in a letter from Hancock to his agents in Holland: [13]

> I have Considered the Difficulty of shipping Tea in Chests, & the often shipping, unshipping, Storeing &c Racks them to pieces by which I lost a great Deal of Tea in the Last & Damaged more. I would propose if Practicable & I think it may be done, that is, to Pack it in good Tite Cask of a suitable size that will hold a Chest or a Chest and a half . . . if this can be done & well Cooper'd, it will Come less liable to Damage & without Suspicion, I'd have Tite Cask that will hold water, and Shipt as Merchandize to the address of Mʳ. Martin Dubrois Godet at Sᵗ. Eustatia. if any NEngland people in Amsterdam please to let no mention be made, they Tell everything here, & our Officers are very Sharp . . .

A further description of the devious methods used to smuggle a cargo of tea from St. Eustatius to Boston is contained in a short letter of advice from Hancock to Godet: [14]

> . . . our mutual friends Messʳˢ. Hopes . . . have Shipt to yoʳ. Address Twelve Cases of Merchandize for my Accoᵗᵗ. I am to beg the favʳˢ. of you when arrive to store them in a dry Secure Store and when any Good Opporʸ. offers for this place will Take three or four of them in a Vessell please to Ship them, I would not have more in one Bottom, they need not know what is in them, I will pay freight to their Satisfaction. They must be Carefull as to Landing them here, which no doubt they are acquainted with . . .

[13] Hancock to the Hopes, May 27, 1755, Hancock Letterbook, 1750–1762.
[14] Hancock to Godet, September 30, 1755, *ibid.* Tea seems to have been the chief article Hancock smuggled from Holland. See also Hancock to the Hopes, January 14, 1753/4. April 17, 1755, *ibid.*

The unscrupulous Godet also managed Hancock's direct trade with St. Eustatius. Horses, lumber, and possibly provisions were shipped to the Dutch island, where Godet exchanged them for illicit consignments of French West India products, according to directions from Hancock, such as the following: [15]

> pleese to ship my Returns for the ne. [net?] proceeds in mol. [molasses?] if Cheep, should it be — above six stivers, then send it in good french Indego if at a moderate price, but if Indego be Scarce & Dear then in mol. [molasses?] as Cheep as you Possibly Can procure it in English hhd . . .

The payment of a cash balance due Hancock from Godet at St. Eustatius required considerable banking ability in those days when modern banking houses of international repute were non-existent. Hancock was his own banker, as was Godet; and the Hopes at Amsterdam, like most other foreign agents, were also bankers. Godet, therefore, with a balance in the hands of the Hopes, was able to draw "sight drafts" on them in Hancock's favor, and the latter forwarded the bills to London, where they were credited to his account with his English agents.[16]

Persons traveling from Boston to London purchased bills of exchange from Hancock, which were redeemable at the office of his English agents, just as today one is able to purchase letters of credit for foreign travel; and New England merchants, who needed funds in Europe, often bought bills from Hancock to settle their accounts with foreign firms.

On the other hand, Hancock's store was practically a bank of deposit for many business men in his immediate locality. Money was left in his care for long intervals, and then suddenly drafts were drawn on him for considerable amounts as it was needed. His partners also often had some funds to their credit on his books, though at times they were considerably overdrawn.

On the European side it was the same. Hancock's agents cashed his drafts, paid bills for him, allowed him to overdraw his account, and charged him a normal rate of interest on all overdrafts. They also drew bills of exchange on Hancock at their convenience. At one time they sent him a bill drawn from Stockholm on Messrs. Lindergreen of London in favor of Rev. C. M. Wrangle, "Pastor of the Swedish Congregation at or near Philadelphia." Hancock had to carry out his end of the affair by sending the bill to an agent at Philadelphia with orders to pay the Rev. Wrangle and have him receipt the bill. The final step was to return it to his agents at London.

It would have been much more difficult for Hancock to settle his accounts with his London agents had it not been for the fact that he did considerable commission buying for them both in partnership and private transactions. Not only did he, as a commission merchant, purchase products of the fisheries

---

[15] Hancock to Godet, February 25, 1742/3, *ibid.* Molasses from the French islands was transferred into English hogsheads in order that it might be passed by the customs officers.

[16] See Godet to Hancock, March 6, 1748/9, *ibid.*

for the English firms, but he also bought logwood and potash for them, charging the usual 5 per cent commission for his services. When the market was favorable his agents were often interested in several speculations in American goods, but at times it appears that their main purpose in ordering Hancock to purchase colonial products was to secure funds long overdue from him.

It is significant that the period in which Hancock first entered foreign trade overlaps the period in which his bookstore and bindery began to be changed into a sort of general warehouse, and the nucleus for a wholesale and retail trade of quite a different type from that carried on when it was first established. The enlargement of his stock took place by easy and natural stages. In 1732 he was selling only a few odd articles such as spectacles, buttons, needles, and garters, at his bookshop; but during the following year he was handling sugar, flour, rum, and tea. Books and paper appear to have remained as the most valuable part of his inventory during the next few years; but, as his enlarged purchases of dry goods and other wares soon changed the nature of his store, the book trade began to make a less prominent showing in his total yearly sales. By 1745 it was clearly unessential to his business.

Hancock did not differentiate between his sales at wholesale and retail. His establishment catered to both retailers and consumers, though he frequently gave dealers a more favorable price on certain commodities. Regardless of the differences that might exist, Hancock commingled sales to the British government, retailers, artisans, and seamen in the same account books in which he also entered items relating to banking, foreign trade, and shipbuilding, as well as purchases of merchandise for his store.

Since we are here interested in analyzing his business, however, we can note that tea was the principal article Hancock sold to retail. Hundreds of one-pound packages were purchased by his customers every year. In addition, they came to his store for many varieties of dry goods, such as serge, broadcloth, linen, taffeta, and calico; for ready-to-wear goods, such as hats and hosiery; as well as for nails, window glass, cordage, bottles, penknives, and paper.

His wholesale market lay all along the New England seaboard, and extended far into the interior of Massachusetts. He had customers at York Harbor, Maine, Exeter, New Hampshire, and Lyme, Connecticut. He pushed his market Rhode-Islandward, into the territory of rival merchants at Providence, and northward, to compete with firms at the enterprising port of Salem; being one of the first who helped bring about trade radiation from the embryo metropolis of Boston.

In Boston itself he supplied many of the merchants of the town, often receiving in return for his wares some necessary articles for export or personal use. In fact, a surprising amount of Hancock's total business came about through the exchange of his merchandise of foreign origin for colonial goods.

Money was scarce, and continually fluctuating in value. And many of Hancock's widespread ventures were based on the export of foodstuffs, rum, lumber, and products of the whaling industry. Under these circumstances, therefore, it was natural that a trade based to a certain extent upon the exchange of articles prevailed.

Payment in kind was rarely made at the time of purchase. Hancock would sell his wholesale customer dozens of knives, combs, handkerchiefs, and necklaces, reams of paper, and a number of bolts of cloth, and some months later would receive several loads of grain or potatoes in return. Accounts were usually balanced only at the end of a long period. The ordinary terms of sale required payment at the end of six months or a year, with interest at 6 per cent on all overdue balances. Though notes were sometimes signed to give additional security, strenuous efforts to collect notes and accounts were rarely made. For this reason, old unpaid notes and uncollectible accounts continued to loom large among Hancock's assets until his death.

Sales experienced sharp fluctuations, which were directly reflected in customer's accounts, for the reason that Hancock received payment on delivery from but a minor portion of those with whom he had dealings. Though figures for total sales in any year are not available, the movement of sales can be approximately ascertained for certain years from entries in Hancock's account books. The monthly variation in his wholesale and retail trade was so great that charge sales in June were often from five to eight times as great as those of January. As an indicaton of what took place the following data may be helpful.

TOTAL CHARGE SALES [17]

(In lawful money of the province)

	1755				1761		
	£	s.	d.		£	s.	d.
January	486	7	$0\frac{1}{4}$		452	14	$10\frac{1}{4}$
February	420	17	$10\frac{3}{4}$		2,100	16	$7\frac{1}{4}$
March	1,612	19	$4\frac{3}{4}$		374	14	$1\frac{3}{4}$
April	846	12	$11\frac{1}{4}$		1,247	9	$11\frac{1}{4}$
May	1,506	13	$4\frac{1}{2}$		611	14	$10\frac{3}{4}$
June	3,420	3	11		704	19	$9\frac{3}{4}$
July	699	5	$7\frac{3}{4}$		1,777	5	
August	674	14	$10\frac{1}{2}$		586	9	7
September	840	1	4		198	11	$\frac{1}{4}$
October	1,020	6	$7\frac{1}{2}$		779	8	$5\frac{3}{4}$
November	1,401	8	$8\frac{1}{2}$		565	10	$3\frac{3}{4}$
December	853	13	$7\frac{1}{4}$		579	5	2
Total	13,783	5	4		9,978	19	$10\frac{1}{4}$

[17] Hancock Journal, 1755–1757; Hancock Waste Book, 1759–1762. These figures are for years in which his business was developed to its highest point. Complete figures for

On the basis of these figures it can be said that Hancock did not have to face the problem of adjusting his business to a highly seasonal variation in sales. January was the one month in which sales usually reached an extremely low point. Wide divergences are shown in figures for the other months, but quarter by quarter sales were about the same, because of the non-seasonal nature of Hancock's business. Customers from distant points seldom purchased more than once a year, but they had no definite period during which they made this purchase; and they often took away merchandise valued at several hundred pounds as the result of a day's buying. Two or three large sales, therefore, were usually responsible for the difference between a good and a poor month. In addition, merchant and whaling vessels required supplies infrequently, but since they were in need of new sails and rigging, as well as provisions, their trade was eagerly sought, as it brought large returns. . . .

For over thirty years [Hancock] continued to advance steadily, and to gain additional respect and honor from the rich merchants and aristocrats of Massachusetts. Petty shopkeepers, farmers, artisans, and seamen fawned upon him, and it is little wonder that at intervals he was able to make great provincial governors, like Edward Cornwallis, stand upon command.

So great was the confidence vested in him by his business associates, that he acted as personal attorney for his agent, Jonathan Barnard of London, and was executor of a number of important New England estates of his day. His father and brothers put their trust in him, and forced him to give serious attention to their affairs on several occasions; while Henchman relied upon his son-in-law from the beginning, and left his fortune to Hancock at his death in 1761.

Thus all the Hancock wealth was not amassed by trade. Large real estate holdings and other property came from the Henchman estate. During his lifetime he invested much and realized comparatively little on his extensive real estate holdings in the town of Boston, in rural Massachusetts, and in New Hampshire, nor did his miles and miles of land along the Kennebec river in Maine ever yield him a worthwhile return.

Circumstances were never favorable enough, however, to give Hancock a chance to put any considerable part of his fortune into enterprises more speculative than those which came his way as merchant and contractor. Although he liked to patronize the London lotteries, he could not very freely indulge his gambling propensity, for his money was tied up in legitimate business during the two decades in which he made the greatest gains.

Because of the effectiveness with which he constantly plowed back the

---

any year previous to 1755 are not available. The table has been compiled from the daily records of charge sales made in those years, each sale being examined separately, as no daily, weekly, or monthly totals could be found. It is possible that the monthly totals are slightly imperfect, because of the difficulty of deciphering the handwriting and discovering the correct meaning of certain entries.

wealth which he amassed, Hancock left a fortune which has been quite reasonably estimated at "about £70,000." His estate stood out prominently as one of the largest ever accumulated in the Province of Massachusetts Bay. □

❖ **24** ❖

The Case of the Planters of Tobacco in Virginia, & C.*

■ *As represented by Themselves; signed by the President of the Council, and Speaker of the House of Burgesses. To which is added, A Vindication of the said Representation.*

We the Council and Burgesses of *Virginia*, the most ancient of the *British* Colonies in *America*, now met in a General Assembly, having under our Consideration the distressed State of the Tobacco Trade, which chiefly employs the Industry of the King's Subjects here, and is their only Support, find ourselves obliged, from a Sense of Duty to His Majesty, and our own Sufferings, to represent, The Progress of that Trade through a long Course of Years; the many Mischiefs that have attended it through the various Changes it has undergone by Several Acts of Parliament; and the particular Hardships which are now imposed upon us by the unjust Dealings of most of our Factors, the Tobacco Merchants in *Great Britain*.

TOBACCO, after the Act of Tonnage and Poundage made in the Twelfth Year of King *Charles* the Second, until the First Year of King *James* the Second, was liable only to the old Subsidy of One Penny, and the additional Duty of another Penny *per* Pound; and during that Time the Duties were no great Burthen upon the Merchants; and the Frauds in the Customs (if there were any) were so inconsiderable, that they did little affect the Planters. But their principal Disadvantage then was, that the Use of Tobacco was not so much grown into Custom, and the Quantity imported into *England*, though it was vastly less than at this Time, did exceed the Consumption; yet it was a more profitable Trade, and perhaps yielded a much better Revenue in Proportion than all the Duties do now.

By the 1st of King James, and Imposition of Three Pence *per* Pound was added, to be paid with several Abatements by the Consumptioner before he should be permitted to receive it from the Merchant; and in the mean Time, the Merchant or Importer was obliged to give Bond with one or more sufficient Securities, or to procure two other Persons to become bound to the King, not to deliver any Tobacco to the Buyer before the Duty should be duly paid;

---

* Adapted from "The Case of the Planters of Tobacco in Virginia, & C." Printed for F. Roberts in Warwick-Lane, London, 1733.

or, in Case he should not sell or export it before the Expiration of Eighteen Months from the Importation, to pay the Duty.

These Bonds were to be discharged by Certificate of the Buyer's having paid the Duty, or giving Bond to export it; and the Merchant or Importer was liable once in Three Months to account upon Oath to the Commissioners of the Customs, and his Warehouses to be searched for all Tobacco remaining in his Hands from Time to Time; and in Case he should fail to make Payment of the Duties which should be found due, his Bonds were to be returned into the Exchequer, there to be prosecuted according to the Course of Law.

Then there arose a sufficient Temptation to defraud the Customs, and the Running of Tobacco became soon a very great Abuse; but in other Respects the Course of the Trade was very little altered, the Price was raised in some Degree in Proportion to the Duties, and this Impost was much better secured to the Crown, than by the Method introduced afterwards by the 7th and 8th of King William, which obliged the Importer to give Bond for the Payment of it at the End of Eighteen Months from the Importation, discounting for prompt Payment Ten, Six, Four, and Two *per* Cent. according to the Time, which was to be discharged by Debentures upon Exportation of the same Tobacco within Twelve Months. It was said that the former Method of paying the Duty by the Consumptioner was found prejudicial to Trade, and grievous to the Merchants; but Experience has not yet discovered any Advantage from the Merchants bonding the Duties; nor were the People of *Virginia* acquainted with the Inconveniencies that were suggested to the Parliament, and were the Grounds upon which that Alteration was made; but many Abuses did soon arise from thence in Regard to the King and People. The Merchants indeed had immediately an apparent Benefit by this Regulation; for in all their Accounts afterwards, they charged their Commissions upon all the Duties, even when the Tobacco was exported, and only the first Penny paid, and the Moiety of that drawn back; Which has been considerably aggravated upon the Planters since the further Subsidy of One Penny by the Act of the 9th and 10th of King *William*, and the one Third Subsidy by the 2d and 3d of Queen Anne were added; So that at this Day, the Merchants Commissions may be generally computed to be above an Eighth Part of the net Produce of the Tobacco, in most of their Accounts, and upon many Sales to more than the whole Balance coming to the Planter. Divers Acts of Parliament have been since made in several Reigns for advancing the Trade; and we conceive that the Prohibition to import Bulk Tobacco was so far useful, as to make the Running of it more difficult; Enlarging the Time for Exportation to Three Years, drawing back the whole Duty upon Exportation, and reducing the several Discounts and Allowances upon the respective Duties to one uniform Abatement, have produced some good Effects. But so long as the Merchant is trusted with the keeping of Tobacco in his own Warehouses, and the Payment of the Duties continues under the present Method, we apprehend no Expedient will be found adequate to the Mischief's designed to be remedied.

For, with respect to the King, it is very obvious from many recent Instances, that many of the Merchants are forced to contract Debts at the Custom-House far exceeding the Value of their Estates, which has occasioned the Loss of vast Sums of Money to the Revenue. The Planters find an unaccountable Difference in the Weights of their Tobacco when it is shipped off here, and when it is weighed again at the Custom-Houses *in Great Britain*, especially in *London*. It will be very clear from an Enquiry into the Balances paid every Year into the Exchequer that not above one half of the Tobacco which must necessarily be consumed in *Great Britain* can have paid the Duties; And it may be worth while to consider by what Means it has been possible for many Merchants who have fail'd, and thereby discovered the ill State of their Affairs, to maintain their Credit for many Years at the Custom-House.

It will be, without Doubt, a very great Difficulty upon us at this Distance, to give any clear Account of the Causes which produce such Evils, and whatever we are able to offer upon the Subject, may possibly amount only to a probable Conjecture. Yet if Recourse be had to the Number of Hogsheads imported and exported, and a just Calculation made of the Weights of one Hogshead with another, (which may now be easily known from the several Custom Houses in *Great Britain*, as to *Virginia* Tobacco, seeing the net Weight when it goes from hence, by a Law lately made here, is marked upon every Hogshead by sworn Inspectors) there will remain a very pregnant Suspicion that a considerable Part of the Frauds must proceed from weighing the Tobacco upon the Landing of it, either through Corruption or Negligence: And if this be probable, the Merchant having the Tobacco in his own Warehouses, or his Servants, Coopers, or Porters, may take out of a great Number of Hogsheads a large Proportion of the whole, and yet by the Favour and Connivance of a corrupt Officer, when it comes to be weighed again for Exportation, may obtain a Debenture for a greater Quantity, and thereby not only defraud the Crown of the Duty which ought to have been paid, but even receive a Drawback for what was never paid: And we think it impossible to account in any Degree for such prodigious Frauds in another Manner.

We conceive it is no hard Matter for a Man of a small Fortune to make a considerable Figure in Trade by a large Credit at the Custom House; for if a Merchant, for Example, enters Five hundred Hogsheads of Tobacco, which he sells for the Home Consumption, and bonds the Duties, though they are payable at the End of Eighteen Months, no Process can issue against him tell after the Time allowed for Exportation, then he cannot be molested upon such a Bond within three Years, and so long he has to contrive a Way to discharge it, which may be done in this Manner: If he can procure the same Quantity every Year, by exporting the Consignment of every Third Year only, the Debenture (if any body will swear it to be for the Same Tobacco that was entered Two Years before) will discharge all the Bonds that can be prosecuted against him, and reimburse him for what he was obliged to pay down for the First Penny: So by such a Management, a Merchant may trade with good Credit a considerable Time upon the Money he really owes to the Crown; and if he is very dexterous, may actually discharge all his Bonds, and by the Frauds in the Weights at the Landing and Shipping off, gain a great deal of Money. A flagrant Instance of this Sort, we are informed, was discovered by the Commissioners of the Customs, in the Case of Mr. *Midford*, and without Doubt many more have remained undiscovered.

As this Method of bonding the Duties turns so much to the Prejudice of the Crown, it is no less injurious to the Planters, not only because it cannot be expected, while such enormous practices subsist in the Trade, that the Tobacco which really pays the Duty can sell at any tolerable Price; but the Merchants, especially in *London*, have it in their Power to oppress the Subjects of the Tobacco Colonies in many grievous Instances. One has been already mentioned in respect to their Commissions, and we must beg Leave to observe several others.

The Merchants, when they sell our Tobacco for the Home Consumption, think themselves under no Obligation to secure the Duties, but deliver it to the Retailer upon a long Credit, as they pretend; and if he happens to become a Bankrupt, they hold the Planter engaged to repay all the Charges of that Tobacco, including the Duties, and even their own Commissions. By this Means, a Man, whose Misfortune it is to have his Tobacco sold to a Bankrupt, will be brought in Debt to the Merchant Eighteen or Nineteen Pounds a Hogshead, besides losing the net Produce; which is so terrible a Circumstance, that some are obliged to make a further Allowance to the Merchant to make good all Debts; and those that will not submit to their Terms are continually exposed to Ruin, and he that has the best Estate is most in Danger.

The Tret and Clough, which is an Allowance to the Freemen of *London* upon all wasting Commodities, is another heavy Article upon us: It is deducted out of the net Tobacco which pays the Duty upon every Sale to any Retailer, and amounts to above Twenty Shillings upon a Hogshead. We are allowed at the Custom House Eight Pounds upon a Hogshead by act of Parliament for Draught, and Two Pounds for Sample; but this the Merchant in most Cases converts to his own Use, and thereby deprives the Planter of about Seven Shillings upon every Hogshead, and very often more. And whereas formerly all the petty Charges upon Tobacco did amount to little more than Five Shillings *per* Hogshead, which we conceive did exceed considerably what was really paid, the present Sett of Merchants have of late contrived to raise that Article to upwards of Ten Shillings in all their Accounts, and very frequently to more than Fifteen Shillings. One extraordinary Charge, among others, in Three Pence a Hogshead, amounting to between Four and Five Hundred Pounds a Year from *Virginia*, and as much from *Maryland*, lately imposed upon us, without our Consent, to defray their

Expences in applying to the Parliament upon any Occasion to relieve us from the Hardships we groan under: How well they deserve this Money, will best appear from the Records of Parliament.

We do admit the Act of Parliament which last settled the Abatements upon prompt Payment of the Duties, was designed for the Good of the Planters, and is so on Account of reducing the Duties to what they are at present; but the Merchants have so determin'd by their own Decrees, as to ingross, in great Measure, the Advantage of this Discount to themselves. For it is the Misfortune of the greatest Part of the Shippers of Tobacco, not to be able to remit Money to pay down the Duties, though some are; but they are obliged by the misterious Rules of Trade, to lodge in the Hands of their Correspondents double the Sum that would be sufficient for that Purpose, or at least a very great Overplus; whereby the Merchant is manifestly in a much better Condition when he allows his Correspondent here the Advantage of the Discounts, than when he takes it to himself, and makes it not worth any Man's while to keep Money to make the prompt Payment of the Duties upon his Tobacco, seeing upon the Merchants Terms of allowing the Discount, and their unreasonable Delays in bringing the Money back to our Credit, nobody can make Four *per* Cent Interest, and very seldom so much, Besides, the Planter without Money, must, in a fair way of Dealing, be very frequently, if not always, entitled to the Discount of Seven *per* Cent *per* Annum, allowed by the 9th of the late King, upon the Payment of the Duties within Eighteen Months: For it is a very great Abuse in the Trade, that the Merchants are too hasty on many Occasions in selling Tobacco, in order to raise ready Money for their own Purposes; and though they keep their Accounts back several Years from their Correspondents, none of them will say that they never receive any Money upon the Sales of Tobacco within Eighteen Months from the Importation. Yet we know not one Instance of any Allowance being made upon this Article by any Merchant in *London*, Though it has been made by some few in the Out-Ports.

This is only an Epitome of some of our Grievances, and there are many other that cannot be properly mentioned upon this Occasion. But lest these should not sufficient by their own Weight to undoe us, we are informed the Merchants have lately obtained an Act of Parliament, whereby an Affidavit before the chief Magistrate of any Town or Borough, is made equal to *viva voce* Evidence, for the Proof of their Accounts, however unjust or mistaken; and the Nature of our Estates (which have from our first Settlement been under the same Circumstances that the like Estates are in *England*) are altered by making our Lands subject to the Payment of their Book Debts, in order to enable them to give us larger Credit. It will not become us, nor do we presume to dispute with the Wisdom of the Parliament; but we are justly alarmed with the Consequences of the additional Power the Merchants will have now to oppress us more than they have ever done before; and are apprehensive they cannot be restrained but by the Laws of their own Consciences, from making themselves Masters of the Estates in both the Tobacco

Colonies, unless we can be relieved by the Parliament. And we persuade ourselves, that these Colonies who employ above Four Hundred Sail of Ships, maintain more than Four Thousand Seamen, consume of the Manufactures of *Great Britain* to the Value of near half a Million yearly, have so considerable a Share in supporting the Balance of Trade with Foreign Nations, and raise so great a Revenue to the Crown, without being one Farthing Expence to our Mother Country, will be thought worthy the Consideration of a *British* Parliament.

To this End we humbly Propose, that the Merchants be no longer solely trusted with the keeping of Tobacco, but that the same be deposited in Warehouses under the Lock and Key of the King and Merchant; that all the Duties be reduced to Four Pence Three Farthings the Pound, which is the net Duty, at present, after discounting the Twenty Five *per* Cent; that no Bonds be taken for securing the Duties upon Importation; that all Tobacco be weighed when it is landed, and weighed again when sold and delivered out to the Retailer or Exporter; that such Retailer pay down the Duty according to the last Weight, and only remain answerable to the Merchant for the Overplus of the Price; that all Tobacco be exported Duty-free, and the same Time allowed for Exportation as is now; and that some severer Penalties be annexed to the relanding of Tobacco delivered out for Exportation, or selling it at home: By this Method no Alteration will be made in respect to the Duty, but that will be better secured, and cannot fail of being encreased by suppressing the Multitude of Frauds, which must needs arise from the Merchant's having the Tobacco in his Power, and bonding the Duties: Many Perjuries will be prevented; the Merchant will then have no Interest in lessening the Weights, but for the sake of his Commissions will see that Justice be done to the King and the Planter, and the Custom-House Books will be a Check upon him if he does any wrong; the Planters will be able to chuse their Merchants for their Probity and kind Treatment, and not for their Riches or Credit; the Sword will be taken out of their Hands, and the Balance held more equally between them and us.

Yet we cannot doubt, but many Objections will be raised by our Enemies to this Scheme, and terrible Consequences must be foretold, to follow upon it, even with Respect to ourselves: But however that may be, we have this Consolation in being assured, that we cannot be in a worse Condition than we are at this Juncture; and if the Trade should not be restored to a better State, we shall at least be secure in our Poverty, and be defended from those who seek to undoe us.

Signed in the Name and Behalf of the Council.

ROBERT CARTER, *President.*

JOHN HOLLOWAY, *Speaker of the House of Burgesses.*
Williamsburg, June 28, 1732. □

An Economic Interpretation of the Constitution
of the United States *

CHARLES A. BEARD

The requirements for an economic interpretation of the formation and adoption of the Constitution may be stated in a hypothetical proposition which, although it cannot be verified absolutely from ascertainable data, will at once illustrate the problem and furnish a guide to research and generalization.

It will be admitted without controversy that the Constitution was the creation of a certain number of men, and it was opposed by a certain number of men. Now, if it were possible to have an economic biography of all those connected with its framing and adoption, — perhaps about 160,000 men altogether, — the materials for scientific analysis and classification would be available. Such an economic biography would include a list of the real and personal property owned by all of these men and their families: lands and houses, with incumbrances, money at interest, slaves, capital invested in shipping and manufacturing, and in state and continental securities.

Suppose it could be shown from the classification of the men who supported and opposed the Constitution that there was no line of property division at all; that is, that men owning substantially the same amounts of the same kinds of property were equally divided on the matter of adoption or rejection — it would then become apparent that the Constitution had no ascertainable relation to economic groups of classes, but was the product of some abstract causes remote from the chief business of life — gaining a livelihood.

Suppose, on the other hand, that substantially all of the merchants, money lenders, security holders, manufacturers, shippers, capitalists, and financiers and their professional associates are to be found on one side in support of the Constitution and that substantially all or the major portion of the opposition came from the non-slaveholding farmers and the debtors — would it not be pretty conclusively demonstrated that our fundamental law was not the product of an abstraction known as "the whole people," but of a group of economic interests which must have expected beneficial results from its adoption? Obviously all the facts here desired cannot be discovered but the data presented in the following chapters bear out the latter hypothesis, and thus a reasonable presumption in favor of the theory is created.

Of course, it may be shown (and perhaps can be shown) that the farmers and debtors who opposed the Constitution were, in fact, benefited by the general improvement which resulted from its adoption. It may likewise be shown, to take an extreme case, that the English nation derived immense advantages from the Norman Conquest and the orderly administrative processes which were introduced, as it undoubtedly did; nevertheless, it does not follow that the vague thing known as "the advancement of general welfare" or some abstraction known as "justice" was the immediate, guiding purpose of the leaders in either of these great historic changes. The point is, that the direct, impelling motive in both cases was the economic advantages which the beneficiaries expected would accrue to themselves first, from their action. Further than this, economic interpretation cannot go. It may be that some larger world process is working through each series of historical events; but ultimate causes lie beyond our horizon.

CONCLUSIONS

At the close of this survey, it seems worth while to bring together the important conclusions for political science which the data presented appear to warrant.

The movement for the Constitution of the United States was originated and carried through principally by four groups of personalty interests which had been adversely affected under the Articles of Confederation: money, public securities, manufactures, and trade and shipping.

The first firm steps toward the formation of the Constitution were taken by a small and active group of men immediately interested through their personal possessions in the outcome of their labors.

No popular vote was taken directly or indirectly on the proposition to call the Convention which drafted the Constitution.

A large propertyless mass was under the prevailing suffrage qualifications, excluded at the outset from participation (through representatives) in the work of framing the Constitution.

The members of the Philadelphia Convention which drafted the Constitution were, with a few exceptions, immediately, directly, and personally interested in, and derived economic advantages from, the establishment of the new system.

The Constitution was essentially an economic document based upon the concept that the fundamental private rights of property are anterior to government and morally beyond the reach of popular majorities.

The major portion of the members of the Convention are on record as recognizing the claim of property to a special and defensive position in the Constitution.

In the ratification of the Constitution, about three-fourths of the adult males failed to vote on the question, having abstained from the elections at which delegates to the state conventions were chosen either on account of their indifference or their disfranchisement by property qualifications.

The Constitution was ratified by a vote of probably not more than one-sixth of the adult males.

It is questionable whether a majority of the voters participating in the elections for the state conventions in New York, Massachusetts, New Hampshire, said; neither was it created by "the states" as Southern nullifiers long constitution.

The leaders who supported the Constitution in the ratifying conventions represented the same economic groups as the members of the Philadelphia Convention; and in a large number of instances they were also directly and personally interested in the outcome of their efforts.

In the ratification, it became manifest that the line of cleavage for and against the Constitution was between substantial personalty interests on one hand and the small farming and debtor interests on the other.

The Constitution was not created by "the whole people" as the jurists have said; neither was it created by "the states" as Southern nullifiers long contended; but it was the work of a consolidated group whose interests knew no state boundaries and were truly national in their scope. □

❖ 26 ❖

Charles Beard and the Constitution *

ROBERT E. BROWN

"CONCLUSIONS"

At the end of Chapter XI Beard summarized his findings in fourteen paragraphs under the heading of "Conclusions" (pp. 324–25). Actually, these fourteen conclusions merely add up to the two halves of the Beard thesis. One half, that the Constitution originated with and was carried through by personal interests — money, public securities, manufactures, and commerce — is to be found in paragraphs two, three, six, seven, eight, twelve, thirteen, and fourteen. The other half — that the Constitution was put over undemocratically in an undemocratic society — is expressed in paragraphs four, five, nine, ten, eleven, and fourteen. The lumping of these conclusions under two general headings makes it easier for the reader to see the broad outlines of the Beard thesis.

Before we examine these two major divisions of the thesis, however, some comment is relevant on the implications contained in the first paragraph. In it Beard characterized his book as a long and arid survey, something in the nature of a catalogue. Whether this characterization was designed to give his book the appearance of a coldly objective study based on the facts we do not know. If so, nothing could be further from reality. As reviewers pointed out in 1913, and as subsequent developments have demonstrated, the book is

* Reprinted by permission of the Princeton University Press. Copyright © 1956, by Princeton University Press. London: Geoffrey Cumberlege, Oxford University Press.

anything but an arid catalogue of facts. Its pages are replete with interpretation, sometimes stated, sometimes implied. Our task has been to examine Beard's evidence to see whether it justifies the interpretation which Beard gave it. We have tried to discover whether he used the historical method properly in arriving at his thesis.

If historical method means the gathering of the data from primary sources, the critical evaluation of the evidence thus gathered, and the drawing of conclusions consistent with this evidence, then we must conclude that Beard has done great violation to such method in this book. He admitted that the evidence had not been collected which, given the proper use of historical method, should have precluded the writing of the book. Yet he nevertheless proceeded on the assumption that a valid interpretation could be built on secondary writings whose authors had likewise failed to collect the evidence. If we accept Beard's own maxim, "no evidence, no history," and his own admission that the data had never been collected, the answer to whether he used historical method properly is self-evident.

Neither was Beard critical of the evidence which he did use. He was accused in 1913, and one might still suspect him, of using only that evidence which appeared to support his thesis. The amount of realty in the country compared with the personalty, the vote in New York, and the omission of the part of *The Federalist* No. 10 which did not fit his thesis are only a few examples of the uncritical use of evidence to be found in the book. Sometimes he accepted secondary accounts at face value without checking them with the sources; at other times he allowed unfounded rumors and traditions to color his work.

Finally, the conclusions which he drew were not justified even by the kind of evidence which he used. If we accepted his evidence strictly at face value, it would still not add up to the fact that the Constitution was put over undemocratically in an undemocratic society by personalty. The citing of property qualifications does not prove that a mass of men were disfranchised. And if we accept his figures on property holdings, either we do not know what most of the delegates had in realty and personalty, or we know that realty outnumbered personalty three to one (eighteen to six). Simply showing that a man held public securities is not sufficient to prove that he acted only in terms of his public securities. If we ignore Beard's own generalizations and accept only his evidence, we would have to conclude that most of the property in the country in 1787 was real estate, that real property was widely distributed in rural areas, which included most of the country, and that even the men who were directly concerned with the Constitution, and especially Washington, were large holders of realty.

Perhaps we can never be completely objective in history, but certainly we can be more objective than Beard was in this book. Naturally the historian must always be aware of the biases, the subjectivity, the pitfalls that confront him, but this does not mean that he should not make an effort to overcome these obstacles. Whether Beard had his thesis before he had his evidence, as some have said, is a question that each reader must answer for himself. Certain it is that the evidence does not justify the thesis.

So instead of the Beard interpretation that the Constitution was put over undemocratically in an undemocratic society by personal property, the following fourteen paragraphs are offered as a possible interpretation of the Constitution and as suggestions for future research on that document.

1. The movement for the Constitution was originated and carried through by men who had long been important in both economic and political affairs in their respective states. Some of them owned personalty, more of them owned realty, and if their property was adversely affected by conditions under the Articles of Confederation, so also was the property of the bulk of the people in the country, middle-class farmers as well as town artisans.

2. The movement for the Constitution, like most important movements, was undoubtedly started by a small group of men. They were probably interested personally in the outcome of their labors, but the benefits which they expected were not confined to personal or, for that matter, strictly to things economic. And if their own interests would be enhanced by a new government, similar interests of other men, whether agricultural or commercial, would also be enhanced.

3. Naturally there was no popular vote on the calling of the convention which drafted the Constitution. Election of delegates by state legislatures was the constitutional method under the Articles of Confederation, and had been the method long established in this country. Delegates to the Albany Congress, the Stamp Act Congress, the First Continental Congress, the Second Continental Congress, and subsequent congresses under the Articles were all elected by state legislatures, not by the people. Even the Articles of Confederation had been sanctioned by state legislatures, not by popular vote. This is not to say that the Constitutional Convention should not have been elected directly by the people, but only that such a procedure would have been unusual at the time. Some of the opponents of the Constitution later stressed, without avail, the fact that the Convention had not been directly elected. But at the time the Convention met, the people in general seemed to be about as much concerned over the fact that they had not elected the delegates as the people of this country are now concerned over the fact that they do not elect our delegates to the United Nations.

4. Present evidence seems to indicate that there were no "propertyless masses" who were excluded from the suffrage at the time. Most men were middle-class farmers who owned realty and were qualified voters, and, as the men in the Convention said, mechanics had always voted in the cities. Until credible evidence proves otherwise, we can assume that state legislatures were fairly representative at the time. We cannot condone the fact that a few men were probably disfranchised by prevailing property qualifications, but it makes a great deal of difference to an interpretation of the Constitution

whether the disfranchised comprised ninety-five per cent of the adult men or only five per cent. Figures which give percentages of voters in terms of the entire population are misleading, since less than twenty per cent of the people were adult men. And finally, the voting qualifications favored realty, not personalty.

5. If the members of the Convention were directly interested in the outcome of their work and expected to derive benefits from the establishment of the new system, so also did most of the people of the country. We have many statements to the effect that the people in general expected substantial benefits from the labors of the Convention.

6. The Constitution was not just an economic document, although economic factors were undoubtedly important. Since most of the people were middle-class and had private property, practically everybody was interested in the protection of property. A constitution which did not protect property would have been rejected without any question, for the American people had fought the Revolution for the preservation of life, liberty, and property. Many people believed that the Constitution did not go far enough to protect property, and they wrote these views into the amendments to the Constitution. But property was not the only concern of those who wrote and ratified the Constitution, and we would be doing a grave injustice to the political sagacity of the Founding Fathers if we assumed that property or personal gain was their only motive.

7. Naturally the delegates recognized that the protection of property was important under government, but they also recognized that personal rights were equally important. In fact, persons and property were usually bracketed together as the chief objects of government protection.

8. If three-fourths of the adult males failed to vote on the election of delegates to ratifying conventions, this fact signified indifference, not disfranchisement. We must not confuse those who could *not* vote with those who *could* vote but failed to exercise their right. Many men at the time bewailed the fact that only a small portion of the voters ever exercised their prerogative. But this in itself should stand as evidence that the conflict over the Constitution was not very bitter, for if these people had felt strongly one way or the other, more of them would have voted.

Even if we deny the evidence which I have presented and insist that American society was undemocratic in 1787, we must still accept the fact that the men who wrote the Constitution believed that they were writing it for a democratic society. They did not hide behind an iron curtain of secrecy and devise the kind of conservative government that they wanted without regard to the views and interests of "the people." More than anything else, they were aware that "the people" would have to ratify what they proposed, and that therefore any government which would be acceptable to the people must of necessity incorporate much of what was customary at the time. The men at Philadelphia were practical politicians, not political theorists. They recognized the multitude of different ideas and interests that had to be reconciled and compromised before a constitution would be acceptable. They were far too practical, and represented far too many clashing interests themselves, to fashion a government weighted in favor of personalty or to believe that the people would adopt such a government.

9. If the Constitution was ratified by a vote of only one-sixth of the adult men, that again demonstrates indifference and not disfranchisement. Of the one-fourth of the adult males who voted, nearly two-thirds favored the Constitution. Present evidence does not permit us to say what the popular vote was except as it was measured by the votes of the ratifying conventions.

10. Until we know what the popular vote was, we cannot say that it is questionable whether a majority of the voters in several states favored the Constitution. Too many delegates were sent uninstructed. Neither can we count the towns which did not send delegates on the side of those opposed to the Constitution. Both items would signify indifference rather than sharp conflict over ratification.

11. The ratifying conventions were elected for the specific purpose of adopting or rejecting the Constitution. The people in general had anywhere from several weeks to several months to decide the question. If they did not like the new government, or if they did not know whether they liked it, they could have voted no and there would have been no Constitution. Naturally the leaders in the ratifying conventions represented the same interests as the members of the Constitutional Convention — mainly realty and some personalty. But they also represented their constituents in these same interests, especially realty.

12. If the conflict over ratification had been between substantial personalty interests on the one hand and small farmers and debtors on the other, there would not have been a constitution. The small farmers comprised such an overwhelming percentage of the voters that they could have rejected the new government without any trouble. Farmers and debtors are not synonymous terms and should not be confused as such. A town-by-town or county-by-county record of the vote would show clearly how the farmers voted.

13. The Constitution was created about as much by the whole people as any government could be which embraced a large area and depended on representation rather than on direct participation. In was also created in part by the states, for as the *Records* show, there was strong state sentiment at the time which had to be appeased by compromise. And it was created by compromising a whole host of interests throughout the country, without which compromises it could never have been adopted.

14. If the intellectual historians are correct, we cannot explain the Constitution without considering the psychological factors also. Men are motivated by what they believe as well as by what they have. Sometimes their actions can be explained on the basis of what they hope to have or hope that their children will have. Madison understood this fact when he said that the

universal hope of acquiring property tended to dispose people to look favorably upon property. It is even possible that some men support a given economic system when they themselves have nothing to gain by it. So we would want to know what the people in 1787 thought of their class status. Did workers and small farmers believe that they were lower-class, or did they, as many workers do now, consider themselves middle-class? Were the common people trying to eliminate the Washingtons, Adamses, Hamiltons, and Pinckneys, or were they trying to join them?

As did Beard's fourteen conclusions, these fourteen suggestions really add up to two major propositions: the Constitution was adopted in a society which was fundamentally democratic, not undemocratic; and it was adopted by a people who were primarily middle-class property owners, especially farmers who owned realty, not just by the owners of personalty. At present these points seem to be justified by the evidence, but if better evidence in the future disproves or modifies them, we must accept that evidence and change our interpretation accordingly.

After this critical analysis, we should at least not begin future research on this period of American history with the illusion that the Beard thesis of the Constitution is valid. If historians insist on accepting the Beard thesis in spite of this analysis, however, they must do so with the full knowledge that their acceptance is founded on "an act of faith" not an analysis of historical method, and that they are indulging in a "noble dream" not history. ◻

[DOCUMENT]   ❖ **27** ❖

Navigation Act of 1651 *

■ *An Act for increase of Shipping and Encouragement of the*
Navigation of this Nation.

For the Increase of the Shipping and the encouragement of the Navigation of this Nation, which under the good Providence and protection of God, is so great a means of the Welfare and Safety of this Commonwealth; Be it Enacted by this present Parliament, and the Authority thereof, That from and after the First day of December, One thousand six hundred fifty one, and from thence-forwards, No Goods or Commodities whatsoever, of the Growth, Production or Manufacture of Asia, Africa or America, or of any part thereof; or of any Islands belonging to them or any of them, or which are described or laid down in the usual Maps or Cards of those places, as well of the English Plantations as others, shall be Imported or brought into this Commonwealth of England, or into Ireland, or any other Lands, Islands, Plantations or Territories to this Commonwealth belonging, or in their Possession, in any

* Taken from Scobell's *Acts of Parliament* (ed. 1653), pp. 165–70.

other Ship or Ships, Vessel or Vessels whatsoever, but onely in such as do truly and without fraud belong onely to the People of this Commonwealth, or the Plantations thereof, as the Proprietors or right Owners thereof: And whereof the Master and Mariners are also for the most part of them, of the People of this Commonwealth, under the penalty of the forfeiture and loss of all the Goods that shall be Imported contrary to this Act; as also of the Ship (with all her Tackle, Guns and Apparel) in which the said Goods or Commodities shall be so brought in and Imported; The one moiety to the use of the Commonwealth, and the other moiety to the use and behoof of any person or persons who shall seize the said Goods or Commodities, and shall prosecute the same in any Court of Record within this Commonwealth.

And it is further Enacted . . . , That no Goods or Commodities of the Growth, Production or Manufacture of Europe, or of any part thereof, shall after the First day of December, One thousand six hundred fifty and one, be Imported or brought into this Commonwealth of England, or into Ireland, or any other Lands, Islands, Plantations or Territories to this Commonwealth belonging, or in their possession, in any Ship or Ships, Vessel or Vessels whatsoever, but in such as do truly and without fraud belong onely to the people of this Commonwealth, as the true Owners and Proprietors thereof, and in no other, except onely such Foreign Ships and Vessels as do truly and properly belong to the people of that Countrey or place, of which the said Goods are the Growth, Production or Manufacture; or to such Ports where the said Goods can onely be, or most usually are first Shipped for Transportation; And that under the same penalty of forfeiture and loss expressed in the former Branch of this Act, the said Forfeitures to be recovered and imployed as is therein expressed.

And it is further Enacted . . . , That no Goods or Commodities that are of Foreign Growth, Production or Manufacture, and which are to be brought into this Commonwealth, in shipping belonging to the people thereof, shall be by them Shipped or brought from any other place or places, Countrey or Countreys, but onely from those of their said Growth, Production or Manufacture; or from those Ports where the said Goods and Commodities can onely, or are, or usually have been first shipped for Transportation; And from none other Places or Countreys, under the same penalty of forfeiture and loss expressed in the first Branch of this Act, the said Forfeitures to be recovered and imployed as it therein expressed.

And it is further Enacted . . . , That no sort of Cod-fish, Ling, Herring, Pilchard, or any other kinde of salted Fish, usually fished for and caught by the people of this Nation; nor any Oyl made, or that shall be made of any kinde of Fish whatsoever; nor any Whale-fins, or Whale-bones, shall from henceforth be Imported into this Commonwealth, or into Ireland, or any other Lands, Islands, Plantations or Territories thereto belonging, or in their possession, but onely such as shall be caught in Vessels that do or shall truly and properly belong to the people of this Nation, as Proprietors and Right

Owners thereof: And the said Fish to be cured, and the Oyl aforesaid made by the people of this Commonwealth, under the penalty and loss expressed in the said first Branch of this present Act; the said Forfeit to be recovered and imployed as is there expressed.

And it is further Enacted . . . , That no sort of Cod, Ling, Herring, Pilchard, or any other kinde of Salted Fish whatsoever, which shall be caught and cured by the people of this Commonwealth, shall be from and after the First day of February, One thousand six hundred fifty three, Exported from any place or places belonging to this Commonwealth, in any other Ship or Ships, Vessel or Vessels, save onely in such as do truly and properly appertain to the people of this Commonwealth, as Right Owners; and whereof the Master and Mariners are for the most part of them English, under the penalty and loss expressed in the said first Branch of this present Act; the said Forfeit to be recovered and imployed as is there expressed.

Provided always, That this Act, nor anything therein contained, extend not, or be meant to restrain the Importation of any of the Commodities of the Streights or Levant Seas, loaden in the Shipping of this Nation as aforesaid, at the usual Ports or places for lading of them heretofore within the said Streights or Levant Seas, though the said Commodities be not of the very Growth of the said places.

Provided also, That this Act nor any thing therein contained, extend not, nor be meant to restrain the Importing of any East-India Commodities loaden in the Shipping of this Nation, at the usual Port or places for lading of them heretofore in any part of those Seas, to the Southward and Eastward of Cabo Bona Esperanza, although the said Ports be not the very places of their Growth.

Provided also, That it shall and may be lawful to and for any of the people of this Commonwealth, in Vessels or Ships to them belonging, and whereof the Master and Mariners are of this Nation as aforesaid, To load and bring in from any of the Ports of Spain and Portugal, all sorts of Goods or Commodities that have come from, or any way belonged unto the Plantations or Dominions of either of them respectively.

Be it also further Enacted . . . , That from henceforth, it shall not be lawful to any person or persons whatsoever, to load or cause to be loaden and carryed in any Bottom or Bottoms, Ship or Ships, Vessel or Vessels whatsoever, whereof any Stranger or Strangers born (unless such as be Denizens or Naturalized) be Owners, part Owners or Master, Any Fish, Victual, Wares, or things of what kinde or nature soever the same shall be, from one Port or Creek of this Commonwealth to another Port or Creek of the same, under penalty to every one that shall offend contrary to the true meaning of this Branch of this present Act, to forfeit all the Goods that shall be so laden or carried, as also the Ship upon which they shall be so laden or carried, the same Forfeit to be recovered and imployed as directed in the First Branch of this present Act.

Lastly, That this Act nor any thing therein contained, extend not to Bullion, nor yet to any Goods taken, or that shall be taken by way of Reprizal by any Ship or Ships, having Commission from this Commonwealth.

Provided, That this Act, or any thing therein contained, shall not extend, nor be construed to extend to any Silk or Silk-wares which shall be brought by Land from any parts of Italy, and there bought with the proceed of English Commodities, sold either for money or in Barter; but that it shall and may be lawful for any of the People of this Commonwealth to ship the same in English Vessels from Ostend, Newport, Rot'erdam, Middleburgh, Amsterdam, or any Ports thereabouts; The Owners and Proprietors first making Oath by themselves, or other credible Witness, before the Commissioners of the Customs for the time being or their Deputies, or one of the Barons of the Exchequer, That the Goods aforesaid were so bought for his or their own proper Accompt in Italy. □

[DOCUMENT] ❖ **28** ❖

Tea Act, July 2, 1767 *

■ *An act for taking off the inland duty of one shilling per pound weight upon all black and singlo teas consumed in Great Britain; and for granting a drawback upon the exportation of teas to Ireland, and the British dominions in America, for a limited time, upon such indemnification to be made in respect thereof by the East India company, as is therein mentioned; for permitting the exportation of teas in smaller quantities than one lot to Ireland, or the said dominions in America; and for preventing teas seized and condemned from being consumed in Great Britain.*

WHEREAS by an act of parliament made in the eighteenth year of the reign of his late Majesty King George the Second, intituled, An Act for repealing the present inland duty of four shillings per pound weight upon all tea sold in Great Britain, and for granting to his Majesty certain other inland duties in lieu thereof; and for better securing the duty upon tea, and other duties of excise; and for pursuing offenders out of one county into another; an inland duty of one shilling per pound weight avoirdupois, and in that proportion for a greater or lesser quantity, was imposed and charged upon all tea to be sold in Great Britain; and also a further duty of twenty five pounds for every one hundred pounds of the gross price at which such teas should be sold at the publick sales of the united company of merchants of England trading to the

---

* Taken and adapted from D. Pickering, *Statutes at Large*, Vol. XXVII, pp. 600–5, 7 Geo. III., c. 56.

East Indies, and proportionably for a greater or lesser sum; which duties were to commence from the twenty fourth day of June, one thousand seven hundred and forty five, over and above all customs, subsidies, and duties, payable to his Majesty for the same, upon importation thereof; to be paid in manner as in the said act is directed: and whereas by an act of parliament made in the twenty first year of his said late Majesty's reign, tea was allowed to be exported from this kingdom to Ireland, and his Majesty's plantations in America, without payment of the said inland duties: and whereas the taking off the said inland duty of one shilling per pound weight upon black and singlo teas, granted by the said act, and the allowing, upon the exportation of all teas which shall be exported to Ireland and his Majesty's plantations in America, the whole of the duty paid upon the importation thereof into this kingdom, appear to be the most probable and expedient means of extending the consumption of teas legally imported within this kingdom, and of increasing the exportation of teas to Ireland, and to his Majesty's plantations in America, which are now chiefly furnished by foreigners in a course of illicit trade: and whereas the united company of merchants of England trading to the East Indies are willing and desirous to indemnify the public, in such manner as is herein after provided, with respect to any diminution of the revenue which shall or may happen from this experiment: . . . be it enacted . . . , That for and during the space of five years, to be computed from the fifth day of July, one thousand seven hundred and sixty seven, the said inland duty of one shilling per pound weight upon teas, shall not be paid for or in respect of any bohea, congo, souchong, or pekoe teas, commonly called Black Teas, or any teas known by the denomination of singlo teas, which shall be cleared for consumption within Great Britain, out of the warehouses of the united company of merchants of England trading to the East Indies, or their successors; but that all such teas so to be cleared, whether the same have been already, or shall be hereafter, sold by the said company, or their successors, shall be and are hereby freed and discharged, during the said term, from the said inland duty.

II. And it is hereby further enacted . . . , That for and during the like space of five years, to be computed from the fifth day of July, one thousand seven hundred and sixty seven, there shall be drawn back and allowed for all teas exported from this kingdom as merchandize to Ireland, or any of the British colonies or plantations in America, the whole duties of customs payable upon the importation of such teas; which drawback or allowance, with respect to such teas as shall be exported to Ireland, shall be made to the exporter in such manner, and under such rules, regulations, securities, penalties, and forfeitures, as any drawback or allowance is now payable out of the duty of customs upon the exportation of foreign goods to Ireland: and with respect to such teas as shall be exported to the British colonies and plantations in America, the said drawback or allowance shall be made in such manner, and under such rules, regulations, penalties, and forfeitures, as any drawback or allowance payable out of the duty of customs upon foreign goods exported to foreign parts, was, could, or might be, made before the passing of this act . . .

VII. And whereas by an act made in the twenty-first year of the reign of his late Majesty, intituled, An act for permitting tea to be exported to Ireland, and his Majesty's plantations in America, without paying the inland duties charged thereupon by an act of the eighteenth year of his present Majesty's reign; and for enlarging the time for some of the payments to be made on the subscription of six millions three hundred thousand pounds, by virtue of an act of this session of parliament; it is enacted, That from and after the first day of June, one thousand seven hundred and forty eight, no tea should be exported to the kingdom of Ireland, or to any of his Majesty's plantations in America, in any chest, cask, tub, or package whatsoever, other than that in which it was originally imported into Great Britain, nor in any less quantities than in the intire lot or lots in which the same was sold at the sale of the said united company, under the penalty of the forfeiture of such tea, and the package containing the same: and whereas the prohibiting the exportation of tea in any less quantity then one intire lot, has been very inconvenient to merchants and traders, and tends to discourage the exportation of tea to Ireland, and the said colonies; be it therefore enacted . . . , That from and after the fifth day of July, one thousand seven hundred and sixty seven, the said recited clause shall be, and is hereby, repealed. . . .

IX. And be it enacted . . . , That from and after . . . (July 24, 1767) . . . , all teas which shall be seized and condemned for being illegally imported, or for any other cause, shall not be sold for consumption within this kingdom, but shall be exported to Ireland, or to the British colonies in America; and that no such teas, after the sale thereof, shall be delivered out of any warehouse belonging to his Majesty, otherwise than for exportation as aforesaid; or be exported in any package containing a less quantity than fifty pounds weight; which exportation shall be made in like manner, and under the same rules, regulations, penalties, and forfeitures, except in respect to the allowance of any drawback, as are by this act prescribed, appointed, and inflicted, in relation to the exportation of teas sold by the said company; and upon the like bond and security as is required by the said act made in the twenty first year of the reign of his late Majesty King George the Second, to be approved of by the commissioners of the customs or excise in England for the time being, or any three of them respectively, or by such person or persons as they shall respectively appoint for that purpose. □

The Quebec Act, June 22, 1774 *

■ An Act for making effectual Provision for the Government
of the Province of Quebec, in North America.

That it may be enacted: . . .

II. Provided always, That nothing herein contained, relative to the boundary of the province of *Quebec*, shall in anywise affect the boundaries of any other colony.

III. Provided always, . . . That nothing in this act contained shall extend, . . . to make void, or to . . . alter any right, title, or possession, derived under any grant, conveyance, or otherwise howsoever, of or to any lands within the said province, or the provinces thereto adjoining; but that the same shall remain and be in force, . . . as if this act had never been made.

IV. . . . And whereas the Provisions made by the said Proclamation, in respect to the Civil Government of the said Province of *Quebec*, and the Powers and Authorities given to the Governor and other Civil Officers of the said Province, by the Grants and Commissions issued in consequence thereof, have been found, upon Experience, to be inapplicable to the State and Circumstances of the said Province, the Inhabitants whereof amounted at the Conquest, to above Sixty five thousand Persons, professing the Religion of the Church of *Rome*. . . .

V. It is hereby declared, That His Majesty's Subjects professing the Religion of the Church of *Rome*, of, and in the said Province of *Quebec*, may have, hold, and enjoy, the free Exercise of the Religion of the Church of *Rome*, . . . and that the Clergy of the said Church may hold, receive, and enjoy their accustomed Dues and Rights, with respect to such Persons only as shall profess the said Religion.

VI. Provided nevertheless, That it shall be lawful for His Majesty, His Heirs of Successors, to make such Provisions out of the rest of the said accustomed Dues and Rights, for the Encouragement of the Protestant Religion, and for the Maintenance and Support of a Protestant Clergy within the said Province, as he or they shall, from Time to Time, think necessary or expedient. . . .

VII. And be it further enacted by the Authority aforesaid, That all his Majesty's *Canadian* Subjects within the Province of *Quebec*, the Religious Orders and Communities only excepted, may also hold and enjoy their Property and Possessions, together with all Customs and Usages, relative thereto, and all other their Civil Rights, in as large, ample and beneficial Manner, as if the said Proclamation, Commissions, Ordinances, and other Acts and Instruments, had not been made, and as may consist with their Allegiance to

* Taken from D. Pickering, *Statutes at Large*, Vol. XXX, p. 549.

His Majesty, and Subjection to the Crown and Parliament of *Great Britain;* and that in all Matters of Controversy relative to Property and Civil Rights, Resort shall be had to the Laws of *Canada,* as the Rule for the Decision of the same; and all Causes that shall hereafter be instituted in any of the Courts of Justice, to be appointed within and for the said Province by His Majesty, shall, with respect to such Property and Rights, be determined agreeably to the said Laws and Customs of *Canada,* . . .

XI. And whereas the Certainty and Lenity of the Criminal Law of *England,* and the Benefits and Advantages resulting from the Use of it, have been sensibly felt by the Inhabitants from an Experience of more than Nine Years, during which it has been uniformly administered; . . . That the same shall continue to be administered, and shall be observed as Law, in the Province of *Quebec,* . . . to the Exclusion of every other Rule of Criminal Law, or Mode of Proceeding thereon, which did or might prevail in the said Province before (1764); any Thing in this Act to the Contrary thereof in any Respect notwithstanding; . . .

XII. And whereas it may be necessary to ordain many Regulations, for the future Welfare and good Government of the Province of *Quebec,* the Occasions of which cannot now be forseen, nor without much Delay and Inconvenience be provided for, without entrusting that Authority for a certain Time and upon proper Restrictions to Persons resident there:

And whereas it is at present inexpedient to call an Assembly; be it therefore enacted by the Authority aforesaid, That it shall and may be lawful for His Majesty, . . . and with the Advice of the Privy Council, to constitute and appoint a Council for the Affairs of the Province of *Quebec,* to consist of such Persons resident there, not exceeding Twenty-three, nor less than Seventeen, as His Majesty, . . . shall be pleased to appoint; . . . which Council, so appointed and nominated, or the major Part thereof, shall have Power and Authority to make Ordinances for the Peace, Welfare, and good Government of the said Province with the Consent of His Majesty's Governor, or, in his Absence, of the Lieutenant Governor, or Commander in Chief for the Time being. . . .

[DOCUMENT]   ❖ **30** ❖

Articles of Confederation *

■ *Adopted November 15, 1777; ratified and enacted March 1, 1781.*

TO ALL TO WHOM these Presents shall come, we the undersigned Delegates of the States affixed to our Names send greeting. Whereas the Dele-

* Taken from James D. Richardson, ed., "Articles of Confederation," *Compilation of the Messages and Papers of the Presidents* (Washington, D. C.: Bureau of National Literature and Art, 1904), 9 ff.

gates of the United States of America in Congress assembled did on the fifteenth day of November in the Year of our Lord One Thousand Seven Hundred and Seventy seven, and in the Second Year of the Independence of America agree to certain articles of Confederation an perpetual Union between the States of Newhampshire, Massachusetts-bay, Rhode-island and Providence Plantations, Connecticut, New York, New Jersey, Pennsylvania, Delaware, Maryland, Virginia, North-Carolina, South-Carolina and Georgia in the Words following, viz. "Articles of Confederation and perpetual Union between the states of Newhampshire, Massachusetts-bay, Rhode-island and Providence Plantations, Connecticut, New-York, New-Jersey, Pennsylvania, Delaware, Maryland, Virginia, North-Carolina, South-Carolina and Georgia.

(Art. I.) The Stile of this confederacy shall be "The United States of America."

(Art. II.) Each state retains its sovereignty, freedom and independence, and every Power, Jurisdiction and right, which is not by this confederation expressly delegated to the United States, in Congress assembled . . .

(Art. IV.) The better to secure and perpetuate mutual friendship and intercourse among the people of the different states in this union, the free inhabitants of each of these states, paupers, vagabonds and fugitives from Justice excepted, shall be entitled to all privileges and immunities of free citizens in the several states; and the people of each state shall have free ingress and regress to and from any other state, and shall enjoy therein all the privileges of trade and commerce, subject to the same duties, impositions and restrictions as the inhabitants thereof respectively, provided that such restriction shall not extend so far as to prevent the removal of property imported into any state, to any other state of which the Owner is an inhabitant; provided also that no imposition, duties or restriction shall be laid by any state, on the property of the united states, or either of them. . . .

(Art. VI.) No state without the Consent of the united states in congress assembled, shall send any embassy to, or receive any embassy from, or enter into any conference, agreement, or alliance or treaty with any King, prince or state; nor shall any person holding any office of profit or trust under the united states, or any of them, accept of any present, emolument, office or title of any kind whatever from any king, prince or foreign state; nor shall the united states in congress assembled, or any of them, grant any title of nobility. . . .

No state shall lay any imposts or duties, which may interfere with any stipulations in treaties, entered into by the united states in congress assembled, with any king, prince or state, in pursuance of any treaties already proposed by congress, to the courts of France and Spain. . . .

(Art. IX.) . . . All controversies concerning the private right of soil claimed under different grants of two or more states, whose jurisdictions as they may respect such lands, and the states which passed such grants are adjusted, the said grants or either of them being at the same time claimed to have originated antecedent to such settlement of jurisdiction, shall on the petition of either party to the congress of the united states, be finally determined as near as may be in the same manner as is before prescribed for deciding disputes respecting territorial jurisdiction between different states.

The united states in congress assembled shall also have the sole and exclusive right and power of regulating the alloy and value of coin struck by their own authority, or by that of the respective states. . . . fixing the standard of weights and measures throughout the united states. . . . regulating the trade and managing all affairs with the Indians, not members of any of the states, provided that the legislative right of any state within its own limits be not infringed or violated . . . establishing and regulating post-offices from one state to another, throughout all the united states, and exacting such postage on the papers passing thro' the same as may be requisite to defray the expences of the said office . . . appointing all officers of the land forces, in the service of the united states, excepting regimental officers. . . .

(Art. XIII.) . . . AND WHEREAS it hath pleased the Great Governor of the World to incline the hearts of the legislatures we respectively represent in congress, to approve of, and to authorize us to ratify the said articles of confederation and perpetual union. . . . In Witness whereof we have hereunto set our hands in Congress. Done at Philadelphia in the state of Pennsylvania the ninth Day of July in the Year of our Lord one Thousand seven Hundred and Seventy-eight, and in the third year of the independence of America.

(Names Omitted) □

[DOCUMENT]   ❖ **31** ❖

The Land Ordinance of May 20, 1785 *

■ *Congress assembled. Present as yesterday.*
Congress proceeded in the third reading of the Ordinance for
ascertaining the mode of disposing of lands in the western
territory, and the same being gone through, was passed
as follows:

Be it ordained by the United States in Congress assembled that the territory ceded by individual States to the United States, which has been purchased of the Indian inhabitants shall be disposed of in the following manner: . . . The Surveyors as they are respectively qualified shall proceed to divide the said territory into townships of six miles square, by lines running due north

* "The Land Ordinance of May 20, 1785," *Journal of the Continental Congress*, Vol. 28, pp. 375–81.

and south and others crossing those at right angles as near as may be, unless where the boundaries of the late Indian purchases may render the same impracticable, and then they shall depart from this rule no farther than such particular circumstances may require. . . . The plats of the townships respectively, shall be marked by subdivisions into lots of one mile square, or 640 acres, in the same direction as the external lines, and numbered from 1 to 36; always beginning the succeeding range of the lots with the number next to that with which the preceding one concluded. And where, from the causes before mentioned, only a fractional part of a township shall be surveyed, the lots, protracted thereone, shall bear the same numbers as if the township had been entire. And the surveyors, in running the external lines of the townships, shall, at the interval of every mile, mark corners for the lots which are adjacent, always designating the same in a different manner from those of the townships. . . .

As soon as seven ranges of townships, and fractional parts of townships, in the direction from south to north, shall have been surveyed, the geographer shall transmit plats thereof to the board of treasury, who shall record the same, with the report, in well bound books to be kept for that purpose. And the geographer shall make similar returns, from time to time, of every seven ranges as they may be surveyed. The Secretary at War shall have recourse thereto, and shall take by lot therefrom, a number of townships, and fractional parts of townships, as well from those to be sold entire as from those to be sold in lots, as will equal to one seventh part of the whole of such seven ranges, as nearly as may be, for the use of the late continental army; and he shall make a similar draught, from time to time, until a sufficient quantity is drawn to satisfy the same, to be applied in manner hereinafter directed. The board of treasury shall, from time to time, cause the remaining numbers, as well as those to be sold entire, as those to be sold in lots, to be drawn for, in the name of the thirteen states respectively, according to the quotas in the last preceding requisition on all the states; provided, that in case more land than its proportion is allotted for sale, in any state, at any distribution, a deduction be made therefor at the next.

The board of treasury shall transmit a copy of the original plats, previously noting thereon, the townships, and fractional parts of townships, which shall have fallen to the several states, by the distribution aforesaid, to the Commissioners of the loan office of the several states, who, after giving notice of not less than two nor more than six months, by causing advertisements to be posted up at the court houses, or other noted places in every county, and to be inserted in one newspaper, published in the states of their residence respectively, shall proceed to sell the townships, or fractional parts of townships, at public vendue, in the following manner, viz: The township, or fractional part of a township, N 1, in the first range, shall be sold entire; and N 2, in the same range, by lots; and thus in alternate order through the whole of the first range. The township, or fractional part of a township, N 1, in the second range, shall be sold by lots; and N 2, in the same range, entire; and so in alternate order through the whole of the second range; and the third range shall be sold in the same manner as the first, and the fourth in the same manner as the second, and thus alternately throughout all the ranges; provided, that none of the lands, within the said territory, be sold under the price of one dollar the acre, to be paid in specie, or loan office certificates, reduced to specie value, by the scale of depreciation, or certificates of liquidated debts of the United States, including interest, besides the expense of the survey and other charges thereon, which are hereby rated at thirty six dollars the township, in specie, or certificates as aforesaid, and so in the same proportion for a fractional part of a township, or of a lot, to be paid at the time of sales; on failure of which payment, the said lands shall again be offered for sale.

There shall be reserved for the United States out of every township, the four lots, being numbered 8, 11, 26, 29, and out of every fractional part of a township, so many lots of the same numbers as shall be found thereon, for future sale. There shall be reserved the lot N 16, of every township, for the maintenance of public schools, within the said township; also one third part of all gold, silver, lead and copper mines, to be sold, or otherwise disposed of as Congress shall hereafter direct.

When any township, or fractional part of a township, shall have been sold as aforesaid, and the money or certificates received therefore, the loan officer shall deliver a deed. . . .

[DOCUMENT] ❖ **32** ❖

Northwest Ordinance (1787) *

■ An Ordinance for the government of the Territory of the United States northwest of the River Ohio.

SEC. 1. *Be it ordained* by the United States in Congress assembled, That the said Territory, for the purposes of temporary government, be one district, subject, however, to be divided into two districts, as future circumstances may, in the opinion of Congress, make it expedient.

SEC. 2. *Be it ordained* by the authority aforesaid, That the estates, both of resident and non-resident proprietors in the said territory, dying intestate, shall descend to, and be distributed among, their children, and the descend-

---

* "Northwest Ordinance of July 13, 1787," *Documents Illustrative of the Formation of the Union of the American States* (Washington, D. C.: Government Printing Office, 1927), pp. I ff.

ants of a deceased child, in equal parts, the descendants of a deceased child or grandchild to take the share of their deceased parent in equal parts among them; and where there shall be no children or descendants, then in equal parts to the next of kin in equal degree; and among collaterals, the children of a deceased brother or sister of the intestate shall have, in equal parts among them, their deceased parents' share; and there shall in no case be a distinction between kindred of the whole and half blood; saving in all cases to the widow of the intestate her third part of the real estate for life, and one-third part of the personal estate; and this law relative to descents and dower, shall remain in full force until altered by the legislature of the district. . . .

SEC. 3. *Be it ordained* by the authority aforesaid, That there shall be appointed from time to time by Congress, a governor, whose commission shall continue in force for the term of three years, unless sooner revoked by Congress; he shall reside in the district, and have a freehold estate therein in one thousand acres of land, while in the exercise of his office.

SEC. 4. *There shall be appointed* from time to time by Congress, a secretary, whose commission shall continue in force for four years unless sooner revoked; he shall reside in the district, and have a freehold estate therein in five hundred acres of land, while in the exercise of his office. . . .

SEC. 14. *It is hereby ordained* and declared by the authority aforesaid, That the following articles shall be considered as articles of compact between the original States and the people and States in the said territory, and forever remain unalterable, unless by common consent, to wit:

ARTICLE IV

The said territory, and the States which may be formed therein, shall forever remain a part of this Confederacy of the United States of America, subject to the Articles of Confederation, and to such alterations therein as shall be constitutionally made; and to all the acts and ordinances of the United States in Congress assembled, conformable thereto. The inhabitants and settlers in the said territory shall be subject to pay a part of the federal debts contracted, or to be contracted, and a proportional part of the expenses of government to be apportioned on them by Congress, according to the same common rule and measure by which apportionments thereof shall be made on the other States; and the taxes for paying their proportion shall be laid and levied by the authority and direction of the legislatures of the district, or districts, or new States, as in the original States, within the time agreed upon by the United States in Congress assembled. The legislatures of those districts or new States, shall never interfere with the primary disposal of the soil to the *bona-fide* purchasers. No tax shall be imposed on lands the property of the United States; and, in no case, shall non-resident proprietors be taxed higher than residents. The navigable waters leading into the Mississippi and St. Lawrence, and the carrying places between the same, shall be common highways, and forever free, as well to the inhabitants of the said territory as to the citizens of the United States, and those of any other States that may be admitted into the confederacy, without any tax, impost, or duty therefor.

ARTICLE V

There shall be formed in the said territory, not less than three nor more than five States; and the boundaries of the States, as soon as Virginia shall alter her act of cession and consent to the same, shall become fixed and established as follows, to wit: The western State in the said territory, shall be bounded by the Mississippi, the Ohio, and the Wabash Rivers; a direct line drawn from the Wabash and Post Vincents, due north, to the territorial line between the United States and Canada; and, by the said territorial line to the Lake of the Woods and Mississippi. The middle State shall be bounded by the said direct line, the Wabash from Post Vincents to the Ohio, by the Ohio, by a direct line, drawn due north from the mouth of the Great Miami, to the said territorial line, and by the said territorial line. The eastern State shall be bounded by the last mentioned direct line, the Ohio, Pennsylvania, and the said territorial line: *Provided, however,* And it is further understood and declared, that the boundaries of these three States shall be subject so far to be altered, that, if Congress shall hereafter find it expedient, they shall have authority to form one or two States in that part of the said territory which lies north of an east and west line drawn through the southerly bend or extreme of Lake Michigan. And, whenever any of the said States shall have sixty thousand free inhabitants therein, such State shall be admitted, by its delegates, into the Congress of the United States, on an equal footing with the original States, in all respects whatever; and shall be at liberty to form a permanent constitution and State government: *Provided,* the constitution and government, so to be formed shall be republican, and in conformity to the principles contained in these articles, and, so far as it can be consistent with the general interest of the confederacy, such admission shall be allowed at an earlier period, and when there may be a less number of free inhabitants in the States than sixty thousand. . . .

Done by the United States, in Congress assembled, the 13th day of July, in the year of our Lord 1787, and of their sovereignty and independence the twelfth. □

PART FOUR

□ The American Economy Between the Revolution and the Civil War

Some of the ensuing articles, mild-mannered though they may seem, constitute a part of the historical materials that emerged from heated academic controversies. It was for a long time argued by historians that the existence of great areas of free or nearly free land constituted a "safety valve" of the American economy, which for many years provided an escape for anyone who wished to leave the teeming cities of the east and the oppression of hostile employers. As you will shortly see, Professor Danhof, like most contemporary historians, takes issue with the old view, leaving the safety-valve doctrine as a notion to be applied, if at all, to the years before 1830, for it was in these early decades that the cost of transporting a family to new lands was not ordinarily prohibitive. In the first of the two articles on slavery we have U. B. Phillips' classical expression of the notion that slavery was not economically justifiable, that sooner or later it would have "fallen of its own weight." The second of this pair of articles (much abbreviated), by Alfred H. Conrad and John R. Meyer, shows how history is continually rewritten, the conclusion of these authors being that the return to money invested in slaves was at least equal to the return on capital in alternative expenditures.

Without belittling the contribution of Eli Whitney to American technology, Robert S. Woodbury suggests that he was by no means the sole innovator of interchangeable parts manufacture. The second of these articles on early American industry is the piece on Dr. Abraham Gesner and the coal oil industry, highly competitive precursor of the flamboyant petroleum industry. The student concludes this section with Douglass C. North's well-known article on the linkage between foreign investment and the opening of the American west, a linkage that must be established if historians are to understand the westward movement.

The documents are for the most part those most frequently cited in historical narratives of the first half of the 19th century. The land acts reprinted here convince us better than any amount of textbook writing of the switch from a conservative to a liberal land policy that occurred in the early years of the 19th century. (Note for example how much easier the terms of land acquisition become beginning in 1820.) The decisions of the Marshall Court established the legal basis of American capitalism, clearly outlining the areas of federal government supremacy and defining the corporate form of business organization. And even without a textbook to guide him, the student who reads the remarks of Andrew Jackson and Daniel Webster and then reads the stark, cold language of the Independent Treasury Act will readily conclude who won the great monetary argument of the first half of the 19th century. □

33

Economic Validity of the Safety-Valve Doctrine *

CLARENCE H. DANHOF

I

The frontier interpretation of American history with which Professor Frederick Jackson Turner captivated and intrigued the observers of American development more than forty years ago still retains its fascination. Professor Turner saw the American frontier as an area in which American society was constantly being rebuilt, each time shaped by special problems: "American social development," he wrote, "has been continually beginning over again on the frontier." [1] It was on this theme that Professor Turner based his most striking contention that "The existence of an area of free land, its continuous recession, and the advance of American settlement westward, explain American development." [2]

It is important in any critical consideration of Professor Turner's thought to distinguish at the outset between the central theme, the broad generalizations employed in stating this fundamental thesis, and the more specific assertions and hypotheses which followed from it and which are subordinate and ancillary to it. With the fundamental thought that the development of the West was of first rank importance in the development of American economic as well as social and political life there can be no quarrel. Professor Turner's active and fertile mind did not confine itself, however, to so modest a claim. He sought rather to illustrate and to particularize, and his essays are rich with sweeping hypotheses of the relation of western development to that of the nation in general.

Among the most prominent of these theories is that one which explains the superior position of American labor and the absence of a class conscious labor movement as a result of the presence of free land. "So long," says Professor Turner, "as free land exists, the opportunity for a competency exists, and economic power secures political power." [3] And likewise, "Whenever social conditions tended to crystallize in the East, whenever capital tended to press upon labor or political restraints to impede the freedom of the mass, there

---

* Clarence H. Danhof, "Economic Validity of the Safety-Valve Doctrine," *The Journal of Economic History*, Vol. I, 1941, pp. 96–106. Used by permission.

[1] "The Significance of the Frontier in American History," originally published in American Historical Association (*Annual Report*, 1893, 199–277), and frequently revised and reprinted. The edition here employed is that contained in *The Early Writings of Frederick Jackson Turner* (Madison, 1938), 187.

[2] *Ibid.*, 186.

[3] *Ibid.*, 221.

was this gate of escape to the free conditions of the frontier. These free lands promoted individualism, economic equality, freedom to rise, democracy. Men would not accept inferior wages, and a permanent position of social subordination, when this promised land of freedom and equality was theirs for the asking. Who would rest content under oppressive legislative conditions when with a slight effort he might reach a land wherein to become a co-worker in the building of free cities and free States on the lines of his own ideal? In a word, then free lands meant free opportunities." [4]

The thought expressed in these excerpts has come to be known as the safety-valve doctrine. It has long enjoyed wide appeal and rather general acceptance. The fascination of this sweeping, simple, and apparently obviously true thesis protected it from critical evaluation for nearly forty years. That fascination has now faded and the doctrine has in recent years been questioned from a number of points of view. . . .

II

The concept of the safety-valve function of the frontier rests upon a number of assumptions whose validity must determine whether the doctrine stands or falls. The theory postulates that significant numbers of laborers once possessed an effective choice between self-employment in agriculture and wage-employment in industry. Otherwise stated, it considers that the supply of labor was to a major degree common to both agricultural and industrial pursuits. The theory takes for granted not only a high degree of residential mobility but also great occupational transferability on the part of wage-earners. Such mobility caused the industrial employee to react quickly to unfavorable employment conditions by moving his home to the West there to undertake tasks quite different from that to which he had been accustomed. It is implied also that the wage-earner as a class possessed the knowledge necessary to shift to the tasks of farm-making and farming and that the financial resources which the wage-earner might be expected to possess were adequate to finance his westward migration whenever such action might seem desirable. The theory affirms also that the ability of frontier attractions to compel desirable industrial conditions was a more important factor in wage determination than the ability of industry to pay such wages, and presumably that the existence of competition between industrial employers was a less significant factor than the competition of agriculture with industry for a given labor supply. The evidence bearing on the validity of these suppositions will be briefly scrutinized.

[4] *The Frontier in American History*, N. Y., 1921, 259–260. Note also the statement in the essay, "Western State Making in the Revolutionary Era": "It is the fact of unoccupied territory in America that sets the evolution of American and European institutions in contrast." In *The Significance of Sections in American History* (New York, 1932), 87.

III

There can be no questioning of the assumption that American labor has always possessed a high degree of residential mobility. The fact is well known though it must not be assumed that such mobility was always or even preponderantly toward the frontier to which Professor Turner referred.[5] The historical accuracy of the assumptions that there was little resistance to a change from urban to rural life or that laborers readily changed their occupations is not so clear. The problem of the turnover of labor has never been absent from American industry, but there is no evidence available to indicate that there existed, at the time when the safety-valve was allegedly operative, any greater shifting from one occupational group to another than exists today. Then as now, occupations of a skilled or semi-skilled character once entered upon tended to be followed for life. Exceptions can be found, of course; farmers became wage-earning employees in industry and mechanics became farmers. It should be noted, however, that western farm-making was by no means the only alternative open to a dissatisfied wage-earner. With the exception of periods of economic depression, the rapid growth of industry, or transportation and of commerce made a shift to some other employer in the same or related occupation a feasible matter. With respect to the movement from industrial to agricultural occupations no evidence has been submitted by the proponents of the safety-value doctrine that such shifting took place on a significant scale. On the contrary a distinct lack of such evidence has been revealed.

On the whole, the eastern wage-earner probably stood to gain little by accepting agricultural wage-employment in the West save only as an opportunity to learn farming and farm-making. Agricultural wages everywhere East and West compared unfavorably with those paid in eastern industry; annual incomes were lower and the problem of seasonal unemployment serious. Moreover wages of certain skilled occupations were distinctly higher on the average in the West than in the East; that was true also to some degree in the South, but such trades were not generally the type which suffered the dangers of wage-exploitation in the East. It was in its opportunity for self-employment coupled with the added possibilities of speculative profits from land ownership (rather than wage-employment) that the western frontier presumably held out attractions to the eastern worker. But for the eastern wage-earner to set himself up as an independent farmer or farm-maker was no easy task. It required the adoption of a distinctly new way of life, the learning of

[5] Professor Turner's concept of the frontier is one of population settlement. Though this frontier is complex and includes that of the Indian trader, the rancher and the farmer, it does not comprehend such factors of economic exploitation as transportation, commerce and industry.

Murray Kane has pointed out that Professor Turner's point of view is essentially that of a geographer and that his interpretation is geographic rather than economic in character. "Some Considerations on the Frontier Concept of Frederick Jackson Turner" *Mississippi Valley Historical Review*, XXVII (1940), 381–394.

the new tasks of agriculture, the surrender of acquired industrial skills, as well as the advantages of the established society of the East, and the acceptance in many cases of a lower standard of living. The assumption that no training or experience were needed to enter farming cannot be defended and the assumption that mechanics entered readily and successfully upon the agricultural life is open to serious question. Successful agriculture required knowledge which a mechanic did not possess and frequently required longer hours of strenuous labor than were asked of the wage-earner in industrial pursuits.

IV

The proponents of the safety-valve doctrine make much of free land. The phrase free land is an inaccurate one whether referring to the cost of land as such or whether it applies more broadly to opportunities for farm-making in general. Until the Homestead Act was passed, the basic price of land was $1.25 per acre. That price was low by modern standards but it does not follow *ipso facto* that land was cheap. Though as Cunynghame pointed out "land per acre and champagne per bottle were equally sold at five shilling each," [6] many a wage-earner must have found either commodity entirely beyond his means. Millions of acres, it is true, were given outright by the federal government to those who qualified for military grants and certain federal lands as well as state lands were frequently available at less than $1.25. The farm-maker searching for desirable locations, however, frequently had to pay far more. The Homestead Act made certain federal lands free, but it did not thereby make the lands accessible to the eastern wage-earner. In the 1850s the making of a farm on virgin prairie land or the purchase and operation of an established western farm required a considerable capital, perhaps about $1,000. The Homestead Act, the product of long agitation based in part on a recognition that western lands were actually out of reach of eastern workers, reduced the sum required only slightly. The fact that the land was now free did not change circumstances materially. It was still raw land requiring a large expenditure of labor and capital to convert it into a productive, remunerative farm. Of all the proposals made to the Congressional Committee of 1878, on Depression in Labor and Business, few were more frequently reiterated than that a loan or subsidy be given by Congress to provide financial assistance to the unemployed so that they could move West, take up a claim and undertake farming.

In the case of agricultural residents of states west of the Appalachians, the capitals required for farm-making might be in the form of equipment and stock. The eastern wage-earner, in contrast, rarely possessed such equipment, moreover the transportation of such goods from the East to the western frontier was generally excessively costly. Hence the capital required of the eastern would-be farm-maker had to be in the form of cash, supplemented by expensive credit. The wages paid unskilled labor in the East during the 'fifties did not average $1.00 per day; in the case of male workers in the factories of

---

[6] A. Cunynghame, *Glimpse of the Great Western Republic* (1851), 7.

Lowell the rate in 1856 approximated 80 cents per day. Annual incomes were thus less than $300 and it obviously required frugality to accumulate wealth at the rate of $50 per year. The possession of such a sum as $1,000 or even as little as $500 by an eastern mechanic, if acquired by saving, postulates long and steady employment; it indicates, moreover, middle or old age, persistent saving, and good fortune in investments. An individual possessed of such qualifications was unlikely to migrate westward. He would undoubtedly have been considered successful in his occupation at home and his probable gain in removing West to farm was nowhere as great as popular description sometimes suggests.

V

Basic to the safety-valve doctrine is the concept of a penniless, poverty-stricken, dissatisfied, possibly unemployed, wage-earner moving westward with his family and possessions, carving a farm out of forest or prairie, and within a very few years acquiring a subsistence and a comfortable homestead which would steadily increase in value. Insofar as this can be accepted as an accurate description of a common occurrence it applies only to the years preceding 1830, to that more self-sufficient, pre-commercial period of agricultural development in the northern states. Since this self-sufficient era of northern agriculture was paralleled by only a slight development of industry and a numerically small wage-earning class, the existence of the frontier as a safety-valve can have had little significance. It is not until American industry developed a large and dissatisfied wage-earning class that the presence or absence of any escape can have had importance. The expansion of industry was paralleled by changes in the character of agriculture. Farming became market-focused and capital-using; a business in which the motive of self-sufficiency was displaced by the desire for quick profits. It is hardly possible that unemployed wage-earners in 1850 could have migrated from Massachusetts to Illinois or Iowa under the same conditions that such a worker might have faced in moving into western New York in 1820.

A wage-earner would obviously be acting in his own self-interest by migrating to the West when employment conditions in the East were particularly unfavorable, assuming that such obstacles to migration as have been noted above did not exist. The agricultural West did not, however, escape the depressions from which the East suffered. In periods of heavy eastern unemployment, western agriculture was generally unprofitable and land purchase unattractive in the face of falling values. Thus, contrary to the assumptions of the safety-valve doctrine, the West was not necessarily attractive when unemployment was severe in the East. Migration was not greatest when unemployment was greatest. The collapse of migration to the West in 1858 following the immense movements of the years from 1854 to 1857 as revealed in newspaper comment, in the passenger traffic of western railroads, and in census data, illustrate the point.

The West did without doubt attract some industrial wage-earners from the

East but such immigrants tended to be the highly paid, self-employed crafts-men rather than wage-employees. They were not the poverty-stricken and in-dustrially oppressed but the successful, skilled, frugal and ambitious. The West attracted them in periods of prosperity when the profits in undertaking farm-making, farming or in establishing their crafts in the new towns and vil-lages were obvious and quick. If this be true then the western frontier was no safety-valve but merely one of a number of areas of economic expansion which shared in the prosperity of the whole nation.

VI

The concept of the frontier as a safety-valve appears in an emasculated form in the argument that since the settling of the frontier reduced the labor supply in the East for wage-earning occupations, wages in the East were nec-essarily higher than would otherwise have been the case. The rôle of the fron-tier is interpreted here as one of the demand factors in the whole labor market and there is nothing of the safety-valve in the theory. In the face of the many dynamic factors in the situation — the development of all phases of industry, commerce, foreign trade, foreign immigration, etc. — the argument is of sec-ondary importance in any explanation of wages. The basic postulate that there existed a demand on the part of both agriculture and industry for the services of a mutual supply of labor is true. The West did attract a signifi-cant part of that eastern agricultural population which, as it increased, found the New England soil inhospitable in the face of western opportunities. A portion of the agricultural population did make a choice between eastern in-dustry and western farm-making and to the degree that it elected the latter some effect upon wage rates may have followed. On the other hand the vol-ume of foreign immigration attracted to these shores in large part by appar-ent agricultural opportunities had quite the opposite effect upon eastern wage levels.

If, finally, the settlement of western lands had some effect upon the charac-ter of eastern industrial conditions, as cannot be doubted, the reverse is cer-tainly equally true. The development of eastern commerce and industry without question influenced the rate and character of western settlement. It was above all the development of an urban industrial market in the East which permitted an expansion far beyond anything that the South could sup-port that made western agriculture profitable and attractive on a large scale. It was eastern transportation agencies which made those profits attainable, eastern financial institutions which to some degree supplied the necessary cap-ital, and eastern industry which supplied the western need for manufactured commodities. And it can be reasonably asserted that to the extent that east-ern wage-earners participated in developing this West they found the oppor-tunity to do so in a wage income that made possible the savings which per-mitted a worker or his sons to go West. □

34

The Economic Cost of Slaveholding in the Cotton Belt *

ULRICH B. PHILLIPS

. . . Whether negro slavery was an advantage in the early colonies and whether it became a burden in the later period, and, if so, how the change occurred, and why the people did not relieve themselves of the incubus — these are a few of the fundamental problems to which the student must address himself. The present essay, based on a study of slave prices, deals with the general economic conditions of slaveholding, and shows the great transformation caused by the opening of the cotton belt and the closing of the African slave trade.

As regards the labor supply, the conditions at the outset in the new world of America were unlike those of modern Europe, but similar to those of Asia and Europe in primitive times. The ancient labor problem rose afresh in the plantation colonies, for land was plentiful and free, and men would not work as voluntary wage-earners in other men's employ when they might as readily work for themselves in independence. There was a great demand for labor upon the colonial estates, and when it became clear that freemen would not come and work for hire, a demand developed for servile labor. At first recourse was had to white men and women who bound themselves to serve three or four years to pay for their transportation across the sea, and to English criminals who were sent to the colonies and bound to labor for longer terms, frequently for five or seven years. Indian slaves were tried, but proved useless. Finally the negroes were discovered to be cheap and useful laborers for domestic service and plantation work.

For above half a century after the first negroes were brought to Virginia in 1620, this labor was considered a doubtful experiment; and their numbers increased very slowly until after the beginning of the golden age of the colony toward the end of the reign of Charles II. But the planters learned at length that the negroes could be employed to very good advantage in the plantation system; and after about 1680 the import of slaves grew steadily larger.

In the West Indies the system of plantations worked by slaves had been borrowed by the English settlers from the Spaniards; and when the South Carolina coast was colonized, some of the West India planters immigrated and brought this system with them. In view of the climate and the crops on the Carolina coast, negro slave labor was thought to be a *sine qua non* of successful colonizing. The use of the slaves was confined always to the lowlands, until after Whitney invented the cotton gin; but in the early years of the nineteenth century the rapid opening of the great inland cotton belt cre-

* Ulrich B. Phillips, "The Economic Cost of Slaveholding in the Cotton Belt," *Political Science Quarterly*, Vol. XX, 1905, pp. 257–75. Reprinted with permission of the *PSQ*.

ated a new and very strong demand for labor. The white farming population already in the uplands was by far too small to do the work; the lowland planters began to move thither with their slaves; the northern and European laboring classes were not attracted by the prospect of working alongside the negroes; and accordingly the demand for labor in the cotton belt was translated into an unprecedented demand for negro slave labor.

Negro slavery was established in the South, as elsewhere, because the white people were seeking their own welfare and comfort. It was maintained for the same economic reason, and also because it was thought to be essential for safety. As soon as the negroes were on hand in large numbers, the problem was to keep their savage instincts from breaking forth, and to utilize them in civilized industry. The plantation system solved the problem of organization, while the discipline and control obtained through the institution of slavery were considered necessary to preserve the peace and to secure the welfare of both races. Private gain and public safety were secured for the time being; but in the long run, as we shall see, these ends were attained at the expense of private and public wealth and of progress.

This peculiar labor system failed to gain strength in the North, because there was there no work which negro slaves could perform with notable profit to their masters. In certain parts of the South the system flourished because the work required was simple, the returns were large, and the shortcomings of negro slave labor were partially offset by the ease with which it could be organized.

Once developed, the system was of course maintained so long as it appeared profitable to any important part of the community. Wherever the immediate profits from slave labor were found to be large, the number of slaves tended to increase, not only through the birth of children, but by importations. Thus the staple-producing areas became "black belts," where most of the labor was done by slaves. With large amounts of capital invested in slaves, the system would be maintained even in times of depression, when the plantations were running at something of a loss; for, just as in a factory, the capital was fixed, and operations could not be stopped without a still greater loss. When property in slaves had become important, the conservative element in politics became devoted, as a rule, to the preservation of this vested interest. The very force of inertia tended to maintain the established system, and a convulsion or crisis of some sort was necessary for its disestablishment in any region.

As a matter of fact it was only in special industries, and only in times of special prosperity, that negro slave labor was of such decided profit as to escape condemnation for its inherent disadvantages. But at certain periods in Virginia and in the lower South, the conditions were unusual: all labor was profitable; hired labor was not to be had so long as land was free; indentured white servants were in various ways unsatisfactory, and negro slaves were therefore found to be of decided profit to their masters. The price of Africans in colonial times was so low that, when crops and prices were good, the labor of those imported repaid their original cost in a few years, and the planters felt a constant temptation to increase their holdings of land and of slaves in the hope of still greater profits.

⌈Thus in Virginia there was a vicious circle: planters bought fresh lands and more slaves to make more tobacco, and with the profits from tobacco they bought more land and slaves to make more tobacco with which to buy yet more land and slaves. The situation in the lower South was similar to that in Virginia, with rice and indigo, or sugar, or in latter times cotton, substituted for tobacco. In either case the process involved a heavy export of wealth in the acquisition of every new laborer.⌋ The Yankee skipper had a corresponding circle of his own: he carried rum to Guinea to exchange for slaves, slaves to the plantation colonies to exchange for molasses, molasses to New England to exchange for more rum, and this rum again to Guinea to exchange for more slaves. ⌈The difference was that the Yankee made a genuine profit on every exchange and thriftily laid up his savings, while the southern planter, as a rule, invested all his profits in a fictitious form of wealth and never accumulated a surplus for any other sort of investment.⌋

From an economic point of view the American system of slavery was a system of firmly controlling the unintelligent negro laborers, and of capitalizing the prospective value of the labor of each workman for the whole of his life. An essential feature of that system was the practice of buying and selling the control over the slave's labor, and one of the indexes to the economic situation at any time may be found in the quotations of slave prices.

The slave trade had no particular local home or "exchange," but it extended throughout all the slaveholding districts of America. Though the number and frequency of slave sales was relatively small, the traffic when once developed had many of the features of modern stock or produce markets. It cannot be forgotten, of course, that the slave trade involved questions of humanity and social organization as well as the mere money problem; but from the financial point of view the slave traffic constituted simply an extensive commodity market, where the article dealt in was life-time labor. As in any other market, the operations in the slave trade were controlled by economic laws or tendencies. There were bull influences and bear influences, and occasional speculative campaigns. And when at times the supply was subjected to monopoly control, the prices tended to go wild and disturb the general system of finance in the whole region.

In the general slave market there was constant competition among those wishing to sell, and among those wishing to buy. The volume of the colonial slave trade and the rate of slave prices tended to fluctuate to some extent with the tides of prosperity in the respective staple-producing areas; but during the colonial period the plantations in the different regions were of such varied interests, producing tobacco, rice, indigo, cotton, sugar and coffee, that depression in one of these industries was usually offset, so far as concerned the slave-trader, by high profits in another. Barbadoes was the information station. The slave ships touched there and gathered news of where their "ebony" was to be sold the highest.[1] The Royal African Company had the best system of intelligence, and about 1770 and 1780 it sold its cargoes at a fairly uniform price of £18 to £22 per head, while the independent traders appear to have obtained from £15 to £25, according to the chances of the market. American-born slaves, when sold, brought higher prices than fresh Africans, because their training in plantation labor and domestic service rendered them more valuable. The prices of the home-raised slaves varied considerably, but so long as the African trade was kept open, the price of field hands of all sorts was kept reasonably near to the price of the savage African imports. . . .

The developments following Whitney's invention of the cotton gin revolutionized the situation. Slave prices entered upon a steady advance, which was quickened by the prohibition of the African trade in 1808. They were then held stationary by the restrictions upon commerce, and were thrown backward by the outbreak of war in 1812. But with the peace of Ghent the results of the new cotton industry and of the cessation of African imports became strikingly manifest. The inland fields of the lower South proved to be peculiarly adapted for the production of cotton. The simplicity of the work and the even distribution of the tasks through the seasons made negro slave labor peculiarly available. With the increasing demand of the world for cotton, there was built up in the South perhaps the greatest staple monopoly the world had ever seen. The result was an enormous demand for slaves in the cotton belt. American ports, however, were now closed to the foreign slave trade. The number of slaves available in America was now fixed, the rate of increase was limited, and the old "tobacco South" had a monopoly of the only supply which could meet the demand of the new "cotton South."

Till 1815 "colonial" conditions prevailed, and the market for slave labor was relatively quiet and steady. In 1815 began the "ante-bellum" régime, in which the whole economy of the South was governed by the apparently capricious play of the compound monopoly of cotton and slave labor. The price of cotton was governed by the American output and its relation to the European demand. And the price of slaves was governed by the profits in cotton and the relation of the labor demand to the monopolized labor supply.[2] . . .

There was always a great difference between the values of individual slaves. When the average price of negroes ranged about $500, prime field hands brought, say, $1,000, and skilled artisans still more. At that rate, an infant would be valued at about $100, a boy of twelve years and a man of fifty at about $500 each, and a prime wench for field work at $800 or $900.

The most feasible comparison of prices is that of prime field hands, who

---

[1] D. McKinnon, Tour Through the British West Indies, p. 8.
[2] *Cf.* De Toqueville, Democracy in America, vol. ii, p. 233.

may be defined as well-grown, able-bodied fellows, with average training and between eighteen and thirty years of age. To find the current price of prime field hands in lists where no classification is given, we take the average of the highest ordinary prices. We ignore any scattering extreme quotations, as applying probably to specially valuable artisans, overseers or domestic servants, and not to field hands. Where ages are given, we take the average of the prices paid for grown fellows too young to have received special training. We leave aside, on the other hand, the exceptionally low quotations as being due to infirmities which exclude the slave from the prime grade. The professional slave traders in the domestic traffic dealt mostly in "likely young fellows and wenches." In the quotations of the sales by these traders, when no details are recorded, we may assume that the average, except for children, will range just a little below the current rate for prime field hands.

In view of all the hindrances, the production of a perfectly accurate table of prices cannot be hoped for, even from the exercise of the utmost care and discrimination. The table which follows is simply an approximation of averages made in a careful study of several thousand quotations in the state of Georgia.[3]

The parallel quotations of cotton prices [4] afford a basis for the study of slave-labor capitalization. In examining these quotations it will be noticed that during many brief periods the prices of slaves and cotton rose and fell somewhat in harmony; but that in the whole period under review the price of cotton underwent a heavy net decline, while slave prices had an extremely strong upward movement. The change which took place in the relative slave and cotton prices was really astonishing. In 1800 a prime field hand was worth in the market about 1500 pounds of ginned cotton; in 1809, about 3000 pounds; in 1818, about 3500; in 1826, about 5400; in 1837, about 10,000; in 1845, about 12,000; in 1860, 15,000 to 18,000. In his capacity for work, a prime negro in 1800 was worth nearly or quite as much as a similar slave in 1860; and a pound of cotton in 1860 was not essentially different from a pound of cotton in 1800. But our table shows that within that epoch of three-score years there was an advance of some 1000 or 1200 per cent in the price of slaves as measured in cotton.

The decline in the price of cotton was due in some measure to a lessening of cost, through improvements in cultivating, ginning and marketing. The advance in slave prices was due in part to the increasing intelligence and abil-

[3] The sources used for this tabulation are the documents in the Georgia state archives and the records of Baldwin, Oglethorpe, Clarke and Troup counties, all lying in the Georgia cotton belt, together with bills of sale in private hands, travelers' accounts, and articles in the newspapers of the period. Instances of sudden rise or fall in slave prices and sales of large and noted estates were often reported in the local press, with comments. There is no printed collection of any large number of slave-price quotations.

[4] The cotton price averages are made from the tables given by E. J. Donnell in his *Chronological and Statistical History of Cotton*, New York, 1872, with the aid of the summaries published by G. L. Watkins, *Production and Price of Cotton for One Hundred Years*, U. S. Department of Agriculture, Washington, 1895.

SLAVE AND COTTON PRICES IN GEORGIA

Year	Average Price of Prime Field Hands	Economic Situation and the Chief Determinant Factors	Average N. Y. Price of Upland Cotton	Years
1755.....	£55			
1773.....	60			
1776–1783	....	War and depression in industry and commerce.		
1784.....	70	Peace and returning prosperity.		
1792.....	$ 300	Depression due to Great Britain's attitude toward American commerce.		
1793.....	....	Cotton gin invented.		
1800 [1]....	450	....	30 cents	1795–1805
1808	....	African slave trade prohibited.		
1809.....	600	Embargo moderates rise in prices.	19 cents	1805–1810
1813.....	450	War with Great Britain........	12 cents	1813
1818.....	1000	Inflation.....................	29 cents	1816–1818
1819.....	....	Financial crisis..............	16 cents	1819
1821.....	700	Recovery from panic..........	14 cents	1821
1826.....	800	Moderate prosperity..........	15 cents	1824–1827
1827.....	....	Depression.		
1828.....	700	....	10 cents	1827–1828
1835.....	900	Flush times.................	17½ cents	1835
1837.....	1300	Inflation — crash.............	13¼ cents	1837
1839.....	1000	Cotton crisis.................	13¼ cents	1839
1840.....	700	Cotton crisis; acute distress....	9 cents	1840
1844.....	600	Depression..................	7½ cents	1844
1845.....	....	Severe depression.............	5½ cents	1845
1848.....	900	Recovery in cotton prices. Texas demand for slaves...........	9½ cents	1847–1848
1851.....	1050	Prosperity...................	12 cents	1851
1853.....	1200	Expansion of cotton industry and simultaneous rise in tobacco prices.[3]...................	11 cents	1850–1860
1859.....	1650			
1860 [2]....	1800			

[1] The quotations down to this point are lowland quotations. There were very few slaves in the uplands before 1800.

[2] In the later fifties there were numerous local flurries in slave valuations. In central Georgia prime negroes brought $2,000 in 1860, while in western Georgia and central Alabama the prices appear not to have run much above $1,500. For prices in the other parts of the South in that decade, see G. W. Weston, "Who are and who may be slaves in the United States," a pamphlet published in 1856. See also Brackett, "The Negro in Maryland"; Ingle, Southern Sidelights; Hammond, "The Cotton Industry," and "De Bow's Review," vol. xxvi, p. 647.

[3] The rise in tobacco prices and the revival of prosperity in Virginia in this decade tended to diminish the volume of the slave trade and contributed to raising slave prices. Cf. W. H. Collins, "The Domestic Slave Trade in the Southern States," N. Y., 1904, p. 57.

ity of the negroes and to improvements in the system of directing their work on the plantations, and also in part to the decline in the value of money. But the ten-fold or twelve-fold multiplication of the price of slaves, when quoted in terms of the product of their labor, was too great to be explained except by reference to the severe competition of the planters in selling cotton and in buying slaves. Their system of capitalized labor was out of place in the modern competitive world, and burdened with that system all the competition of the cotton planters was bound to be of a cut-throat nature. In other words, when capital and labor were combined, as in the American slaveholding system, there was an irresistible tendency to overvalue and overcapitalize slave labor, and to carry it to the point where the financial equilibrium was unsafe, and any crisis threatened complete bankruptcy.

Aside from the expense of food, clothing and shelter, the cost of slave labor for any given period of time was made up of several elements:

(1) Interest upon the capital invested in the slave.

(2) Economic insurance against (a) his death, (b) his illness or accidental injury, and (c) his flight from service.[5] Of course insurance policies were seldom taken out to cover these risks, but the cost of insurance against them must be reckoned in the cost of slave labor for any given period.

(3) The diminishing value of every mature slave by reason of increasing age. Because of the "wear and tear" of his years and his diminishing prospect of life and usefulness, the average slave of fifty-five years of age would be worth only half as much as one of twenty-five years, and after fifty-five the valuation decreased still more rapidly. In computing the cost of any group of slaves it will be necessary to set over against this depreciation the value of the children born; but, on the other hand, the cost by groups would be increased by the need of supporting the disabled negroes who were not in the working gangs.

(4) Taxation assessed upon the capitalized value of the slaves. In the slaveholding region as a whole, in the later ante-bellum period, the total assessed value of slave property was at least as great as that of all the other sorts of property combined.

The rate of slave hire would furnish a good index of the current price of slave labor year by year, if sufficient quotations on a stable basis could be obtained. But on account of the special needs or wishes of the parties to the individual bargains, there were such opportunities for higgling the rate in individual cases that the current rate is very elusive. The following averages, computed from a limited number of quotations for the hire of men slaves in

---

[5] Physicians' and attorneys' fees should perhaps be included under the head of insurance. It may be noted that doctors' charges were generally the same for slaves as for white persons. To illustrate how expensive this charge often was, we may cite an instance given in the records of Troup county, Georgia, where Dr. Ware collected from Col. Truitt's estate $130.50 for medicine and daily visits to a negro child, from November 29, 1858, to January 5, 1859.

middle Georgia, are illustrative: In 1800, $100 per year; in 1816, $110; in 1818, $140; in 1833, $140; in 1836, $155; in 1841, $140; in 1860, $150. These were in most cases the years of maximum quotations in the respective periods. The local fluctuations in short periods were often very pronounced; but in the long run the rate followed a gradual upward movement.

The relation between the price of slaves and the rate of their hire should theoretically have borne, in quiet periods, a definite relation to the rate of interest upon capital; but the truth is that in the matter of slave prices there was, through the whole period after the closing of the African trade, a tendency to "frenzied finance" in the cotton belt. Slave prices were largely controlled by speculation, while slave hire was regulated more largely by the current rate of wages for labor in general. The whole subject of these relations is one for which authentic data are perhaps too scanty to permit of thorough analysis.

Negro slave labor was expensive, not so much because it was unwilling as because it was overcapitalized and inelastic. The negro of himself, by reason of his inherited inaptitude, was inefficient as a self-directing laborer in civilized industry. The whole system of civilized life was novel and artificial to him; and to make him play a valuable part in it, strict guidance and supervision were essential. Without the plantation system, the mass of the negroes would have been an unbearable burden in America; and except in slavery they could never have been utilized, in the beginning, for plantation work. The negro had no love of work for work's sake; and he had little appreciation of future goods when set over against present exemption from toil. That is to say, he lacked the economic motive without which voluntary civilized industry is impossible. It is a mistake to apply the general philosophy of slavery to the American situation without very serious modification. A slave among the Greeks or Romans was generally a relatively civilized person, whose voluntary labor would have been far more productive than his labor under compulsion. But the negro slave was a negro first, last and always, and a slave incidentally. Mr. Cairnes and others make a great mistake when they attribute his inefficiency and expensiveness altogether to the one incident of regulation. Regulation actually remedied in large degree the disadvantages of using negro labor, though it failed to make it as cheap, in most employments, as free white labor would have been. The cotton planter found the negro already a part of the situation. To render him useful, firm regulation was necessary. The forcible control of the negro was in the beginning a necessity, and was not of itself a burden at any time.

In American slaveholding, however, the capitalization of labor-value and the sale and purchase of labor-control were permanent features; and when the supply was "cornered" it was unavoidable that the price should be bid up to the point of overvaluation. And this brings us to the main economic disadvantage of the system.

In employing free labor, wages are paid from time to time as the work is done, and the employer can count upon receiving from the products of that labor an income which will enable him to continue to pay its wages in the future, while his working capital is left free for other uses. He may invest a portion of his capital in lands and buildings, and use most of the remainder as circulating capital for special purposes, retaining only a small percentage as a reserve fund. But to secure a working force of slaves, the ante-bellum planter had to invest all the capital that he owned or could borrow in the purchase of slaves and lands; for the larger his plantation was, within certain limits, the more economies he could introduce. The temptation was very strong for him to trim down to the lowest possible limit the fund for supplies and reserve. The slaveholding system thus absorbed the planter's earnings; and for such absorption it had unlimited capacity, for the greater the profits of the planters the more slaves they wanted and the higher the slave prices mounted. Individual profits, as fast as made, went into the purchase of labor, and not into modern implements or land improvements. Circulating capital was at once converted into fixed capital; while for their annual supplies of food, implements and luxuries the planters continued to rely upon their credit with the local merchants, and the local merchants to rely upon their credit with northern merchants and bankers.

Thus there was a never-ending private loss through the continual payment of interest and the enhancement of prices; and, further, there was a continuous public loss by the draining of wealth out of the cotton belt by the slave trade. With the stopping of the African slave trade, the drain of wealth from the lower South was not checked at all, but merely diverted from England and New England to the upper tier of southern states; and there it did little but demoralize industry and postpone to a later generation the agricultural revival. . . .

Because they were blinded by the abolition agitation in the North and other historical developments which we cannot here discuss, most of the later generation of ante-bellum planters could not see that slaveholding was essentially burdensome. But that which was partly hidden from their vision is clear to us to-day. In the great system of southern industry and commerce, working with seeming smoothness, the negro laborers were inefficient in spite of discipline, and slavery was an obstacle to all progress. The system may be likened to an engine, with slavery as its great fly-wheel — a fly-wheel indispensable for safe running at first, perhaps, but later rendered less useful by improvements in the machinery, and finally becoming a burden instead of a benefit. Yet it was retained, because it was still considered essential in securing the adjustment and regular working of the complex mechanism. This great rigid wheel of slavery was so awkward and burdensome that it absorbed the momentum and retarded the movement of the whole machine without rendering any service of great value. The capitalization of labor and the export of earnings in exchange for more workmen, always of a low degree of efficiency, together with the extreme lack of versatility, deprived the South of the natural advantage which the cotton monopoly should have given. To be rid of the capitalization of labor as a part of the slaveholding system was a great requisite for the material progress of the South. □

✧ **35** ✧

The Economics of Slavery in
the Ante Bellum South *

ALFRED H. CONRAD AND JOHN R. MEYER

OBJECTIVES AND METHODS

The outstanding economic characteristics of southern agriculture before the Civil War were a high degree of specialization and virtually exclusive reliance on a slave labor force. The large-scale, commercial dependence upon slave labor was to distinguish the ante bellum South not only from other regions in its own time but from all regions at all other times in American agricultural history. Because of this unique historical status, ante bellum southern agriculture has been a subject for special historical attention. Above all else, attention has been focused upon the proposition that, even without external intervention, slavery would have toppled of its own weight. This allegation has its source in the assertions of slave inefficiency to be found in the writings of men who lived with slavery: American or English liberals like G. M. Weston, H. R. Helper, or J. E. Cairnes and southern slaveowners who, in a religious, self-righteous age, could find every motive for the protection of the slave system except that it was personally profitable. The argument is to be found most strongly stated in the work of later southern historians, especially C. W. Ramsdell and U. B. Phillips, who take the position that the Civil War, far from being an irrepressible conflict, was an unnecessary blood bath. They argue that slavery had reached its natural limits and that it was cumbersome and inefficient and, probably within less than a generation, would have destroyed itself. To the question why emancipation was not resorted to, they reply that slavery was for the southerners an important (and evidently expensive) duty, part of their "unending task of race discipline." On the other side, Lewis Gray and Kenneth Stampp have strongly contested this view, contending that southern plantation agriculture was at least as remunerative an economic activity as most other business enterprises in the young republic.

The evidence employed in this debate has been provided by the few, usu-

* Reprinted from "The Economics of Slavery in the Ante Bellum South" by Alfred H. Conrad and John R. Meyer, *Journal of Political Economy*, Vol. LXVI, April 1958, pp. 95–122 by permission of The University of Chicago Press. [Copyright 1958 by The University of Chicago.]

ally fragmentary, accounting records that have come down to us from early plantation activities. The opposing parties have arranged and rearranged the data in accordance with various standard and sometimes imaginary accounting conventions. Indeed, the debate over the value of the different constituent pieces of information reconstructs in embryo much of the historical development of American accounting practices. For example, virtually all the accounting valuation problems have been discussed with relation to the slave question, including the role and meaning of depreciation, the nature and accountability of interest charges, and the validity of distinctions between profits and payments of managerial wages. But, despite the fact that the problem is ostensibly one in economic history, no attempt has ever been made to measure the profitability of slavery according to the economic (as opposed to accounting) concept of profitability. This paper is an attempt to fill this void.

Thus this paper is devoted to establishing methodological as well as historical points. Specifically, we shall attempt to measure the profitability of southern slave operations in terms of modern capital theory. In doing so, we shall illustrate the ways in which economic theory might be used in ordering and organizing historical facts. An additional methodological point is also made evident by this exercise, namely, how the very simple statistical concepts of range and central tendency as applied to frequency distributions of data can be employed in interpreting or moderating inferences from historical facts.

In executing these tasks, we must ask first what it is we are talking about and, second, whether we can say anything that can be proved or disproved. For example, we must ask what the slave economy was. Was it cotton culture? Was it cotton and sugar and tobacco? Was it all of ante bellum southern agriculture? In answering, we shall define slavery in terms of two production functions. One function relates inputs of Negro slaves (and the materials required to maintain the slaves) to the production of the southern staple crops, particularly cotton. The second function describes the production of the intermediate good, slave labor — slave-breeding, to use an emotionally charged term which has colored, even determined, most of the conclusions about this problem.

What do we mean by "efficiency"? Essentially, we shall mean a comparison of the return from the use of this form of capital — Negro slaves — with the returns being earned on other capital assets at the time. Thus we mean to consider whether the slave system was being dragged down of its own weight; whether the allocation of resources was impaired by the rigidity of capitalized labor supply; whether southern capital was misused or indeed drawn away to the North; and, finally, whether slavery must inevitably have declined from an inability of the slave force to reproduce itself.

The hypothesis that slavery was an efficient, maintainable form of economic organization is not a new one, of course. Nor are we, by one hundred years, at least, among the first to conclude that Negro slavery was profitable in the ante bellum South. What we do feel to be novel, however, is our approach.

Postulating that American Negro slavery was characterized by two production functions, we argue that an efficient system developed in which those regions best suited to the production of cotton (and the other important staples) specialized in agricultural production, while the less productive land continued to produce slaves, exporting the increase to the staple-crop areas. It is this structure that we are examining.

We propose to test the hypothesis by putting appropriate values on the variables in the production functions and computing the rate of return over cost, the stream of income over the lifetime of the slave. This rate of return, the marginal efficiency of slave capital, must, in turn, be shown to be at least equal to the rate of interest currently available in the American capital markets. It is further necessary to show that appropriate markets existed to make this regional specialization possible and that slavery did not necessarily imply the disappearance or misallocation of capital. Evidence on the ability of the slave force to maintain itself numerically will be had as a corollary result. For these purposes it is necessary to obtain data on slave prices and cotton prices, the average output of male field hands and field wenches, the life-expectancy of Negroes born in slavery, the cost of maintaining slaves during infancy and other non-productive periods, and, finally, the net reproduction rate and the demographic composition of the slave population in the breeding and using areas. . . .

[After careful statistical examination of the variables listed in the preceding paragraph, authors Conrad and Meyer compute the realized returns on prime field hands and wenches, expressed as percentages of capital outlay per hand. They conclude that ". . . slavery was apparently about as remunerative as alternative employments to which slave capital might have been put."]

CONCLUSION

In sum, it seems doubtful that the South was forced by bad statesmanship into an unnecessary war to protect a system which must soon have disappeared because it was economically unsound. This is a romantic hypothesis which will not stand against the facts.

On the basis of the computation of the returns to capital in our model of the ante bellum southern economy and the demonstration of the efficiency of the regional specialization, the following conclusions are offered:

1. Slavery was profitable to the whole South, the continuing demand for labor in the Cotton Belt insuring returns to the breeding operation on the less productive land in the seaboard and border states. The breeding returns were necessary, however, to make the plantation operations on the poorer lands as profitable as alternative contemporary economic activities in the United States. The failure of southern agriculture on these poorer lands in the post bellum period is probably attributable, in the main, to the loss of these capital gains on breeding and not, as is so often suggested, to either the

relative inefficiency of the tenant system that replaced the plantations or the soil damage resulting from war operations. These factors were unquestionably contributing elements to the difficulties of post bellum southern agriculture, but they were of relatively small quantitative importance compared with the elimination of slave-breeding returns.

2. There was nothing necessarily self-destructive about the profits of the slave economy. Neither the overcapitalization argument nor the assertion that slavery must have collapsed because the slaves would not reproduce themselves is tenable. Slave prices did not outpace productivity, and the regional slave price structure would imply a workable transfer mechanism rather than the contrary.

3. Continued expansion of slave territory was both possible and, to some extent, necessary. The maintenance of profits in the Old South depended upon the expansion, extensive or intensive, of slave agriculture into the Southwest. This is sufficient to explain the interest of the Old South in secession and does away with the necessity to fall back upon arguments of statesmanship or quixotism to explain the willingness to fight for the peculiar institution.

4. The available productive surplus from slavery might have been used for economic development or, as in totalitarian regimes in this century, for militarism. In spite of this good omen for development, southern investment and industrialization lagged. It is hard to explain this except on the social ground that entrepreneurship could not take root in the South or on the economic ground that the South did not really own the system but merely operated it. Furthermore, the American experience clearly suggests that slavery is not, from the strict economic standpoint, a deterrent to industrial development and that its elimination may take more than the workings of "inexorable economic forces." Although profitability cannot be offered as a sufficient guaranty of the continuity of southern slavery, the converse argument that slavery must have destroyed itself can no longer rest upon allegations of unprofitability or upon assumptions about the impossibility of maintaining and allocating a slave labor force. To the extent, moreover, that profitability is a necessary condition for the continuation of a private business institution in a free-enterprise society, slavery was not untenable in the ante bellum American South. Indeed, economic forces often may work toward the continuation of a slave system, so that the elimination of slavery may depend upon the adoption of harsh political measures. Certainly that was the American experience. ◻

36

The Legend of Eli Whitney and
Interchangeable Parts *

ROBERT S. WOODBURY

In some legends the story is such that from its very nature we can never establish its truth or falsity; in others patient historical work — usually external to the legend — can ascertain whether the events actually happened or not. The legend of Eli Whitney's part in interchangeable manufacture is, however, unique in that the clues and even much of the evidence for its refutation are part of the legend as customarily recited. It is also unique in that the legend is not merely a popular one nor even a story given "authority" by inclusion in conventional textbooks. This legend has been retold at least twice with all the paraphernalia of historical scholarship — footnotes, elaborate bibliography, discussion of the sources, and even use of archival material. But in both cases we find the same failure to evaluate the evidence critically, to follow leads to other sources, and to question basic presuppositions. These same faults extend back to the origins of the legend.

Poking back into the beginnings of this legend, one finds evidence to show that it was at least partially created consciously by its hero and uncritically accepted by most of his contemporaries. The *editio princeps* of the legend is equally uncritical; in fact it is frankly an *apologia pro vita sua*. In his *Memoir of Eli Whitney*, Denison Olmstead gives us most of the elements of the legend and claims to have based his account upon conversations with those who knew Whitney, as well as upon examination of his correspondence and Miller's. Yet Blake writing in 1887 said: ". . . there have not been wanting persons who have endeavored to take from Mr. Whitney the credit of originating the uniformity system and making it a great practical success at the beginning of this century, thus leading in the van of progress of the mechanical arts, and laying the foundations for the enormous industry development of the nineteenth century." [1] Evidently some of his contemporaries were not taken in by Whitney's claims, but the scholars have not asked either who these other inventors were or what their contributions may have been. Let us examine the principal parts of this legend in some detail.

THE CONTRACT

Whitney's contract of June 14, 1798 to manufacture arms for the Federal Government is the focus of a number of elements of our legend. His mo-

* Reprinted from "The Legend of Eli Whitney and Interchangeable Parts" by Robert S. Woodbury, *Technology and Culture*, Vol. II, No. 1, 1960, pp. 235–53, by permission of The University of Chicago Press. Copyright 1961, Wayne State University Press.

[1] *New Haven Colony Historical Society Papers*, Vol. V, p. 123.

tives in this undertaking have been interpreted as those of a prudent business-man doing his patriotic duty and as those of a genius anxious to put into execution a new scheme of manufacture for the good of his country in a time of crisis. His actual motives were quite different.

In 1798 Miller and Whitney had lost all their suits to obtain their cotton gin patent rights in the courts of the South. What little legal merits these decisions had, stemmed from a defect in the Patent Law of 1793; clearly nothing further could be done until Congress corrected this defect. The efforts of Whitney and others did not finally result in a new patent law until 1800. The intervening years could be seen as a lull in the affairs of Miller and Whitney. But Whitney could hardly look forward to any relaxation, for their financial affairs were in desperate straits. Every source of credit had been exhausted by both partners. Certainly Whitney himself was on the verge of a nervous breakdown. Although some have tried to find in this situation a frustrated love for Catherine Greene, a more careful reading of his letter of October 7, 1797 to Miller indicates rather that Whitney's high hopes of financial security, respected position, and prestige have not only come crashing to the ground, but the disgrace of bankruptcy is staring him in the face. All that winter of 1797–98 Whitney brooded alone, half-heartedly carrying on the affairs of Miller and Whitney. He shut himself off from all his old friends and even unjustly accused his partner and friend Miller.

Whitney needed a new opportunity — any opportunity. But, more important, he needed credit — credit to save Miller and Whitney from bankruptcy, credit to enable him to fight for his rightful profit and for his good name lost in the cotton gin suits. When he heard that the Congress was "about making some appropriations for procuring Arms etc. for the U.S.," here was a heaven-sent opportunity.[2] This would at least keep his manufactory going until he could get his cotton gin rights. The opportunity was so great and Whitney's situation so desperate that he was willing to promise "ten or Fifteen Thousand stand of Arms," a fantastic proposal! Whitney even promised to begin delivering "in a short time" and he "will come forward to Philadelphia immediately. . . ." New hope for a desperate man!

Why was such a rash proposal not rejected at once by such prudent men as President Adams and Timothy Pickering, the Secretary of War? The failure of the Pinckney mission had caused public concern, and French privateers were rumored to be off the coast. Even Washington was called out of retirement to head the armed forces. On the 4th of May, 1798 Congress voted $800,000 for the purchase of cannon and small arms. When on the 24th of May Whitney arrived at the seat of government the plum was not only ripe and juicy but begging to be picked. Public sentiment was aroused, and the highest officials must do something — and that right promptly. Both sides could not close the contract quickly enough. Only the Purveyor of Public

[2] Whitney to Wolcott, May 1, 1798.

Supplies, Tench Coxe, seems to have kept his head — "I have my doubts about this matter and suspect that Mr. Whitney cannot perform as to time." ³ . . .

Certain features of the contract deserve closer examination. The legend makes much of the fact that the actual document was wholly handwritten. It says that all the other contractors of this time received printed contracts, and that there was therefore something special about Whitney's contract. Unfortunately an examination of the actual contracts, including Whitney's, in the National Archives shows that this was by no means the only handwritten contract — there were others, such as that of Owen Evans of Providence, Penn. The fact is that several of the early contracts were handwritten; the later contracts, mostly signed in September, were printed forms. These other contracts, printed or handwritten, were all identical in wording and provisions with Whitney's, except in the terms of the last paragraph. There *was* something special about Whitney's contract — it contained a paragraph six not included in any of the others. It was this paragraph that was crucial for Whitney. Having quickly sized up the situation in which the high officials found themselves, the shrewd Whitney saw his chance, consulted Baldwin as to the form of the contract should take, and at one stroke solved all his immediate problems. This paragraph reads:

> 6th. Five thousand dollars shall be advanced to the party of the second part on closing this contract, and on producing satisfactory evidence to the party of the first, that the said advance has been expended in making preparatory arrangements for the manufacture of arms, Five Thousand dollars more shall be advanced. No further advances shall be demanded until One thousand stands of Arms are ready for delivery, at which time the further sum of Five thousand dollars, shall be advanced. After the delivery of One thousand stands of arms, and the payment of the third advance as aforesaid, further advances shall be made at the discretion of the Secretary of the Treasury in proportion to the progress made in executing this contract. It is however understood and agreed by and between the parties to this instrument, that from time to time, whenever the party of the second part shall have the second thousand ready for delivery he shall be intitled to full payment for the same, so with respect to each and every Thousand until he shall have delivered the said Ten thousand stands.

Here was credit at last! Here was financial standing which assured further credit! Five thousand dollars at once, and five thousand more on terms which could be easily fulfilled by using his cotton gin laborers and machines. And assured payment for each thousand stands of arms upon delivery — to a total of $134,000. Little wonder that Whitney wrote to his friend Stebbins: "Bankruptcy and ruin were constantly staring me in the face and disappointment trip'd me up every step I attempted to take, I was miserable . . . Loaded with a Debt of 3 or 4000 Dollars, without resources, and without any

³ *The Report and Estimate of Tench Coxe, Purveyor of Public Supplies,* June 7, 1798.

business that would ever furnish me a support, I knew not which way to turn . . . By this contract I obtained some thousands of Dollars in advance which saved me from ruin." [4]

No wonder that in his eagerness to read paragraph six of the contract, Whitney evidently skimmed rapidly over the incredible terms of paragraph one. Whitney had contracted to deliver 4000 stands of arms by September 30, 1799, and 6000 more by September 30, 1800. Four thousand stands of arms in 15 months, from a factory yet to be built, and made by laborers as yet untrained, and by methods as yet unknown! And 6000 more in the following year! In his desperation Whitney had thrown all caution to the winds. He was no experienced manufacturer, as his deliveries of the relatively simple cotton gin indicate. He was aware that he knew nothing of arms making. And a prudent man would have expected at least some of the setbacks with which he fills his later letters to Wolcott, together with requests for further credit, contrary to the provisions of the contract. In short, despite his vague claims of new methods and what could be done by "Machinery moved by water," Whitney had only the vaguest idea of how he would actually fulfill the contract. He was not able to deliver even the first 500 muskets until September 26, 1801, and the contract was not actually completed until January 23, 1809. Further, the records of the Springfield Armory, now in the National Archives, show that even during the period 1815 to 1825, when his plant was fully established, Whitney never delivered muskets at the rate promised in his contract of 1798. . . .

It is true that the lull in the affairs of Miller and Whitney from 1798 to 1801, plus the credit advanced him by the federal government, did enable Whitney to devote most of his time in these years to make a beginning on fulfilling his arms contract, and by September of 1801 he did deliver the first 500 muskets. But from this initial delivery until 1807 there is no twelve-month period during which he delivered over 1000 muskets. During this same period he had been given advances from the Treasury such that he was constantly in debt to the United States. In fact, when Whitney finally completed delivery in January 1809 he received a payment of only $2450 as final settlement of the total contract of $134,000. Only on this date was his account up to date. The Whitney account in the Springfield Armory records also shows that in 1806 Whitney delivered 1500 muskets, in 1807 he delivered 2000, and in 1808 and the first few days of 1809 he delivered 1500. What is the explanation of these facts?

I do not wish to imply that Whitney was misrepresenting his troubles in his letters to Wolcott, Dexter, and Dearborn; but he most certainly was not telling the whole story, as his other correspondence clearly shows. In April 1800 the Congress revised the patent law which had been the legal means of defeating Whitney's claims to his cotton gin rights. Under the new law

[4] Whitney to Stebbins, Nov. 27, 1798.

Miller at once started suit against the principal offenders. The "lull" was over. But it became increasingly evident that justice would not be done Miller and Whitney in Georgia under any law. On September 4, 1801, Miller wrote to Whitney of a new possibility — their patent rights were to be purchased by the states legislatures. Here was a greater reward than Whitney could have dreamed of! Miller needs Whitney's help and his "contacts." Whitney can not wait and by November 22, 1801 is dating a letter to Stebbins: "Virginia Nineteen Miles North of the Northern line of North Carolina." He sees a chance that Miller and Whitney may get $100,000 from South Carolina alone for his rights — here was freedom from debt, assured financial security, and a credit reputation of the best. Better still, he will have the fame and prestige of a name officially cleared and full credit for his invention. Is it any wonder that a man of Whitney's ambitions and self-interest rushed off to Columbia and left the troubles and problems of arms manufacturing behind? Whitney had slaved and scrimped to get through Yale that he might become respected and financially secure. Now fortune beckoned, and the arms contract could wait.

From the fall of 1801 until Judge Johnson's decision of December 19, 1806 the ups and downs of cotton gin affairs were certainly far more important in Whitney's mind than the manufacture of arms. This can be definitely established simply by noting the places where Whitney's and others' letters show him to have been in this five-year period. The contents of his correspondence clearly establish a similar conclusion, as does the mere volume of the lawsuits in which Miller and Whitney were engaged. In the final settlement of the partnership in 1818 Whitney was allowed $11,000 for the expenses of six journeys South on these lawsuits. Certainly he was seldom attending full time to the arms manufactory at New Haven.

In short, from 1801 to 1806 Whitney not only failed to fulfill the contract, he regularly substituted long letters of excuse for honest effort to carry out his obligation, while he chased the richer prize of the rewards he expected from the cotton gin. In the light of these facts Dexter can hardly be blamed for his actions, and Jefferson's intervention seems hardly to have been in the interests of the government, whatever effect it may have had upon the future of American industry.

MANUFACTURE BY THE UNIFORMITY PRINCIPLE

The shortage of skilled artisans in the formative years of the American republic has been so often repeated as the source of Yankee mechanical ingenuity that it is now taken as axiomatic, without careful examination of the actual numbers as adequate for the needs of the day. The same axiom has served to "explain" Whitney's use of manufacture by interchangeable parts. In fact, Whitney so explains it himself. But let us look at the facts. The Springfield Armory was opened in 1794, and its payroll records from the beginning are to be found in the National Archives. By 1802 the Armory had

76 skilled armorers employed, and by 1814 it had 225. Although the figures for Harper's Ferry have not been preserved and we know it to have been substantially smaller than Springfield, we would be safe in assuming that Harper's Ferry had at least half this number of armorers. This total is impressive and seems hardly to indicate a scarcity of skilled armorers. In addition, we have the records of deliveries by other private contractors of arms to the Springfield Armory. During the whole period which concerns us, either the Springfield Armory, or Asa Waters of Sutton, Mass., or Lemuel Pomeroy of Pittsfield, Mass., delivered at least as many arms in each year as did Whitney. In fact Springfield manufactured 16,120 in the six years from 1795–1801, a much more impressive record than Whitney's 10,000 in ten and a half years. Both started from nothing. Leaving out of account the deliveries of the smaller manufacturers, Springfield, Waters, and Pomeroy certainly had an ample supply of armorers — or are we to believe that they too had the principle of interchangeable parts which Whitney claimed was unique in his establishment at New Haven?

But where did Whitney get his ideas for manufacture of arms on this new principle? He always claimed that it was his and his alone, and so the legend says, despite strong evidence to the contrary. There can be no doubt that prior to Whitney other men had actually used the principle of manufacture by interchangeable parts. In the 1720's Christopher Polhem, in Sweden, was manufacturing gears for clocks by using machinery and precision measurement to ensure interchangeability.[5] But there is no evidence that Whitney or anyone in the United States knew of Polhem's work, though it could have influenced Blanc in Europe.

The work of Blanc [sic] was clearly known to Thomas Jefferson; in fact our legend always includes a recital of his letter to John Jay in 1785 describing Blanc's work, and Jefferson's letter to Monroe of November 14, 1801, in which he points out that by 1801 Whitney had not developed the method as far as Blanc had in 1788. But the most amazing thing about the Whitney legend is the failure of scholars to follow up this clear lead to answer two questions of first importance: (1) Who was Blanc and what did he do? (2) Did Blanc's work have any influence upon Whitney?

The sources on Blanc are not only easily available, but are very detailed on his methods and results, for much of his work was done in French government arsenals and created controversies which were the subject of several official investigations and reports. Even a cursory examination of these sources would indicate that Whitney was far from being the first to introduce the principle of interchangeable parts in the manufacture of small arms. It is also quite clear that Blanc had carried the technique much further than we have any evidence of Whitney's doing. Furthermore, Blanc's *Mémoire* of 1790 shows a profound understanding of the nature and probable effects of interchangeable manufacture, of which Whitney had only the barest inkling.

[5] C. Polhem, *Patriotiska testamente* (1761).

Whitney's goal was only a system to use unskilled labor to increase output and reduce cost; whatever interchangeability he achieved was only a by-product of his method.

Blanc had problems to meet that Whitney never did. An entrenched officialdom and a threatened craft labor in long established government arsenals, together with the eclipse of the nascent industrial revolution in France under the Revolution and Napoleon, prevented a final fruition and spread of Blanc's ideas and methods in France and on the Continent.

But did the spark fly from Blanc to Whitney? A careful search in the correspondence of Whitney, Jefferson, Monroe, Jay, and Stiles indicates only that there were at least several paths by which it may very well have passed, of which the most likely is through Whitney's numerous conversations with Jefferson. But the only positive evidence seems to be a letter from Wolcott to Whitney dated 9 October 1798 in which he encloses ". . . a pamphlet on manufacture of arms . . . inform me freely and candidly whether the performance appears to you calculated to afford instructions to the workmen in this country. . . ." Whitney replied on 17 October 1798 that it was "misleading." Can this have been a copy of the report by le Roy on Blanc's *Mémoire* of 1790? We know that Jefferson was a regular subscriber to French publications, including the *Encyclopédie* as issued in parts. Did Jefferson's interest in Blanc in 1785 lead to receipt of this publication of the Académie des Sciences? And did he pass it on to Wolcott? One more bit of evidence remains. Writing to Wolcott on December 24, 1800, Whitney regrets that Wolcott does not have the leisure to examine "my whole plan and manner of executing the different branches of the work . . . to . . . compare them with the modes practiced in this and other Countries." Was Whitney actually familiar with the methods in use abroad, and if so, through what means? One must also admit that the language of many of Whitney's letters describing the merits of his methods are strangely reminiscent of Blanc's words. Yet we have nothing conclusive.

We must also ask whether Whitney's contemporaries in America may have influenced him, in particular the work being done at the Springfield Armory. It is most significant that after signing the contract in June 1798 Whitney had gone to Springfield to see their methods and to talk with the superintendent. And we have Whitney's letter in the summer of 1799 in which he had originally written "I might bribe workmen from Springfield to come to make me such tools as they have there." It is clear that Whitney was prepared to copy at least some of the methods already in use at Springfield. What were these machines? Unfortunately a fire in 1801 destroyed many of the records of the Springfield Armory, and the question cannot be answered fully. But we do have one official report [6] that gives clear indications that special machinery was in use by, at the latest, 1799: ". . . the artificers were employed for

[6] *Executive Documents, 6th Congress 1st Session,* January 7, 1800, "Springfield Armory," passim.

some time on the buildings, instead of on the manufactory, and in making the necessary pieces of machinery and tools. . . ." [If we take into account the difficulties of opening a new establishment, such as] "unsuccessful attempts in the proper construction of the machinery," [we should be satisfied with the present cost of muskets]. The report also uses such expressions as "The works now being complete, and labor-saving machines operating to great advantage . . . ," and ". . . improvements in the machinery and system for carrying on the manufactory."

That these improvements in the machines were effective is shown by the fact that in the month of September 1798 the Armory produced 80 muskets, but the following September 1799 it produced 442 muskets. This was accomplished with the same number of workers on the payroll. The report goes on to state that it had previously required 21 man-days to produce a musket; with the improved machinery only 9 man-days were needed. This at a time when Whitney had not yet delivered a single musket!

The later correspondence between Whitney and Roswell Lee, then superintendent at Springfield, although lacking technical details, strongly suggests that, contrary to Whitney's claims, at least a simultaneous development was going on. And there are patents, contracts, and accounts of Simeon North that strongly suggest that he, too, was using interchangeability in making his pistols as early as 1807.[7]

John Hall began work on his rifle designed to be made by interchangeable parts and on machinery to manufacture it prior to his patent of 1811 and was installing his methods and machines in the Harper's Ferry Armory by 1817. In 1827 Hall petitioned the government to give him adequate recompense for his contributions. This resulted in a series of commissions and investigations to establish the facts, by which he was finally compensated in 1840. The most significant for our purposes is one of 1827 — two years after Whitney's death.

> In making this examination our attention was directed, in the first place, for several days, to viewing the operations of the numerous machines which were exhibited to us by the inventor, John H. Hall. Captain Hall has formed and adopted a system of manufacture of small arms, *entirely novel*, and which, no doubt, may be attended with the most beneficial results to the country, especially if carried into effect on a large scale.
>
> His machines for this purpose . . . are used for cutting iron and steel, and for executing woodwork . . . and *differ materially from any other machines we have ever seen in any other establishment . . . By no other process known to us (and we have seen most, if not all, that are in use in the United States) could arms be made so exactly alike as to interchange . . .*[8]) [Italics mine.]

---

[7] See J. E. Hicks, *United States Ordnance* (Mount Vernon, N. Y., 1940), Vol. II, Chap. VII, where much of the material is reprinted.

[8] *Reports of Committees*, No. 375, 24th Congress, 1st Session (1836), John Hall Petition, Document Number 4, "Extracts from Report of Board of Commissioners to the Colonel of Ordnance in 1827 to examine the machinery," pp. 8–9.

All this can hardly be said to justify our legend's categorical statement "In every way Hall profitted by Whitney's work."

MANUFACTURE BY MACHINERY

We have thus far taken the term "manufacture by interchangeable parts" to have a clear meaning, based upon Blanc's, Whitney's, and Hall's dramatic demonstrations in assembling arms out of parts taken at random. This is a concept based upon characteristics of the product. It of course raises the question of how closely the parts must fit to be interchangeable. The usual answer is that the tolerances allowed must be sufficiently small for the product to work as designed and no more, since closer tolerances will merely increase cost. But this is rather vague. A more significant concept of interchangeable parts results from an examination of the actual methods by which such parts are produced. In this sense modern interchangeable parts require these elements: (1) precision machine tools, (2) precision gauges or other instruments of measurement, (3) uniformly accepted measurement standards, and (4) certain techniques of mechanical drawing. We do not, of course, expect Whitney to have all these elements, but we can estimate the contribution he may have made by comparing his work to them.

In what sense were the Whitney firearms interchangeable? A test of a number of known Whitney arms in at least one collection proved that they were *not* interchangeable in all their parts! In fact, in some respects they are not even approximately interchangeable! The answer to this paradox is to be found partly in the actual means of establishment of standards for their manufacture. Each of the contractors of 1798 (and the later contractors as well) was given two or three samples of the Charleville model of 1763, and his contract specified that these were to be followed exactly. This method meant that at best the output of one plant would be interchangeable, but the muskets of a given contractor would not necessarily be interchangeable with those of the other contractors. In short, our third and fourth elements of interchangeable parts — uniform standards of measurement, and working from adequately dimensioned drawings — were absent. In fact, they were not to appear for two more generations.

However, the first steps in this direction were to be taken by John Hall. Writing to Congress February 21, 1840, he says: "And so in manufacturing a limb of a gun so as to conform to a model, by shifting the points, as convenience requires, from which the work is *gauged* and executed; the slight variations are added to each other in the progress of the work, so as to prevent uniformity. The course which I adopted to avoid this difficulty was, *to perform and gauge every operation on a limb from one point,* called a bearing, so that the variation in any operation could only be the single one from that point." [9] [Italics mine.]

[9] *House Reports, No. 453, 26th Congress, 1st Session* (1840), John H. Hall Petition, U. S. Document 671, p, 6,

What about our second element — use of gauges? Polhem had used these, and so had Blanc. There is clear evidence that gauges were being used at the Springfield Armory by 1801. Hall certainly had used them extensively before he went to Harper's Ferry in 1817, but there is not the slightest evidence that Whitney ever did.

A number of visitors went through the Whitneyville plant in Whitney's lifetime. All were properly amazed, but none wrote an account which tells us what Whitney's actual methods were, except that there were "moulds" and "machines." By putting bits of information together, the "moulds" can be interpreted as what would today be called die forging; Blanc had clearly used this method. But "moulds" may also refer to filing jigs. The legend makes much of: (1) the numerous references by Whitney and others to his "machines," (2) the machine tools listed in the inventory made by Baldwin of Whitney's estate, and (3) Whitney's supposed invention of the milling machine.

Let us examine each of these in detail. First, we may ask what did the term "machine" mean in Whitney's day? It most certainly did not mean what it does today. It included a trip hammer and a water wheel, but it also meant almost any kind of device. What machines did Whitney actually employ? In this connection we have the letter of ten-year-old Philos Blake, Whitney's nephew, written after his visit in September 1801: "Thare is a drilling machine and a boureing machine to bour berels and a screw machine and too great large buildings, one nother shop and a stocking shop to stocking guns in, a blacksmith shop and a trip hammer shop and five hundred guns done." This is the only first-hand evidence we have of Whitney's machines at this time. Yet an official inspection of the Springfield Armory in January 1801 says the following: ". . . the number of Files required at the Factory being so great, some Water Machinery is now preparing which will diminish the demand of this expensive article." [10] Even more advanced machinery was used in the national armories by 1817.

Timothy Dwight, one of Whitney's visitors prior to 1823, says: "Machinery moved by water . . . is employed for hammering, cutting, turning, perforating, grinding, polishing, etc." [11] But by this time we have clear evidence that such machinery was in use at both Springfield and Harper's Ferry.

The list of machine tools in the inventory of Whitney's estate is detailed and tells us much about the tools he had in use at the time of his death in 1825, but lists nothing not already in use at Springfield and Harper's Ferry. In fact, the large number of files listed as on hand would suggest that for much of his work Whitney used only a filing jig or fixture to guide a hand operated file as his principal means of producing uniform parts for the locks of his muskets. But Polhem had done this two generations earlier. . . .

---

[10] Lt. Col. John Whiting, *Report on Inspection of Springfield Armories*, to Hon. William Eustis, Esq., Secretary of War, dated Boston, January 13, 1801. Report Number Two.

[11] T. Dwight, *Travels in New England and New York* (Edinburgh, 1823).

The legend includes one specific machine — the milling machine discovered in 1912 by Professor Joseph W. Roe of Yale, and now in the collection of the New Haven Colony Historical Society. It was identified by Eli Whitney's grandson of the same name as having been made by his grandfather and as the first one ever made. His authority for this identification was that he remembered having seen it as a boy and having been told this story by workmen in the old Whitneyville plant. Roe dated this machine as of 1818 merely because of a statement in the *Encyclopaedia Britannica* that "the first milling machine was made in a gun manufactory in 1818." All this hardly seems adequate evidence. The first reference we have to the use of milling by Whitney is in his letter to Calhoun of March 20, 1823. But by 1818 we have clear evidence that milling was in common use in both national armories, and by at least Robert Johnson and Lemuel Pomeroy of the private contractors.

In short, we really know practically nothing of what Whitney actually had in his manufactory at Mill Rock; what little we do know of was clearly not an innovation; and we have good evidence to show that all that Whitney claimed as his own contribution was at least independently innovated by others, particularly in the national armories. Whitney's claims of originality seem to have been the exact opposite of the truth. Certainly no one is justified in stating that Whitneyville was the site of "the birth of the machine tool industry," much less the birthplace, even in America, of manufacture by means of interchangeable parts.

"THE BIRTH OF AMERICAN TECHNOLOGY"

There can be no doubt that what became by the 1850's widely known abroad as the "American system of manufacturing" had its origin in this first quarter of the nineteenth century and that its principal features were developed in the northeastern section of the United States. The American system included mass manufacture, by power-driven machinery, by machinery especially designed to serve its particular purpose, and by the use of the principle of interchangeable parts.

The legend says that all this stems from Eli Whitney. We have seen enough to indicate that we actually know very little of what he really did; hence there is no clear beginning from which we can tell what later developed from Whitney's work. It is also clear that other men were working along these very lines in the manufacture of arms at the same time.

The legend also claims that from Whitney stemmed the application of the American system of manufacture to many light metal-working industries — Colt and his revolver, Jerome's clocks, Waltham watches, Yale's locks, Singer's sewing machines, and so on. Even if we knew exactly what Whitney did, there is little evidence to support this application of the-great-man-in-history hypothesis. About all that can be said is that further applications of interchangeable parts would *logically* seem to follow from Whitney's broad *claims*. But this is not the same as proof that Whitney actually had methods similar to those of later innovators, much less that they really did derive their ideas and methods from his. Certainly many other men contributed as much or more than Whitney, and evidence for their work can be found, far more convincing than Whitney's boasting claims. The legend says, for example, that the influence of Whitney was the basis of the Colt Armory methods of manufacture. In fact, it was E. K. Root who was the technical genius behind the manufacture of the Colt revolver, and his work stems directly from that of John Hall at Harper's Ferry. Whitney's influence on the manufacture of clocks, watches, and sewing machines is equally open to question.

We know so little of Whitney's actual methods of manufacture that his contribution to interchangeable parts is difficult to assess. What little we do know indicates, if anything, that Whitney was on the wrong track anyhow. John Hall's methods can be fairly clearly established, at least sufficiently for us to be sure that modern interchangeable manufacture derives far more from his inventive genius at Harper's Ferry than from Eli Whitney's manufactory at Mill Rock. Actually one is led to find the origins of the "American system of manufacturing" in the culmination of a number of economic, social, and technical forces brought to bear on manufacture by several men of genius, of whom Whitney can only be said to have been *perhaps* one.

CONCLUSION

This analysis of the Legend of Eli Whitney and Interchangeable Parts raises more questions than it answers. We have by no means arrived at the truth about the legend, much less about the advent of manufacture by interchangeable parts. However, I hope it is clear that the whole question needs re-examination — a more critical analysis of presuppositions and of the evidence which is known, and a more careful search for other sources.

But why not let this nice convenient legend go on? Were it Whitney alone that concerns us, that might be well enough. But the issue is larger than that. The history of our industrial growth is of first importance to the understanding of our American heritage. That industrial development cannot be properly understood without careful consideration of its technological basis. Therefore the true story of the "Birth of American Technology" is of prime concern to us. We should make certain that the baby is perfect and legitimate. □

37

Dr. Gesner's Kerosene:
The Start of American Oil Refining *

KENDALL BEATON

I

Oil historians commonly date the birth of the modern petroleum industry from an August afternoon in 1859 when E. L. Drake brought in a small, shallow oil well at Titusville, Pennsylvania. This relatively insignificant event led to the immediate start of a large and flourishing business for one reason only: the facilities to convert petroleum into a salable product already existed in substantial number, and the business of distributing that product to the customer had during the previous five years assumed the proportions of a substantial commerce. It was, indeed, the very profitability of this hydrocarbon oil trade that had led Drake's backers to seek out a "petroleum spring" in the back country of Pennsylvania and provide him with the funds to drill what was, for its day and depth, an expensive oil well.

By the fall of 1859, there were in this country at least 33 "coal-oil" refineries actively engaged in the manufacture of hydrocarbon illuminating oils that differed very little in chemical composition from the petroleum-based illuminants that would shortly displace them. By far the largest of these coal-oil works was the pioneer plant of the New York Kerosene Oil Works, located on the east bank of Newtown Creek in what is now the Borough of Queens. The Kerosene Works had first gone into operation five years earlier, in 1854, and was, at the time Drake completed his oil well, an enterprise of sufficient substance to command a lengthy notice in the New York *Commercial Advertiser*.[1]

Father of this enterprise, which others had been so quick to emulate, was Dr. Abraham Gesner, Nova Scotian by birth, and by turns physician, surgeon, naturalist, geologist, chemist, author, and inventor. . . . To evaluate the importance of Gesner's contribution in providing the push that started this new industry, we need to consider for a moment the state of the illuminating oil trade in the quarter century preceding 1850. For at least 200 years, whale oil had been considered the most satisfactory illuminant available. When burned in the circular-wick Argand lamp, the oil of the sperm whale gave off a fine, clear light. But as the supply of whales diminished and the American whaler found it necessary to go farther and farther in search of his prey, the price of whale oil began the steady climb that brought a temporary "golden

* Taken and adapted from Kendall Beaton, "Dr. Gesner's Kerosene: The Start of American Oil Refining," *Business History Review*, Vol. 29, March 1955, pp. 28–53. Used by permission.
[1] 24 Aug. 1859.

age" to the business of whaling — and concerted efforts on the part of others to find cheaper substitutes for whale oil.

By 1850, the oil of the sperm whale was fetching $2.00 to $2.50 a gallon and the inferior "whale oil" (made from the right whale) $.75 to $1.00. By the early 1800's — when Nantucket captains were erecting stately houses from the profits of a single whaling voyage — the average American householder was turning to lard oil on a large scale. Then, as early as 1825, came the first of the "artificial" hydrocarbon oils, manufactured from a wide range of materials: benzene (1825), a by-product of the new coal-gas works then just getting under way; "rosin oil" and "burning fluid," made from pine pitch and other resins; and camphene, a purified oil of turpentine, distilled over quicklime to free it from resin. Camphene had a tendency to smoke, unless it was burned in a lamp with a strong draft. In order to improve its burning properties and increase its supply, it was generally mixed with alcohol. The resultant mixture (also called camphene) was highly volatile, extremely inflammable, even explosive. To burn it with any degree of safety required a special lamp having two wicks and evaporation caps to cover them when not in use. Even with these drawbacks, camphene became a relatively popular illuminant in the years following 1830, as any antique collector can attest from the multitude of camphene lamps that were made and sold.

There was, obviously, room for a successor to camphene: a hydrocarbon oil that would burn with the brilliance and safety of whale oil, and yet sell for a fraction of whale oil's cost. Beyond doubt, many who left no records of their attempts must have brought forth and sold on a limited scale oils which they hoped would be cheaper, brighter, or less dangerous to use. A chief obstacle in the way of most of these would-be innovators was that they were "practical" men with little schooling and no knowledge of even the first principles of chemistry. Without such knowledge, their efforts were doomed to failure, for any of these oils needed to be "rectified" or "refined" to remove the objectionable substances that caused poor combustion and foul odors in burning. When, finally, satisfactory substitute oils did make their appearance just before the Civil War, they were the work of trained chemists.

Of prime importance in this collective groping for the right answer to a problem posed by economics (a process that seems to be repeated in the case of almost every innovation, as isolated men, working in ignorance of each other, proceed by similar routes to similar solutions) was the work of Dr. Gesner. He provided a satisfactory substitute for existing illuminants; he coined the name by which these oils would be known; and he set in motion the all-important example of a successful commercial venture. . . .

II

In March, 1853, Horatio Eagle, young partner of Eagle & Hazard, ship's agents and brokers, of 40 South Street, issued an eight-page circular entitled "Project for the Formation of a Company to Work the Combined Patent

Rights (for the State of New York) of Dr. Abraham Gesner, of Halifax, N.S., and the Right Hon. The Early of Dundonald, of Middlesex, England." In his prospectus, Eagle set forth some of the articles that the new company proposed to manufacture:

> The *material used* (Asphalte Rock) is an entirely new article of commerce, and is found in inexhaustible quantities in the Province of New Brunswick. Arrangements are being made to insure to the company a full and constant supply of the Rock.

> The *process* of manufacture (chiefly by dry distillation), and the method of extracting the fluids is peculiar, but at the same time very simple, requiring but few hands and no complex machinery.

> Among the various *products* obtained, may be enumerated Mineral Naphtha, Hydraulic Concrete, Burning Fluids, Mineral Tar and Pitch, and Railway Grease; — the whole native material, in fact, being employed for some useful purpose.

The pamphlet then went on to outline (with technical detail that is surprising when one considers that petroleum products would not be used for these purposes for some years yet) the uses of "Mineral Naphtha" as a solvent for India rubber and gutta-percha; the use of petroleum asphalt as a paving material for all manner of walks, roads, pavements, floors and gutter linings; as a waterproofing agent for rendering porous materials such as brick and wood water-tight; as a coating to prevent metals from rusting; and as a perfect insulating agent for telegraph wires run underground. This material would, the prospectus said, make an ideal paint and varnish (as indeed it has), a railway grease, and above all "burning fluids . . . which could be manufactured at a lower cost than the various burning fluids now most in use."

A ton of this "Asphalte Rock" from New Brunswick would make, according to an analysis which had been furnished by Dr. Gesner: 15 gallons of "Kerosine, or Burning Fluid," 15 gallons of "Mineral Naphtha," 5 gallons of railway grease, 880 pounds of "hydraulic concrete" (paving asphalt), 200 pounds of "Mineral Pitch" (semisolid asphalt suitable for paints and caulking), and undetermined amounts of paraffin, coke, gas ("used for lighting manufactory"), and ashes which, because of their ammonia content, were suitable for use as fertilizer.

Dr. Gesner estimated the value of one ton of this raw material at $5.00 and the value of its products, as they came from the still, at $43. To acquaint the New York investor with Dr. Gesner, a brief biographical sketch was appended, occupying a page. At the end of the prospectus, Eagle set forth that "Dr. Gesner's services (it may be as well to observe) have been secured to the company for a term of years, at a moderate salary. It is now proposed to form a Joint Stock Company (for working under the combined patents), of one hundred thousand dollars capital, to be divided into one thousand shares of one hundred dollars each." Specimens of the products to be made were on display at Eagle's office, where stock subscriptions would also be received. Eagle signed the circular as "Assignee of Patentees."

The name tentatively selected for the new company was the Asphalt Mining and Kerosene Gas Company. It was to this company that Gesner's patents were assigned when they finally issued from the patent office on 27 June 1854. The recital of the patents began "I, Abraham Gesner, late of the city and county of New York, now of Williamsburg, in the county of Kings, and State of New York, have invented and discovered a new and useful manufacture or composition of matter, being a new liquid hydrocarbon, which I denominate Kerosene, and which may be used for illuminating or other purposes . . . I obtain this product from petroleum, maltha, or soft mineral pitch, asphaltum, or bitumen wherever found, by dry distillation and subsequent treatment with powerful reagents and redistillation."

Gesner then went on to describe the physical properties of the Kerosene, which he dividede into three fractions: Kerosene "A," Kerosene "B," and Kerosene "C," one patent for each Kerosene. Kerosenes "A" and "B," from the descriptions he gives of them (weight, boiling point, inflammability) can be identified as the light and heavy fractions of what we today call gasoline.

Kerosene "C" offered the best commercial possibilities. "It is not very volatile or inflammable," Gesner wrote in his patent, "but in an Argand lamp, with a button over the wick, it burns with a brilliant white light without smoke or the naphthalous odor so offensive in many hydrocarbons having some resemblance to this but possessing very different properties." It was also "very good as a lubricant for machinery where it has been tried."

The balance of the patent was given over to a careful description of the distilling and treating process. After the liquid had been obtained by dry distillation in a closed retort, it had to be treated to remove undesirable impurities. This, Gesner accomplished by mixing it thoroughly with sulphuric acid, 5 per cent to 10 per cent the volume of the oil being treated, to remove any tars present. The purified oil was then washed with freshly calcined lime, about 2 per cent by volume, to absorb any water present and neutralize the effect of the acid. Following this treatment, the oil was redistilled. As a result of this careful processing, Gesner was able, as he pointed out in his patent, to refine an oil of superior burning qualities. It did not smoke, it burned without an odor, and with a good deal more brilliance than anything which had yet come to the market. His patent was well-drawn, covered the process and not merely the apparatus, and also included, for purposes of protecting it, the trade name which had been chosen — Kerosene.

We are fortunate to have uncovered a first-hand account by one of Dr. Gesner's relatives who was present at the christening of the new product. He tells us: "The writer, a near relative of the patentee, recalls the debate upon the name to be given to the new illuminating oil, and the reason why 'Kerosene' was decided upon. Paraffine, which occurred in the manufacture, has a waxy appearance, and was formerly called tar-wax and it was suggested that Greek words which signified 'wax-oil' might form a proper name. Therefore, *Keros*, wax, and *elain*, oil, were chosen. At that time, camphene, a compound of alcohol and spirits of turpentine, was in use as an illuminator, and it was decided to adopt its termination, the public being familiar with it, and accordingly *Kerosene*, instead of *Keroselain*, was decided upon."

By the time Dr. Gesner's patents were granted in June, 1854, the establishment of a works to make Kerosene, in accordance with the methods he had described, was already under way.

III

Until such time as the incorporation papers, account books, and correspondence of this enterprise turn up (an event which now seems highly unlikely), we shall not be able to say with certainty just who the incorporators of this first Kerosene company were, how much money they furnished to get it started or, indeed, exactly when the works began operation. From land records in the Queens County Register's Office at Jamaica, we learn that on 17 April 1854, Horatio Eagle, merchant, Erastus W. Smith, engineer, and Philo T. Ruggles, lawyer, all of New York, purchased from Neziah Bliss and Samuel Sneden of Greenpoint, a seven-acre tract on the east bank of Newtown Creek, in Queens County, for $17,500. Bliss and Sneden had only recently purchased the land from farmer George Kowenhoven and were busily laying out the development which they had named Blissville. The lots purchased for the site of the new plant were some 800 feet in depth with 327 feet of frontage on the navigable waters of Newtown Creek.

The new company was apparently then in the process of organization. Eagle, Smith, and Ruggles each held a third of the tract in their own names from 17 April until 1 May 1854, at which time they deeded the site, for the same price as they had paid, to the North American Kerosene Gas Light Company. Philo T. Ruggles (1803–1894) was a brother of the rich and famous Samuel B. Ruggles, the man who developed Gramercy Park. Though less well-known to posterity, Philo Ruggles was a prominent New York lawyer of his day, well-to-do in his own right, and was, at 51, in the prime of life. It is reasonable to assume that his interest and activity played an important part in enlisting financial support for the new North American Kerosene Gas Light Company.

The plan to include Dundonald's patents seems to have been dropped at this time, for no attempt was made to file Dundonald's British patents in the United States, and we encounter no further mention of Dundonald among the people in Gesner's circle. The new Kerosene Works on Newtown Creek was quite enough to keep Dr. Gesner and his friends fully occupied for the next several months. Gesner designed the buildings and equipment; Stillman & Allen, doing business as the Novelty Iron Works, foot of 12th Street and East River, fabricated the distilling apparatus to his specifications; the chemicals used to treat the product were supplied by Martin Kalbfleisch, of Bushwick; and the raw material was a cannel coal very similar to the Albert County mineral, from Dorchester, Westmoreland County, New Brunswick, across the bay from Albert County.

From engineers' drawings of the plant which have survived, we can appreciate Dr. Gesner's very real abilities as a practical manufacturing chemist. His plant was laid out in orderly fashion and the individual pieces of equipment, shown in detail drawings, were well planned and well constructed, differing very little from similar pieces of refinery equipment being built as late as the time of the First World War. For all his self-education, Gesner was far better grounded in the theoretical aspects of his business than were the long stream of "practical" refiners who would follow him and dominate the American oil refining business for the next half century.

One might anticipate that the new oil works would encounter technical difficulties in the initial months of operation. Dr. Gesner's son, George W., who was associated with him in the venture, tells us that this was, indeed, the case. We hear very little of the Kerosene Works during the next 12 months, although we can be fairly sure that it began operations in the first half of 1854. A large panoramic view of New York and Brooklyn, published as a supplement to the *Illustrated London News* for 24 November 1855, shows Newtown Creek in the far background, and dimly visible on the Queens bank of the creek are the quite impressive set of buildings of the new Kerosene Oil Works.

By early 1856 at least, the new company was issuing advertising circulars heralding the superior virtue of its product. One of these circular letters tells of extensive tests run in February, 1856, by independent chemists (the "scientific" advertising approach has changed little in a hundred years!) of all the main illuminants then sold in trade: Kerosene, Camphene, Sylvic Oil (a patent rosin oil), rapeseed oil, whale oil, lard oil, sperm oil, and "burning fluid." Kerosene, according to one of these examinations, produced a light 13 times brighter than Sylvic, Lard, and Whale Oils; 6 times as bright as sperm oil; 2½ times as bright as Camphene or rapeseed oil; 26 times as bright as "burning fluid"; and 4 times as bright as even that paragon of the age, the gas light.

An even more telling argument against the other illuminants was expense. Kerosene was then priced at $1.00 a gallon. Camphene ($.63), Sylvic oil ($.50), and "burning fluid" ($.87) were cheaper; the others (except for the oil of the right whale, priced at a dollar) were more expensive: lard oil was $1.25 a gallon, rapeseed oil, $1.50, and sperm oil, $2.25 a gallon. When these figures were reduced to an absolute "cost of an equal amount of light," the economy of Kerosene was impressive. To produce an equal amount of light with the lowly "burning fluid" cost more than seven times as much; with sperm oil, six times as much, with lard oil, four times as much; and so on down the scale. Even gas light was nearly double Kerosene in cost.

"In fact," the pamphlet concluded triumphantly, in an advertising claim destined to prove true, "no material has hitherto been offered to the public capable of producing such a light as Kerosene oil. It gives a better and more brilliant light than any other substance known, at less than one-half the cost of candles or camphene, . . . is extremely cleanly, gives no odor, will not congeal in any climate, and is perfectly safe in any hands. . . . In consequence of the economy and safety of its use, and brilliancy of the light which it emits, [it] must soon be used in every house in the country." [2]

Kerosene, although this may seem strange to us, also found a ready acceptance as a lubricating oil. Such a use for it was, really, not at all unusual, for the other commonly sold illuminants of the day, such as lard oil and whale oil, were normally used to lubricate all sorts of machinery. This early Kerosene circular contains two pages of testimonials from ships' engineers and newspaper pressmen who had words of high praise for Kerosene's properties as a lubricator. The company's New Orleans agents, B. Nautre & Co. (a connection established, no doubt, through Eagle who was ship's agent for New Orleans lines), seem to have been especially zealous in introducing the new oil to newspaper offices.

Following general practice of the time, the Kerosene Works placed its sales in the hands of a firm of selling agents rather than attempt to manage a sales force of its own. General sales agents for the new Kerosene Works were the brothers John H. and George W. Austen, who maintained a sales office at 50 Beaver Street, near Delmonico's corner. The Austen brothers, sons of a well-known New York merchant, were energetic in pushing Kerosene and contributed probably more than any other persons to the new company's commercial success. It was John Austen who introduced an inexpensive lamp for burning the new oil. Kerosene would, as Dr. Gesner had noted in his patent, burn well in an Argand lamp; but the Argand lamp, which had a tall glass chimney and a circular wick, like that of a present-day oil stove, was complicated, expensive, and confined to the well-to-do households able to afford sperm oil. Austen supplied the lack of a satisfactory inexpensive lamp by importing from Vienna a cheap, flat-wick lamp with glass chimney. In it, Kerosene burned cleanly and completely, without smoke or smell. This "Vienna burner," put upon the market as the "Kerosene lamp" by the Austens and their agents, was widely copied. In the ensuing decade, the U.S. Patent office granted literally hundreds of patents for "improvements" in the design of the Vienna burner; but its fundamental features, a flat wick and glass chimney, have never been improved.

This rash of activity in the lamp field is indicative of the success the new oils met once they began to catch on. Horatio Eagle's original prospectus of March, 1853, had confidently predicted the new illuminant would win out over all others; but one must not suppose that this victory was cheap or easy. A relative of Gesner recalled, "The new illuminating oil met with the strongest opposition from the turpentine and alcohol trades. Its odor, which was

---

[2] Gesner, *op. cit.*, p. 1.

not then so well removed as it was later on, gave those interested a weapon against its introduction, which at times seemed likely to be wielded fatally. After a time, however, its soft, steady light and perfect safety, in contrast with the poor light and fiery rays of camphene, gained it friends and enabled its manufacturers to make headway against all opposition." [3]

IV

But by this time (1856–1857), competitors were making their way upon the scene. The two of greatest size and interest were the plants of James Young at Bathgate, in Scotland, and of Samuel Downer, Jr., at South Boston. Both enterprises started out to manufacture lubricants, a class of materials for which there was urgent demand a century ago. The lubricants available in 1850 were natural oils like castor oil, or animal oils such as whale oil and lard. On slow-moving machinery they had been serviceable enough, but in the new high-speed steam-powered machinery such as power looms and steam printing presses, the heat of friction quickly broke down natural oils. Manufacturers (and railroads, too, for they had many of the same problems) were willing to try any lubricant and to pay fancy prices for ones that would work. In response to this demand, the hands of innumerable practical chemists were turned, in the years between 1845 and 1860, to the problem of producing artificial lubricants which would stand up better than natural oils. Most of the numerous patents for distilling or treating hydrocarbon substances taken out in England and America during these years (there were 12 in England in 1853 alone), were for the purpose of manufacturing lubricating oil, for it promised the largest financial rewards.

One of the patentees was James Young (1811–1883), an alert young Scotch chemist working in England who, in December, 1847, had had his attention called to a pretroleum "spring" producing about 300 gallons a day of crude oil in a coal mine at Riddings in Derbyshire. In September, 1848, Young and the mine owners organized a partnership to manufacture lubricants and industrial naphthas for use as solvents. Young theorized (incorrectly) that the crude oil had been formed by the effect of subterranean heat upon the coal deposit. This supposed reaction he set about reproducing in a laboratory in the hope that he could increase the small supply of crude oil available.

"I started an investigation," he later wrote, "with the prospect of procuring petroleum, or [a] substance equivalent to it, from coal and after some time succeeded. . . . The process consists in the distillation of coal at the lowest temperature at which it can be decomposed. By this process we obtain a mixture of several liquids with paraffin dissolved in them. This liquid I named paraffin oil." [4] In a British patent dated 17 October 1850 Young described his method; he filed the same patent in the United States and it was issued to him on 23 March 1852.

[3] *Engineering and Mining Journal, loc. cit.*
[4] Bailey, *loc. cit.*, p. 359.

In 1850–1851, Young moved to Bathgate, West Lothian, Scotland, to be near Torbane Hill, which contained a cannel coal rich in oil. Here, he and his partners, E. W. Binney and James Meldrum, built a large new "Paraffin Oil" works. E. M. Bailey, who wrote a careful account of Young's early work a few years ago from Young's own correspondence and diaries, tells us that the Bathgate works "at first manufactured naphtha and lubricating oil. Paraffin oil for burning and solid paraffin were not sold until 1856, and the demand for it only became considerable in 1859." [5]

This account ties in well with the recollections of Joshua Merrill, for many years superintendent of the Downer works in Boston. Samuel Downer, Jr., had been in the whale oil business in Boston for more than 20 years, building up an oil distributing and candle manufacturing business that was "one of the largest and most prosperous in the trade." [6] Early in the 1850's, Dr. Samuel R. Philbrick and the brothers Luther and William Atwood, manufacturing pharmaceutical chemists of Boston, had become interested in products that could be made by distilling the coal tar left over from the operation of gas works. During 1852, Luther Atwood, the best chemist of the three, succeeded in distilling from coal tar an oil which was, he felt, suitable for lubricating machinery. He christened it "Coup-Oil" in honor of Louis Napoleon's recent *coup d'état*, and applied for a patent which was issued 29 March 1853.

To manufacture their "Coup-Oil," Dr. Philbrick and the Atwoods organized the United States Chemical Manufacturing Co., with a plant at Waltham, Massachusetts. The business prospered indifferently; Downer was induced, about 1854, to buy an interest in it, and once in the company, discovered that its finances were in a sorry state. He paid up the company's debts and took over complete ownership of it, laying out for the purpose some $102,000. Downer retained Dr. Philbrick and the Atwoods in his employ, and they evolved a lubricating oil compounded of castor oil, "Coup-Oil," and animal fats. It had such a trenchant odor that 90 per cent of their customers could not be induced to order a second batch. Downer appeared to be on the verge of losing his investment, when a call from an unexpected quarter completely altered the course of events.

Dr. Philbrick received a letter from Geo. Miller & Co., of Glasgow, saying they wished to install the "Coup-Oil" process. Downer promptly dispatched Luther Atwood to Scotland where he remained a year, building and installing the apparatus. The Miller concern were also large producers of coal-tar naphthas which they sold as a solvent for dissolving rubber then being used for making mackintosh waterproof goods for the Crimean War. The Miller people had such a large demand for this rubber solvent that they bought naph-

---

[5] Young prospered because of his shrewd management and good patent position. He became wealthy, and a benefactor of scientific education and African missions. His best-known effort in the latter category was his financing of some of the expeditions of Dr. Livingstone. His firm, Young's Paraffin Light & Mineral Oil Co., Ltd., is still in existence, since 1919 a wholly owned subsidiary of Anglo-Iranian Oil Company.

[6] Merrill's account, *loc. cit.*, p. 890.

thas from other manufacturers, among them James Young's works. Atwood, an inveterate experimenter, took some of the naphtha from Young's works and by a little treatment made it into a water-white illuminating oil. Some of it was burning in a lamp in the Miller & Co. offices when Young happened in one day. Miller told him, "that is some of your brown Bathgate naphtha that our chemist has been manipulating and refining and this is a sample of the oil." According to Merrill, who witnessed the scene, Young discontinued the sale of his naphtha forthwith, and soon after began to manufacture and sell a paraffin illuminating oil.

Atwood and Merrill returned to Boston in October, 1856, convinced that Downer should begin manufacture of a similar illuminating oil. During 1857, they arranged to obtain supplies of Albert Coal for $25 a ton delivered in Boston, and using it as raw material, got into full-scale manufacture of the new "coal oil." The Downer Works' business went slowly at first but by March of 1859, Downer had a warehouse full of customers' empty cans waiting to be filled with "coal oil" at $1.35 to $1.40 a gallon, and had made a profit, after completely paying off the cost of the plant, of more than $100,000.

This mention of the chief competitors of the "Gesner Works" is for the purpose of showing that they began manufacture of coal-oil illuminants after the start of the Kerosene Works, not before, as several oil industry historians have stated.

V

Meanwhile, how was the Kerosene Works on Newtown Creek prospering? Pending discovery of actual corporate account books, we cannot say definitely, but there is every evidence that this pioneer plant prospered mightily. The Downer works in Boston, paying $25 a ton for its coals and having a daily capacity at the end of 1859, of 1,500 gallons, had cleared by the end of that year, well of $100,000. The Kerosene Company's plant on Newtown Creek had a capacity of 5,000 gallons a day by the end of 1859, more than three times the volume of Downer's plant. The New York works had some years earlier given up the New Brunswick source of coal supply, and instead imported Boghead Coal, from Young's mine on Torbane Hill, in Bathgate. During 1859, the Kerosene Company brought in 20,000 tons of this material at an average cost of $18 a ton, a full one-third less than Downer paid for his raw material. So with raw material costs a third less, and a gross throughput of more than three times the volume of the Downer plant, the Kerosene Company should have made a very handsome profit. It was in addition very favorably located as to markets, with the nation's largest consuming center in its own "front yard."

Some idea of the extent of the New York Kerosene Oil Company's [7] plant

[7] The Kerosene Works were being called by the simpler name, New York Kerosene Oil Co., early in 1859, although Gesner's 1861 book still refers to the company as the North American Kerosene Gas Light Co.

may be had from a descriptive article that appeared in the New York *Com-mercial Advertiser*, 24 August 1859, only three days before the completion of Drake's first oil well at Titusville.

> The land owned by this company is about fourteen acres, seven acres of which are covered with buildings and erections for the purpose of manufac-turing. They have built a bulkhead four hundred and ninety feet long, at which the lighters can discharge their cargo of coal and receive the oil for ship-ment. The Flushing Railroad passes through their grounds. Between the rail-road track and the creek are placed the "pipes," where the oil is extracted from the coal.

Following a detailed description of the distillation process and the under-ground oil storage facilities, the article continued:

> On the grounds back of the railroad are several buildings, where the oil undergoes a process of purification and distillation to purify it and fit it for market. It is then pure white in color, and free from smell or oily feeling. One of these buildings contains thirteen stills. Another building is being con-structed, and will be finished by the first of October, one hundred feet by fifty, to contain eight finishing stills. Still another building, now nearly finished, which is one hundred feet square, and divided into nine rooms, will contain a large number of stills; also two six thousand gallon tanks from which the oil will be drawn off, and barrelled ready for shipment. Other buildings near these are each used for the purpose of purifying the oil.
>
> A large engine house, twenty by fifty feet, and two stories in height, has recently been erected. . . . Attached to this building is a large boiler room with a chimney one hundred and thirty feet high; here are placed two steam boilers forty-two inches in diameter and sixty feet long. Each of these build-ings are fireproof and covered with slate. Two large iron cisterns are being built for this part of the grounds, capable of containing thirty-five thousand gallons each. The company are also about constructing a rail track from this part of the grounds to the docks to facilitate the carrying of oil from the re-fineries to the lighters. The track will be eight hundred feet long.
>
> These works are more extensive than any in this country. The company uses thirty thousand tons of coal per annum; this is unloaded at Greenpoint into canal boats and lighters and thence conveyed by means of the Newtown Creek to the dock. The amount of oil manufactured will average five thousand gal-lons a day for three hundred days in the year. The oil is sold for about one dollar and fifteen cents per gallon. About twelve thousand tons of coal are now on storage on the premises. There are about two hundred men constantly employed in the factories. About twenty-five men find constant employment in erecting buildings and putting up machinery. A coopers' shop is on the premises, where barrels are made and repaired. About one and a quarter mil-lions of dollars are invested in the manufacture.

In conclusion, the *Commercial Advertiser's* reporter detailed the salable prod-ucts then being manufactured, in addition to by-product gas which was flared because it was "at too great a distance from the city" for profitable sale.

These products were Kerosene; "another quality of oil called 'binnacle oil' manufactured for ships' use"; paraffin, which "makes a candle much superior to the spermaceti"; a naphtha called Kerosoline "used for extracting grease from silk, woolen or other fabrics"; and "a superior lubricating oil."

So obvious indeed was the success of these two pioneer firms, the Kerosene Works in New York and Downer in Boston, that a multitude of imitators sprang up during 1858 and 1859. These new oil works were generally staffed by men of little or no experience in oil distilling with the result that the oils they made were inferior in burning qualities and often (through the ignorant inclusion of the fractions we now call gasoline) downright dangerous. The term "coal oil" became an undependable buying guide. Downer, who felt this state of affairs the most, early in 1859 arranged with the Kerosene Co. to be allowed to license their product name, and to incorporate the word in the name of his works at Boston and his new plant at Portland. A trade-mark warning circular dated 28 March 1859 was published advising customers that Kerosene was the registered trade-mark of the New York, Boston, and Portland plants, and that oils made by others must not be called Kerosene.

It would be pleasant to record that Dr. Gesner made a comfortable fortune from the venture which was the child of his brain. This was not, however, the case. Unlike his competitors Young and Downer, Gesner was not a sole proprietor. From the outset he had been the company's salaried chemist; the probability is that he was also given a stock interest in exchange for his patent contributions, but we do not know for sure. Some time between 1856 and 1859, Luther Atwood replaced him as chief chemist of the Kerosene Co. Gesner's patents did not hold up in the courts because of Young's prior filing, and the Kerosene Works, along with Downer and other coal-oil manufacturers, was obliged to take a license and pay royalties to Young.

There was no disputing that it had been Gesner's energy, vision, and enthusiasm that had brought the Kerosene Works into being. But having presided over the birth of the new enterprise and seen it safely through its childhood diseases, he moved on, just as he did in the case of his human patients, to concern himself with other affairs. The city directories of New York and Brooklyn during the late 1850's and early 1860's show him practicing medicine from his home at 16 Bedford Avenue, Brooklyn, and also from an office at 24 William Street, New York. Three of his sons, Brower (1834–1874), John Frederick (1839–1899), and George Weltden (1829–1904), inherited their father's scientific interests and pursued the careers of geologists, mineralogists, chemists, and inventors. The city directory for 1859 shows George W. and Brower in the business of "oils," at 58 Cortlandt Street; and 1860–1861, Geo. W. and Henry as chemists at 24 William Street.

With new coal-oil works being built monthly during 1858–1859, the demand for technical advice was very brisk. Few except the Gesners were competent to supply it. In 1860, Dr. Gesner, reverting to his old role of author, sat down and composed an exhaustive, well-written, extremely lucid guidebook for these refiners, A *Practical Treatise on Coal, Petroleum and Other Distilled Oils*, published early in 1861 by Baillière Brothers of 440 Broadway. This book, 134 pages with illustrations, is remarkable for the sound scientific knowledge the author displayed and for the accuracy of his predictions on the future course the refining business would take. If he had done nothing else, Gesner's *Practical Treatise* would entitle him to a major niche in the early history of petroleum technology. He correctly foresaw that coal-oil refiners must utilize their by-products, if they were to meet the competition of the illuminating oils made from the new petroleum coming from Pennsylvania. He urged in his book that coal-oil refiners use their tar residues to make tar-paper roofing and combine their ammonia water (a by-product) with their waste sulphuric acid to make ammonium sulphate for fertilizer — suggestions which, unfortunately for the future of the coal-oil business, no one saw fit to heed.

To the new business, Dr. Gesner had contributed much, but he was too wise and too well-read to indulge in exaggerated claims. "The progress of discovery," he wrote modestly, "in this case, as in others, has been slow and gradual. It has been carried on by the labors, not of one mind, but of many, so as to render it difficult to discover to whom the greatest credit is due." [8] This was, as it were, his valedictory. Dr. Gesner returned to his native Nova Scotia in 1863, and settled in Halifax, where he was offered the chair of natural history at Dalhousie, but before he could take up these duties, he died, on 29 April 1864, in his sixty-seventh year.

The refining industry he had helped found lived on. The textbook which he had written for it (his son G. W. Gesner brought out a revision in 1865) was sold all over the world, translated into foreign languages and "adapted" by other authors for years to come. The coal-oil refineries, where they were reasonably well-managed, survived the change-over from coal to crude petroleum. The Kerosene Works on Newtown Creek became successively the New-York Kerosene Oil Company, Cozzens & Co., managers, 1863; Queens County Oil Works, R. W. Burke, Agent, 1869–1870; and finally in July, 1876, when the "Best Kerosene Oil" was being advertised at $.16 a gallon,[9] the pioneer Kerosene plant passed quietly into the possession of Chas. Pratt & Co., a subsidiary of the growing Standard Oil Company. Long before this, Dr. Gesner's "Kerosene" had ceased to be a proper noun and passed into the language where it still serves to perpetuate the memory of the hopeful man who with his new illuminant had helped make possible a "long and lasting holiday . . . for . . . the finny monsters of the sea." [10] □

[8] Gesner, *Practical Treatise* (1861), p. 11.
[9] Advertisement, Pratt's Astral Oil, Newtown *Register*, 6 July 1876, p. 1.
[10] Gesner, *Practical Treatise* (1861), p. 32.

38

International Capital Flows and the Development
of the American West *

DOUGLASS C. NORTH

I

. . . The argument of this paper is that surges in westward development were initiated by long-run favorable movements of the prices of key staple commodities. However, an increased supply of these staples could only be obtained by heavy capital expenditure in internal improvements and plantation development. Long-term foreign capital played an important role in meeting this need by directing real resources into the needed social overhead investment and making possible an import surplus of consumer and capital goods during these expansive periods.

A presentation limited to twenty minutes has required some drastic limitations in the scope of this paper. Accordingly, the time span is limited to the period 1820–1860 and the focus is primarily theoretical. In a paper of this length it is clearly impossible to present either the quantitative data or material evidence necessary to substantiate the relationships suggested here.

II

It was the special characteristics of the international economy and conditions in Europe that were critical in the opening up and development of the West, particularly in the first half of the nineteenth century. In the light of the historian's preoccupation with the pervasive influence of the frontier on American development, it perhaps needs stressing that the rate at which the West was developed was basically a function of (1) the changing characteristics of consumer demand in the English and European market, (2) the international mobility of capital and labor that made possible emigration from England, Ireland, and the Continent, and (3) the international flow of technological information, with the particular significance, insofar as this paper is concerned, of the development of the steam engine and its application to land and water transportation. A brief elaboration of the first two factors will serve to clarify their influence upon American development.

The changing characteristics of demand came about as a result of the continuing economic growth of English and European economies and concomitant expansion in population and income. Two factors were particularly significant for American development; they were the growth in cotton textile

* Taken and adapted from Douglass C. North, "International Capital Flows and the Development of the American West," *Journal of Economic History*, Vol. XVI, No. 4, December 1956, pp. 493–505. Used by permission.

manufacturing and the increasing per capita consumption of bread made from wheat flour (reflecting both a rise in income and a shift in taste from rye to wheat flour in leavened bread).

The unprecedented international movement of people appears to have reflected not only differential expectations as to income and employment between the country of emigration and immigration, but also differential expectations as among the alternative countries to which to immigrate. An additional contributing factor was the decline in shipping fares.

The international flow of capital was possible as a result of the earlier growth in income of England and European countries. An aspect of this growth that was important in this capital flow was the substantial income inequality and resultant large volume of savings concentrated in a small segment of the population and responsive to differential rates of return (discounted for risk).

The absence or reduction of government intervention in the movement of goods, people, and capital made the nineteenth century unique in history.

III

In a classic article written more than fifty years ago, G. S. Callender discussed the opening of the West in these terms: "By the opening of the West I do not mean the early settlement of the region west of the Mountains, which took place on a large scale during the thirty years after the Revolution. This in itself, as I shall attempt to show, had very little influence on the economic life of the Country. I refer rather to that improvement in the economic condition of the West which set in about the time of the second war with England, and which in a decade or two entirely changed the relationship of that region to the rest of the country. . . ." [1] The development of the West that Callender had in mind was not the subsistence agriculture of the early pioneer but that which came about as a result of a new region being able to produce goods in demand in existing markets at a cost competitive with alternative sources of supply. The essential requirements for this growth were (1) a market for primary goods and (2) rich land and resources that could be combined with the scarce productive factors of labor and capital to produce these goods at a comparable cost with alternative sources of supply. The limiting factor was the relative inaccessibility of the land and resources.

Under the nineteenth-century conditions of international mobility discussed above, capital and labor can be considered responsive on a world-wide basis to the quality and accessibility of land and resources. An examination of American internal expansion in the first 60 years of the nineteenth century in terms of these considerations will then make possible an assessment of the role of foreign capital in this western expansion.

In striking contrast to present times, the major market for goods in the first

[1] "The Early Transportation and Banking Enterprises of the State in Relation to the Growth of Corporations," *Quarterly Journal of Economics*, XVII (November 1902), 115.

part of the nineteenth century lay outside America. The changing character-istics of demand in the European market, and to a lesser extent in the West Indies, South American, and other external markets, affected fundamentally the fortunes of America. As far as the westward movement was concerned, it was primarily the demand for cotton and then wheat (and flour) that was critical.

It is difficult to exaggerate the role of cotton in American growth in the first half of the nineteenth century. Not only was it the major part of America's external trade, but it was also a fundamental factor influencing internal trade as well. The nature of the trade between the agricultural West and the South and the increasingly industrialized East has been described many times. The importance of this trade, insofar as this paper is concerned, lay in the de-pendence of the West upon cotton expansion in the South during the first half of the nineteenth century. Thus westward expansion during this period was primarily a function of expansion into land for cotton production in the South or into land in the western states capable of producing corn, hogs, and wheat (which would provide pork, lard, bacon, corn, cornmeal, flour, and whisky) to provision the South. While the West Indies, South America, and the eastern seaboard were markets for these staples, the expansion of the cotton South was the most critical determinant of the market for western pro-visions during the period from 1820 to 1850. Although this demand appears to have been somewhat income-inelastic and domestic trade fluctuated less violently than foreign trade, nevertheless the fortunes of the West were tied to the cotton trade.

As early as 1825, with the opening of the Erie Canal, the western trade along the Great Lakes and the northern areas bordering thereon had been di-verted to the East. While the Pennsylvania Canal furthered this east-west trade, it was not until the end of the 1840's that the basic pattern of trade changed. The growth of manufacturing and resultant urbanization in the New England and Middle Atlantic states substantially increased the demand for western staples. This expanded domestic demand was reinforced by in-creased foreign demand for wheat and flour. The rate of expansion of the West became increasingly dependent on the eastern and European market, and the rapid development of the 1850's in Minnesota, Iowa, Michigan, Illi-nois, Wisconsin, and Missouri reflected primarily this expansion in demand for foodstuffs.

Although the development of both the Southwest and Northwest associ-ated with this expanding demand for staple commodities was a continuous process, the pace of the westward movement varied significantly. There were notable surges in this expansion, followed by periods of assimilation in which the pace was markedly slower. Thus the early 1820's, following the land boom of 1818–1819, was a period of slower expansion: there was a gradual acceleration of the tempo in the late 1820's and early 1830's, culminating in the surge of 1835 to 1839. The early years of the 1840's paralleled the 1820's and then gradually the pace quickened and culminated in a sharp surge between 1854 and 1856. The pace was sharply reduced in the intervening years before the Civil War.

An explanation of these surges of expansion is clearly to be found in the expected profitability of western lands. It was the expected return upon cotton in the Southwest and upon the wheat, corn, and hogs (and the manufactures thereof) in the Northwest that was the most fundamental factor affecting the pace of western development. It was actual or anticipated prices of these staple commodities that exercised the most decisive influence. If we take the volume of public land sales as the measure of western development, then we may note a close correlation between the price of cotton on the one hand and the volume of public land sales in the five southern states of Alabama, Louisiana, Mississippi, Arkansas, and Florida on the other hand. A similar correlation exists between the price of wheat (and corn) and public land sales in the seven western states of Ohio, Illinois, Indiana, Michigan, Iowa, Wisconsin, and Missouri. Since the price of cotton on the one hand and of wheat, corn, and provisions on the other did not always move together, although the long-run movements were roughly parallel as indicated above, it is not surprising that accelerated westward movement was at times associated more with the Southwest than the Northwest and vice versa. Thus, while the price of cotton drifted down throughout most of the 1820's, the price of wheat improved after 1827, and the sales of western land in Ohio, Indiana, Illinois, and Michigan picked up markedly after the middle of the 1820's. Cotton prices began to rise after 1832, and only thereafter did public land sales in the southern states increase significantly. Similarly while cotton prices were depressed throughout most of the 1840's, wheat prices improved, and western land sales expanded from the middle forties. Finally, the boom period of the 1850's was primarily associated with the Northwest in which the rising price of wheat and corn was paralleled by a tremendous land boom, whereas cotton prices and land sales in the Southwest increased very moderately.

While the very sharp increases and subsequent declines in prices from 1835 to 1839 and from 1854 to 1857 reflected the speculative boom that overlaid each expansive period, the underlying real factors affecting these price movements were the character of shifts in demand and supply for these commodities. Shifts in demand appear by and large to have been more uniform, reflecting increased demand for cotton textiles and, in the American South and East, fairly steady growth in demand for provisions. Yet there are notable exceptions, such as the expansion in demand for wheat with the Irish famine, which was a critical influence resulting in the rise in wheat prices and the accompanying land expansion in the Northwest in the mid-forties. Moreover, the periods of expansion were accompanied by rising incomes leading to increased demand for consumption goods, once the boom was under way. This rise was reinforced in the 1850's by the volume of immigration. However, it was primarily the response of supply that led to these long-run price movements. The increased supply of these primary commodities was a function of accessibility in the Northwest and of both accessibility and the necessary outlays for land, slaves, clearing the land, buildings, and getting the crop planted in the cotton South. The capital expenditures necessary for transport facilities in the Northwest and for both transport and plantation development in the Southwest were high. In consequence it is not surprising that supply did not shift smoothly with demand. Rather it moved irregularly in spurts, resulting in relative overexpansion, followed by consequent lengthy periods of depressed prices until the gradual increase in demand caught up. This was followed by slowly rising prices which induced another period of accelerated westward expansion and development of new lands.

There were two factors responsible for the radical shifts in supply that took place. The first is inherent in the nature of transport developments to make new land accessible. The opening up of a canal or making a river navigable in the 1830's or the construction of a western railroad in the 1850's did not gradually open up new land but made land available in vast amounts where it had heretofore been simply inaccessible for commercial production.

The second factor involved in the shifts in supply resulted from the impetus of rising prices of these key commodities upon the capital market. The optimism engendered by these favorable price movements in the context of the special characteristics of the banking system and the supply of international capital led to a vast expansion of investment in internal improvements and plantation development during these periods of extensive development.

IV

It should be clear from the preceding discussion that the role of international capital was not in initiating these surges in expansion. The previous analysis suggests that movements in the prices of key staple commodities were the most important impetus in these surges of expansion. Foreign capital, however, did play a vital role in making possible each expansion and in its duration and character. The importance of foreign capital lay in directing real resources into transportation and plantation expansion and sustaining this expansion by making possible an import surplus.

Although there are significant differences in the character of capital inflows in the 1830's as compared with the 1850's the influence upon the balance of trade in each case was similar. In both expansive periods the volume of foreign trade increased substantially and the United States incurred an import surplus typical of a young debtor nation. The increase in imports in the 1830's was in part in capital goods but primarily in consumption goods, with a substantial expansion in the imports of luxury goods. In the 1850's, as one would expect, the import of capital goods, particularly railroad iron, played a far more important part, although there was a significant increase in consumption goods.

Initial expansion in the late 1820's and middle 1840's was at a moderate pace and took place with little rise in prices because of the unemployed and underemployed resources available. Once the expansion had begun, the actual or anticipated development of internal improvements implied a reduction in transfer costs. This made it possible for vast new areas to market their commodities and therefore further to accelerate the westward movement and demand for land. Bank expansion played the most significant role in supplying capital, and foreign investment was selective and limited. The significant flow of foreign funds came later as a result of the increased opportunities associated with each expansive period. These opportunities were associated not only with the favorable prospects of the significant staple commodities but also with the regional expansion that would result from the concomitant development of new cotton areas in the South or new areas producing provisions in the Northwest. The necessary growth of facilities to market these commodities, as well as of those to supply the local needs of planters or settlers in new areas, led to a construction boom. In turn this expansion reacted back upon the East in expanded demand for goods and services, particularly for English imports.

It was the inflow of capital during each expansive period that enabled the expansion to be sustained for a number of years rather than its merely erupting into an inflationary spiral and collapse. Although bank expansion initially provided capital for the crucial investment in transport and plantation expansion that could open up and develop new lands, it was capital inflows that maintained the expansion by permitting a level of imports of consumption goods and capital goods without deterioration of foreign exchanges.

Thus the period from 1830 through 1834 was characterized by a slow but persistent rise in commodity prices, an acceleration in the pace of internal improvements in the West, and an increase in the note issue of state banks from 61 million dollars in 1830 to 103 million dollars in 1835. It was a period of real expansion interrupted only by the interval of contraction by the Second Bank of the United States during Biddle's struggle with Jackson. The bonds issued by the several states in order to build canals in the North or to finance expansion of cotton production in the South found their way for the most part into the hands of English holders of securities. During this period approximately 40 million dollars of American state securities were purchased abroad. At the same time the United States incurred an import surplus of merchandise trade as well as net specie imports of approximately 20 million dollars.

After 1834 the pace increased and was overlaid with speculation, aided and abetted by the uninhibited expansion of the state banks and the policies of the Jacksonian administration. More than 107 million dollars in state securities went abroad and the states pursued an unrestrained expansion in internal improvements, with their bonds finding a ready market among English investors. With the economy already at full employment, the effect was to shift labor out of agriculture and other activities and into construction of canals and other internal improvement. This redirection of productive factors out of consumer goods into social overhead investment was partially offset by the increased importation of consumer goods made possible by English capital. However, the expanded consumer demand associated with rising aggregate income inevitably led to rapidly rising prices. The result was ultimate collapse, yet the extraordinary era between 1835 and 1839 is too often dismissed as one of wild and unproductive speculation without recognizing that substantial real expansion took place during these years. Although land sales were mostly to speculators for resale rather than cultivation, nevertheless this was a part of the process by which land ultimately got in the hands of cultivators and by which the West was developed. Moreover, despite the many half-completed projects that were abandoned in the early 1840's, transport development and plantation expansion had made possible a large increase in the supply of cotton and wheat.

If foreign capital had sustained the boom of the 1830's, the lack of it helped to extend the depressed years of the 1840's. During a number of these years the United States had an export surplus when securities were being returned from Europe and interest payments on existing debt were a significant, if not always honored, obligation. The marked regional differences in economic well-being during the early forties lent support to the arguments presented above. The severely depressed price of cotton and western staples reflected the tremendous increase in supply resulting from the previous expansive era. In contrast, industrial prices in the East declined less severely. The dependence of western expansion upon foreign capital was reflected in almost a cessation of internal improvements. In contrast, railroad construction in the East was significant and, while western railroad and bank stocks were severely depressed, those of the New England area declined only moderately.

The gradual westward expansion that began in the mid-1840's was associated more with the Northwest and wheat than with the Southwest and cotton. The impetus was not only the extraordinary foreign demand for wheat in 1847 but the steady growth in demand by the increasingly urbanized East, reinforced by the first great wave of transatlantic migration that went on from the mid-1840's to 1860 and had its peak from 1849 to 1854. As in the earlier period, initial expansion was mostly effected by domestic capital, with selective purchase of railroad securities by German investors. Beginning in 1850, the United States incurred a large import surplus and a substantial volume of railroad securities went abroad.

Immigration of capital and labor was a prominent feature of the real expansion that took place between 1849 and 1854. Both factors played an important part in the railroad development of the period, providing the additional labor and capital necessary without too significant a redirection of resources from other parts of the domestic economy. The import surplus of consumption goods again provided a cushion against rapid inflation. In addition, the large volume of railroad iron brought in directly contributed to the boom. Railroad mileage tripled from 1849 to 1856. Most of this increase was in the West or in lines connecting the East with the West.

While there is no doubt that the capital inflow during this period was a valuable contributing factor to the extensive expansion of the country, it did not play as important a part as it had in the 1830's. The large volume of gold exports from California, together with the earnings of the merchant marine, were more significant credit items than earlier in balancing the import surplus of the United States. This was particularly true after the advent of the Crimean War. While railroad securities sold abroad may have totaled as much as $160 to 200 million for the decade, the composition of our balance of payments would indicate that most of the purchases after 1854 represented a shift out of mercantile credit rather than a net addition to our aggregate indebtedness. Gold exports alone were sufficient to balance the import surplus of the United States.

While the speculative boom from 1854 to 1857 in some respects paralleled the earlier one, the peak in land sales occurred in 1855–1856. The increase in the supply of wheat had been so substantial that despite record exports the price of wheat was already declining in 1856, and the land boom in the seven western states was over well before the crisis of 1857.

V

This paper has been concerned with the pace of westward development and the influence of the international economy, and particularly the supply of long-term capital, upon that development in the years from 1820 to 1860. The long-run impetus in this economic development was the expanding demand for certain staple commodities in the European and domestic market. The surges in westward expansion were the processes by which the supply of these commodities adjusted to this increasing demand. With the rich quality of the seemingly endless land available in western America, the essential requirement was for social overhead investment to make this land accessible. Although the initial impetus in each period of rapid extensive development was provided by the issuance of bank notes, foreign capital played the important role of directing real resources into the needed social overhead investment and of sustaining an import surplus of consumer and capital goods which made possible the prolonged periods of rapid development. □

✧ **39** ✧

The Land Act of 1796 *

■ An Act providing for the Sale of the Lands of the United
States, in the territory northwest of the river Ohio, and above
the mouth of Kentucky river.

SEC. 2. *Be it further enacted,* That the part of the said lands, which has not
been already conveyed by letters patent, or divided, in pursuance of an ordinance in Congress, passed on the twentieth of May, one thousand seven hundred and eighty-five, or which has not been heretofore, and during the present
session of Congress may not be appropriated for satisfying military land boun-
ties, and for other purposes, shall be divided by north and south lines run according to the true meridian, and by others crossing them at right angles, so
as to form townships of six miles square, unless where the line of the late Indian purchase, or of tracts of land heretofore surveyed or patented, or the
course of navigable rivers may render it impracticable; . . .
SEC. 4. *Be it further enacted,* That whenever seven ranges of townships shall
have been surveyed below the Great Miami, or between the Sciota river and
the Ohio company's purchase, or between the southern boundary of the
Connecticut claims and the ranges already laid off, beginning upon the Ohio
river and extending westwardly, and the plats thereof made and transmitted,
in conformity to the provisions of this act, the said sections of six hundred and
forty acres (excluding those hereby reserved) shall be offered for sale, at
public vendue, under the direction of the governor or secretary of the western
territory, and the Surveyor General: such of them as lie below the Great
Miami shall be sold at Cincinnati; those of them which lie between the
Sciota and the Ohio company's purchase, at Pittsburg; and those between
the Connecticut claim and the seven ranges, at Pittsburg. And the townships remaining undivided shall be offered for sale, in the same manner, at the
seat of government of the United States, under the direction of the Secretary
of the Treasury, in tracts of one quarter of a township lying at the corners
thereof, excluding the four central sections, and the other reservations before
mentioned: *Provided always,* that no part of the lands directed by this act to
be offered for sale, shall be sold for less than two dollars per acre. . . . □

* Taken and adapted from "The Land Act of 1796," *U.S. Statutes at Large,* Vol. I,
pp. 464 ff.

McCulloch v. Maryland (1819) *

Mr. Chief Justice Marshall delivered the opinion of the Court.

In the case now to be determined, the defendant, a sovereign State, denies the obligation of a law enacted by the legislature of the Union, and the plaintiff, on his part, contests the validity of an act which has been passed by the legislature of that State. The constitution of our country, in its most interesting and vital parts, is to be considered; the conflicting powers of the government of the Union and of its members, as marked in that constitution, are to be discussed; and an opinion given, which may essentially influence the great operations of government.

. . . The first question made in the cause is, has Congress power to incorporate a bank? . . .

The government of the United States, . . . though limited in its powers, is supreme; and its laws, when made in pursuance of the Constitution, form the supreme law of the land, "any thing in the Constitution or laws of any State to the contrary notwithstanding."

Among the enumerated powers, we do not find that of establishing a bank or creating a corporation. But there is no phrase in the instrument which, like the Articles of Confederation, excludes incidental or implied powers; and which requires that every thing granted shall be expressly and minutely described. Even the Tenth Amendment, which was framed for the purpose of quieting the excessive jealousies which had been excited, omits the word "expressly," and declares only that the powers "not delegated to the United States, nor prohibited to the States, are reserved to the States or to the people"; thus leaving the question, whether the particular power which may become the subject of contest has been delegated to the one government, or prohibited to the other, to depend on a fair construction of the whole instrument. . . . The men who drew and adopted this amendment had experienced the embarrassments resulting from the insertion of this word in the Articles of Confederation, and probably omitted it to avoid those embarrassments. A constitution, to contain an accurate detail of all the subdivisions of which its great powers will admit, and of all the means by which they may be carried into execution, would partake of the prolixity of a legal code, and could scarcely be embraced by the human mind. It would probably never be understood by the public. Its nature, therefore, requires that only its great outlines should be marked, its important objects designated, and the minor ingredients which compose those objects be deduced from the nature of the objects themselves. That this idea was entertained by the framers of the

* Taken and adapted from "McCulloch v. Maryland," 4 Wheaton 316; 4 L. Ed. 579 (1819).

American Constitution is not only to be inferred from the nature of the instrument, but from the language. Why else were some of the limitations, found in the ninth section of the first article, introduced? . . . considering this question, then, we must never forget that it is a *constitution* we are expounding.

Although, among the enumerated powers of government, we do not find the word "bank" or "incorporation," we find the great powers to lay and collect taxes; to borrow money; to regulate commerce; to declare and conduct a war; and to raise and support armies and navies. The sword and the purse, all the external relations, and no inconsiderable portion of the industry of the nation, are entrusted to its government. It can never be pretended that these vast powers draw after them others of inferior importance, merely because they are inferior. . . .

. . . But the Constitution of the United States has not left the right of Congress to employ the necessary means for the execution of the powers conferred on the government to general reasoning. To its enumeration of powers is added that of making "all laws which shall be necessary and proper, for carrying into execution the foregoing powers, and all other powers vested by this Constitution, in the government of the United States, or in any department thereof." . . .

We admit, as all must admit, that the powers of the government are limited, and that its limits are not to be transcended. But we think the sound construction of the Constitution must allow to the national legislature that discretion, with respect to the means by which the powers it confers are to be carried into execution, which will able that body to perform the high duties assigned to it, in the manner most beneficial to the people. Let the end be legitimate, let it be within the scope of the Constitution, and all means which are appropriate, which are plainly adapted to that end, which are not prohibited, but consist with the letter and spirit of the Constitution, are constitutional.

. . . the choice of means implies a right to choose a national bank in preference to State banks, and Congress alone can make the election.

After the most deliberate consideration, it is the unanimous and decided opinion of this Court that the act to incorporate the Bank of the United States is a law made in pursuance of the Constitution, and is a part of the supreme law of the land. . . .

It being the opinion of the Court that the act incorporating the bank is constitutional; and that the power of establishing a branch in the State of Maryland might be properly exercised by the bank itself, we proceed to inquire —

2. Whether the State of Maryland may, without violating the Constitution, tax that branch?

That the power of taxation is one of vital importance; that it is retained by the States; that it is not abridged by the grant of a similar power to the government of the Union; that it is to be concurrently exercised by the two governments; are truths which have never been denied. But such is that paramount character of the Constitution that its capacity to withdraw any subject from the action of even this power is admitted. The States are expressly forbidden to lay any duties on imports or exports, except what may be absolutely necessary for executing their inspection laws. If the obligation of this prohibition must be conceded — if it may restrain a State from the exercise of its taxing power on imports and exports; the same paramount character would seem to restrain, as it certainly may restrain a State from the exercise of its taxing power on imports and exports; the same paramount character would seem to restrain, as it certainly may restrain a State from such other exercise of this power as is in its nature incompatible with, and repugnant to, the constitutional laws of the Union.

. . . That the power to tax involves the power to destroy; that the power to destroy may defeat and render useless the power to create; that there is a plain repugnance in conferring on one government a power to control the constitutional measures of another, which other, with respect to those very measures, is declared to be supreme over that which exerts the control, are propositions not to be denied. . . .

. . . (T)he States have no power, by taxation or otherwise, to retard, impede, burden, or in any manner control, the operations of the constitutional laws enacted by Congress to carry into execution the powers vested in the general government. This is, we think, the unavoidable consequence of that supremacy which the Constitution has declared.

We are unanimously of opinion, that the law passed by the legislature of Maryland imposing a tax on the Bank of the United States is unconstitutional and void. . . . □

[DOCUMENT] ❖ **41** ❖

The Trustees of Dartmouth College v. Woodward (1819) *

The opinion of the Court was delivered by Mr. Chief Justice Marshall.

. . . It can require no argument to prove that the circumstances of this case constitute a contract. An application is made to the Crown for a charter to incorporate a religious and literary institution. In the application, it is stated that large contributions have been made for the object, which will be conferred on the corporation, as soon as it shall be created. The charter is granted, and on its faith the property is conveyed. Surely in this transaction every ingredient of a complete and legitimate contract is to be found.

* Taken and adapted from "The Trustees of Dartmouth College v. Woodward" (Marshall opinion), 4 Wheaton 518; 4 L. Ed. 629 (1819).

The points for consideration are,

1. Is this contract protected by the Constitution of the United States?
2. Is it impaired by the acts under which the defendant holds?

1. On the first point it has been argued, that the word "contract," in its broadest sense, would comprehend the political relations between the government and its citizens, would extend to offices held within a State for State purposes, and to many of those laws concerning civil institutions which must change with circumstances, and be modified by ordinary legislation; which deeply concern the public, and which, to preserve good government, the public judgment must control. That even marriage is a contract, and its obligations are affected by the laws respecting divorces. . . . Taken in its broad unlimited sense, the clause would be an unprofitable and vexatious interference with the internal concerns of a State, would unnecessarily and unwisely embarrass its legislation, and render immutable those civil institutions which are established for purposes of internal government, and which, to subserve those purposes, ought to vary with varying circumstances. That as the framers of the Constitution could never have intended to insert in that instrument a provision so unnecessary, so mischievous, and so repugant to its general spirit, the term "contract" must be understood in a more limited sense. . . . anterior to the formation of the Constitution, a course of legislation had prevailed in many, if not in all, of the States, which weakened the confidence of man in a faithful performance of engagements. To correct this mischief, by restraining the power which produced it, the State legislatures were forbidden "to pass any law impairing the obligation of contracts," that is, of contracts respecting property, under which some individual could claim a right to something beneficial to himself; and that since the clause in the Constitution must in construction receive some limitation, it may be confined, and ought to be confined, to cases of this description; to cases within the mischief it was intended to remedy.

The general correctness of these observations cannot be controverted. That the framers of the Constitution did not intend to restrain the States in the regulation of their civil institutions, adopted for internal government, and that the instrument they have given us is not to be so construed, may be admitted. The provision of the Constitution never has been understood to embrace other contracts than those which respect property, or some object of value, and confer rights which may be asserted in a court of justice. It never has been understood to restrict the general right of the legislature to legislate on the subject of divorces. Those acts enable some tribunal, not to impair a marriage contract, but to liberate one of the parties because it has been broken by the other. When any State legislature shall pass an act annulling all marriage contracts, or allowing either party to annul it without the consent of the other, it will be time enough to inquire whether such an act be constitutional. . . .

Whence, then, can be derived the idea that Dartmouth College has become a public institution, and its trustees public officers. . . . Not from the source whence its funds were drawn; for its foundation is purely private and eleemosynary. Not from the application of those funds; for money may be given for education, and the persons receiving it do not, by being employed in the education of youth, become members of the civil government. Is it from the act of incorporation? Let this subject be considered.

A corporation is an artificial being, invisible, intangible, and existing only in contemplation of law. Being the mere creature of law, it possesses only those properties which the charter of its creation confers upon it, either expressly, or as incidental to its very existence. These are such as are supposed best calculated to effect the object for which it was created. Among the most important are immortality, and, if the expression may be allowed, individuality; properties, by which a perpetual succession of many persons are considered as the same, and may act as a single individual. They enable a corporation to manage its own affairs, and to hold property without the perplexing intricacies, the hazardous and endless necessity, of perpetual conveyances for the purpose of transmitting it from hand to hand. It is chiefly for the purpose of clothing bodies of men, in succession, with these qualities and capacities, that corporations were invented, and are in use. By these means, a perpetual succession of individuals are capable of acting for the promotion of the particular object, like one immortal being. . . .

(I)t appears, that Dartmouth College is an eleemosynary institution, incorporated for the purpose of perpetuating the application of the bounty of the donors, to the specified objects of that bounty; that its trustees or governors were originally named by the founder, and invested with the power of perpetuating themselves; that they are not public officers, nor is it a civil institution, participating in the administration of government; but a charity school, or a seminary of education, incorporated for the preservation of its property, and the perpetual application of that property to the objects of its creation. . . .

This is plainly a contract to which the donors, the trustees, and the Crown (to whose rights and obligations New-Hampshire succeeds) were the original parties. It is a contract made on a valuable consideration. It is a contract for the security and disposition of property. It is a contract, on the faith of which, real and personal estate has been conveyed to the corporation. It is then a contract within the letter of the Constitution, and within its spirit also. . . .

The opinion of the Court, after mature deliberation, is that this is a contract, the obligation of which cannot be impaired without violating the Constitution of the United States. This opinion appears to us to be equally supported by reason, and by the former decisions of this Court.

2. We next proceed to the inquiry, whether its obligation has been impaired by those acts of the legislature of New-Hampshire, to which the special verdict refers. . . .

The obligations then, which were created by the charter to Dartmouth College, were the same in the new, that they had been in the old government. The power of the government was also the same. A repeal of this charter at any time prior to the adoption of the present constitution of the United States would have been an extraordinary and unprecedented act of power, but one which could have been contested only by the restrictions upon the legislature to be found in the constitution of the State. But the Constitution of the United States had imposed this additional limitation, that the legislature of a State shall pass no act "impairing the obligation of contracts."

It has been already stated, that the act "to amend the charter, and enlarge and improve the corporation of Dartmouth College," increases the number of trustees to twenty-one, gives the appointment of the additional members to the executive of the state, and creates a board of overseers, to consist of twenty-five persons, of whom twenty-one are also appointed by the executive of New-Hampshire, who have power to inspect and control the most important acts of the trustees.

On the effect of this law, two opinions cannot be entertained. Between acting directly, and acting through the agency of trustees and overseers, no essential difference is perceived. The whole power of governing the college is transferred from trustees appointed according to the will of the founder, expressed in the charter, to the executive of New-Hampshire. The management and application of the funds of this eleemosynary institution, which are placed by the donors in the hands of trustees named in the charter, and empowered to perpetuate themselves, are placed by this act under the control of the government of the State. The will of the State is substituted for the will of the donors in every essential operation of the college. . . . The charter of 1769 exists no longer. It is reorganized; and reorganized in such a manner as to convert a literary institution, moulded according to the will of its founders, and placed under the control of private literary men, into a machine entirely subservient to the will of government. This may be for the advantage of literature in general; but it is not according to the will of the donors, and is subversive of that contract, on the faith of which their property was given. . . .

It results from this opinion, that the acts of the legislature of New-Hampshire, which are stated in the special verdict found in this cause, are repugnant to the Constitution of the United States; and that the judgment on this special verdict ought to have been for the plaintiffs. The judgment of the State Court must, therefore, be reversed.

(Mr. Justice Washington and Mr. Justice Story delivered separate concurring opinions. Mr. Justice Duvall dissented.) □

The Trustees of Dartmouth College v. Woodward (1819) *

Justice Story concurred in the opinion of Chief Justice Marshall, the following passages being of special importance to economic historians.

. . . A bank, whose stock is owned by private persons, is a private corporation, although it is erected by the government, and its objects and operations partake of a public nature. The same doctrine may be affirmed of insurance, canal, bridge, and turnpike companies. In all these cases, the uses may, in a certain sense, be called public but the corporations are private; as much so, indeed, as if the franchises were vested in a single person.

. . . When, then, the argument assumes, that because the charity is public, it manifestly confounds the popular with the strictly legal sense of the terms. And if it stopped here, it would not be very material to correct the error. But it is on this foundation that a superstructure is erected which is to compel a surrender of the cause. When the corporation is said at the bar to be public, it is not merely meant that the whole community may be the proper objects of the bounty, but that the government have the sole right, as trustees of the public interests, to regulate, control, and direct the corporation, and its funds and its franchises, at its own good will and pleasure. Now, such an authority does not exist in the government, except where the corporation is in the strictest sense public; that is, where its whole interests and franchises are the exclusive property and domain of the government itself. . . .

Thus far, the rights of the corporation itself, in respect to its property and franchises, have been more immediately considered. But there are other rights and privileges belonging to the trustees collectively, and severally, which are deserving of notice. They are entrusted with the exclusive power to manage the funds, to choose the officers, and to regulate the corporate concerns, according to their own discretion. The *jus patronatus* is vested in them. The visitatorial power, in its most enlarged extent, also belongs to them. When this power devolves upon the founder of a charity, it is an hereditament, descendible in perpetuity to his heirs, and in default of heirs, it escheats to the government.[1] It is a valuable right founded in property, as much so as the right of patronage in any other case. It is a right which partakes of a judicial nature. May not the founder as justly contract for the possession of this right in return for his endowment, as for any other equivalent? and, if instead of holding it as an hereditament, he assigns it in perpetuity to the trustees of the corporation, is it less a valuable hereditament in their hands? The right is not merely a collective right in all the trustees; each of them also has a franchise in it. Lord Holt says, "it is agreeable to

---

* Taken and adapted from "The Trustees of Dartmouth College v. Woodward" (Story opinion), 4 Wheaton 518; 4 L. Ed. 669 (1819).
[1] Rex v. St. Catherine's Hall, 4 T. R. 233.

reason, and the rules of law, that a franchise should be vested in the corporation aggregate, and yet the benefit redound to the particular members, and be enjoyed by them in their private capacities. Where the privilege of election is used by particular persons, it is a particular right vested in each particular man." [2] Each of the trustees had a right to vote in all elections. If obstructed in the exercise of it, the law furnished him with an adequate recompense in damages. If ousted unlawfully from his office, the law would, by a mandamus, compel a restoration. □

[DOCUMENT] ✧ **43** ✧

The Land Law of 1820 *

■ An act making further provision for the sale of the public lands.

Be it enacted by the Senate and House of Representatives of the United States of America, in Congress assembled, That from and after the first day of July next, all the public lands of the United States, the sale of which is, or may be authorized by law, shall, when offered at public sale, to the highest bidder, be offered in half quarter sections; and when offered at private sale, may be purchased, at the option of the purchaser, either in entire sections, half sections, quarter sections, or half quarter sections; . . .

SEC. 2. *And be it further enacted,* That credit shall not be allowed for the purchase money on the sale of any of the public lands which shall be sold after the first day of July next, but every purchaser of land sold at public sale thereafter, shall, on the day of purchase, make complete payment therefore; . . .

SEC. 3. *And be it further enacted,* That from and after the first day of July next, the price at which the public lands shall be offered for sale, shall be one dollar and twenty-five cents an acre; and at every public sale, the highest bidder, who shall make payment as aforesaid, shall be the purchaser; but no land shall be sold, either at public or private sale, for a less price than one dollar and twenty-five cents an acre; and all the public lands which shall have been offered at public sale before the first day of July next, and which shall then remain unsold, as well as the lands that shall thereafter be offered at public sale, according to law, and remain unsold at the close of such public sales, shall be subject to be sold at private sale, by entry at the land office, at one dollar and twenty-five cents an acre, to be paid at the time of making such entry as aforesaid . . . □

---

[2] Ashby v. White, 2 *Ld. Raym.* 938. 952. Attorney General v. Dixie, 13 *Ves.* 519.

* Taken and adapted from "The Land Law of 1820" (April 24, 1820), *U. S. Statutes at Large,* Vol. 3 (1850), 17th Congress, 1st Session, Ch. 51, pp. 566–67.

Pre-emption Act of 1841 *

■ An Act to appropriate the proceeds of the sales of public lands
and to grant pre-emption rights.

SEC. 8. That there shall be granted to each State . . . five hundred thousand
acres of land for . . . internal improvements. *Provided,* that to each of the
States which has already received grants for said purposes, there is hereby
granted no more than a quantity of land which shall, together with the
amount said State has already received . . . made five hundred thousand
acres. . . .
SEC. 9. . . . That the net proceeds of the sale of said lands shall be faithfully applied to objects of internal improvement . . . namely, roads, railways, bridges, canals and improvement of water-courses, and draining of
swamps. . . .
SEC. 10. That from and after the passage of this act, every . . . man, over the
age of twenty-one years, and being a citizens of the United States, or having
filed his declaration of intention to become a citizen . . . who since the first
day of June, A.D. eighteen hundred and forty, has made . . . a settlement in
person on the public lands to which the Indian title had been . . . extinguished, and which . . . shall have been surveyed prior thereto, and who
shall inhabit and improve the same, and who . . . shall erect a dwelling
thereon, . . . is hereby, authorized to enter with . . . the land office . . .
by legal subdivisions, any number of acres not exceeding one hundred and
sixty, or a quarter section of land, . . . upon paying to the United States the
minimum price of such land, subject, however, to the following limitations
and exceptions: No person shall be entitled to more than one pre-emptive
right by virtue of this act; no person who is the proprietor of three hundred
and twenty acres of land in any State or Territory of the United States, and
no person who shall quit or abandon his residence on his own land to reside
on the public land in the same State or Territory, shall acquire any right of
pre-emption under this act; no lands included in any reservation . . . no
lands reserved for the support of schools, nor the lands . . . to which the
title has been or may be extinguished by the United States at any time during
the operation of this act; no sections of land reserved to the United States
alternate to other sections granted to any of the States for the construction of
any canal, railroad, or other . . . public improvement; no sections . . . included within the limits of any incorporated town; no portions of the public
lands which have been selected as the site for a city or town; no parcel or lot
of land actually settled and occupied for the purposes of trade and not agri-

* Taken and adapted from "Pre-emption Act of 1841" (September 4, 1841), *U.S.
Statutes at Large,* Vol. V, p. 453 ff.

culture; and no lands on which are situated any known salines or mines, shall be liable to entry under and by virtue of the provisions of this act. . . .

SEC. 11. That when two or more persons shall have settled on the same quarter section of land, the right of pre-emption shall be in him or her who made the first settlement, provided such persons shall conform to the other provisions of this act; and all questions as to the right of pre-emption arising between different settlers shall be settled by the register and receiver of the district within which the land is situated, subject to an appeal to and a revision by the Secretary of the Treasury of the United States. . . . ▢

[DOCUMENT]   ❖ **45** ❖

Gibbons v. Ogden (1824) *

MR. CHIEF JUSTICE MARSHALL delivered the opinion of the Court.

This instrument (the Constitution) contains an enumeration of powers expressly granted by the people to their government. It has been said that these powers ought to be construed strictly. But why ought they to be so construed? Is there one sentence in the Constitution which gives countenance to this rule? In the last of the enumerated powers, that which grants, expressly, the means for carrying all others into execution, Congress is authorized "to make all laws which shall be necessary and proper" for the purpose. But this limitation on the means which may be used is not extended to the powers which are conferred; nor is there one sentence in the Constitution, which has been pointed out by the gentlemen of the bar, or which we have been able to discern that prescribes this rule. We do not, therefore, think ourselves justified in adopting it. What do gentlemen mean by a strict construction? If they contend only against that enlarged construction which would extend words beyond their natural and obvious import, we might question the application of the term, but should not controvert the principle. If they contend for that narrow construction which, in support of some theory not to be found in the Constitution, would deny to the government those powers which the words of the grant, as usually understood, import, and which are consistent with the general views and objects of the instrument; for that narrow construction, which would cripple the government, and render it unequal to the objects for which it is declared to be instituted, and to which the powers given, as fairly understood, render it competent; then we cannot perceive the propriety of this strict construction, nor adopt it as the rule by which the Constitution is to be expounded. As men whose intentions require no concealment generally employ the words which most directly and aptly express the ideas they intend to convey, the enlightened patriots who framed our Constitution, and the people who adopted it, must be understood to have

* Taken and adapted from "Gibbons v. Ogden," 9 Wheaton 1; 6 L. Ed. 23 (1824).

employed words in their natural sense, and to have intended what they have said. . . .

The words are: "Congress shall have power to regulate commerce with foreign nations, and among the several States, and with the Indian tribes."

The subject to be regulated is commerce; and our Constitution being, as was aptly said at the bar, one of enumeration and not of definition, to ascertain the extent of the power it becomes necessary to settle the meaning of the word. The counsel for the appellee would limit it to traffic, to buying and selling, or the interchange of commodities, and do not admit that it comprehends navigation. This would restrict a general term, applicable to many objects, to one of its significations. Commerce, undoubtedly, is traffic, but it is something more: it is intercourse. It describes the commercial intercourse between nations, and parts of nations, in all its branches, and is regulated by prescribing rules for carrying on that intercourse. The mind can scarcely conceive a system for regulating commerce between nations which shall exclude all laws concerning navigation, which shall be silent on the admission of the vessels of one nation into the ports of the other, and be confined to prescribing rules for the conduct of individuals in the actual employment of buying and selling, or of barter. . . .

. . . The power over commerce, including navigation, was one of the primary objects for which the people of America adopted their government, and must have been contemplated in forming it. The convention must have used the word in that sense, because all have understood it in that sense; and the attempt to restrict it comes too late. . . .

To what commerce does this power extend? The Constitution informs us, to commerce "with the foreign nations, and among the several States, and with the Indian tribes."

It has, we believe, been universally admitted, that these words comprehend every species of commercial intercourse between the United States and foreign nations. No sort of trade can be carried on between this country and any other, to which this power does not extend. It has been truly said that commerce, as the word is used in the Constitution, is a unit, every part of which is indicated by the term. . . .

The subject to which the power is next applied is to commerce "among the several States." The word "among" means intermingled with. A thing which is among others, is intermingled with them. Commerce among the States cannot stop at the external boundary line of each State, but may be introduced into the interior.

It is not intended to say that these words comprehend that commerce which is completely internal, which is carried on between man and man in a State, or between different parts of the same State, and which does not extend to or affect other States. Such a power would be inconvenient, and is certainly unnecessary.

Comprehensive as the word "among" is, it may very properly be restricted to that commerce which concerns more States than one. . . . The completely internal commerce of a State, then, may be considered as reserved for the State itself.

But, in regulating commerce with foreign nations, the power of Congress does not stop at the jurisdictional lines of the several States. It would be a very useless power if it could not pass those lines. The commerce of the United States with foreign nations is that of the whole United States. Every district has a right to participate in it. The deep streams which penetrate our country in every direction pass through the interior of almost every State in the Union, and furnish the means of exercising this right. If Congress has the power to regulate it, that power must be exercised whenever the subject exists. If it exists within the States, if a foreign voyage may commence or terminate at a port within a State, then the power of Congress may be exercised within a State.

This principle is, if possible, still more clear when applied to commerce "among the several States." They either join each other, in which case they are separated by a mathematical line, or they are remote from each other, in which case other States lie between them. What is commerce "among" them; and how is it to be conducted? Can a trading expedition between two adjoining States commence and terminate outside of each? And if the trading intercourse be between two States remote from each other, must it not commence in one, terminate in the other, and probably pass through a third? Commerce among the States must, of necessity, be commerce with the States. In the regulation of trade with the Indian tribes, the action of the law, especially when the Constitution was made, was chiefly within a State. The power of Congress, then, whatever it may be, must be exercised within the territorial jurisdiction of the several States.

. . . We are now arrived at the inquiry — What is this power?

It is the power to regulate; that is, to prescribe the rule by which commerce is to be governed. This power, like all others vested in Congress, is complete in itself, may be exercised to its utmost extent, and acknowledges no limitations other than are prescribed in the Constitution. . . .

The power of Congress, then, comprehends navigation within the limits of every State in the Union; so far as that navigation may be, in any manner, connected with " commerce with foreign nations, or among the several States, or with the Indiana tribes." It may, of consequence, pass the jurisdictional line of New York, and act upon the very waters to which the prohibition now under consideration applies. . . .

Although Congress cannot enable a State to legislate, Congress may adopt the provisions of a State on any subject. When the government of the Union was brought into existence, it found a system for the regulation of its pilots in full force in every State. The act which has been mentioned adopts this system and gives it the same validity as if its provisions had been specially made by Congress. But the act, it may be said, is prospective also, and the adoption of laws to be made in future, presupposes the right in the maker to legislate on the subject.

The act unquestionably manifests an intention to leave this subject entirely to the States, until Congress should think proper to interpose; but the very enactment of such a law indicates an opinion that it was necessary; that the existing system would not be applicable to the new state of things unless expressly applied to it by Congress. . . .

Since, however, in exercising the power of regulating their own purely internal affairs, whether of trading or police, the States may sometimes enact laws, the validity of which depends on their interfering with, and being contrary to, an act of Congress passed in pursuance of the Constitution, the Court will enter upon the inquiry, whether the laws of New York, as expounded by the highest tribunal of that State, have, in their application to this case, come into collision with an act of Congress, and deprived a citizen of a right to which that act entitles him. Should this collision exist, it will be immaterial whether those laws were passed in virtue of a concurrent power "to regulate commerce with foreign nations and among the several States" or in virtue of a power to regulate their domestic trade and police. In one case and the other, the acts of New York must yield to the law of Congress; and the decision sustaining the privilege they confer, against a right given by a law of the Union, must be erroneous.

This opinion . . . is founded as well on the nature of the government as on the words of the Constitution. . . .

But the framers of our Constitution foresaw this state of things, and provided for it by declaring the supremacy not only of itself, but of the laws made in pursuance of it. The nullity of any act inconsistent with the Constitution is produced by the declaration that the Constitution is the supreme law. The appropriate application of that part of the clause which confers the same supremacy on laws and treaties, is to such acts of the State Legislatures as do not transcend their powers, but, though enacted in the execution of acknowledged State powers, interfere with or are contrary to the laws of Congress, made in pursuance of the Constitution, or some treaty made under the authority of the United States. In every such case, the act of Congress, or the treaty, is supreme; and the law of the State, though enacted in the exercise of powers not controverted, must yield to it. . . .

But all inquiry into this subject seems to the Court to be put completely at rest by the act already mentioned, entitled, "An act for the enrolling and licensing of steam boats."

This act authorizes a steam boat employed, or intended to be employed, only in a river or bay of the United States, owned wholly or in part by an alien, resident within the United States, to be enrolled and licensed as if the same belonged to a citizen of the United States.

This act demonstrates the opinion of Congress that steam boats may be enrolled and licensed in common with vessels using sails. They are, of course, entitled to the same privileges, and can no more be restrained from navigating waters, and entering ports which are free to such vessels, than if they were wafted on their voyage by winds instead of being propelled by the agency of fire. The one element may be as legitimately used as the other for every commercial purpose authorized by the laws of the Union; and the act of a State inhibiting the use of either to any vessel having a license under the act of Congress comes, we think in direct collision with that act.

As this decides the cause, it is unnecessary to enter in an examination of that part of the Constitution which empowers Congress to promote the progress of science and the useful arts.

Reversed.

(MR. JUSTICE JOHNSON concurred on the ground that the power of Congress over interstate commerce was intended to be exclusive and that the licensing act did not affect the case.) □

[DOCUMENT]   ❖ **46** ❖

Andrew Jackson's Attitude Toward the Bank in 1829 *

■ *Message of the President to Both Houses of Congress at the commencement of the First Session of the Twenty first Congress, December 8, 1829.*

The charter of the Bank of the United States expires in 1836, and its stockholders will most probably apply for a renewal of their privileges. In order to avoid the evils resulting from precipitancy in a measure involving such important principles, and such deep pecuniary interests, I feel that I cannot, in justice to the parties interested, too soon present it to the deliberate consideration of the Legislature and the People. ⌐Both the constitutionality and the expediency of the law creating this bank, are well questioned by a large portion of our fellow citizens; and it must be admitted by all, that it has failed in the great end of establishing a uniform and sound currency.⌐

Under these circumstances, if such an institution is deemed essential to the fiscal operations of the Government, I submit to the wisdom of the Legislature, whether a National one, founded upon the credit of the Government, and its revenues, might not be devised, which would avoid all constitutional difficulties, and, at the same time, secure all the advantages to the Government and country that were expected to result from the present Bank. □

* Taken from James M. Rix, J. F. Brown, and William White, *Messages of General Andrew Jackson* (Boston: Otis Broaders & Co., 1837), p. 67.

Jackson's Veto of the Bank Bill (1832) *

To the Senate:

The bill "to modify and continue" the act entitled "An act to incorporate the subscribers to the Bank of the United States" was presented to me on the 4th July instant. Having considered it with that solemn regard to the principles of the Constitution which the day was calculated to inspire, and come to the conclusion that it ought not to become a law, I herewith return it to the Senate, in which it originated, with my objections.

. . . Every monopoly and all exclusive privileges are granted at the expense of the public, which ought to receive a fair equivalent. The many millions which this act proposes to bestow on the stockholders of the existing bank must come directly or indirectly out of the earnings of the American people. It is due to them, therefore, if their Government sell monopolies and exclusive privileges, that they should at least exact for them as much as they are worth in open market. . . .

It is not conceivable how the present stockholders can have any claim to the special favor of the Government. The present corporation has enjoyed its monopoly during the period stipulated in the original contract. If we must have such a corporation, why should not the Government sell out the whole stock and thus secure to the people the full market value of the privileges granted? . . .

The bank is professedly established as an agent of the executive branch of the Government, and its constitutionality is maintained on that ground. Neither upon the propriety of present action nor upon the provisions of this act was the Executive consulted. It has had no opportunity to say that it neither needs nor wants an agent clothed with such powers and favored by such exemptions. There is nothing in its legitimate functions which makes it necessary or proper. Whatever interest or influence, whether public or private, has given birth to this act, it can not be found either in the wishes or necessities of the executive department, by which present action is deemed premature, and the powers conferred upon its agent not only unnecessary, but dangerous to the Government and country.

It is to be regretted that the rich and powerful too often bend the acts of government to their selfish purposes. Distinctions in society will always exist under every just government. Equality of talents, of education, or of wealth can not be produced by human institutions. . . . but when the laws undertake to add to these natural and just advantages artificial distinctions, to grant titles, gratuities, and exclusive privileges, to make the rich richer and the po-

---

* Taken from James D. Richardson, *Messages and Papers of the Presidents,* Vol. II, (Washington, D.C.: Government Printing Office, 1896), pp. 576–91.

tent powerful, the humble members of society — the farmers, mechanics, and laborers — who have neither the time nor the means of securing like favors to themselves, have a right to complain of the injustice of their Government. There are no necessary evils in government. Its evils exist only in its abuses. If it would confine itself to equal protection, and, as Heaven does its rains, shower its favors alike on the high and the low, the rich and poor, it would be an unqualified blessing. In the act before me there seems to be a wide and unnecessary departure from these just principles. . . . ☐

[DOCUMENT] ◇ **48** ◇

Commonwealth v. Hunt (1842) *

CHIEF JUSTICE LEMUEL SHAW delivered the opinion of the Court.

. . . Stripped then of these introductory recitals and alleged injurious consequences, and of the qualifying epithets attached to the facts, the averment is this; that the defendants and others formed themselves into a society, and agreed not to work for any person, who should employ any journeyman or other person, not a member of such society, after notice given him to discharge such workman.

The manifest intent of the association is, to induce all those engaged in the same occupation to become members of it. Such a purpose is not unlawful. . . .

Nor can we perceive that the objects of this association, whatever they may have been, were to be attained by criminal means. The means which they proposed to employ, as averred in this count, and which, as we are now to presume, were established by the proof, were, that they would not work for a person, who, after due notice, should employ a journeyman not a member of their society. Supposing the object of the association to be laudable and lawful, or at least not unlawful, are these means criminal? The case supposes that these persons are not bound by contract, but free to work for whom they please, or not to work, if they so prefer. In this state of things, we cannot perceive, that it is criminal for men to agree together to exercise their own acknowledged rights, in such a manner as best to subserve their own interests. . . . ☐

* Taken and adapted from "Commonwealth v. Hunt," (March, 1842), *Massachusetts Reports,* Vol. 45, 4 Metcalf III.

Coinage Act of 1837 *

■ An Act supplementary to the act entitled "An act establishing a mint, and regulating the coins of the United States."

Be it enacted by the Senate and House of Representatives of the United States of America in Congress assembled, That the officers of the mint of the United States shall be a director, a treasurer, an assayer, a melter and refiner, a chief coiner and an engraver, to be appointed by the President of the United States, by and with the advice and consent of the Senate. . . .

SEC. 8. *And be it further enacted,* That the standard for both gold and silver coins of the United States shall hereafter be such, that of one thousand parts by weight, nine hundred shall be of pure metal, and one hundred of alloy; and the alloy of the silver coins shall be of copper; and the alloy of the gold coins shall be of copper and silver, provided that the silver do not exceed one-half of the whole alloy.

SEC. 9. *And be it further enacted,* That of the silver coins, the dollar shall be of the weight of four hundred and twelve and one-half grains; the half dollar of the weight of two hundred and six and one-fourth grains; the quarter dollar of the weight of one hundred and three and one-eighth grains; the dime, or tenth part of a dollar, of the weight of forty-one and a quarter grains; and the half dime, or twentieth part of a dollar, of the weight of twenty grains, and five-eighths of a grain. And that dollars, and quarter dollars, dimes, and half dimes, shall be legal tenders of payment, according to their nominal value, for any sums whatever.

SEC. 10. *And be it further enacted,* That of the gold coins, the weight of the eagle shall be two hundred and fifty-eight grains; that of the half eagle one hundred and twenty-nine grains; and that of the quarter eagle sixty-four and one-half grains. And that for all sums whatever, the eagle shall be a legal tender of payment for ten dollars, the half-eagle for five dollars; and the quarter eagle for two and a half dollars. . . .

SEC. 12. *And be it further enacted,* That of the copper coins, the weight of the cent shall be one hundred and sixty-eight grains, and the weight of the half-cent eighty-four grains. And the cent shall be considered of the value of one hundredth part of a dollar, and the half-cent of the value of one two-hundredth part of a dollar. □

* Taken and adapted from "Coinage Act of 1837," *U.S. Statutes at Large,* Vol. V, p. 136 ff.

Independent Treasury Act (1846) *

■ An Act to provide for the better Organization of the Treasury, and for the Collection, Safe-Keeping, Transfer, and Disbursement of the public Revenue.

Be it enacted . . . , That the rooms prepared and provided in the new treasury building at the seat of government for the use of the treasurer of the United States, his assistants, and clerks, and occupied by them, and also the fireproof vaults and safes erected in said rooms for the keeping of the public moneys in the possession and under the immediate control of said treasurer, and such other apartments as are provided for in this act as places of deposit of the public money, are hereby constituted and declared to be the treasury of the United States. And all moneys paid into the same shall be subject to the draft of the treasurer, drawn agreeably to appropriations made by law. . . . SEC. 6. That the treasurer of the United States, the treasurer of the mint of the United States, the treasurers, and those acting as such, of the various branch mints, all collectors of the customs, all surveyors of the customs acting also as collectors, all assistant treasurers, all receivers of public moneys at the several land offices, all postmasters, and all public officers of whatsoever character, be, and they are hereby, required to keep safely, without loaning, using, depositing in banks, or exchanging for other funds than as allowed by this act, all the public money collected by them, or otherwise at any time placed in their possession and custody, till the same is ordered, by the proper department or officer of the government, to be transferred or paid out; and when such orders for transfer or payment are received, faithfully and promptly to make the same as directed, and to do and perform all other duties as fiscal agents of the government which may be imposed by this or any other acts of Congress, or by any regulation of the treasury department made in conformity to law; and also to do and perform all acts and duties required by law, or by direction of any of the Executive departments of the government, as agents for paying pensions, or for making any other disbursements which either of the heads of these departments may be required by law to make, and which are of a character to be made by the depositaries hereby constituted, consistently with the other official duties imposed upon them. . . . ◻

* Taken and adapted from "Independent Treasury Act," (August 8, 1846), *U.S. Statutes at Large*, Vol. IX, p. 69.

PART FIVE

□ The Transition from Agriculture to Industry, 1865–1920

In 1920 one-third of the American people still took their living from the land. Nevertheless, it was clear by the end of World War I that the United States economy had become industrial rather than agrarian.

The history of economic change after the Civil War must start with some notion of changes taking place on the land. In what follows, Professor Gates tells the reader nearly everything he needs to know about the 19th century land system, and in a poignant vignette John Ise describes the dreary, often hopeless, life of the frontier family. The transition to a modern industrial economy was greatly helped by both a modern transportation system and a sophisticated financial system. Yet the student must beware of jumping to conclusions about the impact of the railroads, as Professor Fogel's clever and imaginative article suggests. Nor were bankers any different from other businessmen when it came to developing schemes for making an honest dollar, as the attempt to make St. Louis a major capital market testifies.

Yet it is to the businessman as creator of great manufacturing and commercial complexes that we must turn for enlightenment about the process of American industrialization. The great entrepreneurs who developed their companies between the Civil War and World War I were the architects and creators of modern society. In their ruthless drive to succeed, these men left an impression of immorality that gave rise to the epithet, "Robber Barons." As Professor Cochrane persuasively argues, these great figures have been much maligned. In any case, they were caught up in a thrust of forces far more powerful than any of the individuals involved, as Alfred D. Chandler's article on development, diversification, and decentralization makes clear.

The documents, beginning with the Homestead Act and ending with the Sherman Antitrust Act, seem strangely dated as we read them today. Yet each stands for a major events in our economic history and, reading them, the student will perceive how a whole host of economic influences takes focus in the unexciting prose of a Congressional statute. □

The Homestead Law in an Incongruous Land System *

PAUL WALLACE GATES

The Homestead Act of 1862 is one of the most important laws which have been enacted in the history of this country, but its significance has been distorted and grossly misinterpreted. An important misconception concerning the Homestead Act is that its adoption marked a more or less complete break with the past, in that the lands which previously had been considered as a source of revenue were now to be given free to settlers. As part of this interpretation it is held that direct land sales virtually ceased except for transactions under the Pre-emption Law, the commutation clause of the Homestead Act, the Timber and Stone Act, and the Desert Land Act. Each of the first three of these acts permitted the purchase by individuals of 160 acres and the Desert Land Act permitted the purchase of an additional 640 acres, making a total which could be acquired under them of 1120 acres. Aside from this maximum which was open to purchasers, the accepted view is that speculators [1] in lands were barred from direct transactions at the land offices and that, to secure large tracts, they were forced to operate through dummy entrymen or buy from states and railroads. . . .

The principle of free homesteads for settlers had long been the goal for which the West had struggled, and as each succeeding land law, more liberal than its predecessor, was passed, that goal came constantly nearer until, in 1862, it was attained. So generous seemed this policy in contrast with the earlier one of regarding the lands as a source of revenue, and so significant did it appear prospectively, that it became the subject of eulogy at the outset. Furthermore, the measure had been sponsored by the Republican party and when this party later accused of representing the interests of large capitalistic combines and of neglecting the farmers, its leaders pointed to the Homestead Act as a refutation of the accusation.[2] Consequently there was built up around the law a halo of political and economic significance which has greatly magnified the importance to be attributed to it and which has mis-

---

* Taken and adapted from Paul W. Gates, "The Homestead Law in an Incongruous Land System," *The American Historical Review*, Vol. XLI, No. 4, July 1936, pp. 652–81. Used by permission of the author and publisher.

[1] The word "speculator", as used in this article, refers to large-scale land operators, and does not include many farmers who speculated in a small way.

[2] The shallowness of this contention was pointed out by George W. Julian in 1884 (*Political Recollections, 1840 to 1872*, Chicago, 1884, p. 218). Speaking of the continuation of cash sales, railroad grants, and disposal of the Indian lands as fatal to the homestead principle, he said that they furnished "a remarkable commentary upon the boasted friendship of the Republican party for the landless poor".

led practically every historian and economist who has dealt with land policies. The Homestead Law has been considered the capstone of an increasingly liberal land policy, and to it has been ascribed the rapid settlement of the West and the large percentage of farmer owners in the United States. It has also been regarded as providing an outlet for the discontented and surplus labor of the East with the result that, as compared with European countries, high wage rates have prevailed in that section. The influence of free land has been blithely discussed by writers who have never taken the time to examine the facts with which they dealt so lightly.[3] . . .

It is the purpose of this paper to show that the Homestead Law did not completely change our land system, that its adoption merely superimposed upon the old land system a principle out of harmony with it, and that until 1890 the old and the new constantly clashed. In presenting this view it will appear that the Homestead Law did not end the auction system or cash sales, as is generally assumed, that speculation and land monopolization continued after its adoption as widely perhaps as before, and within as well as without the law, that actual homesteading was generally confined to the less desirable lands distant from railroad lines, and that farm tenancy developed in frontier communities in many instances as a result of the monopolization of the land. The efforts to abolish cash sales will also be outlined briefly.

The moderate land reformers of the mid-nineteenth century believed that the enactment of a homestead measure would retard if not end speculation in public lands. They argued that once free homesteads were available to settlers speculators would no longer have a market for their lands and all inducements to purchase in advance of settlement would be ended. Parenthetically, similar arguments have been advanced by certain historians to prove that there was little or no profit in land speculation. The land reformers reckoned too lightly, however, with the astuteness of the speculators who in the past had either succeeded in emasculating laws inimical to their interests or had actually flouted such laws in the very faces of the officials appointed to administer them.

From the outset the cards were stacked against the efficient and successful operation of the Homestead Law. Other acts in existence in 1862 greatly limited its application and new laws further restricting it were subsequently enacted. The administration of the law, both in Washington and in the field, was frequently in the hands of persons unsympathetic to its principle,[4] and

---

[3] In contrast, Herbert Heaton ventures the view that the importance of free land in drawing immigrants to America has been overestimated while the influence of high wages has been underestimated. "Migration and Cheap Land — the End of the Two Chapters," *The Sociological Review*, XXVI (July, 1934), p. 237.

[4] Wm. A. J. Sparks, commissioner of the General Land Office, in his *Report* for 1885 (pp. 3–4), writes as follows concerning the administration of the land laws:

I found that the magnificent estate of the nation in its public lands had been to a wide extent wasted under defective and improvident laws and through a laxity of public administration astonishing in a business sense if not culpable in recklessness of official responsibility.

Western interests, though lauding the act, were ever ready to pervert it. The existence of the Pre-emption Law and its later variations, the Desert Land Act, the Timber Culture Act, the Timber and Stone Act, the land grants to railroads and states, the cash sale system, the Indian land policy, the acts granting land warrants to ex-soldiers or their heirs, and the Agricultural College Act of 1862, which granted millions of acres of land scrip to Eastern states, tended to make it practically as easy for speculators to engross huge areas of land after 1862 as before.

The retention of the Pre-emption Law and the commutation clause of the Homestead Law made it possible for timber dealers, cattle graziers, mining interests, and speculators to continue to acquire lands through the use of dummy entrymen, false swearing, and, often, the connivance of local land officers. That this was done on a large scale is evident by the frequent and sometimes pathetic admissions of the apparently helpless land commissioners. The Desert Land Act, the Timber Culture Act, and the Timber and Stone Act provided even greater opportunities for dummy entrymen to enter lands and assign them to hidden land engrossers. The palpable frauds committed and the large areas transferred under these acts and their interference with the homestead principle lead one to suspect that their enactment and retention were the results of political pressure by interested groups.

It was not entirely necessary, however, for speculators to resort to these illegal and fraudulent methods of acquiring land since Congress proceeded to aid their schemes by enacting a series of laws which went far toward vitiating the principle of land for the landless. By continuing after 1862 the policy of granting lands to railroads to encourage their construction, Congress from the outset struck a severe blow at the principle of free homesteads. In the eight years after the passage of the Homestead Law five times as much land was granted to railroads as had been given in the twelve preceding years; 127,-628,000 acres were granted between 1862 and 1871 to aid in the extension of the railroad net and 2,000,000 acres were granted for wagon roads and canals. Such imperial generosity was at the expense of future homesteaders who must purchase the land. As it was necessary to withdraw all lands from entry in the regions through which such roads were projected to prevent speculators from

The widespread belief of the people of this country that the land department has been very largely conducted to the advantage of speculation and monopoly, private and corporate, rather than in the public interest, I have found supported by developments in every branch of the service. It seems that the prevailing idea running through this office and those subordinate to it was that the government had no distinctive rights to be considered and no special interests to protect; hence, as between the government and spoilers of the public domain, the government usually had the worst of it. I am satisfied that thousands of claims without foundation in law or equity, involving millions of acres of public land, have been annually passed to patent upon the single proposition that nobody but the government had any *adverse* interest.

The vast machinery of the land department appears to have been devoted to the chief result of conveying the title of the United States to public lands upon fraudulent entries under strained constructions of imperfect public land laws and upon illegal claims under public and private grants.

anticipating the railroads in making selections of land, and as the routes were rarely definitely established when the grants were made, more than double this amount of land was withdrawn from entry and remained unavailable to settlement for a long period of years.

The railroads were, of course, built through undeveloped regions and, other things being equal, routes were selected which would ensure to the companies the largest amount of what was then considered to be the best agricultural land. When the alternate government sections were finally restored to market settlers were frequently outbid for them by speculators. Moreover, the provision in the Homestead Law which confined the homesteader to eighty acres within the limits of a railroad grant was sufficient to send many homeseekers farther afield. On the railroad sections, of course, no free homesteading was permitted and thus the prospective settler found it necessary to go far from transportation facilities in order to take advantage of the government's bounty. In numerous instances the land policies of the railroads encouraged speculative and large-scale purchases with the result that millions of acres were turned into bonanza farms, such as those found in Dakota Territory, or were rented or leased to incoming settlers who had expected to find free land available to them.

These grants to railroads after 1862 were a limitation on the homestead principle and indicate cynical indifference to the idealistic expressions constantly voiced concerning the principle. That some doubt existed among members of Congress as to the propriety of continuing to make grants for railroads is revealed by a resolution adopted by the House in 1870 [5] which stated:

> That in the judgement of this House the policy of granting subsidies in public lands to railroad and other corporations ought to be discontinued; and that every consideration of public policy and equal justice to the whole people requires that the public lands of the United States should be held for the exclusive purpose of securing homesteads to actual settlers under the homestead and preëmption laws, subject to reasonable appropriations of such lands for the purposes of education.

Although adopted without any debate the resolution was just a bluff, for within the next twelve months Congress made one of the largest and most indefensible of the railroad grants which, together with a number of smaller ones, totaled nearly 20,000,000 acres. The anti-railroad feeling which swept over the West in the early seventies finally brought these grants to an end. After 1871 no more grants were made although various interests were at the time seeking additional grants which, if made, would have required practically all the valuable lands remaining to the government.

The continuation of the policy of granting to the states Federal lands within their borders was likewise contrary to the homestead principle. With the exception of the swamp land grants, the purpose of these donations was to pro-

[5] *Cong. Globe,* 41 Cong., 2 sess., p. 2095.

vide the states with a valuable commodity, the sale of which would produce revenue or endowment for educational and other state institutions. Over 72,000,000 acres were granted to states which came into the Union after 1862 while other states had their grants increased subsequent to the enactment of the Homestead law. It is safe to say that over 140,000,000 acres of land were in the hands of the states for disposition after 1862. The philosophy behind the grants, and frequently the conditions embedded in the donations, required their sale at the highest market price. The states were prevented, therefore, from giving homesteads to settlers and the prices asked for their lands, with the exception of the swamp lands which were generally sold at low prices or granted to railroads, made them the prey of speculators. It is true that limitations were sometimes placed on the amount of land which individuals could purchase, but dummy entrymen were usually employed to circumvent such restrictions. The states, like the railroads, naturally endeavored to secure the best possible lands in order to ensure large returns therefrom. The following table,[6] showing the land sales of and the prices received by representative states, reveals clearly that persons seeking cheap or free lands found little encouragement from state officials.

State	Net Amount of Land Sold to Date	Average Price per Acre
Idaho [7]	838,140	$16.90
Kansas	3,064,547	3.22
Minnesota	2,306,600	6.53
Montana	1,587,488	15.50
North Dakota	1,686,436	16.73
South Dakota	873,960	35.22
Utah	3,448,876	2.44

The maintenance of the cash sale system after the Homestead Law went into operation did even greater violence to the principle of free lands. It is not generally appreciated that there were available in 1862 for cash sale 83,-919,649 acres of land. Contrary to the views of Hibbard and others, this figure was later increased to well over 100,000,000 acres by the opening up of new lands to the auction and cash sale system. Throughout the sixties and seventies and, indeed, until 1888 the government continued to offer land at auction in Oregon, Washington, California, Kansas, Nebraska, Colorado, New Mexico, and in practically all of the states in the Lakes region and in the Mississippi Valley where it still had land. It is true that after 1870 most of the land so offered was timbered but by then a goodly portion of the arable lands had been surveyed and opened to sale. The richest and most fertile sections of Kansas, Nebraska, Missouri, California, Washington, and Oregon were thus open to the cash purchaser after the enactment of the Homestead Law and,

[6] Computed from reports of the land offices of the respective states.
[7] To 1918.

as will be seen later, great landed estates were acquired through outright purchase in these states.

Little attention has been devoted by historians to the Indian lands and yet there is a story involved in their disposition totally at variance with the conventional account of the era of free land. At the time the Homestead Law was passed the government was following the policy of concentrating the Indians on reservations where they would be in less conflict with white settlers. The rights of the Indians in lands claimed by them were recognized and, when they were persuaded to leave a hunting area over which they claimed ownership to dwell in a reservation, they were generally compensated for their lands either by the Federal government or by a purchaser acting with the consent of the government. Some of the lands were ceded outright to the government for a consideration; others were ceded in trust, the lands to be sold for the benefit of the Indians; the disposition of still others to railroads was authorized in a number of treaties. As these Indian lands were frequently the very choicest and contained some improvements they were much desired by speculators. No uniform policy concerning their final disposition was worked out — both legislative and administrative regulations as to their disposal varying widely — and consequently speculators were able to get their grasp on them more easily than if the lands had been subject to a clearly defined policy. The only consistent rule concerning them was that they must be sold for a consideration, which, of course, denied to the homesteader the right to enter them free. The obligation of the government to compensate the Indian for his land did not necessitate a policy of sale to settlers but the revenue complex with reference to the public lands was still prevalent in spite of the Homestead Law, and the Indian lands were reserved for cash sale.

The amount of land in Indian reservations or claimed by the Indians in 1862 was probably 175,000,000 acres.[8] The land was scattered throughout the Western states, but large amounts were concentrated in the states of Kansas and Nebraska and the Dakota and Indian territories into which settlers were eagerly pressing in the sixties, seventies, and eighties, or where they looked longingly for lands. At the outset, these lands were sold in large blocks to groups of capitalists and railroads, as is seen below, without being offered in small lots. Slightly later they were appraised, generally at high valuations, offered at auction and sold to the highest bidders. Still later, some of the Indian lands were sold in small tracts to settlers, a slight concession to the homeseekers.[9] . . .

[8] Indian reservations and claims were not sharply defined in 1862, much of the area not having been surveyed. In 1875 the Commission of Indian Affairs (*Report*, 1875, p. 142) gave the acreage in Indian reservations as 165,729,714 acres. The amount of Indian lands sold directly to individuals and corporations and that sold through the General Land Office during the years 1862–1875 would bring this figure to 175,000,000 acres for 1862.

[9] There is little available information on the Indian lands and their disposition, the most important published source being the *Annual Reports* of the Commissioners of Indian Affairs during the years after the Civil War.

With over 125,000,000 acres of railroad lands, 140,000,000 acres of state lands, 100,000,000 acres of Indian lands, and 100,000,000 acres of Federal lands for sale in large or small blocks, and with the opportunities for evasion of the Homestead and Pre-emption laws and their variations outlined above, it is obvious that there were few obstacles in the way of speculation and land monopolization after 1862. As before, it was still possible for foresighted speculators to precede settlers into the frontier, purchase the best lands, and hold them for the anticipated increase in value which the succeeding wave of settlers would give to them. It has heretofore been maintained that the existence of free land after 1862 greatly diminished the speculators' chances of profit and consequently limited their activities. This view will not bear careful scrutiny. Except for the squatters' claims, the speculators were generally able to secure the most desirable lands, that is, those easily brought under cultivation, fertile and close to timber, water, markets, and lines of communication. The subsequent settler had the choice of buying at the speculators' prices, from the land grant railroads which held their alternate tracts at equally high prices, from the states whose land policies were less generous than those of the Federal government, or of going farther afield to exercise his homestead privilege where facilities for social and economic intercourse were limited. The fact that their lands were more advantageously situated was effectively advertised by the land companies. Thus the American Emigrant Company in advertising its Iowa lands in the sixties summed up under the caption "Better than a Free Homestead" all the disadvantages of free land:

> Under the homestead law the settler must, in order to get a good location, go far out into the wild and unsettled districts, and for many years be deprived of school privileges, churches, mills, bridges, and in fact of all the advantages of society.[10]

Settlers arriving in Kansas — to consider a typical state — between 1868 and 1872 were greeted with advertisements announcing that the choicest lands in the state had been selected by the State Agricultural College which was now offering 90,000 acres for sale on long term credits. The Central Branch of the Union Pacific Railroad offered 1,200,000 acres for prices ranging from $1.00 to $15.00 per acre; the Kansas Pacific Railroad offered 5,000,000 acres for $1.00 to $6.00 per acre; the Kansas and Neosho Valley Railroad offered 1,500,000 acres for sale at $2.00 to $8.00 per acre; the Capital Land Agency of Topeka offered 1,000,000 acres of Kansas land for sale; Van Doren and Havens offered 200,000 acres for $3.00 to $10.00 per acre; T. H. Walker offered 10,000 (or 100,000) acres for $5.00 to $10.00 per acre; Hendry and Noyes offered 50,000 acres; and even the United States government was advertising for bids for approximately 6000 acres of Sac and Fox Indian lands. That virgin lands in Kansas were selling for subtantial prices in this period is shown by the following tables:

[10] Pamphlet: *Two Thousand Families Wanted For Iowa*, n. d., n. p.

■ **TABLE 1   Sales of State Lands** a

		Acres	Average Price per Acre
Common school lands	(1865–1882)	450,764	$4.00
Agricultural college lands	(1868–1882)	48,465	4.78
University lands	(1878–1882)	6,224	2.88
Normal school lands	(1876–1882)	4,966	4.72

a Biennial Report, Auditor of State, Kansas, 1882, pp. 359–360.

■ **TABLE 2   Land Sales of Atchison, Topeka, and Santa Fe Railroad** b

TOTAL SALES FROM MARCH 1, 1871, TO DECEMBER 31, 1879

Year	Acres	Principal	Average Price per Acre
1871	71,801.51	$ 425,013.75	$5.91
1872	45,328.81	269,627.66	5.94
1873	133,507.30	748,977.25	5.61
1874	200,459.96	900,973.30	4.49
1875	75,415.33	416,409.85	5.52
1876	122,201.17	665,455.17	5.44½
1877	85,047.78	423,477.49	4.98
1878	267,122.47	1,206,527.64	4.52
1879	104,744.41	494,353.73	4.72
Total	1,105,628.74	$5,550,815.84	$5.02

b Compiled from Annual Reports of the Atchison, Topeka, and Santa Fe Railroad, 1873–1880.

Such sales — and many others might be cited — are evidence that free homesteads on the most desirable land were not available in this state to incoming settlers. . . .

. . . Homeseekers in the West, being unwilling to go far afield from means of transportation or to settle upon the inferior lands remaining open to homestead, and lacking capital with which to purchase farms and to provide equipment for them, were frequently forced to become tenants on the lands of speculators. Thus farm tenancy developed in the frontier stage at least a generation before it would have appeared had the homestead system worked properly. In the states of Kansas and Nebraska, in which large-scale land monopolization has been revealed, sixteen and eighteen per cent respectively of the farms were operated by tenants in 1880, the first year for which figures are available, and in 1890 twenty-eight and twenty-four per cent respectively were operated by tenants. This continued monopolization of the best lands and the resulting growth of farm tenancy led reformers and others who feared the establishment of a landed aristocracy similar to that existing in many European countries to advocate the ending of the cash sales system entirely. Their demands were expressed in petitions to Congress, agitation in the press, and union of effort with other antimonopoly groups which were coming into prominence in the last third of the nineteenth century. Their agitation and the growing seriousness of the monopoly movement led to a series of halting steps toward the abandonment of cash sales, which frequently were offset by movements in the opposite direction.

The first step in the direction of abolishing the cash sale system was taken in June, 1866, when Congress provided that all public lands in the five Southern states of Alabama, Arkansas, Florida, Louisiana, and Mississippi should be reserved from sale and subject only to entry under the Homestead Law. The avowed purpose of this apparent discrimination against land speculation in the South while it was permitted to flourish elsewhere, was to prevent speculators from monopolizing the land when it was restored to market — all land transactions had of course ceased in these states during the Civil War — and to encourage the growth of small holdings among the freedmen. By the South, the act was regarded, perhaps rightly, as a punitive measure. Certain it is that much of the 46,398,544 acres thus reserved from cash entry was unsuited to small-scale farming and the freedmen showed no great desire to take advantage of the homestead privilege thus safeguarded. Nevertheless, the act was the first attack on the cash sale system.

Two backwards steps were tried the same year, however. In the same month that the law was passed restricting Southern public lands to homestead entry an apparently innocuous measure slipped through Congress without much debate or opposition, giving to the New York and Montana Iron Mining and Manufacturing Company the right to purchase at $1.25 per acre twenty sections — 12,800 acres — of unsurveyed and unopened lands in the territory of Montana, three sections of which might contain iron ore or coal and the remaining sections would presumably be timber lands. This measure was put through by Benjamin Wade of Ohio and Thaddeus Stevens of Pennsylvania of whom it cannot be said that the interests of the homesteaders were nearest to their hearts. It gave a gross extension of privilege to a group of speculators or land monopolists. Never had such a *carte blanche* grant been made before, though frequently petitioned for, and it aroused the indignation of President Johnson who, in a ringing veto message, declared that the privileges conferred by the act "are in direct conflict with every principle heretofore observed in respect to the disposal of the public lands." [11] If the measure had been signed, the principle of granting lands free or for the minimum price to mining companies and other industrial organizations might have been established and the remaining portion of the public domain might have been divided among such capitalistic groups, just as millions of acres were being parceled out among the railroads. In placing himself squarely against the law, President Johnson aided in preserving the lands from speculators. . . . □

The second backward step was a series of Indian treaties and administrative measures by which substantial areas of land in the Great Plains were sold

[11] Message of June 15, 1866, *Senate Journal*, 39 Cong., 1 sess., p. 532.

to railroad companies and other speculative groups. When railroads were projected through Kansas and Nebraska, it was found that they must run through Indian reservations. Congressional land grants did not apply to such lands and the railroad officials therefore sought to purchase the lands which they could not receive as a gift. Instead of asking for alternate sections, however, as in the grants, they sought to purchase solid areas which would enable them to secure the entire benefits resulting from the construction of the railroads. As the Granger period had not yet arrived, railroads were still popular throughout most sections of the country. Furthermore, they possessed great influence at the seat of power and it was not difficult for them to prevail upon the proper officials to make treaties for the cession or sale of Indian lands. The Senate at this time was far more friendly to the railroads than to the homeseekers, as shown by its generous land grants and financial subsidies to the former and its refusal to place restrictions upon speculative purchases of land. Apparently it saw little difference between making donations of alternate sections of the public domain to the railroads and selling solid blocks of Indian lands to them for a low price. It therefore ratified such treaties with little hesitation. . . .

From the date of the repeal of the restrictions on cash entry in the South until 1889 there was not a session of Congress in which the question of reserving all the public lands for homestead entry was not fiercely debated. Continued efforts were made to end the cash sale system. Following 1880, the Pre-emption, Timber and Stone, Timber Culture, and Desert Land acts came in for much criticism since it was apparent that, like the commutation clause of the Homestead Law, they lent themselves to abuse and fraud. In the eighties the movement was given a great impetus by the discovery of enormous frauds in which foreign corporations and titled noblemen were engaged for the purpose of building up vast estates. The fact that most of this alien ownership was English was used effectively by the Anglophobes and, added to the antimonopoly movement which was rapidly gaining in strength, it made easy the conversion of many politicians to the cause of land reform.

President Cleveland's land commissioner, William A. J. Sparks, dramatically brought the issue to the front by revealing with overwhelming evidence that "the public domain was being made the prey of unscrupulous speculation and the worst forms of land monopoly through systematic frauds carried on and consummated under the public land laws." [12]   In cold, biting language, he accused the administration of the General Land Office of being either extraordinarily inept in its management or directly involved in the great frauds which he unearthed. So general were the illegal or fraudulent entries that within a month after his accession to office he suspended all final entries under the Timber and Stone Act and the Desert Land Act, and in Colorado, Dakota, Idaho, Utah, Washington, New Mexico, Montana, Wyoming, Nevada, and parts of Minnesota, Kansas, and Nebraska suspended all entries

[12] G.L.O. *Report*, 1885, p. 48.

except those made with cash and scrip. The evidence of fraud continued to come in, and as the demand for complete suspension of all non-homestead entries stimulated speculators and monopolists to feverish activity, Sparks in desperation, in 1886, ordered the land officers to accept no further application for entries under the Pre-emption, Timber Culture, and Desert Land acts. This precipitate action stirred up a veritable hornets' nest of opposition and the order was rescinded, but its effect remained.

The onslaught of the antimonopolists had the effect of stimulating the speculators, cattlemen, lumber and mining companies to prompt action before the public domain should be closed to them. Land sales and entries under the Pre-emption, Timber Culture, Timber and Stone, and Desert Land acts and the cash sale system shot up to a high point in 1888, exceeding those of any year since 1856 and being surpassed only four times in our entire history.

This enormous speculation, added to the widespread frauds which were being uncovered, produced a demand for reform which swelled to a tremendous volume. Hundreds of petitions with innumerable signatures flooded Congress urging changes in land policy and administration. They made it plain that public opinion had been aroused and could no longer be ignored.

Measure after measure providing for repeal of the objectionable laws passed the House in the eighties only to be defeated in the Senate. Finally, under the stimulus of Spark's dramatic gesture, repeal measures passed both houses in 1886 and again in 1887, but were defeated through failure to harmonize conflicting views. These were to be the last defeats, however, because Congress was rapidly being forced into a position where it had to take action. In May and July, 1888, two measures were passed by which land sales in the five Southern states were temporarily suspended, and the Act of 1876 was reversed. This was followed, on March 2, 1889, by an act ending all cash sales of public lands except in Missouri where the remaining lands were mostly mineral in character or scattered fragments of little value for agriculture. In 1890 a rider was attached to an appropriation act by which it was stipulated that henceforth no person should acquire title to more than 320 acres in the aggregate under all of the land laws. Finally, in 1891 a combination of antimonopoly land reformers and conservationists placed upon the statute books a law which was as far reaching, as important, perhaps, as the Homestead Act of 1862. This law [18] repealed the Pre-emption and Timber Culture acts and placed additional safeguards in the Desert Land Act and the commutation clause of the Homestead Act. Except for Indian lands and small isolated tracts the speculators could no longer purchase whole counties for the minimum price and land engrossment by fraudulent means was at least made more difficult. Unfortunately these land reforms were not enacted until the best of the area suitable for farming without irrigation had passed into private ownership.

The most important section of the Act of 1891 was that which authorized the creation of forest reservations on the public lands. Here was the first

[18] 26 *U.S. Stat.*, 1095–1103.

fundamental break with the underlying philosophy of our land system — the desire to dispose of the lands and hasten their settlement. The conservationists had now convinced the country that a part of our natural resources must be retained in public ownership and preserved for the future. Unfortunately, conservation, when first adopted, was embedded in an outworn laissez-faire land system of a previous age just as the free homestead plan had been superimposed upon a land system designed to produce revenue. In both cases the old and the new clashed with disastrous effects. ☐

◇ **52** ◇

The First Months in the Log Cabin *

JOHN ISE

It was a good summer, Rosie's first summer in the little cabin, with fair rains, and fair crops of spring wheat, oats, sod corn and barley, with late lettuce, beans, cucumbers, tomatoes, and roasting ears for the table. There was not much of the field crops, to be sure — perhaps ten acres altogether — but five acres was sod corn that Henry planted in the sod with a hatchet. It was a back-breaking job, and the field looked big enough before he finished planting. Henry did not get a corn planter or "stabber" until two years later. Very few weeds grew in the sod corn, so there was little hoeing to do the first summer.

Prices were good at first, for what little butter and stuff there was to sell. The first butter Rosie sold brought forty cents a pound, but all prices soon began to decline, and before the end of the summer, butter was worth only ten cents a pound, and eggs scarcely worth taking to town. Some of the local politicians talked about a panic and hard times in the country, but Rosie knew only that butter and eggs were cheap.

A few weeks after Rosie came, Henry took a load of oats to Cawker City, and brought back three chairs and some sugar. Rosie was proud of the new chairs, but later in the year she saw that it had been an extravagance, for they really needed the oats for the horses, and they could have done without the chairs.

In keeping her little cabin, Rosie faced difficulties that would have disheartened a less resolute soul. Her stove was so small that she could bake only two loaves of bread at a time, so she had to bake almost every day. The floor was of cottonwood lumber, which had warped so badly that it was a problem to set the bed so that all four legs would rest on the floor. One day Henry bought some new cottonwood boards for a granary, and Rosie persuaded him to tear up the floor, and put the smooth new boards in the house

* Taken and adapted from John Ise, *Sod and Stubble: The Story of a Kansas Homestead*, Chapter 3 (New York: Wilson-Erickson, Inc., 1936), pp. 17–31.

and the old floor boards in the granary; but this was only a temporary gain, for the new floor was soon as badly warped as the old had been. It was hard to walk about in the house, and Rosie often tripped on the uneven boards, until she got used to them.

There was another discomfort that developed when cold weather came. On windy days the cold wind blew a gale through the cracks in the floor, and it was almost impossible to keep her feet warm. Henry banked the house outside with dirt and straw and manure, covering even the outside cellar entrance. This made the house warmer, but brought another inconvenience, for they then had to clamber into the cellar through a trap-door in the floor.

The cracks in the floor and in the log walls afforded a rendezvous for various pests that kept Rosie in a militant mood much of the time; and the battle front between her and the bedbugs shifted back and forth, with never a decisive victory. Every day she went through the bed, tick and all, and every Saturday searched the house, with a kettle of hot water in one hand and a can of kerosene and a feather in the other. At times she thought she had the enemy beaten, but presently movers would come along and spread their bed on the floor, or perhaps it would be a preacher halt to pass the night, and then the battle had to be fought all over again.

One discomfort that some of the neighbors in sod houses always complained of, she never had to endure. She never had fleas in the house, because the house had a floor with a cellar below. There were fleas in the grass, of course, and every venture out into the grass had to be paid for in considerable physical discomfort, but the fleas did not stay in the house. Frances Athey, who had no cellar, told her one day of the toad she kept under the floor, which not only rid her house of fleas, but served as a pet for the children. She named the toad "Tilden" — it was the time of the Hayes-Tilden campaign.

There were several tragedies in the neighborhood, those first few months. Soon after Rosie came, Henry was called upon one day to help hunt for the body of a woman who had drowned, with her two children, trying to cross the river when it was up. One of the neighbors told Rosie how the poor woman, after she sank, had tried to hold her baby above her head, hoping someone might rescue it. Henry helped hunt for several days, but with no success. A week later the woman's body was found in a pile of driftwood on the State land section, several miles downstream, and several weeks later the body of one of the children was found. The other was never recovered.

A few weeks afterward, a man was killed down on the river. He was hauling logs, and a heavy log rolled off the wagon and struck him, crushing him to death. For some of the sympathizing neighbors there was a touch of consolation in the fact that he was a Democrat — the only one in the community.

Not long afterward Rosie was called upon to help line the coffin of a man named Tipp, who had been shot accidentally. It was a sad task, for the man left his wife and six small children with very little to live on, and he had begun work on his house only a short time before he was killed. The preacher

who delivered the funeral sermon made opportunity for a few pointed morali-
ties regarding the dead man, who was not a church member, declaring that he
"had not loved his Lord." To this Jesse Bender promptly objected, insisting
that Tipp was a good man; and the funeral very nearly closed with a fight over
the merits of the deceased. The next day the neighbors came together and
finished the house he had begun, and built a stable and chicken coop too.
Not long aftrward, Tipp's widow gave birth to a little boy with a mark on his
breast — just where the father had been shot. She never doubted that the
baby's mark was the result of the accident.

In July, the wife of one of the neighbors, John Sibley, died in childbirth.
She was buried the next morning; and that night John called a dance.

Chris drove back to the old home in August to get his cane mill, and Rosie
went along. It was hot and dry, but she enjoyed the trip, enjoyed the freedom
and change, sleeping out in the wagon and cooking over a camp fire. When
they returned with the cane mill, she and Chris made enough molasses to last
all winter, Rosie stripping the cane, while Chris attended to the horse power,
the machine and the boiling pans. They worked hard, sometimes until nearly
midnight; but when it was all done, it seemed good to have so much of their
winter's good supply set away in the cellar.

More women were coming to the new country. Two years earlier, there
had hardly been a woman within miles. Frances Athey and Lizzie Graeber
had come out the year before Rosie arrived; and about the time that Rosie
came, many of the married men went "back east" — which usually meant
Eastern Kansas, Missouri, Iowa, or Illinois — to fetch their wives out to their
new homes. These women soon set about tidying up the primitive dugouts
that dotted the prairie. A few brought children, others soon had them, and
strings of diapers flapped from many a clothes line, or covered the buffalo
grass in the yards.

Frances Athey became the mother of twins soon after Rosie came. Rosie
went over to help, but found hardly enough clothes there for one baby, and
everything so scanty and meager in the little dugout that she hardly knew how
to manage. Afterwards some of the neighbors induced the Cawker merchant,
Parker, to give them some cloth and Rosie helped make it up into diapers and
dresses for the two babies.

"Didn't reelly need two right now, while we're tryin' to git the oxen paid
fer," Frances said one day; "but I reckon the Lord knows what's best." The
Lord was destined to have a lot to account for over at Athey's.

Promising indeed the new country seemed to these settlers; and they were
soon boasting of the wonderful climate, of the mildness of the winters, of the
balmy spring days, of the cool nights of summer, of the heathful and in-
vigorating tonic of the air. It was a common jest that they would never need
a cemetery, that people would probably live forever in such a salubrious climate. And they knew the soil was deep and rich and productive — the finest
in the world. Some of the more sanguine began to feel a sympathy for unfor-

tunate friends and relatives who were enduring the hard life of Iowa or Illinois or Pennsylvania or Eastern Kansas, and wrote back urging them to come to the new Elysium, in the valley of the Solomon. At a party at Mc-Conkeys, one night, Rosie first heard a song which was often sung that year:

> O, give me a home where the buffalo roam,
> Where the deer and the antelope play,
> Where never is heard a discouraging word,
> And the sky is unclouded all day.

When fall came, and the little patch of corn had been husked, there was not a great deal of work to do, for they had only the two horses, a few cows, two pigs, and two dozen chickens to care for. It seemed a life of leisure to Rosie, for in her own home, even as a girl of twelve or thirteen, she had always had to do much of the housework for a family of ten, and had helped her father with the corn husking and other farm work. Henry bought a half-interest in a big cottonwood tree from Chris, and he and Chris together cut a supply of wood for both families.

There were frequent social festivities to attend: Granger parties, taffy parties, surprise parties, and quilting and sewing parties for the women. Henry made a sleigh of two bent saplings, so that he and Rosie could go in style when there was snow on the ground. Occasionally there was a party in the neighborhood where the young people — and they were all young — would prance back and forth to the tuneful melodies of Weevilly Wheat, Old Dan Tucker, Buffalo Girls, Miller Boy, Old Brass Wagon, We'll All Go Down to Rousers, and My Father and Mother were Irish. Dancing to the music of the violin was not deemed a Christian form of amusement by the stricter moralists of the community; but the accordion was not thought to be to the same extent an instrument of the devil, and since Henry played the accordion, he was much in demand. Rosie had been taught that life was for work and not for pleasure, and she was never quite sure that it was right to go to any such light affairs; so she sometimes stayed at home when Henry went out with his accordion. She felt lonesome on such evenings, and even a bit hurt, to think he would leave her alone; but of course Henry could not refuse anyone who wanted him to play.

The refreshments at these parties were usually simple and inexpensive, although sometimes fried cakes were served, or even pie or cake. Once when Henry and Rosie had a party at their house, Rosie served blanc mange, which was thought quite an extravagance. At a surprise party at Benders, the hostess was obliged to bake corn bread and serve it with black coffee. Sometimes no refreshments were served, and to guard against such contingencies, Steve Linge sometimes took bread along in his wagon, and went out between dances to eat.

Then there were literary societies to go to, spelling schools, and lectures on Mormonism; and sometimes Henry and Rosie would visit the neighbors — perhaps go in the morning and stay all day. On New Year's Eve they went up to Bartsch's, who lived two miles up the creek, to watch the old year out, passing the time with visiting, singing and prayer. Chris Bartsch, a German with a face so full of kindly wrinkles that no child could look at him and be afraid, had filed on his claim the year before Rosie came. His claim was not good land — the good land had all been taken before he came. When he brought his wife out a year later, he arrived at his sod dugout during a heavy rain, to find the roof partly caved in, and a foot of water in the house. His wife had hardly expected such accommodations, and refused to enter the house — perhaps not seeing any particular advantage in being there. When he had dipped the water out and got the children in, she was induced to enter, and take up the duties of a homesteader's wife. She and Rosie became fast friends, and many a time, when the latter was sick, she came down to help with the work.

Religious meetings held in the various homes from time to time, served as entertainment too, and there was always a crowd in attendance. There was little in any of the new homes to afford interest or entertainment — few newspapers, or books, or magazines, or musical instruments. Many homes had none of these; and the people were glad to have a place to go, where they could see each other and forget the tedium of their homes.

Most of the preachers were poorly educated, a few of them almost illiterate. The Reverend Mr. Bowers, who preached occasionally at Henry's cabin, was able to read his precious Bible only very slowly and stumblingly, but he had the spirit of evangelism in his heart, and preached with such power that neighbors a mile away could enjoy the message, and even those more than two miles away could sometimes hear him on quiet evenings, when the windows were open. Many of these preachers were sincere and unselfish crusaders, but some were crude and uncultured, others selfish and fleshly, and a few the worst type of rascals, impostors, or even rakes.

Whenever a preacher came into the community, a meeting was arranged at the home of one of the settlers, and someone tried to get word to as many of the neighbors as possible. People would come long distances — ten or twelve miles, or even farther — to attend these meetings, driving in their lumber wagons, or even walking — perhaps barefooted — if they had no teams. One night when a meeting was being held in Henry's cabin, so many crowded in that the floor began to sag dangerously, and in the midst of the services Henry had to ask the worshippers to step outside until he could go down into the cellar and brace up the floor with poles.

One Sunday afternoon, when there was a meeting at Henry's house, during one of the prayers the room suddenly turned dark, and on looking up, the worshippers saw the faces of Indians peering curiously in at the windows. For a moment there was consternation in the little room. Henry seized his revolver and ran to the door, but at a glance he saw that the Indians standing around the cabin carried no weapons, and seemed peaceful enough. They finally made him understand that they only wanted something to eat, and

Rosie had to give them all the bread she had baked for the after church dinner, spread with butter and with some precious citron butter that she had put up for the winter. The Indians seemed dissatisfied, and finally made Rosie understand that they disliked the salted butter on the bread; so she scraped off what she could, and gave them bread spread only with citron butter. This they took without any word or comment, and went away.

The services had scarcely begun again, when the Indians reappeared at the door, and one of them exhibited a dead chicken, that had died of the cholera some time before.

"Heap good," he exclaimed, showing how the skin peeled easily from the decaying flesh. "Heap good," and he pointed to other dead chickens in the hands of other Indians. Henry and Rosie finally understood that they wanted to take all of these with them, and, when they signified their willingness, the noble red men started off again to their camp down by the river.

The post office was established in Henry's cabin that winter, under the name "New Arcadia." Old man Vietz had kept post office in his cave in the creek bank, but Bender coveted his claim, and had threatened to shoot him if he did not leave the country. One day the poor old German came up to Henry's with a bunch of letters, and asked Henry if he would distribute his mail for a few days, as he was leaving for a while. Henry agreed, but Vietz never returned; and so the job of postmaster came to Henry and Rosie.

The pay was small — their percentage receipts from stamps sold and cancelled amounted to only about two dollars a month — and it was a great deal of trouble, for one of them had to be at the house practically all the time. The neighbors came often for their mail — always anxious for letters and news from their old homes — and usually stayed to visit. Sometimes they stayed much too long, or even for meals. If anyone came for mail at dinner time, he was of course invited to eat. The stage driver, who came every day with the mail, usually took his dinner at a station farther up the river, but if he came at dinner time, he was often invited to dinner too. Henry and Rosie, on the other hand, did not need to go anywhere for their own mail; they got a wide variety of stuff through the mail — pictures, magazines, newspapers, samples and advertisements; and they always had interesting news of the outside world from the stage driver.

One day they received a little photograph of Charlie Ross, who had been kidnapped in Philadelphia, with the pathetic request that they help to find him; and for months afterward, whenever an emigrant wagon passed, Rosie could not help wondering if Charlie Ross might be hidden away in it. She was particularly sympathetic because of a kidnapping which her father had once seen, and often told about. Her father and an old friend from Germany had just been admitted as immigrants at New York, and were walking up the street with their families, when a cab with three men in it stopped beside them, two men jumped out of the cab, seized the man's daughter — a young girl of seventeen — threw her into the cab, and drove rapidly away before anyone realized what was happening. Her father never saw her again.

Rosie and Henry once got complimentary tickets to the Ringling Brothers' Show, which was coming to Cawker, so they drove down to Cawker to see the circus. Hundreds of wagons with teams of horses or oxen tied to them stood on the vacant lots about the town; and the crowds of people completely filled the town's single business block. It was a grand circus too, one to be remembered for many long years.

Rosie herself did not read much of the stuff that came through the mails. As a little girl she had never been able to go to winter school, because she had no shoes and no warm clothes; and when a summer term was organized later, she went only half a day — to a teacher who came to school barefooted. Rosie's mother became ill that day, and she never was able to go again. Her father then taught her at home, but with all the work that had to be done, she never developed the habit of reading much — even, from her observations of housewives who read a great deal, got a strong suspicion of the habit. Yet now and then she did take the time to read some of the papers that came to them. Henry always liked to read, and sometimes lost himself in the newspaper when he should have been doing something else — lost himself so completely that he was utterly oblivious to everything going on about him.

Henry was justice of the peace, too, for several years, and the office took time that brought little money returns. Whenever a case came to him for settlement, Rosie usually went down to the cellar to be out of the way. One day two men came in with a quarrel over some cattle, and Rosie went down cellar with her sewing, as usual; but when she overheard all the vile cursing and swearing of the men in the room above, she almost wished she had gone to the stable. On another occasion, a man living several miles away asked Henry to come over and "hitch him up" to the woman of his choice. Since the horses had been working all day, Henry walked over, although it was raining. When the ceremony was over and the man properly "hitched up," he asked Henry what the "damages" were, to which Henry replied that he made no particular charge, expecting of course that the man would give him something for his trouble; but the fellow only thanked him and invited him to supper. Even this Henry could not accept, for his clothes were wet, and it was getting dark, and he wanted to get home. Rosie spent most of the next day cleaning his clothes and boots. It was Henry's usual experience in such matters — and Rosie's too.

Homesick Rosie was, often, for her own people, and for the hills and trees and flowers and fruits of Eastern Kansas; but Henry was kind and considerate, and appreciative of his pretty and efficient young wife. He was not a good manager or business man, and often allowed himself, and incidentally Rosie, to be imposed upon by strangers, and by a few of the neighbors. When he lent out his breaking plow, or his corn sheller, or fanning mill, or his horses, he never could bring himself to ask any rental; he never charged a really fair wage for breaking sod for the neighbors; and of course Rosie had to help make up for his generosity, by skimping in every way. He was generous with Rosie too, though, and never raised any question about her expenditures for herself or for the house; in fact he sometimes bought things for her that she would never have thought of buying for herself. He was a good farmer, always had good crops if anyone had; he was an ingenious mechanic, kept his implements in good working order, and fixed up many little conveniences in and about the house; and, as Rosie often said to herself, he had "good ideas" about almost everything — except money. Rosie soon learned to respect his weather predictions, his skill in treating any kind of illness, and his general information, for he had received a good education in Germany, an education which proved useful not only to her, but to some of the neighbors, who often came to him for help.

Henry's manner of shaving was one of Rosie's greatest surprises. For her father, shaving had always been the rough equivalent of a major operation. His razor had to be stropped at great length, the water had to be heated to just the right temperature, the room must be kept closed, for any draught hurt his face; and even with all conditions favorable, he would grit his teeth as he plied his razor, and would puff out his cheeks and groan and grumble as if he had swallowed a stand of bees. Rosie had learned to think of shaving as a terrible ordeal. What was her surprise to see Henry get out his razor and mug, pour a little water of almost any temperature into the pan, draw the razor a few times across the strop or his boot top, and shave in a few minutes, without any fuss whatever!

Henry was like that in all matters. In the house and outside, he always had his things in order, and with no fuss or noise or irritation. He was scrupulously clean and neat in his personal habits, and gentlemanly in his language and behavior. He never came to the table without first washing and combing his hair and beard with care, he never used tobacco in any form, he never resorted to profanity, and seldom even to slang. "Ach, the deuce!" was his nearest approach to violent language. Most important of all, he was invariably thoughtful and considerate of Rosie. Occasionally he even brought her bouquets of wild flowers when he came in from the field, if he found some that were unusually pretty or fragrant.

It always seemed lonely when Henry went to Russell or Hastings or Waterville. He usually traded at Cawker City, only ten miles away, but Cawker City was sixty miles from the nearest railroad, and prices of goods were high there, while the Cawker City merchant, Parker, paid less for grain and butter and eggs than the dealers in the railroad towns. So Henry sometimes took his stuff to Russell, or even occasionally to Hastings or Waterville.

While he was gone, Rosie had tasks that called for all her capable energy. She had to do the chores, feed and care for the livestock, and attend to the mail. She tried to do as much other work as possible too, while Henry was gone, so she could help him when he was at home. She sorted out corn husks to make a new husk bed tick, to replace the straw tick, which was getting rather hard to sleep on; she braided husks and sewed them together to make little mats for the floor; she made lye of wood ashes, and then used it in hull-ing corn for hominy; she browned rye for coffee. Then she had sewing to do, for she was making a wagon cover, an everyday dress for herself, shirts and mittens and a vest for Henry; and, most important of all, she was making baby clothes, tiny little dresses with hand embroidery and lace, getting the cloth from one of her white skirts and her white polonaise. Rosie worked hard when Henry was gone.

And yet it was lonely, especially at night, when the coyotes barked and howled down along the river and up in the hills, and the owls hooted from the prairie dog town. Then the prairie seemed a vast and lonely place. Although Rosie was almost a stranger to fear, she barred her door, kept Henry's revolver on a chair by her bed, and a few times spent sleepless nights.

Sleeping thus alone one night, she was awakened by a sound of voices in the yard. Henry had just left for Russell that morning, and she knew he could not be back so soon. She held her breath and listened. There were two men outside, talking to each other in low tones. Presently the silhouette of a bearded face darkened the little window across from her bed. For what seemed a long time the face peered into the cabin, while Rosie sat up in her bed, too frightened to think of the revolver that lay on the chair beside her. Presently the face moved from the window, and a moment later she heard a footfall on the door step; a cautious hand fumbled the latch and tried to push the door open. The lock held, and Rosie began to hope that the insistent visitor had gone, when the face appeared at the window, and a hand slowly raised the sash. For a moment she sat there too frightened to move or cry out; but when the intruder started to push his head into the window, Rosie reached for the revolver, aimed above the figure wedged in the opening, and fired. At the report the intruder jerked his head back with such force as to break the window to slivers, and disappeared in the darkness. Very soon she heard a wagon driven rapidly out of the yard. The next morning she saw the wagon tracks left in the grass, but she never knew who her intruders were. They had stolen nothing from the barn or chicken house, but Rosie enjoyed no sound sleep again until Henry returned.

"I'm certainly glad," she said, when he got home, "that you don't have to go down east to work every winter, like Steve Linge. I don't know what I'd do if I had to stay here alone all winter."

The next day after this incident, two passing tramps, perhaps the same ones who had tried to get into Rosie's cabin, outraged the wife of one of the settlers, and this frightened some of the young wives of the neighborhood. Some of them stayed with neighbors when their husbands were away from home; but when Henry, the next time he went to Russell, suggested that Rosie stay with Chris and Louisa, Rosie declared that there was too much work to do, and she thought she could take care of herself. She kept the revolver within easy reach, studied all callers critically, and once had to threaten with the revolver a man who persisted in coming into the house without invitation. ◻

A Quantitative Approach to the Study of Railroads in American Economic Growth: A Report of Some Preliminary Findings *

ROBERT W. FOGEL

Is it legitimate for the historian to consider alternative possibilities to events which have happened? . . . To say that a thing happened the way it did is not at all illuminating. We can understand the significance of what did happen only if we contrast it with what might have happened.

— Morris Raphael Cohen

I

Leland Jenks' article describing the pervasive impact of the railroad on the American economy first as an idea, then as a construction enterprise, and finally as a purveyor of cheap transportation, has become a classic of economic history.[1] The particular contribution of the Jenks article was not the novelty of its viewpoint, but the neat way in which it summarized the conclusions both of those who lived during the "railroad revolution" and those who later analyzed it through the lens of elapsed time. Out of this summary the railroad emerges as the most important innovation of the last two thirds of the nineteenth century. It appears as the *sine qua non* of American economic growth, the prime force behind the westward movement of agriculture, the rise of the corporation, the rapid growth of modern manufacturing industry, the regional location of industry, the pattern of urbanization, and the structure of interregional trade.

Research since the Jenks article has further buttressed the idea that the railroad was an imperative of economic growth. Christopher Savage, in his recent *Economic History of Transport*, states that the influence of the railroad in American development "can hardly be over-emphasized" since "agricultural and industrial development and the settlement of the West would scarcely have been possible" without it.[2] W. W. Rostow has administered an even stronger fillip to this viewpoint. In the projection of his concept of a

---

* Taken and adapted from Robert W. Fogel "Railroads in American Economic Growth," *The Journal of Economic History*, Vol. XXII, No. 2, June 1962, pp. 163–97. Used by permission.

[1] Leland H. Jenks, "Railroads as an Economic Force in American Development," *The Journal of Economic History*, IV, No. 1 (May 1944), 1–20; reprinted in F. C. Lane and J. C. Riemersma, *Enterprise and Secular Change* (Homewood, Ill.: Richard D. Irwin, 1953), pp. 161–80; and in J. T. Lambie and R. V. Clemence, *Economic Change in America* (Harrisburg, Pa.: Stackpole Co., 1954), pp. 52–68.

[2] Christopher I. Savage, *An Economic History of Transport* (London: Hutchinson & Co., 1959), p. 184.

"take-off into self-sustained growth," Rostow assigns railroads a crucial role. The railroad, he argues, was "historically the most powerful single initiator of take-offs." It "performed the Smithian function of widening the market," it was a "pre-requisite in many cases to the development of a major new and rapidly expanding export sector," and most important, it "led on to the development of modern coal, iron and engineering industries." Rostow lists the United States first among the countries in which the influence of the railroad was "decisive." [3]

The idea of a crucial nexus between the railroad and the forward surge of the American economy following 1840 appears to be supported by an avalanche of factual evidence. There is, first of all, the impact of the railroad on the growth of cities. Atlanta was transformed from a spot in the wilderness to a thriving metropolis as a result of the construction of the Western and Atlantic. Chicago eclipsed St. Louis as the commercial emporium of the West by virtue of its superior railroad connections. And Louisville throttled the growth of Cincinnati by its ability to deny the "Porkopolis" rail connection with the South. Further, the decisive victory of the railroads over canals and rivers in the contest for the nation's freight is beyond dispute. One waterway after another was abandoned as a result of its inability to compete with the locomotive. The Pennsylvania Main Line Canal was driven out by the Pennsylvania Railroad, the Blackstone by the Providence and Worcester Railroad, and the Middlesex by the Boston and Lowell line. The Mississippi, which in the early decades of the nineteenth century was the main traffic highway of the center of the continent, had fallen into relative disuse by the end of the century. In 1851–1852 boats carried six times as much freight as railroads; in 1889 the railroads carried five times as much freight as boats.

Finally, there is the high correlation between new railroad construction and both population growth and commercial activity. Illinois, Michigan, and Ohio, for example, experienced a marked increase in population, construction, and manufacturing following the completion of rail lines within and across their borders. For the country as a whole, the undulations in indexes of total output seem to follow closely the cycles in railroad construction. Of particular note is the apparent upsurge in manufacturing output which paralleled the boom in railroad construction. Between 1839 and 1859 railroad mileage in the United States increased by 26,000 miles. The construction of such an immense transportation network required a large volume of manufactured goods, especially iron, lumber, and transportation equipment. Between 1841 and 1850, for example, when railroad mileage increased by 160 per cent, lumber production rose by 150 per cent and pig iron by 100 per cent.

The evidence is impressive. But it demonstrates only an association between the growth of the rail network and the growth of the economy. It fails to establish a causal relationship between the railroad and the regional re-

[3] W. W. Rostow, *The Stages of Economic Growth* (Cambridge: The University Press, 1960), p. 55.

organization of trade, the change in the structure of output, the rise in per capita income, or the various other strategic changes that characterized the American economy of the last century. It does not establish even *prima facie* that the railroad was a necessary condition for these developments. Such a conclusion depends not merely on the traditional evidence, but also on implicit assumptions in its interpretation.

One cannot, for example, leap from data that demonstrate the victory of railroads over waterways in the competition for freight to the conclusion that the development of the railroad network (particularly the trunk lines) was a prerequisite for the rapid, continuous growth of the internal market. The only inference that one can safely draw is that railroads were producing the same (or a similar) service at a lower cost to the buyer. For if rail transportation was a perfect, or nearly perfect, substitute for the canal, all that was required for a large shift from canal to railroad was a small price differential in favor of the latter. Whether the shift produced a significant increase in the size of the internal market depends not on the volume of goods transferred from one medium to the other, but on the magnitude of the associated reduction in transportation costs. If the reduction in cost achieved by the railroads was small, and if canals and rivers could have supplied all or most of the service that railroads were providing without increasing unit charges, then the presence of the railroads did not substantially widen the market, and their absence would not have kept it substantially narrower. The conclusion that the railroad was a necessary condition for the widening of the internal market flows not from a body of observed data, but from the assumption that the cost per unit of transportation service was significantly less by rail than by water.

Other propositions regarding the role of the railroad involve even stronger assumptions than the one just cited. The view that the quantity of manufactured goods used in the construction and maintenance of the railroad was of decisive importance in the upward surge of manufacturing industry during the two decades preceding the Civil War involves a minimum of three assumptions. It not only assumes that the volume of the goods purchased by the railroad was large relative to the total output of the supply industries, but also that railroad purchases were directed toward domestic rather than foreign markets. It assumes further that if there had been no railroad, the demand for manufactured goods by the other forms of transportation would have been significantly less or its impact strategically different from the demand associated with railroads.

The preceding argument is aimed not at refuting the view that the railroad played a decisive role in American development during the nineteenth century. but rather at demonstrating that the empirical base on which this view rests is not nearly so substantial as is usually presumed. The fact that the traditional interpretation involves a number of basic assumptions is not in itself a cause for rejecting it. In the absence of data, the economic historian has no alternative but to make the best possible guess. Without such guesses or assumptions, no analysis is possible. The only question is, "How good are the guesses?" Is there any way of testing them?

It is always easier to point out the need to test a given set of assumptions than to propose a feasible method for testing them. The remainder of this paper deals with the problems involved in evaluating one of the most common presumptions regarding the influence of the railroad on American economic development. The question to be considered is: did the interregional distribution of agricultural products — a striking feature of the American economy of the nineteenth century — depend on the existence of the long-haul railroad? To answer the question, I define a concept of "social saving" in interregional transportation attributable to the existence of the railroad, and propose a method of measuring it. The discussion that follows turns largely on the consistency between the size of this "social saving" and the hypothesis that railroads were a necessary condition for interregional agricultural trade. However, the analytical approach described below transcends the particular hypothesis to which it is applied. The same method is being used to obtain information on such additional questions as the effect of the railroad on the determinants of urbanization, the developmental consequences of various trade rivalries, and the extent to which railroads increased the utilization of land and other resources. The basic issue posed by this paper is the feasibility of applying the analytical techniques of contemporary economics to the reevaluation of one of the major questions in American history — the influence of railroads on economic growth.

II

The massive change in the geographical pattern of agricultural output during the nineteenth century has been a leading theme of American historiography. The meager data at the start of the century strongly suggest that the main sections of the nation were agriculturally self-sufficient. By 1890 the North Atlantic, South Atlantic, and South Central divisions, containing twenty-five states and 60 per cent of the nation's population, had become a deficit area in various agricultural commodities, particularly foodstuffs. The greatest deficits appear in the North Atlantic region, that is, New England, New York, New Jersey, and Pennsylvania. In 1890 this division produced only 36 per cent of its estimated wheat consumption, 45 per cent of the corn requirement, 33 per cent of the beef requirement, and 27 per cent of the pork requirement. The South produced a bigger share of its local needs, but it too had to look outside its borders for a significant part of its food supply. The local supply of foodstuffs in the deficit regions appears even more inadequate when the product needed for the export market is added to domestic consumption. In the North Atlantic division, for example, local production of wheat supplied only 24 per cent of the combined local and export requirement.

In contrast to the decline in regional self-sufficiency in foodstuffs in the

East and South, the North Central division of the country had become a great agricultural surplus area. Virgin territory at the start of the century, these twelve states were producing 71 per cent of the country's cereal grains by 1890 and were also the national center of cattle and swine production. The magnitude of their surpluses is well illustrated by wheat. In the crop year 1890–1891, the twelve states produced 440,000,000 bushels. At five bushels per capita this was enough to feed 88,000,000 people — four times the region's population. Approximately two thirds of the grain surplus of the North Central states was consumed in the East and South, and one third was exported to Europe and South America.

The process by which the agricultural surpluses of the Midwest were distributed can be divided into three stages. In the case of grain, the first stage was the concentration of the surplus in the great primary markets of the Midwest: Chicago, Minneapolis, Duluth, Milwaukee, Peoria, Kansas City, St. Louis, Cincinnati, Toledo, and Detroit. Over 80 per cent of the grain that entered into interregional trade was shipped from the farms to these cities. The second stage involved the shipment of the grain from the primary markets to some ninety secondary markets in the East and South. Among the most important secondary markets were New York City, Baltimore, Boston, Philadelphia, New Orleans, Albany (N. Y.), Portland (Me.), Pittsburgh, Birmingham, and Savannah. The third stage was the distribution of the grain within the territory immediately surrounding the secondary markets, and exportation abroad. The distributional pattern of meat products roughly paralleled that of grain. Perhaps the most important difference was that the first stage of the distribution process — concentration of livestock in the primary markets — was dominated by only four cities: Chicago, St. Louis, Kansas City, and Omaha.

With this background it is possible to give more definite meaning to the term "interregional distribution." For the purposes of this paper, "interregional distribution" is defined as the shipments of commodities from the primary markets of the Midwest to the secondary markets of the East and South. For all other shipments — from farms to primary markets and from secondary markets to the points immediately surrounding them — the term "intraregional distribution" is used. Similarly, the term "interregional railroad" is reserved for lines between primary and secondary markets, and the term "intraregional railroad" is used for all other lines. These terms are useful in distinguishing between the railroad in its role as a long-distance mover of agricultural products and its other functions. It also helps to clarify the hypothesis to be examined in this paper, which can now be stated as follows:

Rail connections between the primary and secondary markets of the nation were a necessary condition for the system of agricultural production and distribution that characterized the American economy of the last half of the nineteenth century. Moreover, the absence of such rail connections would have forced a regional pattern of agricultural production that would have significantly restricted the development of the American economy.

III

In the year 1890, a certain bundle of agricultural commodities was shipped from the primary markets to the secondary markets. The shipment occurred in a certain pattern, that is, with certain tonnages moving from each primary market city to each secondary market city. This pattern of shipments was carried out by some combination of rail, wagon, and water haulage at some definite cost. With enough data, one could determine both this cost and the alternative cost of shipping exactly the same bundle of goods from the primary to the secondary markets in exactly the same pattern without the railroad. The difference between these two amounts I call the social saving attributable to the railroad in the interregional distribution of agricultural products — or simply "the social saving." This difference is in fact larger than what the true social saving would have been.[4] Forcing the pattern of shipments in the nonrail situation to conform to the pattern that actually existed is equivalent to the imposition of a restraint on society's freedom to adjust to a new technological situation. If society had had to ship interregionally by water and wagon without the railroad, it could have shifted agricultural production from the Midwest to the East and South, and shifted some productive factors out of agriculture altogether. Further, the cities entering our set of secondary markets and the tonnages handled by each were surely influenced by conditions peculiar to rail transportation; in the absence of the railroad some different cities would have entered this set, and the relative importance of those remaining would have changed. Adjustments of this sort would have reduced the loss in national income occasioned by the absence of the railroad, but estimates of their effects lie beyond the limits of tools and data. I propose, therefore, to use the social saving, as defined, as the objective standard for testing the hypothesis stated above.

With such a test, one cannot make definite statements about the relationship between the social saving and the geographic structure of agricultural production except for extreme values of the social saving as measured. If the

---

[4] The definition of social saving used in this paper is the difference between the actual level of national income in 1890 and the level of national income that would have prevailed if the economy had made the most efficient possible transport adjustment to the absence of the interregional railroad. As noted in the text, this figure is larger than the more ideal social saving figure, which would take into account the production adjustments that would obtain with a different system of transportation.

In treating the differential in transportation costs as a differential in levels of national income, I am assuming that there would have been no obstacles to an adjustment to a nonrail situation. In other words, I am abstracting from market problems by assuming that national income would have dropped only because it took more productive resources to provide a given amount of transportation, and that all other productive resources would have remained fully employed. The relationship between the railroad and the demand for output is the subject of one of the other essays in my study.

calculation shows the saving to be zero, then obviously the absence of the interregional railroad would not have altered the existing productive pattern. On the other hand, if the social saving turns out to be very large, say on the order of magnitude of national income, it would be equally obvious that in the absence of the interregional railroad all production of surpluses in the Midwest would have ceased. For small differences in the cost differential, there is very little that can be said about the change in the geographic structure of output. It is theoretically conceivable that even a social saving as small as one fourth of 1 per cent of national income would have ended all or most surplus production in the North Central states. But this limitation in the proposed index is not quite so serious as it might seem. For the central concern here is with the influence of the railroad on the course of American economic development. The crucial question is not whether the absence of the railroad would have left agricultural production in a different regional pattern, but whether such a pattern would have significantly restricted economic growth. Sharp regional shifts in production associated with very small values of the social saving would be immaterial from this point of view. They would have served to demonstrate that many geographic patterns of production were consistent with a given rate of economic development, and the geographic pattern of agricultural production could be dismissed as a significant element in the growth of the American economy.

The social saving is calculated in my estimates for only one year, 1890. Yet the hypothesis to be tested refers to a period covering almost half a century. How sound an inference about the significance of the railroad's role with respect to agricultural development over such a period can be made on the basis of only one year's data? The answer depends on the relative efficiency of the railroad in 1890 as compared to earlier periods. If the railroad was relatively more efficient in 1890 than in any previous year, the social saving per unit of transportation in 1890 would have exceeded the saving per unit in all previous years. The available evidence suggests that this was indeed the case. The four decades between 1850 and 1890 were ones of continuous advance in efficiency. The size, speed, and pulling capacity of the locomotive were steadily increased, as was the weight of the load a freight car could carry. At the same time, the scattered rail lines were integrated into a network, thus eliminating or reducing transshipment costs. Terminal facilities were expanded, and such important loading devices as the grain elevator were brought into general operation. Perhaps the most significant indication of the increase in the railroad's relative efficiency is the very considerable shift of heavy, low-value items away from water carriers. In 1852 boats and barges dominated the interregional transportation of these items, while in 1890 they were carried mainly by the railroad. Since the volume of agricultural commodities transported between regions had also increased over the period in question, it seems apparent that the social saving in 1890 exceeded in absolute amount the saving of previous years. While it is true that national income rose over the period, the amount of agricultural goods shipped interregionally appears to have risen just as rapidly. In the case of wheat, population and production figures suggest that local requirements in the deficit states were at least 1.1 million tons less in 1870 than they were in 1890. Export requirements were 1.8 million tons less. These figures indicate that the quantity shipped interregionally increased by 145 per cent over two decades — showing approximately the same rate of growth as real national income. Thus, if it is shown that the social saving of 1890 was quite small relative to national income, the relationship would hold with equal force for the half-century preceding 1890.

The problem posed here would be trivial if the wagon were the only alternative to the railroad in interregional transportation. By 1890 the average cost of railroad transportation was less than a cent per ton-mile. On the other hand, the cost of wagon transportation was in the neighborhood of twenty-five cents per ton-mile. According to estimates made here, approximately 7.7 million tons of corn and 5.0 million tons of wheat entered into interregional transportation. Taking the differential between rail and wagon transportation at twenty-five cents per ton-mile, the social saving involved in moving these 12.7 million tons one mile would have been $3,180,000. Assuming that on the average the corn and wheat shipped interregionally traveled nine hundred miles, the total social saving would have been $2,860,000,-000. Even this figure is low, since wagon rates did not reflect the cost involved in road construction and maintenance. If account were taken of these and other omitted charges, and if a similar calculation were performed for livestock, the figure for the social saving would probably increase by 50 per cent, to four billion dollars, or more than one third of gross national product in 1890. This magnitude exceeds Gallman's 1889 estimate of gross income originating in agriculture by 43 per cent. Such a loss would have pushed the economy back two decades and probably cut the rate of investment by a third. The calculation is very crude, of course, but there seems little doubt that the order of magnitude is correct.

The problem is not trivial, because water transportation was a practical alternative to the railroad in interregional transportation. A glance at a map will show that all of the primary market cities were on navigable waterways. Duluth, Milwaukee, Chicago, Toledo, and Detroit were on the Great Lakes; Omaha and Kansas City were on the Missouri; Minneapolis and St. Louis were on the Mississippi; Cincinnati was on the Ohio; and Peoria was on the Illinois River, midway between the Mississippi and Lake Michigan. The lakes, inland rivers, canals, and coastal waters directly linked the primary market cities to most of the secondary market cities. Of the forty-three most important secondary markets, thirty-two were located on navigable waters still in use in 1890. Seven were on waterways that had been forced into inactivity as a result of railroad competition, but which could have been used in the absence of the railroad. Only four cities were without direct water connection to the Midwest, and each of these was within a relatively short wagon haul of a major water artery.

The importance of a water-route alternative lies in the fact that on a per ton-mile basis, water rates were not only less than wagon rates but also less than railroad rates. The all-rail rate on wheat from Chicago to New York, for example, was about 0.52 cents per ton-mile, or nearly four times as much as the ton-mile rate by water. This fact does not, of course, imply that the social cost or even the private cost on a given tonnage was less when shipped by water. Water routes were much more circuitous than rail routes, and the time in transit was considerably greater. Loss of cargo was more frequent. Terminal charges were higher. These and other problems raised the cost of water transportation to a point where shipments between most primary and most secondary markets were cheaper by rail than by boat. What makes the problem interesting is that the amount by which water costs exceeded railroad costs is far from obvious. As has already been suggested, the massive switch from rail to water transportation by no means implies that the cost differential was large. Consider the hypothetical case of a Chicago wheat shipper who made a profit of 10 per cent on the Chicago price of wheat or nine cents per bushel on a price of ninety cents. If the cost of shipment, all factors considered, was the same by both water and rail, the shipper would be indifferent as to which form he used. Suppose now that technological advances made it possible for the shipper to get his bushel to market for two cents less than before. How strong an inducement to switch from water to rail transportation would such a differential generate? By reducing his cost two cents per bushel, the shipper could increase his profit by 22 per cent. Clearly, the implication of this example is that a differential of two cents per bushel would have created a very strong pressure to shift all wheat that had been transported by water to railroads. Yet the social saving involved in such a shift would have been just $3,300,000 — much too small an amount to prove the indispensability of the interregional railroad to American economic growth.

Until now, the discussion has been carried on as if all the agricultural commodities that entered into interregional trade were to be included in the estimate. In fact, the estimate will be based on only four commodities: wheat, corn, beef, and pork. These four accounted for 42 per cent of income originating in agriculture in 1889. Neglect of the other products is not so serious as it first seems. What is important is not the share of wheat, corn, beef, and pork in total output, but their share in that part of output which entered interregional trade. Obviously, if none of the neglected 58 per cent of output moved interregionally, the restriction is of no real consequence. The most important of the omitted items is cotton, which represented 11 per cent of output. But relatively little cotton entered interregional transportation as here defined, and a large part of the crop shipped interregionally was carried by water. This is illustrated by the distribution of the 1898–1899 crop. Of the output of that season, 79 per cent was shipped from southern farms to southern seaport cities, and carried from there by boat to Europe or to northern ports in the United States. Another 13 per cent was consumed in the South. Hence, at most only 8 per cent or 225,000 tons of cotton (that is, 900,000 bales) could have entered into interregional rail transportation. But 225,000 tons is only 1.8 per cent of the combined wheat-corn tonnage. The case of dairy products, which accounted for 12 per cent of total product, is similar. There are three main dairy products: milk, butter, and cheese. Of these, milk was entirely an intraregional product. Census data on butter and cheese production in the Midwest indicate that the amount entering interregional trade was about 166,000 tons or 1.3 per cent of the wheat-corn tonnage. Again, while virtually all wool was transported from west to east, it was less than 1 per cent (closer to one half of 1 per cent) of the wheat-corn tonnage. In short, neglected items probably do not account for more than 10 per cent of the goods entering into interregional trade, and would not justify the effort required to include them.

The most direct method of determining the social saving is to find the 1890 pattern of the shipments of the four commodities, and then estimate both the actual cost of the pattern and the cost that would have obtained if the pattern had been executed with only boats and wagons. This method requires the following data: the amount of each commodity shipped from each primary market, the amounts received by each secondary market, the routes over which they were shipped, and the transportation costs by each medium. But not all of these data are available. The total volume of shipments from each of the primary markets can be determined, but not their destination and routes. Receipts of the secondary markets can be estimated, but not the markets from which these goods came. The impasse is, of course, only apparent. The gap in the statistics can be bridged by linear programming techniques which yield the solution at a cheaper cost in terms of data requirements. It seems likely, incidentally, that in this case and in others as well mathematical techniques of analysis can reduce the amount of information required to evaluate a given hypothesis. The linear programming problem is not solved in this paper, but a short discussion will indicate its possibilities.

The actual method of analysis is simple. It involves a pair of linear programming models for each commodity. The procedure can be illustrated by considering the case of wheat. In 1890, a certain amount of wheat was shipped from the Midwest to the secondary markets. The first linear programming model will find the least cost of carrying the wheat from the primary to the secondary markets without imposing any restraint on the means of transportation that can be used — that is, allowing the shipments to be made in the cheapest manner, regardless of the transportation medium. The second model imposes the restriction that railroads cannot be used, and then finds the least cost of shipping the same quantity of wheat from the primary to the secondary markets. Presumably these two least-cost figures will differ; but this difference will reflect only the absence of the railroad, since the quantities shipped from each of the primary markets and the requirements of each of the secondary markets will be the same in both models. The difference between the two least-cost figures is the estimate of social saving due to the use of the railroad in the interregional transportation of wheat. The cost differential obtained from such a pair of linear programming models will exceed the true social saving for the reasons specified in Section III, above.

The water rates to be used in the second model must (with some exceptions) be those that actually prevailed in 1890. Even if water rates in 1890 equaled marginal costs, their use in the second model would introduce a bias, since these rates applied to a tonnage which is less than the amount specified in the model. To use them is equivalent to assuming that the marginal cost of water transportation was constant over the relevant range. This assumption probably accentuates the upward bias of the estimate. If all costs except the construction of canals and channels are considered variable, then it seems quite reasonable to assume that marginal costs were constant or declining. The basic operating unit in water transportation was the boat, and boat building may have been subject to economies of scale. In any case, most water routes were greatly under-utilized in 1890 and would have been under-utilized even if they had carried some considerable share of the additional interregional tonnage. Maintenance and other operating costs (for example, dredging, repairing locks, supplying water) would have increased only slightly with additional tonnage. To the extent that these tendencies were operative, the 1890 water rates impart an upward bias to the estimate of social saving. Finally, it is important to note that the published 1890 rates did not reflect all of the costs involved in water transportation. In order to avoid introducing a downward bias into the calculations, it will be necessary to take account of such factors as spoilage, transit time and the unavailability of water routes for five months out of the year. The manner in which these factors will be dealt with is discussed in the final section of this paper.

IV

Use of linear programming would reduce, but does not eliminate, the data problem. An enormous amount of information, some of which cannot be obtained directly, is needed. This section seeks to demonstrate how the necessary estimates can be derived from existing, but largely neglected, bodies of data. What is involved is the application of the estimating techniques usually reserved for the construction of national income accounts to a specific historical problem. It should be emphasized that the results presented below are tentative; many obvious adjustments have not yet been made. Nevertheless, the figures on tonnages entering interregional trade are sufficiently close to the truth for the use to which they are put in the final section of this paper. The problems encountered in translating a theoretically conceived estimate into an actual one can best be discussed by grouping them under four headings: shipments, requirements, railroad rates, and water rates.

Much has been written on the internal agricultural trade of the United States during the nineteenth century. In addition to Schmidt's series of articles in the *Iowa Journal of History and Politics* (1920–1922), there are the studies in the *Census of Agriculture* for 1860 and 1880, the biennial reports on internal commerce issued by the Treasury Department between 1876 and 1891, the volume on the distribution of agricultural products compiled by the Industrial Commission of 1900, and a series of articles which appeared in the *Monthly Summary of Commerce and Finance* in 1900. All of these studies examined the system of primary markets, and they provide a considerable amount of data on the relative importance of the various cities. Surprisingly enough, however, these sources — whether considered separately or together — fail to yield enough data to compile a complete schedule of the shipments of grains and provisions for any year during the nineteenth century. Schmidt comes the closest, giving a schedule of the receipts of grains by primary markets for the year 1890. While there is a relationship between receipts and shipments, Schmidt does not indicate how to convert one into the other. An even more difficult problem is the absence of a complete series on shipments of provisions.

Fortunately, the desired data were relatively easy to obtain. Figures on the shipments of each of the various commodities were taken from the reports of the produce exchanges, the boards of trade or chambers of commerce of each of the primary market cities. These documents contain much highly reliable information, but except in the cases of Chicago, St. Louis, and New York, they have been badly neglected. Table 1 gives the preliminary figures

■ **TABLE 1   Shipments of Corn and Wheat from Primary Markets, 1890**

(*Thousands of tons*)

Primary Market	Wheat [a]	Corn [b]
Chicago	950	2,536
Minneapolis	1,322	53
Duluth-Superior	793	41
Milwaukee	516	7
Peoria	35	211
Kansas City	181	505
St. Louis	522	1,218
Cincinnati	181	70
Toledo	309	463
Detroit	125	32
Total	4,934	5,136

[a] Includes flour converted into wheat at the rate: one barrel of flour equals 0.1430 ton of wheat.
[b] Includes corn meal converted into corn at the rate: one barrel of corn meal equals 0.1262 ton of corn.
Sources: See discussion in text, pp. 169, 178–79.

on the shipments of corn and wheat from the primary markets. The compilation of data on meat shipments is still in process.

The estimation of requirements of the secondary markets is much more difficult than the shipments from the primary markets. The problem here is not merely the absence of a convenient series on the requirements of the various secondary markets; with the exception of such obvious places as New York, Baltimore, and New Orleans, there was no way of knowing which of the various cities of the East and South comprised the relevant set of secondary markets.

The first task, then, was to find some basis for dividing the deficit regions into marketing areas and for determining the cities which served as distributing centers of the area. The basic reference for making this division was a study of wholesale grocery territories carried out by the Department of Commerce in the 1920's. This study divided the country into 183 trading areas. Each of the areas was composed of a group of counties served by a single city. The Boston trading area, for example, was determined by a survey of the wholesale firms situated in Boston, and comprised the six counties immediately surrounding the city.

Since grain and provisions were wholesale grocery products, the Department of Commerce survey provided an appropriate framework for the estimates. That the territories it defined pertained to the economy of the 1920's is not a crucial consideration. The basic rail network, especially in the East, was well established by 1890 and remained stable over the ensuing three decades. In the 1920's, trucks had not yet altered existing geographical patterns of trade. They appeared to have affected the size of the inventories carried by outlying retailers rather than the boundaries of the marketing areas. The impression that motor vehicles conformed to, rather than altered, preexisting patterns is buttressed by a study of wholesale territories made in the late 1930's. The trading areas described by this survey were virtually identical with the earlier set.

This demarcation of trading territories made it possible to devise a procedure for estimating the requirements of each territory by commodity. The area requirement for a given commodity was the difference between the area's total demand for the commodity (including exports) and the amount of the commodity supplied from within the area. Thus, to determine the requirements, estimates of both total demand and local supply were needed. The procedure for arriving at these estimates can be illustrated by the case of wheat.

The total demand for wheat in a given area consisted of two parts: the local demand and the export demand. The export demand was determined directly from export statistics provided by the Treasury Department; the local demand had to be estimated indirectly. The local demand for wheat was almost entirely for human consumption. For the country as a whole, about 10 per cent of the annual wheat crop was set aside for seed and about 2 per cent for animal feed. However, the share of wheat demanded for seed in the deficit regions was considerably less than the national share, since wheat production was quite small. This was especially true in New England, where wheat used as seed was only one half of 1 per cent of the quantity consumed by humans. Similarly, the practice of feeding wheat to animals appears to have been practiced primarily in the areas of surplus production. Hence, the estimate of local demand was largely a matter of determining human consumption.

Total human consumption in a trading area was equal to per capita consumption multiplied by the population of the area. Statistics on area population were obtained from the 1890 census. The tentative estimate of average consumption by regions was calculated from a 1909 survey of urban workers conducted by the British Board of Trade. Based on these data, the estimated per capita consumption of wheat is 4.80 bushels per year in the North and 4.70 bushels per year in the South. These figures do not include an adjustment for urban-rural differences in wheat consumption. However, it does not seem likely that the adjustment, when it is made, will significantly alter the results. A 1913–1914 survey indicates an average per capita wheat consumption of 5.08 bushels among 421 farm families in five North Atlantic states, and an average per capita consumption of 5.13 bushels among 149 families in three southern states.

The local supply of wheat in a trading area was the sum of the annual local production of wheat and the supply (positive or negative) out of local inventories. The Department of Agriculture has published estimates of the production of wheat in 1890 by states but not by counties. However, county data were needed to determine local production in a trading area. The 1889 census production data by counties were multiplied by the 1890:1889 ratio of output for the state in which the particular county was located. Inventories of wheat were held by two main groups: wholesalers in the central cities of the trading areas, and farmers. It was not possible to obtain data on changes in the inventories of wholesalers. However, reports on the inventories in the hands of farmers on March 1, 1890 and March 1, 1891 were published by the Department of Agriculture.[5] It was therefore possible to estimate the change in farmers' inventories which, as a factor in supply, was probably more significant than the change in wholesalers' inventories.

The estimate of total wheat requirements of all the secondary markets in the deficit regions is given in Table 2. It is broken down into a local consumption deficit (obtained by subtracting local production and changes in farm inventories from my estimate of the local demand in each area) and foreign exports. The latter figure is based on the *Commerce and Navigation Reports* of the Treasury Department.

It is possible to test the procedure for estimating local requirements of wheat. Data are available in reports of local boards of trade on the receipts

[5] Baltimore Corn and Flour Exchange, *Annual Report*, 1889, 1890.

■ **TABLE 2   Estimated Requirements of Secondary Markets**

(Thousands of tons)

	1 Local Consumption Deficits	2 Exports	3 Total Requirements (Col. 1 plus Col. 2)
Wheat [a]	3,099	1,916	5,015
Corn [b]	5,415	2,320	7,735
Dressed pork	729	347	1,076
Dressed beef	701	304	1,005

[a] Includes flour converted into wheat at the rate: one barrel of flour equals 0.1430 ton of wheat.
[b] Includes corn meal converted into corn at the rate: one barrel of corn meal equals 0.1262 ton of corn.

Sources: See discussion in text, pp. 181–84.

and foreign exports of the five largest secondary markets. Abstracting from inventory fluctuations, the receipts minus foreign exports will be equal to the local consumption requirement, providing that no wheat is grown locally. This method of estimation cannot be used for three of these largest marketing areas (New York, Philadelphia, and Baltimore) since they grew considerable quantities of wheat, an undetermined amount of which was processed at merchant mills for local consumption, and failed to enter into board of trade statistics. However, only 441 bushels of wheat were grown in the Boston trading area and 120 bushels in the New Orleans trading area, so virtually all the wheat demanded by these markets originated outside the trading areas and was recorded in commercial statistics. To eliminate inventory fluctuations, a nine-year average (centered on 1890) of receipts minus exports was taken. As shown in Table 3, local requirements estimated in this way tend to support the basic estimating procedure. The figure on the New Orleans marketing region (with 64 per cent of the population living in rural areas) lends support to the finding that wheat consumption in the South was considerably higher than has been generally realized.

The procedure followed in estimating corn requirements was similar to that used in the case of wheat. The most important difference was that human consumption represented only 8 per cent of the total demand for corn. Estimates of average animal consumption per head were obtained for each of the main categories of animals. But these averages were only available on a national basis. To the extent that there were regional differences in animal consumption of corn, the estimates tend to overstate requirements of some areas and understate those of others.

In estimating the local demand for beef and pork, national per capita disappearance figures were first obtained, following the method of the Department of Agriculture. The national figures were transformed into regional per capita estimates by using weights taken from a 1901 budget study conducted by the Bureau of Labor. Supply was determined in the manner described by

■ **TABLE 3   A Comparison of the Estimates of the Local Consumption Deficits of Wheat for Two Trading Areas**

(Thousands of bushels)

	1 Method One (local demand minus local supply)	2 Method Two (nine-year average of receipts minus exports)	3 Column One as a Per Cent of Column Two
Boston	6,996	7,215	97
New Orleans	3,504	3,070	114

Strauss and Bean. Table 2 presents tentative estimates of the requirements of meat in the deficit areas. These figures will also have to be adjusted for urban-rural differences in consumption, but the adjustment will not significantly alter the aggregate meat requirement of the deficit areas. Funk's 1913–1914 study indicates that average consumption of beef and pork together in 570 northern and southern farm families was 157 pounds per equivalent adult. Department of Agriculture data indicate that for the population as a whole the corresponding 1913 figure was about 160 pounds per equivalent adult. However, since farm families ate considerably more pork than beef, the urban-rural adjustment will reduce the estimated amount of the aggregate beef deficit and increase the amount of the aggregate pork deficit in about the same proportions.

Standard sources such as the *Annual Reports* of the Interstate Commerce Commission, the Treasury Department *Reports of Internal Commerce,* and the report of the Aldrich Committee provide information on less than 10 per cent of the relevant interregional routes. Fortunately, the tariffs filed with the Interstate Commerce Commission under the Interstate Commerce Act of 1887 are available. These files contain the published rates on all of the desired routes.

To the extent that rebating took place, published rates exceeded actual rates. State and Federal investigations produced voluminous reports and documents on the rebating problem. These contain data that can be used to adjust some of the published rates. Continuing research in archives may yield additional information. However, some procedure will have to be devised by which one can both check the reliability of the evidence in the public record and estimate rebates for which no direct evidence exists. One possible approach involves the use of published rates for a year like 1910, when rebating was rather generally eliminated. Abstracting from changes in the price level, the fall in average published rates between 1890 and 1910 is attributable to two factors: the elimination of rebating and the decline in actual rates. Therefore, the differences between average published rates in 1890 and in 1910 (adjusted for changes in the price level) are the most that the average rebate could have been. Thus, by multiplying appropriate ratios of average 1910 rates to 1890 rates by the actual 1890 rates, one obtains an estimate of the least that average actual rates could have been in 1890.

Water transportation was dominated by three main routes: the Great Lakes and Erie Canal route, the Mississippi route and the intracoastal route. Every movement from a primary to a secondary market can be divided into a movement along one or more of these lines, plus an additional short movement along some other body of water. Rates on the main water highways are available in board of trade reports, tariffs filed with the Interstate Commerce Commission, and other documents. Thus only a small part of the charge to a shipper will have to be estimated. Moreover, possible deviations between published and actual water rates are less troublesome. To the extent that such deviations existed, the upward bias of the estimated social saving will be further accentuated.

V

There is no reliable way to predict the outcome of the linear programming problems. In computations of this sort, surprises are common. Even if all the required data were compiled, it would be difficult to anticipate such results as the efficient patterns of trade in the rail and nonrail situations or the breakdown of the social saving by products, routes, and regions. However, a crude estimate of the *aggregate* social saving is possible. The calculation that follows involves guesses about average transit distances and average freight rates by both water and rail — averages that cannot reliably be calculated until the linear programming problems are solved. Despite its crudity, the calculation is useful for two reasons. First, it provides a convenient format for demonstrating the ways in which a number of costs — costs that have been considered unquantifiable — can be quantified. Second, it provides a rough idea of the magnitude of the aggregate social saving that one can expect to obtain from the models.

The starting point of the calculation is the difference between the average ton-mile transportation rate by water and by rail. Various experts on transportation have pointed out that water rates were generally less than railroad rates. Thus, over the route from Chicago to New York, the average all-rail rate on wheat in 1890 was 0.523 cents per ton-mile while the average all-water rate was 0.139 cents per ton-mile. Casual examination of the available data suggests that the figures are approximately the same as those applying to all grains on this and other routes. Hence, for the purposes of calculation it will be arbitrarily assumed that the New York to Chicago all-water rate per ton-mile on wheat equaled the average all-water rate (per ton-mile) on all grains over all the relevant routes. The assumption to be made on the all-rail rate is symmetric.

For the crude calculation of the social saving, the average national rate at which grain was actually transported in 1890 is needed. This actual rate must have been less than the all-rail rate. Not all grains shipped interregionally were carried exclusively by rail. Considerable quantities were shipped by a combination of rail and water or completely by water. In contrast to the 0.523 cents all-rail rate per ton-mile on wheat transported from Chicago to New York, the lake-and-rail charge was 0.229 cents, and the lake-and-canal charge was 0.186 cents. The average of these three rates, weighted by the quantities of grain shipped under each one, is 0.434 cents (see Table 4). This

■ **TABLE 4   Estimate of the Average Actual Rate**

Type of Transportation	1 Rate per Ton-Mile (cents)	2 Wheat and Corn (millions of tons)	3 Col. 1 × Col. 2 (cents)
1. All-water	0.186	1.254	0.2332
2. Water and rail	0.229	2.423	0.5549
3. All-rail	0.523	9.073	4.7452
4. Sum of columns		12.750	5.5335
5. Average actual rate in cents per ton-mile (sum of Col. 3 ÷ sum of Col. 2)			0.434

Sources and Notes:
    Column 1. The three rates were determined by taking the Chicago-to-New York charges on wheat (including transshipment and insurance costs) and dividing each charge by the appropriate distance. U. S. Congress, House, "Distribution of Farm Products," VI, 142; George G. Tunell, "The Diversion of the Flour and Grain Traffic from the Great Lakes to the Railroad," "Journal of Political Economy" V, No. 3 (June 1897) 345; U. S. Congress, Senate, Select Committee on Transportation—Routes to the Seaboard, Report No. 307, Part 1, 43rd Cong., 1st Sess., p. 17; below, Table 6.
    Column 2, Line 1. This is the total amount of wheat (including the grain equivalent of flour) and corn shipped by canal from the lake ports of Buffalo, Oswego and Tonawanda plus the quantity of the same commodities shipped by river from St. Louis. The amount of flour shipped from St. Louis by boat was obtained by multiplying the proportion of flour shipped by river in 1898 by the total 1890 shipments of flour. Line 2 is the amount of wheat (including the grain equivalent of flour) and corn received at the lake ports of Erie, Buffalo, Oswego and Ogdensburg minus the grain shipped from lake ports by canal. Line 3 is the total quantity of wheat and corn shipped interregionally minus lines 1 and 2. Buffalo Merchants' Exchange, Annual Report, 1891, pp. 71, 106, 108, 109, 112; U. S. Congress, House, Report on the Internal Commerce of the United States for the Year 1891, Executive Doc. No. 6, Part 2, 52nd Cong., 1st Sess., XXVI; U. S. Statistics Bureau, Monthly Summary of Commerce and Finance, 7 (Jan. 1900), pp. 2006–7, 2009, U. S. Congress, Senate, Wholesale Prices, Wages, and Transportation (Aldrich Report), Report No. 1394, Part 1, 52nd Cong., 2nd Sess., p. 558; Table 6, below.

last figure will be taken as the "actual" national average rate on grains per ton-mile in 1890. In passing, it may be noted that the adjustment produced a figure which is less than a mill below the all-rail rate.

In the case of meat and livestock products, the calculation is based on the St. Louis to New Orleans rates on pork. The all-rail rate was 1.07 cents per ton-mile and the all-water rate was 0.45 cents. Again, these rates are comparable to those that prevailed on other meat products shipped on this and other routes. Furthermore, since the quantity of meat shipped by water was a small part of the total interregional tonnage, no further adjustment need be made; that is, the all-rail rate on pork will be assumed to equal the actual average rate on all meat products.

The quantity of corn, wheat, pork, and beef shipped interregionally in 1890 was approximately equal to the net local deficit of the trading areas plus net exports.[6] Assuming that half of the meat products was shipped as livestock and half as dressed meat, the amount transported interregionally was 15,700,-000 tons.[7]

Estimates of average distances are based on a sample of thirty routes (pairs of cities). The sample was randomly drawn from a population of 875 routes. The average rail distance in the sample was 926 miles, and the average water distance was 1,574 miles.[8] Since only small amounts of meat were transported by water, 926 miles will be assumed to be the average distance over which meats were actually shipped in 1890. In the case of grains, an adjustment should be made for the tonnage that was carried partly or wholly by water. The adjusted figure, 1,044 miles, represents the estimate of the average distance over which grains were actually shipped in 1890.[9]

Method	1 Distance (miles)	2 Tons of Grain (millions)	3 Millions of Ton-Miles (Col. 1 × Col. 2)
1. All-rail	926	9.073	8,402
2. Water-and-rail	1,302	2.423	3,155
3. All-water	1,398	1.254	1,753
4. Totals		12.750	13,310
5. Average distance (sum of Col. 3 ÷ sum of Col. 2)			1,044 miles

If rates and ton-miles were the only elements entering into the cost of transportation, it would have been cheaper to have shipped interregionally by water than by rail. As shown in Table 5, the social saving calculated on the basis of these elements is negative by about $38,000,000. This odd result is not difficult to explain. While the estimated actual cost of transportation includes virtually all relevant items, the estimated cost of water transportation does not. In calculating the cost of shipping without the railroad, one must account for six neglected items of cost not reflected in the first approximation: cargo losses in transit, transshipment costs, wagon haulage from water points to secondary markets not on water routes, the cost resulting from the time lost when using a slow medium of transportation, the cost of being unable to use water routes for five months out of the year, and finally, capital costs not reflected in water rates.

When account is taken of the six neglected costs, the loss attributable to the railroad will be transformed into a saving. How big must the neglected

---

[6] See p. 296, Table 2.

[7] A breakdown of this figure is given in Table 6.

[8] The averages are simple arithmetic means.

Water distances between the points in the sample are an average of 70 per cent longer than rail distances. This suggests a somewhat greater degree of circuity in water transportation than was indicated by the study of the Bureau of Railway Economics, *An Economic Survey of Inland Waterway Transportation in the United States*, Special Series, No. 57 (Washington: Bureau of Railway Economics, 1930).

[9] The adjustment was made in the following manner:

■ **TABLE 5** First Approximation of the Social Saving

Com-modity	1 Quantity Shipped (millions of tons)	2 Millions of Ton-Miles of Water Transportation (Col. 1 × 1,574 miles)	3 Water Rate per Ton-Mile (dollars)	4 Cost of Water Transportation in Millions of Dollars (Col. 2 × Col. 3)	5 Average Actual Distance (miles)	6 Millions of Ton-Miles of Actual Transportation (Col. 1 × Col. 5)	7 Actual Rate per Ton-Mile (dollars)	8 Cost of Actual Transportation in Millions of Dollars (Col. 6 × Col. 7)	9 Social Saving in Millions of Dollars (Col. 4 − Col. 8)
Meats	3.000	4,722	.00451	21.296	926	2,778	.01071	29.752	− 8.456
Grains	12.750	20,069	.00139	27.896	1,044	13,311	.00434	57.770	−29.874
Totals	15.750	24,791		49.192		16,089		87.522	−38.330

Sources: See notes to Tables 4, 6, and text, pp. 186–90.

costs be to produce a positive saving of 1 per cent of national income? In 1890 gross national product was about $12,000,000,000, and 1 per cent of this amount is $120,000,000. Without the neglected costs, interregional shipment of the four commodities would have been $38,000,000 cheaper by water than by rail. Consequently, in order to reach a social saving of 1 per cent of gross national product, the neglected costs will have to be approximately $158,-000,000.

The literature on the interregional transportation of agricultural products indicates that cargo losses were greater on water shipments than on rail shipments. Insurance rates can be used to estimate the cost of these water transit losses. Since the average value of a loss on a given shipment was approximately equal to the insurance charge on the shipment, the total value of cargo losses in the absence of the railroad would have been approximately equal to the average insurance charge on a water shipment multiplied by the total value of the goods transported interregionally. Moreover, since railroad rates included insurance, this figure would also represent the neglected cost of cargo losses. The calculation is shown in Table 6. The cost of insurance (cost of cargo losses) in the absence of the railroad would have been approximately $6,000,000. Subtracting this figure from $158,000,000, there is left $152,000,000 to cover the remaining costs.

Transshipping costs were incurred whenever it became necessary to switch a cargo from one type of vessel to another. Grain shipped from Chicago to New York, for example, was transferred at Buffalo from lake steamers to canal barges. In the absence of the railroad there would probably have been an average of two transshipments on each ton carried from a primary to a secondary market. At a cost of fifty cents per ton per transshipment, transshipping charges on the grain and meat products in question would have been $16,000,000. Subtracting this amount from $152,000,000, there is left $136,-000,000 to cover the remaining costs.

The two indirect costs of water transportation most frequently cited are the cost of time lost in shipping by water and the cost of being unable to use water routes for about five months out of each year. Arguments based on the time factor and the limited season of navigation have been decisive in ruling out the possibility that water transportation could have been a good substitute for the railroad. Once invoked, these arguments are invincible, since the costs involved seem to be limited only by the intuition of the disputants. Without a means of quantifying the cost of time and the cost of the limited season of navigation, the hypothesis posed in this paper cannot be tested.

The key to quantifying the cost of the time that would have been lost in water transportation is the nexus between time and inventories. If entrepreneurs could replace goods the instant they were sold, they would, *ceteris paribus*, carry zero inventories. Inventories are necessary to bridge the gap of time required to deliver a commodity from its supply source to a given point. If, on the average, interregional shipments of agricultural commodities re-

■ **TABLE 6   Estimated Cost of Insurance**

	1	2	3	4	5
				Insurance Rate as a Pro-	Cost of Insurance
	Tons Shipped Interregionally	Price per Ton	Value (Col. 1 × Col. 2)	portion of Value	(Col. 3 × Col. 4)
1. Cattle	949,000	$ 97	$ 92,100,000	.01	$ 921,000
2. Dressed beef	503,000	138	69,400,000	.01	694,000
3. Hogs	1,008,000	79	79,600,000	.01	796,000
4. Dressed pork	538,000	110	59,200,000	.01	592,000
5. Corn	7,735,000	13	100,600,000	.01	1,006,000
6. Wheat	5,015,000	30	150,500,000	.01	1,505,000
7. Totals	15,748,000		551,400,000		5,514,000

Sources and Notes:

Column 1. Estimates of tons shipped interregionally are based on the local net deficits of the secondary markets plus exports. In the case of meats, it was assumed that half the deficit was shipped as dressed meats and half as livestock. Dressed pork was converted into a live weight equivalent at the rate of one pound of dressed pork equal to 1.874 pounds of live weight; for beef the conversion factor was one pound of dressed beef equal to 1.887 pounds of live weight. See above, pp. 183–85.

Column 2. The figures cited are the average Chicago wholesale prices except for dressed meats, which are New York quotations. In the case of wheat and corn, the prices represent unweighted averages of the twelve average monthly prices, with averages of missing months determined by linear interpolation. George K. Holmes, "Meat Situation in the United States", U. S. Agriculture Dept., Departmental Report No. 109, Part 1, pp. 289–98; U. S. Congress, Senate, Aldrich Report, Part 2, p. 10; U. S. Census Bureau, Historical Statistics of the United States, Colonial Times to 1957 (Washington: Govt. Printing Office, 1960), p. 123.

Column 4. Insurance rates varied with the distance of a shipment and the route. In 1850, average insurance rates on the Mississippi and Ohio were about 1 per cent of the value of the cargo per thousand miles. In 1870, the rate on the Great Lakes was about the same. However, scattered data suggest that in subsequent years marine insurance rates fell sharply. By the 1890's, insurance on the Lakes was 0.3 per cent per thousand miles. A decade later the rate on cargo from Pittsburgh to New Orleans was about 0.7 cent per thousand miles, while the intracoastal rate was about 0.1 cent. In the absence of the railroad perhaps half of the tonnage would have been carried over the Lakes on intracoastal routes. In view of the foregoing, it seems reasonable to assume that in the absence of the railroad, the average insurance rate probably would not have exceeded the later Mississippi rate, that is, 0.7 cents per thousand miles or approximately 1 per cent for 1,574 miles. Louis C. Hunter, "Steamboats in Western Rivers" (Cambridge: Harvard Univ. Press, 1949), pp. 368–69; U. S. Congress, Senate, Select Committee on Transportation — Routes to the Seaboard, Report No. 307 Part 1, p. 17; George G. Tunell, "The Diversion of Flour and Grain Traffic," p. 345; U. S. Congress, Senate Preliminary Report of the Inland Waterways Commission, pp. 332–33.

quired a month more by water than by rail, it would have been possible to compensate for the time lost through an inventory increase in the secondary markets equal to one twelfth of annual shipments. Hence the cost of the time lost in using water transportation was the 1890 cost of carrying such an additional inventory.

The problems inherent in the limited season of water transportation could also have been met by an increase in inventory. Since water routes were closed for five twelfths of the year, I will assume that the absence of railroads would have increased the inventories of agricultural commodities held in secondary markets by five twelfths of the annual interregional shipment. It should be noted that this assumption overstates the additional inventory requirement. Abstracting from risk considerations, the limited season of navigation would — at least with respect to grains — have had no effect on the inventory requirements of the nation. A crop once harvested was placed in inventory and drawn down throughout the year. A shorter transportation season would only have affected the way in which a fixed total inventory was divided between the Midwest and the secondary markets. Exclusive reliance on water routes would have increased the inventory total only if risk factors were operative. Under conditions of risk, the availability of a central depository reduces the size of the stock that must be held by a given set of cities. Nevertheless, the five-twelfths assumption will be adopted to simplify the computation.

The cost of time lost in water transportation and the limited season of navigation would thus not have exceeded the cost incurred in carrying an inventory equal to one half of the annual amount of agricultural products that were transported interregionally. As shown in Table 6, the Chicago wholesale value of the corn, wheat, beef, and pork shipped interregionally was about $550,000,000. Another $43,000,000 should be added to approximate wholesale value at seaboard.[10] Hence, in the absence of the railroad, the limited season of navigation would have required an increase in the value of inventories of about $297,000,000. The cost of carrying such an additional inventory would have included the foregone opportunity of investing the same amount elsewhere. If it is assumed that on the average capital earned 6 per cent in 1890, the alternative cost of the investment in additional inventory would have been about $18,000,000 per year. To this, one must add about $30,000,000 for storage charges. Subtracting $48,000,000 from $136,000,000 leaves $88,000,000 to account for the two remaining costs.

Cities receiving approximately 10 per cent of the interregional shipments were not on water routes. If these cities were an average of fifty miles from the nearest water point, the cost of wagon haulage (at twenty-five cents per ton-mile) would have been $20,000,000. Subtracting this amount from $88,000,000 leaves $68,000,000 to account for the last item — neglected capital charges.

Water rates failed to reflect capital costs to the extent that rivers and canals were improved or built by the government and financed out of taxes rather than tolls. If a complete statement of these uncompensated expenditures were available, one could easily estimate the neglected capital costs. Data exist on capital expenditures for water transportation, but much work remains to be done to develop a consistent and complete statement of uncompensated investment. Federal expenditures on river improvement over the years between 1802 and 1890 appear to have amounted to $111,000,000. Canals still in operation in 1890 were built at a cost of $155,000,000. In addition, there were abandoned canals which would have been in use in the ab-

---

[10] To the Chicago values shown in Table 6, $2.83 per ton was added for wheat, $2.59 for corn, $4.00 for cattle and $5.00 for hogs. Dressed meats in Table 6 are quoted at the New York prices, so no further adjustment was necessary. U.S. Congress, Senate, *Aldrich Report*, I, 518–19, 526.

sence of the interregional railroad. These were built at a cost of $27,000,000. The total of the three items, $293,000,000, may either overstate or understate the uncompensated capital involved in water transportation. Assuming that the various upward and downward biases, the omitted items and the double counting, cancel each other out, at an interest rate of 6 per cent the neglected capital costs would have been about $18,000,000 — $50,000,000 short of the amount required to bring the social saving to 1 per cent of gross national product.[11]

Thus casual examination of the available data suggests that the social saving attributable to the railroad in the interregional transportation of agricultural products was about 1 per cent of national income. The calculation is, of course, subject to considerable error; but there are grounds for having confidence in the result. Four of the estimates — those dealing with transshipment, wagon haulage, time lost, and the limited season of navigation — probably overstate the actual cost of water transportation. While the estimates of some of the other items may be too low, it does not seem likely that the errors are large enough to alter substantially the magnitude of the indicated social saving. Suppose, for example, that railroad rates on a ton-mile basis were not above water rates, as has generally been assumed. If the initial water-rail rate differential had actually been zero on all commodities, the elimination of this error would increase the estimated social saving by only $56,000,000. Indeed, if railroad rates are assumed to have been zero, the social saving would rise to only $158,000,000, or about 1.3 per cent of gross national product.

This paper has focused on one aspect of the influence of the railroad on American economic development. A small aggregate social saving in the interregional transportation of agricultural products would not prove that the railroad was unimportant in American development. Conclusions regarding the over-all impact of the railroad require, as Simon Kuznets has suggested, a thorough examination of all the avenues through which the most celebrated innovation of the nineteenth century may have exercised a strategic influence on economic growth. In this connection it is important to re-emphasize that the linear programming models referred to earlier will do more than refine the crude estimate of the aggregate social saving. They will provide information on efficient patterns of agricultural distribution both in the rail and non-rail situations, as well as breakdowns of the interregional social saving by regions and commodities. This type of information, supplemented by similar

---

[11] The preceding calculation may be summarized as follows:

First approximation of social saving	$—38,000,000
Neglected cargo losses	6,000,000
Transshipping costs	16,000,000
Additional inventory costs	48,000,000
Supplementary wagon haulage	20,000,000
Neglected capital costs	18,000,000
Total	$ 70,000,000

data on intraregional transportation, will facilitate a re-evaluation of such questions as the developmental significance of various commercial rivalries (for example, the triumph of Chicago over St. Louis and Cincinnati), the determinants of the geographic pattern of urbanization, and the extent to which the railroad promoted a more efficient utilization of certain productive resources.

✧ 54 ✧

St. Louis as a Central Reserve City: 1887–1922 *

ROSS M. ROBERTSON

A hundred years ago her citizens did not doubt that St. Louis would be the principal city of the Midwest, if not of the country. Providentially situated where the trade of the upper Mississippi River terminated and that of the lower river began, St. Louis held a strategic economic position. St. Louis was the northern terminus for the large steamboats of the lower river and the southern terminus for the smaller steamboats of the upper river, and it was here that cargoes were unloaded and reloaded for further shipment. There seemed little doubt that the commerce of the Mississippi Valley would continue in a predominantly north-south direction and that it would hinge on St. Louis. Moreover, it appeared that the future physical expansion of the United States would take place with St. Louis, a natural gateway to the West and Southwest, as the base of operations.

St. Louis' hope of primacy gradually disappeared as technological change removed the great obstacle to the development of Chicago. Possessed of facilities for water transportation eastward, Chicago's chief problem had been to tap the rich territory to the west. The advent of the railroad meant that Chicago, with its more favorable location for east-west rail traffic, could break the commercial hold of St. Louis on the upper Mississippi Valley.[1] Yet despite the economic losses sustained by St. Louis and the impetus given to the growth of Chicago as a result of the Civil War, St. Louis by a narrow margin remained the third largest American city in the census of 1870. During the 1870's, however, as Chicago achieved trade supremacy in the great region to the north, St. Louis was forced to look to the area lying roughly in the quadrant to the southwest for her future markets.

Even thus restricted, St. Louis for more than three decades enjoyed a kind of golden age. That her growth was substantial is evidenced by the fact that St. Louis approximately doubled in population between 1880 and 1910 (to al-

* Ross M. Robertson, "St. Louis as a Central Reserve City: 1887–1922", *Monthly Review*, Federal Reserve Bank of St. Louis, Vol. XXXVI, No. 8, August 1954, pp. 85–92. Used by permission.
[1] Wyatt Winton Belcher, *The Economic Rivalry Between St. Louis and Chicago*, New York: Columbia University Press, 1947.

most 700,000) and during these thirty years remained the fourth city of the country. St. Louis firms specialized in the manufacture of products much in demand in communities on the rapidly closing frontier, and even as the era of the steamboat merged into the railroad age, the city remained a primary transportation center. But it was as a commercial center, her great full-line, full-service wholesalers distributing an endless stream of goods to the whole of the growing Southwest, that St. Louis could lay claim to pre-eminence.

Trade required financing. In a day when the time lapse between investment and return was excessively long by modern standards, St. Louis firms and their customers required large credits. Furthermore, St. Louis financial institutions were asked to provide much of the capital necessary to the growth of young cities of the Southwest like Dallas, Houston, and Oklahoma City. Adequate funds were forthcoming largely because certain St. Louis banks, acting promptly and with foresight, attracted a part of the reserves of other banks. For in those days large commercial banks participated in the central banking function, with resulting increases in their resources and potentialities.

From 1836 until 1914 the United States had no central bank. (Some place the earlier date at 1832, when Andrew Jackson began to withdraw Government deposits from the second Bank of the United States.) Americans generally were fearful of centralized control of the money supply, and until the early years of the twentieth century it was politically impossible to re-establish a central bank. Yet, paradoxically, some central bank functions were performed, for after 1850 the American economy became too complex to muddle along without any monetary guidance or assistance whatsoever. Such central bank control as there was developed by custom within the framework of the Independent Treasury Act of 1846 and the Banking Act of 1864, as amended. To understand the role of St. Louis as a central reserve city, it is helpful to reflect on the central banking operations performed by the Treasury and the commercial banking system itself.

Ironically, monetary responsibilites were accepted by the United States Treasury shortly after the passage of the law which purported to make the Treasury independent of the money market. The main purpose of the act was to put the Government on a strictly cash basis. Under it banks periodically found their reserves dwindling as people paid taxes and replenished as the Government made disbursements from one of the sub-Treasuries. Even before the Civil War so much of the country's cash was at inopportune times locked up in Treasury vaults that in order to replenish the reserves of banks it was necessary to purchase Government bonds in the open market and prepay interest on bonds outstanding. From the close of the Civil War until the establishment of the Federal Reserve System, relations between the Treasury and the banks grew ever less tenuous. Policies varied with different Secretaries, but with only a few exceptions there was a deep consciousness of the effect of Treasury policy on the money market and of the responsibility the Treasury had to the economy as a whole.

Treasury concern with central bank functions was stimulated by Treasury surpluses, which were the rule from 1866 to 1915. The problem of getting back into circulation the cash taken in by the Government reached such proportions that purchase of Government securities and prepayment of interest on the public debt were not sufficient solutions. By liberalizing the interpretation of laws permitting deposits in national banks, successive Secretaries developed a reliable technique of easing the money market. Leslie M. Shaw, who succeeded Lyman Gage as Secretary in 1902, demonstrated remarkable ingenuity in developing control instruments. He ruled that funds might be transferred from Treasury vaults to depositary banks and back again, at the discretion of the Secretary. Deliberately impounding funds during summer months he released them, where needed, to relieve autumn stringencies.[2] When, in 1911, Congress finally authorized the Treasury to accept certified checks drawn on commercial banks in payment of customs duties, there was no remaining hindrance to Treasury influence on the money market.

It was to the commercial banking system itself, however, that bankers looked for most of the services ordinarily performed by a central bank. In the decade before the Civil War a pattern of correspondent relations had become firmly established. The provision of the National Bank Act of 1864 which enabled a bank to maintain part of its reserves as a deposit with a bank in one of seventeen major cities recognized a practice which had developed over many years. As more and more banks secured national charters, banks in the seventeen cities came to be major holders of the system's reserves, with a great concentration of reserves in New York City.[3] Moreover, banks which maintained correspondent accounts with larger institutions expected loan accommodation, and large banks in turn acknowledged their obligation to rediscount the good paper of their correspondent customers. Finally, all the so-called "service" functions of a central bank — providing cash, making collections, effecting large remittances, etc. — were carried out by the intricate correspondent network of commercial banks.

But the structure was faulty. In times of stress large banks necessarily tended to think first of their own stockholders. The entire system was based on cash reserves, and within short periods of time cash was fixed in amount. In the absence of a central bank with the power to create reserves, only the Treasury could afford relief to the New York money market in times of emergency, and such help as the Treasury could give was adequate only during lesser disturbances.

---

[2] In his report of 1906, Shaw proposed that the Secretary be authorized to vary required reserve ratios of national banks and that a fund of $100 million be made available for the sole purpose of easing and tightening bank reserves. However, Shaw argued against the establishment of a central bank on the grounds that Government supervision of monetary operations would be thereby removed, *Annual Report of the Secretary of the Treasury,* 1906, pp. 41–50.

[3] Within New York City there was a further concentration, as six or seven metropolitan banks came to specialize in this business, attracting accounts by offering interest on deposits and rendering services at rates below cost.

Proposals for reform of the commercial banking structure included the suggestion that concentration of reserves could be lessened by establishing more reserve and central reserve cities. To achieve this objective, Congress on March 3, 1887, amended the National Bank Act to permit cities of 50,000 or more to become reserve cities upon the application of three-fourths of their national banks; cities of 200,000 or more could become central reserve cities under the same condition.[4] The amendment made no changes in the basic reserve structure. Against deposit liabilities, country banks had to keep a reserve of 15 per cent, three-fifths of which might be deposits with national banks in reserve *or* central reserve cities. Reserve city banks were required to keep a reserve of 25 per cent against deposits, one-half of which might be balances with banks in central reserve cities. Banks in central reserve cities had no choice but to keep a 25 per cent cash reserve against deposit liabilities. Thus, banks electing to become central reserve city banks would no longer be able to count balances with New York as a part of their reserve.

On March 11, 1887, eight days after the passage of the permissive amendment, the Comptroller of the Currency received from the St. Louis National Bank a letter requesting the proper forms to be used by banks applying for central reserve city status. On March 18 the Comptroller received the application, unanimously signed by the five national banks in the city. Within a few weeks the St. Louis application was approved, shortly before that of Chicago, and both St. Louis and Chicago became central reserve cities.

In seeking to become a group of ultimate holders of bank reserves, St. Louis banks were taking a calculated risk. At one stroke they were required to double their own cash reserves, and balances due from New York would no longer count in the computation of their reserve position. The main objective was to attract balances from reserve cities, which would presumably grow in number; there was the further likelihood that country banks would increase their accounts as St. Louis became a more important money center.

St. Louis had been one of the so-called "redemption cities" — equivalent to a reserve city — since the establishment of the national banking system. But her banks were quite small, even by the standards of the day. As of October 5, 1887, total resources of St. Louis banks were just under $18 million, compared with $188 million for Boston, $136 million for Philadelphia, $47 million for Pittsburgh, and $40 million for Baltimore. Kansas City banks, which had not even reserve city status, had resources of $24 million. As the first city of a great undeveloped trade area, St. Louis could perhaps claim a position of special importance. Yet a study by the Comptroller of the Currency in 1890 revealed that, of the total amount of drafts drawn by national banks on other cities in the preceding year, only 1.64 per cent were drawn on St. Louis, compared with 63 per cent drawn on New York, 9 per cent on Chicago, and 21

---

4 The designation "central reserve city" and "reserve city" did not appear in legislation until 1887; the term "country bank" did not appear in the 1887 law but had by that time become customary.

per cent on other reserve cities. As a great financial center St. Louis had only prospects.

It can be seen from Table 1, however, that St. Louis banks, by requesting central reserve city status, hastened their own growth.[5] St. Louis banks in 1887 reported 3 per cent of all bankers' balances held by the central reserve city group; between 1902 and 1914 the figure was never below 9 per cent and was as high as 11 per cent. How important bankers' balances were to St. Louis institutions may be inferred from the fact that they equalled or exceeded individual deposits on nearly every reporting date in the years 1900 to 1914.[6] Both Chicago and St. Louis banks attracted accounts from banks in contiguous states, and a part of the sharp increase in balances at these cities was attributable to the geographic expansion of the country. It seems apparent, however, that both cities, and especially St. Louis, took business away from New York by gaining accounts in the West and Southwest that had formerly been held in New York.[7]

Table 2 reveals in more striking fashion the rapid rate of growth of St. Louis national banks. Between 1887 and 1914 resources grew nearly eleven-fold, "due to banks" twelve-fold, and "individual deposits" nine-fold. By comparison, Chicago banks, while showing substantially greater increases in these categories than New York, made much smaller gains percentagewise than did those of St. Louis. This was equally true for amounts "due from banks." St. Louis and Chicago banks kept large balances with New York, but St. Louis banks more than Chicago banks appear to have redeposited funds in New York in amounts scarcely in keeping with their central reserve city responsibilities.[8]

Indeed, Sprague argued, with reason, that both Chicago and St. Louis banks behaved under stress like banks of reserve cities rather than of central reserve cities, rapidly drawing down their New York balances, contracting their own loans, and unduly conserving their cash. In fact, during crises some reserve cities accepted more responsibility than did either Chicago or St. Louis, suffering larger reserve losses and expanding their loans as they strove to aid the business community, including other banks.[9] St. Louis banks did make an heroic effort to provide cash during the panic of 1907. Cash reserves of St. Louis banks fell to 20.38 per cent by December 3, 1907, and this was after the

---

[5] The sharp changes in early years were in part the result of a shift by some banks from state to national charters.

[6] Had mid-year reporting dates been used, the differences between "due to banks" and "individual deposits" would have been consistently higher in favor of the former. As fall approached, correspondents of St. Louis banks invariably drew down their accounts. For easily accessible comparative figures, using mid-summer report dates, see Leonard L. Watkins, *Bankers' Balances*, Chicago: A. W. Shaw Company, 1929, pp. 15 and 19.

[7] Compare Margaret G. Myers, *The New York Money Market*, New York: Columbia University Press, 1931, Vol. 1, pp. 240–241.

[8] O. M. W. Sprague, *History of Cases Under the National Banking System*, Washington: Government Printing Office, 1910, pp. 125–126.

[9] *Ibid.*, pp. 309–310.

panic was over.[10] The fact remains, however, that St. Louis, like the reserve cities, responded to both seasonal and cyclical pressures by turning to New York for funds.

It was commonly thought in 1914 that the establishment of the Federal Reserve System would lead to large declines in bankers' balances. Actually they increased during the first decade of System operation, though doubtless less than would have been the case without the central bank. But by 1919 St. Louis banks had experienced a much smaller gain in "due to banks" than had banks in either Chicago or New York; St. Louis increases in bankers' balances were even less than for national banks as a group. (See Tables 1–4.) Meantime, bankers' balances had fallen well below individual deposits, though this was true in Chicago as well as in St. Louis. When, with the onset of the depression of 1920–21, bankers' balances fell well below their 1914 levels, it was apparent that St. Louis banks had suffered a much greater loss of correspondent business than had banks generally. There was no longer a legal reason why reserve city banks should keep balances with central reserve city banks if it were not entirely convenient to do so. No full-fledged money market had developed in St. Louis. In the absence of legal compulsion, many banks in the West and Southwest simply found their interests better served by keeping their correspondent balances in one of the rapidly growing new cities of the area.

St. Louis bankers soon came to the realization that central reserve city status was no longer beneficial. Such additional prestige as the classification afforded was far more than offset by a legal reserve requirement of 13 per cent as compared with 10 per cent for banks in reserve cities.

On April 8, 1919, representatives of the fifteen banks of the St. Louis Clearing House Association which were also members of the Federal Reserve System adopted a resolution requesting termination of the central reserve city classification of St. Louis.[11] On June 30, 1919, Mr. F. O. Watts, President of the Clearing House Association, forwarded the resolution to the Federal Reserve Board. Three principal arguments were advanced in favor of the petition for declassification: (1) since the old order with respect to reserves was changed by passage of the Federal Reserve Act, St. Louis banks were no longer required to keep large cash reserves and the central reserve classification had lost its significance; (2) because the benefits of the central reserve designation had been terminated by law, cities in competition with St. Louis had an unfair competitive advantage in that they did not have to keep such

[10] *Annual Report of the Comptroller of the Currency,* 1908, p. 192. With only one exception cash reserves of St. Louis banks were below the legal 25 per cent minimum on fall report dates between 1897 and 1907.

[11] The petitioning banks were: American Trust Company, Central National Bank, Franklin Bank, United States Bank, Liberty Bank, St. Louis Union Bank, International Bank, Merchants-Laclede National Bank, Mercantile Trust Company, Mississippi Valley Trust Company, National Bank of Commerce, Lafayette-South Side Bank, State National Bank, Third National Bank, and Mechanics-American National Bank.

TABLE 1   Number of Banks, Bankers' Balances, and Individual Deposits for Central Reserve Cities, Selected Fall Dates
(Amounts in millions of dollars)

Year	ST. LOUIS, MISSOURI					CHICAGO, ILLINOIS					NEW YORK, NEW YORK				
	No. of Banks	Total Resources	Due to Banks	Due from Banks	Individual Deposits	No. of Banks	Total Resources	Due to Banks	Due from Banks	Individual Deposits	No. of Banks	Total Resources	Due to Banks	Due from Banks	Individual Deposits
1887	5	$ 17.9	$ 5.5	$ 1.6	$ 6.6	18	$ 103.8	$ 35.2	$ 12.2	$ 35.0	47	$ 469.4	$ 140.2	$ 24.9	$ 228.2
1890	8	45.1	10.4	4.1	21.7	23	135.8	47.0	17.9	59.2	47	533.4	173.4	30.8	227.2
1892	9	49.1	14.8	4.5	20.0	27	175.5	57.7	19.2	77.0	48	601.9	211.3	34.7	254.3
1894	9	46.0	15.9	5.5	16.6	25	170.8	59.1	24.0	74.0	49	691.6	230.5	30.6	323.9
1897	6	57.5	22.6	10.0	21.7	23	180.0	75.3	31.7	71.6	48	733.6	264.9	33.9	312.7
1899	6	90.6	32.5	13.9	37.9	19	243.3	107.4	47.4	101.5	44	985.7	367.2	31.8	401.0
1902	6	146.3	46.4	19.2	44.5	11	321.2	136.4	53.5	131.1	44	1,293.7	316.5	50.8	603.6
1904	8	171.5	57.0	29.2	59.8	13	343.4	146.8	61.0	133.0	44	1,526.0	399.7	52.6	581.1
1906	8	186.7	65.4	27.5	65.0	13	380.2	187.1	60.7	142.6	41	1,474.8	377.9	53.1	659.2
1908	8	200.1	74.4	36.0	66.9	14	432.2	196.1	70.3	151.1	40	1,780.3	471.8	53.7	743.8
1910	10	211.0	76.5	30.7	71.4	14	501.3	207.0	61.9	191.7	37	1,664.8	409.4	67.2	698.1
1912	8	213.8	86.3	38.4	69.3	10	571.8	244.7	90.8	219.6	39	1,762.7	447.7	70.4	767.7
1914	7	193.2	66.2	25.8	60.6	9	588.0	205.0	80.3	224.2	37	1,888.6	422.6	78.7	784.1
1916	7	212.2	85.3	44.0	78.7	10	728.4	306.3	130.2	329.4	33	2,871.6	1,013.6	246.6	1,415.7
1919	5	323.8	84.1	31.2	149.1	9	1,026.7	321.7	136.1	498.8	33	4,345.4	912.1	96.3	2,048.6
1920	5	298.3	71.8	22.3	149.5	8	966.7	278.5	102.6	487.2	31	4,205.9	822.7	47.0	2,051.5
1921	6	239.1	50.1	14.0	126.8	18	838.7	237.6	65.2	426.8	30	3,427.9	686.0	15.7	1,788.6
1922	6	288.6	66.1	20.7	162.0	10	929.6	272.8	81.2	479.6	27	3,924.4	898.4	14.5	2,112.4

Percentages of Total Central Reserve Cities

Year	ST. LOUIS				CHICAGO				NEW YORK			
	Total Resources	Due to Banks	Due from Banks	Individual Deposits	Total Resources	Due to Banks	Due from Banks	Individual Deposits	Total Resources	Due to Banks	Due from Banks	Individual Deposits
1887	3.0	3.0	4.1	2.4	17.6	19.5	31.5	13.0	79.4	77.5	64.4	84.6
1890	6.3	4.5	7.8	7.0	19.0	20.4	33.9	19.2	74.7	75.1	58.3	73.8
1892	6.0	5.2	7.7	5.7	21.2	20.3	39.9	21.9	72.8	74.5	59.4	72.4
1894	5.1	5.2	9.2	4.0	18.8	19.3	39.9	17.9	76.1	75.5	50.9	78.1
1897	5.9	6.2	13.2	5.4	18.5	20.8	41.9	17.6	75.6	73.0	44.9	77.0
1899	6.9	6.4	14.9	7.0	18.4	21.2	50.9	18.8	74.7	72.4	34.2	74.2
1902	8.3	9.3	15.6	5.7	18.2	27.3	43.8	16.8	73.5	63.4	41.1	77.5
1904	8.4	9.5	20.5	7.7	16.8	24.3	42.7	17.2	74.8	66.2	36.8	75.1
1906	9.2	10.7	19.5	7.5	18.6	27.4	42.9	16.5	72.2	61.9	37.6	76.0
1908	8.3	10.0	22.5	7.0	17.9	26.4	43.9	15.7	73.8	63.6	33.6	77.3
1910	8.9	11.0	19.2	7.4	21.1	29.9	38.7	20.0	70.0	59.1	42.1	72.6
1912	8.4	11.1	19.2	6.5	22.4	31.4	45.5	20.8	69.2	57.5	35.3	72.7
1914	7.2	9.6	14.0	5.7	22.0	29.5	43.4	21.0	70.8	60.9	42.6	73.3
1916	5.6	6.1	10.0	4.3	19.1	21.8	34.1	18.1	75.3	72.1	55.9	77.6

Percentages of Total Central Reserve Cities

	ST. LOUIS, MISSOURI					CHICAGO, ILLINOIS					NEW YORK, NEW YORK				
Year	No. of Banks	Total Resources	Due to Banks	Due from Banks	Individual Deposits	No. of Banks	Total Resources	Due to Banks	Due from Banks	Individual Deposits	No. of Banks	Total Resources	Due to Banks	Due from Banks	Individual Deposits
1919		5.7	6.4	11.8	5.5		18.0	24.4	51.6	18.5		76.3	69.2	36.6	76.0
1920		5.5	6.1	13.0	5.6		17.6	23.8	59.7	18.1		76.9	70.1	27.3	76.3
1921		5.3	5.1	14.8	5.6		18.6	24.4	68.7	18.6		76.1	70.5	16.5	75.8
1922		5.6	5.6	17.8	5.9		18.1	23.2	69.8	17.4		76.3	71.2	12.4	76.7

Source (for all tables): Annual reports of the Comptroller of the Currency, 1887–1922.

■ **TABLE 2** **Indexes of Changes in Total Resources, Due to Banks, Due from Banks, and Individual Deposits for Three Central Reserve Cities, Fall Reporting Dates in Selected Years**

1887 = 100.

	ST. LOUIS, MISSOURI				CHICAGO, ILLINOIS				NEW YORK, NEW YORK			
Year	Total Resources	Due to Banks	Due from Banks	Individual Deposits	Total Resources	Due to Banks	Due from Banks	Individual Deposits	Total Resources	Due to Banks	Due from Banks	Individual Deposits
1890	$ 252.0	$ 189.1	$ 256.3	$ 325.8	$130.7	$133.5	$146.7	$169.1	$113.6	$123.7	$123.7	$ 99.6
1892	274.3	260.1	281.3	303.0	168.9	163.9	157.4	220.0	128.2	150.7	139.4	111.4
1897	321.2	410.9	625.0	325.8	173.2	213.9	259.8	204.6	156.3	188.9	136.1	137.0
1902	817.3	843.6	1,200.0	674.2	309.1	387.5	488.5	374.6	275.6	225.7	204.0	264.5
1908	1,117.9	1,352.7	2,250.0	1,015.6	416.0	557.1	576.2	431.7	379.3	336.5	215.7	325.9
1914	1,079.3	1,203.6	1,612.5	918.2	565.9	582.4	658.2	640.6	402.3	301.4	316.1	348.6

1914 = 100.

	ST. LOUIS, MISSOURI				CHICAGO, ILLINOIS				NEW YORK, NEW YORK			
1920	154.4	108.5	86.4	246.7	164.4	135.9	127.8	217.3	222.7	194.7	59.7	261.6
1921	123.8	75.7	54.3	209.2	142.6	115.9	81.2	190.4	181.5	162.3	19.9	221.5
1922	149.4	99.8	80.2	267.3	158.1	133.1	101.1	213.9	207.8	198.4	18.4	269.4

■ **TABLE 3**   Number of Banks, Total Resources, Due to Banks, Due from Banks, and Individual Deposits for All National Banks, Fall Reporting Dates in Selected Years

(*In millions of dollars*)

Date	Number of Banks	Total Resources	Due to Banks	Due from Banks	Individual Deposits
Oct. 5, 1887	3,049	$ 2,620.2	$ 329.6	$ 115.4	$ 1,249.5
Oct. 2, 1890	3,540	3,141.5	426.5	146.8	1,584.8
Sept. 30, 1892	3,773	3,510.1	580.6	173.1	1,765.4
Oct. 5, 1897	3,610	3,705.1	645.7	197.4	1,853.3
Sept. 15, 1902	4,601	6,113.9	934.1	354.6	3,209.3
Sept. 23, 1908	6,853	9,027.3	1,419.8	491.4	4,548.1
Sept. 12, 1914	7,538	11,483.5	1,426.2	602.4	6,139.1
Sept. 12, 1919	7,821	21,615.4	3,053.5	1,707.6	12,672.5
Sept. 8, 1920	8,093	21,885.5	2,770.3	1,424.3	13,595.9
Sept. 6, 1921	8,155	19,014.1	2,101.2	1,039.6	12,033.5
Sept. 15, 1922	8,240	20,926.1	2,614.0	1,363.2	13,439.6

■ **TABLE 4**   Percentage Changes in Total Resources, Due to Banks, Due from Banks, and Individual Deposits for All National Banks, Fall Reporting Dates in Selected Years

1887 = 100.

Date	Total Resources	Due to Banks	Due from Banks	Individual Deposits
Oct. 2, 1890......	119.9	129.4	127.2	125.2
Sept. 30, 1892......	134.0	161.0	150.0	141.3
Oct. 5, 1897......	141.4	195.9	171.1	148.3
Sept. 15, 1902......	233.3	283.4	307.3	256.8
Sept. 23, 1908......	344.5	439.8	425.8	364.0
Sept. 12, 1914......	438.3	432.7	522.0	491.3

1914 = 100.

Date	Total Resources	Due to Banks	Due from Banks	Individual Deposits
Sept. 12, 1919......	188.2	214.1	283.5	206.4
Sept. 8, 1920......	190.6	194.2	236.4	221.5
Sept. 6, 1921......	165.6	147.3	172.6	196.0
Sept. 15, 1922......	182.2	183.3	226.3	218.9

large reserves as St. Louis; and (3) deposits of St. Louis banks were quite as stable as those in reserve cities generally.

There is no indication of the specific action taken by the Board on this petition. However, on July 5 Governor Harding wrote to Mr. Watts indicating that action would not be favorable. The argument that higher reserve requirements put St. Louis at a disadvantage in the competition with Boston, Philadelphia, Kansas City, Cleveland, and other cities could be urged with equal force, he wrote, by banks of Chicago and New York. Further, he said, ". . . the Board has been considering the advisability of classifying cities which are the seat of a Federal Reserve Bank, and perhaps the branch bank cities, on a distinctive basis from all other cities." Governor Harding went on to ask the views of the St. Louis Clearing House Association as to the relative merits of three reserve proposals:

1. Classification of cities having a Federal Reserve Bank as central reserve cities, classification of branch bank cities as reserve cities, and classification of banks in all other towns and cities as country banks.

2. Classification of all Federal Reserve cities and branch bank cities as reserve cities, with cities of a certain minimum population, say 75,000 or 100,000, likewise classified as reserve cities.

3. Amendment of the Federal Reserve Act to provide for uniform reserves in all towns and cities regardless of population; uniform, but presumably different, percentages would apply to time deposits, individual deposits, and interbank deposits.

A few days later the Board sent a letter to the Chairman of each Federal Reserve Bank stating that it was considering the advisability of reclassifying cities in which Federal Reserve Banks and their branches were located as central reserve and reserve cities, respectively. In reply most of the Federal Reserve Banks suggested that, instead of increasing reserve requirements for some cities, it would be better to change St. Louis from a central reserve to a reserve city.

Apparently the St. Louis Clearing House Association shortly withdrew its petition for declassification. A little less than three years later a second petition, dated January 12, 1922, was forwarded to the Federal Reserve Board. The arguments urging favorable action were almost unchanged. This time, however, the St. Louis banks went to considerable lengths to make the strongest possible case. Leading bankers in both Chicago and New York were visited, and assurances were received that neither Chicago nor New York contemplated similar requests for declassification. On January 28, 1922, Mr. William McC. Martin, Chairman of the Federal Reserve Bank of St. Louis and father of the present chairman of the Board of Governors, sent to the Board data showing the effect of declassification on the statement of the Federal Reserve Bank of St. Louis. The effect of reduction in the required reserves of member banks in the city of St. Louis would, he concluded, ". . . have so little effect that it could be done without weakening the general banking situation."

Almost immediately, on January 30, the Board notified Mr. Martin that the St. Louis application for declassification had again been declined. Once more the Board suggested that the inequalities complained of by the St. Louis banks might better be relieved through reclassification of other reserve bank cities as central reserve cities. The Board also called attention to the fact that St. Louis banks had of their own volition asked for classification as a central reserve city and that under the Federal Reserve Act the required reserves were reduced by more than one-half.[12]

Four months later the Federal Reserve Board reconsidered its action, coming this time to a favorable conclusion. On May 31, 1922, the following telegram was sent to Chairman Martin of the St. Louis Federal Reserve Bank: "Board today has reclassified St. Louis a reserve city in lieu of central reserve city, effective July 1, 1922. Please advise interested banks."

Thus was concluded a little known episode in the financial history of America. In an effort to lift themselves by their own bootstraps to positions of greater power and prestige, St. Louis banks requested central reserve city status when the financial importance of the city did not warrant it. As holders of a portion of the ultimate reserves of the banking system, St. Louis banks doubtless experienced a growth which they would not have had as a reserve city. The capital resources thus attracted may well have given impetus to the expansion of the Southwest. Yet St. Louis banks were never able to accept responsibility for guiding and aiding the commercial banking system as New York banks were able to do. Because they could not actually supply central reserve city services, there was no reason for them to bear a greater share of the reserve burden than less venturesome banks in sister cities. □

✧ 55 ✧

The Legend of the Robber Barons *

THOMAS C. COCHRAN

Between business history, which has concentrated attention upon the administration of the firm, and general social or economic history, which has frequently omitted business processes altogether, there is a broad, vacant area. In this twilight zone lie the relations of business leaders with similar men in other firms, the interactions of businessmen with society as a whole, and the economic effects of business decisions. Scholars viewing this area have seen such a host of related problems that a group composed of representatives from some of the East Coast universities has given the study a special name:

---

[12] The Board was correct in this assertion. Under the old rules national banks were required to maintain in vault cash reserves of 25 per cent against net deposits, no distinction for reserve purposes being made between demand and time deposits. A required reserve ratio under the Federal Reserve Act of only 3 per cent against time deposits thus permitted a reduction of more than one half in required reserves.

* Taken and adapted from Thomas C. Cochran, "The Legend of the Robber Barons," *The Pennsylvania Magazine of History and Biography*, Vol. LXXIV, July 1950, pp. 307–21. Used by permission of the author and publisher.

entrepreneurial history.[1] In defining this field, the term entrepreneur has not been restricted to the conventional American textbook meaning of one who risks capital in enterprise. Rather, the older French definitions of Cantillon and Say have been re-expressed in broader language to make entrepreneur roughly equivalent to business executive. In the research of the group, the function of entrepreneurship, or business leadership, is conceived as operating in a broad socio-economic setting.

The systematic pursuit of a new interest of this kind requires a series of assumptions as to what should be examined, some tentative hypotheses about relationships and dynamics, and then historical facts against which to test and expand the original concepts.[2] The major assumption of entrepreneurial history is that it requires the exploration of the economic and social roles played by the entrepreneur: how he did his job, and what doing his particular job meant from the standpoint of his personality, his interests, and his other social roles. To gain adequate perspective, these explorations should take place in various historical settings. . . .

The economists, of course, have recognized the importance of entrepreneurship abstractly; but they have failed to make any satisfactory use of this factor in setting up their equations or developing their theories. The inclusion of this factor in economic history, for example, will unquestionably reorient it in the direction of anthropological and sociological knowledge. It will not necessarily make the businessman a hero, but it will affirm the necessity of seeing economic growth in cultural terms.

For the general historian, it will mean a re-evaluation of the roles and importance of business leaders, particularly in countries such as the United States. Our present history generally has seen business leaders as parasites on a deterministic process. Historians who are in no other way determinists nevertheless seem to assume that our economic development would have gone along in good and productive paths if left to itself, whereas grasping and unscrupulous business leaders deflected this natural progress into antisocial lines for their own advantage. The corrective needed is not a eulogy of business, but real understanding of the social processes which have channeled the economic life of the nation.

An analysis of the period in which many American historians have discussed the businessman, the age of the "robber barons," will illustrate the reinterpretation that may come from entrepreneurial history. The "robber barons" are usually selected from among the railroad, industrial, and financial leaders of the period from about 1865 to 1900, and more often than not are the only businessmen who appear in college textbooks covering this period. According to the present historical mythology, they are seen as "bad" or un-

[1] A Research Center for Entrepreneurial History at Harvard, organized by Arthur H. Cole, is one result of the deliberations of the East Coast group.

[2] It is worth noting that although data may vary in age from six months to five hundred years, any that can be collected are necessarily historical.

usually grasping and unscrupulous types in our culture against the background of a "good" public. The interest in discussing them is to illustrate business malpractices, and, presumably, to convey moralistic warnings against such activities, rather than to understand the business process in society.

In distinction to this pathological approach, the entrepreneurial historian is interested in the culture patterns and social structures which have produced these assumed types, and in whether or not the types have been correctly delineated. In pursuing such a study, the first thing is to decide what some of the major cultural themes were that guided or sanctioned the roles of these men. I think we can pick out three about which there will be little controversy: the concept of the autonomous economy that was self-adjusting; the idea that progress came through competition and the survival of the fittest; and the belief that profit or material gain was the only reliable incentive for action. These themes operated throughout the society as a whole. The truckman delivering dirt for railroad construction was as much motivated by profit and as firm a believer in these themes as was the "robber baron" who was building the road. The dissident element in the society, those who denied the value of these major themes, seem during these years to have been a relatively small, or at least uninfluential, portion of the population. Therefore, if value judgments are to be formed, they should be applied to this type of society or culture. It is rather futile to assert that the culture would have been all right if it were not for the kind of people and activities that resulted directly from its major themes.

If one accepts the additional and continuing American theme that material growth is a reliable index of progress, and its usual corollary that rapid progress is desirable, one question that may be asked of the culture as a whole is whether such progress could have taken place faster if other beliefs had prevailed. Since it is impossible to conceive deductively what the United States would have been like if built up on some other system, such a decision requires the establishment of a comparative standard. But if recourse is had to the history of another nation in order to observe the application of different cultural patterns to economic development, none seems like the United States to offer satisfying parallels. It is interesting, however, to note that in one of the somewhat similar economic situations, that of Australia, where railroads and frontier development went on through more state enterprise, about the same things were complained of that commentators here in the United States blamed upon private enterprise. In other words, a number of the difficulties seem to have been inherent in the rapid development of a pioneer area rather than in the particular means by which the development went on.

Avoiding, therefore, such unanswerable questions, and concentrating on a better understanding of the operation of American culture, let us examine the historical legend of the "robber baron" by analyzing the "case history" of Henry Villard. Villard is an interesting "robber baron" because he was brought up outside the American culture in a German bureaucratic or official family. His father was a German lawyer and judge, who ultimately became a member of the Supreme Court of the Kingdom of Bavaria. Villard, after attendance at three European universities, decided to come to the United States to try his fortune. Supported to some extent by family money, he entered journalism and built himself a successful career as a correspondent for European and American newspapers. The Civil War, particularly, gave prestige to young Villard. He was able to interview Lincoln and to offer many interesting and penetrating views of contemporary events. In the early seventies he went back to Germany, and through his family connections came to know the chief financial men of Frankfort and Munich. These contacts led to his being sent over as a representative of German bondholders in the Oregon railroad and steamship enterprises that had fallen into difficulties during the depression following the panic of 1873.

It is interesting that when Villard was placed in the position of having to make judgments regarding what should be done on the unfinished Oregon and California Railroad and in regard to the river navigation projects, he readily assumed the entrepreneurial role in just about the same form as men who had been brought up in business. In other words, the entrepreneurial role seems to have been so much a part of the cultural pattern of America, and possibly of middle class Germany, at this time, that there was no great gulf between the attitude of the professional intellectual or journalist and that of the businessman. Villard identified himself quickly with the development of the Oregon area, and, instead of advising liquidation and withdrawal for his German clients, he counseled rather the investment of still more capital in order to complete the enterprises. In this way his essential role was that of attracting foreign capital to a frontier development. It is not clear that he was ever deeply interested in problems of technology and management — that is, in just how the capital was applied for productive purposes; rather, he became a public relations man for the area, and an over-all or general enterpreneurial supervisor of where the capital should be allocated.

One factor of great importance in the Villard story is that he started new activities at just about the bottom of the deep depression that lasted from 1873 to 1879, and his ventures from then on, or at least from 1877 on, were first on a gradually rising market, and finally, from 1879 to 1882, on a market that boomed.

Villard saw quickly that the Northern Pacific Railroad, which was being built across the country from Duluth and St. Paul, would have to make, or at least should make, an agreement to connect with whatever road occupied the Columbia River valley. With this long-range plan in mind, he secured foreign and domestic help for the building of the Oregon Railroad and Navigation Company up the Columbia, at a time when Northern Pacific construction was moving very slowly into eastern Montana.

It is from this point on that the most interesting differences occur between the dramatic "robber baron" explanation of Villard's activities and the more sober and socially complex explanation offered by entrepreneurial history. The "robber baron" story is, that as Villard found the Northern Pacific management nearing the Columbia valley but unwilling to agree to make use of his facilities — that is, threatening to build either a parallel line or to cross the Cascade Mountains to Tacoma and Seattle — he decided that he must get control of the Northern Pacific. So great was his prestige for successful operation by this time that he had the boldness to ask a group of his friends in Wall Street to put up $8,000,000 for some project that he would not reveal to them. And, as the story went, he had no difficulty in more than raising the first payment requested for this "blind pool," money which he used secretly to buy control of the Northern Pacific Railroad. The "robber baron" analogy is, of course, obvious and exciting. The "robber baron," Villard, seizes control of a strategic pass and then exacts tribute from the railroad that represents a great, nationally subsidized enterprise.[3] Villard's blind pool has all of the trappings of high drama and shady financial dealings. The "robber baron" story then goes on to assert that Villard robbed the Northern Pacific and his other properties in the course of construction in such a way so that by 1883 they were bankrupt, while he himself had become very rich.

As usual, the actual story is not so dramatic. What appears to have happened is, that when the Northern Pacific secured Drexel Morgan financing in the latter part of the year 1880, and the Drexel Morgan-Winslow Lanier syndicate learned that Frederick Billings, the president of Northern Pacific, was planning to build duplicate facilities to the coast without regard to the already existing Oregon Railroad and Navigation Company, they became worried over the economic loss involved in constructing nearly parallel lines. The bankers, not sharing in the loyalties to individual companies that presidents and other officers almost inevitably develop, could see no reason why Northern Pacific and O.R. & N. could not get together in one co-operating line. But some of the officers of Northern Pacific, particularly Billings, regarded the railroad as their greatest life work; they felt that to compromise and make the final road a joint venture between the "upstart" Villard and the great Northern Pacific enterprise was a personal defeat. Whereupon Morgan, at least, decided that the only way of bringing about a compromise and preventing unnecessary construction was to establish a common control for the two companies. Since Villard, who had, from the financial standpoint, acquitted himself well as receiver for Kansas Pacific, was now anxious to get this joint control, and assured Morgan that he independently had the resources to do so, the syndicate gave him their blessings, and even offered him their help. The "blind pool" was, therefore, chiefly a product of Villard's love of drama, of doing things in a spectacular fashion. Had he been willing to forgo these dramatic frills, control could quietly have been bought through the syndicate over about the same period. Of course, it cannot be overlooked that

---

[3] The Northern Pacific had the largest land grant of any of the western railroads.

successfully doing the job himself gave Villard great personal prestige in Wall Street.

The difficulties from 1881 on to the completion of the road in 1883 seem to have been to some extent inevitable, and to some extent to have resulted from the usual overoptimism of American promoters. Villard formed a holding company, called the Oregon and Transcontinental Company, which was to own stocks in his various enterprises, make the construction contracts, and generally conduct the building which would weld Northern Pacific and O.R. & N. into one system. Undoubtedly, the Oregon and Transcontinental Company stock was a source of large profit for Villard; in fact, it seems probable that all the money Villard made in connection with these enterprises came from floating, buying, and selling the securities in Wall Street. It may be that Villard profited from the constructions contracts, but there is no clear evidence of this, and it is quite possible, by analogy to similar situations, that the profits of construction went largely to local contractors in the West. At all events, the major difficulty was a lack of sufficient traffic to warrant the high construction cost of building railroads through the Rockies and the Oregon coastal regions. The completion of the through-line in August of 1883 was almost simultaneous with the beginning of a steady recession in general business that ended in a crisis the following March. As a result, the difficulties that the system would have experienced in paying returns under any circumstances were accentuated. When the companies were not able to pay dividends and their securities declined, Villard, temporarily losing the confidence of the banking syndicate, was forced to retire from the control of the various enterprises.

One way, therefore, of looking at this whole story is that Villard, a relatively inexperienced entrepreneur, took hold of a series of frontier developments at the bottom of the business cycle, carried them along through his connections and personal enthusiasm during the rise of the cycle, completed them just at the peak of the boom, and was then unable to steer them through the ensuing depression. Viewed from this angle, the whole development was a normal and repetitive one in both big and small business. The general history of even a small retail store or factory enterprise was often just about the same; if the enterprise started at a favorable time in the business cycle, it could last until a major depression. Then, unless it has had farsighted and unusually able management, or had been lucky in making more profit than was possible for most young enterprises, it lapsed into bankruptcy and had to be reorganized with the injection of new capital. The roles that Villard played extremely well were those of a mobilizer of capital resources for pioneer investments, and effective public relations for the development of an area. The roles that he played poorly were those of an expert railroad builder and conservative business forecaster.

What do entrepreneurial historians expect to gain from such a study? In the first place, the study of outstanding examples such as that of Villard may be instructive for the study of the normal practices and operations of business. A detailed study of the Villard enterprises will show more exactly the nature of such practices as the strategic type of entrepreneurship that went into railroad building. The seizing of the transportation route down the Columbia River is merely a dramatic example of the general type of planning done by all western railroad builders. The strategic occupation of territory was like a great game of chess. Each leading entrepreneur had to guess where his rivals were likely to build next, how he could forestall their entrance into an area by throwing a line of track through some valley or across some river, often planning these moves a decade or more ahead. Little is known of the local economic and social results of this process beyond the fact that it extended railroad transportation at an extremely rapid rate.

Trying to assess the larger economic and social effects of Villard's activities, we might note that he mobilized about $60,000,000 in capital, and applied it to western development at a social cost of perhaps one or two million dollars. That is, he may have made more money than that, but the one or two million dollars represent an estimate of what he actually spent on living and personal durable goods during these years. His other money came and went in stock-market operations, and presumably represented a transfer of capital from one set of holders to another. The question remains: granting that this was not a high rate of commission to pay for the mobilization of so much money, was the long-run effect of the development for which the money was spent economically and socially desirable? Undoubtedly, this particular development of transportation was premature, and it was carried on at the cost of some other types of goods or services that could have been produced with the same expenditure. But this in turn raises another question from a purely nationalistic standpoint: could the foreign capital have been attracted for more prosaic and routine operations? To the extent that foreign money was invested unprofitably in western development, it was an economic loss to Germany and the other investing nations, but a net gain to the United States. As to the loss of domestic resources in these developments, it can be noted that, at least, this is what the men of the culture apparently wanted to do with their economic energy. Villard noted in his promotion activities that the word "Oregon" had a kind of popular magic to it in the seventies and early eighties. Then it was the promised land of the American West, and it stimulated the imagination of Americans along entrepreneurial lines. The historian should try to assess the extent to which the dramatic development of natural resources may actually raise the rate of saving in the community, and may increase output of energy in the population as a whole. These are, of course, very difficult and intangible problems, but yet they are just as much a part of the picture of economic development as the old stand-by of assessing the value of natural resources and the cost of getting them to market.

There is a cultural paradox involved in all of this that makes it difficult for the unwary investigator. At the same time that Americans were saving at a high rate for development purposes and investing in railroad securities, they had a distrust of the railroad operator and were inclined to make the railroads a scapegoat for many of their ills. In other words, there was a kind of national Manicheaen heresy, whereby people were willing to sell themselves to the devil, to worship evil, as it were, but at the same time were not ready to forget the fact that it was really the devil and not good that they were supporting. This whole problem of ambiguity of attitude toward business leaders, and the reactions it led to on the part of the executives themselves, is one of the most fruitful fields of American cultural history.

This leads directly to the problem of social sanctions: what codes of conduct, ethics, mores, and folkways were recognized by the railroad entrepreneur? The "robber-baron" approach has implied that there were few sanctions recognized, that these men operated on the basis of nearly complete expediency. To anyone familiar with the study of cultures, this is obviously a very questionable assertion. Actually, there were many but varying sanctions operative upon the business leaders of the period. They varied with types of activity — horse-trading, for instance, having one set of ethics, banking quite another; with the conditioning of the entrepreneur, whereby a man brought up in the strict and staid business community of Philadelphia would have different ethics from one brought up in a less rigidly structured society; and with the geographical region — the frontier, in general, being an area of greater opportunity and larger adherence to the "end-justifies-the-means" philosophy than more settled areas — the mining town of Virginia City and Boston, perhaps, illustrating extreme poles.

Let us take a particular type of social sanction and see how it operated on the basis of these differing situations. One of the most important ones was the feeling of a fiduciary obligation toward stockholders and bondholders — the recognition of the fact that managers were trustees for the real owners of the property. From this standpoint, the distinction between men and regions may be brought out by analyzing the promotion of an extension up the Mississippi River by the directors of the Chicago, Burlington & Quincy Railroad.

But before proceeding to the details of these operations, it is necessary to understand some of the culture patterns of pioneer development and railroad building. The ultimate growth and welfare of the community was a rationalization that to the Westerner justified almost any means that he might employ — particularly in the handling of Easterners' capital. Added to this was the fact that railroad companies were not fitted to do their own construction work and had to let local contractors do the building. That the construction work was not done by contract simply to rob the stockholders is abundantly illustrated by the facts that the most mature and best-managed companies continued to build through contractors, even though they might readily have undertaken the work themselves, and that railroad contractors sometimes bankrupted themselves by bidding too low. The difficulties were that building was a specialized enterprise for which the railroad had no regular staff, that it was occasional rather than continuous and, therefore, did not justify the maintenance of a specialized staff, and that often the work was remote from the railroad offices and could not readily be supervised by the chief executives. In order to facilitate such large-scale work by local interests, it would often be necessary for the road itself, or the directors or large stockholders of the road, to put up cash to assist the local contractor. This would be done by buying stock in a construction company of which the operating executive would usually be a local builder. The construction company took its pay in railroad stocks or bonds, which might in the case of an old road be almost as good as cash, but in the case of many young roads might be of very speculative and dubious value. The par value of securities taken for construction work, therefore, is not a safe guide to the amount of profit actually realized by construction companies. But there is little question that a great deal of eastern stockholders' money went west into construction companies and stayed there as profit to local entrepreneurs, including subcontractors all the way down the line, and even to the owners of local sandbanks and hardware stores. Sometimes the eastern directors and stockholders who had advanced money for construction company stock made handsome profits; at other times, as in the case to be discussed, they lost what they had put in; but in any case, the local people were likely to make a profit. As John Murray Forbes, Boston railroad promoter and conservative financier, put it, "My feeling is . . . that the Landowners and R. Road contractors are the ones who too often get the whole benefit of the money that Capitalists put into the West." [4] Charles E. Perkins, long-time president of the C. B. & Q., went even further: "Iowa people make more money in farms and other industries including contracting and building than in railroads . . . and it is only the eastern capitalist who cannot use his money to advantage at home who is willing to risk it in western railroads and take the low average return which he gets, a return very much lower than the average of other investments in this state [of Iowa]." [5]

This background is necessary to an understanding of the contracts for the so-called River Roads that were to go up the Mississippi from Clinton, Iowa, ultimately to Minneapolis and St. Paul. The central western city involved in this development was Dubuque, Iowa, and the local entrepreneur who undertook to do the construction was J K. Graves. He was a small-scale, general entrepreneur interested in banking, building, and all the wide range of local enterprises usual to the small-city capitalist. In order to undertake construction on these roads, he persuaded a group of the C. B. & Q. directors, headed by ex-president James F. Joy, to put up about half a million dollars cash in return for securities of the construction company. They then entered into a

[4] John Murray Forbes to Charles S. Tuckerman, Apr. 14, 1880. President's Letters, Chicago, Burlington & Quincy Archives, Newberry Library, Chicago, Illinois.

[5] Charles E. Perkins to James W. McDill, Jan. 26, 1885. President's Letters, Chicago, Burlington & Quincy Archives, Newberry Library.

contract with the two railroad companies that were to own and operate the lines after they had been built, whereby the construction company took pay partly in stocks and bonds. The rest of the bonds of these companies were to be marketed to the holders of C. B. & Q. bonds and stock, who would buy them readily because of the endorsement of their own directors; this would in turn provide additional capital that could be used to pay for the construction.

Some of the members of the C. B. & Q. board, particularly John Murray Forbes and J. N. A. Griswold, were not told at the time they endorsed the sale of the bonds that their fellow directors were actually interested in the stock of the construction company. It seems probable that this knowledge was withhheld because Joy and the directors who did buy such stock recognized that Forbes would not approve of their being involved in this kind of relationship. In other words, there appears to have been a difference in the business morality or sanctions recognized by James F. Joy, a western business-man, and those recognized by old, conservative, upper-class Easterners like Forbes and Griswold.

The working out of the pattern has much in common with the Villard story; Graves may or may not have been a good railroad builder. Examination of hundreds of letters to and from Graves, and letters discussing the situation among C. B. & Q. directors, has failed to provide conclusive information on this point. At least, he held the confidence of Joy and the other interested directors right up to the final failure of the enterprise. The contracts were let in the boom of 1871, and, when the depression hit after the panic of 1873, the roads had not been completed. With revenues of all kinds falling off, Graves started borrowing from the funds of the unfinished River Roads to support his other local enterprises. The result was a slowing down of construction, a default on the bonds of the River Roads, and a financial situation that would not bear close scrutiny by accountants. In all this it is very hard to pass moral judgments. Graves had undoubtedly thought that he was doing the best thing possible for Dubuque and the surrounding country by trying to build up many enterprises at once. He had made no plans for a break in the boom and the coming of depression. As a result, he found him-self hopelessly involved in ventures that could not all be kept going; yet the abandonment of any one of them then meant a postponing of all or most of the benefit that was expected to accrue from it. In this situation he tried to borrow from Peter to pay Paul, hoping that Peter would raise additional funds. The same kind of situation has turned pillars of society into scoun-drels time and time again in American business history.

In the case of the River Roads, when the default occurred, Forbes and Griswold became interested in investigating the situation and soon found out the identity of the construction company's stockholders and the nature of the contracts. Forbes denounced Joy, and when the latter refused to assume per-sonal responsibility to the C. B. & Q. investors for the interest in the River

Road bonds — a procedure which would have been highly unusual — Forbes decided that Joy and certain other directors involved must be put off the C. B. & Q. board. Forbes succeeded in doing this in a proxy battle at the next stockholders' meeting and the River Roads passed ultimately into the hands of the Chicago, Milwaukee and St. Paul. This, in the long run, turned out to be a great mistake, as a decade later C. B. & Q. had to build a parallel line under less advantageous circumstances.

The quarrel was due to a conflict in sanctions based upon differences in situation. As one of Joy's followers in the matter, J. W. Brooks, a C. B. & Q. director who had had much experience in the West, put it, "Loosely as these things were done [branch-line contracts and construction in general] they as a whole have proved the salvation of the C. B. & Q. . . . we do not claim to be immaculate beyond expediency, but are content with right intentions and the good results obtained on the whole. . . ." [6]

Perhaps the above examples have demonstrated the difficulty in regarding any particular group of business leaders as "robber barons" without careful analysis of the situation involved, the popular and local codes of ethics, and the general pressure for "justification by profit" that ran all through American culture.

These illustrations have shown only limited aspects of entrepreneurial history. They have touched on, but not elaborated, the political science of the business corporation and the analysis of power within the corporation, showing only in the latter case that it is not easy to put one's finger on the exact location of control in any given instance. Real control over a situation may rest with some contractor or underling in the West, despite the façade of power in the eastern executive officers. Many other relations have not been brought out at all in these two accounts — for example, the relation of business roles to other social roles, which carries with it the discussion of the role of the business elite in relation to cultural leadership. Many railroad men, for example, were active leaders in national or state politics; others were patrons of the arts, or supporters of education. To what extent were these attitudes outgrowths of general social mores, to what extent did business sanctions indicate that these supplementary roles should be played, and to what extent were they peculiarities of the individuals?

Comparative studies need to be made of the place of entrepreneurship in varying national cultures. There seems little doubt that such studies will go further toward explaining the economic progress of different regions than will any assessment of potential natural resources. It is these cultural elements, to a very large extent, that determine who will become entrepreneurs (the quantity and quality of the supply of entrepreneurship), and also the likelihood of entrepreneurial success in various types of endeavor. A culture with feudal standards of lavish living or the support of elaborate ceremonial organ-

---

[6] John W. Brooks to James F. Joy, Mar. 11, 1875. Joy Collection, Michigan Historical Collections, Ann Arbor, Michigan.

izations of church and state will obviously not have the capital to invest in economic development that will be available in a culture where frugal living, saving, and work are the custom.

The resources in theory and scope of interest of all the social sciences may be applied more readily to historical problems in the study of special roles and functions, such as entrepreneurship, than in the general study of the enormous conventional fields of economic, social, political or intellectual history. To learn more about how human beings behave and have behaved in history, it is wise to start with a manageable and definable group of human beings performing certain functions, rather than with the activities of the society as a whole. □

✧ 56 ✧

Development, Diversification and Decentralization *

ALFRED D. CHANDLER, JR.

Decentralization, diversification, and research and development — these have become familiar words in the businessman's vocabulary. Yet their use is comparatively new. A generation ago only a few American industrial firms devoted extensive resources to research and development, made and sold a variety of products, and had decentralized managements. Even today these new forms of business strategy and structure have been adopted in only a relatively small number of industries. Moreover, where a company has taken on one of these new ways, it has usually adopted the other two.

The systematic application of science to industry through organized research and development has never been really widespread. As early as the 1920's three industries — the electrical, chemical, and rubber — accounted for by far the largest amount of money and personnel used in systematic research and development. During the 1920's and 1930's petroleum and power machinery (including automobile and agricultural implements) companies began to build large development organizations. By 1938 three-fourths of the personnel working in organized industrial research were in these five industries. Other basic American businesses, such as steel, non-ferrous metals, paper, textiles, food, and those processing agricultural products, provided well below 25 per cent of the trained men in the nation's industrial laboratories.

The pattern has continued since World War II. The only industries besides the prewar five to devote extensive resources to research and develop-

* "Development, Diversification and Decentralization" by Alfred D. Chandler, Jr., from POSTWAR ECONOMIC TRENDS, edited by Ralph E. Freeman. Copyright © 1960 Massachusetts Institute of Technology. Reprinted by permission of Harper & Row, Publishers.

ment have been aircraft and scientific instruments. As the aircraft industry has been largely government sponsored, it hardly has the same business problems as other industries. The government has also been the market for and has provided over 60 per cent of the funds used in the development of scientific instruments. This same government support has also been true of many of the newer products of the older electrical companies. On the other hand, in the automobile and power machinery industries the government provides less of a market and covers less of the cost of research and development, while in chemicals, petroleum, and rubber, government funds play an even smaller role.

Systematic research has led to the development of new products, new markets, and new processes. It also appears to have stimulated changes in external business strategies and internal management structures. Except in aircraft, the industries which have concentrated on research and development today handle the widest variety of different product lines. Firms in these same industries have tended to be the ones which have replaced the older, functionally departmentalized, centralized management structure with the newer, decentralized form made up of autonomous operating units and a general headquarters with policy-making and coordinating duties.[1] The purpose of this study is, then, to investigate more closely the nature of the connection between decentralization, diversification, and research and development. Or, to put it in the terms of a broad question, what has been the relationship between internal structure, external strategy, and economic and technological change?

In looking for answers to this question, the experience of fifty of the largest American industrial concerns has been examined. These fifty fall into nine major industrial categories. The companies include the forty-four largest by assets in 1948 as listed in the Brookings Institution's study, *Big Enterprise in a Competitive System*. Five other companies from the next fifteen largest have been added to round out the major industrial categories. (See Table 1.) Finally, Sylvania was added in order to include a third electrical company. This sample seems neutral and manageable and at the same time fairly significant. The companies, by any criterion, are among the most influential in American industry.

The nine industrial categories into which these fifty companies fall have, in turn, been classified for the purposes of this paper into three groups: the metals industries and those manufacturing agricultural products, the assembling industries, and the processing industries. Although this study will focus on the last group, since the greatest changes are currently occurring here, the experience of the first will have to be briefly summarized and the second told in more detail if the developments of the more recent period are to be fully understood.

---

[1] The difference between the centralized and decentralized structure is indicated in Charts I and II.

■ **TABLE 1 The Fifty Companies**

(Numbers indicate relative size according to 1948 assets)

• I. METALS AND AGRICULTURAL PROCESSING

Steel	Non-Ferrous	Agricultural Processing
3. U.S. Steel	18. Anaconda Copper	16. American Tobacco
12. Bethlehem	21. Kennecott Copper	23. R. J. Reynolds
26. Republic	25. Aluminum Co. of	24. Swift
32. Jones & Laughlin	America	27. Armour
38. National Steel	39. International Nickel	28. Liggett & Meyer
44. Armco Steel	40. International Paper	34. Distillers—Seagram
	49. American Smelting &	Corporation
	Refining	36. Schenley Industries
	53. Phelps Dodge	Corporation
		41. United Fruit
		42. National Dairy
		Products
		43. Procter & Gamble

• II. ASSEMBLING

Electrical	Power Machinery	Automotive
9. General Electric	17. International Harvester	2. General Motors
15. Westinghouse	57. Deere & Co.	10. Ford
[Sylvania]	59. Allis-Chalmers	22. Chrysler

• III. PROCESS

Rubber	Oil	Chemical
29. Goodyear	1. Standard (N.J.)	8. Du Pont
33. U.S. Rubber	4. Standard (Indiana)	13. Union Carbide
35. Firestone	5. Socony Vacuum	30. Eastman Kodak
56. Goodrich	6. Texas	37. Allied Chemical &
	7. Gulf	Dye
	11. Standard, California	
	14. Sinclair Oil	
	19. Shell Oil	
	20. Phillips Petroleum	
	31. Atlantic Refining	

METALS INDUSTRIES AND THOSE PROCESSING AGRICULTURAL PRODUCTS

The great corporation had its beginnings in the United States in the years after the Civil War. In the 1870's the individual firms in the long-established metals and those in processing agricultural products were small, like those in nearly all American industries, and were concerned almost wholly with manufacturing. Except for what they could buy and sell in the immediate locality, they purchased their raw materials and marketed their finished goods through commission agents and other middlemen. By 1903, the year in which a slight business recession ended the great merger movement at the turn of the century, these and other American industries had become dominated by a few large firms. The great new enterprises now did their own marketing and distribution and purchased their own supplies. Where their supplies came out of the ground rather than from the farmer or another manufacturer, they often obtained control of their raw materials. By 1900 many major American industries had become, to use the words of the economist and sociologist, oligopolistic in their inter-firm relations and bureaucratic in their intra-firm organization.

The strategy that led to the rise of the great corporation was primarily that of vertical integration. The resulting structure usually became a highly centralized one. Both structure and strategy appear to be essentially a response to the coming of the nationwide and increasingly urban market created by the rounding out of the national railroad system in the 1870's and 1880's. The consumer-goods industries were the first to take advantage of the new national market. During the 1880's and 1890's the meat packers (Swift and Armour), the tobacco manufacturers (American Tobacco Company), the soap makers (Procter & Gamble), the distillers (Distillers' Security), the banana merchants (United Fruit), and the refiners of kerosene (Standard Oil) all built nationwide — and often world-wide — distributing and sales organizations and then created large buying departments.

The makers of producers' goods completed their integrated organizations a little later. This was probably because it took longer before the city became such a major market for producers' goods. Until the 1880's the railroad remained their primary market. Then, with the falling off of railroad construction and the rapid growth of the city, the nation's urban and industrial concentrations began to take the great share of the products of the metal industries and also those of the growing machinery industries.

In the new, large, vertically integrated corporations each major function was departmentalized. There was a sales department, a manufacturing department, a purchasing department or one that produced the raw materials. Finally, all these corporations had their financial departments. The vice-presidents who headed these functional units also worked frequently as an executive committee or council with the president in coordinating the work of the different departments and in charting the business course of the corporation as a whole. As the consumer-goods companies required a steady flow of goods from the ground or farm to the market, the control of the central office was tighter and more centralized than in the higher priced, lower volume producers' goods businesses.

In most cases, however, the coordination required to make integration work effectively led to a centralized operating structure. As a result, corporations that began as combinations of firms under the common ownership of a stock-holding company soon consolidated into centralized, functionally departmentalized organizations.[2] International Harvester, for example, tried for three years to maintain its five constituent companies as separate divisions, but then combined into a single centralized operating structure. (See Chart I.) E. I. du Pont de Nemours & Company did the same thing in 1902 when it consolidated the many power-making firms it controlled through stock ownership and a trade association into a very similar centralized organization. Of the fifty largest companies in 1909, all but the United States Steel Corporation and two or three copper companies had some type of functionally departmentalized management structure whose headquarters office was primarily concerned with the flow of materials from mine to market.

By 1903 the typical American industrial corporation handled a single line of products for the national market and had an operating department to carry out each major industrial function. (See Chart I.) Often the manufacturing, marketing, or purchasing of the single line led to the development of by-products. The meat packers manufactured glue and fertilizer and used their marketing organization to distribute poultry and eggs. The steel makers had their cement, the oil refineries their vaseline and medicinal products. Yet these goods remained by-products and received little attention from any of the organization's main operating departments. For these companies, product diversification was not a conscious business strategy.

For the metals, the food, and other agricultural processing industries, the operating pattern set by 1900 has remained little changed over the past half century. Much the same firms make much the same line of goods; they compete with one another and are internally managed in much the same way. In the metals industry the only firms in Table I to be established after 1903 are National Steel (a merger of three older firms) and Kennecott Copper (which was earlier the supplier of raw materials for American Smelting and Refining, both financed largely by the Guggenheims). Actually, in the metals industry the trend has been, if anything, toward increasing centralization to coordinate more efficiently the flow from ground to consumer.

In the agricultural processing industries, political action encouraged a little more change. Two new tobacco companies were formed in 1911, after the dissolution of American Tobacco. The distilling industries were drastically hit by the coming of prohibition in 1920. The only other new firm on the list is National Dairy. In the mid-1950's nearly all the companies in these industries still handled a relatively few lines of closely related goods;

[2] In the steel and copper industry, control of raw material was often obtained primarily for defensive reasons — that is, to have an assured supply of the necessary raw materials. In the early years there was little attempt to include mining within the same managerial organization as processing and marketing. Also, in the metals industry, selling, distributing, and warehousing were relatively simple operations that could be handled by a comparatively small marketing department.

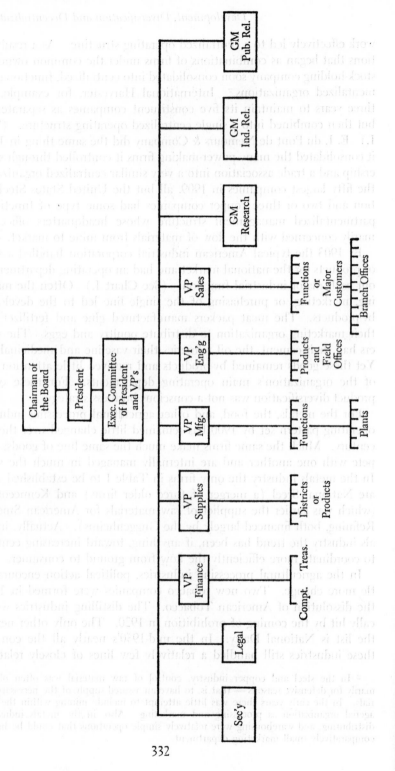

CHART 1

Simplified Chart of a Centralized, Functionally Departmentalized Structure

and by 1955 all but National Dairy and possibly Kennecott and Schenley Industries were still managed through what was essentially a centralized operating structure.

The firms in these industries have been under little real pressure to change. Their basic markets, the sources of their raw materials, and the technology of their manufacturing stayed much the same in the years from 1900 to World War II. Even postwar developments have not caused drastic changes. Just as important, the manufacturing and marketing of primary metals and products based on the output of the American farm were comparatively little affected by the technological innovations resulting from the coming of the new sources of power and the application of physical and natural sciences to industry.

THE ASSEMBLING INDUSTRIES

Basic technological innovations had a great impact on the assembling and process industries. The years after 1900 saw the enormous expansion of the electrical industry, the coming of the automobile industry, and the great changes in the existing power machinery and implement industries. From 1900 until the coming of the Great Depression these new and expanding businesses and the goods that they produced seemed to have been a dominant stimulant for industrial change — change in the sense of the development of new products and processes and of new forms of business structure and strategy.

The manufacturing of engines and vehicles or frames in which the engines were used called for new methods of purchasing, manufacturing, and marketing. Their manufacturing, particularly, required the assembling of a great many parts and components; demanded the working out of a complex production flow, the development of new machine tools, and the devising of new manufacturing methods. Because the loss of one part could delay and actually stop production, the assembling companies felt a need to control parts and accessory firms. On the other hand, as they used relatively few basic materials in relation to their final product, they felt little pressure to go into the production of the primary metals. The marketing of complex power machinery to utilities, manufacturers, and other producers required a technically trained sales and service force, while the selling of durable machinery to the mass consumer market called for the development of new types of consumer financing and servicing facilities. Finally, the new ways of manufacturing and marketing caused the makers of engines and machinery to give more careful attention to systematic research and development. This was particularly true of the two great electrical manufacturers — General Electric and Westinghouse.

The Electrical Firms

General Electric and Westinghouse, beginning as makers of lamps, generating, and other equipment for lighting, quickly moved into the manufacturing of machinery to generate and use electric power in industry and transportation. The scientific nature of their business led both companies to concentrate on technological development. "Competition," as Harold Passer points out, was "in reality between the engineering staffs of the two companies." Each constantly worked to put out more efficient and newer types of engines, transformers, or generators than the other. By 1900 General Electric had gone so far as to set up a research laboratory for basic investigations into electricity which was placed under the direction of Dr. Willis R. Whitney, recruited from the faculty of the Massachusetts Institute of Technology.

Vertical integration, like competition and product improvement, encouraged the taking on of new products. A desire for an assured supply led both companies to purchase or form subsidiaries or departments to make parts and components. As the manufacturing departments did not expect to take all the output of these subsidiaries, the sales departments of both companies were soon marketing many types of switches, fuses, and other electrical engine parts. Similar needs brought General Electric into the plastic business. Unable to purchase satisfactory insulating materials, in 1912 it turned its laboratories to studying the properties of resins. Two years later the company began to make and sell plastic materials.

Development and integration, however, were concentrated in one field — that of developing, manufacturing, and marketing electrical power and lighting machinery. Because both companies remained in this single producers' goods industry, they had comparatively little difficulty in managing their activities through centralized, functionally departmentalized, organizational structures similar to those then coming into use in the metals and agricultural processing industries. The electric companies had smaller purchasing but much larger engineering departments than did the meat packing or steel firms. At headquarters their engineering and sales departments were divided along product lines — indicating the close relation between product development and competition. General Electric's sales department included, by the early 1900's, lighting, railway, power, and supply (parts and accessories) departments as well as its advertising division and its regional sales organization. The engineering department, with comparable product subdivisions, also included the research and the engineering laboratories. All in all, the organizational structure at General Electric and Westinghouse at the time of World War I looked quite similar to that outlined in Chart I.

The one major exception was the lamp business, where both manufacturing and marketing were quite different from the apparatus lines. At General Electric some lamps were made at the Harrison, New Jersey, plant; but the major production was carried on by the National Electric Lamp Association acquired in 1911. NELA operated separately from the rest of the company. Then, in the late 1920's, its activities and those of Harrison were combined. The resulting Lamp Division continued in almost complete independence. Westinghouse, too, had its separate lamp-operating organization by World War I.

When the two companies began, in the years after World War I, to move beyond power machinery, the older structure was unable to meet the new needs, and more autonomous units similar to the lamp organizations began to evolve. At both companies diversification resulted from two basic decisions. The first decision — that to develop consumer appliances — came as part of an effort to increase the demand for power machinery by expanding the nation's needs for electricity and also from a desire to keep the existing plant working more steadily — to avoid the feast-or-famine cycle of the apparatus business. The second decision resulted directly from an agreement to exploit commercially the new and varied products developed in the research laboratories, such as electronic devices, alloys, and chemicals. Soon both of these new types of business were expanded for their own sakes. Continuing diversification, based largely on systematic research and development, became more of an explicit business policy.

The basic problems created by product diversification at the two electrical companies were greater in marketing than in manufacturing. This was true particularly of the new consumer appliances, for these durable goods, unlike power machinery, were sold in volume directly to the ultimate consumer. Their marketing required the creation of a chain of dealers and of retail outlets and the formation of organizations to help finance both customer and dealer. To sell these new products, General Electric formed in the late 1920's, its merchandising department with headquarters at Bridgeport, Connecticut. It long remained almost wholly a marketing department. Refrigerator parts were made at Schenectady and Erie, and the finished product was assembled at Erie; flat irons were manufactured in California, stoves and water heaters in Chicago, and so on. Their design, manufacture, and assembling were supervised by the older functional departments, but all were sold through Bridgeport. So, too, were radios after 1931. This arrangement had its defects, since both the manufacturing and selling units usually had different estimates as to markets and outputs. Moreover, the transferring of parts between plants was costly, and effective over-all control of product flow proved difficult.

Unlike appliances, products that came from the research laboratories tended to be organized in more autonomous units, since their engineering and manufacturing as well as marketing differed from procedures with consumer appliances and power machinery. So General Electric formed a separate subsidiary to handle the making and selling of X-ray equipment and another — Carboloy, Inc. — to handle its alloy business. Its chemical activities were consolidated in 1930 into a separate autonomous unit with headquarters at

Lynn, Massachusetts. At General Electric, too, air-conditioning equipment, developed in the early 1930's, was soon placed within a semi-independent department handling its own sales and manufacturing.

By the early 1930's Westinghouse had similar autonomous units for manufacturing and sales of X-ray equipment and elevators. At Westinghouse the merchandise department came to have more control over other functions than did the one in General Electric. Formed in 1933

> as a separate operation distinct from the other Divisions of the Company. This Division includes not only the sales activities of such products as refrigerators, electric ranges, household appliances, etc., but also related engineering and manufacturing activities, whenever the main outlet for the product is through merchandising channels.[3]

Then came the appointment of "a separate manager" responsible for supervising engineering, manufacturing, and sales in other "main divisions of the Company's products." Vice-presidents in charge of the functional departments now became essentially advisory officers responsible for coordinating engineering, manufacturing, marketing, and other policies of the different product units.

Until after World War II General Electric retained its complex structure which was partly functional and partly along product lines, partly centralized and partly decentralized. The first attempt at simplification came after the retirement of Gerard Swope, its brilliant president who for many years ran the company almost single-handedly. While his successor, Charles E. Wilson, made some tentative beginnings at reorganization, the war delayed his plans. Then, in 1946, he turned over the problem to Ralph Cordiner.

Cordiner quickly redefined the company's activities along product lines by setting up six new major departments — apparatus, lamp, appliances, air conditioning, electronics, and chemical. Each was headed by a senior executive who had all the necessary functions under his control and was responsible for the financial performance of all the products in his department. The older functional departments now became advisory staff units with planning and coordinating duties. Committees of staff and operating men which usually included the three general officers (Wilson, Cordiner, and the chairman of the board) set over-all policies and plans.

When Cordiner became president in 1950, he carried the reorganization still further. He subdivided the product departments into over seventy units and eliminated the coordinating and policy-making committees. The managers of the smaller departments now had the same responsibilities and authority as had the former heads of the six product departments. Supervision and planning for several units were placed under a general divisional manager who, to keep him from interfering with the department heads, was given no staff of his own. At headquarters four new group vice-presidents were ap-

[3] The annual report of the Westinghouse Electric Company for 1934, p. 10.

pointed. Individually they appraised the performance of the various departments and divisions placed under their guidance. Collectively they were — with the president, the chairman, and the head of the service departments — responsible for over-all policies. (See Chart II.)

Westinghouse, under the direction of Mark W. Cresap, Jr., underwent a similar massive reorganization after 1950. The changes there resulted in a structure quite similar to the one Cordiner first set up at General Electric. Operating activities were placed in four groups — apparatus, general industries, consumer products, and defense. The group vice-presidents, assisted by large staffs of their own, were given full responsibility for profit and functions. The older functional departments became explicitly advisory service units. Recently the company has increased the number of general offices at headquarters to five.

In this way, then, the present decentralized structure, consisting of autonomous operating units and a policy-making coordinating headquarters with general officers and staff specialists, evolved at both the great electrical companies out of the older functionally departmentalized centralized organization. Fundamentally the new structure has been the organizational response to the strategy of product diversification developed in the 1920's. The manufacturing, marketing, and engineering of very different lines of products proved extremely difficult to handle within the old organization. The final resolution of the operating problems created by diversification came, however, only when two executives with strong interest in organizational matters — Cordiner and Cresap — devoted their full attention to reorganizing the existing structures. And both men became, once the new structure was completed, the presidents of their respective companies.

The Implement and Power Machinery Firms

The experience of the implement and power machinery firms and the automobile manufacturers had many parallels to that of the electrical companies. The essential difference is that they did not move much beyond the making of implements and power-driven machinery. Also, except for General Motors, they rarely attempted to handle both producers' and consumers' goods. Because they did not diversify much beyond power machinery, their product lines were pretty well completed by the 1930's; and, since they were less diversified than the electrical companies, their later reorganizations were less of a traumatic experience.

Allis-Chalmers and International Harvester, as well as somewhat smaller firms like Worthington (formerly International Steam Pump) and Borg-Warner and, to a much lesser extent, Deere & Company, were changed by the coming of the new sources of power in the early years of the twentieth century. Of these, only Allis-Chalmers exploited the new electrical machinery business. Created in 1901, as a merger of several steam power machinery companies, Allis-Chalmers quickly consolidated the operation of its constitu-

CHART 2

Simplified Chart of a Typical Decentralized Structure

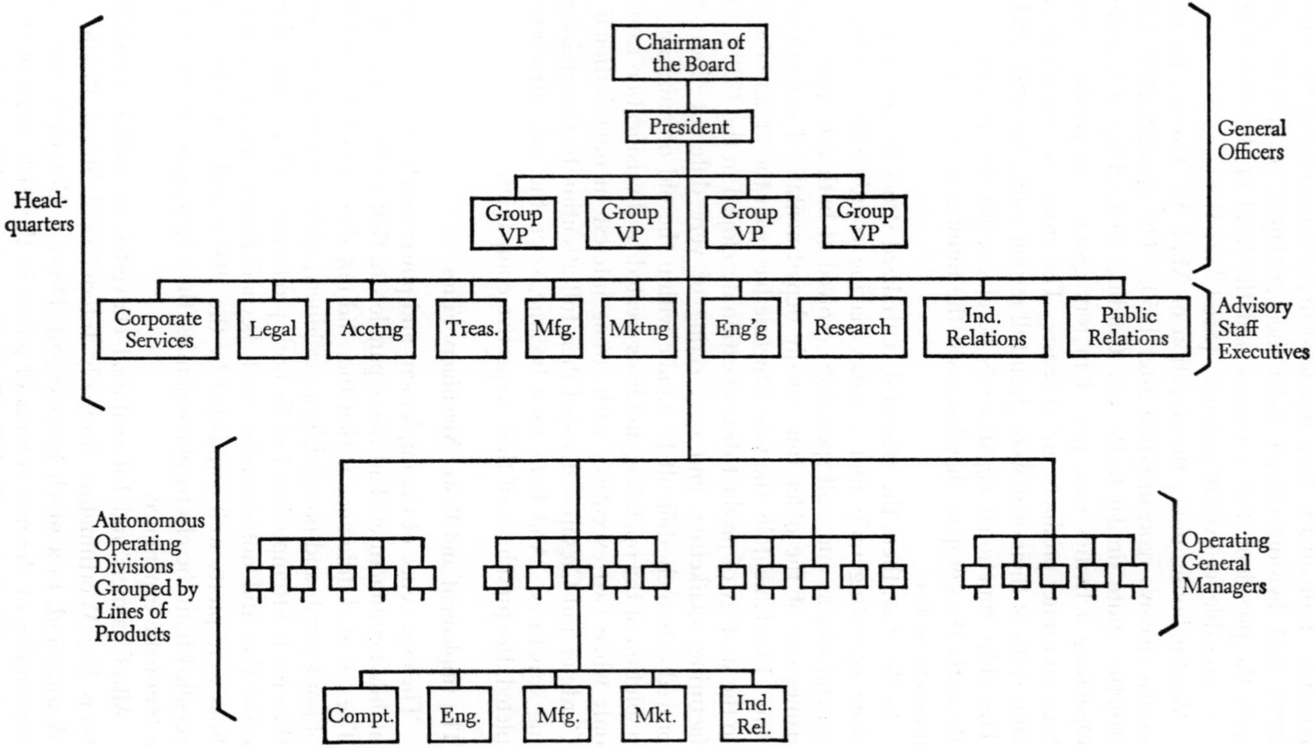

General Officers

Advisory Staff Executives

Operating General Managers

Chairman of the Board

President

Group VP

Group VP

Group VP

Group VP

Corporate Services

Legal

Acctng

Treas.

Mfg.

Mktng

Eng'g

Research

Ind. Relations

Public Relations

Headquarters

Compt.

Eng.

Mfg.

Mkt.

Ind. Rel.

Autonomous Operating Divisions Grouped by Lines of Products

ent firms into a single centralized, functionally departmentalized organization. In 1904 the company, aware of the competitive challenge of the new sources of power, planned to make both electrical and gasoline-driven machinery. This decision called for a great expansion of both its engineering and sales departments which, like those of the electrical companies, quickly became divided along product lines. At first the company concentrated on electrical apparatus; and by 1910 it could report that "of the sales invoiced for the year, about 55 per cent were for the new lines of business which the company has recently developed and, of these new lines, about 75 per cent are electrical." From that time on, Allis-Chalmers remained the third largest manufacturer of electrical machinery and apparatus in the United States.

In the next decade the company shifted its attention to the internal-combustion engine; and by the end of World War I it had developed a line of tractors, earth-moving, and other construction machinery. After the war the company decided to build and sell tractors for farmers as well as for construction companies.

The decision to go into the agricultural tractor business quickly raised marketing difficulties. Allis-Chalmers sold its construction machinery equipment through independent distributors, while it sold directly to the flour, lumber, mining, cement, and utility companies through technically trained salesmen working out of the sales departments' district offices here and abroad. To reach the farmer, however, required warehouses, branch offices, and franchised retail dealers. Also, in order to compete successfully with International Harvester, Deere & Company, and other farm machinery firms, Allis-Chalmers' distributing organization needed a full line of farm implements. The company's engineers were soon hard at work designing harvesters, combines, and other agricultural implements. By 1940 Allis-Chalmers had become the third largest producer of agricultural machinery in the United States.

As the tractor and implement business grew, these activities became more separate from the company's main operating organization. By World War II there was a separate factory and distributing organization, and the company had come to consider its business as being divided into two groups — the Tractor Division and the General Machinery Division. However, although there was a separate sales and manufacturing vice-president for tractors, the company continued to operate through a centralized, functionally departmentalized management structure.

Continued expansion in both tractor and general machinery lines led to a major reorganization in 1954. It started, as did the first changes at General Electric, by making a growing *de facto* situation *de jure*. The operating activities became specifically divided into two groups. The tractor group now included three divisions — construction machinery, farm equipment, and buda (diesel) engine. The industries group included the power equipment, industrial equipment, and general products divisions. As at Westinghouse, each group vice-president had his own staff, including directors of manufacturing, engineering, and sales. With the disbanding of the old major functional departments (manufacturing, engineering, and sales), the other functional activities (research, public relations, industrial relations, and the controller's office) now became "service" departments, with advisory and auditing duties. No general officers were appointed besides the president and the chairman of the board. These two, in consultation with the busy group vice-presidents and senior staff officers, made policy and appraised the activities of the operating divisions.

International Harvester, unlike Allis-Chalmers, never diversified into electrical power machinery. At first it concentrated on adapting the gasoline motor to improve and expand its existing line of farm implements and machinery. In the 1920's, however, as the prolonged postwar depression in agriculture cut down the buying power of the farmer, the company turned increasingly to the making of trucks and power machinery for industry. While this move beyond farm implements raised some new problems of production and of purchasing and control of materials, the major difficulties arose in marketing. Here Harvester's problems were just the reverse of those of Allis-Chalmers. The former had to create marketing and distributing outlets to sell in the cities to industry, just as the latter firm had to develop a rural sales organization. Until World War I the Harvester sales department continued to supervise the marketing of new products. To do this it set up a number of "specialty" departments. As the truck and industrial machinery business grew, the sales organizations became increasingly separated from the department's main organization.

International Harvester did not wait until increasing growth and diversification caused an administrative crisis before it reshaped its organizational structure. Fowler McCormick, who became president in 1941, had developed a strong interest in the problems of organization and had been particularly impressed by the decentralized structure which General Motors used so effectively. In 1943 he set up six new operating divisions — industrial power, motor truck, farm tractor, farm implement, fiber and twine, and Wisconsin steel. The first two — industrial power and motor truck — were completely autonomous. Their managers had full responsibility for profits and sales and soon had under them executives in charge of engineering, manufacturing, sales, supply and inventory, labor relations, and a divisional comptroller. Managers of the next two divisions were responsible for all activities except sales. Since their goods went to the same market, they were sold and distributed through the general line sales department, which was basically the same marketing organization that had been set up shortly after the company's formation in 1902. The sixth division included the steel-making and mining companies that had come into the company with the 1902 merger.

McCormick next carefully redefined the duties of the remaining functional departments. Several were combined into two units — a vice-presidency of supply and inventory and a vice-presidency of merchandising services. The first, divided into three departments (estimate and order review, materials control, order and distribution), was to coordinate the flow of materials or, to use the wording of the 1943 annual report,

> to review orders, to place manufacturing orders, and to control all inventories of raw materials, purchased parts and work in progress, and after manufacture had been completed, to control inventories of finished machines and parts until they reached the hands of the dealers and users.

The vice-presidency of the merchandising services, also divided into three units (customer relations, sales operations research, and credits and collections), was an advisory and service organization. So also were the older engineering and manufacturing departments and the much newer industrial relations and public relations offices.

After the war the general office was more carefully defined. In 1946 three executive vice-presidents were appointed. They were given no specific administrative duties but were to specialize in a major functional area, such as sales, engineering, or finance. The senior staff officers were to assist the general officers to plan, to decide policy, and to appraise and audit divisional and company performance. For the latter task the meetings of the Operations Review Committee, consisting of the executive and staff vice-presidents, came increasingly to be used.

Smaller power machinery and implement firms, such as Worthington, Borg-Warner, Cherry-Burrell, and Thompson Products, have developed the same strategy and, much more recently, the same structure as the two leading companies in this field. Deere & Company has, until almost the present day, remained the exception. Only since the retirement of a president in 1955 ended more than a century of direct family management has attention been turned to development and diversification.

Except for Deere, the coming of the new generators of power had a forceful impact on existing machinery and implement firms as well as creating great new ones. The older policies of vertical integration and having a "full line" led to the production of many new products and to the development of others. Growing product diversification in turn led to *de facto* decentralization by World War II. But not until the late 1940's and early 1950's did such *de facto* structure become *de jure*. When the final reorganizations were made, the managers of the power machinery firms usually took as their model the management structure of the leading automobile company.

The Automobile Companies

The automobile companies differed from the other power machinery firms in their concentration on the mass consumer market. High-volume production called for greater attention to factory layout, production engineering, and the development of highly complex, specialized machine tools. Mass marketing meant more thought had to be given to style, comfort, product differentiation, and advertising. Both marketing and production encouraged vertical integration and management centralization.

Before the gasoline-driven car was over a decade old, Ford and General Motors had become the two leading automobile makers. Their founders, Henry Ford and William C. Durant, more than any other manufacturers, appreciated the potential of the great national market for a moderately priced car. To reach this market, Ford in 1908 put the Model T into production; and Durant, in the same year, formed General Motors. Ford increasingly met the requirements of rapidly growing production by internal expansion. Durant, on the other hand, relied more on external purchases to fill the needs of his car-making units. These differences in growth led to completely different operating structures and, in turn, greatly affected the response of the two companies to the leveling off of demand for new cars in the 1920's.

Ford's decision to concentrate on a single model brought more immediate success in a market where there was an insatiable demand for the inexpensive car. To meet the enormous demand, Ford focused his efforts on improving and expanding production facilities. At his Highland Park works he developed the classic moving assembly line. Then at the River Rouge plant he carried out his dream of building a great factory into which flowed Ford-owned ore, coal, rubber, and glass and from which poured a vast stream of Model T's. With the realization of these plans Ford's manufacturing became, like his marketing and management organization, completely committed to the making of one single model for an ever-expanding market. When the market leveled off, the Ford Company was unable to meet the new situation. It quickly gave way to its more diversified and decentralized rival.

After Durant had formed General Motors as a combination of leading producers of the day — Buick, Cadillac, Oldsmobile, and Oakland — he concentrated, like Ford, on increasing production rather than purchasing new companies. After 1915, when he came into full control of General Motors and enjoyed du Pont financial support, he increased his production facilities at existing and new plants. He also purchased many parts and accessory companies, bought large interests in leather, tire, gear, and body companies, and made long-term contracts with aluminum and steel firms. In these purchases and negotiations his motives were essentially defensive. He wanted to assure his car-making companies of an adequate and certain supply of materials at reasonable prices. Durant made no attempt to coordinate more efficiently the activities of the supplying and manufacturing units. Nor did he try to line up his cars to make the most of different types of demands for automobiles. Like Ford, Durant merely wanted to produce as many units as possible; but, unlike Ford, he preferred to do this through the purchase of facilities rather than through careful rationalization of production.

Durant left General Motors in the fall of 1920 at the time when the sharp postwar recession stopped automobile production and caught General Motors without the necessary operating capital. The du Ponts and J. P. Morgan, who provided the needed funds, installed a new management headed by Pierre du

Pont and Alfred P. Sloan, Jr. The new executives immediately reshaped General Motors' market strategy and management structure. The basic strategic objective became "a car for every purse and purpose," while the new organization was one which Sloan had already suggested to Durant.

Under Durant each operation had been left completely to its own. General Motors was, in fact, almost totally decentralized. To bring some sort of order and unity into the corporation, Sloan had proposed the creation of a central office to coordinate, appraise, and plan policy for the different units and the corporation as a whole. The operating divisions were to remain responsible for market and financial performance. The central office, Sloan suggested, should consist of staff specialists and general officers. The staff would provide the expert services and advice to the operating units and the general officers. These general executives included the president, the chairman of the board, the vice-presidents in charge of the financial and advisory staffs, and the group executives. The latter were made explicitly responsible for appraising the performance and for supervising a group of similar divisions. Sloan recommended separating the divisions into four groups — motor car, parts, accessories, and miscellaneous. This structure, which was changed only in detail after its adoption in January 1921, became a model for structural changes at International Harvester, General Electric, and elsewhere in later years.

Once the strategy of the full line and the decentralized structure had been shaken down, General Motors quickly outdistanced Ford both as to profits and share of the market. In 1925 General Motors had less than 20 per cent of the market and Ford more than 50. By 1940 their positions were almost reversed. Decentralization gave General Motors real advantages in effectively exploiting the variations in the no longer expanding passenger-car market. It also made relatively easy the development of the commercial vehicle, particularly the bus, and the creation of new and the expansion of older nonautomotive lines, such as Frigidaire and Delco. Durant had earlier taken the last two for special reasons. He had purchased Frigidaire in World War I as a means to keep his dealer and some of his manufacturing organization employed if car production was cut down. Delco-Light, manufacturers of electrical equipment, was purchased partly to get the services of Charles F. Kettering.

Kettering, as the head of the first research and development organization in an automobile company, at first concentrated on product improvement. Toward the end of the 1920's, however, his department not only worked on developing household and electrical appliances but also began developing the diesel engine. Soon, through its diesel manufacturing, General Motors was by far the largest maker of railway locomotives in this country. In this way the decentralized organization helped to encourage both development and diversification at General Motors.

Ford had also tried to diversify, but nearly all his ventures failed; and they failed primarily because the Ford organization was set up to handle only a single automobile model. For example, Ford in 1917 enthusiastically developed plans to make a cheap tractor that would revolutionize farming just as the Model T had changed passenger transportation. His tractor was adequately engineered, inexpensive, and popular; but it proved unsuccessful largely because he tried to handle it within his larger organization. As one of his major rivals, Cyrus McCormick III, pointed out:

> He overran his object when he gave his tractor to his dealers to sell. . . . Ford dealers in the country were well acquainted with their customers, but not their farm needs; and Ford dealers in the city had no sales outlet for farm goods.[4]

For a time Ford tried to develop a line of implements which were manufactured on contract to go with his tractor. Even this move was not enough to meet the competition from the established, widespread, fully stocked dealer organizations of International Harvester, Allis-Chalmers, John Deere, and others. Once the Rouge was in operation, the production, like the distribution, of the tractor could not be fitted into the existing organization. So in 1928 Ford stopped making tractors in this country.

Ford also built an excellent airplane; but, again, he was unable to produce and sell it effectively. Although his light truck business, which could be handled through his car-making and selling organization, was profitable, he made almost no attempt to develop other types of commercial vehicles. Nor did he develop a profitable parts and accessory business. Nor was he able to follow General Motors' example and move into diesel and other types of internal-combustion engines. Finally, Ford did not even develop a full line of cars. Until after World War II the Mercury and the Lincoln, accounted for a very small percentage of Ford's sales.

After World War II and the retirement and death of the elder Henry Ford, the company finally began to change its strategy and structure. The younger Henry hired Ernest R. Breech and other General Motors executives to rejuvenate the company. Breech began his new job, in *Fortune's* words,

> by clapping the GM organizational garment onto the Ford manufacturing frame, trimming the garment here and pulling out the frame there. Nobody around Ford makes any bones about this, and indeed one of Breech's first acts was to send around copies of a semi-official GM text on decentralization.[5]

The new organization had its autonomous operating divisions and its group vice-presidents and its advisory and service staff. Since the 1947 change, Ford

---

[4] As a wartime measure Durant had also moved into the tractor business, with the purchase of the Samson Sieve Grip Tractor Company. The venture was liquidated with large inventory loss in 1922, at the time when General Motors was meeting the major crisis created by the postwar recession. *Annual Report of the General Motors Corporation for 1922*, December 31, 1922, pp. 10–11.

[5] *Fortune*, Vol. 35 (May, 1947), p. 88. Other useful articles are *Fortune*, Vol. 45 (March, 1952), p. 97 ff.; Vol. 50 (September, 1945), p. 123 ff. I have also made use of a current organization chart of the company. Keith Sward, *The Legend of Henry Ford* (New York, 1948), especially chap. 14, highlights the business and management costs of the elder Ford's organization methods.

has rounded out its line, devoted more attention to Mercury and Lincoln, and revived its tractor, parts, and accessory businesses. Except for the Edsel fiasco, this imitative strategy and structure appear to have worked quite well.

Chrysler's story is closer to Ford's than General Motors', although Walter Chrysler began the present-day company by imitating the latter. In 1928, with the purchase of Dodge and the creation of the DeSoto and Plymouth, Chrysler fashioned a full line of cars. Until World War II, however, his company concentrated on the Plymouth. Because he began in a time of declining demand, he had little trouble in obtaining his parts, accessories, and materials at a low price. So until World War II the company remained essentially an engine-making and car-assembling organization, operating through a centralized, functionally departmentalized structure. The great increase in demand after the war forced Chrysler to obtain control of some of its supplies. The war also turned the company, like Ford, to the making of products other than automobiles; and since the war the company has continued to produce a larger variety of products. After the retirement of K. T. Keller, Chrysler's successor as chief executive, it began to decentralize along the lines of the General Motors model. By 1955 it had its autonomous divisions, advisory staff, and policy-making general officers.

The experience of the automobile companies stresses how the existence of the volume market encourages product concentration and management centralization. Because of historical circumstances and because of the leading executives' concern with organizational principles and problems, General Motors was able to avoid both concentration and centralization. The decentralized structure permitted it to make the most of the automobile market and, in fact, of the potentials of power machinery used in transportation. Because of it, Kettering's research and development section was encouraged to develop nonautomotive products as well as to improve the automobile. Only after Ford and Chrysler had decentralized too did the first begin to move successfully into nonautomotive products like tractors and implements, and the second into air-conditioning and marine engines.

The limits of diversification for the automobile and power machinery firms seem to have been nearly reached. General Motors, Allis-Chalmers, and International Harvester have added few major products to their lines since World War II. Nor have Westinghouse and General Electric developed much new power machinery or apparatus outside of those needed primarily to meet military demands such as jet aircraft, missiles, and nuclear power. Research and development in the power machinery field have been concentrated on improving existing products and processes and on refining marketing and organizational techniques. As the government has provided the major markets as well as most of the funds for research and development in jet, missiles, and nuclear power, the needs of national defense have been the primary stimulus for technological innovation in the power machinery firms since the 1930's.

In the electrical industry many new nonmilitary products have been developed, and here the systematic application of science in research and development departments appears to have been the major innovating force. The new lines developed at General Electric and Westinghouse in the past twenty-five years have come largely out of the research laboratories. Applied physics has enlarged these companies' offerings in electronics, radio, television, control systems, and a number of scientific instruments. Applied chemistry has increased the offerings, particularly at General Electric, in plastics, silicons, and similar products.

The story of Sylvania Electric Products, Inc., a newer company, stresses how applied chemistry and physics, rather than the demands of electric power, have led to growth and change in the electrical industry in recent years. Sylvania, formed in 1931 as a radio and lamp tube company, never made power machinery. During and after World War II it expanded rapidly into a variety of electronic, electric, and chemical products. Rapid diversification soon led to decentralization.

Sylvania continued with a centralized structure until 1950, when the managers of the different product units were given control over sales and development, as well as manufacturing, and the functional offices at headquarters became advisory and service departments. Then, in 1954, the central headquarters were enlarged by the appointment of three "vice-presidents — operations," one for lighting, one for the other consumer goods businesses (radio and television, radio tubes, picture tubes, and parts), and a third for producers' goods (tungsten and chemical, atomic energy, and electronics). They, with staff vice-presidents, the president, and the chairman, concentrated on over-all supervision and policy making. The story at Sylvania has many parallels in other companies exploiting physics and allied sciences, such as the Radio Corporation of America, the Philco Corporation, and the American Optical Company.

Since the 1930's, then, applied science seems to have encouraged more product diversification than has the exploitation of electrical or petroleum-generated power. Systematic research and development have in fact encouraged many assembling firms, particularly in the electronics business, to make diversification a basic business policy. The laboratories are expected to develop a fairly steady flow of new products which may or may not be integrated into existing manufacturing and marketing organizations. For such a business strategy the decentralized structure has become almost imperative.

SUMMARY AND CONCLUSIONS

Diversification has altered the older ways of inter-firm competition. Competition has grown between firms in different industries making the same product, and it has come to be based more on technological development than on price and product differentiation. Competition has become as much a match between the research and development as between the marketing departments. Consider the differences between the rapidly growing plastics and the older copper industry. Copper mining, smelting, refining, and marketing have been carried out for over half a century by a few large firms which handle little besides copper and closely allied metals; and the primary competitive weapon, when used, has been price. On the other hand, nearly all the chemical, rubber, petroleum, and electrical companies studied here have large and active plastics divisions. Competition in plastics is less concerned with pricing and more with further investigations into the science of polymer chemicals and its commercial applications. It is a competition to develop new types of plastic materials, to locate new uses, new raw materials, and new ways of producing existing products. Moreover, the plastics business is only one of many in which these firms are engaged. In the companies and industries where applied science can be exploited, business strategy has become more concerned with the entering and leaving of different fields, lines of products, and markets. In the older industries like steel, copper, meat packing and, until recently, oil and rubber, such matters rarely concerned the policy makers.

Diversification in multi-industry activities, which is altering the older patterns of oligopolistic competition, has also changed the internal structure of the large corporation. It has helped to break down the huge centralized structures created to manage the vertically integrated corporations handling a single line of goods. The large functional departments have been divided into smaller units based on products. This has permitted more managers to become generalists, rather than specialists, and to become responsible, at an earlier age, for over-all market and financial performance. The shortening of the lines of authority, responsibility, and communication, the reduction in the number of management levels, and the more explicit delegation of decision making have helped to make many a large corporation less of a bureaucracy and more of an enterprise.

Management decentralization appears to have been largely a response to product diversification, and product diversification has been adopted most widely in the industries where the natural and physical sciences can be most effectively applied. Applied science has had its greatest impact in the process industries not only because the products of these industries are usually the result of applied chemistry but also, and even more important, because putting the new products into commercial production is less costly and difficult than in other industries. To say this another way, development, like research, is less risky. Pilot operations are less expensive, as the manufacturing of a new product often requires relatively little more than a change in raw materials or in the ingredient mix rather than, as in the mechanical industries, a heavy outlay for machines and tools. Yet in the assembling and mechanical industries, particularly the power machinery and electrical, there has been still more potential for the application of science to both the development of new products and the requirements of getting these products into production than has been true in the metal and metal-shaping industries. Steel, copper, zinc, and lead and the basic goods fashioned from them can be improved by applied physics and chemistry but not greatly changed. Only in the newer metals, like aluminum and magnesium, has there been the opportunity for much development. Of the metals firms studied here, only the Aluminum Company of America has made a concentrated effort to create new products.

In the industries where the potential of research and development can be applied, concentration on a single line of goods for the mass consumer market has been a major factor inhibiting diversification. This has been true in the oil, tire, camera, and automobile companies and also in the older firms processing agricultural products. Partly because of an increasing use of applied chemistry, Armour, Schenley Industries, and Procter and Gamble in recent years have moved into new business fields such as pharmaceuticals, detergents, chemicals, and cellulose products. All three have begun to reshape their long-established, centralized, functionally departmentalized organizations. Procter and Gamble, for example, set up in 1957 a typical decentralized structure with a central office and seven product divisions. Armour in 1958 and 1959 went through a comparable reorganization. Two somewhat similar food firms — General Mills and Borden — evolved similar structures before 1957, while a third — Quaker Oats — has, like the petroleum companies, a separate autonomous chemical division.

While the decentralized structure has been the normal organizational means to manage a diversified product line, its creation has rarely come automatically. In most cases its introduction required a change in top management. The older executives usually had neither the awareness of the organizational needs caused by diversification nor a specific interest in defining organizational relationships. In nearly every company studied here, the organizational changes were made and carried out by a new set of senior executives.

Decentralization, diversification, and systematic research and development all reflect an increasingly complex technology and economy. Before the railroads had created a national and increasingly urban market, the industrial firm handled only a single line of goods and carried out one commercial function — that of manufacturing. The demands of the new market, with its ever-growing volume, encouraged the industrial concerns to do their own purchasing and even their own mining and their own marketing. The centralized, functionally departmentalized organizations fashioned to handle the new expanding business were still built around a single line of goods. The coming of the new sources of power after 1900 and the application of science to industry in the past twenty-five years not only made procurement, manufacturing, and marketing more complicated but also permitted many firms to increase the number of their offerings. The older centralized structure was unable to carry out the demands of diversification. The decentralized structure evolved, then, largely to meet the growing complexity in all aspects of development, purchasing, manufacturing, and marketing and to help assure the essential coordination between these functions for the individual products within the over-all diversified line. □

Homestead Act *

MAY 20, 1862

■ An Act to secure homesteads to actual settlers on the public domain.

Be it enacted, That any person who is the head of a family, or who has arrived at the age of twenty-one years, and is a citizen of the United States, or who shall have filed his declaration of intention to become such, as required by the naturalization laws of the United States, and who has never borne arms against the United States Government or given aid and comfort to its enemies, shall, from and after the first of January, eighteen hundred and sixty-three, be entitled to enter one quarter-section or a less quantity of unappropriated public lands, upon which said person may have filed a pre-emption claim, or which may, at the time the application is made, be subject to pre-emption at one dollar and twenty-five cents, or less, per acre; or eighty acres or less of such unappropriated lands, at two dollars and fifty cents per acre, to be located in a body, in conformity to the legal subdivisions of the public lands, and after the same shall have been surveyed: *Provided,* That any person owning or residing on land may, under the provisions of this act, enter other land lying contiguous to his or her said land, which shall not, with the land so already owned and occupied, exceed in the aggregate one hundred and sixty acres. □

The Pacific Railway Act †

JULY 1, 1862

■ An Act to aid in the Construction of a Railroad and Telegraph Line from the Missouri River to the Pacific Ocean. . . .

Be it enacted, That Walter S. Burgess [names of corporators]; together with five commissioners to be appointed by the Secretary of the Interior . . . are hereby created and erected into a body corporate . . . by the name . . . of "The Union Pacific Railroad Company" . . . ; and the said corporation is hereby authorized and empowered to lay out, locate, construct, furnish,

---

* Taken and adapted from "Homestead Act" (May 20, 1862), *U.S. Statutes at Large,* Vol. XII, pp. 392 ff.
† Taken and adapted from "The Pacific Railway Act" (July 1, 1862), *U.S. Statutes at Large,* Vol. XII, pp. 489 ff.

maintain and enjoy a continuous railroad and telegraph . . . from a point on the one hundredth meridian of longitude west from Greenwich, between the south margin of the valley of the Republican River and the north margin of the valley of the Platte River, to the western boundary of Nevada Territory, upon the route and terms hereinafter provided. . . .

SEC. 9. . . . The Central Pacific Railroad Company of California are hereby authorized to construct a railroad and telegraph line from the Pacific coast . . . to the eastern boundaries of California, upon the same terms and conditions in all respects [as are provided for the Union Pacific Railroad].

SEC. 10. . . . And the Central Pacific Rail-Road Company of California after completing its road across said State, is authorized to continue the construction of said railroad and telegraph through the Territories of the United States to the Missouri River . . . upon the terms and conditions provided in this act in relation to the Union Pacific Railroad Company, until said roads shall meet and connect. . . .

SEC. 11. That for three hundred miles of said road most mountainous and difficult of construction, to wit: one hundred and fifty miles westerly from the eastern base of the Rocky Mountains, and one hundred and fifty miles eastwardly from the western base of the Sierra Nevada mountains . . . the bonds to be issued to aid in the construction thereof shall be treble the number per mile hereinbefore provided . . . ; and between the sections last named of one hundred and fifty miles each, the bonds to be issued to aid in the construction thereof shall be double the number per mile first mentioned. . . . □

[DOCUMENT] ❖ **59** ❖

The National Bank Act *

JUNE 3, 1864

■ *An Act to provide a National Currency, secured by a Pledge of United States Bonds, and to provide for the Circulation and Redemption thereof.*

. . SEC. 5. That associations for carrying on the business of banking may be formed by any number of persons, not less in any case than five, who shall enter into articles of association, which shall specify in general terms the object for which the association is formed, and may contain any other provisions, not inconsistent with the provisions of this act, which the association may see fit to adopt for the regulation of the business of the association and the conduct of its affairs, which said articles shall be signed by the persons uniting to

* Taken and adapted from "The National Bank Act" (June 3, 1864), *U.S. Statutes at Large*, Vol. XIII, p. 99 ff.

form the association, and a copy of them forwarded to the comptroller of the currency, to be filed and preserved in his office. . . .

SEC. 7. That no association shall be organized under this act, with a less capital than one hundred thousand dollars, nor in a city whose population exceeds fifty thousand persons, with a less capital than two hundred thousand dollars: *Provided,* That banks with a capital of not less than fifty thousand dollars may, with the approval of the Secretary of the Treasury, be organized in any place the population of which does not exceed six thousand inhabitants.

SEC. 8. That every association formed pursuant to the provisions of this act shall . . . transact no business except such as may be incidental to its organization and necessarily preliminary, until authorized by the comptroller of the currency to commence the business of banking. Such association shall have power to adopt a corporate seal, and shall have succession by the name designated in its organization certificate, for the period of twenty years from its organization, unless sooner dissolved according to the provisions of its articles of association, or by the act of its shareholders owning two thirds of its stock, or unless the franchise shall be forfeited by a violation of this act; by such name it may make contracts . . . , and exercise under this act all such incidental powers as shall be necessary to carry on the business of banking by discounting and negotiating promissory notes, drafts, bills of exchange, and other evidences of debt; by receiving deposits; by buying and selling exchange, coin, and bullion; by loaning money on personal security; by obtaining, issuing, and circulating notes according to the provisions of this act. . . .

SEC. 22. That the entire amount of notes for circulation to be issued under this act shall not exceed three hundred millions of dollars. . . .

SEC. 30. That every association may take, receive, reserve, and charge on any loan or discount made, or upon any note, bill of exchange, or other evidences of debt, interest at the rate allowed by the laws of the state or territory where the bank is located, and no more. . . . And when no rate is fixed by the laws of the state or territory, the bank may take, receive, reserve, or charge a rate not exceeding seven per centum . . .

SEC. 31. That every association in the cities hereinafter named shall, at all times, have on hand, in lawful money of the United States, an amount equal to at least twenty-five per centum of the aggregate amount of its notes in circulation and its deposits; and every other association shall, at all times, have on hand, in lawful money of the United States, an amount equal to at least fifteen per centum of the aggregate amount of its notes in circulation, and of its deposits, . . . Provided, That three fifths of said fifteen per centum may consist of balances due to an association available for the redemption of its circulating notes from associations approved by the comptroller of the currency, . . . ▫

Coinage Act of February 12, 1873 *

■ An Act revising and amending the Laws relative to the Mints, Assay-offices, and Coinage of the United States.

SEC. 14. That the gold coins of the United States shall be a one-dollar piece, which, at the standard weight of twenty-five and eight-tenths grains, shall be the unit of value; a quarter-eagle, or two-and-a-half dollar piece; a three-dollar piece; a half-eagle, or five-dollar piece; an eagle, or ten-dollar piece; and a double eagle, or twenty-dollar piece . . . ; which coins shall be a legal tender in all payments at their nominal value when not below the standard weight and limit of tolerance provided in this act for the single piece, and, when reduced in weight, below said standard and tolerance, shall be a legal tender at valuation in proportion to their actual weight. . . .

SEC. 15. That the silver coins of the United States shall be a trade-dollar, a half-dollar, or fifty-cent piece, a quarter-dollar, or twenty-five-cent piece, a dime, or ten-cent piece; . . . and said coins shall be a legal tender at their nominal value for any amount not exceeding five dollars in any one payment.

SEC. 16. That the minor coins of the United States shall be a five-cent piece, a three-cent piece, and a one-cent piece . . . ; which coins shall be a legal tender, at their nominal value, for any amount not exceeding twenty-five cents in any one payment.

SEC. 17. That no coins, either of gold, silver, or minor coinage, shall hereafter be issued from the mint other than those of the denominations, standards, and weights herein set forth. □

Desert Land Act of 1877 †

■ An act to provide for the sale of desert lands in certain States and Territories . . .

Be it enacted by the Senate and House of Representatives of the United States of America in Congress assembled, That it shall be lawful for any citizen of the United States, or any person of requisite age "who may be entitled to become a citizen, and who has filed his declaration to become such" and upon payment of twenty five cents per acre — to file a declaration under oath with the register and the receiver of the land district in which any desert

* Taken and adapted from "Coinage Act of February 12, 1873," U.S. Statutes at Large, Vol. XVII, pp. 242 ff.

† Taken and adapted from "Desert Land Act of 1877," Statutes of the United States of America, 44th Cong., 2nd Session, p. 377.

land is situated, that he intends to reclaim a tract of desert land not exceeding one section, by conducting water upon the same, within the period of three years thereafter, . . . Said declaration shall describe particularly said section of land if surveyed, and, if unsurveyed, shall describe the same as nearly as possible without a survey. At any time within the period of three years after filing said declaration, upon making satisfactory proof to the register and receiver of the reclamation of said tract of land in the manner aforesaid, and upon the payment to the receiver of the additional sum of one dollar per acre for a tract of land not exceeding six hundred and forty acres to any one person, a patent for the same shall be issued to him. *Provided*, that no person shall be permitted to enter more than one tract of land and not to exceed six hundred and forty acres which shall be in compact form. . . .

SEC. 2. That all lands exclusive of timber lands and mineral lands which will not, without irrigation, produce some agricultural crop, shall be deemed desert lands, within the meaning of this act, which fact shall be ascertained by proof of two or more credible witnesses under oath, whose affidavits shall be filed in the land office in which said tract of land may be situated . . .

Approved, March 3, 1877. □

[DOCUMENT] ⬦ **62** ⬦

Chinese Exclusion Act *

MAY 6, 1882

■ *An act to execute certain treaty stipulations relating to Chinese.*

WHEREAS, in the opinion of the Government of the United States the coming of Chinese laborers to this country endangers the good order of certain localities within the territory thereof: Therefore,

Be it enacted, That from and after the expiration of ninety days next after the passage of this act, and until the expiration of ten years next after the passage of this act, the coming of Chinese laborers to the United States be, . . . suspended; and during such suspension it shall not be lawful for any Chinese laborer to come, or, having so come after the expiration of said ninety days, to remain within the United States.

SEC. 14. That hereafter no State court or court of the United States shall admit Chinese to citizenship; and all laws in conflict with this act are hereby repealed.

SEC. 15. That the words "Chinese laborers," whenever used in this act, shall be construed to mean both skilled and unskilled laborers and Chinese employed in mining. □

* Taken and adapted from "Chinese Exclusion Act" (May 6, 1882), *U.S. Statutes at Large*, Vol. XXII, pp. 58 ff.

✧ **63** ✧

The Gold Standard Act of 1900 *

MARCH 14, 1900

■ An act to define and fix the standard of value, to maintain the parity of all forms of money issued or coined by the United States. . . .

Be it enacted, That the dollar consisting of twenty-five and eight-tenths grains of gold nine-tenths fine, as established by section thirty-five hundred and eleven of the Revised Statutes of the United States, shall be the standard unit of value, and all forms of money issued or coined by the United States shall be maintained at a parity of value with this standard, and it shall be the duty of the Secretary of the Treasury to maintain such parity.

SEC. 2. That United States notes, and Treasury notes issued under the Act of July 14, 1890, when presented to the Treasury for redemption, shall be redeemed in gold coin of the standard fixed in the first section of this Act, and in order to secure the prompt and certain redemption of such notes as herein provided it shall be the duty of the Secretary of the Treasury to set apart in the Treasury a reserve fund of one hundred and fifty million dollars in gold coin and bullion, which fund shall be used for such redemption purposes only, and whenever and as often as any of said notes shall be redeemed from said fund it shall be the duty of the Secretary of the Treasury to use said notes so redeemed to restore and maintain such reserve fund. . . .

SEC. 3. That nothing contained in this Act shall be construed to affect the legal-tender quality as now provided by law of the silver dollar, or of any other money coined or issued by the United States. . . .

SEC. 14. That the provisions of this Act are not intended to preclude the accomplishment of international bimetallism whenever conditions shall make it expedient and practicable to secure the same by concurrent action of the leading commercial nations of the world and at a ratio which shall insure, permanence of relative value between gold and silver. ☐

* Taken and adapted from "The Gold Standard Act of 1900" (March 14, 1900), *U.S. Statutes at Large,* Vol. XXXI, pp. 45 ff.

Report of the Pujo Committee *
1913

Section 2 — Fact of Increasing Concentration Admitted

. . . As appears from statistics compiled by accountants for the committee, in 1911, of the total resources of the banks and trust companies in New York City, the 20 largest held 42.97 per cent; in 1906, the 20 largest held 38.24 per cent of the total; in 1901, 34.97 per cent.

Section 3 — Process of Concentration

This increased concentration of control of money and credit has been effected principally as follows:

First, through consolidations of competitive or potentially competitive banks and trust companies, which consolidations in turn have recently been brought under sympathetic management.

Second, through the same powerful interests becoming large stockholders in potentially competitive banks and trust companies. This is the simplest way of acquiring control, but since it requires the largest investment of capital, it is the least used, although the recent investments in that direction for that apparent purpose amount to tens of millions of dollars in present market values.

Third, through the confederation of potentially competitive banks and trust companies by means of the system of interlocking directorates.

Fourth, through the influence which the more powerful banking houses, banks, and trust companies have secured in the management of insurance companies, railroads, producing and trading corporations, and public utility corporations, by means of stockholdings, voting trusts, fiscal agency contracts, or representation upon their boards of directors, or through supplying the money requirements of railway, industrial, and public utilities corporations and thereby being enabled to participate in the determination of their financial and business policies.

Fifth, through partnership or joint account arrangements between a few of the leading banking houses, banks, and trust companies in the purchase of security issues of the great interstate corporations, accompanied by understandings of recent growth — sometimes called "banking ethics" — which have had the effect of effectually destroying competition between such banking houses, banks, and trust companies in the struggle for business or in the purchase and sale of large issues of such securities.

* Taken and adapted from "Report of the Pujo Committee" (1913), U.S. 62d Congress, 3rd. Session, *House Report*, No. 1593, ch. iii.

Section 4 — Agents of Concentration

It is a fair deduction from the testimony that the most active agents in forwarding and bringing about the concentration of control of money and credit through one or another of the processes above described have been and are —

> J. P. Morgan & Co.
> First National Bank of New York
> National City Bank of New York
> Lee, Higginson & Co., of Boston and New York
> Kidder, Peabody & Co., of Boston and New York
> Kuhn, Loeb & Co. □

[DOCUMENT]   ❖ **65** ❖

The Sherman Anti-Trust Act *

JULY 2, 1890

■ An Act To protect trade and commerce against unlawful restraints and monopolies. . . .

Be it enacted

SEC. 1. Every contract, combination in the form of trust or otherwise, or conspiracy, in restraint of trade or commerce among the several States, or with foreign nations, is hereby declared to be illegal. Every person who shall make any such contract or engage in any such combination or conspiracy, shall be deemed guilty of a misdemeanor, and, on conviction thereof, shall be punished by fine not exceeding five thousand dollars, or by imprisonment not exceeding one year, or by both said punishments, in the discretion of the court.

SEC. 2. Every person who shall monopolize, or attempt to monopolize, or combine or conspire with any other person or persons, to monopolize any part of the trade or commerce among the several States, or with foreign nations, shall be deemed guilty of a misdemeanor, . . .

SEC. 3. Every contract, combination in form of trust or otherwise, or conspiracy, in restraint of trade or commerce in any Territory of the United States or of the District of Columbia, or in restraint of trade or commerce between any such Territory and another, or between any such Territory or Territories and any State or States or the District of Columbia, or with foreign nations, or between the District of Columbia and any State or States or foreign nations, is hereby declared illegal. . . .

SEC. 8. That the word "person," or "persons," wherever used in this act shall be deemed to include corporations and associations existing under or authorized by the laws of either the United States, the laws of any of the Territories, the laws of any State, or the laws of any foreign country. . . . □

* Taken and adapted from "The Sherman Anti-Trust Act" (July 2, 1890), *U.S. Statutes at Large*, Vol. XXVI, p. 209.

PART SIX

□ America and the Problems of Economic Maturity, 1920 to the Present

In this closing part, we have tried to identify the problems of a mature economy, of an economy in process of becoming the most powerful in the world by a great margin. We begin with a discussion, by no means the final word on the subject, of the growth of trade unionism since the turn of the century. The failure of the labor movement to thrive in the decade following World War I was in large part the cause of the Great Crash and of the Great Depression that followed. As someone has remarked, the Great Depression was the major historical phenomenon of the past half century, just as the Civil War was the major historical event of the half century before that. We cannot capture the bitterness, the frustration, the total sense of defeat experienced by Americans during the Depression, but Professor Galbraith's "The Great Crash" and David H. Bennett's "The Year of the Old Folks' Revolt" leave the reader with some sense of the emotional upheaval of the time. The three R's of the New Deal, the political response to a foundering economy, have been characterized as "Relief, Recovery, and Reform." One of the reforms introduced in the second Roosevelt administration was in the direction of antitrust policy, which Gene M. Gressley discusses in his article, "Thurman Arnold, Antitrust, and the New Deal."

In the Post World War II era economic historians have been preoccupied with problems of economic stabilization and growth. One of the difficulties requiring solution has been the problem of the international balance of payments, which is reviewed by Frederick L. Deming, Undersecretary of the Treasury for Monetary Affairs, in his address entitled "The International Monetary System — Its Evolution and the Problems Ahead." But recent historical analysis has paid less attention to specific contemporary problems than to the broader question of what drives an economy forward. In Douglass C. North's article, "A Note on Professor Rostow's 'Take-off' into Self-sustained Economic Growth," the student will enjoy the kind of controversy that is

357

presently generating interest and excitement in the field of economic history. In Jonathan Hughes's "Eight Tycoons: The Entrepreneur and American History," we conclude with an article reminiscent of the material in Part I, a perceptive and witty attempt to discern the wellspring of business achievement.

The documents at the end of this part no longer have the pressing relevance that they did to a generation now comfortably middle-aged. But the student may be assured that each of these documents bespeaks a change in public policy that has deeply affected his life and his welfare. They are only a part, but an extremely important part, of the political and economic upheaval that was the Second American Revolution. □

✧ **66** ✧

The Growth of American Unions *

IRVING BERNSTEIN

Casting a gloomy eye over American trade unionism, the labor editor of *Fortune* recently remarked: "U.S. labor has lost the greatest single dynamic any movement can have — a confidence that it is going to get bigger. Organized labor has probably passed its peak strength." [1] He argued that by 1946 unions had "saturated" the readily organizable segment of the labor force, the remainder presenting a more formidable problem — the South, the Mountain States, the small towns, the white-collar workers, the little firms, agricultural labor, and the service occupations.

This dismal analysis, apparently widely held, has only surface plausibility. Since 1946, in fact, the labor movement has been growing steadily. Further, if the factors responsible continue in force — and there are good reasons to expect that they will — unionism will expand in the future.

This conclusion, to be meaningful, must be hung against the backdrop of history. Hence we must determine, first, the actual course of trade union growth in the United States and, second, its causes. Before dealing with these two central problems, however, a few preliminaries concerning sources, method, and scope must be disposed of.

Wolman's series on membership in American unions for the years 1897–1948 supply the critical raw material for this study. I have chosen his data rather than Barnett's, Peterson's, or the Bureau of Labor Statistics' because they are internally consistent and continue over a longer span of time.

Membership, obviously, is not a perfect index of trade union growth and influence. It may, for example, yield an inadequate or erroneous impression at any given moment of the wage job unions are doing for their constituents, of the internal stability of the organizations, of their political effectiveness. Over the long pull, however, it seems reasonable to assume a rough correspondence between membership and factors of this sort. Further, we are confronted with Hobson's choice: there is no statistical substitute.

The manipulation of Wolman's figures includes a concept — "real" membership — that requires explanation. It is the number of union members corrected by the size of the labor force; the concept parallels that of "real" wages. The purpose is to show the growth of the union group over time

---

* Irving Bernstein, "The Growth of American Unions," *American Economic Review*, Vol. DLIV, No. 3, June 1954, pp. 301–18. Used by permission of the author and publisher.

[1] Daniel Bell, "The Next American Labor Movement," *Fortune*, April 1953, XLVII, p. 204.

without the distortion introduced by fluctuations in the number of people available for work. The labor force data are drawn from several sources: the series on gainful workers of the National Industrial Conference Board for 1900–1928 and the civilian labor force series of the Department of Labor and the Bureau of the Census since 1928.

Wolman's figures suffer two deficiencies from the viewpoint of history: they begin too late and end too early. Nothing, unfortunately, can be done about the period prior to 1897. For the years since 1948 a quite clear picture emerges from membership figures provided by other sources, notably the American Federation of Labor and the State of California.

The fact that this paper relies heavily upon statistical techniques requires a word of caution. Although problems that lend themselves to precise measurement are to be viewed statistically, my faith in the usefulness of mathematical methods in social affairs is something short of infinite. Hence, no hesitancy will be shown in drawing conclusions in the absence of numbers.

Exigencies of time, unfortunately, have imposed two limitations of scope. The first is to confine the study to the labor movement as a whole. No attention will be given to particular unions, industries, or localities except in so far as they shed general illumination. The second is to omit experience with unionism in other countries.

THE PATTERN OF GROWTH, 1897–1953

The course of trade union membership in the United States for the period 1897–1953 appears in Table 1. It reveals both actual and "real" membership, year-to-year shifts in each series, and the average annual change.

The data of Table 1 are presented graphically in the accompanying charts. The first shows actual union membership for the period 1897–1948 and the second "real" membership for the years 1900–1948. In both charts the broken lines project membership in the labor movement as a whole for the years 1949–1953. This was done by applying the rate of growth of the A.F. of L. in this period to Wolman's 1948 figure.[2] The trend line in each chart is a hand-smoothed curve which suggests the long-run movement.

[2] A.F. of L. figures are used because they are the only ones to cover the whole period 1949–1953. They suffer three deficiencies for present purposes, none critical. First, the A.F. of L., undoubtedly, has grown faster than the rest of the labor movement since 1948. As a result, the projected figures in Table 1 are somewhat inflated. That they are essentially correct is evident from the fact that A.F. of L. is about sixty per cent of the total and that other sources, notably the reliable California statistics, confirm the growth pattern. A second deficiency with the A.F. of L. figures is that they are affected by the reaffiliation and disaffiliation of unions. In the years 1949–1953, however, only one event of major consequence occurred, the reaffiliation of the Machinists in 1951. Finally, the A.F. of L. figures measure the per capita taxes paid by the internationals rather than the actual number of members. For the period in question the statistics notoriously understate membership. Data for the A.F. of L. and California follow:

Viewed secularly, the transcendent fact of trade union membership between 1897 and 1953 is growth. At the outset there were fewer than half a million unionists; by 1948, according to Wolman, there were more than 14 million and by 1953, BLS reports, the number reached 16½ to 17 million.[3] The average annual accretion was 7.4 per cent. Much the same conclusion stems from an examination of "real" membership. Only 3 per cent of a labor force of 29 million was organized in 1900. By 1953, 26.8 per cent of a working population more than double the size, approximately 63 million, was in the union group. The average annual rate of growth until 1948 was 4.8 per cent.

Although the trend lines in Charts I and II are no more than graphic abstractions, they suggest steadiness in the upwardness of the curves. From the long-run point of view, that is, the fact that the labor movement has grown with relative consistency for fifty-seven years is more impressive than the fact that it has on occasion expanded at a more rapid rate or has actually declined. The only notable deviations from the trends were the periods of the first World War (when growth was at an unusually high rate) and the 'twenties (when this expansion was neutralized by decline).[4]

Turning to the short run, we find that there were four subperiods in which unionism expanded very rapidly: the turn of the century, World War I, the New Deal, and World War II. This becomes evident from an examination of Table 2, which separates out and characterizes ten secondary time intervals on the basis of the average annual rate of change in membership.

The four subperiods that evidenced marked growth in union membership together accounted for nineteen of the fifty-seven years (33 per cent of the total), with adjustments for the exceptional years noted in the table. A fifth subperiod, consisting of three years (5 per cent), produced moderate expan-

	A.F. of L. Membership		California Membership	
	Actual [a]	"Real" [b] (per cent)	Actual [c]	"Real" [d] (per cent)
1949	7,241,290	11.7	—	—
1950	7,142,603	11.3	1,354,500	29.8
1951	7,846,245	12.5	1,443,100	30.9
1952	8,098,302	12.9	1,503,400	30.6
1953	8,654,921	13.7	1,577,900	30.9

[a] Proceedings of the 72nd Convention of the American Federation of Labor, 1953.
[b] Bureau of the Census, civilian labor force.
[c] California Department of Industrial Relations.
[d] California Departments of Industrial Relations and Employment, civilian labor force.

[3] Bureau of National Affairs, *Daily Labor Report*, May 15, 1953. This estimate is not far from the projection based on A.F. of L. data shown in Chart 1, a shade over 17 million.

[4] Union decline in the 'twenties presents a challenging problem of analysis which, unfortunately, cannot be undertaken here. The question is considered at length in Leo Wolman, *Ebb and Flow in Trade Unionism* (New York, 1936), Ch. 4 and Irving Bernstein, *The New Deal Collective Bargaining Policy* (Berkeley, 1950), Ch. 1.

■ **TABLE 1** Union Membership, 1897–1953

	Actual Membership [a]		"Real" Membership [b]	
Year	Number	Per Cent Change from Preceding Year	Union Membership as Per Cent of Civilian Labor Force	Per Cent Change from Preceding Year
1897	447,000	—	—	—
1898	500,700	+12.0	—	—
1899	611,000	+22.0	—	—
1900	868,500	+42.1	3.0	—
1901	1,124,700	+29.5	3.8	+26.7
1902	1,375,900	+22.3	4.5	+18.4
1903	1,913,900	+39.1	6.0	+33.3
1904	2,072,700	+ 8.3	6.4	+ 6.7
1905	2,022,300	− 2.4	6.0	− 6.2
1906	1,907,300	− 5.7	5.5	− 8.3
1907	2,080,400	+ 9.1	5.8	+ 5.5
1908	2,130,600	+ 2.4	5.8	0
1909	2,005,600	− 5.9	5.4	− 6.9
1910	2,140,500	+ 6.7	5.6	+ 3.7
1911	2,343,400	+ 9.5	6.1	+ 8.9
1912	2,452,400	+ 4.7	6.3	+ 3.3
1913	2,716,300	+10.8	6.9	+ 9.5
1914	2,687,100	− 1.1	6.8	− 1.4
1915	2,582,600	− 3.9	6.4	− 5.9
1916	2,772,700	+ 7.4	6.9	+ 7.8
1917	3,061,400	+10.4	7.5	+ 8.7
1918	3,467,300	+13.3	8.4	+12.0
1919	4,125,200	+19.0	10.0	+19.0
1920	5,047,800	+22.4	12.0	+20.0
1921	4,781,300	− 5.3	11.3	− 5.8
1922	4,027,400	−15.8	9.4	−16.8
1923	3,622,000	−10.1	8.3	−11.7
1924	3,536,100	− 2.4	7.9	− 4.8
1925	3,519,400	− 0.5	7.8	− 1.3
1926	3,502,400	− 0.5	7.6	− 2.6
1927	3,546,500	+ 1.3	7.6	0
1928	3,479,800	− 1.9	7.3	− 3.9
1929	3,442,600	− 1.1	7.0	− 4.1
1930	3,392,800	− 1.4	6.8	− 2.9
1931	3,358,100	− 1.0	6.7	− 1.5
1932	3,144,300	− 6.4	6.2	− 7.5

a 1897–1934: Leo Wolman, "Ebb and Flow in Trade Unionism."
1935–1948: Leo Wolman, by correspondence.
1949–1953: Projected from A.F. of L. membership.
b 1900–1928: National Industrial Conference Board, gainful workers.
1929–1948: Department of Labor and Bureau of the Census, civilian labor force.
1949–1953: Projected from A.F. of L. membership.

■ **TABLE 1** (*cont.*)

Year	Actual Membership		"Real" Membership	
	Number	Per Cent Change from Preceding Year	Union Membership as Per Cent of Civilian Labor Force	Per Cent Change from Preceding Year
1933	2,973,000	− 5.4	5.8	− 6.5
1934	3,608,600	+21.4	6.9	+19.0
1935	3,659,300	+ 1.4	6.9	0
1936	4,075,100	+11.4	7.6	+10.1
1937	6,334,300	+55.4	11.7	+53.9
1938	7,342,000	+15.9	13.4	+14.5
1939	7,734,900	+ 5.4	14.0	+ 4.5
1940	8,100,900	+ 4.7	14.6	+ 4.3
1941	8,614,000	+ 6.3	15.4	+ 5.5
1942	9,523,000	+10.6	16.9	+ 9.7
1943	11,320,400	+18.9	20.4	+20.7
1944	12,538,900	+10.8	23.0	+12.7
1945	12,724,700	+ 1.5	23.6	+ 2.6
1946	12,980,800	+ 2.0	22.6	− 4.2
1947	14,119,100	+ 8.8	23.5	+ 4.0
1948	14,186,400	+ 0.5	23.1	− 1.7
1949	14,228,959	+ 0.3	22.9	− 0.8
1950	14,029,754	− 1.4	22.1	− 3.4
1951	15,418,700	+ 9.9	24.4	+10.6
1952	15,912,098	+ 3.2	25.2	+ 3.2
1953	17,010,033	+ 6.9	26.8	+ 6.2
Average yearly change		+ 7.4%		+ 4.8%

■ **TABLE 2** **Periods of Union Membership Change, 1897–1952**

Period	Number of Years	Average Annual Membership Change (per cent)		Characterization	Exceptional Years
		Actual	"Real"		
1897–1903	7	+27.8	+26.1 [b]	sharply up	
1904–1916	13	+ 3.1	+ 1.3	stable, modestly up	1913
1917–1920	4	+16.3	+14.9	sharply up	
1921–1923	3	−10.4	−11.4	sharply down	
1924–1931	8	− 0.9	− 2.6	stable, modestly down	
1932–1933	2	− 5.9	− 7.0	quite sharply down	
1934–1938	5	+21.1	+19.5	sharply up	1935
1939–1941	3	+ 5.5	+ 4.8	modestly up	
1942–1944	3	+13.4	+14.4	sharply up	
1945–1953 [a]	9	+ 3.5	+ 1.8	stable, modestly up	

[a] 1945–1948, all unions; 1949–1953, A.F. of L.
[b] 1900–1903.

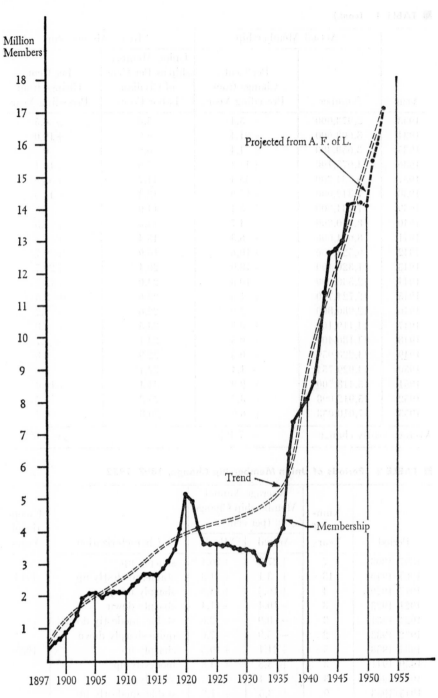

CHART 1   Union Membership, 1897-1953

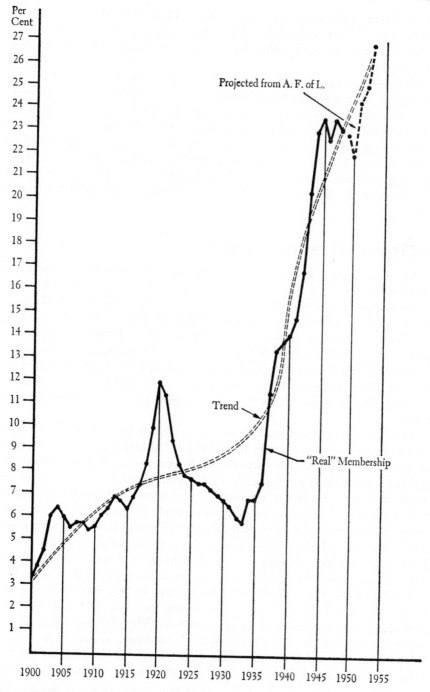

CHART 2 Union Membership as Per Cent of Civilian Labor Force, 1900-1953

sion. Three of the subperiods, comprising, with adjustments for exceptions, thirty years (53 per cent), witnessed relative stability. Two subperiods, providing five years between them (9 per cent), saw a marked retrenchment in membership.

This evidence may be drawn together as follows: In the period 1897–1953 as a whole trade unionism in the United States expanded secularly and quite steadily as measured both by the actual number of members and by that figure corrected by the size of the labor force. Viewed in the short run, four subperiods provided the bulk of the growth. That is, the actual number of trade unionists tended to expand fairly steadily over the time span in its entirety; union membership grew markedly faster than the labor force in four shorter intervals that together comprised one-third of the total number of years.

FACTORS INFLUENCING GROWTH

Any meaningful system of causation must account for both the secular and short-run growth that has occurred. The problem of explaining the emergence and development of trade unionism in our industrial society has given rise to a fair-sized literature. It is rather interesting that most of this writing was done a generation or two ago. The tremendous scholarly activity of the past twenty years in the labor field has, with few exceptions, ignored this issue.

There are two discernible schools that seek to explain the growth of unions: the first relates union expansion to the business cycle and the second relies on a pluralistic conception of the trade union, tying growth to a multiplicity of causes.

The business cycle explanation of union growth has won for itself both wider currency and more eminent authority. Although its exponents have disagreed somewhat among themselves, all have argued that fluctuations in union membership depend directly upon business activity. In 1910, for example, Commons wrote that the movement of wholesale prices for the period 1820–1908 offers "a clue to the labor movements of the time." An upward swing in the curve is an index of prosperity; with good times, unions emerge and grow. When business activity turns down, the organizations suffer defeat; labor either subsides or diverts its attention to political and economic panaceas. "This cycle," he concluded, ". . . has been consistently repeated." [5]

The latest and most sophisticated restatement of this hypothesis is Dunlop's. Viewing American trade union history between 1827 and 1945, he distinguishes seven periods of rapid expansion. They fall into two classes: those associated with wars (Civil, Spanish-American, World War I, and World War II) and those stemming from periods of deep unrest (1827–1836, 1881–1886, and 1933–1937). The growth of union membership in war-

[5] John R. Commons and Helen L. Sumner, *A Documentary History of American Industrial Society* (Cleveland, 1910), V, p. 19.

time "is to be explained almost entirely by developments in the labor market; the rapid rise in the cost of living and the shortage of labor supply relative to demand." The expansions related to unrest, he observes, came at the bottom of the long waves in the Kondratieff cycles. Each upheaval followed a severe depression when workers and unions were severely critical of the social system. Further, in all three cases discontented groups allied themselves with radical political movements — Jacksonian Democracy, Populism, and the New Deal.[6]

The most penetrating exponent of the pluralistic view is Hoxie. American unionism, he tells us, is "one of the most complex, diffuse, and protean of modern social phenomena." Above all else, the labor movement is opportunistic. "For, . . . unionists have been prone to act first and to formulate theories afterward. . . ." Finally, "an interpretation of unionism, not in monistic, but in dualistic or pluralistic terms is required." [7]

Our present task is to test the adequacy of these two analyses in the light of the evidence on union growth. For the economic explanation statistical yardsticks are available; the pluralistic position, however, carries us outside the realm of measurement.

In examining the former, we shall be concerned with a correlation between membership on the one hand and the business cycle as a whole, as well as several of its key components, on the other. The National Bureau of Economic Research offers the generally accepted description of American cycles which is employed for the period 1897–1938, supplemented for the years 1939–1949.[8] This analysis is undertaken with some hesitancy in face of Burns and Mitchell's warning: "The results obtained from annual series are less trustworthy than those from monthly or quarterly." [9] Unfortunately, the only available union membership series are on an annual basis.

For the cycle as a whole it is necessary to distinguish between minor and major fluctuations. That is, secondary business cycles have no observable relationship to the number of trade union members. Hence we must write off for present purposes the contractions of 1899–1900, 1903–1904, 1910–1911, 1913–1914, 1918–1919, 1923–1924, 1926–1927, and 1945, as well as the expansions of 1904–1907, 1908–1910, 1911–1913, 1924–1926, and 1932–1937. On the downside this leaves us with the "Bankers' Panic" of 1907–1908, during

[6] J. T. Dunlop, "The Development of Labor Organization: A Theoretical Framework," in Richard A. Lester and Joseph Shister, eds., *Insights into Labor Issues* (New York, 1948), pp. 190–92. The time span of our data is much too short to permit a test of the Kondratieff cycles.

[7] R. F. Hoxie, *Trade Unionism in the United States* (New York, 1921), pp. 1, 34, 66. See also Wolman, *op. cit.*, Ch. X; W. J. Phillips, Jr., *A Theory of Union Growth* (unpublished Ph.D. dissertation, New York University, 1946), p. 396; and Joseph Shister. "The Logic of Union Growth," *Jour. Pol. Econ.*, Oct. 1953, LXI, p. 413.

[8] The reference cycles through 1938 appear in A. F. Burns and W. C. Mitchell, *Measuring Business Cycles* (New York, 1946), p. 78. Milton Friedman has provided tentative dates for the period 1939–1949, as set forth in Albert Rees, "Industrial Conflict and Business Fluctuations," *Jour. Pol. Econ.*, Oct. 1952, LX, p. 376.

[9] *Ibid.*, p. 202.

which membership rose; the severe postwar depression of 1920–1921, in which unions declined sharply; the Great Depression of 1929–1932, when membership dropped modestly; the recession of 1937–1938, during which the number of unionists rose dramatically; and the downturn of 1948–1949, when unionism grew moderately. The periods of major business expansion also revealed a mixed result: in both 1896–1899 and 1900–1903 membership gained markedly; the same can be said for 1914–1918; unionism, however, suffered its worst decline in the prosperity of 1921–1923; it was relatively stable in 1927–1929; it rose sharply in 1938–1945; and the number of unionists grew modestly in 1945–1948.

Further, the cycle and membership show little correspondence in the direction of movement as measured by year-to-year changes. In twenty (38 per cent) of the fifty-two years in the period 1897–1948, one series rose while the other fell. This leaves entirely aside the more significant matter of the amplitude of fluctuation.

This analysis suggests that the correlation between the National Bureau's cycles and union membership is, at best, remote. The latter, clearly, fluctuates more sluggishly than business conditions. It is evident, therefore, that membership is responsive to several forces and that the cycle does not predominate among them.

In moving from the business cycle as a whole to particular components it is possible to expand the range of analysis. For this purpose four series have been selected: cost of living (consumer prices), employment, wholesale prices, and industrial production. The comparison between year-to-year changes in relative union membership on the one hand and these economic series on the other is shown in Table 3.

Inspection of the data makes it clear that the relationship of "real" membership to these factors is neither direct nor precise. Several statistical manipulations confirm this conclusion without exception. For present purposes we need only rely upon the coefficient of correlation (for whatever it is worth) and the direction of year-to-year movements.[10]

Cost of living is the series whose fluctuations most closely approximate those of union membership. Even here, however, the coefficient of correlation is below any meaningful level of significance, + .39. In fact, in nineteen (40 per cent) of the years the series moved in opposite directions.

[10] The formula from which the coefficient of correlation has been derived is,

$$\frac{\sum \frac{XY - C_x C_y}{N}}{\sigma_x \sigma_y} \quad \text{where} \quad \sigma_x = \sqrt{\frac{X^2}{N} - C_x^2} \quad \text{and} \quad \sigma_y = \sqrt{\frac{Y^2}{N} - C_y^2}.$$

See Frederick C. Mills, *Statistical Methods* (New York, 1924), pp. 428–29. My statistical betters raise doubt over the application of correlation analysis to time series on the ground that the values involved are only a small sample of an unknown universe with no way of testing their representativeness. The results, nevertheless, agree with what is shown by other methods and are supplied so that the reader may give them the weight he thinks they deserve.

■ **TABLE 3** Changes in "Real" Union Membership and Economic Factors, 1900–1948

(*Per cent change from preceding year*)

Year	"Real" Union Membership	Cost of Living [a]	Employment [b]	Wholesale Prices [c]	Industrial Production [d]
1900	—	—	—	—	—
1901	+26.7	+ 2.5	+3.1	− 1.4	+12.7
1902	+18.4	+ 2.4	+7.7	+ 6.5	+12.2
1903	+33.3	+ 4.8	−0.3	+ 1.2	+ 2.3
1904	+ 6.7	− 1.1	+2.8	+ 0.2	− 6.1
1905	− 6.2	0	+6.0	+ 0.7	+19.4
1906	− 8.3	+ 3.4	+5.3	+ 2.8	+ 7.4
1907	+ 5.5	+ 5.6	+0.2	+ 5.5	+ 1.3
1908	0	− 4.2	−1.7	− 3.5	−17.4
1909	− 6.9	0	+7.1	+ 7.5	+18.8
1910	+ 3.7	+ 5.5	+2.3	+ 4.1	+ 6.3
1911	+ 8.9	0	−1.3	− 7.8	− 4.2
1912	+ 3.3	+ 6.3	+2.9	+ 6.5	+14.9
1913	+ 9.5	− 2.0	+0.8	+ 1.0	+ 7.0
1914	− 1.4	+ 1.6	−2.4	− 2.4	− 6.1
1915	− 5.9	+ 1.0	+0.4	+ 2.1	+17.2
1916	+ 7.8	+ 7.4	+6.4	+23.0	+18.8
1917	+ 8.7	+17.6	+6.4	+37.4	− 0.8
1918	+12.0	+17.4	+3.5	+11.7	− 1.2
1919	+19.0	+15.2	−4.9	+ 5.6	−12.6
1920	+20.0	+15.8	−1.6	+11.4	+ 4.2
1921	− 5.8	−10.9	−8.8	−36.8	−22.7
1922	−16.8	− 6.3	+6.3	− 0.9	+25.9
1923	−11.7	+ 1.8	+7.4	+ 4.0	+20.5
1924	− 4.8	+ 0.2	−1.2	− 2.5	− 6.8
1925	− 1.3	+ 2.6	+3.9	+ 5.5	+ 9.8
1926	− 2.6	+ 0.8	+3.0	− 3.4	+ 6.7
1927	0	− 1.9	−0.4	− 4.6	− 1.0
1928	− 3.9	− 1.1	+1.6	+ 1.4	+ 4.2
1929	− 4.1	− 0.1	+4.1	− 1.4	+11.1
1930	− 2.9	− 2.5	−4.5	− 9.3	−17.3
1931	− 1.5	− 9.0	−6.8	−15.5	−17.6
1932	− 7.5	−10.2	−8.2	−11.2	−22.7
1933	− 6.5	− 5.3	−0.5	+ 1.7	+19.0
1934	+19.0	+ 3.6	+5.5	+13.7	+ 8.7
1935	0	+ 2.5	+3.4	+ 6.8	+16.0

[a] 1900–1912: Federal Reserve Bank of New York.
  1913–1948: Bureau of Labor Statistics.
[b] 1900–1928: National Industrial Conference Board.
  1929–1948: Bureau of Labor Statistics and Bureau of the Census.
[c] 1900–1948: Bureau of Labor Statistics.
[d] 1900–1918: National Bureau of Economic Research, manufacturing production.
  1919–1948: Federal Reserve Board, industrial production.

TABLE 3 (*cont.*)

Year	"Real" Union Membership	Cost of Living	Employ- ment	Wholesale Prices	Industrial Production
1936	+10.1	+ 1.0	+5.1	+ 1.0	+18.4
1937	+53.9	+ 3.6	+4.3	+ 6.8	+ 9.7
1938	+14.5	− 1.9	−4.5	− 8.9	−21.2
1939	+ 4.5	− 1.4	+3.5	− 1.9	+22.5
1940	+ 4.3	+ 0.8	+3.9	+ 1.9	+14.7
1941	+ 5.5	+ 5.0	+6.0	+11.1	+29.6
1942	+ 9.7	+10.7	+6.8	+13.2	+22.8
1943	+20.7	+ 6.1	+1.3	+ 4.3	+20.1
1944	+12.7	+ 1.5	−0.9	+ 0.9	− 1.7
1945	+ 2.6	+ 2.3	−2.1	+ 1.7	−13.6
1946	− 4.2	+ 8.5	+4.6	+14.5	−16.3
1947	+ 4.0	+14.3	+5.0	+25.6	+10.0
1948	− 1.7	+ 7.5	+2.3	+ 8.5	+ 2.7

The relationship between "real" membership and employment is nonexistent, the coefficient being + .04. Something may be said, however, for using actual membership in this comparison because employment is the principal component of the labor force, and the latter is the factor by which actual is deflated to find "real" membership. The coefficient for actual, as might be expected, is more favorable, + .25, but still far from significant. In fact, in twenty-two of the years (46 per cent) the two series fluctuated in different directions.[11]

The third of the economic factors, wholesale prices, has an even looser relationship with union membership. The coefficient of correlation is only + .23. Further, in seventeen of the years (35 per cent) the two series moved in opposite directions.

The last economic series, industrial production, exhibits the least connection with union membership. The coefficient of correlation drops here to + .009, suggesting that each responds with virtually complete indifference to the other. In almost half of the years, twenty-three, the two series fluctuated in opposite directions.

In conclusion, the business cycle hypothesis fails to afford us a consistently valid explanation of union growth in the time span covered by this study. This applies both to the cycle as a whole and to several of its key components. The individual instances of relationship are sporadic and are counterbalanced by contrary experiences. So capricious a force can hardly explain the steady

[11] This conclusion is buttressed by a recent empirical study of unemployed workers in the San Francisco Bay area, which revealed that joblessness did not cause the worker to drop his union membership. J. W. Garbarino, "The Unemployed Worker during a Period of 'Full' Employment," Institute of Industrial Relations, University of California, Berkeley, Reprint No. 50, from *A Sourcebook on Unemployment Compensation Insurance in California* (Sacramento, Department of Employment, 1953), p. 29.

long-term growth that we have found. At best, the cycle exerts a contributory influence in specific historical contexts, as indicated below.

A final question remains: Why is it that the growth of American unionism has not been closely linked to the cycle? Here Mitchell has supplied the key. "We cannot expect any activity to respond regularly to business cycles unless it is subject to man's control within the periods occupied by cyclical phases, and unless this control is swayed, consciously or not, by short-period economic considerations." [12] The judgment of a businessman to raise or lower his prices, to expand or contract production, to seek or refrain from seeking a loan is of this sort. The decision of a worker to join or separate himself from a trade union is not. It is, on the whole, not made "within the periods occupied by cyclical phases" and it is only rarely "swayed . . . by short-period economic considerations." By Mitchell's criterion, union membership falls outside the ambit of the business cycle.

Hence we must look to Hoxie's pluralism for a meaningful explanation for the course of trade union growth. Our fundamental problem of analysis is to apply the pluralistic conception to the two quite distinct phenomena of steady secular growth and rapid short-term expansion. As might be expected, the causal factors differ markedly.

The principal secular forces that have shaped the size of the American labor movement are the following:

First, the gradual expansion of the labor force, including employment, has afforded unionism a steadily rising organizable potential. At the end of the nineteenth century the labor force comprised approximately 29 million people; by the middle of the twentieth their number had risen to the neighborhood of 63 million. Moreover, the rate of accretion was remarkably steady at between 1 to 3 per cent annually with few exceptions. It is hardly unreasonable to expect that membership should have advanced at this pace at least.

The second long-run factor has been growing social acceptability of trade unionism. The worker's propensity to join or refrain from joining a labor organization is significantly affected by the attitudes of his normal associates toward this issue. The employee without strong feelings one way or the other (he probably outnumbers those who feel deeply on either side) is inclined "to go along," to accept the prevalent view in his shop or his town. In some industries, for example, construction, it is fashionable to join; in others, such as office work, it is not. In certain towns, like Detroit, signing with the union is the thing to do; in Houston it is not. Over the long run the trade union has become an increasingly accepted institution in American society — in the law, with employers, in the community, and, most important for our purposes, with workers. Hence the act of joining has won growing respectability.

The third force has been the growing homogeneity of the American labor

---

[12] W. C. Mitchell, *What Happens during Business Cycles, A Progress Report* (New York, 1951), p. 95.

force. Obviously, a socially integrated working class is easier to organize than one with divisive elements. In the United States the latter have taken the primary forms of immigrant groups, internal minorities (notably the Negro), religious differences, and sex. Antiunion employers in the past have exploited newly arrived immigrants, Negroes, and women to prevent organization. The marked though slow advances in the direction of homogeneity have made such activities increasingly difficult, or, to turn the coin, have simplified the business agent's task. To take a crude example, he finds it more convenient to organize when all his prospective members speak English. The sharp change in immigration policy in the 'twenties helps to explain the rise of unionism in the following decade. Similarly, the gradual improvement in the status of the Negro in the past generation has permitted his growing participation in all our institutions, including the trade union. Finally, Shister points to the growth of public education as a favorable influence upon the propensity to join.[13]

The last secular factor has been the extension of collective bargaining provisions requiring some version of union security. The membership effect of the closed shop and the union shop is to cause new employees to join and to prevent old employees from withdrawing. Although we have only scrappy statistical information, it is clear that there were many more such agreements in existence in 1950 than in 1900 and that they applied to units with significantly larger numbers of workers. In all likelihood this growth fluctuated prior to the New Deal but has been fairly steady in the past two decades. The linkage of a secular increase in the incidence of union security with a like expansion in employment automatically causes membership to rise.

In analyzing short-run growth, Dunlop's distinction between periods associated with wars and those related to social unrest is helpful. Since 1897, there have been four major stages of rapid expansion — 1897–1903, 1917–1920, 1934–1938, and 1942–1944. The year 1951 may be added to this group. The first of these periods combined the effects of the unrest stemming from the deep depression of the 'nineties and of the Spanish-American War. The years 1917–1920 reflected World War I and post-Armistice conditions. The period 1934–1938 witnessed the expansion set off by the profound social disturbances of the Great Depression. World War II left its imprint upon union growth in 1942–1944. Similarly, the Korean War influenced the development of 1951. In summary, we find three periods related to wars, one to social upheaval, and one to both factors.

Dunlop, in discussing wartime expansion, emphasized labor-market causes exclusively. Here again, the forces at work are more ramified and include, at least, the following:

The first is the business cycle, the impact of which is most significant in wartime. One of the most important of its components is cost of living. It

[13] *Op. cit.*, pp. 421–22.

seems safe to generalize that a very sharp rise in consumer prices, which is characteristic of economic mobilization, is accompanied by a similar increase in membership. This was true during World War I, World War II, and the Korean War. (In the Spanish-American War, however, the increase in prices ran far behind union expansion, suggesting that the latter was primarily a product of social unrest.) The reason for this relationship is simply that the mounting cost of living depreciates real wages, causing workers to join labor organizations in the hope of lifting money wages. The relationship with employment and production, however, is relatively remote.

The second cause of growth during wars has been the enlarged role of the government in the economy, both directly as employer and indirectly as principal consumer of the product of industry. That is, unions find organization easier to achieve when they deal with the government or with an employer who relies primarily or totally upon sales to the government. It is no coincidence that the railway organizations first won general recognition for the nonoperating crafts during the World War I period of federal control and promptly lost it after the Esch-Cummins Act returned the roads to private hands. Nor is it surprising that the shipbuilding industry was unionized in both major conflicts and the airframe industry in the second. The pressures of war, as will be emphasized below, cause the government to seek union support and to influence dependent employers to avoid hostility.

Third, the necessity to achieve unity in prosecuting the war enhances the political power of organized labor. This rests upon the need of a democratic government to enlist all the elements of society in the common effort. Churchill, for example, at once invited Labour to participate in the wartime coalition when he took power in the dark days of 1940. Less dramatically, the Wilson, Roosevelt, and Truman Administrations offered the unions a voice in matters of their interest in our three most recent wars. National War Labor Board I, National War Labor Board II, and the Wage Stabilization Board were all tripartite agencies. In the case of the last the unions exploited that fact to gain wider representation in defense activities. The effect of political power is to raise the prestige, respectability, and acceptability of labor organizations in the eyes of both workers and employers.

A fourth factor is the breakdown of employer hostility in wartime. This has already been noted for the firm dependent upon government contracts. The employer with a private market is under similar, though less severe, pressures. He is operating in an economy of scarcities; he risks exposure to the charge of inciting a recognition strike; his workers are more prone to join unions or to leave him for other employment; he finds it simpler to pass on higher wages in rising prices.

Finally, the social tensions and dislocations that accompany a major war give workers the need to express their discontent. Unionism supplies a vehicle for this purpose. For example, workers who have been denied a wage increase by a stabilization agency are open to joining an organization that points out, and may already have demonstrated, the elasticity of the regulations.

The forces that spur union growth in a period of social unrest are of quite different character. They emerge only in the wake of a depression so severe as to call into question the very foundations of society. In the period with which we are dealing there have been two — the collapse of 1893 and the Great Depression of 1929. Even such important contractions as 1907, 1920, and 1937 do not produce this effect, while the minor fluctuations picked up on the National Bureau's seismograph are, of course, of no consequence in this context. In both relevant cases, moreover, the tremendous expansion of the labor movement began, not when the outlook was darkest, but rather as the upswing got underway — in 1897, and in 1933. This suggests that the cycle exerts a trigger effect under these special circumstances. What, then, were these depression-born forces that caused union ranks to swell so markedly?

The first factor, of course, is labor unrest. A severe and prolonged depression imposes heavy burdens upon workers and their families, causing them to develop sharp grievances against the existing social order. This, in turn, makes them prone to affiliate with instrumentalities of protest, including unions.

The ability of workers to effect organization is, in part, determined by the second consideration, the standing of the employer in the community. As a great slump draws to its close the public is inclined to discredit the businessman. The economic system whose leading protagonist he is, has just demonstrated its ineffectiveness; his voice, no matter how shrill, is not likely to be heard. If he exhibits hostility to unionism, he is less able to implement his views than would be the case in good times.

These two factors combine to permit the third, intervention by the government to protect the right of workers to organize and bargain collectively. At the turn of the century, for example, Congress passed the Erdman Act of 1898, outlawing yellow-dog contracts on the railroads, and created the Industrial Commission, which in 1902, urged restrictions on anti-union practices. In the same year President Roosevelt intervened in the great anthracite strike in a manner that did no harm to the bargaining claims of the United Mine Workers. This era also witnessed a flood of state legislation directed to the same end. For the New Deal period nothing more need be mentioned than the most important of all federal protective ventures, the National Labor Relations Act of 1935.

This framework fails to take account of a final short-run factor, the quality of leadership. It is clear, for example, that the organizing success of the CIO in the late 'thirties was, in part, the personal achievement of John L. Lewis. On a more modest level effective union leaders succeed in expanding their memberships even when external conditions are not favorable. This consideration, however, is of little importance in the long run.

CONCLUSION

The conventional monocausal explanation for fluctuations in union membership, the business cycle, is without general validity. Neither cyclical movements as a whole nor leading components correlate significantly with unionism. They are useless in understanding secular expansion and are only sporadically helpful with respect to short-term changes.

A multicausal system (including the cycle) is necessary to account for the rise of trade unionism. The primary forces that have shaped secular growth are the expansion of the labor force, growing social acceptability of unionism, increasing homogeneity in the working class, and extension of collective bargaining provisions for union security. In the short run membership has expanded sharply as a consequence of wars and very severe depressions. Unions, in other words, have been the beneficiaries of disaster.

Where, now, does this leave *Fortune's* gloomy diagnosis and prognosis? Since 1946, rather than exhibiting "saturation," the labor movement has grown steadily at approximately the long-term rate. Further, in the year 1951, it spurted forward under the impact of the Korean War. If the forces we have emphasized continue at work in the future, unionism will grow steadily in the long run, will suffer little or no loss in bad times, and will expand sharply if we are so unfortunate as to engage in wars or to sustain severe depressions. ☐

◇ **67** ◇

The Great Crash *

JOHN KENNETH GALBRAITH

Purely in retrospect it is easy to see how 1929 was destined to be a year to remember. This was not because Mr. Hoover was soon to become President and had inimical intentions toward the market. Those intentions developed at least partly in retrospect. Nor was it because men of wisdom could tell that a depression was overdue. No one, wise or unwise, knew or now knows when depressions are due or overdue.

Rather, it was simply that a roaring boom was in progress in the stock market and, like all booms, it had to end. On the first of January of 1929, as a simple matter of probability, it was most likely that the boom would end before the year was out, with a diminishing chance that it would end in any given year thereafter. When prices stopped rising — when the supply of people who were buying for an increase was exhausted — then ownership on

* Taken and adapted from John Kenneth Galbraith, *The Great Crash 1929*, Chapters 3 and 6 (Boston: Houghton Mifflin Company, 1961), pp. 29–34, 93–109. Used by permission.

margin would become meaningless and everyone would want to sell. The market wouldn't level out; it would fall precipitately.

All this being so, the position of the people who had at least nominal responsibility for what was going on was a complex one. One of the oldest puzzles of politics is who is to regulate the regulators. But an equally baffling problem, which has never received the attention it deserves, is who is to make wise those who are required to have wisdom.

Some of those in positions of authority wanted the boom to continue. They were making money out of it, and they may have had an intimation of the personal disaster which awaited them when the boom came to an end. But there were also some who saw, however dimly, that a wild speculation was in progress and that something should be done. For these people, however, every proposal to act raised the same intractable problem. The consequences of successful action seemed almost as terrible as the consequences of inaction, and they could be more horrible for those who took the action.

A bubble can easily be punctured. But to incise it with a needle so that it subsides gradually is a task of no small delicacy. Among those who sensed what was happening in early 1929, there was some hope but no confidence that the boom could be made to subside. The real choice was between an immediate and deliberately engineered collapse and a more serious disaster later on. Someone would certainly be blamed for the ultimate collapse when it came. There was no question whatever as to who would be blamed should the boom be deliberately deflated. (For nearly a decade the Federal Reserve authorities had been denying their responsibility for the deflation of 1920–21.) The eventual disaster also had the inestimable advantage of allowing a few more days, weeks, or months of life. One may doubt if at any time in early 1929 the problem was ever framed in terms of quite such stark alternatives. But however disguised or evaded, these were the choices which haunted every serious conference on what to do about the market.

I

The men who had responsibility for these ineluctable choices were the President of the United States, the Secretary of the Treasury, the Federal Reserve Board in Washington, and the Governor and Directors of the Federal Reserve Bank of New York. As the most powerful of the Federal Reserve Banks, and the one with the market at its doorstep, the New York bank both had and assumed responsibilities which were not accepted by the other eleven banks of the system.

President Coolidge neither knew nor cared what was going on. A few days before leaving office in 1929, he cheerily observed that things were "absolutely sound" and that stocks were "cheap at current prices." [1] In earlier years, whenever warned that speculation was getting out of hand, he had comforted himself with the thought that this was the primary responsibility

[1] *The Memoirs of Herbert Hoover*, p. 16.

of the Federal Reserve Board.[2] The Board was a semi-autonomous body precisely because Congress wanted to protect it from excessive political interference by the Executive.

However tender his scruples, President Coolidge could have acted through his Secretary of the Treasury, who served, ex-officio, as a member of the Federal Reserve Board. The Secretary also had the primary responsibility for economic and especially for financial policy. But on this as on other matters of economic policy, the incumbent, Andrew W. Mellon, was a passionate advocate of inaction. The responsibility thus passed to the Federal Reserve Board and the Federal Reserve Banks.

The regulation of economic activity is without doubt the most inelegant and unrewarding of public endeavors. Almost everyone is opposed to it in principle; its justification always relies on the unprepossessing case for the lesser evil. Regulation originates in raucous debate in Congress in which the naked interests of pressure groups may at times involve an exposure bordering on the obscene. Promulgation and enforcement of rules and regulations is by grinding bureaucracies which are ceaselessly buffeted by criticism. In recent times it has become obligatory for the regulators at every opportunity to confess their inadequacy, which in any case is all too evident.

The great exception to this dreary story is the regulatory activity of the central bank — with us, the Federal Reserve System. Here is regulation of a seemly and becoming sort. No one apologizes for it; men of impeccable conservatism would rise to espouse such regulation were they called upon to do so, which they almost never are. This regulation is not the work of thousands of clerks, statisticians, hearing officers, lawyers, and lesser beings in a teeming office building on the Mall. Rather it emerges in the measured and orderly discussion of men of quiet and dignified mien, each at his accustomed place around a handsome table in a richly paneled and richly draperied room. These men do not issue orders; at most they suggest. Chiefly they move interest rates, buy or sell securities and, in doing so, nudge the economy here and restrain it there. Because the meanings of their actions are not understood by the great majority of the people, they can reasonably be assumed to have superior wisdom. Their actions will on occasion be criticized. More often they will be scrutinized for hidden meaning.

Such is the *mystique* of central banking. Such was the awe-inspiring role in 1929 of the Federal Reserve Board in Washington, the policy-making body which guided and directed the twelve Federal Reserve banks. However, there was a jarring difficulty. The Federal Reserve Board in those times was a body of startling incompetence.

For several years, until late in 1927, the Chairman and guiding genius presumptive, was one Daniel R. Crissinger. He had been trained for his task by serving as General Counsel of the Marion Steam Shovel Company of Marion, Ohio. There is no indication that he was an apt student. However, his

[2] *Ibid.*, p. 11.

background seemed satisfactory to another Marion boy, Warren G. Harding, who had brought him to Washington, where he was regarded as a hack politician from Ohio. In 1927 Crissinger was replaced by Roy A. Young, who for eight years had been Governor of the Minneapolis Federal Reserve Bank. Young, a more substantial figure, was undoubtedly aware of what was going on. However, he was a man of caution who sought no fame as a martyr to the broken boom. His colleagues were among the more commonplace of Harding-Coolidge appointees. With one exception — the erstwhile college professor, Adolph C. Miller — they have been conservatively described by Herbert Hoover as "mediocrities." [3]

The New York Federal Reserve Bank was under more vigorous leadership. For several years, until 1928, its governor had been Benjamin Strong, the first American since Nicholas Biddle to make an important reputation as a central banker. Strong's views were regarded throughout the System with only little less awe than the gold standard. However, in the view of Herbert Hoover — and in this instance Hoover's views are widely shared — Strong, so far from being concerned about the inflation, was the man most responsible for it. It was he who took the lead in 1927 in easing money rates to help the hard-pressed Europeans. For this Mr. Hoover later called him "a mental annex to Europe." [4]

This is unfair. Governor Strong's action was entirely reasonable in the circumstances and, as noted in the last chapter, it takes more to start a speculation than a general ability to borrow money. Still, the New York Federal Reserve Bank, under Governor Strong's leadership may not have been sufficiently perturbed by the speculation a block or two away. Nor was it after Governor Strong died in October 1928 and was replaced by George L. Harrison. A reason, no doubt, was the reassurance provided by people in high places who were themselves speculating heavily. One such was Charles E. Mitchell, the Chairman of the Board of the National City Bank who, on January 1, 1929, became a class A director of the Federal Reserve Bank of New York. The end of the boom would mean the end of Mitchell. He was not a man to expedite his own demise. . . .

According to the accepted view of events, by the autumn of 1929 the economy was well into a depression. In June the indexes of industrial and of factory production both reached a peak and turned down. By October, the Federal Reserve index of industrial production stood at 117 as compared with 126 four months earlier. Steel production declined from June on; in October freight-car loading fell. Homebuilding, a most mercurial industry, had been falling for several years, and it slumped still farther in 1929. Finally, down came the stock market. A penetrating student of the economic behavior of this period has said that the market slump, "reflected, in the main, the change which was already apparent in the industrial situation." [5]

[3] *The Memoirs of Herbert Hoover*, p. 9.
[4] *Ibid.*, pp. 9, 10.
[5] Thomas Wilson, *Fluctuations in Income and Employment*, p. 143.

Thus viewed, the stock market is but a mirror which, perhaps as in this instance, somewhat belatedly, provides an image of the underlying or *fundamental* economic situation. Cause and effect run from the economy to the stock market, never the reverse. In 1929 the economy was headed for trouble. Eventually that trouble was violently reflected in Wall Street.

In 1929 there were good, or at least strategic, reasons for this view, and it is easy to understand why it has become high doctrine. In Wall Street, as elsewhere in 1929, few people wanted a bad depression. In Wall Street, as elsewhere, there is deep faith in the power of incantation. When the market fell many Wall Street citizens immediately sensed the real danger, which was that income and employment — prosperity in general — would be adversely affected. This had to be prevented. Preventive incantation required that as many important people as possible repeat as firmly as they could that it wouldn't happen. This they did. They explained how the stock market was merely the froth and that the real substance of economic life rested in production, employment, and spending, all of which would remain unaffected. No one knew for sure that this was so. As an instrument of economic policy, incantation does not permit of minor doubts or scruples.

In the later years of depression it was important to continue emphasizing the unimportance of the stock market. The depression was an exceptionally disagreeable experience. Wall Street has not always been a cherished symbol in our national life. In some of the devout regions of the nation, those who speculate in stocks — the even more opprobrious term gamblers is used — are not counted the greatest moral adornments of our society. Any explanation of the depression which attributed importance to the market collapse would accordingly have been taken very seriously, and it would have meant serious trouble for Wall Street. Wall Street, no doubt, would have survived, but there would have been scars. We should be clear that no deliberate conspiracy existed to minimize the consequences of the Wall Street crash for the economy. Rather, it merely appeared to everyone with an instinct for conservative survival that Wall Street had better be kept out of it. It was vulnerable.

In fact, any satisfactory explanation of the events of the autumn of 1929 and thereafter must accord a dignified role to the speculative boom and ensuing collapse. Until September or October of 1929 the decline in economic activity was very modest. As I shall argue later, until after the market crash one could reasonably assume that this downward movement might soon reverse itself, as a similar movement had reversed itself in 1927 or did subsequently in 1949. There were no reasons for expecting disaster. No one could foresee that production, prices, incomes, and all other indicators would continue to shrink through three long and dismal years. Only after the market crash were there plausible grounds to suppose that things might now for a long while get a lot worse.

From the foregoing it follows that the crash did not come — as some have suggested — because the market suddenly became aware that a serious depression was in the offing. A depression, serious or otherwise, could not be fore-seen when the market fell. There is still the possiblity that the downturn in the indexes frightened the speculators, led them to unload their stocks, and so punctured a bubble that had in any case to be punctured one day. This is more plausible. Some people who were watching the indexes may have been persuaded by this intelligence to sell, and others may then have been en-couraged to follow. This is not very important, for it is in the nature of a speculative boom that almost anything can collapse it. Any serious shock to confidence can cause sales by those speculators who have always hoped to get out before the final collapse, but after all possible gains from rising prices have been reaped. Their pessimism will infect those simpler souls who had thought the market might go up forever but who now will change their minds and sell. Soon there will be margin calls, and still others will be forced to sell. So the bubble breaks.

Along with the downturn of the indexes Wall Street has always attributed importance to two other events in the pricking of the bubble. In England on September 20, 1929, the enterprises of Clarence Hatry suddenly collapsed. Hatry was one of those curiously un-English figures with whom the English periodically find themselves unable to cope. Although his earlier financial history had been anything but reassuring, Hatry in the twenties had built up an industrial and financial empire of truly impressive proportions. The nu-cleus, all the more remarkably, was a line of coin-in-the-slot vending and auto-matic photograph machines. From these unprepossessing enterprises he had marched on into investment trusts and high finance. His expansion owed much to the issuance of unauthorized stock, the increase of assets by the forg-ing of stock certificates, and other equally informal financing. In the lore of 1929, the unmasking of Hatry in London is supposed to have struck a sharp blow to confidence in New York.[6]

Ranking with Hatry in this lore was the refusal on October 11 of the Massa-chusetts Department of Public Utilities to allow Boston Edison to split its stock four to one. As the company argued, such split-ups were much in fash-ion. To avoid going along was to risk being considered back in the corporate gaslight era. The refusal was unprecedented. Moreover, the Department added insult to injury by announcing an investigation of the company's rates and by suggesting that the present value of the stock, "due to the action of speculators," had reached a level where "no one, in our judgment . . . on the basis of its earnings, would find it to his advantage to buy it."

These were uncouth words. They could have been important as, con-ceivably, could have been the exposure of Clarence Hatry. But it could also be that the inherently unstable equilibrium was shattered simply by a spon-taneous decision to get out. On September 22, the financial pages of the New York papers carried an advertisement of an investment service with the arresting headline, OVERSTAYING A BULL MARKET. Its message read as follows:

[6] Hatry pleaded guilty and early in 1930 was given a long jail sentence.

"Most investors make money in a bull market, only to lose all profits made — and sometimes more — in the readjustment that inevitably follows." Instead of the downturn in the Federal Reserve industrial index, the exposure of Hatry, or the unnatural obstinacy of the Massachusetts Department of Public Utilities, it could have been such thoughts stirring first in dozens and then in hundreds, and finally in thousands of breasts which finally brought an end to the boom. What first stirred these doubts we do not know, but neither is it very important that we know.

II

Confidence did not disintegrate at once. As noted, through September and into October, although the trend of the market was generally down, good days came with the bad. Volume was high. On the New York Stock Exchange sales were nearly always above four million, and frequently above five. In September new issues appeared in even greater volume than in August, and they regularly commanded a premium over the offering price. On September 20 the *Times* noted that the stock of the recently launched Lehman Corporation which had been offered at $104 had sold the day before at $136. (In the case of this well-managed investment trust the public enthusiasm was not entirely misguided.) During September brokers' loans increased by nearly $670 million, by far the largest increase of any month to date. This showed that speculative zeal had not diminished.

Other signs indicated that the gods of the New Era were still in their temples. In its October 12 issue, the *Saturday Evening Post* had a lead story by Isaac F. Marcosson on Ivar Kreuger. This was a scoop, for Kreuger had previously been inaccessible to journalists. "Kreuger," Marcosson observed, "like Hoover, is an engineer. He has consistently applied engineer precision to the welding of his far-flung industry." And this was not the only resemblance. "Like Hoover," the author added, "Kreuger rules through pure reason."

In the interview Kreuger was remarkably candid on one point. He told Mr. Marcosson: "Whatever success I have had may perhaps be attributable to three things: One is silence, the second is more silence, while the third is still more silence." This was so. Two and a half years later Kreuger committed suicide in his Paris apartment, and shortly thereafter it was discovered that his aversion to divulging information, especially if accurate, had kept even his most intimate acquaintances in ignorance of the greatest fraud in history. His American underwriters, the eminently respectable firm of Lee, Higginson and Company of Boston, had heard nothing and knew nothing. One of the members of the firm, Donald Durant, was a member of the board of directors of the Kreuger enterprises. He had never attended a directors' meeting, and it is certain that he would have been no wiser had he done so.

During the last weeks of October, *Time* Magazine, young and not yet omniscient, also featured Kreuger on its cover — "a great admirer of Cecil Rhodes." Then a week later, as though to emphasize its faith in the New

Era, it went on to Samuel Insull. (A fortnight after that, its youthful illusions shattered, the weekly newsmagazine gave the place of historic honor to Warden Lawes of Sing Sing.) In these same Indian summer days, *The Wall Street Journal* took notice of the official announcement that Andrew Mellon would remain in the cabinet at least until 1933 (there had been rumors that he might resign) and observed: "Optimism again prevails . . . the announcement . . . did more to restore confidence than anything else." In Germany Charles E. Mitchell announced that the "industrial condition of the United States is absolutely sound," that too much attention was being paid to brokers' loans, and that "nothing can arrest the upward movement." On October 15, as he sailed for home, he enlarged on the point: "The markets generally are now in a healthy condition . . . values have a sound basis in the general prosperity of our country." That same evening Professor Irving Fisher made his historic announcement about the permanently high plateau and added, "I expect to see the stock market a good deal higher than it is today within a few months." Indeed, the only disturbing thing, in these October days, was the fairly steady downward drift in the market.

III

On Saturday, October 19, Washington dispatches reported that Secretary of Commerce Lamont was having trouble finding the $100,000 in public funds that would be required to pay the upkeep of the yacht *Corsair* which J. P. Morgan had just given the government. (Morgan's deprivation was not extreme: a new $3,000,000 *Corsair* was being readied at Bath, Maine.) There were other and more compelling indications of an unaccustomed stringency. The papers told of a very weak market the day before — there were heavy declines on late trading, and the *Times* industrial average had dropped about 7 points. Steel had lost 7 points; General Electric, Westinghouse, and Montgomery Ward all lost 6. Meanwhile, that day's market was behaving very badly. In the second heaviest Saturday's trading in history, 3,488,100 shares were changing hands. At the close the *Times* industrials were down 12 points. The blue chips were seriously off, and speculative favorites had gone into a nosedive. J. I. Case, for example, had fallen a full 40 points.

On Sunday the market was front-page news — the *Times* headline read, "Stocks driven down as wave of selling engulfs the market," and the financial editor next day reported for perhaps the tenth time that the end had come. (He had learned, however, to hedge. "For the time at any rate," he said, "Wall Street seemed to see the reality of things.") No immediate explanation of the break was forthcoming. The Federal Reserve had long been quiet. Babson had said nothing new. Hatry and the Massachusetts Department of Public Utilities were from a week to a month in the past. They became explanations only later.

The papers that Sunday carried three comments which were to become familiar in the days that followed. After Saturday's trading, it was noted, quite a few margin calls went out. This meant that the value of stock which the recipients held on margin had declined to the point where it was no longer sufficient collateral for the loan that had paid for it. The speculator was being asked for more cash.

The other two observations were more reassuring. The papers agreed, and this was also the informed view on Wall Street, that the worst was over. And it was predicted that on the following day the market would begin to receive organized support. Weakness, should it appear, would be tolerated no longer.

Never was there a phrase with more magic than "organized support." Almost immediately it was on every tongue and in every news story about the market. Organized support meant that powerful people would organize to keep prices of stocks at a reasonable level. Opinions differed as to who would organize this support. Some had in mind the big operators like Cutten, Durant, and Raskob. They, of all people, couldn't afford a collapse. Some thought of the bankers — Charles Mitchell had acted once before, and certainly if things got bad he would act again. Some had in mind the investment trusts. They held huge portfolios of common stocks and obviously they could not afford to have them become cheap. Also, they had cash. So if stocks did become cheap the investment trusts would be in the market picking up bargains. This would mean that the bargains wouldn't last. With so many people wanting to avoid a further fall, a further fall would clearly be avoided.

In the ensuing weeks the Sabbath pause had a marked tendency to breed uneasiness and doubts and pessimism and a decision to get out on Monday. This, it seems certain, was what happened on Sunday, October 20.

IV

Monday, October 21, was a very poor day. Sales totaled 6,091,870, the third greatest volume in history, and some tens of thousands who were watching the market throughout the country made a disturbing discovery. There was no way of telling what was happening. Previously on big days of the bull market the ticker had often fallen behind, and one didn't discover until well after the market closed how much richer he had become. But the experience with a falling market had been much more limited. Not since March had the ticker fallen seriously behind on declining values. Many now learned for the first time that they could be ruined, totally and forever, and not even know it. And if they were not ruined there was a strong tendency to imagine it. From the opening on the 21st the ticker lagged, and by noon it was an hour late. Not until an hour and forty minutes after the close of the market did it record the last transaction. Every ten minutes prices of selected bonds were printed on the bond ticker, but the wide divergence between these and the prices on the tape only added to the uneasiness — and to the growing conviction that it might be best to sell.

Things though bad were still not hopeless. Toward the end of Monday's trading the market rallied and final prices were above the lows for the day.

The net losses were considerably less than on Saturday. Tuesday brought a somewhat shaky gain. As so often before, the market seemed to be showing its ability to come back. People got ready to record the experience as merely another setback of which there had been so many previously.

In doing so they were helped by the two men who now were recognized as Wall Street's official prophets. On Monday in New York, Professor Fisher said that the decline had represented only a "shaking out of the lunatic fringe." He went on to explain why he felt that the prices of stocks during the boom had not caught up with their real value and would go higher. Among other things, the market had not yet reflected the beneficent effects of prohibition which had made the American worker "more productive and dependable."

On Tuesday, Charles E. Mitchell dropped anchor in New York with the observation that "the decline had gone too far." (Time and sundry congressional and court proceedings were to show that Mr. Mitchell had strong personal reasons for feeling that way.) He added that conditions were "fundamentally sound," said again that too much attention had been paid to the large volume of brokers' loans, and concluded that the situation was one which would correct itself if left alone. However, another jarring suggestion came from Babson. He recommended selling stocks and buying gold.

By Wednesday, October 23, the effect of this cheer was somehow dissipated. Instead of further gains there were heavy losses. The opening was quiet enough, but toward midmorning motor accessory stocks were sold heavily, and volume began to increase throughout the list. The last hour was quite phenomenal — 2,600,000 shares changed hands at rapidly declining prices. The *Times* industrial average for the day dropped from 415 to 384, giving up all of its gains since the end of the previous June. Tel and Tel lost 15 points; General Electric, 20; Westinghouse, 25; and J. I. Case, another 46. Again the ticker was far behind, and to add to the uncertainty an ice storm in the Middle West caused widespread disruption of communications. That afternoon and evening thousands of speculators decided to get out while — as they mistakenly supposed — the getting was good. Other thousands were told they had no choice but to get out unless they posted more collateral, for as the day's business came to an end an unprecedented volume of margin calls went out. Speaking in Washington, even Professor Fisher was fractionally less optimistic. He told a meeting of bankers that "security values *in most instances* were not inflated." However, he did not weaken on the unrealized efficiencies of prohibition.

The papers that night went to press with a souvenir of a fast departing era. Formidable advertisements announced subscription rights in a new offering of certificates in Aktiebolaget Kreuger and Toll at $23. There was also one bit of cheer. It was predicted that on the morrow the market would surely begin to receive "organized support."

V

Thursday, October 24, is the first of the days which history — such as it is on the subject — identifies with the panic of 1929. Measured by disorder, fright, and confusion, it deserves to be so regarded. That day 12,894,650 shares changed hands, many of them at prices which shattered the dreams and the hopes of those who had owned them. Of all the mysteries of the stock exchange there is none so impenetrable as why there should be a buyer for everyone who seeks to sell. October 24, 1929, showed that what is mysterious is not inevitable. Often there were no buyers, and only after wide vertical declines could anyone be induced to bid.

The panic did not last all day. It was a phenomenon of the morning hours. The market opening itself was unspectacular, and for a while prices were firm. Volume, however, was very large, and soon prices began to sag. Once again the ticker dropped behind. Prices fell farther and faster, and the ticker lagged more and more. By eleven o'clock the market had degenerated into a wild, mad scramble to sell. In the crowded boardrooms across the country the ticker told of a frightful collapse. But the selected quotations coming in over the bond ticker also showed that current values were far below the ancient history of the tape. The uncertainty led more and more people to try to sell. Others, no longer able to respond to margin calls, were sold out. By eleven-thirty the market had surrendered to blind, relentless fear. This, indeed, was panic.

Outside the Exchange in Broad Street a weird roar could be heard. A crowd gathered. Police Commissioner Grover Whalen became aware that something was happening and dispatched a special police detail to Wall Street to insure the peace. More people came and waited, though apparently no one knew for what. A workman appeared atop one of the high buildings to accomplish some repairs, and the multitude assumed he was a would-be suicide and waited impatiently for him to jump. Crowds also formed around the branch offices of brokerage firms throughout the city and, indeed, throughout the country. Word of what was happening, or what was thought to be happening, was passed out by those who were within sight of the board or the Trans-Lux. An observer thought that people's expressions showed "not so much suffering as a sort of horrified incredulity." [7] Rumor after rumor swept Wall Street and these outlying wakes. Stocks were now selling for nothing, The Chicago and Buffalo Exchanges had closed. A suicide wave was in progress, and eleven well-known speculators had already killed themselves.

At twelve-thirty the officials of the New York Stock Exchange closed the visitors gallery on the wild scenes below. One of the visitors who had just departed was showing his remarkable ability to be on hand with history. He was the former Chancellor of the Exchequer, Mr. Winston Churchill. It was

---

[7] Edwin Lefèvre, "The Little Fellow in Wall Street," *The Saturday Evening Post,* January 4, 1930.

he who in 1925 returned Britain to the gold standard and the overvalued pound. Accordingly, he was responsible for the strain which sent Montagu Norman to plead in New York for easier money, which caused credit to be eased at the fatal time, which, in this academy view, in turn caused the boom. Now Churchill was viewing his awful handiwork.

There is no record of anyone's having reproached him. Economics was never his strong point, so it seems most unlikely that he reproached himself.

VI

In New York at least the panic was over by noon. At noon the organized support appeared.

At twelve o'clock reporters learned that a meeting was convening at 23 Wall Street at the offices of J. P. Morgan and Company. The word quickly passed as to who was there — Charles E. Mitchell, the Chairman of the Board of the National City Bank, Albert H. Wiggin, the Chairman of the Chase National Bank, William C. Potter, the President of the Guaranty Trust Company, Seward Prosser, the Chairman of the Bankers Trust Company, and the host, Thomas W. Lamont, the senior partner of Morgan's. According to legend, during the panic of 1907 the elder Morgan had brought to a halt the discussion of whether to save the tottering Trust Company of America by saying that the place to stop the panic was there. It was stopped. Now, twenty-two years later, that drama was being re-enacted. The elder Morgan was dead. His son was in Europe. But equally determined men were moving in. They were the nation's most powerful financiers. They had not yet been pilloried and maligned by New Dealers. The very news that they would act would release people from the fear to which they had surrendered.

It did. A decision was quickly reached to pool resources to support the market.[8] The meeting broke up, and Thomas Lamont met with reporters. His manner was described as serious, but his words were reassuring. In what Frederick Lewis Allen later called one of the most remarkable understatements of all time,[9] he told the newspapermen, "There has been a little distress selling on the Stock Exchange." He added that this was "due to a technical condition of the market" rather than any fundamental cause, and told the newsmen that things were "susceptible to betterment." The bankers, he let it be known, had decided to better things.

Word had already reached the floor of the Exchange that the bankers were meeting, and the news ticker had spread the magic word afield. Prices firmed at once and started to rise. Then at one-thirty Richard Whitney appeared on

[8] The amounts to be contributed or otherwise committed were never specified. Frederick Lewis Allen (*Only Yesterday*, pp. 329–30) says that each of the institutions, along with George F. Baker, Jr., of the First National, who later joined the pool, put up $40 million. This total — $240 million — seems much too large to be plausible. The *New York Times* subsequently suggested (March 9, 1938) that the total was some $20 to $30 millions.

[9] *Op. cit.*, p. 330.

the floor and went to the post where steel was traded. Whitney was perhaps the best-known figure on the floor. He was one of the group of men of good background and appropriate education who, in that time, were expected to manage the affairs of the Exchange. Currently he was vice-president of the Exchange, but in the absence of E. H. H. Simmons in Hawaii he was serving as acting president. What was much more important at the moment, he was known as floor trader for Morgan's and, indeed, his older brother was a Morgan partner.

As he made his way through the teeming crowd, Whitney appeared debonair and self-confident — some later described his manner as jaunty. (His own firm dealt largely in bonds, so it is improbable that he had been much involved in the turmoil of the morning.) At the Steel post he bid 205 for 10,000 shares. This was the price of the last sale, and the current bids were several points lower. In an operation that was totally devoid of normal commercial reticence, he got 200 shares and then left the rest of the order with the specialist. He continued on his way, placing similar orders for fifteen or twenty other stocks.

This was it. The bankers, obviously, had moved in. The effect was electric. Fear vanished and gave way to concern lest the new advance be missed. Prices boomed upward.

The bankers had, indeed, brought off a notable coup. Prices as they fell that morning kept crossing a large volume of stop-loss orders — orders calling for sales whenever a specified price was reached. Brokers had placed many of these orders for their own protection on the securities of customers who had not responded to calls for additional margin. Each of these stop-loss orders tripped more securities into the market and drove prices down farther. Each spasm of liquidation thus insured that another would follow. It was this literal chain reaction which the bankers checked, and they checked it decisively.

In the closing hour, selling orders continuing to come in from across the country turned the market soft once more. Still, in its own way, the recovery on Black Thursday was as remarkable as the selling that made it so black. The *Times* industrials were off only 12 points, or a little more than a third of the loss of the previous day. Steel, the stock that Whitney had singled out to start the recovery, had opened that morning at 205½, a point or two above the previous close. At the lowest it was down to 193½ for a 12-point loss.[10] Then it recovered to close at 206 for a surprising net gain of 2 points for this day. Montgomery Ward, which had opened at 83 and gone to 50, came back to 74. General Electric was at one point 32 points below its opening price and then came back 25 points. On the Curb, Goldman Sachs Trading Corporation opened at 81, dropped to 65, and then came back to 80. J. I. Case, maintaining a reputation for eccentric behavior that had brought much risk

[10] Quotations have normally been rounded to the nearest whole number in this history. The steel quotation on this day seems to call for an exception.

capital into the threshing machine business, made a net gain of 7 points for the day. Many had good reason to be grateful to the financial leaders of Wall Street.

VII

Not everyone could be grateful to be sure. Across the country people were only dimly aware of the improvement. By early afternoon, when the market started up, the ticker was hours behind. Although the spot quotations on the bond ticker showed the improvement, the ticker itself continued to grind out the most dismal of news. And the news on the ticker was what counted. To many, many watchers it meant that they had been sold out and that their dream — in fact, their brief reality — of opulence had gone glimmering, together with home, car, furs, jewelry, and reputation. That the market, after breaking them, had recovered was the most chilling of comfort.

It was eight and a half minutes past seven that night before the ticker finished recording the day's misfortunes. In the boardrooms speculators who had been sold out since morning sat silently watching the tape. The habit of months or years, however idle it had now become, could not be abandoned at once. Then, as the final trades were registered, sorrowfully or grimly, according to their nature, they made their way out into the gathering night. . . . □

⋄ **68** ⋄

The Year of the Old Folks' Revolt *

DAVID H. BENNETT

For Cleveland, Ohio, the summer of 1936 was a time to remember. In the steaming month of July, during which a twelve-day heat wave in the Midwest and East cost 3,000 lives, there came to the great lake-front city a procession of people — gray, simple, sixtyish, and poor — from all across the nation. They came in buses and railroad coaches and brokendown Fords. Carrying their battered suitcases, they found dollar-a-night lodgings on the city's outskirts and travelled to the downtown convention hall in trolleys, eating bananas and oranges out of bags to save lunch money. They had calloused hands and wore clean but threadbare Sears, Roebuck clothing. They were the delegates to the second annual convention of Old Age Revolving Pensions, Ltd. — disciples of Dr. Francis E. Townsend, whom they fervently believed had been sent by God to save the old people of America in their time of deepest need.

The year before, at Chicago, the first national meeting of the organization

* Taken and adapted from David H. Bennett, "The Year of the Old Folks' Revolt," *American Heritage*, December 1964, pp. 48–51, 99, 100. Used by permission.

had attracted 7,000 delegates. The Cleveland convention drew 11,000. Banners proclaimed "The Three Emancipators: Washington, Lincoln, Townsend." One speaker suggested that "God almighty placed this great idea in the mind of one of His servants." Another announced that "the Doctor is the leader of a greater army than any known to history." Yet another wondered why no star had hung over Dr. Townsend's birthplace to "guide Wise Men of that generation to his side."

If the Townsend Plan was an idea so explosive as to merit this kind of response, then in the presidential election year of 1936 it could prove to be political dynamite. Of this the organizers of the meeting were very much aware. Indeed, the Townsendites were assembling in the very hall where, only a month earlier, the Republican party had met to nominate Alfred M. Landon. As one journalist pointed out, Townsend's convention had at least two advantages over Landon's: it was bigger and it was livelier.

The Cleveland gathering of Townsendites marked the high point of one of the most curious and potentially formidable mass movements in modern American history. The road which led to Cleveland began some three years before in Long Beach, California, where Francis Everett Townsend had his great vision. In 1933 Townsend was almost sixty-seven — a country-bred physician who had come to the retirement community of Long Beach in 1919 to recover his health and seek a livelihood. Educated in rural Illinois schools, he was successively a ranch hand and farm laborer in the West; a mucker in Colorado mines; a homesteader, teacher, and salesman in Kansas. Finally, at the age of thirty-one, he entered medical school in Omaha and after graduation practiced medicine in South Dakota, where he was driven out of Belle Fourche for fighting local political corruption. In 1927–28 he was a real-estate promoter in Long Beach. When the Depression struck, most of his savings were wiped out, and he had to accept an appointment as assistant director of the City Health Office. There he could see just how cruelly the economic crisis was ravaging the old people of America. Years later he recalled that "I stepped into such distress, pain and horror as to shake me even today with its memory. . . . They were good men and women, they had done all they could, had played the game as they had been taught to play it, and suddenly, when there was no chance to start over again, they were let down."

In 1933 the Doctor lost his job when the City Health Office ran out of funds; his own crisis seemed only to intensify a growing feeling that something had to be done to help the old people of America.

For most men the years after age sixty-five are the twilight of their careers, but for Dr. Townsend, all the years that went before seemed to serve only as a prelude for the great work he was now to undertake.

For Townsend had a vision of America's elderly people permanently freed from economic privation by means of a substantial pension, disbursed monthly by the federal government to every citizen aged sixty and over. The government was to raise this money through a small "transaction tax," a multiple sales tax, levied not just at the point of ultimate sale but at each point that a commodity changed hands along the way from raw material to finished product.

The Doctor had read somewhere that in 1929 the gross business done in the United States amounted to $935 billion. He deduced that it would be possible, by tapping this enormous business transaction with a sales tax, to produce twenty to twenty-four billion dollars per year, enough to give $150 a month — later he raised it to $200 — to everyone over sixty.

As the months rolled by, Townsend began to advertise his program as a solution to the economic woes of not only the aged but the rest of the population as well. He decided that spending the $200 within thirty days should be made mandatory, and thus began to stress the revolving aspect of his proposal — that twenty to twenty-four billion dollars paid to the elderly every year would tend to stimulate the entire economy as the old people spent their pensions on all manner of consumer goods. He now spoke in terms of the "velocity of money," pointing out, for example, that the dollar spent by an old man for food would be used by his grocer to pay the wholesaler, and so on down the line. In this way, the pension money would "revolve" and would multiply; the pension checks coursing through the economy would stimulate every aspect of American enterprise and finally would end the Depression.

Townsend began to make even more sweeping claims for his plan. Millions of new jobs, he promised, would be made available to younger men by withdrawing the aged from the employment rolls. State and local governments would have the billions of dollars consumed yearly by crime and crime prevention as his plan eliminated poverty and privation; even more billions would be saved which were now spent on charity.

When Townsend described his dream to the aged, it did not seem too farfetched. To them, the economy of abundance of the 1920's had come to be the normal thing; the Depression, a grotesquely atypical phenomenon. When Townsend drew upon these memories of prosperity and added to them his own thesis, few old people challenged his arguments.

Indeed, there were few who would have wanted to doubt the plan's validity, so bleak were the prospects for the elderly during the Depression. In 1934, only twenty-eight of the forty-eight states had any pension plan at all; three of those were bankrupt and the others were woefully inadequate. Allmost three-quarters of a million Americans aged sixty-five and over were on some form of federal relief, and the situation appeared to be getting worse. For, while the elderly were relentlessly being displaced in the job market, they were steadily increasing both in absolute numbers and in percentage of the total population. In 1930 the aged comprised 6.6 million, or 5.4 per cent of all the people in the United States; by 1935 these figures had grown to 7.5 million and 6 per cent.

Thus it was not surprising that when Dr. Townsend first proposed his plan in late 1933, almost immediately support for it sprang up across America.

The plan grew out of a letter Townsend wrote to the "People's Forum" column of a Long Beach newspaper in late September. At the time, he planned no program of action. But within days of the letter's appearance, replies flooded the paper, which soon devoted a daily page to discussion of Townsend's ideas. At the same time he was approached directly by people who wanted concrete proposals for putting his ideas into action. By November, Townsend had decided to devote his life to realizing his plan. When the Doctor advertised for canvassers to obtain signatures on petitions for congressional action, he was overwhelmed by replies. Within a matter of days he had received completed petitions containing the names of 2,000 supporters.

The Doctor now searched about for a promoter, a person to help him set up the organization that would push the Townsend Plan into law. He turned to Robert Earl Clements, a young, driving real-estate broker.

The two men began collecting names and sending out Old Age Revolving Pensions literature. After five weeks, they were getting an average of one hundred replies a day. Physicians and ministers in the Long Beach area became spokesmen for the plan, and a newspaper, *The Townsend Weekly*, was started. As the movement continued to grow, local Townsend clubs began to spring up, and by January, 1935, five months after the first of these had been founded, the leaders proudly announced that more than 3,000 with a total membership approaching one-half million, were operating — actually there were only 1,200 clubs, but even that figure was impressive. Organizers were soon at work across the nation setting up more clubs, and the Doctor had to hire a staff of ninety-five to handle his mounting flow of mail. Almost overnight, the Townsend movement had become a force to be reckoned with.

The fanaticism with which Townsend's growing thousands of followers promoted his plan astounded and finally frightened journalists and politicians throughout the nation. There were ugly rumors that newly organized Townsend clubs in the Pacific Northwest were threatening merchants and newspaper publishers with economic boycotts if they refused to support the plan. "This thing's become a religion," one alarmed editor said. "It holds the whole town in its grasp."

Clearly, Dr. Townsend had struck into a subsoil of fear and discontent which went far deeper than the immediate material privations of the Depression. Most Townsendites had grown to adulthood believing that they were heirs to a tradition of self-reliance and rugged individualism. The America of their youth was a land in which opportunity abounded, in which a man's failure was seen generally as the result of his own inadequacy, in which the thrifty could count on security in their old age. It was also a land of close family ties, where age was respected.

But in the 1930's, these ideas were becoming only memories. Industrialization and urbanization were destroying the nation's traditional rural and small-town way of life. A man was less independent and less secure in the new

America: the factory assembly line robbed him of his individualism and the economics of industrial capitalism subjected him to the vagaries of the business cycle. Family ties were all too often broken as children moved far from their parental homes. Even old age seemed to lose its dignity: the highest premium in the land now seemed to be on youth.

Dr. Townsend appeared on the scene to soothe and comfort the aged. By arguing that a comfortable pension was fully deserved after a lifetime of sacrifice and devotion, he appealed to their hurt pride. He appealed also to their self-esteem, asserting that "people over sixty were selected to be the circulators of large sums of money because they have more buying experience than those of fewer years." He called old people "Civil Veterans of the Republic" and told them that they could become a "research, educational, and corrective force in both a material and spiritual way in the United States."

Thus were the aged offered the best of all possible worlds. They might live in comfort, but they need not feel idle or useless, for as "circulators of money" or, as Townsend preferred to call them, "distributor custodians," they would be serving a vital function.

Furthermore, Townsend did not force his followers to choose between his plan and basic American values. One could be a Townsendite without the risk of being called a foreigner, a "red," or an atheist. The leaders proclaimed their faith in the political and economic system of the nation, and although their solution was clearly a radical one, it was presented in conservative terms. It offered to preserve the "American way of life." It became for its followers, in the words of a contemporary observer, "simply the means of redeeming the promises of the little red school house."

Along with this wholesomely patriotic tone, the movement had a definite religious content. The aura of the evangelist's camp meeting surrounded Townsendism. The leadership included many clergymen; the spokesmen described their cause as being "God-given" and "ordained by the Lord"; well-known religious songs became anthems of the movement; and Bible reading was a part of most of its gatherings.

Aided by this combination of religiosity and patriotism, the Townsend organization, by the start of the election year of 1936, claimed a membership of some 2.2 million in 7,000 local clubs operating across the nation. Dr. Townsend liked to tell his followers that "the movement is all yours, my friends; it belongs to you." In reality, it was very much the property of Francis E. Townsend and the few leaders who surrounded him. Moreover, the old physician began to be affected by his meteoric rise to fame. The speechmaking, the plane trips, the cheering throngs, made him feel, as he confessed to one interviewer, that he "had been chosen by God to accomplish this mission." The movement's newspaper began to compare him to the great men of the past — to Washington and Lincoln, to Columbus and Copernicus, to Franklin and Luther, and even to Christ.

Townsend revelled in the praise, but he did not change his speaking style.

His soft, warm voice was not fitted for oratory, and even after delivering dozens of addresses, the old man still seemed ill at ease on the speaker's platform. This very ineptitude proved to be an asset, for the old folks in the Townsend crusade did not want their leader to be too articulate and dynamic; they wanted him to be like themselves. And this the Doctor knew. His conversation was punctuated with homely phrases such as "dang" and "by gum." His publicists pictured him as the folksy older American who had triumphed over adversity and who was now helping all America overcome its troubles.

But Dr. Townsend was not an organizer. He needed a covey of sleek and efficient proselyters, men who were accustomed to talking for their living, men who were willing to serve as the salesmen of Utopia — men, in short, like Robert E. Clements.

Clements, who insisted on calling himself the "co-founder" of the movement, was its manager and fund-raiser. It was he who devised its authoritarian system of centralized control, which Townsend eventually employed to dispose of those dissidents who rebelled against official policy. Clements made the promotion of the Townsend Plan a big business. He marketed Townsend emblems and stickers for automobiles, pictures, pamphlets, songs, buttons, badges, and banners, all sold at a handsome profit. But of all his lucrative schemes, none was so profitable as the *Townsend Weekly*. Its circulation rose steadily to over 300,000; this and other publications of their Prosperity Publishing Company were soon grossing Townsend and Clements $200,000 a year. The bulk of the income from the *Weekly* came from advertisements, many of which preyed on the fears and anxieties of old people, filling the newspaper with testimonials to the magical qualities of bladder tablets, gland stimulants, and kidney pills.

The intensive campaign to build the organization was paying rich dividends by late 1935. Townsend headquarters announced that in the first fifteen months of its existence, total receipts approached three-quarters of a million dollars. In order to justify this growth the Townsend leaders had to exert political pressure for legislative adoption of the plan. But this presented no problem, for Dr. Townsend eagerly awaited the hour when the whole nation would hail his idea.

The Townsendites entered the national political arena when John Steven McGroarty was elected to Congress from southern California. A seventy-two-year-old dramatist and official poet laureate of his state, McGroarty, though a Democrat, was an ardent anti-New Dealer, and a confirmed believer in the Townsend Plan, and his election was due in large part to a strong campaign waged in his behalf by local O.A.R.P. organizers. In 1935, McGroarty introduced a bill to implement the pension plan, and within three months the movement's leaders claimed they had twenty million signatures urging its passage.

But this massive pressure was not sufficient. When the revised McGroarty bill came to a vote, it lost by almost four to one. Yet Dr. Townsend and his followers were not discouraged. The loss was considered merely a tactical setback; the war was still to be won. When Verner W. Main, a Republican from Michigan, won both a primary and a by-election in the spring of 1935 and attributed his victory to strong backing from the O.A.R.P. organization, the Townsendites were elated. "As Main goes, so goes the nation" became the battle cry as the movement assembled for its first national convention in Chicago. In a remarkable address Francis E. Townsend told cheering thousands:

> We dare not fail. Our plan is the sole and only hope of a confused and distracted nation. . . . We have become an avalanche of political power that no derision, no ridicule, no conspiracy of silence can stem. . . . Where Christianity numbered its hundreds in its beginning years, our cause numbers its millions. And without sacrilege we can say that we believe that the effects of our movement will make as deep and mighty changes in civilization as did Christianity itself.

Now Dr. Townsend was sure that he had power as well as purpose. By late 1935 he was ready to use all of his power to turn his plan into law. . . . □

✧ 69 ✧

The International Monetary System — Its Evolution and the Problems Ahead *

FREDERICK L. DEMING

THE SYSTEM PRIOR TO WORLD WAR II

Before the First World War, the major currencies were tied to gold by fixed exchange rates, and sterling was the major currency used in international transactions. The Bank of England was at the focal point of the whole international monetary system and was able to operate on a remarkably small gold reserve, equivalent to about 5 to 7 percent of the annual imports of the United Kingdom. As the main international banking center, London had at all times large short-term claims on the rest of the world, as well as large liabilities to foreign countries. Changes in the availability and price of credit in London had a very important impact on the attraction of funds to London. The inflow and the outflow of funds from London was a major aspect of the adjustment mechanism under which international settlements were kept within limits that could be met either with a national reserve or borrowings.

* Remarks by the Honorable Frederick L. Deming, Under Secretary of the Treasury for Monetary Affairs at the joint luncheon meeting of the Southern Economic Association and Southern Finance Association at the Deauville Hotel, Miami Beach, Florida, November 12, 1965.

Even before the first World War, there was a considerable variation in the extent to which countries held gold. According to a study made by the International Monetary Fund in 1958, both France and Italy in 1913 had gold reserves equivalent to about 40 percent of annual imports, whereas the Netherlands, Switzerland, and the United Kingdom held gold reserves that were of an entirely different order, equivalent to 4 to 8 per cent of imports.

Excluding countries now in the Communist bloc, the Fund estimated total world gold reserves at about 19 percent of imports in 1913, with an additional 2 percent of imports, or about $400 million, held in the form of foreign exchange reserves.

On the whole, the international monetary system was rather fully loaned up. When pressure developed on the system, credit quickly became tight, leading to the financial panics which accentuated the cyclical down-turns in business activity in those times. At such times, there was not only a drain on gold internationally, but an internal drain on gold reserves could also be expected, because most major currencies could be redeemed in gold coin.

How did the system manage to function — with what, in retrospect, we can see were relatively few periods of stress — with such limited reserves?

First, deficit countries generally were net borrowers on long-term capital account, and surplus countries were net investors of long-term capital. When the capital outflow from the creditor countries tightened up, this probably led rather directly to a shrinkage in the imports of capital equipment and other goods by deficit countries, which were simply not able to raise the capital needed to finance them. Note that this type of adjustment process is a rather stringent one. Second, governmental transactions were much less important in the balance of payments at that time. Finally, and perhaps most important over-all, imports of capital by surplus countries, if they occurred at all, probably took the form of short-term funds.

After the First World War, it was soon realized that the price level was tending to settle down on a plateau about 50 percent higher than prewar prices. There was considerable fear that there would be a shortage of gold, even though a large part of the gold previously circulating among the public in Europe had been called into official reserves during the war. The Genoa Conference in 1921 recommended wide use of the gold exchange standard in order to economize on gold. By the year 1928, world imports had risen about 45 percent above the 1913 level, but the ratio of gold and foreign exchange to imports had approximately doubled, to 42 percent. And, of this total, about one-quarter consisted of foreign exchange reserves. Outside the United States, countries held, on the average, reserves of gold and foreign exchange equal to about 35 percent of annual imports.

During the Twenties, balance of payments data began to be collected and discussed. The dollar became a major world trading and reserve currency. Intergovernmental transfers across the exchanges in the form of reparations and debt payments directed the attention of economists to international exchange and monetary problems.

After 1926, the stabilization of the French franc at an under-valued level was followed by very large receipts of foreign exchange by the French monetary authorities. The management of these funds became a critical aspect of international financial developments of the late Twenties, and the conversion of some of these foreign exchange resources into gold shrank international liquidity. The international financial relationships of this period were noteworthy for a circular flow of funds from the United States to Europe, the outflow representing intergovernmental debt receipts. When it began to be difficult to sell European bonds in the United States, severe exchange pressures soon developed, first in Central Europe and then on the pound sterling.

The great depression brought serious disorganization of the international monetary system, as well as the banking system, in the United States. However liquidity is defined, it was severely shrunk. At least some part of the severity of the depression must probably be attributed to the cumulative weaknesses that became evident in the U. S. financial and monetary system. These weaknesses led to certain important modifications. The internal redeemability of dollar currency into gold was eliminated, thus reserving our gold reserves for international use. The United States also withdrew for some years from the business of extending international credit in the form of bonds and loans to foreign banking systems. The depreciation of sterling in 1931 was followed by dollar depreciation in 1933, and by the eventual collapse of gold bloc exchange rates in 1936.

The record of the Thirties was not a happy one in international trade and finance. It was marked by competitive currency depreciation, by restrictive trade practices, and by a general breakdown in international capital flow. And in the latter years, prior to the War, large amounts of Continental European funds sought refuge in London and in the United States.

In 1936, the first tentative efforts to develop continuing monetary cooperation by the major governments appeared with the Tripartite Agreement of that year. Technically and operationally, this agreement assured temporary official support for the gold market, and thus for the major exchange rates. But it also introduced a general presumption against exchange depreciation among these leading countries.

During the Thirties, world trade fell off in terms of value. In 1938, trade was only about 10 percent higher than it had been in 1913, and was about 25 percent below the 1928 level. Because of this shrinkage, and because currency depreciation raised the price of gold, reserves became very large by comparison with trade. For the world as a whole, reserves rose to 117 percent of trade, and, for the world outside the United States, reserves were 63 percent of trade. However, these very large reserves did not stimulate an effective recovery of world trade under the post-depression conditions.

BRETTON WOODS AND THE PERIOD 1945 TO 1958

While the war was still going on, the Allied nations held an international monetary conference in 1944 at Bretton Woods, New Hampshire. From that conference there emerged certain general principles that have formed the foundation of the international monetary system during the past two decades. And out of this conference came the International Monetary Fund and the International Bank for Reconstruction and Development.

The experience of the inter-war period had vividly impressed the delegates to the conference at Bretton Woods. They, therefore, established the system of so-called "adjustable pegs," or exchange rates, that remained fixed unless a country was considered to be in fundamental disequilibrium. The purpose here was to limit competitive exchange rate depreciation. The second major element was to provide a pool of international credit which could supplement the reserves of individual countries by establishing specified lines of credit availability. The third major principle was that current exchange transactions, as distinguished from capital transactions, should be carried out freely without exchange restrictions.

However, it took some time for reality to overtake these ideals. The world emerged from the war with the dollar as the major key currency. Other currencies were fixed in relation to the dollar, and their value was maintained by official purchase and sale of dollars. Through the convertibility of the dollar into gold, the major currencies were connected with gold. But, for a number of years after the war, restrictions were maintained by European countries, even on current transactions. Many countries did not achieve strong currencies until after the Marshall Plan had poured very large amounts of dollars into their economies. The exchange rates of most European countries were depreciated in terms of the dollar in 1949. Although exchange restrictions began to be relaxed, in the Fifties, and the European Payments Union brought liberalized payments within the Western European group of countries, worldwide convertibility did not come until late in the Fifties. At the end of 1958, fourteen European countries announced de facto convertibility for new acquisitions of their currencies by foreigners, and this was the crucial step in eliminating an important barrier to flows of goods and money between the Western Hemisphere and Western Europe.

Continental Europe recovered its financial strength rapidly after the exchange adjustments of 1949, with the help of the Marshall Plan and large U. S. military expenditures in Europe. However, France was still troubled with currency weakness until 1958. Sterling also came under pressure periodically, and British reserves showed no persistent upward trend. Overall, however, industrial countries other than the United States had already increased their reserves by $14 billion from 1948 to 1958, to nearly $22 billion, a figure almost as large as United States reserves of $22.5 billion.

During this period, the world seemed to be approaching steadily toward carrying out more and more of the objectives of the Bretton Woods Conference. The international monetary system appeared to be making steady progress and to be serving the world well. The postwar recovery of Europe, both economically and financially, was in striking contrast to the difficulties that had been encountered in the first fifteen years after World War I. In Europe, full employment contrasted with the heavy unemployment of the Twenties. Reserves were built up with great rapidity. The burden of postwar indebtedness to the United States was extremely moderate because of the enormous quantity of our resources that was made available to Europe through the Lend-Lease system and the Marshall Plan.

This was the situation at the end of 1958. Why, now, is there so much talk about the need to improve the international monetary system? To find an answer to this question, let us first review some of the elements that make up the international monetary system.

ELEMENTS OF THE INTERNATIONAL MONETARY SYSTEM

Mr. Roosa, my distinguished predecessor as Under Secretary of the Treasury for Monetary Affairs, has pointed out in a recent book that, in a strict sense, there is not really an international monetary system at all. What we have is a set of institutions and procedures which, over time, have become conventionally acceptable arrangements for making international transfers of funds that settle international transactions and for providing reserves that are held by monetary authorities.

The International Monetary Fund and the Articles of Agreement under which it was established provide a certain foundation and basic framework for the system. This is essentially the system of exchange rates that are fixed for considerable periods of time and are changed only when there is a clear case of a fundamental disequilibrium. In addition, there are a number of special arrangements between particular countries and groups of countries, such as the franc area or the sterling area, under which trade or payments are conducted, or reserves are transferred, lent or borrowed.

The system may be likened somewhat to a rather rambling house that has grown up over a considerable period of time, with various additions made from time to time by different builders. It is not necessarily an artistic whole, but it functions rather well and keeps the currencies of the world living together more or less comfortably. At times, however, there is a certain restiveness among the tenants and a feeling that the house needs some further expansion or some major repairs, or both. This is one of those periods.

There appears to be increasing agreement that the world payments system as a whole requires three types of money: (1) national or domestic currencies for internal use; (2) vehicle or transactions currencies that are used by banks and traders of one country in making payments to banks and traders of other countries; and (3) reserve assets that are held by and used by monetary authorities in making payments to monetary authorities of other countries.

Domestically, countries utilize money created by their central banks and their commercial banking systems in the form of currency notes and deposits. The use of domestic money is quite familiar and needs no further comment.

The second type of currency may be called a "trading" or a "vehicle" currency. For this purpose national currencies are normally used in foreign trade, and especially the national currencies of some of the major countries. Most international trade, in practice, utilizes dollars or sterling, though the French franc would be the normal currency for transactions between France and the French-speaking areas of Africa, for example. Along with the use of their currencies in international trade, there is likely to be a substantial amount of financing of trade by banks in New York or in London or Paris in the form of dollar, sterling, and franc credits. During the postwar period, privately held international balances have risen rapidly in the form of dollars to $10.6 billion at the end of 1964, while sterling balances in private hands have grown more slowly to about $4.8 billion.

The third category, reserve assets, are held as reserves by the monetary authorities of the major countries. Although private holdings have their bearing on the over-all liquidity problem, the main questions relate to official reserves. Most of these remarks deal with this category of money.

Internationally, reserve assets are available in case of need to finance deficits in a country's balance of payments. However, central banks cannot replenish their reserves in quite the same way as a commercial bank in the United States. They do have access to certain credit facilities in the International Monetary Fund and they may have arranged bilateral swaps with the United States or other countries, but these credit facilities are usually limited as to the amount that is quickly available without any questions being asked (unconditional credit). Additional borrowing is likely to be accompanied by searching international inquiry into the policies of the borrowing country. Especially important is their inability, in most cases, to sell or discount abroad their assets representing domestic loans or investments.

International reserves may also perform, sometimes in rather severe fashion, the function of exercising restraint upon the lending and investment activities of the national currency system.

But there is no direct and true analogy of the workings of the international monetary system in laying a restraining hand upon the monetary expansion of a country and the workings of domestic monetary systems in restraining the credit expansion of banks within the system. For there is only one monetary authority for a given region or country. Consequently, its reserve position is affected not only in the narrow sense by its own liberality or tightness in credit policy, but also in the broader sense by the vigor and competitive strength of all the business activity that is carried out within the region or country it serves. There is, of course, an important interconnection between the growth of demand and of business activity in the region and the supply and price of credit within the region, but credit cost and availability are by no means the sole factors affecting the relative competitive positions of two currency areas. The efficiency of labor, the availability of natural resources, the many other factors affecting the aggregate levels of demand in the two areas, the structure of savings, consumption and investment, the form and magnitude of public outlays for defense and other purposes, and many other variables will affect the volume of transactions between two currency areas and, hence, the net settlements which must be met out of reserves or out of credit facilities that supplement reserves.

A word must be said here about the applicability of much of what has just been said to reserve currencies. So long as other monetary authorities are prepared to acquire and hold additional deposits or investments denominated in a reserve currency, the monetary authorities of such a reserve country may be able to finance deficits without using reserves or calling upon specific credit facilities. That is, they are in the position of being able to transfer domestic assets to foreign monetary authorities without losing reserves. But this situation lasts only so long as other monetary authorities are prepared to add to their holdings of such assets. And at any time, foreign holders may decide to turn in such assets for conversion and draw down the reserves of the reserve center.

In the last analysis, reserves for the commercial banking system are whatever is defined as reserves and accepted as reserves by national authorities and by the practice of commercial banks. Internationally, in somewhat the same manner, reserves, or reserve assets, represent those assets which major central banks will accept freely from other major central banks.

TYPES OF RESERVE ASSETS

At present, there are three basic forms of international reserve assets: gold, foreign exchange, and virtually unconditional drawing rights on the International Monetary Fund.

The oldest and most firmly established form of reserve is gold. It has served this purpose for many decades, and its use in some form as a basic money goes back for centuries. It is, as someone once pointed out, one of the few commodities that can move in internationl trade without tariffs or restrictions, at least when it is destined for monetary authorities. In effect, it has universal acceptability. The countries of the Free World presently have $41 billion in gold in their international reserves, with about one-third held by the United States, and about 50 percent held by Western European countries.

The foreign exchange component of international reserves consists principally of dollars and sterling. Currencies held as reserves depend partly upon history and practice. A very important factor is confidence in the maintenance of value of the currency in terms of gold and other currencies. But there are other important considerations that lead countries to hold reserves in a particular currency. They like to find assets in which the foreign exchange can be safely invested and which can be sold quickly and easily, with a minimum of possible loss. This means there must be broad and deep markets for the securities in which their reserves are invested. There must be a large supply of foreign exchange available to be widely held by foreign countries. Today, only the dollar and the pound, and, to a more limited extent, the franc, are used as reserve currencies in this way. The pound and the franc are held as reserves largely by countries within the sterling area and the franc area. The foreign exchange component in international reserves now totals about $22 billion, of which about three-fifths is in the form of dollar assets.

The third type of reserve asset has developed more recently, as the Fund has extended credits to its members. It has come to be realized that there is a basic claim on the Fund known as the gold tranche — tranche being French for "slice" or "cut" — which arises initially when a country contributes gold to the Fund in the amount of one-quarter of its quota subscription. But, in addition to this gold tranche, there is also the so-called "super gold tranche," which represents an amount equal to any credit claims that countries may acquire in the Fund in excess of the gold tranche. These credit claims on the Fund arise when the currency of a given country is utilized by the Fund to make loans to other countries. Countries may draw virtually at will on the Fund, so long as they have super gold tranche or gold tranche claims. These "unconditional drawing rights" on the Fund total about $5 billion.

Thus, overall, the countries of the Free World now have about $68 billion in reserve assets — $41 billion in gold, $22 billion in foreign exchange, and $5 billion in unconditional drawing rights on the Fund.

THE U. S. BALANCE OF PAYMENTS DEFICIT AND WORLD RESERVES — 1958 TO 1964

After this survey of the principal types of reserve assets, we may now look at the crowded monetary history of 1959–64 to find the answer to the question as to why there is so much current interest in improving our monetary system. By 1958, the United States had swung sharply into a large deficit, following the somewhat favorable balance of payments position brought about in 1957 by exceptional difficulties of the United Kingdom and France. During the six years beginning with 1959, the United States recorded a series of very large international deficits. It is true that a substantial part of the deficit reported by the Department of Commerce during these years, about $5 billion, took the form of additions to private dollar holdings. Nevertheless, the amount of the deficit which resulted in an increase of officially held reserves in foreign countries was nearly $13 billion. Continental European countries acquired the lion's share of these reserves. We have estimated that nearly three-quarters of the growth in official reserves of the rest of the world was accounted for by the counterpart of United States deficits. Since the over-all growth in reserves of other countries was about $17 billion during these six years, they also derived rather small amounts from new monetary gold supplies or through the net increase of their creditor claims on the International Monetary Fund.

These figures give a quick indication of the two major problems that are faced by the United States and the world in dealing with international reserves in the future. The United States cannot afford to continue to run deficits and supply reserves in this fashion. To do so would mean that our own reserves would be reduced and our own international position impaired, not only financially but in many other ways as well. An internationally strong currency and a strong voice in world affairs tend to go together. Financially, our current assets would be reduced too far relative to our current liabilities. The acceptability of dollar assets to foreign monetary authorities would be weakened, and this could lead to a shrinkage in existing world liquidity, concentrated on our own reserves, which have been declining over quite a long period.

For these reasons, President Johnson has made clear that United States deficits must be stopped. Speaking in Washington on the first of October, he told the Governors of the International Monetary Fund: "I want to be very clear about this. We must, in our own interest and in the interest of those who rely on the dollar as a reserve currency, maintain our payments in equilibrium. This we will do."

But the second part of the problem then faces us with the cessation of U. S. deficits. For this means that a major part of the secular growth in international reserves also stops. New monetary gold supplies are not sufficiently large to meet needs for additional reserves. The world economy is growing rapidly and, while no one sees as necessary an exact or mechanical relationship between the growth in world trade or world activity and the need for additional reserves, it seems quite clear that, sooner or later, more reserves will be required. Thus, some alternative procedures that will provide for additions to world reserves must be established.

In this connection, it is of interest that, in June, 1965, the official reserves of all Free World countries taken together — excluding the United States — stood at about 35 percent of world imports, c. i. f. basis. This means that reserves of other Free World countries were roughly sufficient to cover four months of imports, if fully utilized. Naturally, there were wide differences among countries and regions, but the over-all ratio of 35 percent is the same as it was in 1928, lower than it was in 1958, when it was 41 percent, and as low as at any time since 1948, when the ratio was 43 percent. The ratio of U. S. reserves to imports, at 66 percent, is nearly twice as high as that of other Free World countries taken together. But United States reserves can be called upon by foreign holders of dollars as well as for financing our own imports in case of need. Our own ratio to imports has been halved since 1959.

INTERNATIONAL MONETARY COOPERATION — 1958 TO 1964

Before noting some of the issues that will be faced in trying to find a solution to the problem of reserve creation, it will be helpful to review briefly what has been accomplished in the field of international monetary cooperation during the six years of large U. S. deficits. It is important to do this not only because the progress made in this area makes it now possible to mount an international approach to the new and more difficult task of deliberate reserve creation, but also because the developments of the past six years are, themselves, unprecedented and represent really gigantic steps in international understanding and in determined efforts to organize international activities in the monetary field.

The monetary history of these years is so crowded that it is difficult even to touch upon these achievements in a brief commentary of this type. However, some of the highlights may be mentioned.

First, in 1958–59, quotas in the International Monetary Fund were increased by 50 percent across the board, with additional selective increases for several leading industrial countries. This provided about $2.7 billion in additional gold and European currencies to the Fund, with a total enlargement of its resources of about $5 billion. However, in 1961, it was realized that, even with the quota increase, the resources of the Fund might prove insufficient to meet severe strains on leading currencies and that such strains could threaten to impair the functioning of the monetary system as a whole. After negotiations carried on during 1961, agreement was reached between the Fund and ten leading industrial countries under which these countries contracted to provide loans to the Fund under specified conditions in amounts up to $6 billion. This understanding became known as the General Arrangements to Borrow, and the participants in it became known as the Group of Ten. Parallel arrangements were set up by the Swiss authorities to provide up to about $200 million in Swiss francs directly to the Fund for GAB members.

There is now in process a further increase in the Fund resources, amounting to 25 percent across the board plus additional amounts for a number of individual countries.

Generally speaking, Fund resources make available medium-term credit. Through direct contacts among the monetary authorities of leading countries, short-term credit facilities have also been provided on a very large scale, both on a stand-by basis and through ad hoc arrangements. A network of swap facilities, developed by the Federal Reserve System, has now reached a total of $2.8 billion. The United Kingdom has, from time to time, made use of similar short-term facilities, arranged to meet particular needs. The largest such operation took place at the end of November, 1964, when $3 billion in short-term credits was arranged to strengthen the pound sterling.

In addition to the development of credit facilities, close and frequent consultations between responsible officials of treasuries and central banks are now a regular feature, through the Bank for International Settlements, and through a Working Party of the Organization for Economic Cooperation and Development. This Working Party is now undertaking a thorough study of the process of adjustment of international imbalances under modern conditions.

In the meantime, the Deputies of the Group of Ten bring together responsible officials of these countries to consider the basic problems of the functioning of the international monetary system and future needs for reserves. Under the aegis of this group, a technical study, known as the "Ossola Report," was published in August, 1965. This Report examines a number of possible ways of creating reserve assets.

For its part, the International Monetary Fund has also examined the question of creating reserve assets. In its Annual Report for 1964, the Fund strongly urged that any alterations made in the monetary system be evolutionary and be based on supplementing the existing system, where necessary. The Fund also indicated its belief that further development of international reserves could, and should, be based on the Fund.

THE TASKS AHEAD

Against this background, there are, as mentioned, two basic tasks ahead. *Our first major responsibility* is to reach and maintain a sustained equilibrium in the United States balance of payments. We are well advanced in this task. We know that we can succeed in it, and we will not relax our program for doing so until we succeed.

The second major task, on which I will comment here, is to improve our international monetary arrangements so that they will continue to meet the needs of the rest of the world and of the United States in the future, when reserves are no longer supplied by U. S. deficits because our payments have been brought into equilibrium. We may conveniently divide this into several aspects.

The first aspect is the perfecting of our arrangements for safeguarding the monetary system against abrupt and short-term strains on major currencies. Here, bilateral and other credit arrangements, involving direct action by national monetary authorities, are particularly useful, due to their flexibility and speed of activation.

Secondly, cyclical imbalances of particular countries must be expected, even if we had an all but perfectly adjusted economic world. To deal with such imbalances, medium-term credit is called for, and the Fund has come increasingly to be relied upon for this purpose, supplemented, in appropriate cases, by the General Arrangements to Borrow. To fulfill this function, the Fund needs adequate access to the currencies of surplus countries. How to assure this, to couple the use of the Fund's facilities with appropriate encouragement of correction of the imbalance and to gain the cooperation of surplus countries in correcting imbalances, are the key problems in the cyclical aspect of the over-all task. Whether there is a field for bilateral credits of a medium-term character, through special securities issued to creditor countries directly, could also be explored, since increase in quotas or changes in the scale of the General Arrangements to Borrow may occur only at relatively infrequent intervals.

As in the case of short-term monetary credits, medium-terms credits are likely to create reserve assets on the books of the monetary authorities of the creditor countries. This is now being recognized, and the global statistics on reserves, carried in the publications of the International Monetary Fund, include a category called *Reserve Positions in the Fund.*

It is in considering the longer term, or secular area of creating reserves intended to be more or less permanently or indefinitely carried on the books of monetary authorities, that we encounter the third aspect of the task. This is usually described as the "deliberate creation of additional reserve assets."

There are a number of difficult problems ahead for negotiators. The deliberate creation of additional reserve assets differs from what has been done up to now, in somewhat the same way as our nuclear and space activities in the scientific field differ from conventional weapons and conventional aircraft of the past. The world has never before set about this task deliberately. Monetary authorities are going to be careful before they introduce into balance sheets a reserve asset to be held more or less indefinitely.

I have used the term "additional reserve asset" consciously. There are ways of creating deliberately more reserve assets of the type that we already have, such as reserve positions in the Fund. There are also approaches that would require an entirely new type of asset, such as special reserve units created by a group of countries, either in partnership with the Fund or independently.

The United States has stressed that the interests of all members of the International Monetary Fund must be considered in these negotiations and that countries not members of the Group of Ten must be represented in the second stage of the preparations for formal improvements in the monetary system, after the first stage of negotiations in the Group of Ten has provided some basis for an eventual international understanding. In doing this, however, we fully recognize that there is a conceptual difference between the problem of creating adequate reserves for the world and the capital needs of developing countries.

In the same way, there is a conceptual distinction between the financing of a cyclical or short-term deficit and the creation of reserves of an indefinite duration. But, again, reserves, however created and for whatever purpose, can be spent. Reserves which could only be held and never spent would be strange instruments, indeed, though, in practice, a large proportion of the world's reserves do remain largely inert for long periods of time. □

＊ **70** ＊

Thurman Arnold, Antitrust, and the New Deal *

GENE M. GRESSLEY

In many respects the impact of statutory public policy on business hinges on the way that it is implemented, and in no area is this more true than in antitrust policy. Here, generalized statutes give administrators an opportunity to select certain kinds of problems for emphasis, reserving decisions as to whether specific applications of the law are justified to the courts. In this entire process there is a large element of pragmatism and opportunities exist for experimentation, innovation, and interpretation, as well as reliance on *stare decisis*. Consequently, the tenor of the times and the personalities of public officials have an effort on the vigor and effectiveness with which the antitrust statutes are enforced and the uses to which they are put. For this reason there are always many different perceptions of the objectives, value, and justice of antitrust actions.

At no time in our history, perhaps, more than during the New Deal were these facets of antitrust policy better revealed. And certainly no protagonist of the antitrust approach generated more controversy than Thurman Arnold, chief of the Antitrust Division of the Justice Department from 1938 to 1942. This man and his times serve as a specific example of the general propositions advanced above.

The enforcement of antitrust legislation since the Sherman Act of 1890 has been vacillating and sporadic in approach — confused in policy.[1] This was especially true during the thirty years after 1900. From the well-publicized trust busting of the insurgency period, through the anti-monopolistic views propounded by Wilson, to the business-oriented trade-association movement of the 1920's there was little to suggest that a uniform philosophy of antitrust enforcement had been developed in the United States.

Franklin D. Roosevelt's "New Deal," arriving on the political wave which followed the traumatic shock of the crash of the stock market, did little initially to alleviate the confusion surrounding antitrust enforcement. The first comprehensive legislation to remedy industrial dislocation was the National Industrial Recovery Act (NIRA) which negated the antitrust laws in some areas of industry.

So widespread was the belief that antitrust prosecution would be suspended entirely that Attorney General Homer Cummings issued a statement on

* Gene M. Gressley, "Thurman Arnold, Antitrust, and the New Deal," *Business History Review*, Vol. 38, Summer 1964, pp. 214–31.
[1] Hans B. Thorelli, *The Federal Antitrust Policy* (Baltimore, 1955), provides the best analysis of the origins of antitrust legislation.

July 6, 1933, to counteract the multitude of rumors. Cummings emphatically asserted: [2]

> There seems to be an impression in some quarters that the antitrust laws have been repealed or suspended in whole or in part. This is an entirely erroneous impression. Industrial and other groups must abide by the terms and conditions of the antitrust laws unless and until they obtain actual exemption from certain of the requirements thereof by formulating a code under the National Recovery Act, and obtaining its approval by the President.
>
> A large number of industrial activities and arrangements which are prohibited by the antitrust laws, do not come in any sense whatever within the purview of the exemptions contemplated by the National Recovery Act.

Cummings, as shown later in the revelations of the Temporary National Economic Committee, was whispering in a cave-of-the-winds. A significant element of the business community during the short and unhappy life of the NRA regarded antitrust legislation as nonenforceable. Some large industrial firms exploited the relaxation of the antitrust laws to increase their share of the market at the expense of smaller concerns.

After the 1935 Schechter case nullifying the NIRA, antitrust enforcement reflected the ambivalence of the Roosevelt administration. The President wavered between the trade association-NRA arguments of Henry Wallace, Adolph Berle, Jerome Frank, and Donald Richberg and the increasingly vocal anti-monopolistic position voiced by Felix Frankfurter, Robert Jackson, and Homer Cummings. The Justice Department kept up an unceasing barrage of memoranda which decried the market power of large corporations in the American economy — a situation equated in the public mind with "monopoly."

Slowly the anti-monopoly partisans succeeded in gaining the President's favor. The recession of 1937 greatly assisted their case. Roosevelt's political antennae sensed the general discontent in the country. Why not spotlight the monopoly issue? Public uneasiness at the economic conditions in the country had been increased by a segment of the intellectuals who were producing a spate of tomes on economic concentration in the United States. Politically, it appeared to be an opportune time to launch an investigation.

A most effective pressure on the President for renewed emphasis on antitrust policy came from Congress, where the Progressive bloc, albeit disorganized, was in open revolt. Senators O'Mahoney, Nye, Borah, and La Follette had all contested presidential leadership on a variety of issues. Borah and O'Mahoney especially were attempting to gain political advantage over the Chief Executive on the monopoly issue by again proposing the old idea of a federal licensing bill for all interstate corporations. Indeed, O'Mahoney

---

[2] Statement to the Press, Homer Cummings, July 6, 1933, Franklin D. Roosevelt Papers, Franklin Delano Roosevelt Library, Hyde Park, New York. Hereafter cited, Roosevelt Papers.

seemingly never gave up his hope that a licensing act would be passed. Well along into the Temporary National Economic Committee (TNEC) hearings, O'Mahoney wrote the President: [3]

> Nothing has transpired since I had the honor of talking with you a day or so after the NRA decision of the Supreme Court to change my belief that the answer to the economic problem lies in a simple recognition of the fact that the corporations which carry on interstate and foreign commerce should be required to take their charters from the federal government. This solution has been feared by many business leaders because they have seen in it only another effort to strengthen discretionary government control over business . . .
>
> It can, however, be demonstrated that the result of a wise system of federal charters would be to set business free from government domination and to set the people free from both the danger of monopoly on the one hand and of the totalitarian state upon the other.

Roosevelt, with his usual political adeptness, had no desire to surrender the initiative on the monopoly issue to Congress; just the opposite, he determined to steal the thunder of the Progressive bloc.

It was against this background of dissent that two events occurred which signaled a radical departure from the NRA philosophy. On October 22, 1937, Roosevelt wrote Attorney General Robert Jackson: [4]

> One of the problems that continues to require attention is the inadequacies and defects in our anti-monopoly laws, which I have often reviewed informally with you and others. I want to ask you to undertake, with the help of such others in government service as you wish from time to time to enlist, to assemble for me the following:
>
> 1. The important facts bearing upon the success or failure of our present anti-monopoly laws, their economic and social results, and the necessity for revision or amendment.
>
> 2. The different proposals or alternatives worthy of practical consideration, with the advantages and disadvantages of each.

This letter marked a significant step, which finally resulted in Roosevelt's famous anti-monopoly speech of April 29, 1938,[5] and the subsequent TNEC investigation.

Six months after the letter to Jackson, Roosevelt appointed Thurman Arnold as Assistant Attorney General in charge of the Anti-trust Division. Arnold had previously been a Wyoming lawyer and professor at the University of Wyoming Law School, Dean of the University of West Virginia Law School, and most recently a professor in the Yale Law School. When Arnold left New Haven, he did not journey south as a neophyte in the New Deal scene. He had already served as special counsel to the Agricultural Adjust-

---

[3] Joseph C. O'Mahoney to Franklin D. Roosevelt, June 19, 1939, Roosevelt Papers.
[4] Franklin D. Roosevelt to Robert Jackson, October 22, 1937, Roosevelt Papers.
[5] The text of Roosevelt's address is in Samuel I. Rosenman (ed.), *The Public Papers and Addresses of Franklin D. Roosevelt: The Continuing Struggle for Liberalism, 1938* (New York, 1941), pp. 305–320.

ment Administration and as trial examiner with the Securities and Exchange Commission. Further, he was a confidant of many New Dealers such as Robert Jackson, Benjamin Cohen, and Thomas Corcoran. The general public knew him as the highly successful author of two disturbing works, *The Folklore of Capitalism* and *The Symbols of Government.*[6]

A main thesis of this essay is that soon after Thurman Arnold arrived in Washington, a folklore developed around his public image — a folklore which clouded Arnold's aims as interpreted by his contemporaries and has yet to be dispelled by historians. In sum, there has been a failure to understand what Arnold was attempting to accomplish in the field of antitrust enforcement. While many of his objectives have been treated superficially it is the distortion of his aims which requires explanation.

First of all, there was the unusual Arnold personality. Alsop and Kinter in one of the more memorable sketches of Arnold describe him thus:[7]

> Thurman Wesley Arnold is a large, somewhat paunchy, middle-aged man with a yellowish face and overflowing human gusto, who looks like a small-town storekeeper and talks like a native of Rabelais. He enjoys the distinction of being the only New Dealer who is also an Elk, and very likely the only Elk who is also an iconoclast.

Arnold was always good journalistic copy, whether he was lecturing to his Yale classes or expounding a witticism at one of Washington's innumerable social affairs. That Arnold was eminently quotable, as well as an excellent subject for anecdotes, did little to ensure accurate assessment of his philosophy and role as a government administrator.

As an author, the Yale professor was viewed as an iconoclast. Iconoclasts and suspicion have a habit of being part of the same syllogism. Senator William Borah, in the hearing conducted on Arnold's nomination for Assistant Attorney General, announced that he was convinced, after reading *The Folklore of Capitalism*, that Arnold did not have "any faith in the antitrust laws." While admittedly this may have been more a reflection on Borah than Arnold, the senator from Idaho was not alone in misreading Arnold's books. Arnold's early works, interwoven with a plethora of allegories and analogies, frequently puzzled readers. Reviewers were prone to find a variety of theses, many of which were seemingly never intended by the author.

If Arnold's literary work led to confusion, certainly his enforcement of the antitrust laws did not clarify his public image. Just when big business was convinced of his unquenchable hostility, Arnold launched a massive suit against labor unions with the same intensity that he demonstrated in his direction of the proceedings against the petroleum industry. In spite of Arnold's repeated assurances — that he was not opposing big business because of

[6] Thurman W. Arnold, *The Folklore of Capitalism* (New Haven, 1937), *The Symbols of Government* (New Haven, 1935).

[7] Joseph Alsop and Robert D. Kinter, "Trust Buster — the Folklore of Thurman Arnold," *Saturday Evening Post*, vol. CCXII (August 12, 1939), p. 5.

size *per se,* but only attacking monopolistic tendencies — business leaders in general remained aloof, skeptical, and uncomprehending.

Another element which obscured the true proportions of the antitrust picture for outside observers was the divided counsels in the administration. In response to press queries, Arnold made several pronouncements that the administration was unified in its antitrust approach. Nevertheless, seeds of dissent sown by a few remnants of the old believers in NRA, still played upon Roosevelt's latent faith in the trade-association philosophy. In April, 1938, Donald Richberg, during one of the moments he was in temporary favor, wrote Roosevelt: [8]

> The philosophy of the NRA was wholly consistent with the New Deal. The philosophy of the fanatic trust busters, their hostility to all large enterprise, their assumption that co-operation is always a cloak for monopolistic conspiracy, this philosophy is wholly inconsistent with the New Deal.

Three months after Richberg wrote Roosevelt that the antitrust program was the antithesis of the NRA, the *United States News* carried a column refining the position outlined by Richberg. The antitrust philosophy was not diametrically opposed to the NRA, according to the *News,* it was the NRA in reverse: [9]

> President Roosevelt, reversing the tactics of earlier years, now is turning loose the Department of Justice in a quest for industrial recovery.
>
> The Department's quest consists of searching for what it determines to be criminal practices on the part of business men. The attack on these practices — the White House is convinced — will improve the chance for achieving prosperity through the program of spending that is about to be started.
>
> All of this is in sharp contrast to the procedure followed in 1933. At that time business men were encouraged to forget the nation's 45-year-old antitrust laws and to get together to plan their operations through consultation.

Besides the opposition Arnold inevitably met within the government bureaucracy, his definition of the role he should play as an enforcer of antitrust laws confused even some of his close associates. They were apparently imbued with the belief that he proposed to remake the structure of American industry in conformity with some economist's competitive model. Arnold, however, insisted both in *The Folklore of Capitalism* and in public utterances that he was a diagnostician of institutional decay and not an economic practitioner. Arnold had an innate skepticism of "preachers" with manufactured economic panaceas.

While Arnold was more than a legal and economic technician he definitely was against using his influence in a legislative capacity. His function, as he saw it, was to enforce and recommend corrective measures. Whether his im-

---

[8] Donald R. Richberg to Franklin D. Roosevelt, April 23, 1938, Roosevelt Papers.

[9] *United States News,* June 6, 1938; Professor Freidel concludes that the antitrust program was more of a negative NRA than it was in direct disagreement. *America in the Twentieth Century* (New York, 1960), pp. 348–49.

mediate success in antitrust suits would have been greater had he followed more of a policy-making role is a moot question; that his influence on New Deal economic policy might have been greater is another matter.

While associates, fellow bureaucrats, and the general public may have been hazy on the specific outlines of the Arnold antitrust policy, the Assistant Attorney General had a well-defined conceptual framework of what he desired to accomplish. Writing to Charles Seymour, President of Yale, on July 4, 1939, Arnold stated that he was not interested in "trust busting for the sake of trust busting"; quite the contrary, he intended to give the Antitrust Division a constructive purpose. The creation of a positive antitrust program had three facets, according to Arnold: (1) a statement of a uniform well-publicized policy was essential; (2) the building up of an effective antitrust organization; and (3) "the elimination of partisan politics from the Division was desired." "I have refused to make a single political speech during my term of office, or to become identified with any exclusively New Deal group." [10]

During his first year in office Arnold made amazing progress in maneuvering to accomplish these goals. He quickly admitted to one and all that the Sherman Act was an imperfect tool at best, but that he was convinced that the "sole weakness of the enforcement of the Sherman Act in the past has been the lack of an enforcement organization." [11] Revision of the law was not the answer, Arnold maintained, but more funds for personnel in the Antitrust Division were essential. In the first two years, his sizeable budget requests received generous congressional support.

In effect, admitting the inadequacy of his organizational analysis of the enforcement problem, Arnold also blamed the general climate of opinion which historically had regarded the antitrust laws as a moral and emotional problem rather than one deserving of economic significance. It was this ignorance of the economic ramifications of the antitrust laws which particularly piqued the head of the Antitrust Division.

The social aspects of the antitrust policy, the remnants of the Progressive attitude toward trusts incorporating moralistic and ethical considerations, annoyed the Arnold of 1937. He believed that these were attitudes outmoded by the complex industrial system of the twentieth century; the United States could no longer afford to be a nation of economic illiterates. Arnold's good friend, H. L. Mencken, perhaps in silent sympathy with Arnold's reasoning, thought this analysis far too sophisticated. For Mencken the solution to the antitrust problem was characteristically simple and clear: the men who wrote the Sherman Act made just one mistake — they forgot to provide for capital punishment.

Accepting the Sherman Act as a workable one, Arnold formulated a pro-

---

[10] Thurman, Arnold to Charles Seymour, July 4, 1939, Arnold Papers.

[11] "Free Trade Within the Borders of the United States," Address before the South Carolina Bar Association, Columbia, April 11, 1940, unpublished manuscript, Arnold Papers.

cedure for handling antitrust cases. Utilizing the machinery which had long been available for enforcement he undertook two courses. First, he revived use of the consent decree which involved the dropping of indictments in return for the adoption of basic remedial practices by the industry in question, and second, he stepped up criminal prosecution. Arnold contended that the consent decree as employed in previous years, was nothing more than a subterfuge. Historically, the government had used the consent decree to accomplish the objective of litigation without going through a lengthy court proceeding. Having secured evidence of an antitrust violation, the government would give the potential defendant an opportunity to make a private compact, whereby, in return for the government's dropping a criminal indictment, the subject of the action would promise not to commit specific violations in the future. Arnold deemed this use of the consent decree "absurd." Instead, Arnold developed a new approach to the consent decree more properly termed a civil decree. In the future no prosecution would be dismissed categorically on the basis of announced good intentions. Instead, Arnold advanced a plan whereby the defendant would present, as formerly, a plan to the court, but this scheme now must incorporate not only sufficient redress of the indictment but, more importantly, offer genuine reorganization on a company or industry-wide basis which would be more beneficial to the general public than would the results of a criminal prosecution.

A crucial technique in this application of a civil decree was that all proceedings must be public, thereby providing the consumers, public commissioners, or competitors an opportunity to object. As Arnold wrote, this utilization of the civil decree offered in substance, "a reward to the businessmen who really desire to clean up their industry and to prevent a situation arising in the future which would lead to a violation of the law." [12] Modified consent decrees of this type were used with success in the gas, automobile, typewriter, and container industries.

Although the consent decree, as conceived by Arnold, was a novel contribution to the over-all flexibility of the antitrust laws, it was in the regular enforcement of the antitrust laws that Arnold devised his most concrete and permanent contribution to antitrust enforcement. In the preceding forty years, the Justice Department had launched mercurial attacks on industrial giants, with some degree of success but without accomplishing the eradication of violations in the entire industry. Arnold saw the crux of the monopolizing power in the system of distribution. Speaking to the Advertising Federation of America in Detroit, Arnold noted the adverse effects of the power of producers over distribution. "Incredible as it may seem, in order to keep prices up, industry is choking off its own avenues of distribution, decreasing employment and widening the disparity of prices." [13] The solution prescribed

---

[12] "Statement of Thurman W. Arnold before the Temporary National Economic Committee," Washington, D. C., July 7, 1939, p. 20.

[13] "What is Monopoly?" Address before the Advertising Federation of America, Detroit, June 15, 1938, unpublished manuscript, Arnold Papers.

was a comprehensive prosecution at the distribution level in an attempt to remove the artificial "roadblocks." Joseph Alsop and Robert Kinter described the Arnold attack on distribution as one of "hit hard, hit everyone and hit them all at once." [14]

There just was no over-all magic potion which could be administered in one massive dose by the Justice Department to the industrial economy. The most rewarding prosecution formula promised to be the case-by-case indictment. Arnold logically contended that restraints of trade in the movie industry would have little relevance to restraints in the steel industry, while artificial "tolls" in the milk industry in Detroit would differ often from the abuses in the same industry in Chicago. The basic requirement was a pliable policy molded to the necessities of the individual prosecution. Arnold's imaginative ability at selecting prototype cases and administering the antitrust laws in a kaleidoscopic fashion, instead of being bound by inflexible precedents, was one of his most brilliant achievements.

A practical task of undertaking a case-by-case approach was the necessity of a huge legal staff. Arnold was able during the first two years to obtain sufficient appropriations to increase the number of lawyers in the Antitrust Division from 48 to over 300. Congressional approval of the antitrust program was in large measure due to the tremendous publicity resulting from the indictments — plus Arnold's unabashed demonstration that for every dollar appropriated to his Division, two or three dollars flowed into the Treasury in fines received from indicted defendants.

The widespread publicity buttressed Arnold's program in a variety of ways, not only by stimulating consumer pressure on congressional delegations for increased appropriations, but as a powerful catharsis on industry in general. Arnold saw nothing surprising about the fact that often a successful suit in one sector of business resulted in lower prices in other sectors. In an article in the *New Republic*, he wrote: [15]

> We do not think there is anything mysterious about our results. An antitrust proceeding suddenly confronts the members of an industry with an appraisal of the industry's performance from the point of view of the public interest. It is sharp enough to shock, to induce self-questioning; and there is no reason for surprise that business men with public spirit and imagination sometimes alter their pricing policies as a result of such examination.

The very scope of the Justice Department's suits was justification enough for such business reactions.

Within three years the Antitrust Division had sought indictments in the movie, construction, tire, fertilizer, newspaper, tobacco, shoe, and petroleum industries, not to mention suits against trade unions, the American Medical

---

[14] Joseph Alsop and Robert D. Kinter, "Trust Buster — The Folklore of Thurman Arnold," *Saturday Evening Post*, vol. CCXII (August 12, 1939), p. 7.

[15] "National Defense and Restraints of Trade," manuscript draft of an article in *New Republic*, May 19, 1941, Arnold Papers.

Association and various agricultural marketing agencies. In all, Arnold and his colleagues instigated 215 investigations and brought 93 suits.

Concurrently with the antitrust campaign, a broad congressional inquiry had been launched concerning the character and extent of economic concentration in America. The idea for the Temporary National Economic Committee germinated in the recession of 1937 but originated directly from President Roosevelt's famous April 29, 1938, message to Congress on monopoly. The President's message ended with the frequently quoted phrase, "idle factories and idle workers profit no man." This expression set the tone of the TNEC probe; the Committee was assigned the implied task of uncovering the causes of the depression. Leon Henderson, on the staff of the TNEC, offered a more precise definition of the Committee's goals in a memorandum to Roosevelt on September 3, 1939. "The committee plans to outline, in detail, the facts about control in finance, insurance, industry, natural resources — the methods and devices of control — instances of abuses, and to recommend proper legislation." [16]

The TNEC hearings began on December 1, 1938, and lasted until March 11, 1941. The testimony of 552 witnesses filled thirty-seven impressive volumes; the various economic studies by the TNEC staff were collected in another forty-three volumes. As in other investigations of this type, the recommendations were feeble indeed in relation to the comprehensiveness of the inquiry. The main prescription, which had been pointed to from the beginning of the hearings, was the necessity of a vigorous and militant enforcement of the antitrust laws. This was an anti-climactic conclusion for over two years of questioning and cross-examination. Yet there was a significant by-product of the hearings in that American economic strengths and weaknesses were widely publicized. As David Lynch has pointed out, at least the Committee brought up-to-date our knowledge of competitive practices.

Arnold's relationship to the TNEC investigation provides a revealing insight into his conception of antitrust enforcement. As a member of the Committee, Arnold was deeply involved in the hearings, provided his Division's assistance for specialized studies, presented memoranda to the Attorney General and the President on the direction that the investigation should take, and testified on antitrust procedures and practices before the Committee. Nevertheless, while Arnold sympathized with the TNEC objectives, there was a dichotomy between his personal relationship to the Committee and that of the Antitrust Division.

Arnold, understandably, gave most of his time and energy to the task of antitrust enforcement. The TNEC probe, on the other hand, was a committee appointed by Congress and aimed at revision of the antitrust laws. Arnold, of course, desired a more effective statutory basis for antitrust, yet officially he restricted his primary attention to the enforcement, not the development of this legislative structure. While he could have taken a more active

[16] Leon Henderson to Franklin D. Roosevelt, September 3, 1939, Roosevelt Papers.

role in the TNEC query at the policy-making level, it is difficult to see how he could have chosen any other interpretation of his duties as Assistant Attorney General.

A more practical consideration which limited his relationship with the TNEC hearings was simply the lack of time. The rapid expansion of the Antitrust Division plus Arnold's numerous speech-making forays, designed to outline his antitrust views in detail across the country, left few hours for any other enterprise, including TNEC.

Just as Arnold's program was producing dramatic results, he was effectively undermined. Support was withdrawn by the administration for his increased budget requests of 1941 and again in 1942. In three short years the Antitrust Division had been remarkably successful, in fact, too successful perhaps for its own perpetuation. One does not have to ferret the subsurface motives for the administration's severely diminished enthusiasm for the antitrust program. The most crucial and obvious explanation was the war in Europe. As early as July 6, 1940, Arnold was cognizant of the political and economic pressures which would utilize the war as a lever to impede antitrusts suits. In a letter to a Scripps-Howard columnist, Arnold succinctly stated his position: [17]

> If some combination is imperative to the interest of national defense, it is a reasonable combination which requires no waiver of the law to get this result, fine. However, I fail to see any possibility of the things we are now prosecuting standing the test.

Arnold concluded his letter by noting that the President was in agreement with this statement.

By the fall of 1940, Arnold was not as sanguine regarding the administration's attitude. It became increasingly clear that attack on monopoly was being given a holiday. Attorney General Francis Biddle made a mild protest over the suspension of the antitrust program in the spring of 1942, which was promptly lost in the noise of creating an arsenal of democracy. Arnold for his part became quite vocal on the relaxation of antitrust enforcement. In the Baxter Memorial Lectures delivered at the University of Omaha in 1942, he presented the case for wartime surveillance of monopoly. Because of cartel tendencies inherent in any national emergency, Arnold argued that antitrust prosecution should be increased not abated.

Three years after the war terminated, Arnold was still bitter about being forsaken by the President. Writing on the subject, "Must 1929 Repeat Itself?" Arnold commented: [18]

> . . . F. D. R. recognizing that he could have only one war at a time, was content to declare a truce in the fight against monopoly. He was to have his foreign war; monopoly was to give him patriotic support — on its own terms.
>
> And so more than 90% of all war contracts went to a handful of giant em-

[17] Thurman Arnold to John T. Flynn, July 6, 1940, Arnold Papers.
[18] Thurman Arnold, "Must 1929 Repeat Itself?" *Harvard Business Review*, vol. XXVI (January, 1948), p. 43.

pires, many of them formerly linked by strong ties with the corporations of the Reich. The big fellows got the contracts, the little fellows were dependent upon subcontracts with the big boys.

The European combat alone would have resulted in a drastic alteration of the anti-monopoly attack. Yet there were other cumulative influences which abetted the war psychosis. Arnold in his attempt at an application of the antitrust laws had made numerous enemies. Subjected to unceasing lobbying, the administration, as well as some congressmen, undoubtedly hoped some morning to find Arnold's program miraculously transformed into a mirage. Aware of these pressures, Arnold considered the best antidote was the one he had utilized many times before — publicity. But this time publicity was not enough to counteract the opposition.

Disillusioned, Arnold resigned and accepted Roosevelt's appointment as Judge of the United States Circuit Court of Appeals. *Business Week*, inter-viewing Arnold in 1949, asked,

> "Judge Arnold, although you are in private law practice now, your ideas haven't changed a great deal since you were in the Dept. of Justice?" Arnold retorted, "Well, I don't know why they should."

Although Arnold's ideas on antitrust policy may have remained stable, certainly his political beliefs during the 1940's underwent a metamorphosis. In the early 1930's, he bridged the philosophies of Justices Holmes and Brandeis. Arnold agreed with Holmes that economic concentration was not intrinsically a curse; however, he deviated from Holmes' doctrine of the totality of countervailing power. Arnold was not convinced that the public interest was adequatey safeguarded by competition of industrial giants. On the other hand, he sympathized with Brandeis as to the desirability of humanizing competition with modifications. He wrote the editor of the *Saturday Evening Post* in 1942: [19]

> When our whole thinking is dominated by a search for security, I believe that we have lost the greatest stimulus to industrial activity that exists, and that is the belief . . . the driving force of a society must be based on the preservation of opportunities to succeed or to fail. I am committed to a politics of opportunity versus a politics of security.

Arnold dissented from the Brandeis opinion that big business was an evil to be destroyed and small business a positive good to be preserved.

By the early 1940's Arnold was beginning to sound like a resurrected Western Progressive, the tinge of Wilsonianism was there, but fading. In an amazing letter to William Allen White, he summed up his philosophy: [20]

> I expect you have little realization of how you have caught the imagination of that peculiar brand of liberal who comes from the Middle West and who

[19] Thurman Arnold to Benjamin Hibbs, October 1, 1942, Arnold Papers.

[20] Thurman Arnold to William Allen White, September 9, 1943, Arnold Papers. The writer is indebted to Robert O'Neill, Harvard University, for bringing to his attention this significant letter.

believes in the simple philosophy that our institutions are fundamentally sound and, therefore, all we need to do is to attack entrenched special privileges. The economic planners are always too complicated for me. They were bound to get in power during a period of frustration when people were afraid to face a world in which they had to take a chance of failure on their own efforts. But now, in spite of all the reactionary influences, I begin to feel a new spirit rising in this country. I believe that men like Henry Kaiser, who I got to know very well in my efforts to prosecute the steel companies for preventing him from getting into production on the Pacific Coast, are going to get strong enough through this war that they cannot be stopped. If they do, liberalism in this country is going to change from faith in Government bureaucracy to the sort of thing that you have represented for so many years.

Whether the shift in Arnold's political philosophy was the result of five years of give-and-take in Washington politics, from the estrangement with the administration regarding antitrust programs, or from the fact that he was forced to assume an increasingly defensive position which terminated in an inflexible stand, it is obvious that the Arnold of 1937 was not the Arnold of 1943. By the time he donned judicial robes, Arnold was for sustaining twentieth-century industrialism, at the same time protesting strongly the loss of economic individualism — a stand which a young Hiram Johnson, of three decades past, would have applauded.

In retrospect, it appears that a folklore around Arnold often obscured his antitrust objectives. What then was Arnold's antitrust ideal? The answer is surprisingly simple: his entire antitrust program was oriented toward the benefit of the consumer. In one sentence he summed up his aim: "The idea of antitrust laws is to create a situation in which competition compels the passing on to the consumers the savings of mass distribution and production." [21] It is mystifying that Arnold's goal should have been so largely ignored by so many commentators. Perhaps its very simplicity confused those who were in search of a more sophisticated or complex motivation. On the first page of *The Bottlenecks of Business*, the purpose of the book was outlined as an exploration of how the consumer could benefit from an equitable distribution of goods. In fact, the whole book was an economic and political platform for the consumer.

The question remains: what was Arnold's motivation in raising the consumer placard? Undoubtedly he was aware of the political advantage of casting the consumer in the role of the forgotten man. Roosevelt most certainly was conscious of the political promise of an anitrust crusade. Yet Arnold was enough of a political pragmatist to know, as well as the President, that the amorphous body of consumers was a capricious political force at best, its whims frequently shaped by special interest lobbies. Furthermore, it is difficult to accuse Arnold of courting popularity; the wide-ranging indictments against industry and labor alike belie any attempt to be among the political

[21] "The War on Monopoly," Address before the Oregon Bar Association, Gearhart, Oregon, September 29, 1939, unpublished manuscript, Arnold Papers.

elect. The only clear rationale is that Arnold was sincerely convinced that proper enforcement of the antitrust laws provided the means for economic and social justice.

The political philosophy of Thurman Arnold had evolved into a composite of moralistic individualism, "politics of opportunity," and economic reform — all good tenets of the Western Progressive in pre-World War I America. ◻

❖ **71** ❖

A Note on Professor Rostow's "Take-off" into Self-sustained Economic Growth *

DOUGLASS C. NORTH

Professor Rostow has provided us with many suggestive ideas about economic growth, and his latest contribution, which attempts to isolate the "take-off" into self-sustained economic growth, is indeed an attractive notion.[1] It figured recently as part of the argument of Professor P. S. M. Blackett in his Presidential Address to the British Association in Dublin in September, 1957. The purpose of this Note is to examine the validity of Professor Rostow's thesis in the case of the United States and to assess the usefulness of the concept of "take-off" in the analysis of economic growth.

I

Professor Rostow's hypothesis may be briefly summarized as follows: He suggests that ". . . the process of economic growth can usefully be regarded as centering on a relatively brief time interval of two or three decades when the economy and the society of which it is a part transform themselves in such ways that economic growth is, subsequently, more or less automatic."[2]

This period of take-off is preceded by a lengthy period when the pre-conditions for take-off are established and a subsequent period when growth becomes automatic. Rostow distinguishes two kinds of societies; the first is one in which fundamental social, political and cultural changes are an essential part of establishing the pre-conditions of take-off, and the second is one where more narrowly economic changes initiate the take-off. Whether society is "traditional" (the first case) or "acquisitive" (the second case), take-off is usually initiated by some particularly sharp stimulus. The resultant

* From Douglass C. North, "A Note on Professor Rostow's 'Take-off' into Self-sustained Economic Growth," *Manchester School of Economics and Social Studies*, Vol. 26, January 1958, pp. 68–75. Reprinted by Kraus Reprint Limited and with permission of the author.
   [1] "The Take-off into Self-sustained Economic Growth," *The Economic Journal*, Vol. LXVI, March, 1956, pp. 25–48.
   [2] *Ibid.*, p. 25.

changes which are defined as take-off are a rise in the rate of productive investment from 5 per cent. of national income or less to 10 per cent. or more, the development of a significant manufacturing sector(s) with a rapid rate of growth, and the accompaniment of these economic changes with social, political and institutional modifications favorable to the perpetuation of this economic expansion. The rise in capital formation comes either from shifts in control over income flows or from capital imports. The leading sectors in the take-off (evidently not the same as the development of a significant manufacturing sector which was part of the definition of take-off) have been diverse ranging from textiles (England) to railroads (the United States, Germany, and Russia). In conclusion Rostow states that ". . . this hypothesis is, then, a return to a rather old-fashioned way of looking at economic development. The take-off is defined as an industrial revolution, tied directly to radical changes in methods of production, having their decisive consequence over a relatively short period of time." [3]

This hypothesis is illustrated with respect to the take-off in a number of countries. I shall confine my remarks to the case of the United States, a country which figures rather prominently in the exposition.

The ambiguities in his illustration make it difficult to come to grips with the case he presents for take-off in the United States. The period of acceleration in growth is given as the years 1843–60 which sub-divide into two periods — the 1840's, confined primarily to railroad and manufacturing development in the east, and the 1850's with rail-road expansion into the middle west (p. 31). However, in a footnote it is suggested that, if New England is considered independently, take-off would be between 1820 and 1850 (p. 45). The sharp stimulus initiating take-off is said to be capital imports (p. 29). However, this stimulus did not come until the end of the 40's (p. 29), six years after take-off was under way in the east. Also a footnote assigns an important role to the tariffs of 1828 and 1841–42 (p. 29). In addition capital imports played a critical role in increasing the rate of productive investment (pp. 31, 32, 40). The railroad was the leading sector (p. 45), although in the case of New England it was the cotton textile industry (p. 45).

Far more serious to Rostow's case is the degree to which his evidence is consistent with what we know of the American economy during the period. First, with respect to capital imports, which figure so prominently both in initiating the take-off and in the increased rate of investment, the evidence available is not consistent with Rostow's interpretation. As pointed out in the preceding paragraph (and acknowledged by Rostow) the expansion in the east in the 1840's was accomplished without any significant capital imports. In fact capital was returning to Europe during most of the decade. Clearly railroad construction in the east could be undertaken without capital imports. What Rostow does not appear to be aware of is that (1) the boom in the mid-west was well under way at the end of the 40's before any significant

[3] *Ibid.,* p. 47.

amount of capital was imported and (2) the total capital imports for the entire period 1847–60 were very modest. The expanded foreign demand for wheat in 1846–47 led to a revival in westward expansion and stimulus to extension of railroads. After a brief setback in 1848, the boom really got going in 1849. Capital imports were not significant until 1850. The following table, giving the net position of the United States with respect to merchandise trade and specie flows from 1847 to 1860, will help to illustrate both the timing and quantity of capital flows.

■ **TABLE 1 Net United States Commodity Trade and Specie Balance, 1847–1860**

(*In millions of dollars*)

1847	...	...	...	...	+12
1848	...	...	...	...	− 1
1849	...	...	...	...	− 2
1850	...	...	...	...	−26
1851	...	...	...	...	+ 2
1852	...	...	...	...	− 3
1853	...	...	...	...	−37
1854	...	...	...	...	−26
1855	...	...	...	...	+14
1856	...	...	...	...	+12
1857	...	...	...	...	+ 2
1858	...	...	...	...	+42
1859	...	...	...	...	+18
1860	...	...	...	...	+37

Source: U. S. Bureau of the Census, Historical Statistics of the United States, 1789–1945, Washington, D.C., 1949, figures are rounded off. Pp. 244–45.

It remains to see to what extent invisible items modify this picture. Unlike the last quarter of the nineteenth century when large scale capital imports and an export surplus were balanced by very substantial debit items of shipping, immigrant remittances, interest, and tourists, the 1850's were characterized by very large shipping earnings estimated by Bullock, Williams, and Tucker as a net credit of $243 million for the decade. Other credit items have been estimated as net immigrant (funds less remittances) $100 million, sale of ships, $17 million against which are debited interest, $203 million, and tourist expenses, $165 million.

While these items are rough estimates they nevertheless made clear that invisible items almost balance out during the decade. I do not mean to imply that capital imports played no part in the expansion of the 1850's. On the contrary I think that they did direct more real investment into railroads than would have otherwise taken place, and helped to finance an import surplus in 1853–54, but this is very different from saying that they set-off industrialization or were instrumental in raising the rate of investment from 5 per cent. to 10 per cent. of national income. On the latter point, it is clear that foreign capital was far more important in the expansion of the 1830's than it was in the 1850's and was certainly a greater percentage of national income. Clearly gold exports played a far more important role in the years 1848 to 1860 than capital imports and if we return to the expansion of merchandise trade as a factor enabling the American economy to finance the importation of capital goods it was obviously cotton and not grain as Rostow maintains (p. 40) which was of fundamental importance during this period.

I shall not dwell at length on the effect of the tariffs of 1828 and 1841–42 except to say that Rostow's argument conflicts with the view generally prevailing from Taussig,[4] on that they exerted no such critical stimulus. The fact that America was exporting cheap cotton textiles by 1830 and that Manchester merchants were complaining of American competition in the cotton trade of Mexico and South America as early as 1833 makes me doubtful that the 1828 tariff had much influence on the expansion of the cotton textile industry.

The railroad, according to Rostow, played a revolutionary role for three reasons. It lowered transport costs; it was essential to the development of a new and expanding export sector which became important in providing capital for internal expansion; and it induced expansion in other industries (notably coal, iron, and engineering). There certainly can be no quarrel with assigning to the railroad an important role in American expansion in the nineteenth century. However, Rostow's second reason as specifically applied to the United States in the 1850's (p. 45) is misleading if not incorrect. Cotton played the key role in the expansion of American exports up to the Civil War and its expansion was accomplished with little aid from railroads. Wheat and flour, which presumably Rostow had in mind, accounted for only 13 per cent. of American exports in the years 1846–50, 10 per cent. from 1850–55, and 11 per cent. from 1856–60. Moreover, the five-year interval during which wheat made up the greatest percentage of the value of exports, 1846–50, was before the great extension of railroads into the mid-west.

My last point is to suggest a need for clarification. Rostow says that New England's take-off began in 1820, twenty-three years before the economy as a whole experienced a similar phenomenon. While it is certainly evident in American development that regions experienced varying rates of growth, it would seem from the very chain reaction implicit in Rostow's concept that this should imply take-off for the economy as a whole. I am sure that Rostow does not mean to imply that the whole economy must industrialize since this was clearly untrue of either the south or the west during his period of take-off for the U.S. as a whole. We are still left uncertain about the relationship between regional industrialization and the expansion of the economy as a whole.

We now turn to the usefulness and general applicability of the concept. As I indicated above, the idea of isolating a take-off period is an attractive notion and I should be happy to see such a concept cleared of the difficulties

---

[4] F. W. Taussig, *The Tariff History of the United States* (New York: G. P. Putnam and Sons, 8th ed.. 1931), Ch. III and pp. 57, 128–38.

discussed in the preceding section. But such a conceptual framework involves implications about the nature of economic growth which at this stage
of our knowledge are highly questionable, of doubtful general applicability,
and therefore liable to lead subsequent investigation astray. I shall confine
myself to two implications of such a conceptual framework, the transition
from pre-take-off to take-off (to use Rostow's suggested terminology, p. 31) in
"acquisitive" type economies, and the nature of the acceleration which may
take place.

As Rostow points out, the idea of a succession of stages is a return to an
old-fashioned framework in which industrialization occurs only after a set of
preconditions have been achieved. The barriers in traditional underdeveloped
countries are social, political, and cultural as well as economic, but in acquisitive cultures ". . . take-off fails to occur mainly because the comparative advantage of exploiting productive land and other natural resources delays the
time when self re-enforcing industrial growth can profitably take place." [5]

In a footnote to this quotation, Rostow admits the possibility of a very
different sort of development where agricultural innovations may counter diminishing returns and where increased agricultural productivity will lead on
to self re-enforcing industrial growth. However, this argument need not be
confined to increases in agricultural productivity. It applies to the exploitation of new land and resources in the "empty" countries of the nineteenth
century. The expansion of the New England cotton textile industry, as Rostow points out, came from expanding demand without the region. An important part of this increasing demand came from the south which was expe-
riencing rapid expansion with the development of cotton, and from the west
whose population and income were growing with the export out of the area
of wheat, corn, and livestock products. Furthermore, it was the rich land and
primary production of the west which made the railroad boom of the 1850's
feasible. In short, one could advance a hypothesis which is the reverse of
Rostow's, namely, that the opening up and development of new areas capable of producing primary goods in demand in existing markets induced the
growth of industrialization.

It is doubtful whether the diverse paths by which economies may expand
and/or industrialize can be encompassed into any framework of universal applicability, at least in the present state of knowledge. We need to discover a
good deal more about the complex phenomena which lead to rapid growth,
and, strangely enough, our knowledge is least satisfactory about countries
which have experienced most rapid development, as Rostow's illustrative mate
rial gives abundant evidence (albeit inadvertently).

There is also reason to doubt the universal applicability of a rapid acceleration in economic growth characterized by an abrupt expansion in the rate of
investment. This may have happened in some countries, but it is likely that
in others an increased rate of expansion took place rather gradually. The pos-

[5] Rostow, *op. cit.*, p. 28.

sibility of long swings in the rate of growth and investment may make the evidence adduced for rapid take-off indeed illusory. Certainly international migration, which does not figure at all in Rostow's framework, seems to have behaved in this fashion. So did many other series of obvious importance in economic growth. In the United States, for example, the rate of expansion in a period of rapid growth like the 1830's was not markedly different from that of Rostow's take-off period in the 1850's. It is also doubtful whether investment as a proportion of net national product jumped from 5 per cent. to 10 per cent. (or any other such abrupt change) as between the two periods. I do not deny that the rate of growth and investment may have been increasing as between the two periods, but not in the discontinuous fashion that Rostow's hypothesis implies. There appear to be many possible combinations in the timing and pace of accelerated growth and industrialization, of which Rostow's example of take-off within a space of two or three decades is but one variation. ◻

❖ 72 ❖

Eight Tycoons: the Entrepreneur and American History *

J. R. T. HUGHES

It is customary in certain circles to preface a methodological essay with apologies. Mine are offered, even though I will put some factual flesh on my methodological bones as we go along and thus hope to lighten the offense to good taste. But it seems to me that now is an opportune time to look into certain basic methodological problems of Entrepreneurial History. The journal, *Explorations in Entrepreneurial History*, has been resurrected, and new interest seems to be building up in the use of the entrepreneur as a vehicle for the study and comprehension of American economic history and of economic development generally. It is to this view of the uses of Entrepreneurial History that I shall address my remarks.

I

Doubtless, the main difficulty in the study and writing of Entrepreneurial History is the choice of an appropriate frame of reference within which study is to be conducted. The social geography of the entrepreneurial domain, as it stands at any moment, is primarily a map of social artifacts, a map of the results of past actions. And there are, and have been, an enormous number of entrepreneurs involved in the creation of those artifacts. How does one decide who is worth studying? Some of the most successful business and in-

* J. R. T. Hughes, "Eight Tycoons: The Entrepreneur and American History," *Explorations in Entrepreneurial History*, Research Center in Entrepreneurial History, Harvard University Press, Vol. 1, No. 3, Spring/Summer, 1964, pp. 213–23. Used by permission.

dustrial leaders led uninspiring careers, and some of the most dramatic and original leaders in entrepreneurial activity have been relatively unsuccessful. The situation is reminiscent of the statement of the Victorian scholar, Arnold Toynbee, who argued that the roll of English landholding was scarcely susceptible to pure economic analysis.[1] It was the singular product of centuries of intrigue, violence, political favoritism, accidents of birth and economic upheaval held tightly within the grip of primogeniture and entail. It was a history of individual cases, the landscape at any moment being inhabited by survivors of a process that was anarchistic from the point of view of vigorous economic analysis.

Can Entrepreneurial History do better than this? On what general grounds do certain entrepreneurial achievements emerge from the whole universe of them and come into the historian's focus? Surely we can do better than merely measure entrepreneurial achievement by the index of lifetime net dollar earnings. In the long pull of the nation's life many financial failures had important effects. I would argue, in fact, given the record of successes, the failures are important information; William Penn's colony (a loss to him) and Edison's electric light company (he claimed to have lost money on it) are cases in point.

If failures are important, then one indicator of appropriate subjects of study in the whole entrepreneurial galaxy is not too useful, and that, of course, is price theory. It does not inform the scholar much in a general way if profits are negative and the index of efficiency is successful, non-negative, profit maximization. And, moreover, *all* failures were not important; failure, no more than financial success, illuminates the contributions of the entrepreneur to the nation's economic development. There must be some more meaningful frame of reference. Aggregative economic theory also is not too useful initially, as it tends to blot out the achievements of individuals. Even if the individual contributions could be measured on a current basis, the larger contributions at any moment of time are not necessarily the most fruitful in the long run; sailing ships were making greater contributions than the steamships in the "transportation sector" in the early 1850's, but the smallness of the steam sector is misleading as an indicator of the growth path. Steam, after all, was the wave of the future, however diminutive and unprofitable were the activities of the entrepreneurs launching that innovation.

The standard gauges of the importance of the industry in question are of course useful, except that the focus is again upon success alone, and, as I said before, failures can be important information about the direction of the nation's growth. Here I am thinking, for example, of the canals in the antebellum period, or perhaps railroads today. In such cases it can be argued that the record of failures in entrepreneurial activity can be as informative of the nation's economic growth pattern over time as is the customary catalogue of

---

[1] *The Industrial Revolution* (Boston), 1956, pp. 2–3 and Chapter V.

entrepreneurial triumph. For example, I think that Henry Villard's failures with the Northern Pacific tell us a great deal about which of James J. Hill's methods were crucial in the success of the Great Northern.

The problem of the appropriate "unit of history" in entrepreneurial studies is so inordinately complex and difficult primarily because it encompasses two sets of historical information: (1) economic criteria, such as markets and technology, and (2) personalities. Each set of information has members in common with the other, and each would be difficult to comprehend in isolation. The two kinds of information taken together condemn the student of entrepreneurial activity to the life of the proverbial "lion-taming snake charmer." The fine old notion that one need merely find and study "forces of history" is muddled by the undoubted influence of personality; and the *simpliste* grandeur of Carlylian hero is subverted by the need of each hero to deal with a complex economic world in order to come into the historian's focus at all. Each entrepreneur in history faced the others, and none acted except in response to the others, all of whom employed skills and techniques determined by the "market" and by the "state of the arts." I think this is a sufficient statement of the problem to underscore the unhappy fact that realistic entrepreneurial history cannot be a simple enterprise.

I do not mean to present a cry of despair, or a blueprint for historiographical anarchy in which each man is a "thing in himself." But I do not think that some careful methodological thinking is warranted by the difficulties of the problem.

II

If "economic theory" is not a sufficient guide, and if I consider financial success by itself to be an excessively facile and superficial approach, what alternatives are open? I think there are many alternatives, and they constitute a problem of simple taxonomy — a problem, initially, of basic classification.

The efforts of men in economic life can be classified according to the nature of their historical achievements in their economic environments. The environment needs to be defined, and this can be done by sub-dividing the whole entrepreneurial domain on a functional basis. We ask ourselves not "how much money did they make," but rather, "how, and in what circumstances, did they make, or lose, their money?" Each student of entrepreneurial activity is not only considering men, but the whole ecological world of the men in question. Whether it be on a micro or macro level, both the selection of men and the "interesting" actions of these men are determined by our notions of what facts were important ones in the relevant historical segment we are considering. The facts, as always in historical studies, are illumined by bias, preference, theory or what have you. Enough ink has been spilled on this last issue to render nugatory any fresh remarks I might have to make. But a rigorous application of this method to the economic history which is the ecology of any entrepreneur provides some bench marks for study. After that, theory and ingenuity inform the student in his analyses of individual entrepreneurial actions.

III

I would like to illustrate the usefulness of this taxonomic approach by out-lining a somewhat grandiose but simple scheme wherein the biographies of eight entrepreneurial figures were used to illuminate some broad channels of American economic development. Here I am using the entrepreneur as my vehicle to study American economic development, which is my main interest. I could have chosen any number of historical figures for this purpose, but I selected eight well-known figures for purposes of simplicity. It is my conten-tion that an explicit ordering of these men on the basis of their functional contributions throws a bright and different light upon our history. The ini-tial question I asked was simple "What goes on in economic life, at any time, in the broadest sense?" Out of the infinity of possible answers I constructed an inclusive five part "stage system" in which the stages are functional. Events flow through the stages, but the stages are the framework of analysis, and they do the job of selection of "facts." Time is passive, to be used as suits the analysis. This arbitrary stage system is thus a functional, and not a chronological one. Nations do not pass through these stages in sequence; economic life is enmeshed in these functional stages constantly, simultane-ously.

My justification for this approach is a simple one. *Men*, after all, make "history," not changes in rates of capital formation, or other quantitative of qualitative measures of change. One needs a method of analyzing men them-selves, *their* contributions to some general aspect of development form the important set of questions.

The American economy is the deliberate product of the sum of individual human actions. I think it is vital for the entrepreneurial historian to be most explicit about this. Otherwise, why bother with individual enterpre-neurs at all?

The five simultaneous "stages of history," or, if you prefer, "conceptual cat-egories," are: (1) idealism, (2) invention, (3) innovation, (4) organization, and (5) stagnation and decline. Allow me to explain these categories for a moment.

1. It is clear that every identifiable economic product or sustained activity represents some vested interest, weak or powerful, that will likely oppose change, since change implies that other products or activities will be pro-duced. Competition will thus exist to confront virtually any new idea, even ideas of a wholly abstruse nature. To overcome resistance to change, then, is almost by necessity to fly in the face of some "convention." To press ideas against existing reality in the face of argument, and perhaps threat, is to be idealistic or fanatical (I'm not sure there is really any difference). A vast and

largely unplumbed region of American economic life and history is the role of systematic idealism about such non-economic matters as religion and social organization in provoking change. The wholly recondite can be, and has been, burning reality to men who built empires, but whose metaphysics could not be comprehended by mere reason.

2. Invention must supply the wares of economic change. Viable growth in a nation usually depends upon some self-generating inventive activity, even if there is a great deal of borrowing from others. Inventors are mainly creatures of the "state of the arts." [2] But invention also advances the arts, and economic change crucially depends at any time upon the flow of invention that changes the technology and produces a new range of choice to the seller or user of economic products.

3. As Schumpeter emphasized, the man who changes the stream of the allocation of resources over time by introducing new departures into the flow of economic life is not necessarily an inventor of anything. He is an innovator, and plays a vital role in the economy. Andrew Carnegie, for example, invented nothing in the technology of the steel industry, and is credited with the remark "Pioneering don't pay." What he meant by "pioneering" was activity in which the probability of failure seemed to him to be high. Yet he was a real pioneer in the steel industry and his pioneering paid off in astronomical figures. He was an innovator *par excellence*, and American history has many like him.

4. A significant feature, in many ways a singular feature in American economic life, is the presence of great size of enterprises at crucial junctures in manufacturing, communications and transportation. In many cases access to internal economies of scale meant that the nation's pool of wealth and the flow of current savings had to be tapped through capital markets. To organize and tap capital and money markets some men had to develop the means of reconciling the demand for resources and available supplies of those resources on a massive scale. In any nation there is a pool of wealth and a flow of savings. But it may take organizational genius to effect even the simplest markets for securities and transfer buying power from savers to users of resources, especially where the individual sources of wealth and savings are widely dispersed.

5. Finally, as Simon Kuznets and A. F. Burns [3] demonstrated more than three decades ago, the history of separate firms and industries shows that their rate of growth tends to slow down, and, moreover, that they tend to stagnate and decline once the retardation has advanced. Because of the power of ideas and technology in individual cases these stagnating tendencies do not neces-

---

[2] A singular little essay on the general question of inventiveness (in this case, architecture), its technical antecedents, and the influence of contemporary environment, is: Aldous Huxley, "Faith, Taste, and History," *Encounter*, Feb., 1954.

[3] Simon Kuznets, "The Retardation of Industrial Growth," reprinted in *Economic Change* (London, 1954); A. F. Burns, *Production Trends in the United States* (New York, 1934).

sarily find expression in aggregative measures of growth; youth replaces age in economic life. Bureaucracy presides over retardation and decline. But, bureaucracy performs useful and necessary functions. After all, someone needs to replace the burnt out light bulbs at the River Rouge, but the job hardly requires a Henry Ford. In fact, one wonders how an enterpreneurial historian would approach the problem of the role of bureaucracy. I haven't tried, but someone should. I'm certain that many tired economic activities have had their Robert McNamaras. The post-1945 history of the Ford Motor Company shows clearly enough that the arts of management contain certain powers of corporate rejuvenation.

IV

I would not like to put some flesh on this framework. It follows that if I really think that these arbitrary categories can be sufficiently bent and twisted to cover, roughly, all facets of economic activity, the whole history of the American economy could be squeezed within this framework. Moreover, because I am using actual entrepreneurial action as the basis for constructing the history, and those entrepreneurial actions are chosen by my framework, I ought to be able to provide a new and more meaningful interpretation of both sides of my problem, the history itself and the contributions of the men in question. If these categories form an operational taxonomy of the main species, who are the fishes that reflect the wealth of individuals in the entrepreneurial ocean? Remember that I have defined "species" arbitrarily to include only a minimal number. Instead of selecting a large number of historical figures suggested by this framework, I have kept the number of individuals to a minimum, deliberately choosing men in these categories whose functional contributions cover the main part of the historical canvas, the economic growth of the United States. To gain the advantages of contrast and comparison, I have chosen my men in pairs. As I said earlier, the "stage" of stagnation and decline was not treated in this way since it is growth that presently concerns me.

The way our individuals operated within their environments illustrates the importance of personality in the shaping of actions. The framework within which the men operated explains, given the personalities, why each contribution came in the form it did. It is important to recall that the men acted upon each other, and the whole environment at any time contained men acting in all categories. One of my men, John Pierpont Morgan, acted partly as a lover of order (mathematics) with the rules of an ancient art (finance) to change a world of vigorous activity created by men of elemental and sometimes undisciplined force. His achievements reflected largely the power of technique systematically applied to a hostile world. Another of my men, Andrew Carnegie, had Morgan in his environment. After he went into steel, Carnegie gave up his activities as a seller of securities, and even became highly and socially contemptuous of bankers and " finance." Morgan I count as an organizer, and Carnegie as innovator. They lived in the same waters and made common cause just as the whale and the shark both contribute to ecological balance in the ocean. To simply lump the two together as "entrepreneurs" is to miss the crucial parts of the mosaic; all "big business" is not the same, and entrepreneurial activity is not a set with a single member.

My choice of men in my problem are as follows:

1. Idealists: William Penn and Brigham Young
2. Inventors: Eli Whitney and Thomas Edison
3. Innovators: Andrew Carnegie and Henry Ford
4. Organizers: Edward Harriman and Pierpont Morgan

In the first category the choice of men was easy enough. Given the supply of manpower, America required two things initially, a viable and developable institutional system and the land itself. Our institutions are largely descendants of the upheavals of seventeenth-century England, and in fact, largely the outgrowth of the Charter of Liberties and Frame of Government of Penn's colony. The selection of basically democratic institutions from the chaos of seventeenth-century English autarchy was the gift of history, and was due in large part to Penn's single-minded, perhaps even simple-minded, devotion to a set of religious beliefs which brought death, maiming, imprisonment and banishment to thousands. Much of the Leveller doctrine had permeated the Quakers, and Penn's thinking. It was Penn's largely egalitarian democracy (allowed to operate within a private fief), and not the bigotry of the New England theocracy that found expression in the basic American documents, and finds a home today in typical American organizational structures, economic as well as political. Penn's decisions were a product of a fanatical adherence to a system of theology. This country scarcely knows a more profound entrepreneurial contribution to its development. As a business venture Pennsylvania was a disaster to Penn, but it was a great legacy to future generations.

From the time of the first settlement the taking of the Continent engaged all sorts of people. But from Plymouth onwards, systematic idealization of thought — national, religious, racial, economic and political — and mixtures of all played critical roles. At the end of the trail, in the mountain deserts of the West were Brigham Young and the Mormons. They were not only acting out the closing of the American geographical frontier, but were themselves a kind of distillation of several main strains of American utopianism. The New England village, the Puritan millenialism, the social experimentation of Oneida, Brook Farm, New Harmony and a hundred other frontier settlements, and the movement of the physical frontier across the middle west into the acquisitions of the Mexican War. Young's radical pragmatism, mixed with self-effacing devotion to his singular religious principles were a reflection of a main stream of American life of the ante-bellum period, which was permanently deflected after the 1840's. Young's successes as well as his failures were partly the results of his personality, partly the outcome of the movement he represented, and partly were compromises with an alien environment. He represented a multitude of individuals whose lives were fulfilled on the American frontier. In the cases of both Penn and Young the contribution of the individual to the historical outcome was striking, yet their environment was "given" by the actions of others. Adherents to systematic idealism today make the same sorts of impacts on the flow of events, even though, in our time, the idealism is not so likely to be a religious one.

2. Through the life of Eli Whitney (and others like him in his time) ran two fundamental threads of American development: the rise of the antebellum South with its slave economy, and the nascent industrial and commercial power of the North. Whitney contributed to both developments, as did scores of other men who converted the "state of the arts" to American needs. Whitney's early career, from the cotton gin, financed by expropriated British crown property, through his weary negotiations and battles over his government musket contracts, was deeply concerned with the growth of governmental power and methods in the new nation. The proliferation of invention from his hands and those of his colleagues in the armament field, into a broader spectrum of industrial uses mirrored a remarkable chapter of American industrial history.

Edison's career, on the other hand, was not importantly connected to government, but straddled a more complex technological world developed primarily in the private sector after the Civil War. The vast new world of electricity and chemistry went from crude beginnings to a powerful adolescence in the lifetime of Edison, and he participated in the new technology at its beginnings. Edison dealt with most of the great inventors of this crucial time in American history on terms that ranged from open patent infringements (the telephone) to the more subtle oligopolistic jostling of the old motion picture cartel.

The study of Edison's role as an inventor raises an interesting line of inquiry for entrepreneurial historians. His dictum, "A patent is an invitation to a lawsuit" would have found a welcome "Amen" from Whitney, and from other inventors all the way down to our own times. I think that the history of patent infringement is by itself an illuminating view of the permeation of new technology into the nation's economic life over time. The entrepreneurs involved might sometimes seem to be slightly disreputable but ours is the study of facts, and not the judging of ethics.

Both Edison and Whitney made their contributions in a certain way because of properties of their own personalities and private circumstances, and subtly influenced the course of economic history in the process. But they also were reacting to a changing world created not only by men like themselves, but by men in our other "stages" of development, entrepreneurs like Westinghouse and Morgan, men whose visions were part of circumstances which only touched the inventor tangentially.

3. Schumpeterian innovators have, of course, held the center of the stage

from the very beginning of entrepreneurial studies. These were men who invented nothing, but adapted and forced new technology and products into economic life. Carnegie and Ford were two such men. Their careers not only determined important departures in the course of economic change, their personalities powerfully determined their contributions — and, I hasten to add, the nature of the reaction, especially the violence and single-mindedness of labor-union action in America from Homestead to the River Rouge and after.

Carnegie's great contribution, from the establishment of the Edgar Thomson works at Braddock Field in 1873 until Pierpont Morgan loosened the aged Spencerian grip in 1900, was to make the American steel industry one of the wonders of industrial history. His methods were those of ruthless and unremitting competition. Carnegie Steel was the cutting edge of progress in the basic industry during the great industrial transformatic of 1873–1900, an epoch in which the United States outstripped all others in industrial development. Carnegie himself was a product of two deeper and older economic phenomena. His father, Thomas, was actually a hand-loom weaver, a master weaver of linen in Dunfermline, displaced by the power loom. The classic Industrial Revolution was thus one progenitor of Carnegie Steel. The other was the Atlantic migration of the nineteenth century, to which was added, in 1848, the little Scottish family of Thomas Carnegie. Andrew Carnegie's contributions to his new country were many-sided, ranging from steel to philanthropy, and remain with us. But the entire story is most clearly framed by the single fact that, in the growth of the American economy in the late nineteenth century, the poor lad from Dunfermline became the Schumpeterian entrepreneur *par excellence*. Carnegie's own development was a microcosm of much of American experience in economic affairs in the last half of the nineteenth century.

Perhaps the greatest change in American economic history thus far in the twentieth century has been due to the transformation of a European "invention" into an American innovation — the automobile. And the automobile industry was almost spelled Ford in its vital formative years, when a rich man's plaything became the basic mode of American transport. The automobile set off a vast change in the demographic and social structure of the country that still shows few signs of stabilizing. To really understand this phenomenon, and its main instrument, the Model T, one must begin by looking closely into the character of the tyrant of Dearborn, the Napoleon of the River Rouge, and oppressor of the worker, who probably brought more freedom to more people than all the liberators of history. Ford was a corn-fed Bolivar to the twentieth century. His greatest contribution to American life was to free the common man from his geography. After Ford, no man needed to stay in any locale if he had the few dollars it cost to buy some sort of an automobile. And here I do not mean to include only inter-regional mobility in the national economy, but also, and perhaps mainly, the local freedom of movement which has diminished the farmtown and made the new shopping-center world of suburbia a threat to the conventional city itself. Model T was Ford's religion and the mass-produced world of the automobile his monument. His own life and work take American history from the horse-drawn plough to the mechanical farm, from the wagon road to the superhighway. Oddly enough, both of these men, Carnegie and Ford, are now associated in the public mind with vast philanthropics. It was not always so. The details of these careers in industrial revolution comprise a key which unlocks a rich understanding of this country's past and its present.

4. I chose Harriman and Morgan as my men of organization to illustrate a singular and continuous thread in economic history, the essentially conservative power of the financial art. Finance imposes a logic of its own upon both the borrower and the lender. Even financial frauds and chicaneries follow identifiable, almost predictable patterns. There is great continuity in techniques in arts and crafts over time, and the mind follows the action of the hand. Pierpont Morgan was like the Medicis in more ways than his personal tastes; over the gulf of centuries, they were essentially in the same trade. If the users of savings, the tycoons of a new technology, wanted contact with accumulated wealth and with current flows of savings, that contact had to come from an intermediary whose rules were fixed by customs far older than the Newtonian science from which that new technology had developed. Financiers set terms for repayment of debt. To meet those terms, borrowers had to regulate their own activity according to schedules of repayment and even, commonly, to accept bankers into direct management in order to guarantee the necessary safeguards. The decisions of industry were thus powerfully influenced by the needs of the manipulators of engraved paper. Hence, men like Carnegie and Ford, who did not use the capital markets, had a freedom of action quite different from those like Gary and Durant who did need to come to terms with the world of high finance.

In the late nineteenth century, as certain American transportation and industrial ventures generated ambitions which outstripped their own current earning capacities, the builders of these systems sought contractual partnerships with those who wanted earning assets in place of cash hoards. The resulting unions were arranged for and sanctified by the financial organizers. The result has been called such names as the "age of finance capitalism," the "age of trusts," and the like. These phrases described a reality, and a vital one, in American economic history. Without the union of finance and industry the massive size of many of our great companies might well not have developed. There is no evidence that most of these are not based upon efficiency. The charge of "monopoly power" sounded good, but it has not held up as the origin of economic strength among the industrial giants. Internal economies made access to the capital markets desirable. In industry after industry in the late nineteenth century, the union of technology and the capital market provided an opening for growth, where reliance upon current earnings for expansion seemed to constrain management.

I chose Harriman as one of my financial organizers to illustrate the contribution of the specialist. He is the paragon of the railroad financier. From his reorganization of the Ontario and Southern through the Northern Pacific Trust (in which Morgan had a hand) and on to the post-humous liquidation of the Southern Pacific empire under the Sherman Act, Harriman's activities showed a consistent pattern of rationalization, conservative reorganization, and expansion. Men like Villard built the railroads, but they didn't run them. Time after time it seemed that the empire-builders had to "hand over" to the financial organizers. Harriman, like Carnegie, was both thoughtful and ruthless. He also represented Thomas Mun's ideal, the man whose private ambitions embraced the public interest, or at least advanced the public interest. Harriman was apparently not an attractive person in business, and historians have gleefully followed the unsubstantiated and bitter charges of Harriman's defeated enemies. Yet a careful study of Harriman's career as an organizer provides a vivid lesson in the mechanics of transportation finance at the turn of the century. Harriman was no hero to the historians, but he was a whale of a financial organizer, and his volcanic and controversial career creates a bright light on the American past when that career is viewed as an example of a particular kind of contribution; viewed merely as a "Robber Baron," as he traditionally has been treated, Harriman has almost been lost to the history books.

My final entrepreneur is John Pierpont Morgan himself. Sometimes it seems that all roads led to the Morgan library until Morgan died in 1913. Personally he was an enigma, but as a financial organizer he knew no peer. We have not seen his like since, nor, in my opinion, are we likely to. Almost every facet of his life was a side of American economic history. One part of Morgan's personality, the hard-eyed Yankee moralist studying the imperfections of his fellow tycoons, is an essay in Americana. One imagines the astonished forefather of our race, in his threadbare suit and mud-covered boots looking upon his affluent progeny with both dismay and disapproval — yet recognizing his own. On the other hand, Morgan's tastes in matters of personal consumption, and his aesthetic senses, were extravagant in his time, and perhaps foreshadowed a future when affluence came within the reach of millions. Morgan had a passion to impose discipline and order upon everything he touched. When men came to him for help they took away orders. In fact, when Wall Street's elite came voluntarily to the old man for help, as they did that Sunday half a century ago in the panic of 1907, they knew that orders would come which would be painful but effective. The portly old gentleman with the blazing eyes, long cigar, whose words were few, who reorganized a vast portion of the nation's industry during his endless games of solitaire, was a one-man segment of American financial history. His banking house grew out of the older tradition of merchant banking, and he presided over the growth of American investment banking practice virtually from its beginning. His actions in national emergencies from 1877 to 1907 were examples for those who yearned for the restoration of central banking to the United States. His promotion of the arts was a great beginning of the infusion of high quality into everyday American life — the Metropolitan Museum of Art is as much his monument as is United States Steel, but few remember that today.

In my scheme of organization of American economic development the Morgans are as essential as the Penns, and if neither kind is identifiable today on such a heroic scale, it is the scale of the national framework that has changed, not the basic economic functions of idealism, invention, innovation and organization. We sometimes overlook the extent to which our society automatically systematizes useful art. Entrepreneurship of the Morgan or Harriman variety was most rare in their time. The *talent* is still rare enough, but business schools now teach the skills those men had.

V

I have outlined this view of American economic development in order to underscore two points: (1) the entrepreneur can quite properly be used as a focal point in the interpretation of American economic history generally, but (2) the entrepreneurial role can be made coherent *only* within some sort of explicit analytical framework. Because I chose to try this scheme on the grandest scale, my analytical framework is one of desperate simplicity. One presumes that more specific problems would yield more complex analytical systems. As any experienced economist is aware, it is in disaggregation that complications develop. But I want to insist upon the view that the entrepreneurial historian should be as much concerned with *what* he is talking about as with *whom* he is dealing. Sub-division of the entrepreneurial function into conceptual categories is a useful device for clarification. If his work is to be a coherently integrated part of the whole fabric of American history, the entrepreneurial historian owes it to his reader to commit himself as much to identifying and analyzing his problem as to getting his biographical facts straight. This is so, even if for no other reason than this simple one: *it is the underlying problem that determines which facts shall be chosen.* My conceptual framework determined how I was to pick my men, and why. The "facts" themselves are silent, unless ordered by ideas. Brigham Young was a financier, and Pierpont Morgan was a religious enthusiast. But, given my frame of reference, I argue that Young's great contribution, including even his banking, came primarily from his religious commitment, and Pierpont Morgan's from his financial acumen (perhaps soothed by appropriate scripture).

Let me add two points. First, I doubt that there will ever be any single, generally accepted way to write Entrepreneurial History, because there will be as many analytical frames of reference as there are ideas about what is important in economic life. That will always be a large number indeed. Second, there is more, much more, than economic motivation in the lives of men. For example, let me make a "far out" but entirely serious suggestion about these men in particular, and Entrepreneurial History in general. It seems to me that my men could have been studied most profitably indeed from a type of Freudian analysis. What were the effects upon Penn, Brigham Young and Morgan of their all-powerful fathers? Whitney was a "solitary," a bachelor into his fifties. Were these facts, together with his inventiveness, and with the secretiveness of his actions, all related in an important way? Did they have important effects? Did Harriman, the "Little Giant," act out the part in a defensive reaction to his small stature? What was the impact of strong mothers and weak fathers upon Carnegie, Harriman, Ford and Edison? I am almost asking what was the effect of family life on American history *through* these men. Yet, if we are seriously interested in understanding the individual entrepreneur's impact, I don't really see how we can avoid the problems of the determination of personality.

It also seems to me that the "lessons" of history aren't really very easily found by entrepreneurial historians. For the Victorian period especially, there were powerful motivations which might not seem reasonable to our age, but these must be learned and taken into account if the historian is to make any sense of some Victorian entrepreneurs. I'm not saying that unvarnished greed — or profit maximization — was not important. But I am saying that profit maximization isn't a sufficient identification of motivation. For example, there was millennialism in both Penn and Young, there was a powerful belief in inexorable *moral* progress in both Carnegie and Morgan. In Edison and Ford there was a rich strain of what might be called cracker-barrel chauvinism — disdain for formal science and for expertise. The chauvinism was sincere, and partly armed those two classic "country boys" to triumph over a world in which science and expertise were both largely hostile. Of the men I've studied here, possibly only Whitney and Harriman were sufficiently examples of *homo oeconomicus* to satisfy the most mundane model of human motivation. But even in these two it can be shown that the "public interest" intruded at times.

Our hideous age of wars and atrocities, the impact of income taxes upon the aggregation and control of great wealth by individuals, remorseless inflation adding to the persistent social disorganization of our times, may make the Victorian world more obsolete as a model of basic motivation and behavior than the passage of time alone might indicate. The student of entrepreneurship, no less than any other variety of historian, needs to acclimate himself in the culture of the period he is studying, and this is an added burden.

All such considerations lead me back to one of my earliest statements: informed Entrepreneurial History is difficult and complex, and must necessarily be so. The biographer-historian-economist-social psychologist-philosopher who scales all these heights in a really professional way will indeed be worthy of our admiration. But what is most difficult of all, is that this lion-taming snake charmer needs the broad as well as the narrow view. And this is an unkind fate. □

National Industrial Recovery Act *
JUNE 16, 1933

TITLE I — INDUSTRIAL RECOVERY

SEC. 1. A national emergency productive of widespread unemployment and disorganization of industry, which burdens interstate and foreign commerce, affects the public welfare, and undermines the standards of living of the American people, is hereby declared to exist. It is hereby declared to be the policy of Congress to remove obstructions to the free flow of interstate and foreign commerce which tend to diminish the amount thereof; and to provide for the general welfare by promoting the organization of industry for the purpose of cooperative action among trade groups, to induce and maintain united action of labor and management under adequate governmental sanctions and supervision, to eliminate unfair competitive practices, to promote the fullest possible utilization of the present productive capacity of industries, to avoid undue restriction of production (except as may be temporarily required), to increase the consumption of industrial and agricultural products by increasing purchasing power, to reduce and relieve unemployment, to improve standards of labor, and otherwise to rehabilitate industry and to conserve natural resources. . . .

TITLE II — PUBLIC WORKS AND CONSTRUCTION PROJECTS

SEC. 201. (a) To effectuate the purposes of this title, the President is hereby authorized to create a Federal Emergency Administration of Public Works, all the powers of which shall be exercised by a Federal Emergency Administrator of Public Works, . . . □

The Clayton Anti-Trust Act †
OCTOBER 15, 1914

. . . SEC. 2. That it shall be unlawful for any person engaged in commerce, in the course of such commerce, either directly or indirectly to discriminate in price between different purchasers of commodities . . . where the effect of

* Taken and adapted from "National Industrial Recovery Act" (June 16, 1933), *U.S. Statutes at Large* (73rd Cong., 1933–34), Vol. XLVIII, pp. 195 ff.

† Taken and adapted from "The Clayton Anti-Trust Act" (October 15, 1914), *U.S. Statutes at Large*, Vol. XXXVIII, pp. 730 ff.

such discrimination may be to substantially lessen competition or tend to create a monopoly in any line of commerce: . . .

SEC. 6. That the labor of a human being is not a commodity or article of commerce. Nothing contained in the anti-trust laws shall be construed to forbid the existence and operation of labor, agricultural, or horticultural organizations, instituted for the purposes of mutual help, . . . nor shall such organizations or the members thereof, be held or construed to be illegal combinations or conspiracies in restraint of trade, under the anti-trust laws.

SEC. 7. That no corporation engaged in commerce shall acquire, directly or indirectly, the whole or any part of the stock or other share capital of another corporation engaged also in commerce, where the effect of such acquisition may be to susbtantially lessen competition . . . or to restrain such commerce in any section or community, or tend to create a monopoly of any line of commerce. . . . □

[DOCUMENT]   ✧ **75** ✧

The Transportation Act of 1920 *

FEBRUARY 28, 1920

SEC. 200. (a) Federal control shall terminate at 12:01 A.M., March 1, 1920; and the President shall then relinquish possession and control of all railroads and systems of transportation then under Federal control and cease the use and operation thereof. . . .

SEC. 209. . . . (c) The United States hereby guarantees —

(1) With respect to any carrier with which a contract . . . has been made . . . that the railway operating income of such carrier for the guaranty period as a whole shall not be less than one-half the amount named in such contract as annual compensation, . . .

SEC. 407. . . . (4) The Commission shall as soon as practicable prepare and adopt a plan for the consolidation of the railway properties of the continental United States into a limited number of systems. In the division of such railways into such systems under such plan, competition shall be preserved as fully as possible and wherever practicable the existing routes and channels of trade and commerce shall be maintained. . . .

SEC. 422. . . . (2) In the exercise of its power to prescribe just and reasonable rates the Commission shall initiate, modify, establish or adjust such rates so that carriers as a whole . . . will, under honest, efficient and economical management and reasonable expenditures for maintenance of way, structures and equipment, earn an aggregate annual net railway operating income equal, as nearly as may be, to a fair return upon the aggregate value of the railway

* Taken and adapted from "The Transportation Act of 1920" (February 28, 1920), *U.S. Statutes at Large*, Vol. XLI, pp. 456 ff.

property of such carriers held for and used in the service of transportation. . . .

(6) If, under the provisions of this section, any carrier receives for any year a net railway operating income in excess of 6 per centum of the value of the railway property held for and used by it in the service of transportation, one-half of such excess shall be placed in a reserve fund established and maintained by such carrier, and the remaining one-half thereof shall, within the first four months following the close of the period for which such computation is made, be recoverable by and paid to the Commission for the purpose of establishing and maintaining a general railroad contingent fund as hereinafter described. . . . □

[DOCUMENT]   ❖ **76** ❖

Coolidge's Veto of the McNary-Haugen Bill *

FEBRUARY 25, 1927

To the Senate:

. . . A board of 12 men are granted almost unlimited control of the agricultural industry and can not only fix the price which the producers of five commodities shall receive for their goods, but can also fix the price which the consumers of the country shall pay for these commodities. The board is expected to obtain higher prices for the American farmer by removing the surplus from the home market and dumping it abroad at a below-cost price. To do this, the board is given the authority by implication to fix the domestic price level, either by means of contracts which it may make with processors or cooperatives, or by providing for the purchase of the commodities in such quantities as will bring the prices up to the point which the board may fix.

Except as it may be restrained by fear of foreign importations, the farm board, composed of representatives of producers, is given the power to fix the prices of these necessities of life at any point it sees fit. The law fixes no standards, imposes no restrictions, and requires no regulation of any kind. There could be no appeal from the arbitrary decision of these men, who would under constant pressure from their constituents to push prices as high as possible. To expect moderation under these circumstances is to disregard experience and credit human nature with qualities it does not possess. It is not so long since the Government was spending vast sums and through the Department of Justice exerting every effort to break up combinations that were raising the cost of living to a point conceived to be excessive. This bill, if it accomplishes its purpose, will raise the price of the specified agricultural commodities to the highest possible point and in doing so the board will op-

* Taken and adapted from "Coolidge's Veto of the McNary-Haugen Bill" (February 25, 1927), *Congressional Record*, 69th Congress, 2d Session, Vol. LXVIII, pp. 4771 ff.

erate without any restraints imposed by the antitrust laws. The granting of any such arbitrary power to a Government board is to run counter to our traditions, the philosophy of our Government, the spirit of our institutions, and all principles of equity. . . .

The main policy of this bill is an entire reversal of what has been heretofore thought to be sound. Instead of undertaking to secure a method of orderly marketing which will dispose of products at a profit, it proposes to dispose of them at a loss. . . . It runs counter to the well-considered principle that a healthy economic condition is best maintained through a free play of competition by undertaking to permit a legalized restraint of trade in these commodities and establish a species of monopoly under Government protection. . . . For many generations such practices have been denounced by law as repugnant to the public welfare. It can not be that they would now be found to be beneficial to agriculture. . . . □

[DOCUMENT] ❖ **77** ❖

Norris-Laguardia Anti-Injunction Bill *

MARCH 20, 1932

■ *An Act to amend the Judicial Code and to define and limit the jurisdiction of courts sitting in equity, and for other purposes.*

Be it enacted, That no court of the United States, as herein defined, shall have jurisdiction to issue any restraining order or temporary or permanent injunction in a case involving or growing out of a labor dispute, except in a strict conformity with the provisions of this Act; nor shall any such restraining order or temporary or permanent injunction be issued contrary to the public policy declared in this Act.

SEC. 2. . . . Whereas, under prevailing economic conditions, . . . the individual unorganized worker is commonly helpless to exercise actual liberty of contract and to protect his freedom of labor, and thereby to obtain acceptable terms and conditions of employment, wherefore, though he should be free to decline to associate with his fellows, it is necessary that he should have full freedom of association, self-organization, and designation of representatives of his own choosing, to negotiate the terms and conditions of his employment, and that he shall be free from the interference, restraint, or coercion of employers of labor, or their agents, in the activities for the purpose of collective bargaining or other mutual aid or protection; therefore, the following defi-

---

* Taken and adapted from "Norris-Laguardia Anti-Injunction Bill" (March 20, 1932), *U.S. Statutes at Large,* Vol. XLVII, pp. 70 ff.

nitions of, and limitations upon, the jurisdiction and authority of the courts of the United States are hereby enacted. . . .

SEC. 5. No court of the United States shall have jurisdiction to issue a restraining order or temporary or permanent injunction upon the ground that any of the persons participating or interested in a labor dispute constitute or are engaged in an unlawful combination or conspiracy because of the doing in concert of the acts enumerated in section 4 of this Act. . . .

SEC. 13. . . . (c) The term "labor dispute" includes any controversy concerning terms or conditions of employment, or concerning the association or representation of persons negotiating, fixing, maintaining, changing, or seeking to arrange terms or conditions of employment, regardless of whether or not the disputants stand in approximate relation of employer and employee. . . . □

[DOCUMENT] ⟡ **78** ⟡

The Agricultural Adjustment Act *
MAY 12, 1933

■ *An Act to relieve the existing national economic emergency by increasing agricultural purchasing power, . . . to provide for the orderly liquidation of joint-stock land banks, and for other purposes.*

TITLE I — AGRICULTURAL ADJUSTMENT

Declaration of Emergency

That the present acute economic emergency being in part the consequence of a severe and increasing disparity between the prices of agricultural and other commodities, which disparity has largely destroyed the purchasing power of farmers for industrial products, has broken down the orderly exchange of commodities, and has seriously impaired the agricultural assets supporting the national credit structure, it is hereby declared that these conditions in the basic industry of agriculture have affected transactions in agricultural commodities with a national public interest, have burdened and obstructed the normal currents of commerce in such commodities, and render imperative the immediate enactment of title I of this Act.

Declaration of Policy

SEC. 2. It is hereby declared to be the policy of Congress —

(1) To establish and maintain such balance between the production and

* Taken and adapted from "The Agricultural Adjustment Act" (May 12, 1933), *U.S. Statutes at Large*, Vol. XLVIII, p. 31.

consumption of agricultural commodities, and such marketing conditions therefor, as will re-establish prices to farmers at a level that will give agricultural commodities a purchasing power with respect to articles that farmers buy, equivalent to the purchasing power of agricultural commodities in the base period. The base period in the case of all agricultural commodities except tobacco shall be the prewar period, August 1909–July 1914. In the case of tobacco, the base period shall be the postwar period, August 1919–July 1929. . . .

PART 2 — COMMODITY BENEFITS

General Powers

sec. 8. In order to effectuate the declared policy, the Secretary of Agriculture shall have power —

(1) To provide for reduction in the acreage or reduction in the production for market, or both, of any basic agricultural commodity, through agreements with producers or by other voluntary methods, and to provide for rental or benefit payments in connection therewith or upon that part of the production of any basic agricultural commodity required for domestic consumption, in such amounts as the Secretary deems fair and reasonable, to be paid out of any moneys available for such payments. . . .

(2) To enter into marketing agreements with processors, associations of producers, and others engaged in the handling, in the current of interstate or foreign commerce of any agricultural commodity or project thereof, after due notice and opportunity for hearing to interested parties. The making of any such agreement shall not be held to be in violation of any of the antitrust laws of the United States, and any such agreement shall be deemed to be lawful. . . . □

[DOCUMENT]   ✧ **79** ✧

Reciprocal Trade Agreements Act, 1934 *

■ *An Act to amend the Tariff Act of 1930.*

Be it enacted by the senate and house of representatives of the united states of america in congress assembled, that the tariff act of 1930 is amended by adding at the end of title III the following:

PART III — PROMOTION OF FOREIGN TRADE

sec. 350. (a) For the purpose of expanding foreign markets for the products of the United States (as a means of assisting in the present emergency in re-

---

* Taken and adapted from "Reciprocal Trade Agreements Act, 1934," Public — No. 316 — 73D Congress, H.R. p. 8687.

storing the American standard of living, in overcoming domestic unemployment and the present economic depression, in increasing the purchasing power of the American public, and in establishing and maintaining a better relationship among various branches of American agriculture, industry, mining, and commerce) by regulating the admission of foreign goods into the United States in accordance with the characteristics and needs of various branches of American production so that foreign markets will be made available to those branches of American production which require and are capable of developing such outlets by affording corresponding market opportunities for foreign products in the United States, the President, whenever he finds as a fact that any existing duties or other import restrictions of the United States or any foreign country are unduly burdening and restricting the foreign trade of the United States and that the purpose above declared will be promoted by the means hereinafter specified, is authorized from time to time —

(1) To enter into foreign trade agreements with foreign governments or instrumentalities thereof; and

(2) To proclaim such modifications of existing duties and other import restrictions, or such additional import restrictions, or such continuance, and for such minimum periods, of existing customs or excise treatment of any article by foreign trade agreements, as are required or appropriate to carry out any foreign trade ageement that the President has entered into hereunder. No proclamation shall be made increasing or decreasing by more than 50 per centum any existing rate of duty or transferring any article between the dutiable and free lists. . . . □

[DOCUMENT]   ❖ **80** ❖

The National Labor Relations Act *

JULY 5, 1935

■ An Act to diminish the causes of labor disputes burdening or obstructing interstate and foreign commerce, to create a National Labor Relations Board, and for other purposes.

FINDINGS AND POLICY

SECTION 1. The denial by employers of the right of employees to organize and the refusal by employers to accept the procedure of collective bargaining lead to strikes and other forms of industrial strife or unrest, which have the intent or the necessary effect of burdening or obstructing commerce by (a) impairing the efficiency, safety, or operation of the instrumentalities of commerce;

* Taken and adapted from "The National Labor Relations Act" (July 5, 1935), *U.S. Statutes at Large,* Vol. XLIX, p. 449.

(b) occurring in the current of commerce; (c) materially affecting, restraining, or controlling the flow of raw materials or manufactured or processed goods from or into the channels of commerce, or the prices of such materials or goods in commerce; or (d) causing diminution of employment and wages in such volume as substantially to impair or disrupt the market for goods flowing from or into the channels of commerce.

The inequality of bargaining power between employees who do not possess full freedom of association or actual liberty of contract, and employers who are organized in the corporate or other forms of ownership association substantially burdens and affects the flow of commerce, and tends to aggravate recurrent business depressions, by depressing wage rates and the purchasing power of wage earners in industry and by preventing the stabilization of competitive wage rates and working conditions within and between industries.

Experience has proved that protection by law of the right of employees to organize and bargain collectively safeguards commerce from injury, impairment, or interruption, and promotes the flow of commerce by removing certain recognized sources of industrial strife and unrest, by encouraging practices fundamental to the friendly adjustment of industrial disputes arising out out of differences as to wages, hours, or other working conditions, and by restoring equality of bargaining power between employers and employees.

It is hereby declared to be the policy of the United States to eliminate the causes of certain substantial obstructions to the free flow of commerce and to mitigate and eliminate these obstructions when they have occurred by encouraging the practice and procedure of collective bargaining and by protecting the exercise by workers of full freedom of association, self-organization, and designation of representatives of their own choosing, for the purpose of negotiating the terms and conditions of their employment or other mutual aid or protection. . . . ◻

[DOCUMENT]   ◇ **81** ◇

Labor Management Relations Act of 1947 *

■ An Act to amend the National Labor Relations Act, to provide additional facilities for the mediation of labor disputes affecting commerce, to equalize legal responsibilities of labor organizations and employers, and for other purposes.

Be it enacted by the Senate and House of Representatives of the United States of America in Congress assembled.

* Taken and adapted from "Labor Management Relations Act of 1947," Public Law 101 — 80th Congress, Chapter 120 — 1st Session, H.R. p. 3020.

SHORT TITLE AND DECLARATION OF POLICY

SEC. 1. (a) This Act may be cited as the "Labor Management Relations Act, 1947."

(b) Industrial strife which interferes with the normal flow of commerce and with the full production of articles and commodities for commerce, can be avoided or substantially minimized if employers, employees, and labor organizations each recognize under law one another's legitimate rights in their relations with each other, and above all recognize under law that neither party has any right in its relations with any other to engage in acts or practices which jeopardize the public health, safety, or interest.

It is the purpose and policy of this Act, in order to promote the full flow of commerce, to prescribe the legitimate rights of both employees and employers in their relations affecting commerce, to provide orderly and peaceful procedures for preventing the interference by either with the legitimate rights of the other, to protect the rights of individual employees in their relations with labor organizations whose activities affect commerce, to define and proscribe practices on the part of labor and management which affect commerce and are inimical to the general welfare, and to protect the rights of the public in connection with labor disputes affecting commerce.

Title I — Amendment of National Labor Relations Act

SEC. 101. The National Labor Relations Act is hereby amended to read as follows: . . .

"RIGHTS OF EMPLOYEES

"SEC. 7. Employees shall have the right to self-organization, to form, join, or assist labor organizations, to bargain collectively through representatives of their own choosing, and to engage in other concerted activities for the purpose of collective bargaining or other mutual aid or protection, and shall also have the right to refrain from any or all of such activities except to the extent that such right may be affected by an agreement requiring membership in a labor organization as a condition of employment as authorized in section 8 (a) (3). . . .

"(d) . . . no party to such contract shall terminate or modify such contract, unless the party desiring such termination or modification —

"(1) serves a written notice upon the other party to the contract of the proposed termination or modification sixty days prior to the expiration date thereof, or in the event such contract contains no expiration date, sixty days prior to the time it is proposed to make such termination or modification; . . .

"SEC. 9. . . . (f) No investigation shall be made by the Board of any question affecting commerce concerning the representation of employees, raised by a labor organization under subsection (c) of this section, no petition under section 9 (e) (1) shall be entertained, and no complaint shall be issued pursuant to a charge made by a labor organization under subsection (b) of section 10, unless such labor organization and any national or international labor organization of which such labor organization is an affiliate or constituent unit (A) shall have prior thereto filed with the Secretary of Labor copies of its constitution and bylaws and a report, in such form as the Secretary may prescribe, showing — . . .

"(6) a detailed statement of, or reference to provisions of its constitution and bylaws showing the procedure followed with respect to, (a) qualification for or restrictions on membership, (b) election of officers and stewards, (c) calling of regular and special meetings, (d) levying of assessments, (e) imposition of fines, (f) authorization for bargaining demands, (g) ratification of contract terms, (h) authorization for strikes, (i) authorization for disbursement of union funds, (j) audit of union financial transactions, (k) participation in insurance or other benefit plans, and (l) expulsion of members and the grounds therefor; and (B) can show that prior thereto it has —

"(1) filed with the Secretary of Labor, in such form as the Secretary may prescribe, a report showing all of (a) its receipts of any kind and the sources of such receipts, (b) its total assets and liabilities as of the end of its last fiscal year, (c) the disbursements made by it during such fiscal year, including the purposes for which made; . . .

"(h) No investigation shall be made by the Board of any question affecting commerce concerning the representation of employees, raised by a labor organization under subsection (c) of this section, no petition under section 9 (e) (1) shall be entertained, and no complaint shall be issued pursuant to a charge made by a labor organization under subsection (b) of section 10, unless there is on file with the Board an affidavit executed contemporaneously or within the preceding twelve-month period by each officer of such labor organization and the officers of any national or international labor organization of which it is an affiliate or constituent unit that he is not a member of the Communist Party or affiliated with such party, and that he does not believe in, and is not a member of or supports any organization that believes in or teaches, the overthrow of the United States Government by force or by any illegal or unconstitutional methods. . . .

"sec. 14. . . . (b) Nothing in this Act shall be construed as authorizing the execution or application of agreements requiring membership in a labor organization as a condition of employment in any State or Territory in which such execution or application is prohibited by State or Territorial law. . . .

NATIONAL EMERGENCIES

sec. 206. Whenever in the opinion of the President of the United States, a threatened or actual strike or lock-out affecting an entire industry or a substantial part thereof engaged in trade, commerce, transportation, transmission, or communication among the several States or with foreign nations, or engaged in the production of goods for commerce, will, if permitted to occur or to continue, imperil the national health or safety, he may appoint a board of inquiry to inquire into the issues involved in the dispute and to make a written report to him within such time as he shall prescribe. . . .

SEC. 208. (a) Upon receiving a report from a board of inquiry the President may direct the Attorney General to petition any district court of the United States having jurisdiction of the parties to enjoin such strike or lock-out or the continuing thereof, . . .

SEC. 209. . . . (b) Upon the issuance of such order, the President shall reconvene the board of inquiry which has previously reported with respect to the dispute. At the end of a sixty-day period (unless the dispute has been settled by that time), the board of inquiry shall report to the President the current position of the parties and the efforts which have been made for settlement, and shall include a statement by each party of its position and a statement of the employer's last offer of settlement. The President shall make such report available to the public. The National Labor Relations Board, within the succeeding fifteen days, shall take a secret ballot of the employees of each employer involved in the dispute on the question of whether they wish to accept the final offer of settlement made by their employer as stated by him and shall certify the results thereof to the Attorney General within five days thereafter. . . . □